Tenth Edition / ALL NEW

The **No. 1** Price Guide to
M.I. HUMMEL®
Figurines, Plates, More . . .

- accurate prices
- easy-to-use
- pocket size

by renowned expert
ROBERT L. MILLER

Special contributors
Don and Beth Woodworth
Specialists in
Goebel Hummels

Reverie
PUBLISHING COMPANY

*This book is dedicated to my wife Ruth, the
"Original" M.I. Hummel Figurine Collector.*

The 10th Edition Price Guide is dedicated to special contributors Don
and Beth Woodworth, for all your time, energy and help in putting this
10th edition together, and also to M.I. Hummel Collectors worldwide who
have shared with us their passion and love in collecting.

We thank you for all your caring and sharing in our hobby.

Tenth edition/ First printing

*M.I. Hummel® and Hummel®, in signature and block forms, are registered trademarks of W. Goebel Porzellanfabrik,
Germany.*

M.I. Hummel figurines, plates and bells are copyrighted products of W. Goebel Porzellanfabrik, Germany.

*M.I. Hummel ® and Hummel® are used under license from Goebel.
© ARS AG, Zug/Switzerland.*

This book was originally published by Portfolio Press Corporation.

To purchase additional copies of this book, please contact:
Reverie Publishing Company, 130 South Wineow Street, Cumberland, MD 21502
888-721-4999 • www.reveriepublishing.com

Library of Congress Control Number 2006932444

ISBN-13: 978-1-932485-35-6

ISBN-10: 1-932485-35-X

Production Director: Tammy S. Blank

Printed and bound in the United States of America

Introduction

This price guide is designed to meet the growing needs of dealers and insurance underwriters, as well as the collector-enthusiast. It is primarily intended as an aid in identifying, dating and pricing both current and older "M.I. Hummel" figurines, along with plates, bells, lamps, and other related "M.I. Hummel" items produced through the years by W. Goebel Porzellanfabrik of Rödental, Germany.

The publication of this book has been approved by W. Goebel Porzellanfabrik, the sole manufacturers of the "M.I. Hummel" figurines, plates, and bells.

The format of this guide provides a flexible bracket or price range, rather than one arbitrary price for each item. It is extremely difficult to assign an exact value for each figurine since many factors can affect this valuation. Prices do vary from one section of the country to another—and even sales within a given area may be at different figures. General economic conditions prevailing at the time of sale can affect valuations too. Exact values on older specimens of Hummel figurines are impossible to ascertain, because so many factors must be taken into consideration. In such instances, the rarity of the piece, its general condition (whether mint, restored, damaged), its color, its authenticity, and finally, its appeal to the collector, must be considered.

The price ranges quoted in this book reflect the current retail prices as opposed to wholesale or dealer prices. Thus a person selling a certain item cannot expect to receive the top bracket price in most instances. Some dealers use the price ranges in this guide as a "bench mark," and offer the seller a percentage of either the high or the low figure. Again the rarity of the piece enters into the actual value determination. After reading the above, you may question the worth of any price guide in the first place. However, the author firmly believes the growth in Hummel collecting over many years dictates the necessity for such a yardstick of value. More and more collectors, novices and veterans alike, have been asking, "What should I expect to pay for this or that figurine?" "What should I sell my figurines for?" "What should I insure my collection for?" These questions are answered intelligently in this up-to-date list of values. The easy-to-read format provides simple and understandable information which reflects prices on today's market.

The author, having years of experience in buying, selling and collecting "M.I. Hummel" figurines and related items, would be the first to admit that there are wide fluctuations or variations in market prices today. It would be foolhardy and misleading to think that this or any other price guide could assign exact values for each and every Hummel piece. What has been provided in this guide is an accurate and reasonable range or "norm" so that the collector, dealer, or insurance agent can intelligently place a true valuation on each item. When it comes to a matter of worth, you must remember: it is "what the buyer is willing to pay, and the seller is willing to accept" that really sets the price. It takes two to strike a bargain!

Robert L. Miller

—Robert L. Miller

We solicit your questions, suggestions, opinions and criticisms. If we can be of help in making your collecting more complete and enjoyable, or if you just want to say "hello"— call or write:

Robert L. Miller
112 Woodland Drive
P.O. Box 210
Eaton, OH 45320-0210
1-937-456-3735
E-mail: hummelking@voyager.net

Beth & Don Woodworth
5866 W. Sweden Road
Bergen, NY 14416

1-585-494-2337

The Remarkable Story of Sister M.I. Hummel

C hildren are children the world over, impish or shy, saucy or quiet, mischievous or thoughtful . . . language differences don't matter, nor do variances in national custom. The innocence of childhood produces a universality that is loved and understood everywhere.This is perhaps the key to the remarkable and enduring popularity of the wonderful creations of Sister Maria Innocentia Hummel.

Berta Hummel was born in the town of Massing in Lower Bavaria, Germany, on May 21, 1909, one of six children of Adolph and Viktoria Hummel. Although a closely knit family, the children were not carbon copies of one another. While her older sisters were industriously helping their mother with household chores, Berta was busy drawing, making costumes for her dolls, and putting on theatricals for family and friends.

War broke out when she was only six. Hor father was drafted into the army and the family was left without his guiding influence. Berta, whose artistic talents he had always encouraged, began to show signs of willfulness and lack of discipline, often taxing the patience of her teachers. Fortunately, her creativity was to be recognized early; due to the efforts of one of her teachers, she was enrolled at a fine religious boarding school at Simbach, near Massing, the Institute of English Sisters.

It was here that she first received artistic direction. Her flair for scenic and costume design fostered just for fun in the family's backyard, now began to emerge as a genuine talent. Soon she was designing for school productions. In four years, she progressed from only sketching the friends of her childhood and illustrating folk tales to painting landscapes in watercolor.

The religious training at the school proved to be good discipline, and her development into a young lady and a promising artist was a delight to behold.

In 1927, when she was 18, Berta's proud father went with her to Munich where she was enrolled in the Academy of Fine Arts, to be on some familiar ground in otherwise strange territory, she took up residence outside the Academy in a dormitory run by a religious order.

The Academy, a prestigious center of design and applied arts, provided her with still more extensive training. Soon she began to paint in oils, and her experience with costumes was now expanded to include weaving of fabrics and designing clothing.

She was soon under the wing of a leading artist and teacher, who hoped she would remain at the Academy after graduation as his assistant. But a conflict was developing within Berta. Although she was gaining a great knowledge of art, its history, its scope and an exciting awareness of what travel and study in other cities, perhaps even other lands, might offer a young student, she was still the simple Bavarian girl from a warm, loving family, and her ties to her background were strong. Her feelings of religion were profound, and through a warm friendship at the dormitory with two Franciscan nuns who were also studying at the Academy, became even more important.

Her wonderful sense of fun never left her, and to the delight of her fellow students (and often the chagrin of the Mother Superior) she would play pranks at the residence. But more than anything, she was a gentle, emotional person, deeply affected by people and events.

In 1929, Hitler's National Socialist Party was on the rise in Munich, making specific promises of employment within the party. It offered an economic stability in depression years for sympathizers among the students of the Academy. But the militarism and politics of the Nazis were counter to Berta's sensitivities, and she turned with even greater need to the quiet, withdrawn life of her two religious friends.

With graduation drawing near, the pressures were becoming stronger for her to make a decision. On the one hand were her professors, eager for her to remain with them and continue her promising development. But on the other hand, with the frightening political atmosphere growing, there was the draw of fulfillment to be found behind the cloistered walls of a convent where she could continue her art while serving humanity through her devotion to God.

By the time of graduation in March 1931, she had made her decision. On April 22, she entered the convent of Siessen at Saulgau, and two years later was ordained Sister Maria Innocentia of the Sisters of the Third Order of St. Francis.

While a novice, she had taught art to children in kindergarten, and by late 1933 had so developed that she exhibited her work in a nearby town. In March 1933, the convent at Siessen sent a letter with proof sheets of sketches of the artist Berta Hummel to the publishing company in Munich named "Ars Sacra Josef Mueller Verlag," who specialized in the printing of religious art and books. Ars Sacra was very appreciative of the first pictures and asked for more sketches. Thus started a prosperous relationship between Sister Maria Innocentia Hummel and the publishing house "Ars Sacra Josef Mueller." The artwork of Sister

Maria Innocentia was first known to the public in the two-dimensional form. The postcards with the Hummel motifs became very popular and found their way into the United States shortly before World War II. Franz Goebel, fourth-generation head of W. Goebel, first became aware of her in 1934, and sought permission from her and the convent to translate her sketches of sparkling children and serene religious figures into three-dimensional form. This marked the beginning of a relationship between Sister Maria Innocentia, the convent and W. Goebel that continues to endure, long years after her death.

But dark clouds were hovering everywhere, and soon the sisters began to live in dread, for the Nazi government was determined to close the convent. In late 1940, the convent became a repatriation center for German nationals from other countries, and a small group of nuns, Sister Maria Innocentia included, remained to care for them.

It was a time of great deprivation. No longer able to remain in her spacious studio because of the terribly overcrowded conditions, Sister Maria Innocentia lived in a small, damp, basement room. Food and fuel were scarce, and she became terribly weakened by a lung infection. True to her dominant spirit, however, she tried to continue to work.

By November 1944 she was so ill that she was admitted to a sanitarium for treatment where her illness was finally diagnosed as chronic tuberculosis. In April 1945, the war ended and, feeling somewhat strengthened, Sister Maria Innocentia returned to the convent to help with the enormous task of rebuilding. Her spirit as ever was strong, but her physical condition had deteriorated so that she was forced to enter another sanitarium the following September, leaving it in late September 1946 to return to her beloved convent.

On November 6, 1946, at the hour of noon, the chapel bells rang out in solemn proclamation of the death of Sister Maria Innocentia at the age of 37.

A young life, full of spirit and love, came to a tragic end. But the youthful, loving spirit lives on in the pert faces of the Hummel children and the gentle bearing of the madonnas that are with us in ceramic. If we look at them a certain way, we can almost hear them breathe!

You Won't Believe This, But. . . .

Some very early "M.I. Hummel" figurines were not marked "Hum" in their original form! It has been discovered that the figurines we know today as Hum 1, Hum 2 and Hum 3 were once marked "FF 15, FF 16 and FF 17," respectively!

According to factory records, when "Puppy Love, Little Fiddler and Book Worm" were originally sculpted the series designation had not yet been determined. They were assigned these markings on an interim basis and were provisionally registered on 2 January 1935. When the licensing agreement with the Convent of Siessen was signed at the end of January 1935, the system was changed. Sister Maria Innocentia Hummel was now an acknowledged Goebel artist, and her artwork was designated its own series' reference. As was customary, it became the first three letters of her last name. Therefore, any figurines based on her art done before that date had to be remarked. Since these three were the first to be sculpted, they became "Hum 1, Hum 2 and Hum 3." The figurine FF 17, according to factory records, must be one of the first samples from the mother mold. Probably no more than six samples were made.

"Double Crown" Trademark

Incised Crown   1935-1949   Stamped Crown

This term is used to describe the Goebel Company trademark found on some "M.I. Hummel" figurines. On "double crown" pieces the "crown" trademark is usually found both incised and stamped.

According to information from the Goebel Factory, they state: "We have not yet been able to locate 'undoubted' records. With some certainty it can be assumed that the incised crown mark was used until 1945. Afterwards, supposedly, the crown mark was stamped on all figurines. However, it could happen that figurines with the incised crown mark from stock on hand were additionally provided with the stamped crown mark. It is quite unascertainable today which figurines and how many were marked in this way, i.e., with both incised and stamped crown mark. The years from 1945 to 1948 can be regarded as the transition period."

..... PRICES IN THIS GUIDE .....

We are in a period of DISCOUNTING of many items in our society. "M.I. Hummel" figurines are no exception. The prices in this guide give the relative values in relationship to new or current prices of (TM 8) trademark items. If the new figurines are discounted, the older models will likely be discounted, too, but possibly in a lesser degree. This guide reduces all items to one common denominator.

History and Explanation of Marks and Symbols

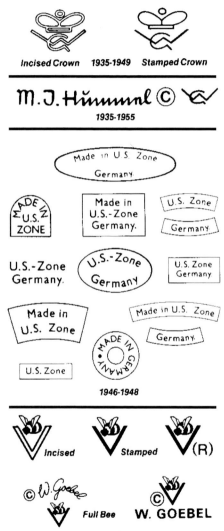

Incised Crown   1935-1949   Stamped Crown

M.J.Hümmel © 🐝
1935-1955

Made in U.S. Zone Germany

MADE IN U.S. ZONE

Made in U.S.-Zone Germany.

U.S. Zone
Germany.

U.S.-Zone Germany.

U.S.-Zone Germany

U.S. Zone Germany

Made in U.S. Zone

U.S. Zone

Made in U.S. Zone

Germany.

MADE IN GERMANY

1946-1948

Incised   Stamped   (R)

© W. Goebel   © Full Bee   © W. GOEBEL

1950-1955

The "wide-crown-WG" trademark was used on the first "M.I. Hummel" figurines produced in 1935. On the earliest figurines it was incised on the bottom of the base along with the "M.I. Hummel" signature on the top or side of the base. Between 1935 and 1955, the company occasionally used a © 🐝 mark on the side or top of the base of some models. It is seen occasionally to the right of the "M.I. Hummel" signature. The "crown" appears either incised or stamped. When both are used on the same piece it is known as a "double crown" mark.

From 1946 through 1948 it was necessary to add the stamped words "Made in the U.S. Zone Germany." This mark was used within various types of frames or without a frame, underglazed or stamped over the glaze in black ink.

In 1950, four years after Sister M.I. Hummel's death, Goebel wished in some way to pay tribute to her fine artistry. They radically changed the trademark, instituting the use of a bee flying high with a "V." (Hummel means "bumble bee" in German, and the "V" stands for "Verkaufsgesellschaft" or distribution company.) This mark, known as the full bee trademark, was used until 1955 and appeared — sometimes both incised and underglazed—in black or blue and occasionally in green or magenta. In addition, the stamp "Germany" and later "West Germany" appeared. An (R) appearing beside the trademark stands for "Registered."

Sometimes the molds were produced with a lightly incised circle on the bottom of the base in which the trademark was centered. It has no significance other than as a target for the location of the decal. Some current production figurines still have this incised circle even though it is no longer used for that purpose.

Always searching for a mark that would blend aesthetics with professionalism, the company continued to modify the trademark. In 1956, the company—still using the bee inside the "V"—made the bee smaller, with its wing tips parallel with the top of the "V." In 1957, the bee remained, although once again rising slightly above the "V." In 1958, the bee was smaller still and it flew deep within the "V", reflecting the changing trends of modern design. The year 1959 saw the beginning of stylization and the wings of the bee became sharply angular.

In 1960, the completely stylized bee with "V" mark came into use, appearing with "W. Germany." It was used in one form or another until 1979. In addition to its appearance with "W. Germany" to the right (1960–1963), it appeared above the "West Germany" (1960–1972), and to the left of the "three line mark" (mid-1960' to 1972). The three line mark was used intermittently and sometimes concurrently with the small, stylized 1960–1972 mark. It was the most prominent trademark in use prior to the "Goebel bee" trademark.

It became apparent that the public was equating the "V and Bee" mark only with "M.I. Hummel" items, not realizing that the mark included the full scope of Goebel products. It was decided to experiment further with marks. In 1972, satisfied that it now had a mark designating a quality Goebel product, the company began using a printed "Goebel" with the stylized bee poised between the letters "b" and "e."

Since 1976, the Goebel trademark on Hummel figurines has been affixed by a decal on top of the glaze. It is possible for two figurines on the primary market to have differing decals.

In 1979, the stylized bee was dropped and only the name Goebel appears. The year of production will be on the base next to the initials of the chief decorator.

In 1991, the W. (West) was deleted, with only the word Germany remaining, since Germany is once again a united country. The original "crown" has been added to the (TM 7) trademark.

In the Year 2000, the beginning of a new millennium, the trademark was once again changed. The "bumblebee" symbol, to honor the memory of Sister Maria Innocentia Hummel was reinstated to the (TM 8) current trademark.

The above information is a concise documentation of all W. Goebel trademarks authorized for use on "M.I. Hummel" figurines. In searching for accurate documentation on all W. Goebel trademarks used in conjunction with "M.I. Hummel" figurines, the author made a thorough investigation of the W. Goebel archives and queried the world's leading collectors. But it is always possible that a few rare and undocumented variations may exist.

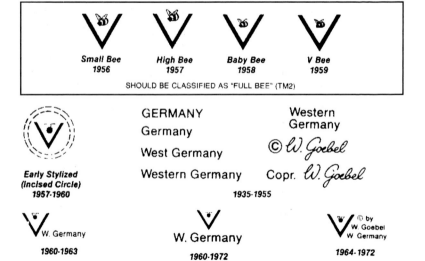

| Small Bee 1956 | High Bee 1957 | Baby Bee 1958 | V Bee 1959 |

SHOULD BE CLASSIFIED AS "FULL BEE" (TM2)

Early Stylized (Incised Circle) 1957-1960

GERMANY
Germany
West Germany
Western Germany

Western Germany

© W. Goebel
Copr. W. Goebel

1935-1955

W. Germany
1960-1963

W. Germany
1960-1972

© by W. Goebel W Germany
1964-1972

Evolution of Goebel Bee Trademark in use since 1972
(The copyright symbols © ® are found in various sizes and locations)

Goebel trademark
(since 1979)

Goebel trademark
(since 1991)

Current trademark
(since 2000)

Ⓜ.J. Hummel © ⌇

Between 1935 and 1955, the company occasionally used a © ⌇ mark on the side or top of the base of some models, before or after the "M.I. Hummel" signature. This is *NOT* considered a (TM 1) or "crown" trademark! It only means "copyright by W. Goebel".

DOUBLE TRADEMARK FIGURINES

Occasionally an older "M.I. Hummel" figurine will be found with an incised "crown" trademark as well as a stamped "full bee" trademark on the same figurine. It is neither a crown nor a full bee; it is a combination. A figurine with this double mark would have been sold in the very early 1950s. The incised crown was in the mold, and the figurine itself was quite possibly produced in the late 1940s, but then actually painted and sold in the early 1950' during the change over from one trademark to the other.

When using the No. 1 Price Guide to determine the value of a figurine with both the crown and the full bee trademark, we recommend using the high side of the full bee price bracket and the low side of the crown bracket. For example, HUM 1 "Puppy Love" with full bee (TM 2) is listed at $600 to $700, and the same with a crown (TM 1) is valued at $800 to $1000. The new bracket value would be $700 to $800.

This double marking makes it a distinctive piece and puts it in a class by itself. It is better (or earlier) than a double full bee or a plain full bee, but not quite as good (or as early) as the crown or double crown marking. This combination of two different trademarks normally occurred only during this brief change over period and has not happened since, to my knowledge. Not all models can be found with this combination marking, and it is good to have an example of this in your collection.

EXAMPLE: ❶ $800—1000 ❷ $600—700 } 700—800

A "double crown" trademark—a term used to describe the Goebel Company trademark found on some M.I. Hummel figurines, both incised as well as stamped, are usually very nice examples, but will not usually add greatly to their value. This is compensated for in the high side of the price bracket.

The Collection

Here is the revised and fully-authorized documentation of the complete collection of "M.I. Hummel" figurines, plates, plaques and all other art objects. This is the most definitive listing and photographic collection ever assembled. This list, compiled from the W. Goebel production journal in Rödental, West Germany, constitutes a record of all "M.I. Hummel" figurines. Identification numbers run in ascending order from 1 to 2248. English names of the figurines, as well as their sizes, notes, and most models, will be found in the special annotated listing.

All sizes are approximate and depend upon exact method of measurement. Minor variations occur frequently and therefore should not be considered significant.

"M.I. Hummel" figurine identification numbers and their corresponding figurines are divided into eight distinct categories:

Open Edition (OE): Pieces currently in W. Goebel's production program.

Closed Edition (CE): Pieces formerly in W. Goebel production program but no longer produced. Also, models that are still being produced, but have a trademark that is no longer used, are shown as (CE) Closed Editions.

Open Number (ON): An identification number, which in W. Goebel's numerical identification system has not yet been used, but which may be used to identify new "M.I. Hummel" figurines as they are released in the future.

Closed Number (CN): An identification number in W. Goebel's numerical identification system that was used to identify a design or sample models for possible production, but then for various reasons never authorized for release.

Possible Future Edition (PFE): Pieces that have been designed and approved for production and possible release in future years.

Temporarily Withdrawn (TW): Pieces that have been suspended or withdrawn from Goebel's current production program, but may be reinstated and produced at some future date.

Exclusive Edition (EE): Pieces that are originally sold only to members of the M.I. Hummel Club.

PREVIEW EDITION (PE): Figurines with an M.I. Hummel Club backstamp offered exclusively to members for a special preview period. After its first two years of production, it may become an open edition (OE) available to the general public, bearing a regular Goebel backstamp only. (This term is no longer used.)

Many collectors are interested in the trademarks that were used on "M.I. HUMMEL" figurines; therefore, we have used the numbering system shown below:

MARK		FIRST USED
❶ =	(CROWN)	1935
❷ =	(FULL BEE)	1950
❸ =	(STYLIZED)	1957
❹ =	© by W. Goebel W. Germany (THREE LINE)	1964
❺ =	Goebel (GOEBEL BEE)	1972
❻ =	Goebel W Germany	1979
❼ =	Goebel Germany	1991
❽ =	Goebel (CURRENT)	2000

SOME VARIATIONS AND COMBINATIONS USED IN BETWEEN ABOVE DATES

This numbering system is used to identify each mark that can be found on a particular figurine. There will be some exceptions to this rule. Some early figurines will be found with no trademark or model numbers at all. This fact does not lessen their value to any great extent, but does make it more difficult to determine their age. When figurines vary greatly in size, we will use the "bracket" system, showing the smallest to the largest size, i.e. 5.50" to 6.00". Your measurement may vary depending on what means you use to measure. To properly measure a figurine, you should place it on a flat surface, then stand a ruler beside it.

Place another ruler or straight object horizontally touching the highest point of the figurine and the perpendicular ruler. You will then have an accurate measurement.

Decoration-designations for "M.I. Hummel" figurines

All "M.I. Hummel" figurines are hand-painted according to "M.I. Hummel's" original design. The decoration techniques had to be numbered because the factory uses so many.

The "M.I. Hummel" decor is done in painting method number eleven. A stroke-eleven (/11) is added to the model number following the size indicator in the factory's literature and price lists. It does not, however, appear incised on the base. In this book we only refer to incised numbers.

Decor. No.	Marked	Description
11	/11	all matte-finish colors in rich variety of pastels inspired by rural surroundings
11 blue	/11 blue	madonna with dark blue cloak; rest of figurine in pastels
13	/13	ivory decoration in pastels
6 blue	/6 blue	madonna with pastel blue cloak; rest of figurine in matching pastels
6 red	/6 red	madonna with light red cloak; rest of figurine in matching pastels
83	/83	matte-finish shading on bisque body
H	/H	brown matte decor, very rare—not made after 1955
W	/W	white overglaze

..... SPECIAL NOTE .....

WIn previous price guides we listed trademark 1, 2, 3, 4, 5 and 6 items as Open Editions (OE), which was not quite accurate. We wanted to indicate that a certain model was still being produced, even though the trademark had changed.

With this edition, we show each former trademark as a Closed Edition (CE).The only Open Editions (OE) will be items with trademark eight (TM 8) that are currently in W. Goebel's production program.

Alphabetical Listing

NAME	HUM No.
A Budding Maestro	477
A Fair Measure	345
A Flower For You	2077/B
A Four Leaf Clover	2068/B
A Free Flight	569
A Gentle Glow CH	439
A Heartfelt Gift	856
A Nap	534
A Personal Message	(PFE) 446
A Salute to the U.S.A	2074/A
A Star for You	2222
A Story From Grandma	620
A Sweet Offering	549
Accompanist, The	453
Accordion Ballad	857
Accordion Boy	185
Adoration	23
Adoration with Bird	105
Adoring Children	903
Adventure Bound	347
African Wanderer	2062
Afternoon Nap	836
All Aboard	2044
All Bundled Up	2221
All By Myself	2079/A
All Smiles	498
Alpine Dancer	2108/B
American Spirit	2197
American Wanderer	2061
An Apple a Day	403
An Emergency	(PFE) 436
Angel CH	Page 571
Angel Cloud Font	206
Angel Duet	261
Angel Duet Ceramic Ball Ornament	3016
Angel Duet CH	193
Angel Duet Font	146
Angel Lights CH	241
Angel Looking Left Font	91A
Angel Looking Right Font	91B
Angel Serenade	214D, 260E, 718
Angel Serenade Ceramic Ball Ornament	3017
Angel Serenade with Lamb	83
Angel Shrine Font	147
Angel Sitting with Bird Font	167
Angel with Accordion	238B
Angel with Accordion CH	39
Angel with Bird Font	22
Angel with Children At Feet	108
Angel with Cross and Bird Font	354C
Angel with Lantern Font	354A
Angel with Lute	238A
Angel with Lute CH	38
Angel with Triangle	2135/K
Angel with Trumpet	238C
Angel with Trumpet CH	40
Angel with Trumpet Font	354B
Angel, Joyous News w/Lute Font	241
Angel, Joyous News w/Trumpet Font	242
Angela	2230/L
Angelic Conductor	2096/A
Angelic Drummer	2135/A
Angelic Guide Ornament	571
Angelic Sleep CH	25
Angelic Song	144
Angelic Trumpeter	2135/H
Angler, The	566
Apple Tree Boy	142
Apple Tree Girl	141
April Showers	610
Arithmetic Lesson	(PFE) 303
Art Critic	318
Artist, The	304
Asian Wanderer	2063
At Grandpa's	621
At Play	632
At the Fence	(PFE) 324
Attached Pots and Bowls	Pages 546-547
Auf Wiedersehen	153 & Page 551
Australian Wanderer	2064
Autumn Harvest	355
Autumn Time	2200
Baker	128
Baker's Delight (2004)	2162
Baking Day	330
Baking Time	2116/B
Band Leader	129
Barnyard Hero	195
Bashful Serenade	2133
Bashful!	377
Basket Of Gifts	618
Bath Time	412
Be Mine	2050/B
Be Patient	197

NAME	HUM No.
Bee Hopeful	2107/A
Begging His Share	9
Begging His Share (before 1964) CH	9
Behave	339
Being Punished, Wall Plaque	(PFE) 326
Bells On High	2096/V
Benevolent Birdfeeder, The	2187
Berlin Airlift Memorial	Page 551
Best Buddies	(PFE) 794
Best Friends	731
Best Wishes	540
Big Announcement	2153
Big Housecleaning	363
Bird Duet	169
Bird Watcher	300
Birthday Cake CH	338
Birthday Candle CH	440
Birthday Present	341
Birthday Serenade	218
Blessed Child	78
Blessed Event	333
Blessed Mother	(PFE) 372
Blossom Time	608
Book Worm	3 & 8
Boots	143
Botanist Vase, The	638
Botanist, The	351
Boy with Accordion	390
Boy with Horse	239C
Boy with Horse CH	117
Boy with Toothache	217
Boy's Best Friend, A	2101/B
Brave Soldier	802
Brave Voyager	(PFE) 796
Brother	95
Builder, The	305
Bumblebee Blossom	2068/A
Bumblebee Friend	837
Bunny's Mother	547
Bust of Sr. M.I. Hummel	Page 538
Busy Student	367
Calendars	Pages 557-570
Call to Glory	739
Call to Worship, clock	441
Camels, Goebel	Page 540
Camera Ready	2132
Can I Play? (2006)	2097
Can't Catch Me	2228
Candlelight CH	192
Carefree	490

NAME	HUM No.
Carnival	328
Carnival Fun	239/E
Catch of the Day	2031
Cat's Meow, The	2136
Celebrate with Song	790
Celebration of Freedom	2154/B
Celestial Dreamer	2135/E
Celestial Drummer	2096/C
Celestial Musician	188
Celestial Musician Ceramic Ball Ornament	3012
Celestial Musician Ornament	646
Celestial Reveille	2096/G
Celestial Strings	2096/F
Chapel Time, clock	442
Checkpoint Charlie	Page 551
Cheeky Fellow	554
Chick Girl	57
Chicken-Licken	385
Child Jesus Font	26
Child with Flowers Font	36
Children's Prayer	(PFE) 448
Chimney Sweep	12
Christ Child	18
Christmas Angel	301
Christmas Angel Ball Ornament	3015
Christmas By Candlelight	838
Christmas Carol	2073/B
Christmas Delivery	2014
Christmas Delivery Puff Ornament	3023
Christmas Gift	2074
Christmas Song	343
Christmas Song Ball Ornament	3018
Christmas Song Ornament	645
Christmas Surprise	536
Christmas Time	2106
Christmas Wish	2094
Cinderella	337
Circus Act	2166
Clear As A Bell	2181
Close Harmony	336
Coffee Break	409
Come Back Soon	545
Come On	(PFE) 468
Comfort And Care	2075
Companions	(PFE) 370
Concentration	(PFE) 302
Confidentially	314
Congratulations	17
Copies From Around the World	Pages 544-545
Coquettes	179

NAME	HUM No.	NAME	HUM No.
Count Me In	2084/B	Feathered Friends	344
Country Devotion	(PFE) 572	Feeding Time	199
Country Song, clock	(PFE) 443	Festival Harm/Flute Ornament	648
Country Suitor	760	Festival Harm/Mandolin Ornament	647
Cowboy Corral	2021	Festival Harmony (Flute)	173
Crossroads	331	Festival Harmony (Mandolin)	172
Crystal Figurines	Page 550	Festival Harmony Flute Ball Orn	3019
Cuddles	2049/A	Festival Harmony Mandolin Ball Orn	3020
Culprits	56A	Final Issues	xxviii
Cymbals of Joy	2096/U	Final Sculpt, The	2180
Daddy's Girls	371	Fire Fighter	2030
Daisies Don't Tell	380	First Bloom	2077/A
Darling Duckling	2019	First Flight	2173
Daydreamer Plaque	827	First Love	765
Dearly Beloved	2003	First Mate	2148/B
Declaration of Freedom	2114	First Snow	2035
Delicious	435	First Solo	2182
Divine Drummer	2096/M	First Violin	2184
Do I Dare	411	Fishing Adventure	885
Do You Love It!	2217/A	Flag Day	2077/B
Doctor	127	Florist	349
Doll Bath	319	Flower For You, A	2077/B
Doll Mother	67	Flower Girl	548
Dolls	Pages 573-580	Flower Madonna	10
Don't Be Shy	(PFE) 379	Flower Vendor	381
DoReMi	(PFE) 466	Flowers for Mother	2193
Dove Font	(PFE) 393	Flute Song	(PFE) 407
Duet	130	Flying Angel	366
Duty Calls	2194	Flying Full Dee Display	Page 552
Easter Greetings	378	Flying High Ornament	452
Easter Time	384	Follow the Leader	369
Easter's Coming	2027	Fond Goodbye	660
Echoes of Joy	642	For Father	87
Echoes of Joy Ornament	597	For Keeps	630
Elephant, Goebel	Page 541	For Me	2067/B
European Wanderer	2060	For Mother	257
Evening Prayer	495	For My Sweetheart	(PFE) 732
Eventide	99	Forest Shrine	183
Expressions of Youth	Page 570	Forever Yours	793
Extra! Extra!	2113	Forget Me Not	362
Factory Workers Plate	Page 539	Forty Winks	401
Faience Pieces	Pages 548-549	Four Seasons Music Boxes	Page 553
Fancy Footwork	2211	Free Flight, A	569
Fanfare	1999	Free Spirit	564
Farewell	65	Freedom Day	2069/A
Farm Boy	66	Fresh Blossoms	624
Farm Days (2003)	2165	Friend or Foe Doll	514
Fascination	649	Friend or Foe?	434
Father Christmas (Ruprecht)	473	Friendly Feeding	2231
Favorite Pet	361	Friends	136
Favorite Pet Easter Egg	858/A	Friends Together	662

NAME	HUM No.
Frisky Friends	2008
From Me to You	629
From My Garden	795
From The Heart	761
From the Pumpkin Patch	2175
Full Speed Ahead	2157
Garden Gift	619
Garden Splendor	835
Garden Treasures	727
Gay Adventure	356
Gentle Care	(PFE) 474
Gentle Fellowship	628
Gift from a Friend	485
Gifts of Love	909
Girl with Accordion	259
Girl with Doll	239B
Girl with Fir Tree	239D
Girl with Fir Tree CH	116
Girl with Mandolin	254
Girl with Nosegay	239A
Girl with Nosegay CH	115
Girl with Sheet of Music	389
Girl with Trumpet	391
Girl's Best Friend, A	2101/A
Globe Trotter	79
Going Home	383
Going to Grandma's	52
Gone A-Wandering	908
Good Friends	182
Good Hunting	307
Good Luck Charm	2034
Good Luck!	(PFE) 419
Good News	539
Good Night	260D, 214C
Good Shepherd	42
Good Shepherd Font	35
Good Tidings	2026
Goose Girl	47
Goose Girl Anniversary Clock	750
Goose Girl Doll	517
Goose Girl Vase	625
Goose Girl Wooden Case Clock	Page 421
Gotcha!	2215
Grandma's Girl	561
Grandpa's Boy	562
Guardian Angel Font	248
Guardian Angel Font	29
Guardian, The	455
Guiding Angel	357
Halt!	2039
Happiness	86

NAME	HUM No.
Happy Birthday	176
Happy Days	150
Happy Pastime	69
Happy Returns	(PFE) 763
Happy Traveller	109
Harmonica Player	(PFE) 614
Harmony in Four Parts	471
Harvest Time	2190
Hear Ye, Hear Ye	15
Heart and Soul	559
Heart of Hope	2240
Heart's Delight	698
Heaven and Nature Sing	2096/Q
Heavenly Angel	21
Heavenly Angel Ball Ornament	3021
Heavenly Angel Font	207
Heavenly Angel Tree Topper	755
Heavenly Angels	718 & 214 D/0
Heavenly Harmony	2096/L
Heavenly Harpist	2096/B
Heavenly Horn Player	2096/J
Heavenly Hubbub	2096/P
Heavenly Lullaby	262
Heavenly Prayer	815
Heavenly Protection	88
Heavenly Rhapsody	2096/E
Heavenly Song CH	113
Heavenly Time	2096/T
Hello	124
Hello World	429
Helping Mother	(PFE) 325
Herald Angels CH	37
Herald on High Ornament	623
Here's My Heart	766
Hitting the High Note	846
Holiday Dreaming Collector Set	2241
Holiday Fun	2204
Holy Child	70
Holy Cross (Cross w/Doves) Font	77
Holy Family Font	246
Holy Offering	718/C
Home from Market	198
Homecoming	2216
Homeward Bound	334
Honey Lover	312
Honor Student	2087/B
Hope	2203
Horse Trainer	423
Horse, Goebel	Page 541
Hosanna	480
Hummele	365

NAME	HUM No.	NAME	HUM No.
Hummel-Hummel	Page 586	Letter To Santa Claus	340
Hummelnest	822	Light of Hope	2233
Hush-A-Bye	718/B	Light The Way	715
I Brought You A Gift	479	Light The Way Ornament	599
I Didn't Do It	626	Light Up the Night Ornament	622
I Wonder	486	Little Architect, The	410
I'll Protect Him	483	Little Band (on base)	392
I'm Carefree	633	Little Band CH	388
I'm Here	478	Little Bookkeeper	306
I'm Sorry	(PFE) 543	Little Cellist	89
In "D" Major	430	Little Drummer	240
In The Kitchen	2038	Little Farm Hand	2085
In The Meadow	459	Little Fiddler	2
In The Orchard	(PFE) 461	Little Fiddler	4
In Tune	414	Little Fiddler Doll	513
Infant of Krumbad	78	Little Fisherman	803
International Hummel		LIttle Flag Bearer	239/E
Figurines	Pages 429-434	Little Gabriel	32
Is It Raining?	420	Little Gardener	74
It's Cold	421	Little Goat Herder	200
Join in Song	718/D	Little Guardian	145
Joyful	53	Little Helper	73
Joyful Noise	643	Little Hiker	16
Joyful Noise Ornament	598	Little Knitter	2107/B
Joyful Recital	2096/K	Little Landscaper	2011
Joyous News	27	Little Maestro	826
Joyous News CH	27	Little Miss Mail Carrier	2120
Jubilee	416	Little Nurse	376
Jump For Joy	2084/A	Little Pair	449
Just Dozing	451	Little Patriot	2048
Just Fishing	373	Little Pharmacist	322
Just Resting	112	Little Scholar	80
Keeping Time	2183	Little Scholar Doll	522
Kindergartner, The	467	Little Shopper	96
Kiss Me	311	Little Sweeper	171
Kiss Me Doll	515	Little Tailor	308
Kitty Kisses	2033	Little Thrifty Bank	118
Knit One, Purl One	432	Little Toddler	(PFE) 805
Knitting Lesson	256	Little Tooter	214H, 260K
Lamplight Caroler	847	Little Troubadour	558
Land in Sight	530	Little Velma	219
Lantern Fun	2115	Little Visitor	563
Latest News	184	Little Visitor Plaque	722
Lazybones	612	Littlest Angel	365
Let It Shine	718/A	Look What I Made!	2217/B
Let It Snow	2036	Looking Around	2089/A
Let's Be Friends	2232	Lost Sheep	68
Let's Play	2051/B	Lost Stocking	374
Let's Sing	110	Love from Above Ornament	481
Let's Take to the Ice	2143/B	Love in Bloom	699
Let's Tell the World	487	Love Petals	804

NAME	HUM No.	NAME	HUM No.
Love's Bounty	751	My Toy Train	2078
Loving Wishes	573	My Wish is Small	463
Lucky Boy	335	Nap, A	534
Lucky Charmer	2071	Nature's Gift	729
Lucky Fellow	560	Night Before Christmas	2234
Lucky Friend	2235	Nimble Fingers	758
Lullaby CH	24	No Thank You	535
Lute Song	(PFE) 368	Not for You!	317
Madonna and Child Font	243	Nutcracker Sweet	2130
Madonna Holding Child	151	Off to School	(PFE) 329
Madonna with Halo	45	Old Man Reading Newspaper	181
Madonna without Halo	46	Old Man Walking to Market	191
Maid to Order	2091	Old Woman Knitting	189
Mail Is Here, The	226	Old Woman Walking to Market	190
Make a Wish	475	On Holiday	350
Make Me Pretty	2092	On Our Way	472
Making New Friends	2002	On Parade	720 & Page 572
March Winds	43	On Secret Path	386
Max and Moritz	123	Once Upon A Time	2051/A
May Dance	791	One Coat or Two	2040
Me and My Shadow	2164	One Cup of Sugar	2116/A
Meditation	13	One For You, One For Me	482
Mel Items	Pages 542-543	One Plus One	556
Melodic Mandolin	2135/D	One, Two, Three	555
Melody - Conductor	2198	Ooh, My Tooth	533
Merry Wanderer	7 & 11	Out of Danger	56B
Merry Wanderer Doll	516	Over The Horizon	828
Merry Wandress	2059	Parade of Lights	616
Messages of Love	2050/A	Patade of States	2153
Millennium Bliss	2096/H	Patriotic Spirit	2154/A
Millennium Madonna	855	Pay Attention	426
Miniature Annual Plates	971-995	Peace on Earth Ornament	484
Miniature Annual Plates in Frame	Page 589	Peaceful Blessing	814
Miniatures	Pages 581-585	Peaceful Offering	2066
Mischief Maker	342	Peaceful Sounds	718/E
Miss Beehaving	2105	Pen Pals	Page 554
Miss Patriot	2077/A	Photographer, The	178
Mission Madonna	(PFE) 764	Picture Perfect	2100
Mixing the Cake	2167	Pigtails	2052
Monkey Business	2069/A	Pixie	768
Morning Call	2227	Playful Blessing	658
Morning Concert	447	Playful Pals	2053
Morning Stroll	375	Playing Around	2088/A
Mother's Darling	175	Playmates	58
Mother's Helper	133	Pleasant Journey	406
Mountaineer	315	Pleasant Moment	(PFE) 425
Musik, Please	2108/A	Pledge to America	2068/B
My Best Friend	2049/B	Pocket Full of Posies	2174/B
My Favorite Pony	2019	Poet, The	397
My Heart's Desire	2102/A	Postman	119
My Little Lamb	661	Practice Makes Perfect, Boy	771

NAME	HUM No.
Practice Makes Perfect, Girl	2223
Prayer Before Battle	20
Precious Pianist	2135/C
Pretty As A Picture	(PFE) 667
Pretty Performer	2171/A
Pretty Please	489
Pretty Posey	2174/A
Pretzel Boy	2093
Pretzel Girl	2004
Private Conversation	615
Proclamation	2095
Professor, The	320
Proud Moments	800
Puppet Love	2209/A
Puppet Pal	2209/B
Puppet Prince	2103/B
Puppet Princess	2103/A
Puppy Love	1
Puppy Pal	2229
Puppy Pause	2032
Rainy Day Bouquet	(PFE) 797
Rare Variations	Pages 555-556
Rejoice	2135/G
Relaxation	316
Retired Figurines	Page xxviii
Retreat to Safety	201
Ride into Christmas	396
Ride Into Christmas Doll	519
Ride Into Christmas Puff Ornament	3022
Riding Lesson	2020
Ring Around the Rosie	348
Ring In The Season	2073/A
Rock-A-Bye	574
Rolling Around	2088/B
Roses Are Red	762
Run-A-Way, The	327
Ruprecht	473
Sad Song	404
Saint George	55
Saint Nicholas' Day	2012
Scamp	553
School Boy	82
School Boys	170
School Days	2220
School Girl	81
School Girl Doll	521
School Girls	177
School's Out	538
Scooter Time	2070
Season's Best	2143/A
Secret Admirer	2102/B
Sensitive Hunter	6
Seraphim Soprano	2096/R
Serenade	85
Serenade of Songs	2171/B
Seventieth Anniversary Collection	Page 580
Shall We Dance	2177
Sharpest Student	2087/A
She Loves Me, She Loves Me Not!	174
Shepherd Boy	395
Shepherd's Apprentice	2226
Shepherd's Boy	64
Shining Light	358
Signs of Spring	203
Silent Night CH	54
Silent Night with Black Child CH	31
Silent Vigil	(PFE) 723
Sing Along	433
Sing With Me	405
Singing Lesson	63
Singing Lesson (without base)	41
Sister	98
Skate In Stride	2058/B
Skating Lesson	2058/A
Skier	59
Sleep Tight	424
Sleep, Little One, Sleep	(PFE) 456
Sleigh Ride	2236
Smart Little Sister, The	346
Smiling Through	408
Soap Box Derby (2002)	2121
Solder Boy Plaque	726
Soldier Boy	332 & Page 531
Soloist	135
Song of Praise	454
Sound the Trumpet	457
Sounds of Joy	2135/F
Sounds of the Mandolin	438
Special Delivery	2248
Spirit of Liberty	2049/A
Spirited Saxophonist	2135/J
Spring Bouquet	(PFE) 398
Spring Cheer	72
Spring Dance	353
Spring Sowing	2086
Springtime Friends	2218
St. Nicholas' Day	2012
Standing Madonna w/child	247
Star Gazer	132
Star Gazer (wall plaque)	237
Star Light, Star Bright	2037
Starting Young	(PFE) 469

NAME	HUM No.
Steadfast Soprano	848
Stitch in Time	255
Stormy Weather	71
Storybook Time	458
Street Singer	131
Strike Up the Band	668
String Symphony	2096/D
Strolling Along	5
Strum Along	557
Summer Adventure	2124
Summertime Surprise	428
Sunday Stroll	2237
Sunflower Boy	2219
Sunflower Friends	2104
Sunflower Girl	2195
Sunflowers, My Love?	902
Sunny Morning	313
Sunny Song	(PFE) 611
Sunshower	634
Supreme Protection	364
Surprise	94
Surprise Visit	2013
Sweet As Can Be	541
Sweet Freedom	2067/A
Sweet Greetings	352
Sweet Music	186
Sweet Treats	2067/A
Teacher's Pet	2125
Teddy Tales	2155
Telling Her Secret	196
Tender Love	2007
Thanksgiving Prayer	641
Thanksgiving Prayer Ornament	596
The Guardian	455
The Little Pair	449
The Surprise	431
Thoughtful	415
Time Out	(PFE) 470
Timid Little Sister	394
Tit for Tat	462
To Keep You Warm	759
To Market	49
Today's Recipe	2168
Togetherness	753
Too Shy To Sing	845
Toyland Express	2018
Traveling Trio	787
Trio of Wishes	721
Triumphant Trumpeter	2096/S
Troublemaker (2005)	2205
True Friendship	402
Trumpet Boy	97
Tuba Player	437
Tuneful Angel	359
Tuneful Trio, A	757
Two Hands, One Treat	493
Umbrella Boy	152A
Umbrella Boy Doll	518
Umbrella Girl	152B
Umbrella Girl Doll	512
Vagabond	(PFE) 799
Valentine Gift	387
Valentine Gift Doll	524
Valentine Gift Plaque	717
Valentine Joy	399
Village Boy	51
Visiting An invalid	382
Volunteers	50
Wait For Me	2148/A
Waiter	154
Waiting Around	2089/B
Wanderers, The	Page 459
Wash Day	321
Watchful Angel	194
Wayside Devotion	28
Wayside Harmony	111
We Come In Peace	754
We Congratulate	214/E & 260F
We Congratulate (with Base)	220
We Wish You the Best	600
Weary Wanderer	204
Well Done!	(PFE) 400
Welcome Spring	635
What A Smile	2214
What Now?	422
What's New?	418
What's That?	488
What's Up	(PFE) 613
When I Grow Up	2157
Where Are You?	427
Where Did You Get That?	(PFE) 417
Where Shall I Go?	(PFE) 465
Where To Go?	829
Which Hand?	258
Whistler's Duet	413
White Angel Font	75
Whitsuntide	163
Will It Sting?	450
Will You Be Mine?	573
Windy Wishes	2079/B
Winter Adventure	2028
Winter Days	2072

NAME	HUM No.
Winter Sleigh Ride	2047
Winter Song, A	476
Winter Time Duet	2134
Winter's Here	2185
Wishes Come True	2025/A
With Loving Greetings	309
Wonder of Christmas	2015
Wooden Dealer Plaque	Page 552
Worldwide Wanderers	2000
Worship	84
Worship Font	164
Young Scholar	(PFE) 464
Zealous Xylophonist	2096/N

AMBASSADORS OF FREEDOM SERIES
Brave Soldier	802
Declaration of Freedom	2114
Duty Calls	2194
Homecoming	2216
Little Patriot	2048

ANGEL ORCHESTRA
Angel with Triangle	2135/K
Angelic Conductor	2096/A
Angelic Drummer	2135/A
Angelic Trumpeter	2135/H
Bells On High	2096/V
Celestial Dreamer	2135/E
Celestial Drummer	2096/C
Celestial Reveille	2096/G
Celestial Strings	2096/F
Cymbals of Joy	2096/U
Divine Drummer	2096/M
Heaven and Nature Sing	2096/Q
Heavenly Harmony	2096/L
Heavenly Harpist	2096/B
Heavenly Horn Player	2096/J
Heavenly Hubbub	2096/P
Heavenly Rhapsody	2096/E
Heavenly Time	2096/T
Joyful Recital	2096/K
Melodic Mandolin	2135/D
Millennium Bliss	2096/H
Precious Pianist	2135/C
Rejoice	2135/G
Seraphim Soprano	2096/R
Sounds of Joy	2135/F
Spirited Saxophonist	2135/J
String Symphony	2096/D
Triumphant Trumpeter	2096/S
Zealous Xylophonist	2096/N

NAME	HUM No.

ANGELS OF CHRISTMAS ORNAMENT SERIES
Angel on Cloud	585
Angel with Lute	580
Angel with Trumpet	586
Celestial Musician	578 & 578 FD
Festival Harmony w/Flute	577 & 577 FD
Festival Harmony w/Mandolin	576 & 576 FD
Gentle Song	582
Heavenly Angel	575 & 575 FD
Prayer of Thanks	581
Song of Praise	579

ANIMAL FRIENDS COLLECTION
Be Patient	197 4/0
Bunny's Mother	547
Can't Catch Me	2228
Friendly Feeding	2231
Friends	136 4/0
Let's Be Friends	2232
Morning Call	2227
My Little Lamb	661
Puppy Pal	2229
Shepherd's Apprentice	2226
Springtime Friends	2218

ANNIVERSARY PLATES
1975, Stormy Weather	280
1980, Spring Dance	281
1985, Auf Wiedersehen	282

ANNUAL ANGEL
Millennium Bliss	(2000)	2096/H
Joyful Recital	(2001)	2096/K
Cymbals of Joy	(2002)	2096/U
Rejoice	(2003)	2135/G
Angelic Trumpeter	(2004)	2135/H
Spirited Saxophonist	(2005)	2135/J
Angel with Triangle	(2006)	2135/K

ANNUAL BELLS
Annual Bell 1978, Let's Sing	700
Annual Bell 1979, Farewell	701
Annual Bell 1980, Thoughtful	702
Annual Bell 1981, In Tune	703
Annual Bell 1982, She Loves Me	704
Annual Bell 1983, Knit One	705
Annual Bell 1984, Mountaineer	706
Annual Bell 1985, Sweet Song	707
Annual Bell 1986, Sing Along	708
Annual Bell 1987, With Loving Greetings	709
Annual Bell 1988, Busy Student	710

NAME	HUM No.

Annual Bell 1989, Latest News 711
Annual Bell 1990, What's New?.............712
Annual Bell 1991, Favorite Pet 713
Annual Bell 1992, Whistler's Duet (FE) 714
Anniversary Bell 730

ANNUAL FIGURAL CHRISTMAS PLATES
1995-Festival Harmony/Flute 693
1996-Christmas Song.............................692
1997-Thanksgiving Prayer 694
1998-Echoes of Joy 695
1999-Joyful Noise.....................................696
2000-Light The Way 697

ANNUAL MINIATURE ORNAMENTS
1993-Celestial Musician 646
1994-Festival Harm/Mandolin..................647
1995-Festival Harm/Flute 648
1996-Christmas Song.............................645
1997-Thanksgiving Prayer 596
1998-Echoes of Joy 597
1999-Joyful Noise....................................598
2000-Light The Way 599

ANNUAL ORNAMENTS
1988-Flying High.......................................452
1989-Love from Above 481
1990-Peace on Earth 484
1991-Angelic Guide 571
1992-Light Up the Night 622
1993-Herald on High 623

ANNUAL PLATES
Annual Plate 1971, Heavenly Angel 264
Annual Plate 1972, Hear Ye, Hear Ye 265
Annual Plate 1973, Globe Trotter 266
Annual Plate 1974, Goose Girl 267
Annual Plate 1975, Ride into Christmas 268
Annual Plate 1976, Apple Tree Girl 269
Annual Plate 1977, Apple Tree Boy........270
Annual Plate 1978, Happy Pastime 271
Annual Plate 1979, Singing Lesson........272
Annual Plate 1980, School Girl 273
Annual Plate 1981, Umbrella Boy 274
Annual Plate 1982, Umbrella Girl 275
Annual Plate 1983, Postman 276
Annual Plate 1984, Little Helper 277
Annual Plate 1985, Chick Girl 278
Annual Plate 1986, Playmates................279
Annual Plate 1987, Feeding Time 283

NAME	HUM No.

Annual Plate 1988, Little Goat Herder ..284
Annual Plate 1989, Farm Boy 285
Annual Plate 1990, Shepherd's Boy 286
Annual Plate 1991, Just Resting 287
Annual Plate 1992, Wayside Harmony ..288
Annual Plate 1993, Doll Bath 289
Annual Plate 1994, Doctor 290
Annual Plate 1995, Come Back Soon (FE)....291
Miniature Annual Plates 971-995
Millennium Plate 2000, Star Gazer 920
Annual Plate 2000, Garden Splendor 921
Annual Plate 2001, Afternoon Nap 922
Annual Plate 2002, Bumblebee Friend ..923
Annual Plate 2003, The Florist 924
Annual Plate 2004, Garden Gift (FE)......925

ARS-AG CHRISTMAS PLATES
1987 Celestial Musician ....Page 553
1988 Angel Duet ....Page 553
1989 Guiding Light ....Page 553
1990 Tender Watch.......................Page 553

ASH TRAYS
Boy with Bird...166
Happy Pastime 62
Joyful 33
Joyful (without rest for cigarette) 216
Let's Sing 114
Prayer Before Battle 19
Singing Lesson 34

BAS RELIEF CHRISTMAS ORNAMENTS
Christmas Delivery 2110/A
Christmas Song....................................879/A
Cymbals of Joy ....(2002) 2098/C
Dearly Beloved 2163/A
Hear Ye, Hear Ye 880/A
Heavenly Angel 876/A
Joyful Recital ....(2001) 2098/B
Making New Friends 2111/A
Millennium Bliss ....(2000) 2098/A
Rejoice ....(2003) 2098/D
Ride Into Christmas...............................877/A
Ring In The Season 2129/A
Saint Nicholas Day 2099/A
Sleep Tight 878/A
Guardian, The 881/A

BOOKENDS
Apple Tree Girl & Boy ....252A & B
Book Worm Boy & Girl ....14A & B

NAME	HUM No.	NAME	HUM No.
Doll Mother & Prayer Before Battle	76A & B	It's Cold	735
Eventide & Adoration (w/out shrine)	90A & B	Valentine Gift	738
Farm Boy & Goose Girl	60A & B	Valentine Joy	737

Good Friends & She Loves Me,
    She Loves Me Not! ....251A & B
Joyful and Let's Sing 120
Little Goat Herder & Feeding Time ..250A & B
Playmates & Chick Girl ....61A & B
Puppy Love and Serenade with Dog 122
Wayside Harmony & Just Resting 121

CENTURY COLLECTION
1986 Chapel Time, Clock 442
1987 Pleasant Journey 406
1988 Call To Worship, Clock 441
1989 Harmony In Four Parts 471
1990 Let's Tell The World 487
1991 We Wish You the Best 600
1992 On Our Way 472
1993 Welcome Spring 635
1994 Rock-A-Bye 574
1995 Strike Up the Band 668
1996 Love's Bounty 751
1997 Fond Goodbye.................................660
1998 Here's My Heart 766
1999 Fanfare 1999

CALENDARS
Hello (Perpetual) 788A
Sister (Perpetual) 788B
Calendars (Annual, paper)....Pages 557-570

CENTURY COLLECTION MINI PLATES
Call To Worship 888
Chapel Time 886
Fanfare 899
Fond Goodbye 897
Harmony in Four Parts 889
Here's My Heart 898
Let's Tell The World 890
Love's Bounty 896
On Our Way 892
Pleasant Journey 887
Rock-A-Bye..894
Strike Up The Band 895
We Wish You The Best 891
Welcome Spring 893

CANDLE HOLDERS
A Gentle Glow 439
Angel ....Page 571
Angel Duet 193
Angel Lights 241
Angel with Accordion 39
Angel with Lute 38
Angel with Trumpet...................................40
Angelic Sleep 25
Begging His Share (before 1964) 9
Birthday Cake 338
Birthday Candle 440
Boy with Horse 117
Candlelight 192
Girl with Fir Tree 116
Girl with Nosegay 115
Heavenly Song 113
Herald Angels 37
Joyous News 27/1
Little Band...388
Lullaby..24
Silent Night 54
Silent Night with Black Child 31

CHRISTMAS BELLS
1989 Ride Into Christmas........................775
1990 Letter to Santa Claus 776
1991 Hear Ye, Hear Ye 777
1992 Harmony In Four Parts 778
1993 Celestial Musician 779
1994 Festival Harmony Mandolin 780
1995 Festival Harmony Flute 781
1996 Christmas Song 782
1997 Thanksgiving Prayer 783
1998 Echoes of Joy 784
1999 Joyful Noise...................................785
2000 Light The Way 786

CANDY BOXES
Chick Girl III/57
Happy Pastime III/69
Happy Pastime, old style 221
Joyful III/53
Let's Sing III/110
Playmates III/58
Singing Lesson III/63

CELEBRATION PLATE SERIES
Daisies Don't Tell 736

CLOCKS

NAME	HUM No.
Call to Worship 441
Chapel Time 442
Country Song ....(PFE) 443
Goose Girl Anniversary............750
Goose Girl Wooden Case ....Page 421
In Tune Wooden Case 970
Puppy Love Wooden Case 969

DANBURY MINT CANDLEHOLDERS
Apple Tree Boy.........................677
Apple Tree Girl 676
Good Friends 679
She Loves Me, She Loves Me Not 678

FOUR SEASONS PLATE SERIES
1996 Winter Melody 296
1997 Springtime Serenade 297
1998 Summertime Stroll 298
1999 Autumn Glory 299

FRIENDS FOREVER PLATE SERIES
1992 Meditation 292
1993 For Father 293
1994 Sweet Greetings 294
1995 Surprise 295

HEART OF HUMMEL COLLECTION
Fresh Blossoms 624
Gone A-Wandering 908
Lucky Friend 2235
Sunday Stroll..........................2237

HOLY WATER FONTS
Angel Cloud 206
Angel Duet 146
Angel with Bird 22
Angel, Joyous News w/Lute...........241
Angel, Joyous News w/Trumpet..........242
Angel looking left 91A
Angel looking right 91B
Angel Shrine 147
Angel Sitting with Bird 167
Angel with Cross and Bird.............354C
Angel with Lantern 354A
Angel with Trumpet 354B
Child Jesus.............................26
Child with Flowers 36
Dove Font.....................(PFE) 393
Good Shepherd 35
Guardian Angel 29
Guardian Angel.......................248

NAME	HUM No.
Heavenly Angel.......................207
Holy Cross (Cross w/Doves) 77
Holy Family 246
Madonna and Child 243
White Angel............................75
Worship.................................164

HOPE SERIES
Hope ....(2004)..........2203
Light of Hope ....(2005).........2233
Heart of Hope ....(2006)..........2240

HUMMEL/SWAROVSKI COLLABORATION
A Heartfelt Gift ....(2003)............856
Sunflowers, My Love? ......(2004)............902
A Star For You ....(2005).........2222
Special Delivery ....(2006).........2248

INTERNATIONAL HUMMEL FIGURINES
806	Bulgarian Boy	Page 430
807	Bulgarian Girl	Pages 429, 430
808	Bulgarian Boy	Page 430
809	Bulgarian Girl	Pages 429, 431
810/A	Bulgarian Girl	Page 431
810/B	Bulgarian Girl	Page 431
811	Bulgarian Boy	Page 431
812/A	Serbian Girl	Page 431
812/B	Serbian Girl	Page 431
813	Serbian Boy	Page 431
824/A	Swedish Boy	Page 431
824/B	Swedish Boy	Page 431
825/A	Swedish Girl	Page 432
825/B	Swedish Girl	Page 432
831	Slovak Boy	Page 432
832/A	Slovak Girl	Page 429
832/B	Slovak Girl	Page 432
833	Slovak Boy	Page 432
834	Slovak Boy	Page 434
841	Czech Boy	Pages 430, 432
842/A	Czech Girl	Page 432
842/B	Czech Girl	Page 432
851	Hungarian Boy	Pages 430, 432
852/A	Hungarian Girl	Page 433
852/B	Hungarian Girl	Page 433
853/A	Hungarian Boy	Page 433
853/B	Hungarian Boy	Page 433
854	Hungarian Girl	Pages 429, 433
904	Serbian Boy	Pages 430, 433, 434
913	Serbian Girl	Page 433
947	Serbian Girl	Page 433
968	Serbian Boy	Page 433

NAME		HUM No.

KINDER CHOIR

Too Shy To Sing	2003-2004	845
First Solo	2003-2004	2182
Clear As A Bell	2004-2005	2181
Hitting the High Note	2004-2005	846
Steadfast Soprano	2005-2006	848
First Violin	2005-2006	2184
Keeping Time	2006-2007	2183
Lamplight Caroler	2006-2007	847
Melody – Conductor	2006-2007	2198

KITCHEN MOLD COLLECTION

A Fair Measure	670
Baker	674
Baking Day	669
For Father	672
Going to Grandma's	673
Happy Birthday	671

LITTLE HOMEMAKERS PLATE SERIES

1988 Little Sweeper	745
1989 Wash Day	746
1990 Stitch In Time	747
1991 Chicken Licken	748

LITTLE MUSIC MAKERS PLATE SERIES

1984 Little Fiddler	744
1985 Serenade	741
1986 Soloist	743
1987 Band Leader	742

M.I. HUMMEL PEN PALS

For Mother	257 5/0
March Winds	43 5/0
One For You, One For Me	482 5/0
Sister	98 5/0
Soloist	135 5/0
Village Boy	51 5/0

M.I.H. CLUB ANNIVERSARY FIGURINES

Flower Girl (5 years)	548
Sunflower Friends (5 years)	2104
Little Pair (10 years)	449
Miss Beehaving (10 years)	2105
Honey Lover (15 years)	312
Behave (20 years)	339
Relaxation (25 years)	316
Forget Me Not (30 years)	362

M.I.H. CLUB ANNUAL EXCLUSIVE EDITIONS

NAME	HUM No.
A Story From Grandma	620
A Sweet Offering	549 3/0
April Showers	610
At Grandpa's	621
At Play	632
Birthday Candle	440
Bust of Sister M.I. Hummel	HU 3
Celebrate with Song	790
Clear As A Bell	2181
Coffee Break	409
Country Suitor	760
Daisies Don't Tell	380
Daisies Don't Tell Plate	736
Extra, Extra – 25th Anniversary	2113
First Love	765
First Mate	2148/B
First Solo	2182
First Violin	2184
For Keeps	630
Forever Yours	793
From Me To You	629
Garden Treasures	727
Gift from a Friend	485
Gifts of Love	909
Hello World	429
Hitting the High Note	846
Honey Lover Pendant	Pages 581, 595
Honor Student	2087/B
Hummele	365
I Brought You A Gift	479
I Didn't Do It	626
I Wonder	486
It's Cold	421
It's Cold Plate	735
Keeping Time	2183
Lamplight Caroler	847
Little Visitor	563
Looking Around	2089/A
Lucky Charmer	2071
Lucky Fellow	560
Melody — Conductor	2198
Merry Wanderer Pendant	Page 595
Merry Wanderer Plaque w/Bumblebee	900
Morning Concert	447
Morning Concert Vignette	Pages 583-584
My Wish Is Small	463
Nature's Gift	729
Picture Perfect	2100
Pigtails	2052
Playful Blessing	658
Playing Around	2088/A

NAME	HUM No.
Puppet Prince	2103/B
Puppet Princess	2103/A
Private Conversation	615
Rolling Around	2088/B
Sad Song	404
Scooter Time	2070
Sharpest Student	2087/A
Smiling Through	408
Smiling Through Plaque	690
Steadfast Soprano	848
Summer Adventure	2124
The Surprise	431
Togetherness	753
Too Shy To Sing	845
Two Hands, One Treat	493
Valentine Gift	387
Valentine Gift Doll	524
Valentine Gift Pendant	Pages 581, 595
Valentine Gift Plaque	717
Valentine Gift Plate	738
Valentine Joy	399
Valentine Joy Plate	737
Wait For Me	2148/A
Waiting Around	2089/B
What Now?	422
What Now Pendant	Pages 581, 595
Will It Sting?	450
Wishes Come True	2025/A

MILLENNIUM COLLECTION

African Wanderer	2062
American Wanderer	2061
Asian Wanderer	2063
Australian Wanderer	2064
European Wanderer	2060
Worldwide Wanderers	2000

MINIATURE BELLS

Mini Bell 1978, Let's Sing	860
Mini Bell 1979, Farewell	861
Mini Bell 1980, Thoughtful	862
Mini Bell 1981, In Tune	863
Mini Bell 1982, She Loves Me	864
Mini Bell 1983, Knit One	865
Mini Bell 1984, Mountaineer	866
Mini Bell 1985, Sweet Song	867
Mini Bell 1986, Sing Along	868
Mini Bell 1987, With Loving Greetings	869
Mini Bell 1988, Busy Student	870
Mini Bell 1989, Latest News	871
Mini Bell 1990, What's New?	872

NAME	HUM No.
Mini Bell 1991, Favorite Pet	873
Mini Bell 1992, Whistler's Duet (FE)	874

MOMENTS IN TIME SERIES

Soap Box Derby (2002)	2121
Farm Days (2003)	2165
Baker's Delight (2004)	2162
Troublemaker (2005)	2205
Can I Play? (2006)	2097

MUSIC BOXES

Blossom Time	IV/608
Boy with Accordion	IV/390
Celestial Dreamer	IV/2135/E
Chick Girl	(Anri) Page 553
Chick Girl	IV/57
Girl with Sheet Music	IV/389
In Tune	(Anri) Page 553
Joyful	IV/53
Little Band	392M
Little Band, Candleholder	388M
Playmates	IV/58
Ride into Christmas	(Anri) Page 553
Singing Lesson	IV/63
Umbrella Girl	(Anri) Page 553

NATIVITY FIGURINES
Small:

Madonna	214 A/M/0
Infant Jesus	214 A/K/0
Joseph	214 B/0
Angel Serenade	214 D/0
Donkey	214 J/0
Ox	214 K/0
Lamb	214 0/0
King Standing	214 L/0
King on One Knee	214 M/0
King on Two Knees	214 N/0
Shepherd Standing	214 F/0
Shepherd Kneeling	214 G/0
Little Tooter	214 H/0
Flying Angel	366/0

Standard:

Madonna	214 A/M
Infant Jesus	214 A/K
Joseph	214 B
Good Night	214 C
Angel Serenade	214 D
We Congratulate	214 E
Shepherd, Standing	214 F
Shepherd, Kneeling	214 G

NAME	HUM No.	NAME	HUM No.
Little Tooter	214 H	Caribbean Collection	820
Donkey	214 J	Child in Bed	137
Ox	214 K	Daydreamer	827
King Standing	214 L	Dearly Beloved Certificate	2179/A
King on One Knee	214 M	Dearly Beloved Framed Picture	2178/A
King on Two Knees	214 N	Early Goebel Plaque	Page 539
Lamb	214 0	Flitting Butterfly	139
Flying Angel	366/I	Guardian, The - Birth Certificate	883/A
Large:		Guardian, The - Framed Picture	882/A
Madonna	260 A	Hummelnest	822
St. Joseph	260 B	Little Fiddler	93
Infant Jesus	260 C	Little Fiddler (Wood Frame)	107
Good Night	260 D	Little Visitor	722
Angel Serenade	260 E	Madonna and Child (in relief)	249
We Congratulate	260 F	Madonna	48
Shepherd, Standing	260 G	Madonna (Metal Frame)	222
Sheep, standing w/lamb	260 H	Mail is Here	140
Shepherd Boy, kneeling	260 J	Merry Christmas	323
Little Tooter	260 K	Merry Wanderer	92
Donkey	260 L	Merry Wanderer (Wood Frame)	106
Ox	260 M	Merry Wanderer (in relief)	263
Moorish King	260 N	M.I. Hummel Display Plaque (redesigned	
King, Standing	260 0	from older model)	187A
King, Kneeling	260 P	M.I. Hummel Store Plaque	
Sheep, Lying	260 R	(in English)	187 & 900
Children's:		M.I. Hummel Store Plaque (Schmid)	210
Mary	2230/A	M.I. Hummel Store Plaque	
Joseph	2230/B	(British Version)	460
Baby Jesus With Straw Manger	2230/C	M.I. Hummel Store Plaque	
Shepherd with Staff	2230/D	(In Dutch)	460
Shepherd with Milkjug	2230/E	M.I. Hummel Store Plaque	
Shepherd with Flute	2230/F	(In English, Oeslau)	211
King Melchior	2230/G	M.I. Hummel Store Plaque	
King Balthazar	2230/H	(in French)	208 & 460
King Gaspar	2230/J	M.I. Hummel Store Plaque	
Angel with Lantern	2230/K	(in German)	205 & 460
Angela	2230/L	M.I. Hummel Store Plaque	
Adoring Children	903	(In Italian)	460
Young Calf	2230/M	M.I. Hummel Store Plaque	
Donkey	2230/N	(In Japanese)	460
Sheep, Laying	2230/O	M.I. Hummel Store Plaque	
Sheep, Standing	2230/P	(In Spanish)	213 & 460
Children's Nativity Stable and Accessories:		M.I. Hummel Store Plaque	
Bridge and Five Trees	2230/S	(In Swedish)	209 & 460
		M.I. Hummel Store Plaque	
PLAQUES		(U.S. Version)	460
Artist	756	Over the Horizon	828
Authorized Retailer	460 & 900	Puppy Love	767
Australian Dealer	Page 590	Quartet	134
Ba-Bee Ring	30A & B	Retreat to Safety	126
Being Punished	(PFE) 326	Searching Angel	310

NAME	HUM No.
Smiling Through Plaque	690
Soldier Boy	726
Standing Boy	168
Star Gazer	237
Swaying Lullaby	165
Tiny Baby in Crib	138
Tuneful Goodnight	180
U.S. Military	Page 572
Vacation Time	125
Valentine Gift	717
Wall picture with sitting Woman and child	156

RETIREMENT MOTIF MINI-PLATES

Puppy Love - 1988	1/T
Strolling Along - 1989	5/T
Signs of Spring - 1990	203/T
Globe Trotter - 1991	79/T
Lost Sheep - 1992	68/T
Farewell - 1993	65/T
Accordion Boy - 1994	185/T
Duet - 1995	130/T
Happy Pastime - 1996	69/T
Mother's Darling - 1997	175/T
Boots - 1998	143/T
Congratulations - 1999	17/T
Carnival - 2000	328/T
Auf Wiedersehen - 2000	153/T
Hello - 2001	124/T
Little Hiker - 2002	16/T
Autumn Harvest - 2002	355/T
Little Fiddler - 2003	4/T

SEVENTIETH ANNIVERSARY COLLECTION

Bookworm Bookend, Boy	14 A
Bookworm Bookend, Girl	14 B
Bust of Sr. M.I. Hummel	HU2
Chimney Sweep	12/I
Hear Ye, Hear Ye	15/0
Latest News - Leipzig Fair	184
Lullaby	24/I
Madonna with Halo	45/III
March Winds	43
Merry Wanderer	11/0
Prayer Before Battle	20
Puppy Love Clock	969
Sensitive Hunter	6/0
Wayside Devotion	28/III

TABLE LAMPS

Apple Tree Boy	230

NAME	HUM No.
Apple Tree Girl	229
Birthday Serenade	231 & 234
Culprits	44A
Eventide	104
Farewell	103
Good Friends	228
Happy Days	232 & 235
Just Resting	II/112 & 225
Old Man Reading Newspaper	202
Out of Danger	44B
She Loves Me, She Loves Me Not	227
Shrine	100
To Market	101 & 223
Volunteers	102
Wayside Harmony	II/111 & 224

TRINKET BOXES

Thoughtful	(round)	684
Bookworm	(round)	685
Dearly Beloved	(heart)	2152/A
Guardian, The	(oval)	884
Pixie	(oval)	997
Scamp	(oval)	996
She Loves Me	(heart)	687
Sweet Greetings	(heart)	686
Umbrella Boy	(round)	688
Umbrella Girl	(round)	689

WALL VASES

Boy and Girl	360A
Boy	360B
Girl	360C

WINTERTIME WONDERS SERIES

All Bundled Up	2221
First Snow	2035 4/0
It's Cold	421 4/0
Let It Snow	2036 4/0
Skier	59 4/0
Sleigh Ride	2236

WONDER OF CHILDHOOD SERIES

Wishes Come True	2000-2001	2025
Scooter Time	2001-2002	2070
Summer Adventure	2002-2003	2124

Permanently Retired
M.I. Hummel Figurines
Final Issue

1988	Puppy Love	HUM 1
1989	Strolling Along	HUM 5
1990	Signs of Spring	HUM 203 2/0–203/1
1991	Globe Trotter	HUM 79 (Final Issue decal)
1992	Lost Sheep	HUM 68 2/0 & 68/0 (Final Issue decal)
1993	Farewell	HUM 65 (Final Issue decal)
1994	Accordion Boy	HUM 185 (Final Issue decal)
1995	Duet	HUM 130 (Final Issue decal)
1996	Happy Pastime	HUM 69 (Final Issue decal)
1997	Mother's Darling	HUM 175 (Final Issue decal)
1998	Boots	HUM 143/0–143/I (Final Issue decal)
1999	Congratulations	HUM 17/0 (Final Issue decal)
2000	Auf Wiedersehen	HUM 153/0–153/I (Final Issue decal)
2000	Carnival	HUM 328 (Final Issue decal)
2001	Favorite Pet	HUM 361 (Final Issue decal)
2001	Hello	HUM 124/0–124/I (Final Issue decal)
2002	Autumn Harvest	HUM 355 (Final Issue decal)
2002	Little Hiker	HUM 16 2/0–16/I (Final Issue decal)
2003	Little Fiddler	HUM 4 (Final Issue decal)
2004	Going To Grandmas	HUM 52/0-52/I (Final Issue decal)
2004	Happiness	HUM 86 (Final Issue decal)
2005	Farm Boy	HUM 66 (Final Issue decal)
2005	Celestial Drummer	HUM 2096/C (Final Issue decal)
2005	Little Helper	HUM 73 (FInal Issue decal)
2005	Small Nativity Set	HUM 214/0 (No Final Issue decal)
2006	Little Gardener	HUM 74 (FInal Issue decal)
2006	Celestial Strings	HUM 2096/F (Final Issue decal)
2006	Little Sweeper	HUM 171 4/0–171/0–171 (Final Issue decal)

Beginning in 1990 the factory initiated the practice of applying a "FINAL ISSUE" (plus the year) backstamp on all permanently retired figurines. The final issue figurines usually have a small gold commemorative medallion attached by string to each figurine being retired.

Beginning in 1991 the factory initiated the practice of applying a "FIRST ISSUE" (plus the year) backstamp on all newly released figurines during the first year of production.

While working on the 8th Edition of the No. 1 Price Guide to M.I. Hummel Figurines, I was given the following history of HUM 78 "Blessed Child," formerly called "Infant of Krumbad." I decided to share it with all of you M.I. Hummel figurine collectors. Cheryl Gorski, of Goebel North America, researched the entire history of this figurine through both the Factory and the Convent of Siessen, including a personal interview with Sister Antje. The results of her study was provided for publication in the 9th edition of the Price Guide. Cheryl states that this is the true and complete history of this special figurine.

Hope you enjoy! Thank you, Cheryl.

Blessed Child (Hum 78) (formerly Infant of Krumbad)

W. Goebel Porzellanfabrik in Roedental, Germany has been creating figurines inspired by the artwork of Fransiscan Sister Maria Innocentia Hummel for more than 60 years. During her lifetime, Sister Maria Innocentia reviewed each figurine inspired by her creative vision. Tody, figurines are sculpted by a Master Sculptor and then approved by the Artistic Board of the Convent of Siessen (to which Sister Hummel belonged). Each authentic M.I. Hummel figurine created by W. Goebel Porzellanfabrik is given a Hum or mold number for identification and cataloguing purposes. The Hum number is consistent throughout the world and is incised on the underside of the base of each figurine. Figurines are also given names; however, these names may differ between markets—such as Europe and North America.

The M.I. Hummel figurine Hum 78, depicting the infant Jesus, was named Christkind in the European market and has never had any other name. Literally translated from German, Christkind means Christ Child. However, in the North American market, the figurine was first named Infant of Krumbad. This name was changed to Blessed Child in 1985 and remains so today.

In order to understand the significance of the Infant of Krumbad name, it is important to become familiar with the relationship between two charitable institutions: the Sanatorium of Krumbad and the Convent of Siessen. A Sanatorium is a convalescent or rehabilitation facility.

The Sanatorium of Krumbad is a center for convalescence and recuperation following long bouts with illness or disease. Located in Krumbach some 60 miles north and east of Siessen, the Sanatorium has been in existence for more than 500 years. (The town was originally called Krumbad but was eventually changed—the facility retains this original name.)

Beginning in 1937, Sister Maria Innocentia had several periods of convalescence at the facility to offset the influence of tuberculosis. She enjoyed the company of the patients, the visitors and the staff at the facility. As she would regain her strength, she would return to the Convent of Siessen. In gratitude for the many kindnesses bestowed upon her during her visits to Krumbad, Sister Maria Innocentia decided to send a gift to the Mother Superior there.

One of the works in production at W. Goebel Porzellanfabrik at the time was the Christkind (Hum 78). Sister Maria Innocentia requested a number of these figurines for her use as personal gifts. Since the factory could not produce as many as she required in a timely manner, plaster figurines were created for her instead. The sometimes still-wet figurines were given to the Sister who then hand-painted the pieces and sent them to friends and institutions as gifts.

One such piece was Sister Maria Innocentia's thank you to the Sanatorium of Krumbad. Being so moved, the sisters of Krumbad treated the very special gift of Sister Maria Innocentia with great reverence. This moving legacy gave birth to the name, Infant of Krumbad, used in North America for many years. Since this story was not well-known to casual M.I. Hummel collectors, the name was changed to Blessed Child as it is more descriptive of the figurine.

UNDERSTANDING THE "M.I. HUMMEL" NUMBERING SYSTEM

An M.I. Hummel figurine with a plain or whole number, (no size designator) indicates that this model was made in one size only. Any figurine that is made in a larger size will have a Roman numeral from /I to /X. The larger the Roman numeral, the greater the size of the figurine.

Figurines smaller than the standard size are designated by Arabic numbers, followed by a slash "/" zero. The general rule is, the larger the Arabic number, the smaller the figurine size. The presence of this zero to the right of the designator indicates that the figurine is smaller than the standard size.

Here are a couple of examples of incised model numbers:

    195 2/0 HUM 195 "Barnyard Hero"   4.00 inches
    195/I   HUM 195 "Barnyard Hero"   5.50 inches

The size designation system can be best demonstrated by this key:

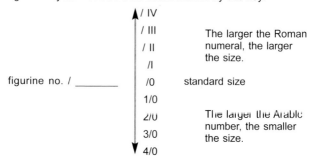

There are exceptions to all rules! This does not guarantee that two figurines of the same model number will be the same height. This variation can be the results of "mold growth" of the old plaster working molds used prior to 1954. It is also possible that a figurine has been restyled slightly and will still have the same model number and size designator. An example would be HUM 10/III "Flower Madonna" which was restyled in 1956 and reduced in size by approximately 1.50 inches, but still retained the same model number. Sometimes in the early years, an Arabic 10/3 was used instead of 10/III or 136/5 instead of 136/V. In some cases an Arabic or Roman numeral will appear to the left of the model number, such as on old lamp bases (II/112) or (2/112) or on candy boxes (III/53). Another example: HUM 153 "Auf Wiedersehen" was made originally in one size only. In the early 1950s a smaller size was created and numbered 153/0 or "standard" size for this model, while the original size became 153/I indicating it was larger than the new "standard" size 153/0.

In understanding the size designation system of "M.I. Hummel" figurines, it is important to remember that the designations apply differently to each specific figurine model, but that generally the larger and smaller sizes of the same model will follow this system.

Rare old style (TM 1)   **(TM 1+1)**   **New style (TM 3)**

HUM 1 — Puppy Love (CE)

First modeled by master sculptor Arthur Moeller in 1935. A very few early models were made with the head tilted at a different angle and without the tie. This old style is considered extremely rare and would command a premium of $4000 to $5000. Always featured with a black hat. In old catalog listed as the "Little Violinist." "Puppy Love" was permanently retired by Goebel in the fall of 1988 and will not be produced again. The original issue price was 35¢ in 1935! Old 1955 price list shows a price of $6.50 while 1988 price list shows a price of $125, the last year it was sold on the primary market. A rare terra cotta "Puppy Love" was found in Florida. It has an incised (TM 1) crown trademark and an incised number "T-I." Value would be $5000 to 10,000 in terra cotta finish. According to old Goebel product book, a sample was produced by Arthur Moeller in 1935 of "Puppy Love" with an attached "pot," similar to HUM 16/I "Little Hiker" with attached "pot." Value $5000 to 10,000 if found. For more information, see: Rare/Unique Sample Variations of "M. I. Hummel" Figurines in back of this book.

☐ FF 15	(Original Number)			$5000—10,000	(Early Sample)
☐ II/1	(With Attached "Pot")			$5000—10,000	(Early Sample)
☐ T-1	(Terra Cotta Material)			$5000—10,000	(Early Sample)
☐ 1	(No Tie-Head tilted right)			$4000—5000	(Early Sample)
☐ 1	5.00 to 5.25"	(CE)	❶	$800—1000	
☐ 1	5.00 to 5.25"	(CE)	❷	$600—700	
☐ 1	5.00 to 5.25"	(CE)	❸	$500—550	
☐ 1	5.00 to 5.25"	(CE)	❹	$400—500	
☐ 1	5.00 to 5.25"	(CE)	❺	$375—400	
☐ 1	5.00 to 5.25"	(CE)	❻	$350—375	

FINAL ISSUE
1988

HUM 2 — Little Fiddler

Also modeled by master sculptor Arthur Moeller in 1935, this figurine differs from the boy in "Puppy Love" in the fact that it always has a brown hat with an orange hat band. There are many size variations and all sizes have now been restyled with the new textured finish. Old name: "Violinist" or "The Wandering Fiddler." Same as HUM 4 except for the color of hat. Sometimes incised 2/3 instead of 2/III. A new miniature size figurine was issued in the fall of 1984 with a suggested retail price of $39 to match a new miniature plate series called the "Little Music Makers"—one each year for four years. This is the first in the series. This miniature size figurine has an incised 1984 copyright date. The large sizes (2/II and 2/III) were (TW) "Temporarily Withdrawn" from production on 31 December 1989, but may be reinstated at some future date. A few sample pieces have been found decorated with bright colors and glossy finish of the "Faience" technique—value would be $5000 to $6000 depending on size and condition. In 1985 Goebel produced a (LE) Limited Edition of 50 pieces of Hum 2/I (7.50") with a gold painted base for a Goebel sponsored contest in Europe celebrating 50 years of M. I. Hummel figurines. It has a special round backstamp: "50 Jahre M. I. Hummel-Figuren 1935–1985"—value would be $1500 to $2000. The miniature size (2 4/0) was (TW) "Temporarily Withdrawn" from the North American market on 31 December 1997, but may be reinstated at some future date.

☐ FF 16	(Original Number)			$5000—10,000 (Early Sample)
☐ 2 4/0	3.00"	(CE)	❻	$125—140
☐ 2 4/0	3.00"	(TW)	❼	$115—120
☐ 2/0	5.75 to 6.50"	(CE)	❶	$750—900
☐ 2/0	5.75 to 6.50"	(CE)	❷	$450—525
☐ 2/0	5.75 to 6.50"	(CE)	❸	$375—400
☐ 2/0	5.75 to 6.50"	(CE)	❹	$350—375
☐ 2/0	5.75 to 6.50"	(CE)	❺	$300—310
☐ 2/0	5.75 to 6.50"	(CE)	❻	$280—300
☐ 2/0	5.75 to 6.50"	(CE)	❼	$270—275
☐ 2/0	5.75 to 6.50"	(OE)	❽	$270
☐ 2/I	7.50"	(CE)	❶	$1100—1500
☐ 2/I	7.50 to 8.00"	(CE)	❷	$650—925
☐ 2/I	7.50 to 8.00"	(CE)	❸	$560—650
☐ 2/I	7.50 to 8.00"	(CE)	❹	$460—550
☐ 2/I	7.50 to 8.00"	(CE)	❺	$420—430
☐ 2/I	7.50 to 8.00"	(CE)	❻	$410—420
☐ 2/I	7.50 to 8.00"	(TW)	❼	$400—410
☐ 2/II	10.75"	(CE)	❶	$2500—3500
☐ 2/II	10.75"	(CE)	❷	$1800—2300
☐ 2/II	10.75"	(CE)	❸	$1500—1600
☐ 2/II	10.75"	(CE)	❹	$1300—1500
☐ 2/II	10.75"	(CE)	❺	$1200—1300
☐ 2/II	10.75"	(TW)	❻	$1100—1200
☐ 2/III	12.25"	(CE)	❶	$3500—4000
☐ 2/III	12.25"	(CE)	❷	$2500—3000
☐ 2/III	12.25"	(CE)	❸	$2000—2300
☐ 2/III	12.25"	(CE)	❹	$1700—1800
☐ 2/III	12.25"	(CE)	❺	$1600—1700
☐ 2/III	12.25"	(CE)	❻	$1550—1600
☐ 2/III	12.25"	(CE)	❼	$1550
☐ 2/III	12.50"	(OE)	❽	$1550

HUM 3 — Book Worm

This figurine was modeled by master sculptor Arthur Moeller in 1935. Old name: "Little Book Worm." Size 3/I has only one flower on page, while sizes 3/II and 3/III have two flowers on page. Sometimes incised 3/2 instead of 3/II and 3/3 instead of 3/III but does not affect the value as Arabic or Roman size indicators were used interchangeably for no basic reason. Same design was used for HUM 8. "Book Worm" was restyled by master sculptor Gerhard Skrobek in 1972 with the new textured finish. Size 3/II has an incised 1972 copyright date. Size 3/III has no incised copyright date at all. The large sizes (3/II and 3/III) were (TW) "Temporarily Withdrawn" from production on 31 December 1989, but may be reinstated at some future date. A few sample pieces have been found decorated with bright colors and glossy finish of the "Faience" technique—value would be $3000–$5000 depending on size and condition. See "Faience" article in back of Price Guide.

3/I

☐ FF 17	(Original Oumber)			$5000—10,000	(Early Sample)
☐ 3/I	5.50"	(CE)	❶	$1000—1200	
☐ 3/I	5.50"	(CE)	❷	$600—750	
☐ 3/I	5.50"	(CE)	❸	$500—525	
☐ 3/I	5.50"	(CE)	❹	$450—500	
☐ 3/I	5.50"	(CE)	❺	$400—425	
☐ 3/I	5.50"	(CE)	❻	$390—400	
☐ 3/I	5.50"	(CE)	❼	$380—390	
☐ 3/I	5.50"	(**OE**)	❽	$380	
☐ 3/II	8.00"	(CE)	❶	$2500—3500	
☐ 3/II	8.00"	(CE)	❷	$1800—2300	
☐ 3/II	8.00"	(CE)	❸	$1500—1600	
☐ 3/II	8.00"	(CE)	❹	$1300—1500	
☐ 3/II	8.00 to 9.00"	(CE)	❺	$1200—1300	
☐ 3/II	8.00 to 9.00"	(**TW**)	❻	$1100—1200	
☐ 3/III	9.00 to 9.50"	(CE)	❶	$3500—4000	
☐ 3/III	9.00 to 9.50"	(CE)	❷	$2300—2800	
☐ 3/III	9.00 to 9.50"	(CE)	❸	$1600—1800	
☐ 3/III	9.00 to 9.50"	(CE)	❹	$1450—1600	
☐ 3/III	9.00 to 10.00"	(CE)	❺	$1350—1450	
☐ 3/III	9.00 to 10.00"	(**TW**)	❻	$1250—1350	

Notice great variations In sizes

HUM 4 — Little Fiddler

Same as HUM 2 except it has a charcoal black hat. Many size variations. Old name: "Violinist" or "The Wandering Fiddler." First modeled by master sculptor Arthur Moeller in 1935 but current production models have been restyled with the new textured finish. One of several figurines that make up the Hummel orchestra. A very few early models were made with the head tilted at a different angle and without tie. This old-style is considered extremely rare and would command a premium of $3000–$4000. See old style "Puppy Love" HUM 1. A few sample pieces have been found made of hard porcelain material–value $2000–$3000. The original issue price was 40¢ in 1935! According to old Goebel product book, a sample was produced by Arthur Moeller in 1935 of "Little Fiddler" with an attached "pot," similar to HUM 16/I "Little Hiker" with attached "pot." Value $5000 to 10,000 if found. "Faience" finish—value $4000 to $5000. Permanently retired in 2003.

☐ 4	4.75 to 5.75"	(CE)	❶	$700—900
☐ 4	4.75 to 5.75"	(CE)	❷	$450—550
☐ 4	4.75 to 5.75"	(CE)	❸	$350—400
☐ 4	4.75 to 5.75"	(CE)	❹	$325—350
☐ 4	4.75 to 5.75"	(CE)	❺	$290—310
☐ 4	4.75 to 5.75"	(CE)	❻	$270—280
☐ 4	4.75 to 5.75"	(CE)	❼	$260—270
☐ 4	4.75 to 5.75"	(CE)	❽	$260

FINAL ISSUE
2003

Old style (TM 1)   "Faience" (TM 1)   New style (TM 6)   Hard Porcelain (TM 1)

4

New style ZZ,5O   Old style

HUM 5 — Strolling Along (CE)

Originally modeled by master sculptor Arthur Moeller in 1935. Older models have eyes that glance off to one side. Restyled by Gerhard Skrobek in 1962 with eyes looking straight ahead. Color of dog will vary. "Strolling along" was permanently retired by Goebel in the fall of 1989 and will not be produced again. Old 1955 price list shows a price of $6.00 while 1989 price list shows a price of $120, the last year it was sold on the primary market. Original issue price was 50¢ in 1935! According to old Goebel product book, a sample was produced by Arthur Moeller in 1935 of "Strolling Along" with an attached "pot," similar to HUM 16/I "Little Hiker" with attached "pot." Value $5000 to $10,000 if found.

☐ 5 ....4.75 to 5.75"......(CE) ....❶ ....$700—950
☐ 5 ....4.75 to 5.75"......(CE) ....❷ ....$500—600
☐ 5 ....4.75 to 5.75"......(CE)...............❸ ....$450—500
☐ 5 ....4.75 to 5.75"......(CE)...............❹ ....$350—450
☐ 5 ....4.75 to 5.75"......(CE) ....❺ ....$300—350
☐ 5 ....4.75 to 5.75"......(CE) ....❻ ....$275—300

FINAL ISSUE
1989

.... HUM TERM ....

DOUBLE CROWN: This term is used to describe the Goebel Company trademark found on some "M. I. Hummel" figurines. On "double crown" pieces the crown trademark is found both incised and stamped.

TM 1   TM 3   TM 6

HUM 6 — Sensitive Hunter

Modeled by master sculptor Arthur Moeller in 1935. Was originally called "The Timid Hunter." The lederhosen straps on older models of size 6 or 6/0 are parallel in back. Newer models have crossed-strap suspenders. Model 6/0 in TM 3 straps are found both ways. All other sizes have crossed straps in all time periods. Sometimes incised 6/2 instead of 6/II. All sizes were restyled in 1981 and now have a more natural-looking brown rabbit instead of the original orange-colored rabbit. Some variations in the position of the ears of the rabbit in older models. A new small size "Sensitive Hunter" was issued in 1985 at a suggested retail price of $60. It has an incised 1984 copyright date. This small size (6 2/0) was listed as (TW) "Temporarily Withdrawn" from production in January 1999. The large size (6/II) was listed as (TW) "Temporarily Withdrawn" from production on 31 December 1984 but could possibly be reinstated at some future date. The small size (6/0) "Sensitive Hunter" sold for $6.00 in 1955.

TM 1   TM 3   TM 6

	TM 1	*TM 3*	*TM 6*

Size (6/I) was listed as (TW) "Temporarily Withdrawn" in January 1999. Size (6/0) was listed as (TW) "Temporarily Withdrawn" in June 2002. Note: Red ring on base indicates this was a painter's sample and should not have left the factory. Part of 70th Anniversary Collection.

☐	6 2/0	4.00"	(CE)	❻	$175—180
☐	6 2/0	4.00"	**(TW)**	❼	$170—175
☐	6/0	4.75"	(CE)	❶	$700—900
☐	6/0	4.75"	(CE)	❷	$450—550
☐	6/0	4.75"	(CE)	❸	$350—400
☐	6/0	4.75"	(CE)	❹	$325—350
☐	6/0	4.75"	(CE)	❺	$290—310
☐	6/0	4.75"	(CE)	❻	$270—280
☐	6/0	4.75"	(CE)	❼	$260—270
☐	6/0	4.75"	**(TW)**	❽	$260—270
☐	6/0	4.75"	**(LE)**	❽	$339 (70th Anniversary)
☐	6/I	5.50 to 6.00"	(CE)	❶	$850—1000
☐	6/I	5.50 to 6.00"	(CE)	❷	$500—600
☐	6/I	5.50 to 6.00"	(CE)	❸	$375—425
☐	6/I	5.50"	(CE)	❹	$350—375
☐	6/I	5.50"	(CE)	❺	$325—350
☐	6/I	5.50"	(CE)	❻	$300—325
☐	6/I	5.50"	**(TW)**	❼	$280—285
☐	6/II	7.00 to 7.50"	(CE)	❶	$1500—2000
☐	6/II	7.00 to 7.50"	(CE)	❷	$950—1250
☐	6/II	7.00 to 7.50"	(CE)	❸	$550—650
☐	6/II	7.00 to 7.50"	(CE)	❹	$475—550
☐	6/II	7.00 to 7.50"	(CE)	❺	$425—475
☐	6/II	7.00 to 7.50"	**(TW)**	❻	$350—425
☐	6	5.00"	(CE)	❶	$850—1000

Just a few of the many size variations

HUM 7 — Merry Wanderer

Can be found in more size variations than any other figurine. A six-foot model was placed in front of the Goebel factory in Roedental in 1971 to commemorate Goebel's 100th Anniversary, and in 1987 an eight-foot model was unveiled in front of the former headquarters of the Goebel Collectors' Club (now The M. I. Hummel Club) in Tarrytown, New York. First modeled by master sculptor Arthur Moeller in 1935. Was restyled by master sculptor Gerhard Skrobek in size 7/II with the new textured finish in 1972, with an incised copyright date. Size 7/III was restyled in 1978 but without an incised copyright date. Older models of size 7/I have what collectors call a "double base" or "stair step" base. This accounts for the wide price variation of 7/I in trademark 3 since it was produced with either normal or "double base.' All sizes and all time periods of HUM 7 usually have only five buttons on vest. Sometimes incised 7/2 instead of 7/II. The 32-inch model (HUM 7/X) was first sold in the U.S. market in 1976 and "temporarily withdrawn" (TW) from production as of 1 January 1991, but was reinstated on the May 15, 1995 price list. The large sizes (7/II and 7/III) were (TW) "Temporarily Withdrawn" from production on 31 December 1989, but may be reinstated at some future date. The small size "Merry Wanderer" (7/0) sold for $6.00 in 1955. A few sample pieces have been found decorated with bright colors and glossy finish of the "Faience" technique—value would be $4000–$7000 depending on size and condition. See "Faience" article in back of Price Guide. In 1996 a promotional figurine with a bright red satchel was produced for a chain of gift shops in the Caribbean Islands. Bears a special backstamp "Exclusively for Little Switzerland" in size 7/0. Original retail price was $249 plus shipping charges.

☐ 7/0	6.00 to 6.25"	(CE)	❶	$800—1000	
☐ 7/0	6.00 to 6.25"	(CE)	❷	$500—650	
☐ 7/0	6.00 to 6.25"	(CE)	❸	$450—475	
☐ 7/0	6.00 to 6.25"	(CE)	❹	$400—425	
☐ 7/0	6.00 to 6.25"	(CE)	❺	$375—390	
☐ 7/0	6.00 to 6.25"	(CE)	❻	$370—375	
☐ 7/0	6.00 to 6.25"	(CE)	❼	$360—370	
☐ 7/0	6.00 to 6.25"	(OE)	❽	$359	
☐ 7/I	7.00 to 8.00"	(CE)	❶	$1500—1750	(Double base)
☐ 7/I	7.00 to 8.00"	(CE)	❷	$1300—1500	(Double base)
☐ 7/I	7.00 to 8.00"	(CE)	❸	$1200—1300	(Double base)
☐ 7/I	7.00 to 8.00"	(CE)	❸	$600—750	(Plain base)
☐ 7/I	7.00 to 8.00"	(CE)	❹	$500—600	
☐ 7/I	7.00 to 8.00"	(CE)	❺	$475—500	
☐ 7/I	7.00 to 8.00"	(CE)	❻	$450—475	

☐ 7/I	..........7.00 to 8.00”	......(TW)	.... ❼	.........$425—450
☐ 7/II	..........9.50 to 10.25”	....(GE)	.... ❶	.........$3000—3500
☐ 7/iI	..........9.50 to 10.25”	....(CE)	.... ❷	.........$1900—2750
☐ 7/II	..........9.50 to 10.25”	....(CE)	.... ❸	.........$1700—1800
☐ 7/II	..........9.50 to 10.25”	....(CE)	.... ❹	.........$1500—1700
☐ 7/II	..........9.50 to 10.25”	....(CE)	.... ❺	.........$1250—1275
☐ 7/II	..........9.50 to 10.25”	....(CE)	.... ❻	.........$1225—1250
☐ 7/II	..........9.50 to 10.25”	....(TW)	.... ❼	.........$1200—1225
☐ 7/III	..........11.00 to 12.00”	..(CE)	.... ❶	.........$3300—4000
☐ 7/III	..........11.00 to 12.00”	..(CE)	.... ❷	.........$2500—3000
☐ 7/III	..........11.00 to 12.00”	..(CE)	.... ❸	.........$1700—2000
☐ 7/III	..........11.00 to 12.00”	..(CE)	.... ❹	.........$1400—1500
☐ 7/III	..........11.00 to 12.00”	..(CE)	.... ❺	.........$1300—1350
☐ 7/III	..........11.00 to 12.00”	..(TW)	.... ❻	.........$1250—1300
☐ 7/III	........11.25”	................(OE)	.... ❽	.........$1550
☐ 7/X	.........32.00”	................(CE)	.... ❺	.........$20,000—25,000
☐ 7/X	.........32.00”	................(CE)	.... ❻	.........$20,000—25,000
☐ 71X	.........32.00 to 33.00”	..(CE)	.... ❼	.........$20,000—25,000
☐ 7/X	.........32.00 to 33.00”	..(OE)	.... ❽	.........$26,550

*Faience style painting
7/I "double base"
variation*

Little Switzerland

HUM 8 — Book Worm

Same as HUM 3 except smaller in size. Has only one flower on page. Old name: "Little Book Worm." Factory records indicate that this figurine was modeled by master sculptor Reinhold Unger in 1935. This figurine sold for $8.00 in 1955.

☐ 8	.............4.00 to 4.50”	......(CE)	.... ❶	.........$750—900
☐ 8	.............4.00 to 4.50”	......(CE)	.... ❷	.........$450—525
☐ 8	.............4.00 to 4.50”	......(CE).	.... ❸	.........$375—400
☐ 8	.............4.00 to 4.50”	......(CE)	.... ❹	.........$350—375
☐ 8	.............4.00 to 4.50”	......(CE)	.... ❺	.........$300—310
☐ 8	.............4.00 to 4.50”	......(CE)	.... ❻	.........$285—300
☐ 8	.............4.00 to 4.50”	......(CE)	.... ❼	.........$280—265
☐ 8	.............4.00 to 4.50”	......(OE)	.... ❽	.........$279

New   Very old

New style   **Old style**

HUM 9 — Begging His Share

There is much size variation in this figurine. Originally modeled by master sculptor Arthur Moeller in 1935 as a candleholder. Restyled in 1964, reduced slightly in size and made with a solid cake rather than with a hole for a candle. Can be found in trademark 3 with or without hole for candle. Called "Congratulatory Visit" in some old catalogues. Very early models have brightly colored striped socks. Has also been found in "crown" trademark without hole for candle. Listed as (TW) "Temporarily Withdrawn" in January 1999.

☐ 9 ....5.25 to 6.00".........(CE) ....❶ ....$750—950
☐ 9 ....5.25 to 6.00".........(CE) ....❷ ....$500—600
☐ 9 ....5.25 to 6.00".........(CE) ....❸ ....$375—400
☐ 9 ....5.25 to 6.00".........(CE).............❹ ....$340—360
☐ 9 ....5.25 to 6.00".........(CE).............❺ ....$320—330
☐ 9 ....5.25 to 6.00".........(CE) ....❻ ....$310—320
☐ 9 ....5.25 to 6.00".........(**TW**).............❼ ....$300—310

This very rare example of "Begging His Share" without the normal base was found in Europe—value $7000–$8000. Has also been found with "Faience" technique of painting.

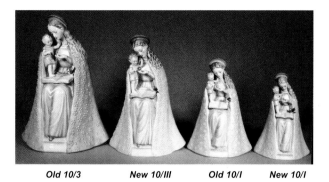

Old 10/3	*New 10/III*	*Old 10/I*	*New 10/I*

HUM 10 — Flower Madonna

First created in 1935 by master sculptor Reinhold Unger. In 1956 the mold was renewed (restyled) by Theo A. Menzenbach and made approximately 2 inches smaller. The halo was changed at that time from the open style to the flat style. It has been produced in white over-glaze, pastel blue cloak, brown cloak, ivory cloak and pastel yellow. Also has been found in reddish brown terra cotta finish, signed "M. I. Hummel" with the "crown" trademark in both 10/I and 10/3 size. The older color variations will usually range from $2500 to $3500 depending on color, condition and other variations. Old catalogues list it as large as 14 inches. Some earlier models appear with only the number 10 (no size designator). Also called "Sitting Madonna with Child" or "Virgin With Flowers" in old catalogues. Sometimes incised 10/3 instead of 10/III. (See page 12) Both 10/I and 10/III are (TW) "Temporarily Withdrawn."

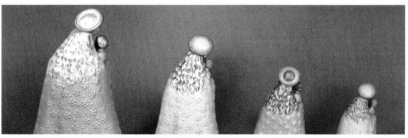

Old 10/3	*New 10/III*	*Old 10/I*	*New 10/I*
	Note variation in halo		

				Color	White
10/I	7.50 to 9.50"	(CE)	❶	☐ $800—950	☐ $500—600
10/I	7.75 to 9.50"	(CE)	❷	☐ $700—800	☐ $300—475
10/III	12.00 to 13.00"	(CE)	❶	☐ $900—1300	☐ $450—750
10/III	12.00 to 13.00"	(CE)	❷	☐ $800—900	☐ $450—650
10/I	7.75 to 8.25"	(CE)	❸	☐ $575—675	☐ $275—300
10/I	7.75 to 8.25"	(CE)	❹	☐ $525—575	☐ $250—275
10/I	7.75 to 8.25"	(CE)	❺	☐ $500—525	☐ $225—250
10/I	7.75 to 8.25"	(CE)	❻	☐ $475—500	☐ $200—225
10/I	7.75 to 8.25"	(TW)	❼	☐ $470—480	☐ $175—200
10/III	11.00 to 11.50"	(CE)	❷	☐ $650—900	☐ $425—500
10/III	11.00 to 11.50"	(CE)	❸	☐ $600—650	☐ $400—450
10/III	11.00 to 11.50"	(CE)	❹	☐ $550—600	☐ $375—400
10/III	11.00 to 11.50"	(CE)	❺	☐ $525—550	☐ $325—350
10/III	11.00 to 11.50"	(TW)	❻	☐ $500—525	☐ $300—325

HUM 11 — Merry Wanderer

Same style as HUM 7. Also modeled by master sculptor Arthur Moeller in 1935. Most models of "Merry Wanderer" have five buttons on vest. Some models in size 11 2/0 have six or seven buttons, and usually command a slight premium of 10–15 percent. According to old Goebel product book, a sample was produced by Arthur Moeller in 1935 of HUM 11/0 "Merry Wanderer" with an attached "pot," similar to HUM 16/I "Little Hiker" with attached "pot." Value $5000 to $10,000 if found. Part of the 70th Anniversary Collection.

☐ 11	4.75"	(CE)	❶	$650—750	
☐ 11 2/0	4.25 to 4.50"	(CE)	❶	$500—600	
☐ 11 2/0	4.25 to 4.50"	(CE)	❷	$275—325	
☐ 11 2/0	4.25 to 4.50"	(CE)	❸	$240—260	
☐ 11 2/0	4.25 to 4.50"	(CE)	❹	$210—225	
☐ 11 2/0	4.25 to 4.50"	(CE)	❺	$200—210	
☐ 11 2/0	4.25 to 4.50"	(CE)	❻	$190—200	
☐ 11 2/0	4.25 to 4.50"	(CE)	❼	$180—190	
☐ 11 2/0	4.25 to 4.50"	(OE)	❽	$179	
☐ 11/0	4.75 to 5.00"	(CE)	❶	$550—700	
☐ 11/0	4.75 to 5.00"	(CE)	❷	$400—500	
☐ 11/0	4.75 to 5.00"	(CE)	❸	$325—375	
☐ 11/0	4.75 to 5.00"	(CE)	❹	$300—325	(Difficult to find in TM 4)
☐ 11/0	4.75 to 5.00"	(CE)	❺	$275—300	
☐ 11/0	4.75 to 5.00"	(CE)	❻	$250—275	
☐ 11/0	4.75 to 5.00"	(CE)	❼	$225—230	
☐ 11/0	5.00"	(LE)	❽	$339	(70th Anniversary)

| 12 (TM 1) | 12/1 (TM 2) | 12 2/0 (TM 2) | 12 2/0 (TM 5) |

HUM 12 — Chimney Sweep

Originally modeled by master sculptor Arthur Moeller in 1935, but has been restyled several times through the years. There is much size variation in both sizes. Many old crown (TM 1) trademark pieces have a high gloss finish. A 1992 Sampler kit contained a special ceramic chimney and rooftop display base for use with the small size 12 2/0 "Chimney Sweep". Called "SMOKY" in old catalogue. Part of the 70th Anniversary Collection.

☐ 12 4/0 ....3.00 to 3.25".......(OE) ....❽ $99
☐ 12 2/0 ....4.00 to 4.25".......(CE) ....❷ ....$275—350
☐ 12 2/0 ....4.00 to 4.25".......(CE) ....❸ ....$190—210
☐ 12 2/0 ....4.00 to 4.25".......(CE) ....❹ ....$180—190
☐ 12 2/0 ....4.00 to 4.25".......(CE) ....❺ ....$170—180
☐ 12 2/0 ....4.00 to 4.25".......(CE) ....❻ ....$160—170
☐ 12 2/0 ....4.00 to 4.25".......(CE) ....❼ ....$150—160
☐ 12 2/0 ....4.00 to 4.25".......(OE) ....❽ $149
☐ 12/I ....5.50 to 6.50".......(CE) ....❶ ....$700—850
☐ 12/I ....5.50 to 6.50".......(CE) ....❷ ....$425—500
☐ 12/I ....5.50 to 6.50".......(CE) ....❸ ....$350—400
☐ 12/I ....5.50 to 6.50".......(CE) ....❹ ....$325—350
☐ 12/I ....5.50 to 6.50".......(CE) ....❺ ....$270—300
☐ 12/I ....5.50 to 6.50".......(CE) ....❻ ....$260—270
☐ 12/I ....5.50 to 6.50".......(CE) ....❼ ....$255—260
☐ 12/I ....5.50 to 6.50".......(TW).............❽ $255
☐ 12/I ....6.00"..................(LE) ....❽ ....$379   (70th Anniversary)
☐ 12 ....6.00 to 6.25".......(CE) ....❶ ....$750—900
☐ 12 ....6.00 to 6.25".......(CE) ....❷ ....$450—525

| 13/V | 13/2 | Old 13/2 | 13/II New |

HUM 13 — Meditation

First modeled by master sculptor Reinhold Unger in 1935 in two sizes: 13/0 and 13/2. Size 13/2 was originally styled with flowers in the back half of basket, but in 1978 was restyled by master sculptor Gerhard Skrobek with no flowers in basket. Large size (13/V) was modeled by Theo A. Menzenbach in 1957 with full basket of flowers. The small size (13/2/0) was modeled by master sculptor Gerhard Skrobek in 1962. A 1962 copyright date appears on newer models of size 13/2/0. Also called "The Little Messenger." Sometimes 13/2 instead of 13/II and 13/5 instead of 13/V. The larger size (13/II) was listed as (TW) "Temporarily Withdrawn" from production on 31 December 1984 and (13/V) was listed as (TW) "Temporarily Withdrawn" on 31 December 1989, but may be reinstated at some future date in the U.S. market. Available in (TM 8) in the European market with retail price of $1500.

Information located in an old Goebel product book indicates that master sculptor Reinhold Unger in 1935 produced samples of "Meditation" in the 13/0 size with a round attached "pot" and another with an oblong attached "bowl." The "pot" has no markings other than a "crown" (TM 1) trademark and the "M. I. Hummel" signature on the figurine. The piece with the "bowl" is marked "KZ 27/I," a "double crown" (TM 1 +1) trademark and a signature on the figurine. The "KZ 27/I" indicates that he used a bowl that had been designed for Goebel figurine KZ 27. For more information, see Rare/Unique Sample Variations of "M. I. Hummel" Figurines in the back of this book. Both sizes (13 2/0) and (13/0) were listed as (TW) "Temporarily Withdrawn" in January 1999. New small size (13 4/0) "First Issue 2005" with 2004 (CRD) copyright date. The 13/0 and 13/V size are available in (TM 8). In 2000 the 13/II size was included in the "Millennium Revival" Collection.

- ☐ 13 4/0 ....3.00 to 3.50" ....(**OE**) ......❽ $99
- ☐ 13 2/0 ....4.25" ....(CE) ......❷ ....$250—350
- ☐ 13 2/0 ....4.25" ....(CE) ......❸ ....$225—250

☐ 13 2/0	....4.25"	(CE)	❹	$190—225
☐ 13 2/0	....4.25"	(CE)	❺	$175—190
☐ 13 2/0	....4.25"	(CE)	❻	$160—175
☐ 13 2/0	....4.25"	(TW)	❼	$160—165
☐ 13/0	........5.00 to 6.00"	(CE)	❶	$700—850
☐ 13/0	........5.00 to 6.00"	(CE)	❷	$425—500
☐ 13/0	........5.00 to 6.00"	(CE)	❸	$350—400
☐ 13/0	........5.00 to 6.00"	(CE)	❹	$325—350
☐ 13/0	........5.00 to 6.00"	(CE)	❺	$270—300
☐ 13/0	........5.00 to 6.00"	(CE)	❻	$260—270
☐ 13/0	........5.00 to 6.00"	(CE)	❼	$245—250
☐ 13/0	........5.00"	(TW)	❽	$240
☐ 13	..........7.00 to 7.25"	(CE)	❶	$4000—5000
☐ 13/I	........5.25"	(CE)	❶	$1500—2000
☐ 13/II	........7.00 to 7.25"	(CE)	❶	$4000—5000
☐ 13/II	........7.00 to 7.25"	(CE)	❷	$3500—4000
☐ 13/II	........7.00 to 7.25"	(CE)	❸	$3000—3500
☐ 13/II	........7.00 to 7.25"	(CE)	❺	$400—450
☐ 13/II	........7.00 to 7.25"	(CE)	❻	$350—400
☐ 13/II	........7.00"	(TW)	❽	$325
☐ 13/V	........13.25 to 14.00"	(CE)	❶	$4000—5000
☐ 13/V	........13.25 to 14.00"	(CE)	❷	$3000—3500
☐ 13/V	........13.25 to 14.00"	(CE)	❸	$1700—2200
☐ 13/V	........13.25 to 14.00"	(CE)	❹	$1350—1500
☐ 13/V	........13.25 to 14.00"	(CE)	❺	$1300—1350
☐ 13/V	........13.25 to 14.00"	(CE)	❻	$1200—1300
☐ 13/V	........13.25 to 14.00"	(CE)	❼	$1100—1200
☐ 13/V	........13.25"	(OE)	❽	$1500

13/0 with "Pot" (TM 1)   *13/0 with "Bowl" (TM 1+1)*

14/B   14/A (TM 1 + 1)

HUM 14 — Book Worm, Bookends, Boy and Girl

These figurines are weighted with sand through a hole on the bottom and closed with a cork or plastic plug. Sometimes sealed with a paper sticker and inscription "75 Years Goebel." The girl is the same as HUM 3 and HUM 8 except that the pictures on book are black and white rather than in color. Modeled by master sculptor Reinhold Unger in 1935. The boy was made only as part of bookend set and not normally sold separately. This policy, however, was changed and the boy could be purchased alone and unweighted. This was done mainly to satisfy collectors who desired a figurine to match the 1980 Annual Bell that had a motif similar to the bookend boy. Then in 1981 HUM 415 "Thoughtful" was released in the U.S. market to match the annual bell. "Bookworm" bookends were (TW) "Temporarily Withdrawn" from production on 31 December 1989. Listed at $315.00 a pair on the 1989 price list, the last year sold on the primary market. "Bookworm" bookends were listed at $15.00 a pair on 1955 price list. In 1993 "Bookworm" bookends could be purchased from Danbury Mint, Norwalk, Connecticut by mail order only, but they are no longer available from them. Bookworm boy has been found with number "14" only (NO "A") incised on the bottom. Boy was called "Learned Man" in very old catalogues. Wooden bookend displays are included in 70th Anniversary Collection editions.

☐ 14	5.50"	(CE)	❶	$600—800	
☐ 14 A&B	5.50"	(CE)	❶	$1200—1600	
☐ 14 A&B	5.50"	(CE)	❷	$650—750	
☐ 14 A&B	5.50"	(CE)	❸	$600—650	
☐ 14 A&B	5.50"	(CE)	❹	$550—600	
☐ 14 A&B	5.50"	(CE)	❺	$500—550	
☐ 14 A&B	5.50"	(CE)	❻	$450—500	
☐ 14 A&B	5.50"	(CE)	❼	$400—450	
☐ 14 A&B	4.50 to 5.00"	(LE)	❽	$858	(70th Anniversary)
☐ 14 A	5.50"	(CE)	❺	$250—275	
☐ 14 A	5.50"	(CE)	❻	$225—250	

HUM 15 — Hear Ye, Hear Ye

Old name: "Night Watchman." There are some variations in color of mittens. Right hand facing photo (left hand of figurine) shows fingers on older models. Originally modeled by master sculptor Arthur Moeller in 1935. Older models usually incised 15/2 instead of 15/II. A new small size (15 2/0) "Hear Ye, Hear Ye" was first issued in 1985 with a suggested retail price of $60. It has an incised 1984 copyright date. The 6.00" size 15/I sold for $7.50 on 1955 price list. A few sample pieces have been found decorated with bright colors and glossy finish of the "Faience" technique–valued $3000–$5000. Size (15/I) was listed as (TW) "Temporarily Withdrawn" from production in January 1999. Part of 70th Anniversary Collection.

15/0 (TM 2) 6"   15/0 (TM 2) 5.25" 15 2/0 (TM 6)
(Note size variation)

☐ 15 2/0 ....4.00" ....(CE) ....❻ ....$205—210
☐ 15 2/0 ....4.00" ....(CE) ....❼ ....$200—205
☐ 15 2/0 ....4.00" ....(**OE**) ....❽ $199
☐ 15/0 ....5.00 to 5.50"......(CE) ....❶ ....$600—750
☐ 15/0 ....5.25 to 6.00"......(CE) ....❷ ....$350—450
☐ 15/0 ....5.00 to 5.50"......(CE) ....❸ ....$300—325
☐ 15/0 ....5.00 to 5.50"......(CE) ....❹ ....$275—300
☐ 15/0 ....5.00 to 5.50"......(CE) ....❺ ....$250—270
☐ 15/0 ....5.00 to 5.50"......(CE) ....❻ ....$240—250
☐ 15/0 ....5.00 to 5.50".....(CE) ....❼ ....$235—240
☐ 15/0 ....5.00 to 5.50"......(CE) ....❽ ....$235—240
☐ 15/0 ....5.75" ....(**LE**) ....❽ ....$339   (70th Anniversary)
☐ 15/I ....6.00 to 6.25"......(CE) ....❶ ....$700—900
☐ 15/I ....6.00 to 6.25"......(CE) ....❷ ....$450—600
☐ 15/I ....6.00 to 6.25"......(CE) ....❸ ....$375—400
☐ 15/I ....6.00 to 6.25"......(CE) ....❹ ....$350—375
☐ 15/I ....6.00 to 6.25"......(CE) ....❺ ....$310—340
☐ 15/I ....6.00 to 6.25"......(CE) ....❻ ....$290—310
☐ 15/I ....6.00 to 6.25"......(CE) ....❼ ....$280—285
☐ 15/II ....7.00 to 7.50"......(CE) ....❶ ....$1200—1500
☐ 15/II ....7.00 to 7.50"......(CE) ....❷ ....$750—1000
☐ 15/II ....7.00 to 7.50"......(CE).............❸ ....$650—750
☐ 15/II ....7.00 to 7.50"......(CE) ....❹ ....$550—650
☐ 15/II ....7.00 to 7.50"......(CE) ....❺ ....$500—525
☐ 15/II ....7.00 to 7.50"......(CE) ....❻ ....$475—500
☐ 15/II ....7.00 to 7.50".....(**TW**) ....❼ ....$450—475
☐ 15 ....7.25" ....(CE) ....❶ ....$1400—1700

16/I (TM 2)   16/I with "Pot" (TM 1)

HUM 16 — Little Hiker

This figurine was originally modeled by master sculptor Arthur Moeller in 1935. The old name of "Happy-Go-Lucky" was used in early catalogues. Slight changes can be noticed when comparing older models with new. Many old crown trademark pieces have a high gloss finish. An early sample painting variation is found with green jacket and blue hat—value $1500–$2000. The large size (16/I) "Little Hiker" was (TW) "Temporarily Withdrawn" from the U.S. market at the end of 1997. According to old Goebel product book, a sample was produced by Arthur Moeller in 1935 of "Little Hiker" with an attached "pot." Value $5000 to $10,000 when found. For more information, see Rare/Unique Sample Variations of "M. I. Hummel" Figurines in back of this book. Both sizes permanently retired in 2002.

☐	16 2/0	3.75 to 4.25"	(CE)	❶	$375—450
☐	16 2/0	3.75 to 4.25"	(CE)	❷	$275—300
☐	16 2/0	3.75 to 4.25"	(CE)	❸	$180—200
☐	16 2/0	3.75 to 4.25"	(CE)	❹	$165—170
☐	16 2/0	3.75 to 4.25"	(CE)	❺	$160—165
☐	16 2/0	3.75 to 4.25"	(CE)	❻	$155—160
☐	16 2/0	3.75 to 4.25"	(CE)	❼	$150—155
☐	16 2/0	3.75 to 4.25"	**(CE)**	❽	$145—150
☐	16	5.50 to 5.75"	(CE)	❶	$650—750
☐	16	5.50 to 5.75"	(CE)	❷	$450—550
☐	16/I	5.50 to 6.00"	(CE)	❶	$600—700
☐	16/I	5.50 to 6.00"	(CE)	❷	$400—500
☐	16/I	5.50 to 6.00"	(CE)	❸	$350—400
☐	16/I	5.50 to 6.00"	(CE)	❹	$300—350
☐	16/I	5.50 to 6.00"	(CE)	❺	$275—300
☐	16/I	5.50 to 6.00"	(CE)	❻	$260—275
☐	16/I	5.50 to 6.00"	**(TW)**	❼	$245—250
☐	16/I	5.50 to 6.00"	(CE)	❽	$245—250

FINAL ISSUE
2002

Size differences   *Rare sample (TM 1)*

HUM 17 — Congratulations

First modeled by master sculptor Reinhold Unger in 1935. Called "I Congratulate" in old catalogues. Older models do not have socks. Restyled in 1971 by master sculptor Gerhard Skrobek, who added socks, new hair and textured finish. Larger size (17/2) is no longer produced and considered rare. Early crown mark pieces are marked 17 with either a zero or a 2 directly underneath. Old catalogue dated 1955 lists size of 3.75" which is believed to be in error. Crown and some full bee pieces have the handle of the horn pointing to the back. Since the larger size is (CE) Closed Edition and will not be produced again in the future, the size designator on the remaining size will eventually be eliminated, according to factory information, and will be incised 17 only. (This has not happened.) "Congratulations" (17/0) was permanently retired in the fall of 1999 and will not be produced again. According to old Goebel product book, a sample was produced by Reinhold Unger in 1935 of "Congratulations" with an attached "pot," but was not approved for production by Siessen Convent. Value $5000 to $10,000 when found. For more information, see Rare/Unique Sample Variations of "M. I. Hummel" Figurines in back of this book.

☐ 17/0 ....5.50 to 6.00"......(CE) ....❶ ....$600—750
☐ 17/0 ....5.50 to 6.00"......(CE) ....❷ ....$350—450
☐ 17/0 ....5.50 to 6.00"......(CE) ....❸ ....$300—325
☐ 17/0 ....5.50 to 6.00"......(CE) ....❹ ....$275—300
☐ 17/0 ....6.00".................(CE) ....❺ ....$250—275
☐ 17/0 ....6.00".................(CE) ....❻ ....$240—250
☐ 17/0 ....6.00".................(CE) ....❼ ....$230—235
☐ 17/2 ....7.75 to 8.25"......(CE) ....❶ ....$6500—8000
☐ 17/2 ....7.75 to 8.25"......(CE) ....❷ ....$5500—6500
☐ 17/2 ....7.75 to 8.25"......(CE) ....❸ ....$4500—5500

FINAL ISSUE
1999

.... HUM TERM ....

HUM NO.: Mold number or model number incised on the bottom of each "M.I. Hummel" figurine at the factory. This number is used for identification purposes.

Early models larger than newer models

HUM 18 — Christ Child

Early models measure 3.75 x 6.50". Old name: "Christmas Night." At one time this piece was sold in Belgium in the white overglaze finish and would now be considered extremely rare. These white pieces usually bring about double the price of a colored piece. Originally modeled by master sculptor Reinhold Unger in 1935. Christ Child in white overglaze finish listed at $4.00 on 1955 price list. Christ Child was (TW) "Temporarily Withdrawn" from production on 31 December 1990, but was reinstated on 1997 price list, but is once again listed as (TW) "Temporarily Withdrawn" in January 1999.

☐ 18	3.75 x 6.50"	(CE)	❶	$400—550
☐ 18	3.75 x 6.50"	(CE)	❷	$250—300
☐ 18	3.75 x 6.50"	(CE)	❸	$225—250
☐ 18	3.25 x 6.00"	(CE)	❹	$200—225
☐ 18	3.25 x 6.00"	(CE)	❺	$175—200
☐ 18	3.25 x 6.00"	(CE)	❻	$170—175
☐ 18	3.25 x 6.00"	(TW)	❼	$165—170

HUM 19 — Prayer Before Battle, Ashtray (CN)

Factory book of models indicates: "Big round tray with praying child (with flag and trumpet) standing at wooden (toy) horse. Prayer Before Battle, modeled by A. Moeller—June 20, 1935." An additional note states that this item was not accepted by the Convent at Siessen. An example of this rare piece was located on the East Coast of the U.S. This is the best photograph we could obtain. The piece is actually an ashtray and does have the "M. I. Hummel" signature, scratched in by hand. It is different material than the normal "M. I. Hummel" figurines. The owner washed it in an automatic dishwasher and much of the paint washed off. It is likely that this piece had not been fired after the painting process, thus the paint washed off. The final firing normally locks on the paint in a normally completed figurine. Caution should always be used when cleaning a figurine.

☐ 19	5.50"	(CN)	❶	$5000—10,000

20

TM 1 Normal   *TM 1 Reversed horn*

HUM 20 — Prayer Before Battle

Created in 1935 by master sculptor Arthur Moeller. Only slight variations between old and new models. Some color variations, but most noticeable difference is in size. Newer models are smaller. Some older pieces of HUM 20 will have a little paint or highlight inside the handle of the horn; most newer ones do not. Also, another interesting variation appears on the front of the horn. Sometimes this area is recessed on older examples; most newer figurines will be almost flat and will have a little paint for highlight in this area. These are interesting variations, but they will not affect the value. "Prayer Before Battle" listed for $7.50 on old 1955 price list. Found with handle of horn reversed or upside down. Painting of little flag will also vary—either with light color or dark color on top of flag. Has been found with horn missing completely. Also found decorated with bright colors and glossy finish of the "Faience" technique style of painting—value $3000 to $4000. In 2005 a sequentially numbered (LE) Limited Edition of 1935 was made available commemorating the 70th Anniversary of Hummels (1935-2005), cast using copies of the 1935 molds and painted in the original painting style and colors; priced $259. The 70th Anniversary Edition has inscribed crown mark and stamped TM 8, "70th Anniversary" backstamp, and a crimped on 70th Anniversary ceramic plaque.

☐ 20 ....4.00 to 4.50".....(CE) ....❶ ....$550—650
☐ 20 ....4.00 to 4.50".....(CE) ....❷ ....$375—400
☐ 20 ....4.00 to 4.50".....(CE) ....❸ ....$275—300
☐ 20 ....4.00 to 4.50".....(CE) ....❹ ....$250—275
☐ 20 ....4.00 to 4.50".....(CE) ....❺ ....$220—235
☐ 20 ....4.00 to 4.50".....(CE) ....❻ ....$215—220
☐ 20 ....4.00 to 4.50".....(CE) ....❼ ....$205—215
☐ 20 ....4.00 to 4.50".....(OE) ....❽ $205
☐ 20 ....4.50"................(LE)............❽ ....$259   (70th Anniversary)

HUM 21 — Heavenly Angel

First figurine to have ".50" size designator. Much variation in size. Old name: "Little Guardian" or "Celestial Messenger." First modeled by master sculptor Reinhold Unger in 1935. Sometimes incised 21/2 instead of 21/II. According to factory information, this figurine was also sold in white overglaze at one time. "Heavenly Angel" motif was used for the first annual plate in 1971 (HUM 264), and as a "tree topper" in 1994 (HUM 755). The only other "M. I. Hummel" figurine with ".50" size designator is "Blessed Child" HUM 78/II½ sold only at the Siessen convent. The large size 21/II was listed as (TW) "Temporarily Withdrawn" on the 1993 price list, while the 1992 price list shows a price of $390, the last year it was sold on the primary market. Size (21/I) was listed as (TW) "Temporarily Withdrawn" in January 1999.

☐ 21/0	4.00 to 4.75"	(CE)	❶	$450—500
☐ 21/0	4.00 to 4.75"	(CE)	❷	$225—275
☐ 21/0	4.00 to 4.75"	(CE)	❸	$200—225
☐ 21/0	4.00 to 4.75"	(CE)	❹	$190—195
☐ 21/0	4.00 to 4.75"	(CE)	❺	$190—195
☐ 21/0	4.00 to 4.75"	(CE)	❻	$185—190
☐ 21/0	4.00 to 4.75"	(CE)	❼	$180—185
☐ 21/0	4.00 to 4.75"	(OE)	❽	$179
☐ 21/0½	5.75 to 0.50"	(CE)	❶	$760 860
☐ 21/0½	5.75 to 6.50"	(CE)	❷	$450—500
☐ 21/0½	5.75 to 6.50"	(CE)	❸	$375—400
☐ 21/0½	5.75 to 6.50"	(CE)	❹	$350—375
☐ 21/0½	5.75 to 6.50"	(CE)	❺	$300—325
☐ 21/0½	5.75 to 6.50"	(CE)	❻	$285—300
☐ 21/0½	5.75 to 6.50"	(CE)	❼	$280—285
☐ 21/0½	5.75 to 6.50"	(OE)	❽	$279
☐ 21/I	6.75 to 7.25"	(CE)	❶	$800—1000
☐ 21/I	6.75 to 7.25"	(CE)	❷	$500—600
☐ 21/I	6.75 to 7.25"	(CE)	❸	$425—475
☐ 21/I	6.75 to 7.25"	(CE)	❹	$350—400
☐ 21/I	6.75 to 7.25"	(CE)	❺	$340—350
☐ 21/I	6.75 to 7.25"	(CE)	❻	$330—340
☐ 21/I	6.75 to 7.25"	(TW)	❼	$320—330
☐ 21/II	8.50 to 8.75"	(CE)	❶	$1400—1600
☐ 21/II	8.50 to 8.75"	(CE)	❷	$800—1000
☐ 21/II	8.50 to 8.75"	(CE)	❸	$650—700
☐ 21/II	8.50 to 8.75"	(CE)	❹	$550—600
☐ 21/II	8.50 to 8.75"	(CE)	❺	$475—500
☐ 21/II	8.50 to 8.75"	(CE)	❻	$460—470
☐ 21/II	8.50 to 8.75"	(TW)	❼	$450—460

22/I (TM 1)   *22/0 (TM 1)*

HUM 22 — Holy Water Font, Angel With Bird (Angel Sitting)

First modeled by master sculptor Reinhold Unger in 1935. Old name: "Sitting Angel." Variations in size, color and design of bowl are found on other models. This small size font sold for $1.35 on 1955 price list. Current 2005 price list name: "Angel Sitting."

- ☐ 22 ....3.125 to 4.50" ......(CE) ....**❶** ....$300—325
- ☐ 22/0 ....3.00 x 4.00".........(CE) ....**❶** ....$275—300
- ☐ 22/0 ....3.00 x 4.00".........(CE) ....**❷** ....$140—160
- ☐ 22/0 ....3.00 x 4.00".........(CE) ....**❸** ....$90—95
- ☐ 22/0 ....3.00 x 4.00".........(CE) ....**❹** ....$85—90
- ☐ 22/0 ....3.00 x 4.00".........(CE) ....**❺** ....$80—85
- ☐ 22/0 ....3.00 x 4.00".........(CE) ....**❻** ....$75—80
- ☐ 22/0 ....3.00 x 4.00".........(CE) ....**❼** ....$70—75
- ☐ 22/0 ....3.00 x 4.00".........(**OE**) ....**❽** $69.50
- ☐ 22/I ....3.50 to 4.875" ......(CE) ....**❶** ....$500—600
- ☐ 22/I ....3.50 to 4.875" ......(CE) ....**❷** ....$400—500
- ☐ 22/I ....3.50 to 4.875" ......(CE) ....**❸** ....$300—400

.... HUM TERM ....

SCARCE: (Webster) Infrequently seen or found. Not Plentiful or abundant.

| 23/3 (TM 1) | 23/I (TM 1+1) | 23/I (TM 3) |

HUM 23 — Adoration

This ever popular design was modeled by master sculptor Reinhold Unger in 1935. Size 23/I was restyled in 1978, with new textured finish, by master modeler Gerhard Skrobek. Some models can be found with either Arabic (23/3) or Roman (23/III) three. Both sizes were sold in white overglaze at one time in Belgium and would be considered rare today—value would be $1500 to $2000 for the small size and $3000 to $4000 for the large, depending on trademark and condition. Old name: "Ave Maria." Most older models have rounded corners on the base of the large size while newer models are more square. Early double crown marked, large size found without size designator—23 only. Early crown-marked, small size usually found without flowers on base. The small size Adoration (23/I) sold for $12.00 on 1955 price list. Large size (23/III) was listed as (TW) "Temporarily Withdrawn" in January 1999.

☐ 23/I	........6.25 to 7.00"	........(CE)	........❶	.........$1200—1400
☐ 23/I	........6.25 to 7.00"	........(CE)	........❷	.........$700—800
☐ 23/I	........6.25 to 7.00"	........(CE)	........❸	.........$525—600
☐ 23/I	........6.25 to 7.00"	........(CE)	........❹	.........$475—525
☐ 23/I	........6.25 to 7.00"	........(CE)	........❺	.........$450—475
☐ 23/I	........6.25 to 7.00"	........(CE)	........❻	.........$440—450
☐ 23/I	........6.25 to 7.00"	........(CE)	........❼	.........$400—440
☐ 23/I	........6.25 to 7.00"	........**(OE)**	........❽	.........$399
☐ 23	..........8.75 to 9.00"	........(CE)	..........❶	.........$1600—2100
☐ 23/III	......8.75 to 9.00"	........(CE)	..........❶	.........$1500—2000
☐ 23/III	......8.75 to 9.00"	........(CE)	..........❷	.........$900—1250
☐ 23/III	......8.75 to 9.00"	........(CE)	..........❸	.........$800—900
☐ 23/III	......8.75 to 9.00"	........(CE)	..........❹	.........$675—775
☐ 23/III	......8.75 to 9.00"	........(CE)	..........❺	.........$625—675
☐ 23/III	......8.75 to 9.00"	........(CE)	..........❻	.........$600—625
☐ 23/III	......8.75 to 9.00"	.......**(TW)**	..........❼	.........$595—600

24/III (TM 1+1)   *24/I (TM 2)*

HUM 24 — Lullaby, Candleholder

Records show that this figurine was first modeled in 1935. Both Arthur Moeller and Reinhold Unger are given credit—possibly one created the small size while the other the larger size. Variations are found in size and construction of socket for candle on size 24/I. Old name: "Cradle Song." Also made without hole for candle—see HUM 262. Sometimes incised 24/3 instead of 24/III. In the spring of 1982 the large size (24/III) was listed by Goebel as (TW) "Temporarily Withdrawn," to be possibly reinstated at a future date. The small size (24/I) also was (TW) "Temporarily Withdrawn" from production on 31 December 1989, but was once again listed on the 1997 price list for $210. Both the large size (24/3) and the small (24/I) have been found in Belgium in white overglaze in the (TM 2) and (TM 3) trademarks. Value $2000 to $4000 each. The small size (24/I) was again listed as (TW) "Temporarily Withdrawn" in January 1999. Part of 70th Anniversary Collection.

☐ 24/I	.....3.50 x 5 to 5.50"	......(CE)	........**❶**	.........$550—700	
☐ 24/I	.....3.50 x 5 to 5.50"	......(CE)	........**❷**	.........$350—425	
☐ 24/I	.....3.50 x 5 to 5.50"	......(CE)	........**❸**	.........$275—300	
☐ 24/I	.....3.50 x 5 to 5.50"	......(CE)	........**❹**	.........$250—275	
☐ 24/I	.....3.50 x 5 to 5.50"	......(CE)	........**❺**	.........$230—250	
☐ 24/I	.....3.50 x 5 to 5.50"	......(CE)	........**❻**	.........$220—230	
☐ 24/I	.....3.50 x 5.00"	.............(CE)	........**❼**	.........$210—215	
☐ 24/I	.....3.50"	.........................(**LE**)	........**❽**	.........$329	(70th Anniversary)
☐ 24/III	....6.25 x 8.75"	.............(CE)	........**❶**	.........$1500—1900	
☐ 24/III	....6.25 x 8.75"	.............(CE)	........**❷**	.........$950—1250	
☐ 24/III	....6.25 x 8.75"	.............(CE)	........**❸**	.........$600—700	
☐ 24/III	....6.25 x 8.75"	.............(CE)	........**❹**	.........$525—600	
☐ 24/III	....6.25 x 8.75"	.............(CE)	........**❺**	.........$500—525	
☐ 24/III	....6.25 x 8.75"	.............(**TW**)	........**❻**	.........$475—500	

Crown (TM 1)   *Full bee (TM 2)*

HUM 25 — Angelic Sleep, Candleholder

Records indicate that this figurine was first modeled in 1935 and that both Arthur Moeller and Reinhold Unger were involved with the design. At one time this figurine was sold in Belgium in the white overglaze finish and would now be considered rare. Listed as "Angel's Joy" in some old catalogues. In some old, as well as new catalogues and price lists, shown as 25/I in error. Made only one size and incised 25 only. (Candleholder figures are not always photographed with candles with this guide.) This figurine was (TW) "Temporarily Withdrawn" from production on 31 December 1989 and again later in (TM 8), but may be reinstated at some future date. Available in (TM 8).

- ☐ 25 ......3.50 x 5.00 to 5.50"..........(CE) ......❶ ....$550—700
- ☐ 25 ......3.50 x 5.00 to 5.50"..........(CE) ......❷ ....$350—425
- ☐ 25 ......3.50 x 5.00 to 5.50"..........(CE) ......❷ ....$1500—2000 (White Overglaze)
- ☐ 25 ......3.50 x 5.00 to 5.50"..........(CE) ......❸ ....$285—290
- ☐ 25 ......3.50 x 5.00 to 5.50"..........(CE) ......❺ ....$280—285
- ☐ 25 ......3.50 x 5.00 to 5.50"..........(CE) ......❻ ....$275—280
- ☐ 25 ......3.50 x 5.00 to 5.50"..........(CE) ......❼ ....$270—275
- ☐ 25 ......3.50 x 5.00 to 5.50"..........(OE) ......❽ $270

.... HUM TERM ....

OUT OF PRODUCTION: A term used by the Goebel Company to designate items that are not currently in production, yet have not been given an official classification as to their eventual fate. Some items listed as out of production may become closed editions, remain temporarily withdrawn, or ultimately return to current production status.

26/0 (TM 2)   *26/I (TM 2)*

HUM 26 — Holy Water Font, Child Jesus

Originally modeled by master sculptor Reinhold Unger in 1935. The normal color for the gown is a dark red but is occasionally found in a light blue color or green color. All that I have ever seen with the blue gown were in the small (26/0) size and with the small stylized (TM 3) trademark. Old crown mark and full bee pieces in both sizes usually have scalloped edge on bowl of font. This "Christ Child" font listed for $1.35 on 1955 price list. The large size 26/I was found in (TM 2) in white overglaze in the Netherlands. Listed as (TW) "Temporarily Withdrawn" from production in January 1999.

- ☐ 26/0 ....2.75 x 5.25" ....(CE) ....❶ ....$225—275
- ☐ 26/0 ....2.75 x 5.25" ....(CE) ....❷ ....$125—150
- ☐ 26/0 ....2.75 x 5.25" ....(CE) ....❸ ....$90—95
- ☐ 26/0 ....2.75 x 5.25" ....(CE) ....❹ ....$85—90
- ☐ 26/0 ....2.75 x 5.25" ....(CE) ....❺ ....$80—85
- ☐ 26/0 ....2.75 x 5.25" ....(CE) ....❻ ....$75—80
- ☐ 26/0 ....2.75 x 5.25" ....(**TW**) ....❼ ....$70—75
- ☐ 26 ....3.00 x 5.75" ....(CE) ....❶ ....$350—550
- ☐ 26/I ....3.25 x 6.00" ....(CE) ....❶ ....$300—500
- ☐ 26/I ....3.25 x 6.00" ....(CE) ....❷ ....$250—300
- ☐ 26/I ....3.25 x 6.00" ....(CE) ....❸ ....$200—250

27/I (TM 1)   *27/3 (TM 1)*

HUM 27 — Joyous News

This figurine was made in two sizes. The small size is a candleholder while the larger size is a figurine. Both were modeled by master sculptor Reinhold Unger in 1935. 27/I is so similar to III/40/I that it is extremely difficult to tell the difference unless they are clearly marked. The small size "Joyous News" candleholder (27/I) is no longer produced and is considered rare. Usually found only in crown trademark. Can be found with the candleholder on the front side or on the back side. 27/I is also sometimes found with light purple shoes. Some models designed to hold .6 cm size candles while others designed to hold 1 cm size candles. The small size also found with incised number III/27/1 which indicates made for larger 1 cm size candles. The larger size "Joyous News" is rare in the older trademarks; TM 1, TM 2 and TM 3 but was reinstated in 1978 using the original molds, and the original number 27/3 (Arabic 3). In 1979 when it was restyled with the new textured finish the number was changed to 27/III (Roman III). Both 27/3 (old mold) and 27/III (new mold) can be found in TM 5. Large size (27/III) was listed as (TW) "Temporarily Withdrawn" in January 1999.

☐ 27/I	2.75"	(CE)	❶	$300—500
☐ 27/I	2.75"	(CE)	❷	$250—400
☐ 27/3	4.25 x 4.75"	(CE)	❶	$1500—2000
☐ 27/3	4.25 x 4.75"	(CE)	❷	$1000—1500
☐ 27/3	4.25 x 4.75"	(CE)	❸	$750—1000
☐ 27/3	4.25 x 4.75"	(CE)	❺	$260—280
☐ 27/III	4.25 x 4.75"	(CE)	❺	$260—280
☐ 27/III	4.25 x 4.75"	(CE)	❻	$250—260
☐ 27/III	4.25 x 4.75"	(TW)	❼	$245—250

28/III (TM 3)   *28/II (Double crown)*

HUM 28 — Wayside Devotion

First modeled by master sculptor Reinhold Unger in 1935. Old name: "The Little Shepherd" or "Evensong." According to factory information, this figurine was also sold in white overglaze finish at one time. Sometimes incised 28/2 instead of 28/II or 28/3 instead of 28/III. Also found without a size designator on the large size—incised 28 only. The small size 28/II was restyled by Gerhard Skrobek in the early 1970s. Made without the shrine (see HUM 99) and was named "Eventide." The small size "Wayside Devotion" listed for $16.50 on 1955 price list. The large size (28/III) was listed as (TW) "Temporarily Withdrawn" in January 1999. Then in 2005 the 28/III size was part of 70th Anniversary Collection.

☐ 28/II	7.00 to 7.50"	(CE)	❶	$1300—1500
☐ 28/II	7.00 to 7.50"	(CE)	❷	$800—900
☐ 28/II	7.00 to 7.50"	(CE)	❸	$650—700
☐ 28/II	7.00 to 7.50"	(CE)	❹	$575—600
☐ 28/II	7.00 to 7.50"	(CE)	❺	$550—575
☐ 28/II	7.00 to 7.50"	(CE)	❻	$525—550
☐ 28/II	7.00 to 7.50"	(CE)	❼	$510—525
☐ 28/II	7.00 to 7.50"	(CE)	❽	$510—525
☐ 28	8.75"	(CE)	❶	$1700—1900
☐ 28/III	8.75"	(CE)	❶	$1400—1700
☐ 28/III	8.75"	(CE)	❷	$1000—1200
☐ 28/III	8.75"	(CE)	❸	$800—900
☐ 28/III	8.75"	(CE)	❹	$700—800
☐ 28/III	8.75"	(CE)	❺	$650—700
☐ 28/III	8.75"	(CE)	❻	$625—650
☐ 28/III	8.75"	(CE)	❼	$600—615
☐ 28/III	8.75"	(LE)	❽	$799 (70th Anniversary)

| 29 Crown (TM 1) | 29/0 Full bee (TM 2) | 248/0 (TM 4) |

HUM 29 — Holy Water Font, Guardian Angel

(CE) Closed Edition. Modeled by master sculptor Reinhold Unger in 1935 in two sizes. Because of the fragile wing design, it was discontinued in 1958 and replaced with a new design by Gerhard Skrobek and given the new model number HUM 248.

☐ 29 ....2.50 x 5.75"..........(CE) ....❶ ....$1300—1500
☐ 29/0 ....2.875 x 6.00"........(CE) ....❶ ....$1300—1500
☐ 29/0 ....2.875 x 6.00"........(CE) ....❷ ....$1000—1250
☐ 29/0 ....2.875 x 6.00"........(CE) ....❸ ....$950—1000
☐ 29/I ....3.00 x 6.375"........(CE) ....❶ ....$1750—2000
☐ 29/I ....3.00 x 6.375"........(CE) ....❷ ....$1500—1750

.... HUM TERM ....

DECIMAL POINT: This incised "period" or dot was used in a somewhat random fashion by the W. Goebel Porzellanfabrik over the years. The decimal point is and was primarily used to reduce confusion in reading the incised numbers on the underside of the figurines. Example: 66. helps one realize that the designation is sixty-six and not ninety-nine.

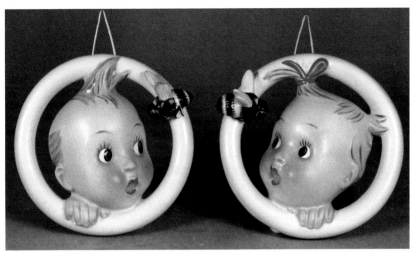

30/0 A   30/0 B

30/0 A   30/I A

30/0 B   30/I B

HUM 30 — Ba-Bee-Ring

Old name: "Hummel Rings." Originally modeled in 1935 by master sculptor Reinhold Unger. There is some size variation between old and new pieces. Early red color rings are extremely rare. Now produced in tan color only. The girl, 30 B always has orange color hair ribbon, except on red color rings, then it is blue. Although now made in only one size, current production models still have incised "O" size designator. Factory representatives state that this "will possibly disappear sometime in the future." Priced by the set of two. Also found unpainted in white overglaze finish. "Ba-Bee-Rings" sold for $4.00 a pair on 1955 price list.

☐ 30/0 A&B ....4.75 x 5.00" ....(CE) ....❶ ....$550—700
☐ 30/0 A&B ....4.75 x 5.00" ....(CE) ....❷ ....$350—450
☐ 30/0 A&B ....4.75 x 5.00" ....(CE) ....❸ ....$325—350
☐ 30/0 A&B ....4.75 x 5.00" ....(CE) ....❹ ....$300—325
☐ 30/0 A&B ....4.75 x 5.00" ....(CE) ....❺ ....$260—280
☐ 30/0 A&B ....4.75 x 5.00" ....(CE) ....❻ ....$250—260
☐ 30/0 A&B ....4.75 x 5.00" ....(CE) ....❼ ....$245—250
☐ 30/0 A&B ....4.75 x 5.00" ....(OE) ....❽ $245
☐ 30/I A&B ....5.25 x 6.00" ....(CE) ....❶ ....$2000—3500
☐ 30/0 A&B ....Red Rings ....(CE) ....❶ ....$6000—7000
☐ 30/I A&B ....Red Rings ....(CE) ....❶ ....$8000—9000

31

Note black child on left

(TM 1+1) Double crown   *Stamped with "Hummel" family crest*

HUM 31 — Silent Night with Black Child/Advent Group with Candle (CE)

Similar to HUM 54 except embossed earring and bare feet of black child. Modeled in 1935 by master sculptor Arthur Moeller but not produced in quantity. HUM 31 was also produced and sold with all white children and also considered extremely rare. HUM 31 was still listed in old German price lists as late as 1956. That does not necessarily mean that it was produced and sold at that time. It could possibly have been listed in error since so very, very few have been located. According to factory representatives, a few HUM 54 were produced with a black child, but wearing shoes instead of bare feet or without shoes with white marks to indicate toes. The figurine photographed here is particularly unique since it was originally purchased from Mrs. Victoria Hummel, the mother of Sister Hummel. Her mother died on 24 October 1983 at the age of 98. This figurine is part of the Robert L. Miller collection.

☐ 31 ....3.50 x 5.00" ......(CE) ....❶ ....$10,000—15,000 (White children)
☐ 31 ....3.50 x 5.00" ......(CE) ....❶ ....$20,000—25,000 (Black child)

.... **HUM TERM** ....

CURRENT PRODUCTION: The term used to describe those items currently being produced by the W. Goebel Porzellanfabrik of Roedental, West Germany.

32/0 (TM 1+1)   *32/0 (TM 2)*   *32/I (TM 1)*

HUM 32 — Little Gabriel

There are many size variations in this figurine that was first modeled by master sculptor Reinhold Unger in 1935. Called "Joyous News" in some old catalogues. Newer models have no size designator since it is now produced in only the small size. The large size is found incised 32/I or 32 only and is considered rare. "Little Gabriel" was restyled in 1982 with several changes—arms are now apart, angle of the wings is longer and the incised "M. I. Hummel" signature is on the top of the base rather than on the side, as in the past. Listed as (TW) "Temporarily Withdrawn" in January 1999.

☐	32/0	5.00 to 5.50"	(CE)	❶	$450—550
☐	32/0	5.00 to 5.50"	(CE)	❷	$300—375
☐	32/0	5.00 to 5.50"	(CE)	❸	$225—250
☐	32/0	5.00 to 5.50"	(CE)	❹	$200—225
☐	32/0	5.00"	(CE)	❺	$180—200
☐	32	5.00"	(CE)	❺	$180—200
☐	32	5.00"	(CE)	❻	$170—180
☐	32	5.00"	(TW)	❼	$165—170
☐	32/I	5.75 to 6.00"	(CE)	❶	$2000—2500
☐	32/I	5.75 to 6.00"	(CE)	❷	$1500—2000
☐	32/I	5.75 to 6.00"	(CE)	❸	$1200—1500
☐	32	5.75 to 6.00"	(CE)	❶	$2000—2500
☐	32	5.75 to 6.00"	(CE)	❷	$1500—2000

New (TM 6)   *Old (TM 5)*

"FAIENCE" (TM 1)   *(TM 2)*

HUM 33 — Ashtray, Joyful

First modeled by master sculptor Reinhold Unger in 1935. Older models have slightly different construction of ashtray and are usually slightly larger. HUM 33 "Joyful Ashtray" was listed as (TW) "Temporarily Withdrawn" from production on 31 December 1984, but may be reinstated at some future date. It is very unlikely, in our opinion, that this item will ever be made again. Also found decorated in the "Faience" technique with bright colors and glossy finish—value would be $3000 to $5000. An unusual example was found with orange dress and blue shoes, which is the reverse of the normal colors—value $2000 to $3000.

☐ 33........3.75 x 6.00" ....(CE) ....❶ ....$400—650
☐ 33........3.75 x 6.00" ....(CE) ....❷ ....$300—350
☐ 33........3.75 x 6.00" ....(CE) ....❸ ....$220—250
☐ 33........3.75 x 6.00" ....(CE) ....❹ ....$200—220
☐ 33........3.75 x 6.00" ....(CE) ....❺ ....$190—200
☐ 33........3.75 x 6.00" ....(**TW**) ....❻ ....$175—190

HUM 34 — Ashtray, Singing Lesson

First modeled by master sculptor Arthur Moeller in 1935. Slight variation in colors of older models. Several variations in construction on bottom of ashtray. The "M.I. Hummel" signature is usually found under the lip of the ashtray on most older models, and on top of rim on newer models. "Singing Lesson" ashtray was (TW) "Temporarily Withdrawn" from production on 31 December 1989, but may be reinstated at some future date.

☐ 34........3.50 to 6.25" ....(CE) ....❶ ....$450—650
☐ 34........3.50 to 6.25" ....(CE) ....❷ ....$300—350
☐ 34........3.50 to 6.25" ....(CE) ....❸ ....$220—250
☐ 34........3.50 to 6.25" ....(CE) ....❹ ....$200—220
☐ 34........3.50 to 6.25" ....(CE) ....❺ ....$190—200
☐ 34........3.50 to 6.25" ....(**TW**) ....❻ ....$175—190

HUM 35 — Holy Water Font, Good Shepherd

First modeled by master sculptor Reinhold Unger in 1935. There are slight variations in size as well as variations in the construction of the bowl of font. Also found in the large size without a size designator—incised 35 only. Found with yellow lambs and green grass by angel's feet. Both sizes have been found made in porcelain rather than the normal ceramics.

35/I (TM 1)   35/0 (TM 1)

☐ 35/0	2.50 x 4.75"	(CE)	❶	$275—300
☐ 35/0	2.50 x 4.75"	(CE)	❷	$140—160
☐ 35/0	2.50 x 4.75"	(CE)	❸	$90—95
☐ 35/0	2.50 x 4.75"	(CE)	❹	$80—90
☐ 35/0	2.50 x 4.75"	(CE)	❺	$80—85
☐ 35/0	2.50 x 4.75"	(CE)	❻	$75—80
☐ 35/0	2.50 x 4.75"	(CE)	❼	$70—75
☐ 35/0	2.50 x 4.75"	(TW)	❽	$69.50
☐ 35	2.75 x 5.75"	(CE)	❶	$400—450
☐ 35/I	2.75 x 5.75"	(CE)	❶	$375—425
☐ 35/I	2.75 x 5.75"	(CE)	❷	$275—375
☐ 35/I	2.75 x 5.75"	(CE)	❸	$175—225

HUM 36 — Holy Water Font, Child with Flowers

First modeled by master sculptor Reinhold Unger in 1935. There are slight variations in size, color and in the construction of the bowl of the font. Also called "Flower Angel" or "Angel with Flowers."

36/I (TM 1)   36/0 (TM 1)

☐ 36/0	3.50 x 4.50"	(CE)	❶	$275—300
☐ 36/0	3.50 x 4.50"	(CE)	❷	$140—160
☐ 36/0	3.50 x 4.50"	(CE)	❸	$90—95
☐ 36/0	3.50 x 4.50"	(CE)	❹	$85—90
☐ 36/0	3.50 x 4.50"	(CE)	❺	$80—85
☐ 36/0	3.50 x 4.50"	(CE)	❻	$75—80
☐ 36/0	3.50 x 4.50"	(CE)	❼	$70—75
☐ 36/0	3.50 x 4.50"	(OE)	❽	$69.50
☐ 36	3.50 x 4.50"	(CE)	❶	$400—450
☐ 36/I	3.50 x 4.50"	(CE)	❶	$375—425
☐ 36/I	3.50 x 4.50"	(CE)	❷	$275—375
☐ 36/I	3.50 x 5.00"	(CE)	❸	$175—225

New model (TM 5)   *Old model (TM 1)*

HUM 37 — Herald Angels, Candleholder

Many variations through the years. On older models the candleholder is much taller than on the newer ones. The order of placement of the angels may vary on the older models. Current production pieces have a half-inch wider base. Originally modeled in 1935 by master sculptor Reinhold Unger. Early "crown" mark examples are sometimes found with light purple shoes rather than the dark brown shoes found on newer models. "Herald Angels" candleholder was (TW) "Temporarily Withdrawn" from production on 31 December 1989, but may be reinstated at some future date. A few sample pieces have been found decorated with bright colors and glossy finish of the "Faience" technique—value would be $3000 to $5000.

☐ 37 ....2.75 x 4.00" ....(CE)...........❶ ....$600—800
☐ 37 ....2.75 x 4.00" ....(CE)...........❷ ....$400—450
☐ 37 ....2.75 x 4.00 to 4.50" ......(CE)...........❸ ....$250—275
☐ 37 ....2.75 x 4.00 to 4.50" ......(CE)...........❹ ....$225—250
☐ 37 ....2.75 x 4.00 to 4.50" ......(CE)...........❺ ....$200—225
☐ 37 ....2.75 x 4.00 to 4.50" ......(TW) ....❻ ....$180—200

.... HUM TERM ....

MOLD GROWTH: In the earlier days of figurine production the working molds were made of plaster of paris. As these molds were used, the various molded parts became larger due to the repeated usage. With modern technology at the Goebel factory and the use of acrylic resin molds, this problem has been eliminated and today the collector finds very few size differences within a given size designation.

38/0 (TM 3)   *39/0 (TM 3)*   *40/0 (TM 3)*

HUM 38 — Angel, Joyous News with Lute, Candleholder

HUM 39 — Angel, Joyous News with Accordion, Candleholder

HUM 40 — Angel, Joyous News with Trumpet, Candleholder

Roman numerals to the left of the HUM number indicate the size of the candle that fits into the figurine. Size I is .6 cm, size III is 1 cm. (Note: Not all figurines which hold candles are photographed with candles in this book, but they are usually sold with candles.) Also called "Little Heavenly Angel" in old catalogues. Also known as "Angel Trio" candleholders. Candleholders are always on right side of angel. These three figurines were originally modeled in 1935 by master sculptor Reinhold Unger. Very early pieces do not have a size designator—incised 38. 39. 40. only. Since these figurines are relatively small in size, the signature may be only "Hum" on the back or on the leg of the angel. HUM 38/0 sometimes found with green shoes.

☐ 1/38/0 ....2.00 to 2.50".......(CE) ....❶ ....$175—200
☐ 1/38/0 ....2.00 to 2.50".......(CE) ....❷ ....$120—140
☐ 1/38/0 ....2.00 to 2.50".......(CE) ....❸ ....$100—110
☐ 1/38/0 ....2.00 to 2.50".......(CE) ....❹ ....$90—95
☐ 1/38/0 ....2.00 to 2.50".......(CE) ....❺ ....$85—90
☐ 1/38/0 ....2.00 to 2.50".......(CE) ....❻ ....$80—85
☐ 1/38/0 ....2.00 to 2.50".......(CE) ....❼ ....$75—80
☐ 1/38/0 ....2.00 to 2.50"......**(TW)** ....❽ ....$75—80
☐ III/38/0 ...2.00 to 2.50".......(CE) ....❶ ....$175—200
☐ III/38/0 ...2.00 to 2.50".......(CE) ....❷ ....$120—140
☐ III/38/0 ...2.00 to 2.50".......(CE) ....❸ ....$100—110
☐ III/38/0 ...2.00 to 2.50".......(CE) ....❹ ....$90—95
☐ III/38/0 ...2.00 to 2.50".......(CE) ....❺ ....$85—90
☐ III/38/0 ...2.00 to 2.50"......**(TW)** ....❻ ....$80—85
☐ III/38/I ...2.50 to 2.75".......(CE) ....❶ ....$300—350
☐ III/38/I ...2.50 to 2.75".......(CE) ....❷ ....$250—300

☐ III/38/I ....2.50 to 2.75”......(CE) ....**❸** ....$200—250
☐ 1/39/0 ....2.00 to 2.50”......(CE) ....**❶** ....$150—200
☐ 1/39/0 ....2.00 to 2.50”......(CE) ....**❷** ....$100—125
☐ 1/39/0 ....2.00 to 2.50”......(CE) ....**❸** ....$95—100
☐ 1/39/0 ....2.00 to 2.50”......(CE) ....**❹** ....$90—95
☐ 1/39/0 ....2.00 to 2.50”......(CE) ....**❺** ....$85—90
☐ 1/39/0 ....2.00 to 2.50”......(CE) ....**❻** ....$80—85
☐ 1/39/0 ....2.00 to 2.50”......(CE) ....**❼** ....$68—70
☐ 1/39/0 ....2.00 to 2.50”......(**TW**) ....**❽** ....$75—80
☐ III/39/0 ....2.00 to 2.50”......(CE) ....**❶** ....$150—200
☐ III/39/0 ....2.00 to 2.50”......(CE) ....**❷** ....$100—125
☐ III/39/0 ....2.00 to 2.50”......(CE) ....**❸** ....$90—100
☐ III/39/0 ....2.00 to 2.50”......(CE) ....**❹** ....$80—90
☐ III/39/0 ....2.00 to 2.50”......(CE) ....**❺** ....$70—80
☐ III/39/0 ....2.00 to 2.50”......(**TW**) ....**❻** ....$60—70
☐ III/39/I ....2.50 to 2.75”......(CE) ....**❶** ....$300—350
☐ III/39/I ....2.50 to 2.75”......(CE) ....**❷** ....$250—300
☐ III/39/I ....2.50 to 2.75”......(CE) ....**❸** ....$200—250

☐ 1/40/0 ....2.00 to 2.50”......(CE) ....**❶** ....$150—200
☐ 1/40/0 ....2.00 to 2.50”......(CE) ....**❷** ....$100—125
☐ 1/40/0 ....2.00 to 2.50”......(CE) ....**❸** ....$95—100
☐ 1/40/0 ....2.00 to 2.50”......(CE) ....**❹** ....$90—95
☐ 1/40/0 ....2.00 to 2.50”......(CE) ....**❺** ....$85—90
☐ 1/40/0 ....2.00 to 2.50”......(CE) ....**❻** ....$80—85
☐ 1/40/0 ....2.00 to 2.50”......(CE) ....**❼** ....$75—80
☐ 1/40/0 ....2.00 to 2.50”......(**TW**) ....**❽** ....$75—80
☐ III/40/0 ....2.00 to 2.50”......(CE) ....**❶** ....$150—200
☐ III/40/0 ....2.00 to 2.50”......(CE) ....**❷** ....$100—125
☐ III/40/0 ....2.00 to 2.50”......(CE) ....**❸** ....$90—100
☐ III/40/0 ....2.00 to 2.50”......(CE) ....**❹** ....$80—90
☐ III/40/0 ....2.00 to 2.50”......(CE) ....**❺** ....$70—80
☐ III/40/0 ....2.00 to 2.50”......(**TW**) ....**❻** ....$60—70
☐ III/40/I ....2.00 to 2.75”......(CE) ....**❶** ....$300—350
☐ III/40/I ....2.00 to 2.75”......(CE) ....**❷** ....$250—300
☐ III/40/I ....2.00 to 2.75”......(CE) ....**❸** ....$200—250

HUM 41 — Singing Lesson (without base) (CN)
Factory book of models indicates this piece is similar to HUM 34 (Singing Lesson, Ashtray). Closed 31 October 1935. No known examples.

☐ 41 ....(CN)...........................$5000—10,000

| 42/0 (TM 1) | 42/0 (TM 2) Blue | 42/I (TM 1) |

HUM 42 — Good Shepherd

First modeled by master sculptor Reinhold Unger in 1935. Normally has a rust-colored gown. Factory sample of small size 42/0 has light blue gown. Several examples are now in private collections, including the Robert L. Miller collection, value $2000–$3000. Size 42/I is considered rare and no longer produced in large size. Factory information states that (0) size designator will eventually be dropped from number. Current production still incised 42/0. Small size (42/0) was listed as (TW) "Temporarily Withdrawn" in January 1999.

☐ 42/0	5.75 to 6.25".....(CE)	❶	$750—900
☐ 42/0	6.25 to 6.50".....(CE)	❷	$425—600
☐ 42/0	6.25 to 6.50".....(CE)	❸	$375—425
☐ 42/0	6.25 to 6.50".....(CE)	❹	$325—375
☐ 42/0	6.25"................(CE)	❺	$300—325
☐ 42/0	6.25"................(CE)	❻	$290—300
☐ 42/0	6.25"................(TW)	❼	$280—290
☐ 42/I	7.25 to 7.75".....(CE)	❶	$7000—8000
☐ 42/I	7.25 to 8.00" ....(CE)	❷	$6000—7000
☐ 42/I	7.25 to 8.00" ....(CE)	❸	$5000—6000

(TM 2)   (TM 1)   (TM 3)

HUM 43 — March Winds

Many size variations with older pieces slightly larger. First modeled by master sculptor Reinhold Unger in 1935. Called "Urchin" in some old catalogues. There is some variation in the front "flap" of boy's trousers; sometimes this is in the mold, other times made with white paint—not attributed to any certain time period. In 1996 a 2.75" size (3.25" with base) with incised model number 43 5/0 was produced as part of the "Pen Pals" series of personalized name card table decorations. The original issue price was $55 in 1996. In the fall of 2001 a "March Winds" Progression Set was issued in a (LE) Limited Edition of 1,000 sets worldwide. Each piece has the incised model number 43/0, the (TM 8) trademark, and Special Edition — "ARBEITSMUSTER Series" on the bottom of each of the three figurines. HUM 43 "March Winds" is part of 70th Anniversary Collection.

☐ 43 5/0	....2.75"	(CE)	❼	$55—60
☐ 43	4.75 to 5.50"	(CE)	❶	$500—600
☐ 43	4.75 to 5.50"	(CE)	❷	$290—375
☐ 43	4.75 to 5.50"	(CE)	❸	$260—280
☐ 43	4.75 to 5.50"	(CE)	❹	$210—250
☐ 43	4.75 to 5.50"	(CE)	❺	$200—210
☐ 43	4.75 to 5.50"	(CE)	❻	$195—200
☐ 43	4.75 to 5.50"	(CE)	❼	$190—195
☐ 43	5.25"	**(LE)**	❽	$289 (70th Anniversary)
☐ 43/0	4.75 to 5.50"	**(OE)**	❽	$190
☐ 43/0	5.25"	(LE)	❽	$425 (Progression Set)

*March Winds
Progression Set*

44 A   *44 B*

HUM 44 A — Culprits, Table Lamp

Originally modeled by master sculptor Arthur Moeller in 1935. Older models have a half-inch larger base, and hole for electrical switch on top of base. They usually have a 1935 copyright date incised. "Culprits" table lamp was (TW) "Temporarily Withdrawn" from production on 31 December 1989, but may be reinstated at some future date.

☐ 44 ....8.50 to 9.50"......(CE) ....❶ ....$650—750
☐ 44A ....8.50 to 9.50"......(CE) ....❶ ....$500—650
☐ 44A ....8.50 to 9.50"......(CE) ....❷ ....$425—475
☐ 44A ....8.50 to 9.50"......(CE) ....❸ ....$400—425
☐ 44A ....8.50" ....(CE) ....❹ ....$375—400
☐ 44A ....8.50" ....(CE) ....❺ ....$350—375
☐ 44A ....8.50" ....(TW) ....❻ ....$325—350

Hum 44 B — Out of Danger, Table Lamp

Originally modeled by master sculptor Arthur Moeller in 1935. Older models have a half-inch larger base, and hole for electrical switch on top of base. They usually have a 1936 copyright date incised. Variation in color of the girl's dress. Old "crown" trademark (TM 1) examples are found with girl in black dress while the normal blue dress is found on all others. "Out of Danger" table lamp was (TW) "Temporarily Withdrawn" from production on 31 December 1989, but may be reinstated at some future date.

☐ 44B ....8.50 to 9.50"......(CE) ....❶ ....$500—650
☐ 44B ....8.50 to 9.50"......(CE) ....❷ ....$425—475
☐ 44B ....8.50 to 9.50"......(CE) ....❸ ....$400—425
☐ 44B ....8.50" ....(CE) ....❹ ....$375—400
☐ 44B ....8.50" ....(CE) ....❺ ....$350—375
☐ 44B ....8.50" ....(TW) ....❻ ....$325—350

Many size and color variations   *Terra Cotta*

HUM 45 — Madonna With Halo

HUM 46 — Madonna Without Halo

These beautiful Madonnas were first modeled by master sculptor Reinhold Unger in 1935. Sometimes called "The Holy Virgin" in old catalogues. There are many size variations as well as color variations. Produced in white overglaze, pastel blue, pastel pink, heavy blue and ivory finish. Also has been found in reddish brown terra cotta finish signed "M. I. Hummel" but without incised number— height 11 inches. Value $2000 to $3000. Some pieces have been mismarked 45 instead of 46, etc. Some pieces have been found with both 45 and 46 on the same piece. In the spring of 1982 the large sizes (45/III and 46/III) (both white overglaze finish as well as color) were listed by Goebel as (TW) "Temporarily Withdrawn," to be possibly reinstated at a future date. Sometimes an Arabic size designator is used on older models. The small sizes (45/0 and 46/0), both in white overglaze finish as well as color, were (TW) "Temporarily Withdrawn" from production on 31 December 1984, but may be reinstated at some future date. The medium size (46/I), both in white overglaze finish and in color, were (TW) "Temporarily Withdrawn" from production on 31 December 1989, but may be reinstated at some future date. This leaves only the 45/I "Madonna With Halo" in color as an (OE) "Open Edition" in this series at this time. Some "crown" (TM 1) trademark pieces have been found without the usual "M. I. Hummel" signature, but do have the normal 45 or 46 model number. In 2005 the color 45/III size was part of the 70th Anniversary Collection.

```
                                           Color ............ White
45/0 ......10.50" ...............(CE)........❶ ......☐ $200—275 ....☐ $125—175
45/0 ......10.50 to 11.75" .....(CE)........❷ ......☐ $95—175 ......☐ $85—125
45/0 ......10.50" ...............(CE)........❸ ......☐ $85—95 ......☐ $55—70
45/0 ......10.50" ...............(CE)........❹ ......☐ $70—85 ......☐ $50—55
45/0 ......10.50" ...............(CE)........❺ ......☐ $65—70 ......☐ $45—50
45/0 ......10.50" ...............(TW)........❻ ......☐ $60—65 ......☐ $40—45

                                           Color ............ White
45/I .....11.50 to 13.25" ......(CE)........❶ ......☐ $300—400 ....☐ $150—200
45/I .....11.50 to 13.25" ......(CE)........❷ ......☐ $210—225 ....☐ $100—150
45/I .....11.50 to 13.25" ......(CE)........❸ ......☐ $200—210 ....☐ $90—100
45/I .....11.50 to 13.25" ......(CE)........❹ ......☐ $195—200 ....☐ $85—95
45/I .....11.50 to 13.25" ......(CE)........❺ ......☐ $180—185 ....☐ $80—85
45/I .....11.50 to 13.25" ......(CE)........❻ ......☐ $185—190 ....☐ $75—80
45/I .....11.50 to 13.25" ......(CE)........❼ ......☐ $180—185 ....☐ $75—80
45/I .....11.50 to 13.25" ......(OE)........❽ ......☐ $119 ........☐
45/III ...15.50 to 16.75" ......(CE)........❶ ......☐ $400—600 ....☐ $250—350
45/III ...15.50 to 16.75" ......(CE)........❷ ......☐ $275—375 ....☐ $175—225
45/III ...15.50 to 16.75" ......(CE)........❸ ......☐ $175—220 ....☐ $140—165
45/III ...15.50 to 16.75" ......(CE)........❹ ......☐ $165—175 ....☐ $115—140
45/III ...15.50 to 16.75" ......(CE)........❺ ......☐ $155—165 ....☐ $110—115
45/III ...15.50 to 16.75" ......(TW)........❻ ......☐ $150—155 ....☐ $105—110
45/III ...16.00" ...............(LE)........❽ ......☐ $429   (70th Anniversary)

                                           Color ............ White
46/0 ......10.25" ...............(CE)........❶ ......☐ $200—275 ....☐ $125—175
46/0 ......10.25" ...............(CE)........❷ ......☐ $95—175 ......☐ $85—125
46/0 ......10.25" ...............(CE)........❸ ......☐ $85—95 ......☐ $55—70
46/0 ......10.25" ...............(CE)........❹ ......☐ $70—85 ......☐ $50—55
46/0 ......10.25" ...............(CE)........❺ ......☐ $65—70 ......☐ $45—50
46/0 ......10.25" ...............(TW)........❻ ......☐ $60—65 ......☐ $40—45
46/I .....11.25 to 13.00" ......(CE)........❶ ......☐ $300—400 ....☐ $200—250
46/I .....11.25 to 13.00" ......(CE)........❷ ......☐ $170—225 ....☐ $125—175
46/I .....11.25 to 13.00" ......(CE)........❸ ......☐ $160—170 ....☐ $110—125
46/I .....11.25 to 13.00" ......(CE)........❹ ......☐ $155—160 ....☐ $100—110
46/I .....11.25 to 13.00" ......(CE)........❺ ......☐ $145—150 ....☐ $90—100
46/I .....11.25 to 13.00" ......(TW)........❻ ......☐ $140—145 ....☐ $85—90
46/III ...15.25 to 16.25" ......(CE)........❶ ......☐ $400—600 ....☐ $250—350
46/III ...15.25 to 16.25" ......(CE)........❷ ......☐ $275—375 ....☐ $175—225
46/III ...115.25 to 16.25" .....(CE)........❸ ......☐ $175—220 ....☐ $140—165
46/III ...15.25 to 16.25" ......(CE)........❹ ......☐ $165—175 ....☐ $115—140
46/III ...15.25 to 16.25" ......(CE)........❺ ......☐ $155—165 ....☐ $110—115
46/III ...15.25 to 16.25" ......(TW)........❻ ......☐ $150—155 ....☐ $105—110
```

NOTE: HUM 1 through HUM 46 were all put
on the market in 1935.

HUM 47 —
Goose Girl
First modeled by master sculptor Arthur Moeller in 1936. There are many size variations between the older and newer models. Sometimes called "Little Gooseherd" in old catalogues. Older models have a blade of grass between the geese. This has been eliminated completely or reduced in size on newer models. The large size 47/II was restyled with the new textured finish in the early 1970s. Sometimes incised 47/2 or 47.2. instead of 47/II. Large size (47/II) was listed as (TW) "Temporarily Withdrawn" on 1993 price list. Information located in an old Goebel product book indicates that master sculptor Arthur Moeller in 1935 produced samples of "Goose Girl" in the 47/0 size with a round attached "pot" and another with an oblong attached "bowl." The sample with the "bowl" is now in the collection of a collector in the Midwest. An example with the attached round "pot" was found in Europe. For more information, see: Rare/Unique Sample Variations of "M. I. Hummel" Figurines in back of this book. New 12.5" size released in 2004 has three geese.

☐ 47 3/0	....4.00 to 4.25"	......(CE)	............❶	.........$550—700
☐ 47 3/0	....4.00 to 4.25"	......(CE)	............❷	.........$300—400
☐ 47 3/0	....4.00 to 4.25"	......(CE)	............❸	.........$275—300
☐ 47 3/0	....4.00 to 4.25"	......(CE)	............❹	.........$230—260
☐ 47 3/0	....4.00 to 4.25"	......(CE)	............❺	.........$220—230
☐ 47 3/0	....4.00 to 4.25""	....(CE)	............❻	.........$210—220
☐ 47 3/0	....4.00 to 4.25"	......(CE)	............❼	.........$205—210
☐ 47 3/0	....4.00 to 4.25"	......(OE)	............❽	.........$219
☐ 47	.........5.00"	.................(CE)	............❶	.........$800—900
☐ 47/0	....4.75 to 5.25"	......(CE)	............❶	.........$750—900
☐ 47/0	....4.75 to 5.25"	......(CE)	............❷	.........$500—700
☐ 47/0	....4.75 to 5.25"	......(CE)	............❸	.........$375—400
☐ 47/0	....4.75 to 5.25"	......(CE)	............❹	.........$350—375
☐ 47/0	....4.75 to 5.25"	......(CE)	............❺	........$335—350
☐ 47/0	....4.75 to 5.25"	......(CE)	............❻	........$325—335
☐ 47/0	....4.75 to 5.25"	......(CE)	............❼	.........$320—325
☐ 47/0	....4.75 to 5.25"	......(OE)	............❽	.........$319
☐ 47/II	.......7.00 to 8.00"	......(CE)	............❶	.........$1000—1300
☐ 47/II	.......7.00 to 8.00"	......(CE)	............❷	.......$700—900
☐ 47/II	.......7.00 to 7.50"	......(CE)	............❸	.......$600—700
☐ 47/II	.......7.00 to 7.50"	......(CE)	............❹	.........$500—600
☐ 47/II	.......7.00 to 7.50"	......(CE)	............❺	.........$420—440
☐ 47/II	.......7.00 to 7.50"	......(CE)	............❻	.........$410—420
☐ 47/II	.......7.00 to 7.50"	......(TW)	............❼	.........$400—410
☐ 47/III	......12.50"	.................(LE)	............❽	.........$2000

47/II (TM 5)   47/0 (TM 2)   47/0 (TM 5)   47 3/0 (TM 1)

Current Model

HUM 48 — Madonna Plaque

This bas-relief plaque was first modeled by master sculptor Reinhold Unger in 1936. Old crown mark pieces are slightly smaller in size. Newer models have hole on back for hanging while older models have two small holes to use for hanging on wall with cord. Sometimes incised 48/2 instead of 48/II and 48/5 instead of 48/V. Also sold in white overglaze finish at one time in Belgium but are now considered rare. Very early models have a flat back while all others have a recessed back. Large size 48/II was listed as (TW) "Temporarily Withdrawn" from production on 31 December 1984, and the small size 48/0 was (W) "Temporarily Withdrawn" from production on 31 December 1989, but may be reinstated at some future date.

☐ 48/0	3.25 x 4.25"	(CE)	❶	$325—375
☐ 48/0	3.25 x 4.25"	(CE)	❷	$175—225
☐ 48/0	3.25 x 4.25"	(CE)	❸	$110—135
☐ 48/0	3.25 x 4.25"	(CE)	❹	$95—110
☐ 48/0	3.25 x 4.25"	(CE)	❺	$90—95
☐ 48/0	3.25 x 4.25"	(TW)	❻	$85—90
☐ 48	4.75 x 5.75"	(CE)	❶	$650—850
☐ 48/II	4.75 x 5.75"	(CE)	❶	$550—800
☐ 48/II	4.75 x 5.75"	(CE)	❷	$375—525
☐ 48/II	4.75 x 5.75"	(CE)	❸	$190—250
☐ 48/II	4.75 x 5.75"	(CE)	❹	$160—190
☐ 48/II	4.75 x 5.75"	(CE)	❺	$135—145
☐ 48/II	4.75 x 5.75"	(TW)	❻	$130—135
☐ 48/V	8.75 x 10.75"	(CE)	❶	$1500—2000
☐ 48/V	8.75 x 10.75"	(CE)	❷	$1250—1500
☐ 48/V	8.75 x 10.75"	(CE)	❸	$1000—1250
☐ 48/II	4.75 x 5.75"	(CE)	❸	$500—600 (white overglaze)

Early sample with bowl

White variation of 48/0

HUM 49 — To Market
First modeled by master sculptor Arthur Moeller in 1936. Sometimes called "Brother and Sister" in old catalogues. Small size 49 3/0 never has bottle in basket. Some newly produced figurines in 6.25" size have appeared without a size designator. Only the number 49 is incised on the bottom along with the 5 trademark. This was corrected on later production. Girl is same as HUM 98 "Sister." The large size (49/I) was listed as (TW) "Temporarily Withdrawn" on 31 December 1984, but may be reinstated at some future date. The suggested retail price on the large size (49/I) on the 1984 price list was $240. Information located in an old Goebel product book indicates that master sculptor Arthur Moeller in 1935 produced a sample of "To Market" in the 5-inch size with an attached "bowl" similar to HUM 13/0 "Meditation" with attached "bowl." An example of this rare piece has NOT been found, as of this writing. For more information, see: Rare/Unique Sample Variations of "M. I. Hummel" Figurines in back of this book. Size (49/0) was listed as (TW) "Temporarily Withdrawn" in January 1999. In 2000 the 49/I size was included in the "Millenium Revival" collection.

49/I (TM 1+1)   49/0 (TM 1+1)   49 3/0 (TM 1)

☐ 49 3/0	4.00"	(CE)	❶	$500—650
☐ 49 3/0	4.00"	(CE)	❷	$300—375
☐ 49 3/0	4.00"	(CE)	❸	$250—275
☐ 49 3/0	4.00"	(CE)	❹	$220—240
☐ 49 3/0	4.00"	(CE)	❺	$210—220
☐ 49 3/0	4.00"	(CE)	❻	$200—210
☐ 49 3/0	4.00"	(CE)	❼	$195—200
☐ 49 3/0	4.00"	(CE)	❽	$195—200
☐ 49/0	5.00 to 5.50"	(CE)	❶	$750—1000
☐ 49/0	5.00 to 5.50"	(CE)	❷	$450—625
☐ 49/0	5.00 to 5.50"	(CE)	❸	$425—450
☐ 49/0	5.00 to 5.50"	(CE)	❹	$375—425
☐ 49/0	5.00 to 5.50"	(CE)	❺	$350—375
☐ 49/0	5.00 to 5.50"	(CE)	❻	$335—350
☐ 49/0	5.00 to 5.50"	(TW)	❼	$325—335
☐ 49/I	6.25 to 6.50"	(CE)	❶	$1400—1700
☐ 49/I	6.25 to 6.50"	(CE)	❷	$1200—1400
☐ 49/I	6.25 to 6.50"	(CE)	❸	$550—700
☐ 49/I	6.25 to 6.25"	(CE)	❹	$500—550
☐ 49/I	6.25 to 6.25"	(CE)	❺	$450—475
☐ 49/I	6.25 to 6.25"	(CE)	❻	$425—450
☐ 49/I	6.25 to 6.25"	(LE)	❽	$475
☐ 49	6.25 to 6.50"	(CE)	❶	$1400—1700
☐ 49	6.25 to 6.50"	(CE)	❷	$1200—1400
☐ 49	6.25 to 6.50"	(CE)	❺	$600—700

50/I (TM 5)   *50/0 (TM 5)*   *50 2/0 (TM 3)*

HUM 50 — Volunteers

Originally modeled by master sculptor Reinhold Unger in 1936. Listed as "Playing Soldiers" in old catalogues. Sizes 50/0 and 50/I are difficult to find in older trademarks but were reinstated in 1979 with (TM 5) trademark. The original drawing for this figurine was used by Ars Sacra Herbert Dubler on small note paper bearing a 1943 copyright date. The large size (50/I) was listed as (TW) "Temporarily Withdrawn" from production on 31 December 1984, but may be reinstated at some future date. The small size (50 2/0) was produced with special commemorative backstamp in limited quantity and was available only through U.S. Military Exchanges; retail price was $150—175. The suggested retail price on the large size (50/I) on the 1984 price list was $240.

☐ 50 2/0 ....4.75 to 5.00"......(CE) ....❷ ....$425—500
☐ 50 2/0 ....4.75 to 5.00"......(CE) ....❸ ....$350—400
☐ 50 2/0 ....4.75 to 5.00"......(CE) ....❹ ....$325—350
☐ 50 2/0 ....4.75 to 5.00"......(CE) ....❺ ....$290—300
☐ 50 2/0 ....4.75 to 5.00"......(CE) ....❻ ....$285—290
☐ 50 2/0 ....4.75 to 5.00"......(CE) ....❼ ....$280—285
☐ 50 2/0 ....4.75 to 5.00"......(OE) ....❽ $279
☐ 50/0 ....5.50 to 6.00"......(CE) ....❶ ....$850—1100
☐ 50/0 ....5.50 to 6.00"......(CE) ....❷ ....$500—650
☐ 50/0 ....5.50 to 6.00"......(CE) ....❸ ....$475—500
☐ 50/0 ....5.50 to 6.00"......(CE) ....❹ ....$425—450
☐ 50/0 ....5.50 to 6.00"......(CE) ....❺ ....$390—400
☐ 50/0 ....5.50 to 6.00"......(CE) ....❻ ....$380—385
☐ 50/0 ....5.50 to 6.00"......(CE) ....❼ ....$375—380
☐ 50/0 ....4.75 to 6.00"......(TW) ....❽ $375

HUM 50 2/0 (TM 7)
Commemorative

☐ 50/I ....6.50 to 7.00"......(CE) ....❶ ....$1200—1500
☐ 50/I ....6.50 to 7.00"......(CE) ....❷ ....$750—950
☐ 50/I ....6.50 to 7.00"......(CE) ....❸ ....$600—750
☐ 50/I ....6.50 to 7.00"......(CE) ....❹ $550-600
☐ 50/I ....6.50 to 7.00"......(CE) ....❺ ....$475—500
☐ 50/I ....6.50 to 7.00"......(TW) ....❻ ....$450—475
☐ 50 ....7.00".................(CE) ....❶ $1250–1550

51/I (TM1)   **51/0 (TM 1) 51 2/0 (TM 5) 51 3/0 (TM 1)**

HUM 51 — Village Boy

First modeled by master sculptor Arthur Moeller in 1936. Has been slightly restyled several times through the years. Size 51/0 was restyled by Theo R. Menzenbach in 1960. Some newer models have a 1961 incised copyright date. Called "Country Boy" in old catalogues. Many size variations in the older pieces. Occasionally found in the small size 51 3/0 in crown trademark with red or yellow tie and blue jacket—value: $1500—2000. The large size (51/I) was listed as (TW) "Temporarily Withdrawn" from production on 31 December 1984, but could possibly be reinstated at some future date. The small size 51 3/0 are also found with orange socks in (TM 1) & (TM 2) trademarks. In 1996 a new 2.75" size (3.25" with base) with incised model number 51 5/0 was produced as part of the six piece set of "Pen Pals" series of personalized name card table decorations. The original issue price was $55 in 1996. Size 51 2/0 listed as (TW) "Temporarily Withdrawn" in June 2002.

☐ 51 5/0	....3.00"	(CE)	❼	$55—60
☐ 51 3/0	...4.00"	(CE)	❶	$400—450
☐ 51 3/0	...4.00"	(CE)	❷	$250—300
☐ 51 3/0	...4.00"	(CE)	❸	$200—225
☐ 51 3/0	...4.00"	(CE)	❹	$165—185
☐ 51 3/0	...4.00"	(CE)	❺	$160—165
☐ 51 3/0	...4.00"	(CE)	❻	$155—160
☐ 51 3/0	...4.00"	(CE)	❼	$160 155
☐ 51 3/0	...4.00"	(TW)	❽	$150—155
☐ 51 2/0	....5.00"	(CE)	❶	$450—550
☐ 51 2/0	...5.00"	(CE)	❷	$300—350
☐ 51 2/0	...5.00"	(CE)	❸	$235—275
☐ 51 2/0	...5.00"	(CE)	❹	$210—235
☐ 51 2/0	...5.00"	(CE)	❺	$195—210
☐ 51 2/0	...5.00"	(CE)	❻	$190—195
☐ 51 2/0	...5.00"	(CE)	❼	$185—190
☐ 51 2/0	...5.00"	(TW)	❽	$185—190
☐ 51/0	......6.00 to 6.75"	(CE)	❶	$700—900
☐ 51/0	......6.00 to 6.75"	(CE)	❷	$450—550
☐ 51/0	......6.00 to 6.75"	(CE)	❸	$375—400
☐ 51/0	......6.00 to 6.75"	(CE)	❹	$325—375
☐ 51/0	......6.00 to 6.75"	(CE)	❺	$300—325
☐ 51/0	......6.00 to 6.75"	(CE)	❻	$290—300
☐ 51/0	......6.00 to 6.75"	(TW)	❼	$280—285
☐ 51/I	.......7.25 to 8.00"	(CE)	❶	$800—1100
☐ 51/I	.......7.25 to 8.00"	(CE)	❷	$500—600
☐ 51/I	.......7.25 to 8.00"	(CE)	❸	$400—475
☐ 51/I	.......7.25 to 8.00"	(CE)	❹	$350—400
☐ 51/I	.......7.25 to 8.00"	(CE)	❺	$320—350
☐ 51/I	.......7.25 to 8.00"	(TW)	❻	$300—320
☐ 51	.........8.00"	(CE)	❶	$900—1150

Old   52/I   New   Old   52/0   New

HUM 52 — Going to Grandmas

Originally modeled in 1936 by master sculptor Reinhold Unger. Called "Little Mothers of the Family" in old catalogues. All large size and older small size figurines were produced with rectangular base. Small size was restyled in the early 1960s and changed to an oval base. The objects protruding from the cone represent candy and sweets rather than flowers. The cone appears empty on the large size models. In 1979 size 52/I was restyled with a new textured finish, an oval base and sweets in the cone. Both the old and new styles are found with (TM 5) trademark. The large size (52/I) was listed as (TW) "Temporarily Withdrawn" from production on 31 December 1984, but could possibly be reinstated at some future date. The suggested retail price on the large size 52/I on the 1984 price list was $240. On most older figurines, the girl with the basket has a pink colored petticoat painted under her dress. The other girl has only a blue hemline showing. Newer models in trademarks 4, 5, 6 and 7 do not have this area painted. In 2000 the 52/I size was included in the "Millenium Revival" collection. "Going to Grandmas" was permanently retired in both sizes in 2004.

☐ 52/0	4.50 to 5.00"	(CE)	❶	$800—1000
☐ 52/0	4.50 to 5.00"	(CE)	❷	$500—600
☐ 52/0	4.50 to 5.00"	(CE)	❸	$425—475
☐ 52/0	4.50 to 5.00"	(CE)	❹	$350—400
☐ 52/0	4.50 to 5.00"	(CE)	❺	$325—350
☐ 52/0	4.50 to 5.00"	(CE)	❻	$310—320
☐ 52/0	4.50 to 5.00"	(CE)	❼	$305—310
☐ 52/0	4.50 to 5.00"	(CE)	❽	$305—310
☐ 52/I	6.00 to 6.25"	(CE)	❶	$1250—1500
☐ 52/I	6.00 to 6.25"	(CE)	❷	$800—950
☐ 52/I	6.00 to 6.25"	(CE)	❸	$650—800
☐ 52/I	6.00 to 6.25"	(CE)	❺	$550—800 old style (rectangular)
☐ 52/I	6.00 to 6.50"	(CE)	❺	$475—525 new style (oval)
☐ 52/I	6.00 to 6.25"	(CE)	❻	$455—500
☐ 52/I	6.00 to 6.25"	(CE)	❽	$450—500
☐ 52	6.25"	(CE)	❶	$1300—1600
☐ 52	6.25"	(CE)	❷	$850—1000

FINAL ISSUE
2004

HUM 53 — Joyful

First modeled by master sculptor Reinhold Unger in 1936. Many size variations—older pieces usually much larger. Listed as "Singing Lesson" in old catalogues, but also called "Banjo Betty" in an old 1950 catalogue. Some early crown (TM 1) trademark examples have orange dress and blue, purple or brown shoes. Value: $2000 to $3000. Newer models have a brown banjo. A sample was produced by Reinhold Unger in 1936 of "Joyful" with an attached "pot" but was not approved by the Siessen Convent for production. Value: $5000 to $10,000. For more information, see: Rare/Unique Sample Variations of "M. I. Hummel" figurines in back of this book. Listed as (TW) "Temporarily Withdrawn" in January 1999.

☐ 53	3.50 to 4.25"	(CE)	❶	$350—450
☐ 53	3.50 to 4.25"	(CE)	❷	$225—300
☐ 53	3.50 to 4.25"	(CE)	❸	$190—220
☐ 53	3.50"	(CE)	❹	$170—190
☐ 53	3.50"	(CE)	❺	$150—170
☐ 53	3.50"	(CE)	❻	$145—150
☐ 53	3.50"	(TW)	❼	$110 145

Old bowl style   *New jar style*   *New music box*

HUM III/53 — Joyful, Box

Bowl style box first produced in 1936. Jar style first produced and sold in 1964. Model number is found on underside of lid. "M. I. Hummel" signature is found on topside of lid directly behind figure. "Joyful" candy box was (TW) "Temporarily Withdrawn" from production on 31 December 1989, but may be reinstated at some future date. In 1996 a new music box was produced with model number IV/53 applied by decal on the bottom. This is one of four in a series of music boxes produced for the European market only at this time. May be sold in the U.S. market at some future date. Newer models have a brown banjo. IV/53 produced with German graphics on bottom in a (LE) Limited Edition of 29,900.

☐ III/53	.....6.50"	.............(CE)	...........❶	........$750—850	
☐ III/53	.....6.50"	.............(CE)	...........❷	........$575—650	
☐ III/53	.....6.50"	.............(CE)	...........❸	........$475—550	(Old Style)
☐ III/53	.....5.75"	.............(CE)	...........❸	........$300—350	(New Style)
☐ III/53	.....5.75"	.............(CE)	...........❹	........$250—275	
☐ III/53	.....5.75"	.............(CE)	...........❺	........$225—250	
☐ III/53	.....5.75"	.............(**TW**)	...........❻	........$200—225	
☐ IV/53	.....5.75"	.............(CE)	...........❼	........$250—260	(Music Box)

HUM 54 — Silent Night, Candleholder

This candleholder was first modeled by master sculptor Reinhold Unger in 1936. There are some color variations in the wings of angel. Early crown mark figurines are usually very light in color. Older pieces have smaller socket for candle. Almost identical to the model used for HUM 31 with the exception of the embossed earring and bare feet. Factory representatives state that a small quantity of HUM 54 were painted with a black child in the standing position—usually wearing shoes, but also found with bare feet and painted toes,

and a painted rather than an embossed earring. An unusual painting variation found painted with two black children. Listed as (TW) "Temporarily Withdrawn" in January 1999.

☐ 54	..........3.50 x 4.75"	......(CE)	..........❶	........$850—1100	
☐ 54	..........3.50 x 4.75"	......(CE)	..........❷	........$550—700	
☐ 54	..........3.50 x 4.75"	......(CE)	..........❸	........$475—500	
☐ 54	..........3.50 x 4.75"	......(CE)	..........❹	........$425—475	
☐ 54	..........3.50 x 4.75"	......(CE)	..........❺	........$400—425	
☐ 54	..........3.50 x 4.75"	......(CE)	..........❻	........$375—395	
☐ 54	..........3.50 x 4.75"	......(CE)	..........❶	........$10,000—12,000	(with Black Child)
☐ 54	..........3.50 x 4.75"	......(CE)	..........❷	........$7500—10,000	(with Black Child)
☐ 54	..........3.50 x 4.75"	......(CE)	..........❷	........$10,000—15,000	(two Black Children)
☐ 54	..........3.50 x 4.75"	......(**TW**)	..........❼	........$360—370	

Old style   *New style*

Old style   *New style*

HUM 55 — Saint George

First modeled by master sculptor Reinhold Unger in 1936. Early crown mark models are sometimes found with bright orange-red saddle on horse. Old name: "Knight St. George" or "St. George and Dragon." The original drawing by Sister Hummel for this figurine was reproduced in the 1934 German edition of "Das Hummel Buch," published by Emil Fink of Stuttgart, Germany. Restyled in 1986. Variations in the wings of the dragon and minor changes in the tail of horse. It appears that the factory was probably experiencing excessive breakage in this figurine. Was listed as (TW) "Temporarily Withdrawn" from production in January 1999, but could possibly be reinstated at some future date. Known to exist in (TM 8).

☐ 55	..........6.75".................(CE)	...........❶	..........$2500—3000 (with Red saddle)
☐ 55	..........6.75".................(CE)	...........❶	..........$1000—1300
☐ 55	..........6.75".................(CE)	...........❷	..........$600—750
☐ 55	..........6.75".................(CE)	...........❸	..........$450—525
☐ 55	..........6.75".................(CE)	...........❹	..........$400—450
☐ 55	..........6.75".................(CE)	...........❺	..........$375—400
☐ 55	..........6.75".................(CE)	...........❻	..........$360—375
☐ 55	..........6.75".................(CE)	...........❼	..........$350—360
☐ 55	..........6.75".................(TW)	...........❽	..........$350—360

56A (TM 3)   *56B (TM3)*

HUM 56 A — Culprits

Originally modeled in 1936 by master sculptor Arthur Moeller but has been restyled in later years. Restyled figurines have an extra branch by boy's feet. Variations in height and size of base. Old name "Apple Thief." Crown mark and early full bee trademarked pieces incised 56 only. Older models have the boy's eyes open while newer version eyes are looking down at dog. (TW) "Temporarily Withdrawn" in June 2002.

☐ 56	6.25 to 6.75"	(CE)	❶	$900—1100
☐ 56/A	6.25 to 6.75"	(CE)	❷	$600—650
☐ 56/A	6.25 to 6.75"	(CE)	❸	$450—500
☐ 56/A	6.25 to 6.75"	(CE)	❹	$390—450
☐ 56/A	6.25 to 6.75"	(CE)	❺	$380—390
☐ 56/A	6.25 to 6.75"	(CE)	❻	$370—380
☐ 56/A	6.25 to 6.75"	(CE)	❼	$365—370
☐ 56/A	6.25 to 6.75"	(TW)	❽	$365—370

HUM 56 B — Out of Danger

This companion figurine was first modeled by master sculptor Arthur Moeller in March of 1952, therefore will not be found with the crown trademark. Variation in height, and size of base. On older models the girl's eyes are open; on the newer version her eyes are looking down at dog. Full bee models have an extra flower on base. (TW) "Temporarily Withdrawn" in June 2002.

☐ 56/B	6.25 to 6.75"	(CE)	❷	$600—650
☐ 56/B	6.25 to 6.75"	(CE)	❸	$450—500
☐ 56/B	6.25 to 6.75"	(CE)	❹	$390—450
☐ 56/B	6.25 to 6.75"	(CE)	❺	$380—390
☐ 56/B	6.25 to 6.75"	(CE)	❻	$370—380
☐ 56/B	6.25 to 6.75"	(CE)	❼	$365—370
☐ 56/B	6.25 to 6.75"	(TW)	❽	$365—370

57/1   57/0   57 2/0

HUM 57 — Chick Girl

First modeled by master sculptor Reinhold Unger in 1936 and later remodeled by master sculptor Gerhard Skrobek in 1964. Small size has two chicks in basket while large size has three chicks. Old name: "Little Chicken Mother" or "The Little Chick Girl." There are three different styles of construction that have been used on bottom of base: quartered, doughnut and plain. A new small size (57 2/0) was issued in 1985 with a suggested retail price of $60. Has an incised 1984 copyright date. According to old Goebel product book, a sample was produced by Arthur Moeller in 1936 of "Chick Girl" with an attached "pot," similar to HUM 16/I "Little Hiker" with attached "pot." Value: $5000 to $7000 if found. For more information, see: Rare/Unique Sample Variations of "M. I. Hummel" figurines in back of this book. Retired in 3.25" size in April 2006 (CE) Closed Edition.

☐ 57 2/0	3.00"	(CE)	❻	$210—220
☐ 57 2/0	3.00"	(CE)	❼	$200—210
☐ 57 2/0	3.00 to 3.25"	(CE	❽	$200—210
☐ 57/0	3.50"	(CE)	❶	$550—700
☐ 57/0	3.50"	(CE)	❷	$325—400
☐ 57/0	3.50"	(CE)	❸	$260—300
☐ 57/0	3.50"	(CE)	❹	$235—260
☐ 57/0	3.50"	(CE)	❺	$220—230
☐ 57/0	3.50"	(CE)	❻	$220—230
☐ 57/0	3.50"	(CE)	❼	$220—230
☐ 57/0	3.50"	(OE)	❽	$219
☐ 57/I	4.25"	(CE)	❶	$750—1000
☐ 57/I	4.25"	(CE)	❷	$450—600
☐ 57/I	4.25"	(CE)	❸	$400—450
☐ 57/I	4.25"	(CE)	❹	$350—400
☐ 57/I	4.25"	(CE)	❺	$340—350
☐ 57/I	4.25"	(CE)	❻	$320—340
☐ 57/I	4.25"	(TW) Jan '99	❼	$310—320
☐ 57	4.00 to 4.625"	(CE)	❶	$800—1050
☐ 57	3.74 x 4.625"	(CE)	❷	$500—650

Old bowl style

New jar style

New music box

HUM III/57 — Chick Girl, Box

Bowl style first produced in 1936. Jar style first produced and sold in 1964. Sometimes found with the incised number III 57/0 on the bowl style pieces. Model number is found on underside of lid. "M. I. Hummel" signature is found on topside of lid directly behind figure. "Chick Girl" candy box was (TW) "Temporarily Withdrawn" from production on 31 December 1989, but may be reinstated at some future date. In 1996 a new music box was produced with model number IV/57 applied by decal on the bottom. This is one of four in a series of music boxes produced for the European market only at this time. May be sold in the U.S. market at some future date.

☐ III/57	.....6.00 to 6.25".....(CE)	...........**❶**	.........$750—850	
☐ III/57	.....6.00 to 6.25".....(CE)	...........**❷**	.........$575—650	
☐ III/57	.....6.00 to 6.25".....(CE)	...........**❸**	.........$475—550	(Old Style)
☐ III/57	.....5.00"................(CE)	...........**❸**	.........$300—350	(New Style)
☐ III/57	.....5.00"................(CE)	...........**❹**	.........$250—275	
☐ III/57	.....5.00"................(CE)	...........**❺**	.........$225—250	
☐ III/57	.....5.00"................(**TW**)	...........**❻**	.........$200—225	
☐ IV/57	.....6.00"................(CE)	...........**❼**	.........$250—260	(music box)

HUM 58 — Playmates

Originally modeled by master sculptor Reinhold Unger in 1936 and later restyled by master sculptor Gerhard Skrobek in 1964. Some size and color variations between old and new figurines. Both ears of rabbit pointing up on large size 58/I. Ears are separated on small size 58/0. Old name: "Just Friends." Three different styles of construction on bottom of base:

58/I   58/0   58 2/0

quartered, doughnut and plain. A new small size (58 2/0) "Playmates" was issued in 1986 with a suggested retail price of $68. Has an incised 1984 copyright date. According to old Goebel product book, a sample was produced by Reinhold Unger in 1936 of "Playmates" with an attached "pot," similar to HUM 16/I "Little Hiker" with attached "pot." Value: $5000 to $7000 if found. No known examples. For more information, see: Rare/Unique Sample Variations of "M. I. Hummel" figurines in back of this book.

☐ 58 2/0	....3.50"................(CE)	...............**❻**	.........$210—220
☐ 58 2/0	....3.50"................(CE)	...............**❼**	.........$200—210
☐ 58 2/0	....3.50"................(**OE**)	...............**❽**	.........$199
☐ 58/0	.......4.00"................(CE)	...............**❶**	.........$550—700
☐ 58/0	.......4.00"................(CE)	...............**❷**	.........$325—375
☐ 58/0	.......4.00"................(CE)	...............**❸**	.........$275—300
☐ 58/0	.......4.00"................(CE)	...............**❹**	.........$250—275
☐ 58/0	.......4.00"................(CE)	...............**❺**	.........$230—235
☐ 58/0	.......4.00"................(CE)	...............**❻**	.........$225—230
☐ 58/0	.......4.00"................(CE)	...............**❼**	.........$220—225
☐ 58/0	.......4.00"................(**OE**)	...............**❽**	.........$219
☐ 58/I	......4.25"................(CE)	...............**❶**	.......$750—1000
☐ 58/I	......4.25"................(CE)	...............**❷**	.......$450—600
☐ 58/I	......4.25"................(CE)	...............**❸**	.......$400—450
☐ 58/I	......4.25"................(CE)	...............**❹**	.......$350—400
☐ 58/I	......4.25"................(CE)	...............**❺**	.......$340—350
☐ 58/I	......4.25"................(CE)	...............**❻**	.......$320—340
☐ 58/I	......4.25"................(**TW**) Jan '99	.....**❼**	.........$310—320
☐ 58	.........4.00 to 4.50"......(CE)	...............**❶**	.........$800—1050
☐ 58	.........4.00 to 4.50"......(CE)	...............**❷**	.........$500—650

Old bowl style   New jar style   New   New

HUM III/58 — Playmates, Box

Bowl style first produced in 1936. Jar style first produced and sold in 1964. Sometimes found with the incised number III 58/0 on the old bowl style pieces. Model number is found on underside of lid. "M. I. Hummel" signature is found on topside of lid directly behind figure. "Playmates" candy box was (TW) "Temporarily Withdrawn" from production on 31 December 1989. In 1996 a new music box was produced with model number IV/58 applied by decal on the bottom. This is one of four in a series of music boxes produced for the European market only at this time. In 1996 a new "M. I. Hummel" collector box was issued. It is the same as the "jar" style box. The only difference is that color graphics have been added.

☐ III/58 ......6.75" ....(CE) ....❶ ....$750—850
☐ III/58 ......6.75" ....(CE) ....❷ ....$575—650
☐ III/58 ......6.75" ....(CE) ....❸ ....$475—550   (Old Style)
☐ III/58 ......5.50" ....(CE) ....❸ ....$300—350   (New Style)
☐ III/58 ......5.50" ....(CE) ....❹ ....$250—275
☐ III/58 ......5.50" ....(CE) ....❺ ....$225—250
☐ III/58 ......5.50" ....(CE) ....❻ ....$200—225
☐ III/58 ......5.50" ....(CE) ....❼ ....$200—225
☐ IV/58 ......6.50" ....(CE) ....❼ ....$250—260   (Music Box)

Wooden poles   Plastic poles   Metal poles

HUM 59 — Skier

First modeled by master sculptor Reinhold Unger in 1936. Older models were sold with wooden poles and fiber disks; newer models with plastic poles for a short period of time. The metal poles have been used since 1970. Many size variations; the full bee pieces usually are the largest. Original wooden poles are reflected in the prices of the older models. Original plastic poles are the most difficult to locate and some avid collectors would probably pay a premium for them. New small size (59 4/0) "Skier" was released in 2006.

☐ 59 4/0 ....3.5" ....(OE) ....❽ $129
☐ 59 ....5.00 to 6.00" ......(CE) ....❶ ....$750—900

(prices continued on next page)

☐ 59	.........5.00 to 6.00".....(CE)	...........❷	.........$450—550
☐ 59	.........5.00 to 6.00".....(CE)	...........❸	.........$350—400
☐ 59	.........5.00 to 6.00".....(CE)	...........❹	.........$275—300
☐ 59	.........5.00 to 6.00".....(CE)	...........❺	.........$270—275
☐ 59	.........5.00 to 6.00".....(CE)	...........❻	.........$265—270
☐ 59	.........5.00 to 6.00".....(CE)	...........❼	.........$260—265
☐ 59	.........5.00 to 6.00".....(OE)	...........❽	.........$259

60 B   *60 A*

HUM 60 A — Farm Boy

HUM 60 B — Goose Girl, Bookends
First produced in September 1936. Trademarks usually stamped on wood base rather than on figurine. The number 60 A is found incised on bottom of feet of "Farm Boy" in crown and full bee trademarks. Have been unable to find a similar number on any "Goose Girls" that have been separated from wooden base. See HUM 148 and HUM 149 for additional information. This pair of bookends was listed as (TW) "Temporarily Withdrawn" from production on 31 December 1984, but may be reinstated at some future date. Note: 60/A and 60/B have "Hummel" incised on back of slippers on some (TM 1) and (TM 2) examples.

☐ 60 A&B	........4.75"	............(CE)	............❶	.........$950—1250
☐ 60 A&B	........4.75"	............(CE)	............❷	.........$650—950
☐ 60 A&B	........4.75"	............(CE)	............❸	.........$425—500
☐ 60 A&B	........4.75"	............(CE)	............❹	.........$425—500
☐ 60 A&B	........4.75"	............(CE)	............❺	.........$400—425
☐ 60 A&B	........4.75"	............(TW)	............❻	.........$400—425

HUM 61 A — Playmates
HUM 61 B — Chick Girl, Bookends
First produced in November 1936. Trademarks stamped on wood base rather than on figurine. This pair of bookends was listed as (TW) "Temporarily Withdrawn" on 31 December 1984, but may be reinstated at some future date.

- ☐ 61 A&B....4.00" ..(CE) ..❶ ....$950—1250
- ☐ 61 A&B....4.00" ..(CE) ..❷ ....$650—950
- ☐ 61 A&B....4.00" ..(CE) ..❸ ....$425—500
- ☐ 61 A&B....4.00" ..(CE) ..❹ ....$425—500
- ☐ 61 A&B....4.00" ..(CE) ..❺ ....$400—425
- ☐ 61 A&B....4.00" ..(TW) ..❻ ....$400—425

HUM 62 — Happy Pastime, Ashtray
Slight difference in construction of ashtray on older models. Crown mark piece has "M. I. Hummel" signature on back of ashtray while newer models have signature on back of girl. First modeled by master sculptor Arthur Moeller in 1936. "Happy Pastime" ashtray was (TW) "Temporarily Withdrawn" from production on 31 December 1989, but may be reinstated at some future date.

- ☐ 62 ..3.50 x 6.25"....(CE) ..❶ ....$450—650
- ☐ 62 ..3.50 x 6.25"....(CE) ..❷ ....$300—350
- ☐ 62 ..3.50 x 6.25",...(CE) ..❸ ....$225—250
- ☐ 62 ..3.50 x 6.25"....(CE) ..❹ ....$200—225
- ☐ 62 ..3.50 x 6.25"....(CE) ..❺ ....$175—200
- ☐ 62 ..3.50 x 6.25"....(TW) ..❻ ....$150—175

HUM 63 — Singing Lesson
First modeled by master sculptor Arthur Moeller in 1937. Some variations in size between old and new models. Sometimes a slight variation in tilt of boy's head and position of hand. Old name: "Duet" or "Critic." "Singing Lesson" is the motif used on the 1979 Annual Plate, HUM 272. Sometimes found with no "dots" on horn. Older models have a donut base while newer models have a plain base. Also found with either one, two or three flowers on hat.

- ☐ 63 ....2.75 to 3.00".......(CE) ....❶ ....$450—550
- ☐ 63 ....2.75 to 3.00".......(CE) ....❷ ....$275—375
- ☐ 63 ....2.75 to 3.00".......(CE) ....❸ ....$190—210
- ☐ 63 ....2.75 to 3.00".......(CE) ....❹ ....$170—190
- ☐ 63 ....2.75 to 3.00".......(CE) ....❺ ....$165—170
- ☐ 63 ....2.75 to 3.00".......(CE) ....❻ ....$160—165
- ☐ 63 ....2.75 to 3.00".......(CE) ....❼ ....$155—160
- ☐ 63 ....2.75 to 3.00".......(OE) ....❽ $149

HUM III/63 —
Singing Lesson, Box

Bowl style first produced in 1937. Jar style first produced and sold in 1964. Old name: "Duet" box. Model number is found on underside of lid. "M. I. Hummel" signature is found on topside of lid directly behind figure.

Old bowl style   *New jar style*   *New music box*

"Singing Lesson" candy box was (TW) "Temporarily Withdrawn" from production on 31 December 1989, but may be reinstated at some future date. In 1996 a new music box was produced with model number IV/63 applied by decal on the bottom. This is one of four in a series of music boxes produced for the European market only at this time. May be sold in the U.S. market at some future date.

☐ III/63 ......5.75"..................(CE) ....❶ ....$750—850
☐ III/63 ......5.75"..................(CE) ....❷ ....$575—650
☐ III/63 ......5.75"..................(CE) ....❸ ....$475—550   (Old Style)
☐ III/63 ......4.75"..................(CE) ....❸ ....$300—350   (New Style)
☐ III/63 ......4.75"..................(CE) ....❹ ....$250—275
☐ III/63 ......4.75"..................(CE) ....❺ ....$225—250
☐ III/63 ......4.75"..................(**TW**) ....❻ ....$200—225
☐ IV/63 ......4.75"..................(CE) ....❼ ....$250—260   (Music Box)

HUM 64 — Shepherd's Boy

First modeled by master sculptor Arthur Moeller in 1937. Restyled with the new textured finish in the late 1970s by master sculptor Gerhard Skrobek. Many size variations—note photo. Old name: "The Good Shepherd." "Shepherd's Boy" sold for $9.00 on old 1955 price list. Older figurines have a donut base while newer models have a plain base. "Shepherd's Boy" was (TW) "Temporarily Withdrawn" in 2005, then reissued in 13" size in 2006.

(TM 2)   *Double crown (TM 1+1)*   *(TM 3)*

☐ 64 ....5.50 to 6.25"......(CE) ....❶ ....$750—900
☐ 64 ....5.50 to 6.25"......(CE) ....❷ ....$450—650
☐ 64 ....5.50 to 6.25"......(CE) ....❸ ....$400—450
☐ 64 ....5.50"..................(CE) ....❹ ....$360—400
☐ 64 ....5.50"..................(CE) ....❺ ....$350—360
☐ 64 ....5.50"..................(CE) ....❻ ....$340—350
☐ 64 ....5.50"..................(CE) ....❼ ....$330—340
☐ 64 ....5.50"..................(**TW**) ....❽ ....$319—325
☐ 64/III ......13.00"............ ..(**LE**)..............❽ $1200

65 (TM 2)   *65/I (TM 3)*   *65/0 (TM 2)*

HUM 65 — Farewell

First modeled by master sculptor Arthur Moeller in 1937. Restyled in 1964 by master sculptor Gerhard Skrobek. The small size (65/0) was modeled in 1955 by Gerhard Skrobek. 65/0 is extremely rare since only a few sample pieces were produced. Called "So Long" or "Good Bye" in some old catalogues. Many size variations. Currently produced in only one size with incised number 65 only. A new variation of "Farewell" was created by error in the early 1980s. During the assembly process, the basket was improperly placed, giving the appearance that part of the handle was missing. This "missing handle" variation now commands a premium of $50 to $100. The error was never corrected. Examples can be found in most time periods. "Farewell" was permanently retired at the end of 1993 and will not be produced again. The 1993 production bears a special "FINAL ISSUE" backstamp and a small gold "FINAL ISSUE" commemorative tag.

☐ 65	4.75"	(CE)	❺	$325—350
☐ 65	4.75"	(CE)	❻	$300—325
☐ 65	4.75"	(CE)	❼	$275—300
☐ 65/0	4.00"	(CE)	❷	$6000—8000
☐ 65/0	3.75"	(CE)	❸	$5000—6000
☐ 65/I	4.50 to 4.875"	(CE)	❶	$750—1000
☐ 65/I	4.50 to 4.875"	(CE)	❷	$450—575
☐ 65/I	4.50 to 4.875"	(CE)	❸	$400—450
☐ 65/I	4.50 to 4.875"	(CE)	❹	$350—400
☐ 65/I	4.50 to 4.875"	(CE)	❺	$325—350
☐ 65	4.75 to 5.00"	(CE)	❶	$750—1000
☐ 65	4.75 to 5.00"	(CE)	❷	$450—575

FINAL ISSUE
1993

HUM 66 — Farm Boy
Many size variations. Old name: "Three Pals " or "Happy-Go-Lucky Fellow." Originally modeled in 1937 by master sculptor Arthur Moeller. Also called "Little Pig-Driver" in some catalogues. "Farm Boy" sold for $9.00 on old 1955 price list. Permanently retired in 2005.

Double crown (TM 1+1)   *Full bee (TM 2)*

☐ 66	5.00 to 5.75"	(CE)	❶	$750—900
☐ 66	5.00 to 5.75"	(CE)	❷	$450—550
☐ 66	5.00 to 5.75"	(CE)	❸	$375—400
☐ 66	5.00 to 5.75"	(CE)	❹	$325—375
☐ 66	5.00 to 5.75"	(CE)	❺	$305—320
☐ 66	5.00 to 5.75"	(CE)	❻	$300—305
☐ 66	5.00 to 5.75"	(CE)	❼	$290—300
☐ 66	5.00 to 5.75"	(CE)	❽	$290—300

FINAL ISSUE
2005

HUM 67 — Doll Mother
First modeled by master sculptor Arthur Moeller in 1937 but has been restyled in recent years. Slight difference in hair ribbon on girl. Old name: "Little Doll Mother" or "Little Mother of Dolls" in some catalogues. "Doll Mother" sold for $8.00 on old 1955 price list. An unusual painting variation has been found with a white blanket with red cross stripes instead of the normal pink color and red stripes, in (TM 1) trademark. Value: $750–$1000. A special "60th Anniversary" figurine of "Doll Mother" was issued in 1997 with a special backstamp

Full bee (TM 2)   *Crown (TM 1)*

and a round gold medallion with: "HUM 67 Doll Mother 1937–1997 (and) 60th" in a round circle. This figurine was first introduced at the Leipzig Trade Fair in 1937.

☐ 67	4.25 to 4.75"	(CE)	❶	$700—900
☐ 67	4.25 to 4.75"	(CE)	❷	$450—550
☐ 67	4.25 to 4.75"	(CE)	❸	$350—375
☐ 67	4.25 to 4.75"	(CE)	❹	$300—350
☐ 67	4.25 to 4.75"	(CE)	❺	$270—290
☐ 67	4.25 to 4.75"	(CE)	❻	$265—270
☐ 67	4.25 to 4.75"	(CE)	❼	$260—265
☐ 67	4.25 to 4 75"	(OE)	❽	$259

| 68 2/0 | 68/0 | 68 Crown | 68 Full bee | 68 Double crown |

HUM 68 — Lost Sheep

Originally modeled by master sculptor Arthur Moeller in 1937 and later restyled by a combination of several modelers. Many size and color variations. Older models have dark brown or gray trousers. Similar to HUM 64 "Shepherd's Boy" except for single lamb and different colors. "Lost Sheep" sold for $7.50 on old 1955 price list. Both sizes of "Lost Sheep" were permanently retired by Goebel in the fall of 1992 and will not be produced again. The suggested retail prices for "Lost Sheep" on the 1992 price list were $125 and $180.

☐ 68 2/0 ....4.25 to 4.50"......(CE) ....❷ ....$250—350
☐ 68 2/0 ....4.25 to 4.50"......(CE) ....❸ ....$225—250
☐ 68 2/0 ....4.25 to 4.50"......(CE) ....❹ ....$190—225
☐ 68 2/0 ....4.25 to 4.50"......(CE) ....❺ ....$180—190
☐ 68 2/0 ....4.25 to 4.50"......(CE) ....❻ ....$170—180
☐ 68 2/0 ....4.25 to 4.50"......(CE) ....❼ ....$160—170
☐ 68/0 ....5.50".................(CE) ....❷ ....$350—450
☐ 68/0 ....5.50".................(CE) ....❸ ....$300—350
☐ 68/0 ....5.50".................(CE) ....❹ ....$275—300
☐ 68/0 ....5.50".................(CE) ....❺ ....$250—275
☐ 68/0 ....5.50".................(CE) ....❻ ....$225—250
☐ 68/0 ....5.50".................(CE) ....❼ ....$200—225
☐ 68 ....5.50 to 6.50".....(CE) ....❶ ....$600—750
☐ 68 ....5.50 to 6.50".....(CE) ....❷ ....$400—500
☐ 68 ....5.50 to 6.50".....(CE) ....❸ ....$350—400

FINAL ISSUE
1992

.... HUM TERM ....

OVERSIZE: This description refers to a piece that has experienced "mold growth" size expansion. A figurine that measures larger than the standard size is said to be "oversized."

HUM 69 — Happy Pastime

First modeled by master sculptor Arthur Moeller in 1937. Very little difference between old and new models. Older models slightly larger and usually do not have dots or head scarf. Called "Knitter" in old catalogues. The "M.I. Hummel" signature is very faint or difficult to see on some old models. Occasionally found with a stamped "M. I. Hummel" signature on the bottom. "Happy Pastime" is the motif used on the 1978 Annual Plate, HUM 271. "Happy Pastime" was permanently retired by Goebel as of 31 December 1996 and will not be produced again. The 1996 production bears a special "Final Issue" backstamp and a small gold "Final Issue" commemorative tag. The suggested retail price on the 1996 price list was $175.

☐ 69	3.25 to 3.50"	(CE)	❶	$500—650
☐ 69	3.25 to 3.50"	(CE)	❷	$300—400
☐ 69	3.25 to 3.50"	(CE)	❸	$250—275
☐ 69	3.25 to 3.50"	(CE)	❹	$225—250
☐ 69	3.25 to 3.50"	(CE)	❺	$210—225
☐ 69	3.25 to 3.50"	(CE)	❻	$200—210
☐ 69	3.25 to 3.50"	(CE)	❼	$190—200

FINAL ISSUE
1996

HUM III/69 — Happy Pastime, Box

Bowl style first produced in 1937. Jar style first produced and sold in 1964. Model number is found on underside of lid. "M.I.Hummel" signature is found on topside of lid directly behind figure. "Happy Pastime" candy box was (TW) "Temporarily Withdrawn" from production on 31 December 1989, but may be reinstated at some future date.

Old bowl style

New jar style

☐ III/69	6.50"	(CE)	❶	$750—850	
☐ III/69	6.50"	(CE)	❷	$575—650	
☐ III/69	6.50"	(CE)	❸	$475—550	(Old Style)
☐ III/69	5.25"	(CE)	❸	$300—350	(New Style)
☐ III/69	5.25"	(CE)	❹	$250—275	
☐ III/69	5.25"	(CE)	❺	$225—250	
☐ III/69	5.25"	(TW)	❻	$200—225	

(Note size variation)

HUM 70 — Holy Child

Factory records indicate this was originally modeled in 1937 by a combination of modelers. Was sold in white overglaze (unpainted) finish at one time in Belgium and would be considered rare today. Has been restyled in later years with newer models having the textured finish on gown and robe. Many size variations. Also listed as "Child Jesus" in some old catalogues. "Holy Child" was (TW) "Temporarily Withdrawn" from production on 31 December 1990, but was once again back on current price lists (TM 7) trademark. The suggested retail price for "Holy Child" on the 1990 price list was $130. Listed as (TW) "Temporarily Withdrawn" in January 1999. Not listed on current 2006 price list.

☐ 70 ....6.75 to 7.50" ....(CE) ....❶ ....$750—850
☐ 70 ....6.75 to 7.50"......(CE) ....❷ ....$375—500
☐ 70 ....6.75 to 7.50"......(CE) ....❸ ....$350—375
☐ 70 ....6.75 to 7.50"......(CE) ....❹ ....$325—350
☐ 70 ....6.75 to 7.50"......(CE) ....❺ ....$300—325
☐ 70 ....6.75 to 7.50"......(CE) ....❻ ....$290—300
☐ 70 ....6.75"................(TW) ....❼ ....$280—285

71 (TM 2)   71/I (TM 6)   71 2/0 (TM 6)

HUM 71 — Stormy Weather

Originally modeled by master sculptor Reinhold Unger in 1937. Has been restyled several times through the years. Many size variations. Full bee models are usually the largest size. Old name "Under One Roof." Slight difference between old and new models other than size. Several variations in structure of bottom of base design. This motif was used for the first Anniversary Plate, HUM 280 in 1975. A new small size (71 2/0) was issued in the spring of 1985 at a suggested retail price of $120. The large size has now been renumbered 71/I. There are two variations of the new small size. The first production appeared with the inside of the umbrella hand-painted with obvious brush strokes while later production has the inside painted by air brush. These early pieces usually sell for $500–$750. "Stormy Weather" sold for $16.50 on old 1955 price list. A special painting variation of the small size HUM 71 2/0 was produced in 1997. The price was $279.50. It was painted with a yellow umbrella with tan colored highlights, a decal signature on back of umbrella and a special "60th Anniversary" backstamp.

☐ 71 2/0 ....4.50 to 5.00".....(CE) ....❻ ....$370—380
☐ 71 2/0 ....4.50 to 5.00".....(CE) ....❼ ....$365—370
☐ 71 2/0 ....4.50 to 5.00".....(OE) ....❽ $359
☐ 71 ....6.00 to 7.00".....(CE) ....❶ ....$1200—1350
☐ 71 ....6.00 to 7.00".....(CE) ....❷ ....$850—950
☐ 71 ....6.00 to 7.00".....(CE) ....❸ ....$675—700
☐ 71 ....6.00 to 6.25".....(CE) ....❹ ....$625—675
☐ 71 ....6.00 to 6.25".....(CE) ....❺ ....$575—600
☐ 71 ....6.00 to 6.25".....(CE) ....❻ ....$560—575
☐ 71/I ....6.00 to 6.25".....(CE) ....❻ ....$550—560
☐ 71/I ....6.00 to 6.25".....(CE) ....❼ ....$540—550
☐ 71/I ....6.00 to 6.25".....(OE) ....❽ $529

NOTE: See RARE VARIATIONS in back of book for an unusual variation of this figurine.

| (TM 1) | (TM 3) | (TM 6) |

HUM 72 — Spring Cheer

First modeled in 1937 by master sculptor Reinhold Unger. Older models have yellow dress and no flowers in right hand. Restyled in 1965 by master sculptor Gerhard Skrobek who added flowers to right hand and changed color of dress to dark green. Both mold variations can be found with (TM 3) stylized trademark. Older style can also be found with dark green dress. This variation would be considered rare and would bring a premium usually anywhere from $1500 to $2000. Old name: "Spring Flowers". Crown mark pieces have a flower on reverse side. Later production pieces omitted this flower. "Spring Cheer" was listed as (TW) "Temporarily Withdrawn" from production on 31 December 1984, but may be reinstated at some future date. The suggested retail price for "Spring Cheer" on the 1984 price list was $55.

☐ 72 ....5.00 to 5.50".......(CE) ....❶ ....$500—650
☐ 72 ....5.00 to 5.50".......(CE) ....❷ ....$325—400
☐ 72 ....5.00 to 5.50".......(CE) ....❸ ....$300—325
☐ 72 ....5.00 to 5.50".......(CE) ....❹ ....$250—300
☐ 72 ....5.00 to 5.50".......(CE) ....❺ ....$225—250
☐ 72 ....5.00 to 5.50".......(TW) ....❻ ....$200—225

.... HUM TERM ....

WHITE OVERGLAZE: The term used to designate an item that has not been painted, but has been glazed and fired. These pieces are completely white. All "M. I. Hummel" items are produced in this finish before being individually hand-painted.

HUM 73 — Little Helper
Originally modeled in 1937 by master sculptor Reinhold Unger. Very little variation between old and new pieces. Older figurines are usually slightly larger. Old name: "Diligent Betsy" or "The Little Sister" in some old catalogues. "Little Helper" sold for $4.00 on old 1955 price list. Was permanently retired by Goebel in 2005 and will not be produced again.

(TM 2)   *(TM 2)*   *(TM 1)*   *(TM 3)*

☐ 73 ....4.25 to 4.50".....(CE) ....❶ ....$450—500
☐ 73 ....4.25 to 4.50"......(CE) ....❷ ....$275—350
☐ 73 ....4.25 to 4.50"......(CE) ....❸ ....$200—210
☐ 73 ....4.25 to 4.50"......(CE) ....❹ ....$165—200
☐ 73 ....4.25 to 4.50"......(CE) ....❺ ....$160—165
☐ 73 ....4.25 to 4.50"......(CE) ....❻ ....$155—160
☐ 73 ....4.25 to 4.50"......(CE) ....❼ ....$150—155
☐ 73 ....4.25 to 4.50"......**(CE)** ....❽ $150

FINAL ISSUE
2005

HUM 74 — Little Gardener
Originally modeled by master sculptor Reinhold Unger in 1937 but has undergone many changes through the years. Older models have an oval base. Restyled in the early 1960s and changed to a round base and smaller flower. Many color variations on girl's apron. "Little Gardener" sold for $4.00 on old 1955 price list. Used as a *demonstration promotion* piece for 1992 *with a special*

Crown   *Crown*   *Full bee*   *Stylized*
(TM 1)   *(TM 1)*   *(TM 2)*   *(TM 3)*

backstamp–sold only at stores having a Goebel "M. I. Hummel" promotion in 1992. Not sold at other stores for two years. Then back in current production. "Little Gardener" has *not* been found with (TM 4) "three line" trademark at time of printing. Permanently retired in 2006.

☐ 74 ....4.00 to 4.50"......(CE) ....❶ ....$450—550
☐ 74 ....4.00 to 4.50"......(CE) ....❷ ....$250—350
☐ 74 ....4.00 to 4.50"......(CE) ....❸ ....$200—225
☐ 74 ....4.00 to 4.50"......(CE) ....❹ ....$500—750
☐ 74 ....4.00 to 4.50"......(CE) ....❺ ....$160—165
☐ 74 ....4.00 to 4.50"......(CE) ....❻ ....$155—160
☐ 74 ....4.00 to 4.50"......(CE) ....❼ ....$150—155
☐ 74 ....4.00 to 4.50"......**(CE)** ....❽ $149

FINAL ISSUE
2006

(TM 1)   (TM 3)

HUM 75 — Holy Water Font, White Angel

First modeled by master sculptor Reinhold Unger in 1937. Newer models have hole for hanging font. Older models provide a hole only on back. Variation in construction of bowl. Also called "Angelic Prayer" in some catalogues. Also found in terra cotta finish. Value $1000–$1500. Listed as (TW) "Temporarily Withdrawn" in January 1999.

☐ 75 ....3.25 to 4.50".......(CE) ....❶ ....$225—275
☐ 75 ....3.25 to 4.50".......(CE) ....❷ ....$125—150
☐ 75 ....3.25 to 4.50".......(CE) ....❸ ....$100—125
☐ 75 ....3.25 to 4.50".......(CE) ....❹ ....$75—100
☐ 75 ....3.25 to 4.50".......(CE) ....❺ ....$70—75
☐ 75 ....3.25 to 4.50".......(CE) ....❻ ....$70—75
☐ 75 ....3.25 to 4.50".......(TW) ....❼ ....$70—75

HUM 76 A — Doll Mother

HUM 76 B — Prayer Before Battle, Bookends

No known examples other than this half of set which was located in Goebel factory. Originally modeled by master sculptor Arthur Moeller. Factory note indicates: "Not produced after 28 February 1938."

☐ 76 .... A & B ....(CE) ....❶ ....$10,000—15,000

HUM 77 — Holy Water Font, Cross With Doves

First modeled by master sculptor Reinhold Unger in 1937 but according to factory information was made as samples only and never in production. Listed as a (CE) Closed Edition on 21 October 1937. As of this date, ten examples are known to exist. One is now in the Robert L. Miller collection, thanks to a collector from California. Has also been found in white overglaze (unpainted) finish.

☐ 77 ....1.75 x 6.25" ......(CN) ....❶ ....$5000—10,000

Bisque   Color   White

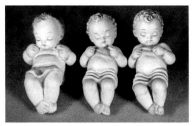

Old style   New style   Current style

HUM 78 — Blessed Child (Infant of Krumbad)

In 1985 the official name was changed from "Infant of Krumbad" to the "Blessed Child." It was also listed as "In the Crib" in an old 1950 catalogue. This figurine has been produced in three different finishes. Produced in brownish bisque finish (U.S. Market); full color and white overglaze (various other countries), sometimes found in Belgium. Note variations in older models. First modeled by master sculptor Erich Lautensack in 1937. (Lautensack died during the Second World War.) Restyled by master sculptor Gerhard Skrobek in 1965. The two small holes on the back are designed to hold a wire halo. Full color and white overglaze pieces command varied premiums. Also found with the incised number 78/6 (arabic) in (TM 1) "crown" and (TM 2) "full bee" trademarks only.

Factory records for Blessed Child indicate the following:

Originally modeled by:			Restyled:	
78/0	Lautensack	1937	Skrobek	1962 (discontinued 1983)
78/I	Skrobek	1964	Skrobek	1965
78/II	Skrobek	1964	Skrobek	1965
78/III	Lautensack	1937	Skrobek	1965
78/V	Skrobek	1963	Skrobek	1965
78/VI or 78/6	Lautensack	1937	Skrobek	1965
78/VIII	Lautensack	1937	Skrobek	1965

(prices continued on next page)

B.C.W. ....

☐☐☐	78/0	2.25"	(CE)	❷	$200—300
☐☐☐	78/0	2.25"	(CE)	❸	$150—200
☐☐☐	78/I	2.25"	(CE)	❸	$40—50
☐☐☐	78/I	2.25"	(CE)	❹	$35—40
☐☐☐	78/I	2.25"	(CE)	❺	$30—35
☐☐☐	78/I	2.25"	(TW)	❻	$30—35
☐☐☐	78/II	3.50"	(CE)	❸	$50—60
☐☐☐	78/II	3.50"	(CE)	❹	$45—50
☐☐☐	78/II	3.50"	(CE)	❺	$40—45
☐☐☐	78/II	3.50"	(TW)	❻	$35—40
☐☐☐	78/III	4.50 to 5.25"	(CE)	❶	$350—400
☐☐☐	78/III	4.50 to 5.25"	(CE)	❷	$250—350
☐☐☐	78/III	4.50 to 5.25"	(CE)	❸	$60—70
☐☐☐	78/III	4.50 to 5.25"	(CE)	❹	$55—60
☐☐☐	78/III	4.50 to 5.25"	(CE)	❺	$50—55
☐☐☐	78/III	4.50 to 5.25"	(TW)	❻	$45—50
☐☐☐	78/V	7.50 to 7.75"	(CE)	❸	$125—175
☐☐☐	78/V	7.50 to 7.75"	(CE)	❹	$115—170
☐☐☐	78/V	7.50 to 7.75"	(CE)	❺	$110—165
☐☐☐	78/V	7.50 to 7.75"	(CE)	❻	$105—160
☐☐☐	78/V	7.50 to 7.75"	(TW)	❽	$90—150
☐☐☐	78/VI	10.00 to 11.25"	(CE)	❶	$600—850
☐☐☐	78/VI	10.00 to 11.25"	(CE)	❷	$400—600
☐☐☐	78/VI	10.00 to 11.25"	(CE)	❸	$200—250
☐☐☐	78/VI	10.00 to 11.25"	(CE)	❹	$200—250
☐☐☐	78/VI	10.00 to 11.25"	(CE)	❺	$150—175
☐☐☐	78/VI	10.00 to 11.25"	(TW)	❻	$150—175
☐☐☐	78/VIII	13.25 to 14.25"	(CE)	❶	$750—1000
☐☐☐	78/VIII	13.25 to 15.00"	(CE)	❷	$500—750
☐☐☐	78/VIII	113.25 to 14.25"	(CE)	❸	$350—400
☐☐☐	78/VIII	13.25 to 14.25"	(CE)	❹	$350—400
☐☐☐	78/VIII	13.25 to 14.25"	(CE)	❺	$300—325
☐☐☐	78/VIII	13.25 to 14.25"	(TW)	❻	$300—325
☐☐☐	78/II½	4.25"	(CE)	❻	$100—150
☐☐☐	78/II½	4.25"	(OE)	❼-❽	$75—100

A new small size "Blessed Child" is now being produced for the exclusive sale of the Siessen Convent in Germany. It has an incised 78/II½ model number, incised 1987 copyright date and the current (TM 6) trademark. This is only the second time a "Hummel" figurine has been produced using the "1/2" size designator. (The other figurine is "Heavenly Angel" HUM 21/0½.) This new "Blessed Child" reverts back to the old original style modeled by Lautensack rather than the newer Skrobek design. The price at the Siessen Convent was for approximately $30 in U.S. currency. The Siessen Convent sometimes have an old style 2.25" "Blessed Child" for sale with TM 7 for approximately $60 in U.S. currency in 2006.

HUM 79 — Globe Trotter

Originally modeled by master sculptor Arthur Moeller in 1937. Remodeled in 1955 at which time the basket weave was changed from a double weave to a single weave. Crown mark pieces usually have a tan-colored handle on umbrella while others are black. Some variation of color on the inside of basket. Some old catalogues list name as "Happy Traveller." Some older models have dark green hat. This motif is used on the 1973 Annual Plate, HUM 266. "Globe Trotter" was permanently retired by Goebel in the fall

New (TM 3)   *Old (TM 1)*

of 1991 and will not be produced again. The 1991 price list shows a price of $170, the last year it was sold on the primary market. Both (TM 6) and (TM 7) can be found with "Final Issue" decal, and "Final Issue" medallion.

☐	79	5.00 to 5.25"	(CE)	❶	$600—750
☐	79	5.00 to 5.25"	(CE)	❷	$375—500
☐	79	5.00 to 5.25"	(CE)	❸	$300—350
☐	79	5.00 to 5.25"	(CE)	❹	$275—300
☐	79	5.00 to 5.25"	(CE)	❺	$250—275
☐	79	5.00 to 5.25"	(CE)	❻	$225—250
☐	79	5.00 to 5.25"	(CE)	❼	$200—225

FINAL ISSUE
1991

New   *Old*

71

(TM 1+1)   *(TM 2)*   *New 80 2/0 size*

HUM 80 — Little Scholar

Original model made by master sculptor Arthur Moeller in 1937. Some color variations. Old models have brown shoes. The cone in boy's right arm is called Schultute or Zuckertute, a paper cone containing school supplies and other goodies, which German parents traditionally give their children on the first day of school. "Little Scholar" sold for $7.00 on old 1955 price list. "Crown" and some early "full bee" pieces have a hole in the pretzel on the top of the cone. Later pieces are solid. A new small size (80 2/0) 4.25" was released in mid-2001 with (TM 8) trademark and a "First Issue 2002" backstamp.

- ☐ 80 2/0 ....4.25" ....(**OE**)......❽ $179
- ☐ 80 ....5.25 to 5.75".........(CE)......❶ ......$700—800
- ☐ 80 ....5.25 to 5.75".........(CE)......❷ ......$450—525
- ☐ 80 ....5.25 to 5.75".........(CE)......❸ ......$350—375
- ☐ 80 ....5.25 to 5.75".........(CE)......❹ ......$300—350
- ☐ 80 ....5.25 to 5.75".........(CE)......❺ ......$290—300
- ☐ 80 ....5.25 to 5.75".........(CE)......❻ ......$285—290
- ☐ 80 ....5.25 to 5.75".........(CE)......❼ ......$280—285
- ☐ 80 ....5.25 to 5.75".........(**OE**)......❽ $279

| 81 (TM 1) | 81/0 (TM 2) | 81 2/0 (TM 2) | 81 2/0 (TM 3) |

HUM 81 — School Girl

Old name: "Primer Girl" or "Little Scholar." Original model made by master sculptor Arthur Moeller in 1937. Many size variations as well as color variations. Size 81 2/0 basket filled; all others, baskets empty. Old catalogue listing of 7.75" is in error. This motif is used on the 1980 Annual Plate, HUM 273. Early "crown" trademark examples are sometimes found with orange color skirt and blouse rather than the normal dark colored blouse. Large size (81/0) was (TW) "Temporarily Withdrawn" in January 1999.

- ☐ 81 2/0 ....4.25 to 4.75"..........(CE)...... ❶ ....$500—600
- ☐ 81 2/0 ....4.25 to 4.75"..........(CE)...... ❷ ....$250—350
- ☐ 81 2/0 ....4.25 to 4.75"..........(CE)...... ❸ ....$225—250
- ☐ 81 2/0 ....4.25 to 4.75"..........(CE)...... ❹ ....$200—225
- ☐ 81 2/0 ....4.25 to 4.75"..........(CE)...... ❺ ....$190—200
- ☐ 81 2/0 ....4.25 to 4.75"..........(CE)...... ❻ ....$185—190
- ☐ 81 2/0 ....4.25 to 4.75"..........(CE)...... ❼ ....$180—185
- ☐ 81 2/0 ....4.25 to 4.75"..........(**OE**)...... ❽ $179
- ☐ 81/0 ....4.75 to 5.25"..........(CE)...... ❶ ....$550—700
- ☐ 81/0 ....4.75 to 5.25"..........(CE)...... ❷ ....$325—450
- ☐ 81/0 ....4.75 to 5.25"..........(CE)...... ❸ ....$300—325
- ☐ 81/0 ....4.75 to 5.25"..........(CE)...... ❹ ....$270—300
- ☐ 81/0 ....4.75 to 5.25"..........(CE)...... ❺ ....$245—270
- ☐ 81/0 ....4.75 to 5.25"..........(CE)...... ❻ ....$235—245
- ☐ 81/0 ....4.75 to 5.25"..........(**TW**)..... ❼ ....$225—230 60th Anni Decal 1998
- ☐ 81 ....5.125 to 5.50".......(CE)...... ❶ ....$600—750
- ☐ 81 ....5.125 to 5.50".......(CE)...... ❷ ....$350—475

| 82/2 | 82/0 | 82/0 | 82 2/0 | 82 2/0 |

HUM 82 — School Boy

First modeled by master sculptor Arthur Moeller in 1938. Many size variations. Old name: "Little Scholar," "School Days" or "Primer Boy." The larger size 82/II (82/2) has been considered rare but is once again back in current production. See HUM 329. To my knowledge, the large size (82/II) was not produced in (TM 4) "three line" trademark. Large size (82/II) was (TW) "Temporarily Withdrawn" in January 1999. Size (82/0) was not listed on the January 2001 price list.

- ☐ 82 2/0 ....4.00 to 4.50".......(CE) ....❶ ....$500—600
- ☐ 82 2/0 ....4.00 to 4.50".......(CE) ....❷ ....$250—350
- ☐ 82 2/0 ....4.00 to 4.50".......(CE) ....❸ $225 250
- ☐ 82 2/0 ....4.00 to 4.50".......(CE) ....❹ ....$200—225
- ☐ 82 2/0 ....4.00 to 4.50".......(CE) ....❺ ....$190—200
- ☐ 82 2/0 ....4.00 to 4.50".......(CE) ....❻ ....$185—190
- ☐ 82 2/0 ....4.00 to 4.50".......(CE) ....❼ ....$180—185
- ☐ 82 2/0 ....4.00 to 4.50".......(OE) ....❽ $179
- ☐ 82 ....5.00"..................(CE) ....❶ ....$625—775
- ☐ 82/0 ....4.75 to 6.00".......(CE) ....❶ ....$600—750
- ☐ 82/0 ....4.75 to 6.00".......(CE) ....❷ ....$350—500
- ☐ 82/0 ....4.75 to 6.00".......(CE) ....❸ ....$325—350
- ☐ 82/0 ....4.75 to 6.00".......(CE) ....❹ ....$275—325
- ☐ 82/0 ....4.75 to 6.00".......(CE) ....❺ ....$250—270
- ☐ 82/0 ....4.75 to 6.00".......(CE) ....❻ ....$240—250
- ☐ 82/0 ....4.75 to 6.00".......(CE) ....❼ ....$235—240
- ☐ 82/0 ....4.75 to 6.00"......(TW) ....❽ $235
- ☐ 82/II ....7.50".................(CE) ....❶ ....$1200—1600
- ☐ 82/II ....7.50".................(CE) ....❷ ....$900—1100
- ☐ 82/II ....7.50".................(CE) ....❸ ....$600—700
- ☐ 82/II ....7.50".................(CE) ....❺ ....$550—600
- ☐ 82/II ....7.50".................(CE) ....❻ ....$525—550
- ☐ 82/II ....7.50".................(TW) ....❼ ....$500—510

Left to right, Angel Serenade (TM 1), (TM 2), (TM 3), and (TM 5) from an angle looking down on the base of each figurine.

Left to right, Angel Serenade (TM 1), (TM 2), (TM 3), and (TM 5) from the front.

HUM 83 — Angel Serenade (with Lamb)

Old name: "Psalmist" in some early Goebel catalogues. First modeled by master sculptor Reinhold Unger in 1938. In the 1950s and 1960s, "Angel Serenade" was considered rare or hard-to-find, but, according to Goebel terminology, it was not in their "current production program" for quite a few years. In the late 1970s "Angel Serenade" was put back into the Goebel current production program, and it probably was at this time that the change was made in the position of the figure on the base. The details of the angel and the lamb remained almost identical. The "Angel Serenade" name is also used for HUM 214/D (part of the small Nativity set) and HUM 260/E (part of the large Nativity set). To my knowledge, it has been produced in all eight trademark periods—although I do not have a (TM 4) "three line" trademark example in our personal collection. Not listed on the current 2006 price list.

☐ 83 ....5.50 to 5.75"......(CE) ....❶ ....$650—750
☐ 83 ....5.50 to 5.75"......(CE) ....❷ ....$550—600
☐ 83 ....5.50 to 5.75"......(CE) ....❸ ....$400—500
☐ 83 ....5.50 to 5.75"......(CE) ....❹ ....$300—400
☐ 83 ....5.50 to 5.75"......(CE) ....❺ ....$280—300
☐ 83 ....5.50 to 5.75"......(CE) ....❻ ....$275—280
☐ 83 ....5.50 to 5.75"......(CE) ....❼ ....$270—275   60th Anni Decal 1998
☐ 83 ....5.50 to 5.75"......(TW) ....❽ $270

(TM 2)   **(TM 3)**

HUM 84 — Worship
Originally modeled by master sculptor Reinhold Unger in 1938. Old name: "At The Wayside" or "Devotion" in some catalogues. The small size 84/0 was also sold in white overglaze at one time in Belgium and would be considered rare. Current models of the large size 84/V have "M.I. Hummel" signature on back of shrine while older models have signature on back of base. Sometimes incised 84/5 instead of 84/V. The large size (84/V) was (TW) "Temporarily Withdrawn" from production on 31 December 1989, but may be reinstated at some future date.

☐ 84	White 5.25"	(CE)	❶	$1200—1500	
☐ 84	5.25"	(CE)	❶	$525—625	
☐ 84/0	5.00 to 5.50"	(CE)	❶	$500—600	
☐ 84/0	5.00 to 5.50"	(CE)	❷	$325—400	
☐ 84/0	5.00 to 5.50"	(CE)	❸	$300—325	
☐ 84/0	5.00"	(CE)	❹	$235—300	
☐ 84/0	5.00"	(CE)	❺	$230—2135	
☐ 84/0	5.00"	(CE)	❻	$225—230	
☐ 84/0	5.00"	(CE)	❼	$220—225	60th Anni Decal 1998
☐ 84/0	5.00"	(OF)	❽	$219	
☐ 84/V	12.50 to 13.25"	(CE)	❶	$2000—3000	
☐ 84/V	12.50 to 13.25"	(CE)	❷	$1700—2000	
☐ 84/V	12.50 to 13.25"	(CE)	❸	$1650—1675	
☐ 84/V	12.50 to 13.25"	(CE)	❹	$1625—1650	
☐ 84/V	12.50 to 13.25"	(CE)	❺	$1600—1625	
☐ 84/V	12.50 to 13.25"	(CE)	❻	$1575—1600	
☐ 84/V	12.50 to 13.25"	(CE)	❼	$1550—1575	
☐ 84/V	12.50 to 13.25"	(OE)	❽	$1550	

.... **HUM TERM** ....

OPEN EDITION: Pieces currently in W. Goebel's production program.

Note fingers

HUM 85 — Serenade
First modeled by master sculptor Arthur Moeller in 1938. Many size variations. Note variation of boy's fingers on flute—cannot be attributed to any one time period. Old model with 85/0 number has fingers up. Size 85/0 has recently been restyled with a new hair style and textured finish. Normal hat color is dark gray or black. Older models also found with light gray hat. Old large size figurine with crown trademark has 85 number. Also found with incised number 85.0. or 85. in crown trademark in the small size. Sometimes incised 85/2 instead of 85/II. One of several figurines that make up the Hummel orchestra. Old name: "The Flutist." A new miniature size figurine was issued in 1985 with a suggested retail price of $39 to match a new mini size plate series called the "Little Music Makers"—one each year for four years. This is the second in the series. 85 4/0 has an incised 1984 copyright date. 85 4/0 was (TW) "Temporarily Withdrawn" on 31 December 1997. A large 24-inch "Serenade" is currently on display at the factory showroom in Rödental.

☐	85 4/0	....3.50"	(CE)	❻	$130—135
☐	85 4/0	....3.50"	**(TW)**	❼	$125—130
☐	85/0	........4.75 to 5.25"	(CE)	❶	$400—500
☐	85/0	........4.75 to 5.25"	(CE)	❷	$225—300
☐	85/0	........4.75 to 5.25"	(CE)	❸	$210—225
☐	85/0	........4.75 to 5.25"	(CE)	❹	$200—210
☐	85/0	........4.75 to 5.25"	(CE)	❺	$190—195
☐	85/0	........4.75 to 5.25"	(CE)	❻	$185—190
☐	85/0	........4.75 to 5.25"	(CE)	❼	$180—185
☐	85/0	........4.75 to 5.25"	**(OE)**	❽	$179
☐	85	.........7.00 to 7.50"	(CE)	❶	$1250—1550
☐	85	.........7.00 to 7.50"	(CE)	❷	$775—975
☐	85/II	.......7.00 to 7.50"	(CE)	❶	$1200—1500
☐	85/II	.......7.00 to 7.50"	(CE)	❷	$750—950
☐	85/II	.......7.00 to 7.50"	(CE)	❸	$650—700
☐	85/II	.......7.00 to 7.50"	(CE)	❹	$600—650
☐	85/II	.......7.00 to 7.50"	(CE)	❺	$550—600
☐	85/II	.......7.00 to 7.50"	(CE)	❻	$525—550
☐	85/II	.......7.00 to 7.50"	**(TW)**	❼	$500—510
☐	85/III	......12.50"	**(OE)**	❽	$1550

HUM 86 — Happiness

First modeled by master sculptor Reinhold Unger in 1938. Many size variations. Made with either square or rectangular base. Old name: "Wandersong" or "Traveller's Song" in early Goebel catalogue. Occasionally found with both pig tails down on older models. "Happiness" was permanently retired by Goebel in 2004 and will not be producted again.

☐ 86 ....4.50 to 5.00"....(CE) .... ❶ ..$400—500
☐ 86 ....4.50 to 5.00"....(CE) .... ❷ ..$250—350
☐ 86 ....4.50 to 5.00"....(CE) .... ❸ ..$200—225
☐ 86 ....4.50 to 5.00"....(CE) .... ❹ .$185—210
☐ 86 ....4.50 to 5.00"....(CE) .... ❺ .$180—185
☐ 86 ....4.50 to 5.00"....(CE) .... ❻ .$175—180
☐ 86 ....4.50 to 5.00"....(CE) .... ❼ ..$170—175
60th Anniversary Decal 1998
☐ 86 ....4.50 to 5.00"....(CE) .... ❽ ..$170

FINAL ISSUE
2004

HUM 87 — For Father

First modeled in 1938 by master sculptor Arthur Moeller. Some size and color variations between old and new models. Boy is carrying white (with brownish-tan highlights) radishes and beer stein. Some models have orange-colored vegetables that would appear to be carrots—usually found only with "full bee" (TM 2) or early stylized (TM 3) trademarks. The orange carrot variation normally sells in the $2500 to $4000 price range. Old name: "Father's Joy." Stein can be personalized by a Goebel artist.

☐ 87 2/0......4.25" ....(OE) ....❽ $179
☐ 87 ....5.50" ....(CE) ....❶ ....$700—800
☐ 87 ....5.50" ....(CE) ....❷ ....$400—525
☐ 87 ....5.50" ....(CE) ....❸ ....$350—400
☐ 87 ....5.50" ....(CE) ....❹ ....$300—350
☐ 87 ....5.50" ....(CE) ....❺ ....$290—300
☐ 87 ....5.50" ....(CE) ....❻ ....$285—290
☐ 87 ....5.50" ....(CE) ....❼ ....$280—285 60th Anni Decal 1998
☐ 87 ....5.50" ....(TW) ....❽ $279

| 88 (TM 1) | 88/II (TM 3) | 88/I (TM 4) |

HUM 88 — Heavenly Protection

Originally modeled by master sculptor Reinhold Unger in 1938. Some size and color variations between old and new models. Small size 88/I first put on the market in early 1960s. Some pieces have an incised 1961 copyright date on bottom. Older pieces sometimes incised 88/2 instead of 88/II. Some variation in the location of the "M.I. Hummel" signature on the back side of this figurine. Sometimes on the base, sometimes on the bottom of the robe or sometimes in a diagonal position on the robe. The large size 88/II was listed on the 1993 and 1994 price lists as (TW) "Temporarily Withdrawn," but is once again back on the 1995 and succeeding price lists. Has also been found in white overglaze (unpainted) finish. Large size (88/II) was (TW) "Temporarily Withdrawn" in January 1999. HUM 88 in (TM 1 + TM 2) was found in white overglaze in the Netherlands.

☐ 88	.........9.25"	.............(CE)	...........❶	........$1800—2400	
☐ 88	.........9.25"	.............(CE)	...........❷	........$1300—1600	
☐ 88	.........8.75 to 9.25"	......(CE)	...........❸	........$1100—1200	
☐ 88/I	........6.25 to 6.75"	......(CE)	...........❸	........$650—750	
☐ 88/I	........6.25 to 6.75"	......(CE)	...........❹	........$575—650	
☐ 88/I	........6.25 to 6.75"	......(CE)	...........❺	........$560—575	
☐ 88/I	........6.25 to 6.75"	......(CE)	...........❻	........$550—560	
☐ 88/I	........6.25 to 6.75"	......(CE)	...........❼	........$530—550	60th Anni Decal 1998
☐ 88/I	........6.25 to 6.75"	......(OE)	...........❽	........$529	
☐ 88/II	........8.75 to 9.00"	......(CE)	...........❷	........$1100—1300	
☐ 88/II	........8.75 to 9.00"	......(CE)	...........❸	........$1000—1100	
☐ 88/II	........8.75 to 9.00"	......(CE)	...........❹	........$900—1000	
☐ 88/II	........8.75 to 9.00"	......(CE)	...........❺	........$850—900	
☐ 88/II	........8.75 to 9.00"	......(CE)	...........❻	........$825—850	
☐ 88/II	........8.75 to 9.00"	......(TW)	...........❼	........$800—825	

89/I New (TM 3)   *89/I Old (TM 1)*

HUM 89 — Little Cellist

Modeled by master sculptor Arthur Moeller in 1938. Restyled in the early 1960s. Many size variations through the years. Older examples of size 89/I have eyes open and looking straight ahead. Newer pieces have eyes looking down. Older pieces have rectangular base while newer pieces have rectangular base with corners squared off. Found with either 89/2 or 89/II on older models. Name listed as "Musician" in some old catalogues. The large size 89/II was listed on the 1993 price list as (TW) "Temporarily Withdrawn" and is still not back on current price lists.

☐	89/I	5.25 to 6.25"	(CE)	❶	$750—850
☐	89/I	5.25 to 6.25"	(CE)	❷	$450—550
☐	89/I	5.25 to 6.25"	(CE)	❸	$350—400
☐	89/I	5.25 to 6.25"	(CE)	❹	$300—350
☐	89/I	5.25 to 6.25"	(CE)	❺	$290—300
☐	89/I	5.25 to 6.25"	(CE)	❻	$285—290
☐	89/I	5.25 to 6.25"	(CE)	❼	$280—285 60th Anni Dcal 1998
☐	89/I	5.25 to 6.25"	(OE)	❽	$279
☐	89/II	7.50 to 7.75"	(CE)	❶	$1200—1500
☐	89/II	7.50 to 7.75"	(CE)	❷	$800—1000
☐	89/II	7.50 to 7.75"	(CE)	❸	$650—750
☐	89/II	7.50 to 7.75"	(CE)	❹	$600—650
☐	89/II	7.50 to 7.75"	(CE)	❺	$500—550
☐	89/II	7.50 to 7.75"	(CE)	❻	$475—500
☐	89/II	7.50 to 7.75"	(TW)	❼	$450—475
☐	89	7.50"	(CE)	❶	$1250—1600

Factory sample

HUM 90 (A) — Eventide

HUM 90 (B) — Adoration (without Shrine), Bookends
Records indicate that this set of bookends was made in 1938 by a team of artists, which possibly included Reinhold Unger. Factory sample only. Extremely rare. Not produced after 28 February 1938. Listed as a (CE) Closed Edition. One half of this rare bookend (minus the wood base) was located in Michigan. This piece does not have the "M.I. Hummel" signature nor any identifying numbers—only a little dried glue remaining, indicating it had originally been attached to another object. Keep looking! Maybe you can locate the other half! Note position of lambs in photo, then see HUM 99 "Eventide" for interesting comparison.

☐ 90 A & B ....(CE)............................$10,000—15,000
☐ 90 B ....4.00" ....(CE)............................$5000—7500

Found in Michigan

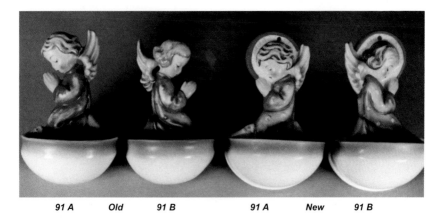

| 91 A | Old | 91 B | | 91 A | New | 91 B |

HUM 91 A & B — Holy Water Font, Angels at Prayer

Angel facing left was apparently made first since early crown mark pieces are incised 91 only (not part of set). Angel facing right (91 B) was probably introduced slightly later. Now listed as a pair—91 A & B. First modeled by master sculptor Reinhold Unger in 1938. Older models (left) do not have halos while more recent designs have halos and a redesigned water bowl. Trademarks 1, 2 and 3 are without halos, 3, 4, 5 and 6 with halos. Note: trademark 3 can be found either way.

Priced for pair.
- ☐ 91 ....3.25 x 4.50"..........(CE) ......❶ ......$400—500
- ☐ 91 A & B ....3.625 x 5.00"........(CE) ......❶ ......$400—500
- ☐ 91 A & B ....3.625 x 5.00"........(CE) ......❷ ......$200—250
- ☐ 91 A & B ....3.625 x 5.00"........(CE) ......❸ ......$160—165
- ☐ 91 A & B ....3.625 x 5.00"........(CE) ......❹ ......$155—160
- ☐ 91 A & B ....3.625 x 5.00"........(CE) ......❺ ......$150—155
- ☐ 91 A & B ....3.625 x 5.00"........(CE) ......❻ ......$145—150
- ☐ 91 A & B ....3.625 x 5.00"........(CE) ......❼ ......$140—145
- ☐ 91 A & B ....3.625 x 5.00"........(OE) ......❽ $139

.... HUM TERM ....

UNDERGLAZE: The term used to describe especially the number 5 trademark that appears actually underneath the glaze as opposed to the later version of the number 5 trademark that appears on the top of the glaze.

.... HUM TERM ....

SAMPLE MODEL: Generally a figurine that was made as a sample only and not approved by the Siessen Convent for production. Sample models (in the true sense of the term) are extremely rare items and command a premium price on the secondary market.

HUM 92 — Merry Wanderer, Plaque

Many size variations. Crown mark pieces can be found in both sizes. Some have incised 1938 copyright date, others do not. Some pieces have "M.I. Hummel" signature on both front and back, while others have signature on back only. Some TM 2 plaques have

Old (TM 2)   *New (TM 4)*

copyright (©WG) on front lower right, signature on back. Originally modeled by master sculptor Arthur Moeller in 1938 but restyled several times in later years. The "Merry Wanderer" plaque was (TW) "Temporarily Withdrawn" from production on 31 December 1989, but may be reinstated at some future date.

☐ 92	.........4.50 x 5.00 to 5.00 x 5.50"	....(CE)........	❶	.......$450—575
☐ 92	.........4.50 x 5.00 to 5.00 x 5.50"	....(CE)........	❷	.......$275—350
☐ 92	.........4.50 x 5.00"	.............................(CE)........	❸	.......$225—275
☐ 92	.........4.50 x 5.00"	.............................(CE)........	❹	.......$175—225
☐ 92	.........4.50 x 5.00"	.............................(CE)........	❺	.......$160—170
☐ 92	.........4.50 x 5.00"	.............................(TW)	❻	.......$150—160

HUM 93 — Little Fiddler, Plaque

Originally modeled by master sculptor Arthur Moeller in 1938. Many size variations. Two different backgrounds as noted in photograph. Older model (left) extremely rare. Some models have 1938 copyright date. Some pieces have "M.I. Hummel" sig-

Rare old style (TM 1+1)   *New (TM 1)*

nature on both front and back, while others have signature on back only, or front only. Also sold in white overglaze at one time. The background on the left is similar to HUM 107. The "Little Fiddler" plaque was (TW) "Temporarily Withdrawn" from production on 31 December 1989, but may be reinstated at some future date.

☐ 93	.........4.50 x 5.00 to 5.00 x 5.50"	....(CE)	❶	.......$450—575
☐ 93	.........4.50 x 5.00 to 5.00 x 5.50"	....(CE)	❷	.......$275—350
☐ 93	.........4.50 x 5.00"	.............................(CE)	❸	.......$225—275
☐ 93	.........4.50 x 5.00"	.............................(CE)	❹	.......$175—225
☐ 93	.........4.50 x 5.00"	.............................(CE)	❺	.......$160—170
☐ 93	.........4.50 x 5.00"	.............................(TW)	❻	.......$150—160
☐ 93	.........Rare old style	.......................(CE)	❶	.......$3000—4000

| 94/I (TM 2) | 94/I (TM 3) | 94 3/0 (TM 2) |

HUM 94 — Surprise

Records indicate this model was produced by a team of sculptors in 1938. Old name: "The Duet" or "Hansel and Gretel." Also found listed with name of: "What's Up?" Older pieces marked "94" or "94/I" have rectangular base. All newer models have oval base. Slight variation in suspender straps on older models. Numbering errors occur occasionally—as an example, we have size 94/I that is marked 94/II in trademark 3. This trademark, however, has been "slashed" indicating that it was probably sold to a factory employee. The small size 94 3/0 does not have the detail that the larger sizes have. Large size (94/I) was (TW) "Temporarily Withdrawn" in January 1999.

☐ 94 3/0	....4.00 to 4.25"......(CE)	...........❶ ....$450—550
☐ 94 3/0	....4.00 to 4.25"......(CE)	...........❷ ....$275—375
☐ 94 3/0	....4.00 to 4.25"......(CE)	...........❸ ....$225—250
☐ 94 3/0	....4.00 to 4.25"......(CE)	...........❹ ....$215—225
☐ 94 3/0	....4.00 to 4.25"......(CE)	...........❺ ....$210—215
☐ 94 3/0	....4.00 to 4.25"......(CE)	...........❻ ....$205—210
☐ 94 3/0	....4.00 to 4.25"......(CE)	...........❼ ....$200—205
☐ 94 3/0	....4.00 to 4.25"......(OE)	...........❽ $199
☐ 94/I	........5.25 to 5.50"......(CE)	...........❶ ....$750—950
☐ 94/I	........5.25 to 5.50"......(CE)	...........❷ ....$500—650
☐ 94/I	........5.25 to 5.50"......(CE)	...........❸ ....$425—475
☐ 94/I	........5.25 to 5.50"......(CE)	...........❹ ....$400—425
☐ 94/I	........5.25 to 5.50"......(CE)	...........❺ ....$350—390
☐ 94/I	........5.25 to 5.50"......(CE)	...........❻ ....$335—350
☐ 94/I	........5.25 to 5.50"......(TW)	...........❼ ....$325—335
☐ 94	........5.75".................(CE)	...........❶ ....$800—1000
☐ 94	........5.75".................(CE)	...........❷ ....$550—700

| (TM 1) | (TM 2) | (TM 6) |

HUM 95 — Brother Tm 3 $26,00

Many size and color variations. Old name: "Our Hero" or "Hero of The Village." Same boy as used in HUM 94 "Surprise." Records indicate this figurine was first modeled in 1938 by a team of sculptors. "Brother" sold for $6.50 on old 1955 price list. A special 60th Anniversary decal and metal tag was used on 1998 production. "Temporarily Withdrawn" (TW) in 2005.

☐ 95 ....5.25 to 5.75"......(CE) ....❶ ....$700—800
☐ 95 ....5.25 to 5.75"......(CE) ....❷ ....$400—500
☐ 95 ....5.25 to 5.75"......(CE) ....❸ ....$300—350
☐ 95 ....5.25 to 5.75"......(CE) ....❹ ....$295—300
☐ 95 ....5.25 to 5.75"......(CE) ....❺ ....$290—295
☐ 95 ....5.25 to 5.75"......(CE) ....❻ ....$285—290
☐ 95 ....5.25 to 5.75"......(CE) ....❼ ....$280—285 60th Anni Decal 1998
☐ 95 ....5.25 to 5.75"......(TW) ....❽ ....$279—280

.... HUM TERM ....

RÖDENTAL: The town in Germany where the W. Goebel Porzellanfabrik is situated. Rödental is located near Coburg and lies only a few miles from the former East German border. In 1981 Rödental became the official Sister City of Eaton, Ohio, due to the longtime "Hummel" relationship with Robert L. & Ruth Miller.

| (TM 1) | (TM 2) | (TM 6) |

HUM 96 — Little Shopper
Many size variations. Old name: "Errand Girl," "Gretel" or "Meg" in some older catalogues. Some catalogues and price lists indicate size as 5.50". This is believed, by this author, to be in error. I have never seen it over 5 inches in over thirty years of collecting. Records indicate this figurine was first modeled in 1938 by a team of sculptors possibly including master sculptor Reinhold Unger. Same girl as used in HUM 94 "Surprise." "Little Shopper" sold for $5.50 on old 1955 price list. (TW) "Temporarily Withdrawn" in 2005.

☐	96	4.50 to 5.00"	(CE)	❶	$450—550
☐	96	4.50 to 5.00"	(CE)	❷	$300—350
☐	96	4.50 to 5.00"	(CE)	❸	$220—250
☐	96	4.50 to 5.00"	(CE)	❹	$195—220
☐	96	4.50 to 5.00"	(CE)	❺	$190—195
☐	96	4.50 to 5.00"	(CE)	❻	$185—190
☐	96	4.50 to 5.00"	(CE)	❼	$180—185
☐	96	4.50 to 5.00"	(**TW**)	❽	$180—185

.... HUM TERM ....

SECONDARY MARKET: The buying and selling of items after the initial retail purchase has been transacted. Often times this post-retail trading is also referred to as the "after market." This very publication is intended to serve as a guide for the secondary market values of "M. I. Hummel" items.

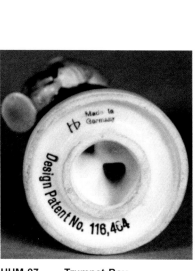

HUM 97 — Trumpet Boy

Originally modeled by master sculptor Arthur Moeller in 1938. Many size variations. Boy's coat is normally green. Old "U.S. Zone" specimen has blue coat shaded with green. Old name: "The Little Musician." There are a few rare pieces with the inscription "Design Patent No. 116,464" stamped on the bottom. This indicates that this piece was originally sold in England to comply with an English requirement that each figurine carry the respective design patent number. This variation valued from $1000—1500. "Trumpet Boy" sold for $5.50 on old 1955 price list. "Trumpet Boy" was (TW) "Temporarily Withdrawn" from the U.S. market 31 December 1997, but may be reinstated at some future date. Available in "Trumpet Boy" Progression Set.

☐ 97 ....4.50 to 4.75".......(CE) ....❶ ....$400—525
☐ 97 ....4.50 to 4.75"......(CE) ....❷ ....$250—300
☐ 97 ....4.50 to 4.75"......(CE) ....❸ ....$200—225
☐ 97 ....4.50 to 4.75"......(CE) ....❹ ....$180—200
☐ 97 ....4.50 to 4.75"......(CE) ....❺ ....$170—180
☐ 97 ....4.50 to 4.75"......(CE) ....❻ ....$165—170
☐ 97 ....4.50 to 4.75"......(CE) ....❼ ....$150—160
☐ 97 ....4.50" ....(LE)..............❽ .... (Progression set)

| 98/0 (TM 3) | 98 (TM 1) | 98 2/0 (TM 4) |

HUM 98 — Sister

When first modeled in 1938 by master sculptor Arthur Moeller, this figurine was produced in one size only with the incised number 98. A smaller size was issued in the early 1960s with the incised number 98 2/0. At the same time, the large size was changed to 98/0. Many size variations; otherwise very little change between old and new models. Old name: "The Shopper" or "The First Shopping" in some old catalogues. Some small size pieces have an incised 1962 copyright date. In 1996 a 2.875" size (3.125" with base) with incised model number 98 5/0 was produced as part of the "Pen Pals" series of personalized name card table decorations. The original issue price was $55. "Sister" is same girl as used on HUM 49 "To Market." "Sister" sold for $6.50 on old 1955 price list. Large size (98/0) was (TW) "Temporarily Withdrawn" in January 1999. Small size (98 2/0) had special 60th Anniversary decal on 1998 production. Small size (98 2/0) "Sister" was (TW) "Temporarily Withdrawn" in 2005.

☐ 98 5/0	....2.875"	...............(CE)	............❼	.........$55—60	
☐ 98	..........5.75"	..................(CE)	............❶	.........$600—700	
☐ 98	..........5.75"	..................(CE)	............❷	.........$400—450	
☐ 98	..........5.75"	..................(CE)	............❸	.........$325—350	
☐ 98 2/0	....4.50 to 4.75"	......(CE)	,,...........❸	.........$225—250	
☐ 98 2/0	....4.50 to 4.75"	......(CE)	............❹	.........$195—225	
☐ 98 2/0	....4.50 to 4.75"	......(CE)	............❺	.........$190—195	
☐ 98 2/0	....4.50 to 4.75"	......(CE)	............❻	.........$185—190	
☐ 98 2/0	....4.50 to 4.75"	......(CE)	............❼	.........$180—185	60th Anni Decal 1998
☐ 98 2/0	....4.50 to 4.75"	......(TW)	............❽	.........$179—180	
☐ 98/0	........5.25 to 5.50"	......(CE)	............❸	.........$300—325	
☐ 98/0	........5.25 to 5.50"	......(CE)	............❹	.........$275—300	
☐ 98/0	........5.25 to 5.50"	......(CE)	............❺	.........$250—275	
☐ 98/0	........5.25 to 5.50"	......(CE)	............❻	.........$240—250	
☐ 98/0	........5.25 to 5.50"	......(TW)	............❼	.........$230—235	

HUM 99 — Eventide

Records indicate this model was produced in 1938 by a combination of modelers. Almost identical with "Wayside Devotion" HUM 28 but without the shrine. Many size variations. Note photo of rare crown mark piece with lambs in different position directly in front of children. At one time this figurine was sold in Belgium in the white overglaze finish and would now be considered rare. Eventide was listed as (TW) "Temporarily Withdrawn" in January 1999.

Normal (TM 1)　　　　　　　　　　*Rare version (TM 1)*

☐ 99	4.25 x 5.00"	(CE)	❶	$950—1250
☐ 99	4.25 x 5.00"	(CE)	❷	$600—750
☐ 99	4.25 x 5.00"	(CE)	❸	$500—550
☐ 99	4.25 x 5.00"	(CE)	❹	$425—500
☐ 99	4.25 x 5.00"	(CE)	❺	$390—425
☐ 99	4.25 x 5.00"	(CE)	❻	$370—390
☐ 99	4.25 x 5.00"	**(TW)**	❼	$360—370
☐ 99	Rare version	(CE)	❶	$3000—3500

Rare   *Extremely Rare*

HUM 100 — Shrine, Table Lamp (CE)

This extremely rare lamp is similar to the figurine "Adoration" HUM 23. First modeled by Erich Lautensack in 1938 and produced in very limited quantities. Only a few examples known to exist. The example in our collection has a light beige-colored post, an incised crown trademark plus the stamped "U.S. Zone". Another example had a dark brown post, an incised crown trademark plus stamped "full bee." Also had 6/50 painting date. Pictured on the right is this extremely rare variation that was found in England in a damaged conditoin. Incised model number: 2/100 on the bottom, has a "double crown" trademark. Note the bird on post in place of Madonna Shrine and NO kneeling bench at bottom similar to HUM 105. Both lamps were modeled by master sculptor Erich Lautensack in 1937-1938.

☐ 100 ....7.50" ....(CE)..........❶ ....$8000—10,000
☐ 2/100 ......7.50" ....(CE)..........❶ + ❶ ....$8000—10,000

Plain post   *Tree trunk post*

HUM 101 — To Market, Table Lamp (CE)

Originally modeled by master sculptor Arthur Moeller in 1937. Listed as a (CE) Closed Edition on factory records 20 April 1937. Redesigned and limited quantity produced in early 1950s with "tree trunk" post. Some incised with number II/101, III/101 and others with 101 only. Lamp was adapted from figurine "To Market" HUM 49. Master sculptor Arthur Moeller redesigned this lamp in 1952 into the 9.50" size HUM 223.

☐ 101 ....6.50" ....(CE)..............❶ ....$8000—10,000 Plain Post
☐ 101 ....6.50" ....(CE)..............❷ ....$6000—8000 Plain Post
☐ 101 ....7.50" ....(CE)..............❶ ....$1500—2000 Tree trunk post
☐ 101 ....7.50" ....(CE)..............❷ ....$750—1000
☐ 101 ....7.50" ....(CE)..............❸ ....$500—750

HUM 102 — Volunteers, Table Lamp (CE)
Originally modeled by Erich Lautensack in 1937.
Listed as a (CE) Closed Edition in factory records
20 April 1937. In 1979 a rare specimen was found
in Seattle, Washington, and is now in the Robert L.
Miller collection. This piece has a double crown
(incised and stamped) trademark. Since 1979 several other specimens have been found and the
Goebel factory now has one in their archives.

☐ 102 ....7.50" ......(CE) .... ❶......$8000—10,000

HUM 103 — Farewell, Table Lamp (CE)
Originally modeled by Erich Lautensack in 1937.
Listed as a (CE) Closed Edition on factory records
20 April 1937. Several examples of this extremely
rare lamp have been found and one is now in the
Robert L. Miller collection. A second specimen was
presented to the Goebel factory for their archives in
Rödental, Germany. Since 1983 several other specimens have been found, but is still considered
extremely rare.

☐ 103 ....7.50" ......(CE) .... ❶......$8000—10,000

HUM 104 — Eventide, Table Lamp (CE)
Originally modeled by Reinhold Unger in 1938.
Listed as a (CE) Closed Edition on factory records
3 March 1938. This lamp was originally called
"Wayside Devotion" in our earlier books but is now
correctly named "Eventide." The first known example of this extremely rare lamp base was purchased from its original owner in northern Indiana
and is now in the Robert L. Miller collection. The
lamp was located through the help of Ralph and
Terry Kovel and their syndicated news-paper column on antiques. Notice the position of lambs in
this photo and then compare with photo of "Eventide" HUM 99.

☐ 104 ....7.50" ......(CE) .... ❶......$8000—10,000

HUM 105 — Adoration With Bird (CE)

Very limited production. Listed as a (CE) Closed Edition on factory records 24 May

1938. All known examples have double crown (incised and stamped) trademark. Notice difference in pigtail of little girl in this comparative photograph. Unable to locate information on original sculptor or date of original model; probably master sculptor Reinhold Unger who created model for "Adoration" HUM 23 which is similar in design. This figurine is considered extremely rare.

Double crown (TM1 + 1)   *Double crown (TM 1 + 1)*

☐ 105 ....4.75" ....(CE) ....❶ ....$7000—8000

106 (TM 1)   *107 (TM 1)*

HUM 106 — Merry Wanderer, Plaque with wood frame (CE)

Very limited production. Listed as a (CE) Closed Edition on factory records 1 August 1938. First modeled by master sculptor Arthur Moeller in 1938. Similar to all-ceramic plaque of "Merry Wanderer" HUM 92 except for wood frame. Some variation in frames. Considered extremely rare.

☐ 106 ....6.00 x 6.00" ......(CE) ....❶ ....$3000—4000

HUM 107 — Little Fiddler, Plaque with wood frame (CE)

Very limited production. Listed as a (CE) Closed Edition on factory records 1 August 1938. First modeled by master sculptor Arthur Moeller in 1938. Similar to the all-ceramic plaque of "Little Fiddler" HUM 93 (rare old style background) except for the wood frame. Some variation in frames. Considered extremely rare.

☐ 107 ....6.00 x 6.00" ......(CE) ....❶ ....$3000—4000

(TM 1+USZ)   HS 01 (Not 108)   (TM 1+2)

HUM 108 — Angel With Two Children At Feet (CN)

Originally modeled by master sculptor Reinhold Unger in 1938. No known examples. Listed on factory records of 14 October 1938 as a wall decoration. Pictured here is Goebel item HS 01 listed in 1950 Goebel catalogue. Factory representatives state that it is possibly a Hummel design—probably rejected by Siessen Convent and then later marketed as a Goebel item. When and if found with the "M. I. Hummel" signature and incised 108 would have a value of $10,000—$15,000. Note hair on boy: blonde on left while dark hair on right as we face photo. Several examples of Goebel HS 01 have been found and are now in private collections—including the Robert L. Miller collection.

☐ 108 ....(CN) ......❶ ....$10,000—15,000
☐ Goebel HS 01 ....10.25" ....(CE) ......❶ ....$3000—5000
☐ Goebel HS 01 ....10.25" ....(CE) ......❶ + ❷ ....$2500—4500

.... HUM TERM ....

SAMPLE MODEL: Generally a figurine that was made as a sample only and not approved by the Siessen Convent for production. Sample models (in the true sense of the term) are extremely rare items and command a premium price on the secondary market.

109/II (TM 3)   *109 (TM 1 + 1)*   *109/0 (TM 2)*

HUM 109 — Happy Traveller

First modeled by master sculptor Arthur Moeller in 1938 and has been produced in all trademark periods. The large size was permanently retired by Goebel in the spring of 1982. Early pieces were usually incised 109/2 instead of 109/II. Small size only is still in current production. Sometimes the small size is found without the size designator in trademarks 3, 4 and 5. Listed as "Wanderer" in old catalogues. Small size was restyled in 1980 with the new textured finish. The small size normally has black handles on the umbrella while the large size has tan. 109/0 listed as (TW) "Temporarily Withdrawn" from production in June 2002.

☐ 109/0 ......4.75 to 5.00"......(CE) ....❷ ....$275—350
☐ 109/0 ......4.75 to 5.00"......(CE) ....❸ ....$225—250
☐ 109 ....4.75 to 5.00"......(CE) ....❸ ....$225—250
☐ 109/0 ......4.75 to 5.00"......(CE) ....❹ ....$210—225
☐ 109 ....4.75 to 5.00"......(CE) ....❹ ....$210—225
☐ 109/0 ......4.75 to 5.00"......(CE) ....❺ ....$195—200
☐ 109 ....4.75 to 5.00"......(CE) ....❺ ....$195—200
☐ 109/0 ......4.75 to 5.00"......(CE) ....❻ ....$190—195
☐ 109/0 ......4.75 to 5.00"......(CE) ....❼ ....$185—190
☐ 109/0 ......4.75 to 5.00"......(TW) ....❽ ....$185—190
☐ 109 ....7.75".................(CE) ....❶ ....$1200—1500
☐ 109 ....7.50".................(CE) ....❷ ....$800—900
☐ 109/II ......7.50".................(CE) ....❸ ....$500—550
☐ 109/II ......7.50".................(CE) ....❹ ....$450—500
☐ 109/II ......7.50".................(CE) ....❺ ....$400—425
☐ 109/II ......7.50".................(CE) ....❻ ....$375—400

110 (TM 1)   *110/0 (TM 3)*

HUM 110 — Let's Sing

Originally modeled by master sculptor Reinhold Unger in 1938. There are many size variations. Some have an incised 1938 copyright date. Sometimes found with "©W. Goebel." Some incised model numbers are difficult to read because of the extremely small bases. "Let's Sing" sold for $6.00 on old 1955 price list. See: HUM 114 "Let's Sing" ashtray.

☐ 110..........4.00"......................(CE)..........❶ ....$500—600
☐ 110..........4.00"......................(CE)..........❷ ....$350—400
☐ 110/0 .....3.00 to 3.25" ....(CE)..........❶ ....$400—500
☐ 110/0 .....3.00 to 3.25" ....(CE)..........❷ ....$250—300
☐ 110/0 .....3.00 to 3.25" ....(CE)..........❸ ....$200—250
☐ 110/0 .....3.00 to 3.25" ....(CE)..........❹ ....$190—195
☐ 110/0 .....3.00 to 3.25" ....(CE)..........❺ ....$185—190
☐ 110/0 .....3.00 to 3.25" ....(CE)..........❻ ....$180—185
☐ 110/0 .....3.00 to 3.25" ....(CE)..........❼ ....$179—180
☐ 110/0 .....3.00 to 3.25" ....(OE)..........❽ $179
☐ 110/I........3.50 to 4.00" ....(CE)..........❷ ....$300—375
☐ 110/I........3.50 to 4.00" ....(CE)..........❸ ....$250—300
☐ 110/I........3.50 to 4.00" ....(CE)..........❹ ....$225—250
☐ 110/I........3.50 to 4.00" ....(CE)..........❺ ....$205—225
☐ 110/I........3.50 to 4.00" ....(CE)..........❻ ....$200—205
☐ 110/I........3.50 to 4.00" ....(CE)..........❼ ....$195—200
☐ 110/I........3.50 to 4.00" ....(TW) ....❽ ....$195—200

Old bowl style   *New jar style*

HUM III/110 — Let's Sing, Box

Bowl style first produced in 1938. Jar style first produced and sold in 1964. Model number is found on underside of lid. The "M .I. Hummel" signature is found on topside of lid directly behind figure. "Let's Sing" candy box was (TW) "Temporarily Withdrawn" from production on 31 December 1989, but may be reinstated at some future date.

☐ III/110 ....6.25" ....(CE) ....❶ ....$750—850
☐ III/110 ....6.25" ....(CE) ....❷ ....$575—650
☐ III/110 ....6.25" ....(CE) ....❸ ....$475—550 (Old Style)
☐ III/110 ....5.25" ....(CE) ....❸ ....$300—350 (New Style)
☐ III/110 ....5.25" ....(CE) ....❹ ....$250—275
☐ III/110 ....5.25" ....(CE) ....❺ ....$225—250
☐ III/110 ....5.25" ....**(TW)** ....❻ ....$200—225

111/I (TM 1)   *111 3/0 (TM 4)*

HUM 111 — Wayside Harmony

First modeled in 1938 by master sculptor Reinhold Unger. There are many size variations. Normally has green-colored socks, but some crown and full bee trademark pieces have yellow socks in the small (111 3/0) size. Old name: "Just Sittin-Boy." Some models have a 1938 incised copyright date. The small size "Wayside Harmony" listed for $5.00 while the large size listed for $10.00 on 1955 price list. Large size (111/I) was (TW) "Temporarily Withdrawn" in January 1999.

☐ 111 3/0 ..3.75 to 4.00" ......(CE) ....❶ ....$450—550
☐ 111 3/0 ..3.75 to 4.00" ......(CE) ....❷ ....$300—350
☐ 111 3/0 ..3.75 to 4.00" ......(CE) ....❸ ....$235—250
☐ 111 3/0 ..3.75 to 4.00" ......(CE) ....❹ ....$210—235
☐ 111 3/0 ..3.75 to 4.00" ......(CE) ....❺ ....$195—200
☐ 111 3/0 ..3.75 to 4.00" ......(CE) ....❻ ....$190—195
☐ 111 3/0 ..3.75 to 4.00" ......(CE) ....❼ ....$185—190
☐ 111 3/0 ..3.75 to 4.00" ......**(OE)** ....❽ $185
☐ 111/I ....5.00 to 5.50" ......(CE) ....❶ ....$650—800
☐ 111/I ....5.00 to 5.50" ......(CE) ....❷ ....$450—550
☐ 111/I ....5.00 to 5.50" ......(CE) ....❸ ....$400—450
☐ 111/I ....5.00 to 5.50" ......(CE) ....❹ ....$350—400
☐ 111/I ....5.00 to 5.50" ......(CE) ....❺ ....$340—350
☐ 111/I ....5.00 to 5.50" ......(CE) ....❻ ....$330—340
☐ 111/I ....5.00 to 5.50" ......**(TW)** ....❼ ....$320—330
☐ 111 ....5.50" ....(CE) ....❶ ....$700—850

II/111 (TM 2)   *224/I (TM 4)*

HUM II/111 — Wayside Harmony, Table Lamp (CE)
This number was used briefly in the early 1950s. Later changed to 224/I. The only difference is that the boy is slightly larger. Some models have been found with number III/111/I.

☐ II/111 ....7.50" ....(CE)....... ❶ ....$600—800
☐ II/111 ....7.50" ....(CE)....... ❷ ....$450—550
☐ II/111 ....7.50" ....(CE)....... ❸ ....$375—525

112/I (TM 2)   *112 3/0 (TM 4)*

HUM 112 — Just Resting

First modeled in 1938 by master sculptor Reinhold Unger. Many size variations. Old name: "Just Sittin-Girl." Some models have a 1938 incised copyright date. There is an unusual example of size 112/I without a basket in front of the girl (not shown). The direction of the basket handle varies on old "crown" trademark examples. Large size (112/I) was (TW) "Temporarily Withdrawn" from production in January 1999.

☐ 112 3/0 ....3.75 to 4.00".........(CE) ...... ❶ ....$450—550
☐ 112 3/0 ....3.75 to 4.00".........(CE) ...... ❷ ....$300—350
☐ 112 3/0 ....3.75 to 4.00".........(CE) ...... ❸ ....$235—250
☐ 112 3/0 ....3.75 to 4.00".........(CE) ...... ❹ ....$210—235
☐ 112 3/0 ....3.75 to 4.00".........(CE) ...... ❺ ....$195—210
☐ 112 3/0 ....3.75 to 4.00".........(CE) ...... ❻ ....$190—195
☐ 112 3/0 ....3.75 to 4.00".........(CE) ...... ❼ ....$185—190
☐ 112 3/0 ....3.75 to 4.00".........(**OE**) ...... ❽ $179
☐ 112/I ....4.75 to 5.50".........(CE) ...... ❶ ....$650—800
☐ 112/I ....4.75 to 5.50".........(CE) ...... ❷ ....$450—550
☐ 112/I ....4.75 to 5.50".........(CE) ...... ❸ ....$400—450
☐ 112/I ....4.75 to 5.50".........(CE) ...... ❹ ....$350—400
☐ 112/I ....4.75 to 5.50".........(CE) ...... ❺ ....$340—350
☐ 112/I ....4.75 to 5.50".........(CE) ...... ❻ ....$330—340
☐ 112/I ....4.75 to 5.50".........(**TW**) ..... ❼ ....$320—330
☐ 112 ....5.50"...................(CE) ...... ❶ ....$700—850

II/112 (TM 2)	225/I (TM 5)	112 (TM 1+1)

HUM II/112 — Just Resting, Table Lamp (CE)

This number was used briefly in the early 1950s. Later changed to 225/I. The only difference is that the girl is slightly larger. Some models have a 1938 incised copyright date. Some models have been found with numbers III/112/I and 2/112/I. Very hard to find with these numbers. An unusual variation was found in Sweden in 1991 with a "double crown" trademark, incised "M. I. Hummel" signature on back of tree trunk and incised number 112 only. It is now in the Robert L. Miller collection. Possibly a "prototype" or at least a "mother mould sample." The base is too small to be used successfully as a lamp and was re-designed with a larger round base. The history of this lamp is still unknown and I have not been able to locate another sample like this one, nor any information on it at the factory. A similar variation of the companion lamp of "Wayside Harmony" HUM 111 is yet to be found.

☐ II/112 ......7.50" ....(CE) ....❶ ....$600—800
☐ II/112 ......7.50" ....(CE) ....❷ ....$450—550
☐ II/112 ......7.50" ....(CE) ....❸ ....$375—525
☐ 112..........7.00" ....(CE) ....❶ + ❶ ......$5000—6000

HUM 113 — Heavenly Song, Candleholder (CE)

Originally modeled by master sculptor Arthur Moeller in 1938 but was produced in very limited quantities. Sometimes mistaken for HUM 54 "Silent Night;" which is similar. Was scheduled for production again in 1978 and listed in some catalogues and price lists, but because of its similarity to HUM 54 "Silent Night" the factory decided it should not be produced again. In 1980 it was listed as a (CE) Closed Edition. At least one piece is known to exist with the 5 trademark. All specimens would now be considered extremely rare. Also found decorated in bright colors and glossy finish of the "Faience" technique. Usually sell for $3000—$5000.

☐ 113 ....3.50 x 4.75" ....(CE)......❶ ......$6000—10,000
☐ 113 ....3.50 x 4.75" ....(CE)......❷ ......$4500—5500
☐ 113 ....3.50 x 4.75" ....(CE)......❸ ......$3500—4500
☐ 113 ....3.50 x 4.75" ....(CE)......❺ ......$3000—3500

Old style (TM 2)   *New style (TM 2)*

HUM 114 — Let's Sing, Ashtray

First modeled in 1938 by master sculptor Reinhold Unger with the ashtray on the left as we face the figurine (boy's right). Restyled in 1959 by master sculptor Theo R. Menzenbach with the ashtray on the right as we face the figurine (boy's left). Old style would be considered difficult to find today. Both styles can be found with the (TM 2) full bee trademark. This accounts for the wide price variation in TM 2 trademark prices.

☐ 114 ....3.50 x 6.25" ....(CE)......❶ ......$850—1000   (Old Style)
☐ 114 ....3.50 x 6.25" ....(CE)......❶ ......$750—1000   (New Style)
☐ 114 ....3.50 x 6.25" ....(CE)......❷ ......$600—850   (Old Style)
☐ 114 ....3.50 x 6.25" ....(CE)......❷ ......$250—350   (New Style)
☐ 114 ....3.50 x 6.25" ....(CE)......❸ ......$225—250
☐ 114 ....3.50 x 6.25" ....(CE)......❹ ......$170—225
☐ 114 ....3.50 x 6.25" ....(CE)......❺ ......$160—170
☐ 114 ....3.50 x 6.25" ....(TW)......❻ ......$150—160

115 / Mel 1   *116 / Mel 2*   *117 / Mel 3*

HUM 115 — Advent Candlestick, Girl With Nosegay
HUM 116 — Advent Candlestick, Girl With Fir Tree
HUM 117 — Advent Candlestick, Boy with Horse
These three figurines were first modeled by master sculptor Reinhold Unger in 1939. They are similar to HUM 239 A, B & C (without candleholders). Very early models were incised with "Mel"

instead of "M. I. Hummel." Reportedly sold only in Germany. Note: "Mel" is the last three letters of Hummel. Some "Mel" pieces have been found with the early stylized trademark indicating that both "Hummel" and "Mel" pieces were being produced and marketed at the same time. Mel 1, Mel 2, and Mel 3 usually sell for $300 to $350 each depending on the condition. HUM 115, 116 and 117 were listed as (TW) "Temporarily Withdrawn" in June 2002.

☐	115	3.50"	(CE)	❶	$225—275
☐	115	3.50"	(CE)	❷	$125—150
☐	115	3.50"	(CE)	❸	$95—100
☐	115	3.50"	(CE)	❹	$90—95
☐	115	3.50"	(CE)	❺	$85—90
☐	115	3.50"	(CE)	❻	$80—85
☐	115	3.50"	(CE)	❼	$75—80
☐	115	3.50"	(TW)	❽	$72.50
☐	116	3.50"	(CE)	❶	$225—275
☐	116	3.50"	(CE)	❷	$125–150
☐	116	3.50"	(CE)	❸	$95—100
☐	116	3.50"	(CE)	❹	$90—95
☐	116	3.50"	(CE)	❺	$85—90
☐	116	3.50"	(CE)	❻	$80—85
☐	116	3.50"	(CE)	❼	$75—80
☐	116	3.50"	(TW)	❽	$72.50
☐	117	3.50"	(CE)	❶	$225—275
☐	117	3.50"	(CE)	❷	$125—150
☐	117	3.50"	(CE)	❸	$95—100
☐	117	3.50"	(CE)	❹	$90—95
☐	117	3.50"	(CE)	❺	$85—90
☐	117	3.50"	(CE)	❻	$80—85
☐	117	3.50"	(CE)	❼	$75—80
☐	117	3.50"	(TW)	❽	$72.50

New style (TM 3)   **Old style (TM 1+2)**

HUM 118 — Little Thrifty, Bank
This figurine is actually a bank. Made with a metal lock & key on bottom. Originally modeled by master sculptor Arthur Moeller in 1939. Restyled by Rudolf Wittman in 1963. Older models have a slightly different base design as noted in photograph. The object into which "Little Thrifty" is putting her coin is a medieval form of a poor box, something which can still be found in old European churches. "Little Thrifty" sold for $6.00 on old 1955 price list. Found with either gold or silver coin. "Little Thrifty" was found in (TM 4) trademark. (TW) "Temporarily Withdrawn" from production in January 2005

☐ 118 ....5.00 to 5.50".........(CE).......❶ ....$600—650
☐ 118 ....5.00 to 5.50".........(CE).......❷ ....$425—475
☐ 118 ....5.00 to 5.50".........(CE).......❸ ....$250—275
☐ 118 ....5.00 to 5.50".........(CE).......❹ ....$500—600
☐ 118 ....5.00 to 5.50".........(CE).......❺ ....$205—210
☐ 118 ....5.00 to 5.50".........(CE).......❻ ....$200—205
☐ 118 ....5.00 to 5.50".........(CE).......❼ ....$195—200
☐ 118 ....5.00 to 5.50".........(**TW**) ......❽ ....$195—200

.... HUM TERM ....

THREE LINE TRADEMARK: The symbol used by the W. Goebel Porzellanfabrik from 1964 until 1972 as their factory trademark. The name for this trademark was adopted to recognize that the V and bee was accompanied by three lines of print to the right of the V. Also known as TM 4.

119 (TM 2)   *119 (TM 2)*   *119 2/0 (TM 6)*

HUM 119 — Postman

Many size variations although officially made in one size only. First modeled by master sculptor Arthur Moeller in 1939. Later restyled by master sculptor Gerhard Skrobek in 1970 giving it the new textured finish. Newer models have four letters in the mail bag while older models have five letters. A new small size "Postman" (119 2/0) was released in 1989 with a suggested retail price of $90. It was modeled by master sculptor Gerhard Skrobek in 1985. It has an incised 1985 copyright date. Note letters on (119 2/0). The large size has been renumbered 119/0 and the old 119 is now classified as a (CE) Closed Edition because of this change. In the spring of 2002 a "Postman" Progression Set was issued in a (LE) Limited Edition of 1000 sets worldwide. Each piece has the incised model number 119/0, the (TM 8) trademark, and Special Edition — "ARBEITSMUSTER Series" on the bottom of each of the three figurines. Available from Europe only at present time. New small size (119 4/0) released in 2005.

☐ 119 4/0	3.50"	**(OE)**	❽	$99	
☐ 119 2/0	4.50"	(CE)	❻	$200—210	
☐ 119 2/0	4.50"	(CE)	❼	$199—200	
☐ 119 2/0	4.50"	**(OE)**	❽	$199	
☐ 119	5.00 to 5.50"	(CE)	❶	$600—750	
☐ 119	4.75 to 5.50"	(CE)	❷	$350—450	(small hat)
☐ 119	4.75 to 5.50"	(CE)	❸	$300—350	(small hat)
☐ 119	5.00 to 5.50"	(CE)	❹	$300—325	
☐ 119	5.00 to 5.50"	(CE)	❺	$265—270	
☐ 119	5.00 to 5.50"	(CE)	❻	$260—265	
☐ 119/0	5.00 to 5.50"	(CE)	❻	$255—260	
☐ 119/0	5.50"	(CE)	❼	$250—255	
☐ 119/0	5.50"	**(TW)**	❽	$250—255	

HUM 120 — Joyful and Let's Sing (on wooden base), Bookends (CE)
No known examples. Listed as a (CE) Closed Edition on factory records 16 June 1939. Records indicate this was made in 1939 by a combination of sculptors. Probably similar in design to Hum 122.

☐ 120 ....(CE).....................❶ ....$10,000—20,000

HUM 121 — Wayside Harmony and Just Resting (on wooden base), Bookends (CE)
Listed as a (CE) Closed Edition on factory records 16 June 1939. Records indicate this was made in 1939 by a combination of sculptors. This bookend (half only) was located in central Europe and is now part of the Robert L. Miller collection.

☐ 121 A..........(CE).....................❶ ....$5000—10,000
☐ 121 B..........(CE).....................❶ ....$5000—10,000

Factory prototypes

HUM 122
Puppy Love and Serenade With Dog (on wooden base), Bookends (CE)
Factory sample only. Listed as a (CE) Closed Edition on factory records 16 June 1939. Records indicate this was made in 1939 by a combination of sculptors.

☐ 122 ....(CE).....................❶ ....$10,000—20,000

Old style (TM 2)   *New style (TM 5)*

HUM 123 — Max and Moritz

First modeled by master sculptor Arthur Moeller in 1939. Color variations found in early "Crown" (TM 1) pieces—"Max" with black hair and black shoes;—"Moritz" with brown shoes instead of black. Restyled in the early 1970s with the new textured finish. Color of boys' hair will vary. Old name: "Good Friends" in some catalogues. "Max and Moritz" sold for $8.00 on old 1955 price list. See: HUM 553 "Scamp" and HUM 554 "Cheeky Fellow"—how one old figurine has been made into two new ones!

☐ 123 ....5.00 to 5.50".........(CE).......❶ ......$700—800
☐ 123 ....5.00 to 5.50".........(CE).......❷ ......$450—550
☐ 123 ....5.00 to 5.50".........(CE).......❸ ......$350—400
☐ 123 ....5.00 to 5.50".........(CE).......❹ ......$325—350
☐ 123 ....5.00 to 5.50".........(CE).......❺ ......$290—300
☐ 123 ....5.00 to 5.50".........(CE).......❻ ......$285—290
☐ 123 ....5.00 to 5.50".........(CE).......❼ ......$280—285
☐ 123 ....5.00 to 5.50".........(OE).......❽ $279

| 124/0 (TM 7) | 124/I (TM 2) | 124 (TM 1) |

HUM 124 — Hello

Many size variations. Earliest models produced had grey coat, grey trousers and pink vest. Changed to brown coat, green trousers and pink vest in early 1950s. Changed to dark brown coat, light brown trousers and blue-white vest in mid-1960s. Originally modeled by master sculptor Arthur Moeller in 1939. Has been restyled several times through the years. Old name: "The Boss" or "Der Chef." The large size 124/I had been difficult to find but was put back on the market in 1978, then in the spring of 1982 was listed as (TW) "Temporarily Withdrawn" by Goebel, to be reinstated at a later date. Some models have been painted with open eyes while most models have eyes looking down. Both sizes of "Hello" were permanently retired on 31 December 2001 and will not be produced again. They both have a "Final Issue 2001" backstamp and small gold "Final Issue" medallion.

☐ 124 ....6.50" ....(CE)...... ❶ ......$800—1000
☐ 124 ....6.50" ....(CE)...... ❷ ......$450—600
☐ 124/0 ....5.75 to 6.25" ....(CE)...... ❷ ......$400—450
☐ 124/0 ....5.75 to 6.25" ....(CE)...... ❸ ......$350—400
☐ 124/0 ....5.75 to 6.25" ....(CE)...... ❹ ......$290—350
☐ 124/0 ....5.75 to 6.25" ....(CE)...... ❺ ......$265—290
☐ 124/0 ....5.75 to 6.25" ....(CE)...... ❻ ......$260—265
☐ 124/0 ....5.75 to 6.25" ....(CE)...... ❼ ......$255—260
☐ 124/0 ....5.75 to 6.25" ....(CE)...... ❽ ......$255—260
☐ 124/I ....6.75 to 7.00" ....(CE)...... ❶ ......$800—1000
☐ 124/I ....6.75 to 7.00" ....(CE)...... ❷ ......$450—600
☐ 124/I ....6.75 to 7.00" ....(CE)...... ❸ ......$400—450
☐ 124/I ....6.75 to 7.00" ....(CE)...... ❹ ......$350—400
☐ 124/I ....6.75 to 7.00" ....(CE)...... ❺ ......$330—350
☐ 124/I ....6.75 to 7.00" ....(CE)...... ❻ ......$325—330

FINAL ISSUE
2001

New style (TM 3)   *Old style (TM 1)*

HUM 125 — Vacation Time, Plaque

First modeled in 1939 by master sculptor Arthur Moeller. Restyled in 1960 by master sculptor Theo R. Menzenbach. Slight color variations on older models. The newer model has five fence posts while the older one has six. Old name: "Happy Holidays" or "On Holiday." Newer models produced without string for hanging, only a hole on back for hanging. Both old style and new style can be found with the stylized (TM 3) trademark. "Vacation Time" plaque was (TW) "Temporarily Withdrawn" from production on 31 December 1989 in (TM 6). Reissued with (TM 7) trademark in 1998 in a combination package with "Vacation Time" Hummelscape (Mark #1002-D). Retail price for both pieces $445 on 2003 price list.

☐ 125 ....4.375 x 5.25" ....(CE)...... ❶ ......$600—750
☐ 125 ....4.375 x 5.25" ....(CE)...... ❷ ......$450—550
☐ 125 ....4.375 x 5.25" ....(CE)...... ❸ ......$375—450 (Old Style)
☐ 125 ....4.00 x 4.75" ....(CE)...... ❸ ......$275—350 (New Style)
☐ 125 ....4.00 x 4.75" ....(CE)...... ❹ ......$255—275
☐ 125 ....4.00 x 4.75" ....(CE)...... ❺ ......$245—255
☐ 125 ....4.00 x 4.75" ....(CE)...... ❻ ......$235—245
☐ 125 ....4.00 x 4.75" ....(TW) ...... ❼ ......$225—235

With Hummelscape

HUM 126 — Retreat to Safety, Plaque

First modeled by master sculptor Arthur Moeller in 1939. Older plaques are slightly larger. Slight color variations on older models. This same motif is also produced as a figurine by the same name although the colors are different. See "Retreat to Safety" HUM 201. "Retreat to Safety" plaque was (TW) "Temporarily Withdrawn" from production on 31 December 1989, but may be reinstated at some future date.

☐ 126..........4.75 x 4.75" to 5.00 x 5.00".......(CE)........❶........$550—700
☐ 126..........4.75 x 4.75" to 5.00 x 5.00".......(CE)........❷........$400—500
☐ 126..........4.75 x 4.75"..................................(CE)........❸.......$275—350
☐ 126..........4.75 x 4.75"..................................(CE)........❹.......$225—275
☐ 126..........4.75 x 4.75"..................................(CE)........❺.......$190—200
☐ 126..........4.75 x 4.75"..................................(**TW**) ....❻........$185—190

(TM 2)　　*(U.S. Zone)*　　*(TM 1+1)*　　*(TM 3)*

HUM 127 — Doctor

Originally modeled by master sculptor Arthur Moeller in 1939. Has been restyled several times during the years. Many variations in size through the years with older examples slightly larger. Old name: "The Doll Doctor." Legs of doll sometimes protrude over edge of base. Newer models now have the "textured" finish.

☐ 127 ....4.75 to 5.25".........(CE)......❶ ......$500—650
☐ 127 ....4.75 to 5.25".........(CE)......❷ ......$300—350
☐ 127 ....4.75 to 5.25".........(CE)......❸ ......$250—300
☐ 127 ....4.75 to 5.25".........(CE)......❹ ......$220—250
☐ 127 ....4.75 to 5.25".........(CE)......❺ ......$210—220
☐ 127 ....4.75 to 5.25".........(CE)......❻ ......$205—210
☐ 127 ....4.75 to 5.25".........(CE)......❼ ......$200—205
☐ 127 ....4.75 to 5.00".........(**OE**)......❽ $199

HUM 128 — Baker

This figurine was first modeled in 1939 by master sculptor Arthur Moeller. Has been restyled several times during the years—most recently in the mid-1970's with the new textured finish. Slight color variations can be noticed. Some older "crown" examples have eyes open. The little baker is holding a "Gugelhupf" round pound cake, a popular Bavarian treat.

(TM 1)   *(TM 2)*   *(TM 3)*   *(TM 5)*

- [ ] 128 ....4.75 to 5.00"........(CE)......❶ ......$650—750
- [ ] 128 ....4.75 to 5.00"........(CE)......❷ ......$375—450
- [ ] 128 ....4.75 to 5.00"........(CE)......❸ ......$325—350
- [ ] 128 ....4.75 to 5.00"........(CE)......❹ ......$300—325
- [ ] 128 ....4.75 to 5.00"........(CE)......❺ ......$270—280
- [ ] 128 ....4.75 to 5.00"........(CE)......❻ ......$265—270
- [ ] 128 ....4.75 to 5.00"........(CE)......❼ ......$260—265
- [ ] 128 ....4.75 to 5.00"........(**OE**)......❽ $259

HUM 129 — Band Leader

First modeled by master sculptor Arthur Moeller in 1939. Many size and color variations. Old name: "Leader." One of several figurines that make up the Hummel orchestra. A new miniature size was issued in 1987 with a suggested retail price of $50 to match a new mini plate series called the "Little Music Makers"—one each year for four years. This is the fourth and last in the series. This miniature figurine has an incised 1985 copyright date. The miniature "Band Leader" is made without a

(TM 2)   *(TM 1)*   *(TM 6)*   *(TM 3)*

music stand. The miniature size (129 4/0) was (TW) "Temporarily Withdrawn" from production on 31 December 1997 and as a (CE) "Closed Edition" on 1 January 1999.

- [ ] 129 4/0 ......3.25" ....(CE)......❻ ......$130—140
- [ ] 129 4/0 ......3.25" ....(CE)......❼ ......$125—130
- [ ] 129 ....5.00 to 5.875" ....(CE)......❶ ......$650—750
- [ ] 129 ....5.00 to 5.875" ....(CE)......❷ ......$400—500
- [ ] 129 ....5.00 to 5.875" ....(CE)......❸ ......$325—350
- [ ] 129 ....5.00 to 5.875" ....(CE)......❹ ......$300—325
- [ ] 129 ....5.00 to 5.875" ....(CE)......❺ ......$270—275
- [ ] 129 ....5.00 to 5.875" ....(CE)......❻ ......$265—270
- [ ] 129/0 ....5.00 to 5.875" ....(CE)......❻ ......$265—270
- [ ] 129/0 ....5.00 to 5.25" ....(CE)......❼ ......$260—265
- [ ] 129/0 ....5.00 to 5.25" ....(**OE**)......❽ $259
- [ ] 129/III ....13.50" ....(CE)......❼ ......$1550 (Special Edition)
- [ ] 129/III ....13.50" ....(**OE**)......❽ $1550

(Lip base)

Normal model   (TM 2)   (Without ties)   (TM 3)

HUM 130 — Duet

Many size variations—from 5 to 5.50". Originally modeled in 1939 by master sculptor Arthur Moeller. Early crown mark pieces have incised notes as well as painted notes on sheet music. Some early crown mark examples have a small "lip" on top edge of base. This variation should be valued from $1000 to $1500. Old name: "The Songsters." One of several figurines that make up the Hummel orchestra. "Duet" is similar to a combination of "Street Singer" HUM 131 and "Soloist" HUM 135. Occasionally found without tie on either boy. This variation would command a premium of over $3000. "Duet" was permanently retired by Goebel in the fall of 1995 and will not be produced again.

☐ 130 ....5.00 to 5.50" ....(CE)...... ❶ ....$800—1000
☐ 130 ....5.00 to 5.50" ....(CE)...... ❷ ....$550—650
☐ 130 ....5.00 to 5.50" ....(CE)...... ❸ ....$400—450
☐ 130 ....5.00 to 5.50" ....(CE)...... ❹ ....$335—400
☐ 130 ....5.00 to 5.50" ....(CE)...... ❺ ....$325—335   FINAL ISSUE
☐ 130 ....5.00 to 5.50" ....(CE)...... ❻ ....$310—325   1995
☐ 130 ....5.00 to 5.50" ....(CE)...... ❼ ....$300—310
☐ 130 ....(without ties).........(CE)...... ❷ or ❸ ...$2000—3500
☐ 130 ....(with "lip" base) ....(CE)...... ❶ ....$1000—1500

.... **HUM TERM** ....

DOUGHNUT BASE: A term used to describe the raised circular support on the underside of a figurine. Many figurine bases with a circle inside the regular circular base gave rise to the term, but has now been used to describe many bases with the circular support on the underside.

| (TM 2) | (TM 3) | (TM 1) |

HUM 131 — Street Singer

Many size variations as well as some slight color variations of this popular figurine. Originally modeled by master sculptor Arthur Moeller in 1939. Old name: "Soloist." One of several figurines that make up the Hummel orchestra. "Street Singer" was (TW) "Temporarily Withdrawn" in 2005.

- ☐ 131 ....5.00 to 5.50"..........(CE)....... ❶ ....$600—700
- ☐ 131 ....5.00 to 5.50"..........(CE)....... ❷ ....$400—450
- ☐ 131 ....5.00 to 5.50"..........(CE)....... ❸ ....$325—375
- ☐ 131 ....5.00 to 5.50"..........(CE)....... ❹ ......$275—325
- ☐ 131 ....5.00 to 5.50"..........(CE)....... ❺ ......$270—275
- ☐ 131 ....5.00 to 5.50"..........(CE)....... ❻ ......$265—270
- ☐ 131 ....5.00 to 5.50"..........(CE)....... ❼ ......$260—265
- ☐ 131 ....5.00 to 5.50"..........(TW) ...... ❽ $259

.... HUM TERM ....

An authentic Goebel "M.I. Hummel" Figurine will always have a plain incised model number. It will *never* have an alphabetical prefix in front of the number (such as: HM, FE, HX etc.) *If* it *has* an alphabetical pre-fix—it is a *Goebel* item and not "M.I. Hummel." Alphabetical letters may appear <u>after</u> a HUM number (such as: A, B, C etc.)—this indicates that it is part of a set. Example: HUM 239 A, 239 B, or 239 C. This is a good "rule of thumb" guide to remember when looking at a figurine with a *Goebel* trademark.

New model (TM 6)   *Old model (TM 2)*

HUM 132 — Star Gazer

A very few older models have blue shirt. Most models in all trademark periods have purple shirts. Also some color variations on telescope. No cross-strap on boy's lederhosen on older models. "M. I. Hummel" signature is straight on early models; curved on later models. First modeled by master sculptor Arthur Moeller in 1939. Restyled by master sculptor Gerhard Skrobek in 1980 with the new textured finish and slightly rounded corners on the base. A special figurine was produced for sale to the U.S. military stationed in Bosnia in 1996. Inscribed on base: "Looking for a Peaceful World." Value $250–$300. Listed as (TW) "Temporarily Withdrawn" from production in June 2002.

☐ 132 ....4.75" ....(CE)....... ❶ ......$700—800
☐ 132 ....4.75" ....(CE)....... ❷ ......$400—500
☐ 132 ....4.75" ....(CE)....... ❸ ......$350—375
☐ 132 ....4.75" ....(CE)....... ❹ ......$300—350
☐ 132 ....4.75" ....(CE)....... ❺ ......$270—275
☐ 132 ....4.75" ....(CE)....... ❻ ......$265—270
☐ 132 ....4.75" ....(CE)....... ❼ ......$260—265
☐ 132 ....4.75 to 5.00"........(TW) ...... ❽ ....$260—265

| TM 1 | TM 2 | TM 6 |

HUM 133 — Mother's Helper

At one time this was the only figurine (in current production) that was produced with a cat. A similar figurine with a cat, named "Helping Mother" HUM 325, now classified as a (PFE) Possible Future Edition, may be released at a later date. At present there are several newer figurines with cats now on the market. Older figurines are slightly larger in size. Originally modeled in 1939 by master sculptor Arthur Moeller. Note variations in photo. Some examples have legs of stool reversed—valued $750—$1000. "Mother's Helper" was (TW) "Temporarily Withdrawn" from production in 2004. Other figurines with cats include: HUM 2007 "Tender Love"; HUM 2033 "Kitty Kisses"; HUM 2101/A A "Girl's Best Friend"; HUM 2107/B "Little Knitter"; and HUM 2136 "The Cat's Meow."

☐ 133 ....4.75 to 5.00".........(CE).......❶ ......$700—800
☐ 133 ....4.75 to 5.00".........(CE).......❷ ......$400—500
☐ 133 ....4.75 to 5.00".........(CE).......❸ ......$350—375
☐ 133 ....4.75 to 5.00".........(CE).......❹ ......$300—350
☐ 133 ....4.75 to 5.00".........(CE).......❺ ......$270—275
☐ 133 ....4.75 to 5.00".........(CE).......❻ ......$265—270
☐ 133 ....4.75 to 5.00".........(CE).......❼ ......$260—265
☐ 133 ....4.75 to 5.00".........(**TW**) ......❽ ......$250—260

Reversed legs

113

(TM 1+2)   *(TM 3)*

HUM 134 — Quartet, Plaque

First modeled by master sculptor Arthur Moeller in 1939. Older models have "M.I. Hummel" signature on back while newer models have signature incised on front. Older models provided with two holes for cord to hang on wall while newer models have a centered hole on back for hanging. Quartet, Plaque was (TW) "Temporarily Withdrawn" from production on 31 December 1990, but may be reinstated at some future date.

☐ 134 ....5.50 x 6.25" ....(CE).......❶ ......$800—1000
☐ 134 ....5.50 x 6.25" ....(CE).......❷ ......$525—625
☐ 134 ....5.50 x 6.25" .   .(CE).......❸ ......$375—425
☐ 134 ....5.50 x 6.25" ....(CE).......❹ ......$325—375
☐ 134 ....5.50 x 6.25" ....(CE).......❺ ......$260—270
☐ 134 ....5.50 x 6.25" ....(**TW**) ......❻ ......$250—260

.... HUM TERM ....

REINSTATED: The term used to indicate that a figurine has been placed back into production by the W. Goebel Porzellanfabrik after some prior classification of non-production.

| 135 (TM 1) | 135 (TM 3) | 135/0 (TM 8) | 135 4/0 (TM 6) |

HUM 135 — Soloist

Many size variations between old and new figurines. Originally modeled in 1940 by master sculptor Arthur Moeller. Old name "High Tenor." Similar to singer in figurine "Duet" HUM 130. One of several figurines that can be used to make up the Hummel orchestra. A new miniature size figurine was issued in 1986 with the suggested retail price of $45. Designed to match a new mini plate series called the "Little Music Makers"—one each year for four years. This is the third in the series. This miniature figurine has an incised 1985 copyright date. The large size has been renumbered 135/0 and the old 135 is now classified as a (CE) Closed Edition because of this change. The miniature size (135 4/0) was (TW) "Temporarily Withdrawn" from production on 31 December 1997. In 1996 a 2.75 size (3.25" with base) with incised model number 135 5/0 was produced as part of the "Pen Pals" series of personalized name card table decorations. The original issue price was $55. Recently released in 13.00" size.

- ☐ 135 5/0......2.75".....................(CE).......❼.......$55—60
- ☐ 135 4/0......3.00".....................(CE).......❻.......$145—150
- ☐ 135 4/0......3.00".....................(CE).......❼.......$140—145
- ☐ 135 4/0......3.00".....................(**OE**).......❽.......$139
- ☐ 135...........4.50 to 5.00".........(CE).......❶.......$450—550
- ☐ 135...........4.50 to 5.00".........(CE).......❷.......$325—375
- ☐ 135...........4.50 to 5.00".........(CE).......❸.......$210—250
- ☐ 135...........4.50 to 5.00".........(CE).......❹.......$195—210
- ☐ 135...........4.50 to 5.00".........(CE).......❺.......$190—195
- ☐ 135...........4.50 to 5.00".........(CE).......❻.......$185—190
- ☐ 135/0.........4.75".....................(CE).......❻.......$185—190
- ☐ 135/0.........4.75".....................(CE).......❼.......$180—185
- ☐ 135/0.........4.75".....................(**OE**).......❽.......$179
- ☐ 135/III.......13.00".....................(**OE**).......❽.......$1550

136/I (TM 5)　　　　*136 Terra cotta (TM 1)*

HUM 136 — Friends
Originally modeled by master sculptor Reinhold Unger in 1940. Spots on deer will vary slightly—sometimes three rows rather than two rows. Old name: "Good Friends" or "Friendship." The small size 136/I usually has an incised 1947 copyright date. Sold at one time in reddish-brown terra cotta finish in size 136 (10.00") with incised crown trademark. Very limited production in this finish; would be considered extremely rare. Value: *$10,000–15,000.* Also old crown trademark example (large size) found in white overglaze finish, but probably not sold that way. Sometimes incised 136/5 instead of 136/V. Also found in a smaller 9.75" size in a dark chocolate brown finish. The large size (136/V) was listed as (TW) "Temporarily Withdrawn" in January 1999. New small size 136 4/0 released in 2006 with an incised 2005 copyright date.

☐	136 4/0	3.50"	(OE)	❽	$129
☐	136/I	5.00 to 5.375"	(CE)	❶	$850—950
☐	136/I	5.00 to 5.375"	(CE)	❷	$450—500
☐	136/I	5.00 to 5.375"	(CE)	❸	$350—400
☐	136/I	5.00 to 5.375"	(CE)	❹	$300—350
☐	136/I	5.00 to 5.375"	(CE)	❺	$270—300
☐	136/I	5.00 to 5.375"	(CE)	❻	$265—270
☐	136/I	5.00 to 5.375"	(CE)	❼	$260—265
☐	136/I	5.00 to 5.375"	(OE)	❽	$259
☐	136/V	10.75 to 11.00"	(CE)	❶	$3000—4000
☐	136/V	10.75 to 11.00"	(CE)	❷	$1750—2500
☐	136/V	10.75 to 11.00"	(CE)	❸	$1600—1750
☐	136/V	10.75 to 11.00"	(CE)	❹	$1500—1600
☐	136/V	10.75 to 11.00"	(CE)	❺	$1450—1500
☐	136/V	10.75 to 11.00"	(CE)	❻	$1400—1450
☐	136/V	10.75 to 11.00"	(TW)	❼	$1350—1380
☐	136	10.50"	(CE)	❶	$3000—4000
☐	136	10.50"	(CE)	❷	$2000—3000
☐	136	10.00"	(CE)	❶	$10,000—15,000 (terra cotta)
☐	136	9.75"	(CE)	❶	$10,000—15,000 (dark chocolate brown)

137 A (TM 1)   137 B (TM 2)

HUM 137 — Child in Bed, Wall Plaque
HUM 137 A — (Child looking left) (CE)
HUM 137 B — (Child looking right) (CE)
Originally modeled by master sculptor
Arthur Moeller in 1940 as a set of two
small wall plaques—one child looking left
and one child looking right. Pictured here
is the first known example of 137 A which
was found hanging on a kitchen wall
somewhere in Hungary in 1986. Since
that time several other examples have
been found in Europe. The child looking
right (HUM 137 B) has been on the market for years and can be found in all trademark periods. Current production models
are numbered 137 only, incised on the
back along with the "M.I. Hummmel" sig-

137A Rear view

nature. Also called "Baby Ring with Ladybug" or "Ladybug Plaque" in old catalogues. A
rare "Mel 14" was found in Amsterdam, Holland. It is identical in size, color and construction to HUM 137 B "Child in Bed" wall plaque. This piece has no "M. I. Hummel"
signature, but is clearly incised "Mel 14" along with a "double crown" trademark. Factory
records indicate it was sculpted on 18 July 1940. HUM 137 was listed as (TW) "Temporarily Withdrawn" in January 1999.

☐ 137 A	3.00 x 3.00"	(CE)	❶	$5000—7000
☐ 137 B	3.00 x 3.00"	(CE)	❶	$350—550
☐ 137 B	3.00 x 3.00"	(CE)	❷	$200—225
☐ 137 B	3.00 x 3.00"	(CE)	❸	$110—135
☐ 137 B	3.00 x 3.00"	(CE)	❹	$85—110
☐ 137 B	3.00 x 3.00"	(CE)	❺	$80—85
☐ 137	3.00 x 3.00"	(CE)	❺	$75—80
☐ 137	3.00 x 3.00"	(CE)	❻	$70—75
☐ 137	3.00 x 3.00"	(TW)	❼	$70—75
☐ Mel 14	3.00 x 3.00"	(CN)	❶	$2000—2500

HUM 138 — Tiny Baby In Crib, Wall Plaque (CN)

According to factory information this small plaque was never produced for sale. The original model was made by master sculptor Arthur Moeller in 1940. Now listed on factory records as a (CN) Closed Number meaning that this design was produced as a sample model, but then for various reasons never authorized for release. Apparently, a very few examples left the factory and have been found in Germany. This plaque would be considered extremely rare. Factory records indicate this was originally produced as "Mel 15" in 1940. Color variations have been found in (TM 1) examples.

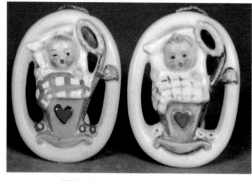

(TM 1+1)   *(TM 3)*

- ☐ 138 ....2.25 x 3.00" ....(CN)....... ❶ ......$4000—5000
- ☐ 138 ....2.25 x 3.00" ....(CN)....... ❷ ......$3000—3500
- ☐ Mel 15 ....2.25 x 3.00" ....(CN)....... ❶ ......$2000—2500

Crown (TM 1)   *Stylized (TM 3)*   *Full Bee (TM 2)*

HUM 139 — Flitting Butterfly, Wall Plaque

First modeled by master sculptor Arthur Moeller in 1940, this plaque is also known as "Butterfly Plaque." Early crown mark pieces have no dots on girl's dress. The "M.I. Hummel" signature has been on the back during all time periods. Redesigned in the 1960s with no air space behind girl's head. Some design and color variations have evolved through the years of production. To my knowledge, not produced in trademark 4. Factory records indicate this was originally produced as "Mel 16" in 1940. Listed as (TW) "Temporarily Withdrawn" in January 1999.

- ☐ 139 ....2.50 x 2.50" ....(CE)...... ❶ ......$350—550
- ☐ 139 ....2.50 x 2.50" ....(CE)...... ❷ ......$200—250
- ☐ 139 ....2.50 x 2.50" ....(CE)...... ❸ ......$100—150
- ☐ 139 ....2.50 x 2.50" ....(CE)...... ❺ ......$78—80
- ☐ 139 ....2.50 x 2.50" ....(CE)...... ❻ ......$75—78
- ☐ 139 ....2.50 x 2.50" ....(TW) ...... ❼ ......$75—78
- ☐ Mel 16 ....2.50 x 2.50" ....(CN)....... ❶ ......$2000—2500

118

*All (TM 6) (Note horn, doors and
windows)*

HUM 140 — The Mail is Here, Plaque

Originally modeled by master sculptor Arthur Moeller in 1940, this plaque can be found in all trademark periods. At one time it was sold in Belgium in the white overglaze finish and would now be considered rare. Old name: "Post Carriage." Also known to collectors as "Mail Coach" plaque. In 1952 this same motif was made into a figurine by the same name (HUM 226) by master sculptor Arthur Moeller. "The Mail is Here" plaque was (TW) "Temporarily Withdrawn" from production on 31 December 1989, but may be reinstated at some future date. Several variations can be found in the doors and windows of the coach as well as the handle of the horn—sometimes down instead of up. This cannot be attributed to any one time period.

- ☐ 140 ....4.25 x 6.75" ....(CE).......❶ ......$1000—1500 (white overglaze)
- ☐ 140 ....4.25 x 6.75" ....(CE).......❶ ......$650—950
- ☐ 140 ....4.25 x 6.75" ....(CE).......❷ ......$450—550
- ☐ 140 ....4.25 x 6.75" ....(CE).......❸ ......$325—350
- ☐ 140 ....4.25 x 6.75" ....(CE).......❹ ......$300—325
- ☐ 140 ....4.25 x 6.75" ....(CE).......❺ ......$275—300
- ☐ 140 ....4.25 x 6.75" ....(TW) ......❻ ......$250—275

HUM 141 — Apple Tree Girl

First modeled by master sculptor Arthur Moeller in 1940 and has been restyled many times during the years that it has been produced. There are many size variations and early models have a tapered brown base. The smaller models have always been made without the bird in the tree. Size 141/V

141/V   *Old   141/*   *New*   *Old 141 3/0 New*

was first produced in the early 1970s and is found in 4, 5, 6 and 7 trademarks only. Size 141/X was first produced in 1975. Old name: "Spring" or "Springtime." This same motif is used on the 1976 Annual Plate, HUM 269; Table Lamp, HUM 229; and Bookends, HUM 252 A. Size 141/X was (TW) "Temporarily Withdrawn" from production on 31 December 1990, but may be reinstated at some future date. New 3.5" size in 2004.

☐ 141 4/0	3.50"	(OE)	❽	$99
☐ 141 3/0	4.00 to 4.25"	(CE)	❶	$450—550
☐ 141 3/0	4.00 to 4.25"	(CE)	❷	$325—375
☐ 141 3/0	4.00 to 4.25"	(CE)	❸	$240—275
☐ 141 3/0	4.00 to 4.25"	(CE)	❹	$210—240
☐ 141 3/0	4.00 to 4.25"	(CE)	❺	$190—195
☐ 141 3/0	4.00 to 4.25"	(CE)	❻	$185—190
☐ 141 3/0	4.00 to 4.25"	(CE)	❼	$180—185
☐ 141 3/0	4.00 to 4.25"	(OE)	❽	$179
☐ 141	6.00 to 6.75"	(CE)	❶	$850—950
☐ 141	6.00 to 6.75"	(CE)	❷	$650—750
☐ 141/I	6.00 to 6.75"	(CE)	❶	$750—800
☐ 141/I	6.00 to 6.75"	(CE)	❷	$550—650
☐ 141/I	6.00 to 6.75"	(CE)	❸	$450—500
☐ 141/I	6.00 to 6.75"	(CE)	❹	$380—450
☐ 141/I	6.00 to 6.75"	(CE)	❺	$370—380
☐ 141/I	6.00 to 6.75"	(CE)	❻	$365—370
☐ 141/I	6.00 to 6.75"	(CE)	❼	$360—365
☐ 141/I	6.00 to 6.75"	(OE)	❽	$359
☐ 141/V	10.25"	(CE)	❹	$1650—1700
☐ 141/V	10.25"	(CE)	❺	$1600—1650
☐ 141/V	10.25"	(CE)	❻	$1550—1600
☐ 141/V	10.25"	(CE)	❼	$1500—1550
☐ 141/V	10.25"	(TW)	❽	$1495—1500
☐ 141/X	32.00"	(CE)	❺	$15,000—30,000
☐ 141/X	32.00"	(CE)	❻	$15,000—30,000
☐ 141/X	32.00"	(CE)	❼	$15,000—30,000
☐ 141/X	32.00"	(OE)	❽	$29,900

HUM 142 — Apple Tree Boy

This companion figurine to "Apple Tree Girl" was also modeled by master sculptor Arthur Moeller in 1940, and has been restyled many times during the years. There are many size variations and early models have a tapered brown base. The small size 142 3/0 with trademark 2 usu-

142/V   Old   142/I   New   Old 142 3/0 New

ally has a red feather in the boy's hat. Size 142/V was first produced in the early 1970s and is found in 4, 5, 6 and 7 trademarks only. Old name: "Autumn" or "Fall." Smaller models have always been made without the bird in the tree. The same motif is used on the 1977 Annual Plate, HUM 270; Table Lamp, HUM 230; and Bookends, HUM 252 B. Found with (TM 3) small "stylized" (1960–1972) trademark.

(continued on next page)

☐	142 4/0	3.50"	(OE)	❽	$99
☐	142 3/0	4.00 to 4.25"	(CE)	❶	$450—550
☐	142 3/0	4.00 to 4.25"	(CE)	❷	$325—375
☐	142 3/0	4.00 to 4.25"	(CE)	❸	$240—275
☐	142 3/0	4.00 to 4.25"	(CE)	❹	$210—240
☐	142 3/0	4.00 to 4.25"	(CE)	❺	$190—195
☐	142 3/0	4.00 to 4.25"	(CE)	❻	$185—190
☐	142 3/0	4.00 to 4.25"	(CE)	❼	$180—185
☐	142 3/0	4.00 to 4.25"	(OE)	❽	$179
☐	142	6.00 to 6.875"	(CE)	❶	$850—950
☐	142	6.00 to 6.875"	(CE)	❷	$650—750
☐	142/I	6.00 to 6.875"	(CE)	❶	$750—800
☐	142/I	6.00 to 6.875"	(CE)	❷	$550—650
☐	142/I	6.00 to 6.875"	(CE)	❸	$450—500
☐	142/I	6.00 to 6.875"	(CE)	❹	$380—450
☐	142/I	6.00 to 6.875"	(CE)	❺	$370—380
☐	142/I	6.00 to 6.875"	(CE)	❻	$360—370
☐	142/I	6.00 to 6.875"	(CE)	❼	$360—370
☐	142/I	6.00 to 6.875"	(OE)	❽	$359
☐	142/V	10.25"	(CE)	❸	$1800—2000
☐	142/V	10.25"	(CE)	❹	$1650—1700
☐	142/V	10.25"	(CE)	❺	$1600—1650
☐	142/V	10.25"	(CE)	❻	$1550—1600
☐	142/V	10.25"	(CE)	❼	$1500—1550
☐	142/V	10.25"	(TW)	❽	$1495—1550

Old style

New style

HUM 142 — Apple Tree Boy *(continued from previous page)*
According to factory information, size 142/X (also known as "Jumbo" size) was first produced in the early 1960s with number 142/10 incised and the stylized trademark incised rather than stamped. A Canadian collector has a very early "Jumbo" Apple Tree Boy with the "full bee" (TM 2) trademark but no model number incised on it. The "Jumbo" size 142/X was restyled in the mid-1970's by master sculptor Gerhard Skrobek. Notice that the older model has two apples while the restlyed version has four apples. The newer version is slightly larger because of the extended branch on the boy's right. Size 142/X was (TW) "Temporarily Withdrawn" from production on 31 December 1990, but may be reinstated at some future date. New 3.5" size in 2004.

☐ 142/X..........30.00" ....(CE)....... ❷ ......$26,000—30,000
☐ 142/X..........30.00" ....(CE)....... ❸ ......$17,000—26,000
☐ 142/X..........30.00" ....(CE)....... ❹ ......$16,000—25,000
☐ 142/X..........30.00 to 32.00".....(CE)....... ❺ ......$15,000—25,000
☐ 142/X..........30.00 to 32.00".....(CE)....... ❻ ......$15,000—25,000
☐ 142/X..........30.00 to 32.00".....(CE)....... ❼ ......$15,000—25,000
☐ 142/X..........30.00 to 32.00".....(**OE**)....... ❽ $29,900

| 143 (TM 1) | 143/0 (TM 2) | 143/0 (TM 5) |

HUM 143 — Boots

When first modeled by master sculptor Arthur Moeller in 1940 this figurine was produced in one size only with the incised model number 143. A smaller size was issued in the mid-1950s with the incised model number 143/0. At the same time, the large size was changed to 143/I. There have been many size variations—from 5.00 to 5.50" on the small; from 6.00 to 6.75" on the large. Old name: "Shoemaker." Both sizes were restyled with the new "textured" finish by master modeler Gerhard Skrobek in the late 1970s. Both sizes of "Boots" were permanently retired by Goebel on 31 December 1998 and will not be produced again.

☐ 143/0 ....5.00 to 5.50" ....(CE)....... ❶ ....$550—700
☐ 143/0 ....5.00 to 5.50" ....(CE)....... ❷ ....$370—450
☐ 143/0 ....5.00 to 5.50" ....(CE)....... ❸ ....$300—325
☐ 143/0 ....5.00 to 5.50" ....(CE)....... ❹ ....$270—300
☐ 143/0 ....5.00 to 5.50" ....(CE)....... ❺ ....$245—270
☐ 143/0 ....5.00 to 5.50" ....(CE)....... ❻ ....$235—245
☐ 143/0 ....5.00 to 5.50" ....(CE)....... ❼ ....$225—235
☐ 143/I ....6.50 to 6.75" ....(CE)....... ❶ ....$850—1000
☐ 143/I ....6.50 to 6.75" ....(CE)....... ❷ ....$600—700
☐ 143/I ....6.50 to 6.75" ....(CE)....... ❸ ....$450—525
☐ 143/I ....6.50 to 6.75" ....(CE)....... ❹ ....$425—450
☐ 143/I ....6.50 to 6.75" ....(CE)....... ❺ ....$390—425
☐ 143/I ....6.50 to 6.75" ....(CE)....... ❻ ....$370—390
☐ 143/I ....6.50 to 6.75" ....(CE)....... ❼ ....$360—370
☐ 143 ....6.75" ....(CE)....... ❶ ....$900—1050
☐ 143 ....6.75" ....(CE)....... ❷ ....$650—750

FINAL ISSUE
1998

HUM 144 — Angelic Song

Originally modeled in 1941 by master sculptor Reinhold Unger. Little variation between old and new models. Old names: "Angels" or "Holy Communion." "Angelic Song" was (TW) "Temporarily Withdrawn" from production early in 2005.

☐ 144.......4.00" ....(CE)...... ❶ .....$450—550
☐ 144.......4.00" ....(CE)...... ❷ .....$275—325
☐ 144.......4.00" ....(CE)...... ❸ .....$235—260
☐ 144.......4.00" ....(CE)...... ❹ .....$210—235
☐ 144.......4.00" ....(CE)...... ❺ .....$195—200
☐ 144.......4.00" ....(CE)...... ❻ .....$190—195
☐ 144.......4.00" ....(CE)...... ❼ .....$185—190
☐ 144.......4.00" ....(TW).....❽ $185

HUM 145 — Little Guardian

This figurine was first modeled by master sculptor Reinhold Unger in 1941. The only noticeable difference would be in size, with the older pieces slightly larger. "Little Guardian" was (TW) "Temporarily Withdrawn" from production early in 2006.

☐ 145 ....3.75 to 4.00" ...(CE) .... ❶ ...$450—550
☐ 145 ....3.75 to 4.00" ...(CE) .... ❷ ...$275—325
☐ 145 ....3.75 to 4.00" ...(CE) .... ❸ ...$235—260
☐ 145 ....3.75 to 4.00" ...(CE) .... ❹ ...$215—235
☐ 145 ....3.75 to 4.00" ...(CE) .... ❺ ...$210—215
☐ 145 ....3.75 to 4.00" ...(CE) .... ❻ ...$205—210
☐ 145 ....3.75 to 4.00" ...(CE) .... ❼ ...$200—205
☐ 145 ....3.75 to 4.00" ...(TW)....❽ ...$199

Old (TM 2)   *New (TM 3)*

HUM 146 — Holy Water Font, Angel Duet

First modeled by master sculptor Reinhold Unger in 1941. This font has been restyled several times through the years with noticeable variations in the shape of angels' wings, construction of the back, holes between angels' heads and wings. Newer examples are completely solid and have the new textured finish. Listed as (TW) "Temporarily Withdrawn" in January 1999.

☐ 146 ....3.50 x 4.75" ....(CE) .... ❶ ..$175—225
☐ 146 ....3.50 x 4.75".....(CE) .... ❷ ...$125—150
☐ 146 ....3.50 x 4.75".....(CE) .... ❸ ...$80—100
☐ 146 ....3.50 x 4.75".....(CE) .... ❹ ...$75—80
☐ 146 ....3.50 x 4.75".....(CE) .... ❺ ...$70—75
☐ 146 ....3.50 x 4.75".....(CE) .... ❻ ...$65—70
☐ 146 ....3.50 x 4.75".....(TW)....❼ ...$60—65

Old (TM 1)   *New (TM 3)*

HUM 147 — Holy Water Font, Angel Shrine

Originally modeled in 1941 by master sculptor Reinhold Unger and has been produced in all trademark periods. Older models are usually larger. Some variation in construction of back of font and water bowl. Old name: "Angel Devotion." No longer on current price list.

☐ 147 ....3.00 x 5.00 to 3.125 x 5.25" ....(CE)......**❶**...........$225—275

☐ 147 ....3.00 x 5.00 to 3.125 x 5.25" ....(CE)......**❷**...........$125—175

☐ 147 ....3.00 x 5.00"................................(CE)......**❸**...........$85—100

☐ 147 ....3.00 x 5.00"................................(CE)......**❹**...........$80—85

☐ 147 ....3.00 x 5.00"................................(CE)......**❺**...........$75—80

☐ 147 ....3.00 x 5.00"................................(CE)......**❻**...........$70—75

☐ 147 ....3.00 x 5.00"................................(CE)......**❼**...........$68—70

☐ 147 ....3.00 x 5.00"................................**(TW)**.....**❽**...........$67.50

HUM 148 (CN)

Factory records indicate this was the same as the boy from HUM 60/A (Farm Boy, Bookend). Modeled in 1941 by a combination of the modelers. Listed as a Closed Number on 28 February 1941. No known examples or photographs.

☐ 148...(CN) ....

HUM 149 (CN)

Factory records indicate this was the same as the girl from HUM 60/B (Goose Girl, Bookend). Modeled in 1941 by a combination of modelers. Listed as a Closed Number on 28 February 1941. No known examples or photographs. A (CN) Closed Number: an identification number in W. Goebel's numerical identification system, used to identify a design or sample model intended for possible production but then for various reasons never authorized for release.

☐ 149...(CN)..................

150 (TM 1)   *150/0 (TM 2)*   *150 2/0 (TM 5)*

HUM 150 — Happy Days

"Happy Days" was the very first "M.I. Hummel" figurine my wife, Ruth, acquired to start her collection. It reminded her of our daughter and son. We no longer have this first piece, as one of the children broke it; has since been replaced by an intact piece! "Happy Days" was first modeled in 1942 by a combination of modelers. All large size and older pieces have an extra flower on the base. The large size in the crown trademark usually does not have a size designator; incised 150 only. Sizes (150/0) and (150/I) had been in very limited production, but were both put back on the market in the 1970s. Sizes 150/0 and 150/I both listed as (TW) "Temporarily Withdrawn" in January 1999. Size 150 2/0 retired in April 2006 (CE) Closed Edition.

☐	150 2/0	4.25"	(CE)	❷	$325—400
☐	150 2/0	4.25"	(CE)	❸	$260—285
☐	150 2/0	4.25"	(CE)	❹	$235—260
☐	150 2/0	4.25"	(CE)	❺	$225—235
☐	150 2/0	4.25"	(CE)	❻	$220—225
☐	150 2/0	4.25"	(CE)	❼	$219—220
☐	150 2/0	4.25"	(CE)	❽	$219—220
☐	150/0	5.00 to 5.25"	(CE)	❷	$525—625
☐	150/0	5.00 to 5.25"	(CE)	❸	$425—475
☐	150/0	5.00 to 5.25"	(CE)	❹	$390—425
☐	150/0	5.00 to 5.25"	(CE)	❺	$360—390
☐	150/0	5.00 to 5.25"	(CE)	❻	$340—360
☐	150/0	5.00 to 5.25"	(TW)	❼	$330—340
☐	150/I	6.25 to 6.50"	(CE)	❶	$1250—1550
☐	150/I	6.25 to 6.50"	(CE)	❷	$850—950
☐	150/I	6.25 to 6.50"	(CE)	❸	$675—775
☐	150/I	6.25 to 6.50"	(CE)	❹	$600—675
☐	150/I	6.25 to 6.50"	(CE)	❺	$550—600
☐	150/I	6.25 to 6.50"	(CE)	❻	$525—550
☐	150/I	6.25 to 6.50"	(TW)	❼	$500—510
☐	150	6.25"	(CE)	❶	$1300—1600
☐	150	6.25"	(CE)	❷	$900—1000

HUM 151 — Madonna Holding Child

Known as the "Madonna with the Blue Cloak." Modeled by master sculptor Reinhold Unger in 1942. Was produced in five color variations: white overglaze, pastel blue cloak, dark blue cloak, brown cloak, and ivory finish. This figurine had not been produced for many years but was put back into production in 1977 and was produced in white overglaze and pastel blue only. Can now be found in (TM 5) and (TM 6) trademarks. This figurine sold for $44.00 on old 1955 price list. "Madonna Holding Child" in both color and white overglaze finish were (TW) "Temporarily Withdrawn" from production on 31 December 1989, but may be reinstated at some future date. I have never seen this figurine with (TM 3) "stylized" or (TM 4) "three line" trademark. Has recently been sold in European market in (TM 8) trademark for $1200 retail. Not listed on U.S. price lists.

☐ 151	12.50" Blue	(CE)	❶	$2000—3000
☐ 151	12.50" Blue	(CE)	❷	$2000—2500
☐ 151	12.50" Blue	(CE)	❺	$925—950
☐ 151	12.50" Blue	(CE)	❻	$900—925
☐ 151	12.50"	(TW)	❽	$1200
☐ 151	12.50" White	(CE)	❶	$1500—2500
☐ 151	12.50" White	(CE)	❷	$1000—2000
☐ 151	12.50" White	(CE)	❺	$425—450
☐ 151	12.50" White	(TW)	❻	$400—425
☐ 151	12.50" Brown	(CE)	❶	$9000—12,000
☐ 151	12.50" Ivory	(CE)	❶	$9000—12,000
☐ 151	12.50" Dk. Blue	(CE)	❶	$9000—12,000

152 (TM 1)   152/0 A (TM 2)

HUM 152 A — Umbrella Boy

Originally modeled by master sculptor Arthur Moeller in 1942. The crown mark piece in our collection is incised 152 only and is considered rare with that trademark. The large size was restyled in 1972 with a thin umbrella and new textured finish. Older models usually have the umbrella handle fastened on boy's right shoe while in newer models the handle is fastened to his left shoe. The 4.75" size was first produced in 1954 and can be found in all trademarks except the crown. Some 4.75" size examples have a stamped 1951 or 1956 copyright date while others have an incised 1957 date. Old name: "In Safety" or "Boy Under Umbrella." A new small size: 152/A 2/0 with 1996 copyright date, "First Issue 2002" decal and (TM 8) trademark was released in the fall of 2001. Issue price $300.

- ☐ 152/A 2/0....3.50".....................(OE)......❽ $329
- ☐ 152/0 A.......4.75".....................(CE)......❷ ....$1200—1600
- ☐ 152/0 A.......4.75".....................(CE)......❸ ....$900—1100
- ☐ 152/0 A.......4.75".....................(CE)......❹ ....$775—875
- ☐ 152/0 A.......4.75".....................(CE)......❺ ....$750—775
- ☐ 152/0 A.......4.75".....................(CE)......❻ ....$725—750
- ☐ 152/0 A.......4.75".....................(CE)......❼ ....$720—725
- ☐ 152/0 A.......4.75".....................(OE)......❽ $719
- ☐ 152 ....8.00".....................(CE)......❶ ....$5000—7000
- ☐ 152 ....8.00".....................(CE)......❷ .....$2500—3000
- ☐ 152 A.........8.00".....................(CE)......❷ .....$2300—2800
- ☐ 152 A.........8.00".....................(CE)......❸ .....$1900—2100
- ☐ 152 A.........8.00".....................(CE)......❹ .....$1825—1900
- ☐ 152/II A......8.00".....................(CE)......❹ .....$1825—1900
- ☐ 152/II A......8.00".....................(CE)......❺ ....$1800—1825
- ☐ 152/II A......8.00".....................(CE)......❻ ....$1775—1800
- ☐ 152/II A......8.00".....................(CE)......❼ ....$1750—1775
- ☐ 152/II A......8.00".....................(OE)......❽ $1750

152/II B (TM 4)   *152/0 B (TM 3)*

HUM 152 B — Umbrella Girl

Originally modeled by master sculptor Arthur Moeller in 1949. We have never been able to locate "Umbrella Girl" with the crown trademark for our collection. It would be considered extremely rare, if it actually does exist. The large size was restyled in 1972 with a thin umbrella and new textured finish. The 4.75" size was first produced in 1954 and can be found in all trademarks except the crown. Some 4.75" size examples have an incised 1951 copyright date while others have an incised 1957 date. Old name: "In Safety" or "Girl Under Umbrella." A new small size: 152/B 2/0 with 1996 copyright date, "First Issue 2002" decal and (TM 8) trademark was released in the fall of 2001. Issue price $300.

☐ 152/B 2/0....3.50" ....(**OE**)......❽ $329
☐ 152/0 B.......4.75" ....(CE).......❷ ....$1200—1600
☐ 152/0 B.......4.75" ....(CE).......❸ ....$900—1100
☐ 152/0 B.......4.75" ....(CE).......❹ ......$775—875
☐ 152/0 B.......4.75" ....(CE).......❺ ......$750—775
☐ 152/0 B.......4.75" ....(CE).......❻ ......$725—750
☐ 152/0 B.......4.75" ....(CE).......❼ ......$720—725
☐ 152/0 B.......4.75" ....(**OE**)......❽ $719
☐ 152 B.........8.00" ....(CE).......❶ ......$5000—7000
☐ 152 B.........8.00" ....(CE).......❷ ......$2300—2800
☐ 152 B.........8.00" ....(CE).......❸ ......$1900—2100
☐ 152 B.........8.00" ....(CE).......❹ ......$1825—1900
☐ 152/II B......8.00" ....(CE).......❹ ......$1825—1900
☐ 152/II B......8.00" ....(CE).......❺ ......$1800—1825
☐ 152/II B......8.00" ....(CE).......❻ ......$1775—1800
☐ 152/II B......8.00" ....(CE).......❼ ......$1750—1775
☐ 152/II B......8.00" ....(**OE**)......❽ $1750

| 153/0 | 153/I | 153/0 Boy with hat (CE) |

HUM 153 — Auf Wiedersehen

Originally modeled by master sculptor Arthur Moeller in 1943. First produced in the large size only with plain 153 incised number. The small size was introduced in the early 1950s with the boy wearing a hat and waving his hand—always with full bee trademark and "0" size designator directly under the number "153"—considered rare. This style was made in the small size only. Both sizes have been restyled in recent years. Both styles of the small size can be found in full bee trademark. Also called "Good Bye" in old catalogues. In 1993 the small size 153/0 was used as part of a special limited edition memorial to the Berlin Airlift. (See photo in back of this book.) Both sizes of "Auf Wiedersehen" were permanently retired by Goebel on 31 December 2000 and will not be produced again. They both have a "Final Issue 2000" backstamp and small gold "Final Issue" medallion in addition to the new (TM 8) trademark. The large size (153/I) is available with "Mildstones" Hummelscape (Mark #1011-D) in a (LE) Limited Edition of 6500 pieces.

☐	153/0	5.50 to 6.00".....(CE)	❷	$425—525
☐	153/0	5.50 to 6.00".....(CE)	❸	$350—400
☐	153/0	5.50 to 6.00".....(CE)	❹	$320—350
☐	153/0	5.50 to 6.00".....(CE)	❺	$300—320
☐	153/0	5.50 to 6.00".....(CE)	❻	$280—300
☐	153/0	5.50 to 6.00".....(CE)	❼	$285—290
☐	153/0	5.50 to 6.00".....**(CE)**	❽	$285—290
☐	153/0	5.25"...................(CE)	❷	$3000—4000 (with hat)
☐	153	6.75 to 7.00".....(CE)	❶	$900—1200
☐	153	6.75 to 7.00".....(CE)	❷	$650—750
☐	153/I	6.75 to 7.00".....(CE)	❶	$750—1050
☐	153/I	6.75 to 7.00".....(CE)	❷	$600—700
☐	153/I	6.75 to 7.00".....(CE)	❸	$475—525
☐	153/I	6.75 to 7.00".....(CE)	❹	$425—475
☐	153/I	6.75 to 7.00".....(CE)	❺	$360—390
☐	153/I	6.75 to 7.00".....(CE)	❻	$350—360
☐	153/I	6.75 to 7.00".....(CE)	❼	$340—350
☐	153/I	6.75 to 7.00".....**(CE)**	❽	$340—350

FINAL ISSUE
MILLENNIUM
2000

| 154/0 | 154/0 | 154/I | 154 (CE) |

HUM 154 — Waiter

Originally modeled by master sculptor Arthur Moeller in 1943. Was first produced in the 6.50" size and incised number 154 only, with gray coat and gray striped trousers. In the early 1950s the colors were changed to blue coat and tan striped trousers, and "Waiter" was produced in two sizes: 154/0 and 154/I. Has been produced with various names on bottle. "Rhein-wine" or "Rhein Wine" are the most common. "Whisky," "Hiher Mchie" and other illegible names have been used. Old name: "Chef of Service" or "Little Waiter" in some old catalogues. Both sizes have recently been restyled with the new "textured" finish. Large size (154/I) was listed as (TW) "Temporarily Withdrawn" in January 1999. Small size (151/0) was listed as (TW) "Temporarily Withdrawn" in March 2005.

☐	154/0	....6.00 to 6.25".....(CE)	........❶	........$700—800
☐	154/0	....6.00 to 6.25".....(CE)	........❷	........$400—500
☐	154/0	....6.00 to 6.25".....(CE)	........❸	........$350—375
☐	154/0	....6.00 to 6.25".....(CE)	........❹	........$325—350
☐	154/0	....6.00 to 6.25".....(CE)	........❺	........$290—295
☐	154/0	....6.00 to 6.25".....(CE)	........❻	........$285—290
☐	154/0	....6.00 to 6.25".....(CE)	........❼	........$280—285
☐	154/0	....6.00 to 6.25".....(TW)	........❽	........$279—280
☐	154/I	......6.50 to 7.00".....(CE)	........❶	........$750—1000
☐	154/I	......6.50 to 7.00".....(CE)	........❷	........$500—600
☐	154/I	......6.50 to 7.00".....(CE)	........❸	........$450—500
☐	154/I	......6.50 to 7.00".....(CE)	........❹	........$375—450
☐	154/I	......6.50 to 7.00".....(CE)	........❺	........$350—375
☐	154/I	......6.50 to 7.00".....(CE)	........❻	........$340—350
☐	154/I	......6.50 to 7.00".....(TW)	........❼	........$325—335
☐	154	........6.50".................(CE)	........❶	........$850—1150
☐	154	........6.50".................(CE)	........❷	........$550—700
☐	154/0	....6.50".................(CE)	........❷	........$1600—2100 (with whisky)

HUM 155 (CN)

Factory records indicate: Madonna with cloak, sitting with child on her lap, Reinhold Unger in 1943. Listed as (CN) Closed Number on 18 May 1943. No known examples or photographs.

☐ 155...(CN).................

HUM 156 (CN)

Factory records indicate: Wall picture with sitting woman and child, Arthur Moeller in 1943. Listed as (CN) Closed Number on 18 May 1943. No known examples or photographs.

☐ 156...(CN).................

HUM 157 (CN)

Factory records indicate: Boy standing with flower basket. Sample model sculpted by Arthur Moeller in 1943. Considered for production but was never made. This factory sample does not have "M. I. Hummel" signature. Listed as (CN) Closed Number on 17 September 1943. No known examples in private collections—factory archive samples only.

☐ 157...(CN).................

HUM 158 (CN)

Factory records indicate: Girl standing with dog in her arms. Sample model sculpted by Arthur Moeller in 1943. Considered for production but was never made. This factory sample does not have "M. I. Hummel" signature. Listed as (CN) Closed Number on 17 September 1943. No known examples in private collections—factory archives samples only.

☐ 158...(CN).................

.... **HUM TERM** ....

STYLIZED TRADEMARK: The symbol used by the Goebel Company from 1957 until 1964. It is recognized by the V with a bumblebee that has triangular or "stylized" wings.

HUM 159 (CN)
Factory records indicate: Girl standing with flowers in her arms. Sample model sculpted by Arthur Moeller in 1943. Considered for production but was never made. This factory sample does not have "M.I. Hummel" signature. Listed as (CN) Closed Number on 17 September 1943. No known examples in private collections—factory archives samples only.

☐ 159..(CN)..................

HUM 160 (CN)
Factory records indicate: Girl standing in tiered dress and bouquet of flowers. Sample model sculpted by Reinhold Unger in 1943. Considered for production but was never made. This factory sample does not have "M. I. Hummel" signature. Listed as (CN) Closed Number on 17 September 1943. No known examples in private collections—factory archive samples only.

☐ 160..(CN)..................

HUM 161 (CN)
Factory records indicate: Girl standing with hands in her pockets. Sample model sculpted by Reinhold Unger in 1943. Considered for production but was never made. This factory sample does not have "M. I. Hummel" signature. Listed as (CN) Closed Number on 17 September 1943. No known examples in private collections—factory archive samples only.

☐ 161..(CN)..................

133

HUM 162 (CN)

Factory records indicate: Girl standing with pocket-book (handbag). Sample model sculpted by Reinhold Unger in 1943. Listed as (CN) Closed Number on 11 October 1943. No known examples or photographs.

☐ 162...(CN).................

Old style (TM 1)   *New style (TM 3)*

HUM 163 — Whitsuntide

Originally modeled by master sculptor Arthur Moeller in 1946. Can be found in all trademarks except (TM 4) and (TM 8). Older models are larger than newer models. Old name: "Christmas." Sometimes referred to as "Happy New Year." Angel on base holds red or yellow candle on older models. Unusual variation has small hole in angel's cupped hands where candle should be. Had been considered rare at one time, but was put back into current production in 1978 and can be found with TM 5, TM 6 and TM 7. Listed as (TW) "Temporarily Withdrawn" in January 1999.

☐ 163.............6.50 to 7.00"........(CE)......❶ ......$1000—1200
☐ 163.............6.50 to 7.00"........(CE)......❷ ......$850—1000
☐ 163.............6.50 to 7.00"........(CE)......❸ ......$650—800
☐ 163.............6.50 to 7.00"........(CE)......❺ ......$350—390
☐ 163.............6.50 to 7.00"........(CE)......❻ ......$340—350
☐ 163.............6.50 to 7.00"........(TW)......❼ ......$330—340

Old   **New**

HUM 164 — Holy Water Font, Worship
First modeled by master sculptor Reinhold
Unger in 1946. There are variations in
construction of this font in that older models do not have a rim on back side of bowl
while newer models do. Also color variations on lip of water bowl—older ones
were hand-painted; newer ones are
shaded with airbrush.

☐ 164 ....3.25 x 5.00” ....(CE)....... ❶ ......$250—300
☐ 164 ....3.25 x 5.00” ....(CE)....... ❷ ......$150—200
☐ 164 ....3.25 x 5.00” ....(CE)....... ❸ ......$90—110
☐ 164 ....3.25 x 5.00” ....(CE)....... ❹ ......$85—90
☐ 164 ....3.25 x 5.00” ....(CE)....... ❺ ......$80—85
☐ 164 ....3.25 x 5.00” ....(CE)....... ❻ ......$75—80
☐ 164 ....3.25 x 5.00” ....(CE)....... ❼ ......$70—75
☐ 164 ....3.25 x 5.00” ....(OE)....... ❽ $69.50

**HUM 165 — Swaying Lullaby,
Wall Plaque**
Originally modeled by master sculptor Arthur Moeller in 1946. Not pictured in older catalogues; most
collectors were not aware of the existence of this plaque until the early
1970s. Our first purchase came
through an American soldier who had
been stationed in Panama. Put back
into current production in 1978 and
was available in (TM 5) and (TM 6).
Older models have the “M.I. Hummel” signature on the back while
newer models have signature on
front lower right corner. Old name:
“Child in a Hammock.” Inscription
reads: “Dreaming of better times.”
Restyled in 1979. Current production
models are slightly thicker in depth,
with signature on back. Was (TW)
“Temporarily Withdrawn” from pro-

(TM 3) “Stylized” trademark

duction on 31 December 1989. Reissued in 1999 with (TM 7) trademark and a “Sweet
Dreams” (Mark #1012-D) Hummelscape in a collectors set for $325.

☐ 165 ....4.50 x 5.25” ....(CE)....... ❶ ......$800—1100
☐ 165 ....4.50 x 5.25” ....(CE)....... ❷ ......$550—800
☐ 165 ....4.50 x 5.25” ....(CE)....... ❸ ......$375—525
☐ 165 ....4.50 x 5.25” ....(CE)....... ❺ ......$225—250
☐ 165 ....4.50 x 5.25” ....(CE)....... ❻ ......$200—225
☐ 165 ....4.50 x 5.25” ....(CE)....... ❼ ......$325   (with Hummelscape)

HUM 166 — Boy With Bird, Ashtray

This ashtray was modeled by master sculptor Arthur Moeller in 1946. Only slight variations in color and construction through the years; no major differences between old and new models. "Boy with Bird" ashtray was (TW) "Temporarily Withdrawn" from production on 31 December 1989, but may be reinstated at some future date.

☐ 166	3.25 x 6.00"	(CE)	❶	$450—650
☐ 166	3.25 x 6.00"	(CE)	❷	$275—325
☐ 166	3.25 x 6.00"	(CE)	❸	$190—210
☐ 166	3.25 x 6.00"	(CE)	❹	$160—190
☐ 166	3.25 x 6.00"	(CE)	❺	$150—160
☐ 166	3.25 x 6.00"	(TW)	❻	$140—150

Old-crown (TM 1)   *Old (TM 2)*   *New (TM 3)*

HUM 167 — Holy Water Font, Angel with Bird

Also referred to as: "Angel-Bird" or "Angel Sitting" font. Newer models have a hole at top of font for hanging. Older models have hole on back of font for hanging. We found old crown (TM 1) font that has both hole at top and on back, is smaller in size and has no rim on back edge of bowl. Variations in color on lip of water bowl—older ones were hand-painted; newer ones are shaded with airbrush. First modeled by Reinhold Unger in 1945.

☐ 167	3.25 x 4.125"	(CE)	❶	$250—300
☐ 167	3.25 x 4.125"	(CE)	❷	$150—200
☐ 167	3.25 x 4.125"	(CE)	❸	$90—110
☐ 167	3.25 x 4.125"	(CE)	❹	$85—90
☐ 167	3.25 x 4.125"	(CE)	❺	$80—85
☐ 167	3.25 x 4.125"	(CE)	❻	$75—80
☐ 167	3.25 x 4.125"	(CE)	❼	$70—75
☐ 167	3.25 x 4.125"	(OE)	❽	$69.50

Stylized trademark (TM 3)   *Goebel Bee (TM 5)*

HUM 168 — Standing Boy, Wall Plaque

Originally modeled by master sculptor Arthur Moeller in 1948. Not pictured in older catalogues; most collectors were not aware of the existence of this plaque until the early 1970s. Very limited early production, probably sold mostly in European market. Put back into current production in 1978 and was available in TM 5 and TM 6. Older models have only "Hummel" on front, lower left, along with "© WG" in lower right corner. Newer models have "M.I. Hummel" signature incised on back. This same motif was made into a figurine in 1979 by master sculptor Gerhard Skrobek; see HUM 399 "Valentine Joy." "Standing Boy" wall plaque was (TW) "Temporarily Withdrawn" from production on 31 December 1989, but may be reinstated at some future date. To my knowledge, not produced in (TM 4) "three line" trademark.

- ☐ 168 ....4.125 x 5.50" ....(CE)...... ❶ ....$800—1100
- ☐ 168 ....4.125 x 5.50" ....(CE)...... ❷ ......$550—800
- ☐ 168 ....4.125 x 5.50" ....(CE)...... ❸ ......$375—525
- ☐ 168 ....4.125 x 5.50" ....(CE)...... ❺ ......$225—250
- ☐ 168 ....4.125 x 5.50" ....(**TW**) ...... ❻ ....$200—225

.... HUM TERM ....

BAS RELIEF: Sculptural relief in which the projection from the surrounding surface is slight. This type of raised work is found on the annual and anniversary "M.I. Hummel" plates.

Old style (TM 1)   **New style (TM 3)**

HUM 169 — Bird Duet

Originally modeled in 1945 by master sculptor Arthur Moeller; later restyled in 1967 by master sculptor Gerhard Skrobek. Many variations between old and new figurines. Variations are noted in angel's wings, gown and position of baton. Color variation in birds, angel's hair and gown, as well as music stand. "Bird Duet" can be personalized with a name or date by a Goebel artist. Also sold with "Celestial Harmony" Hummelscape (Mark #1021-D) gift set at $205.

☐ 169 ....3.75 to 4.00".........(CE).......❶ ....$450—550
☐ 169 ....3.75 to 4.00".........(CE).......❷ ......$275—350
☐ 169 ....3.75 to 4.00".........(CE).......❸ ......$225—250
☐ 169 ....3.75 to 4.00".........(CE).......❹ ......$215—225
☐ 169 ....3.75 to 4.00".........(CE).......❺ ......$210—215
☐ 169 ....3.75 to 4.00".........(CE).......❻ ......$205—210
☐ 169 ....3.75 to 4.00".........(CE).......❼ .....$200—205
☐ 169 ....3.75 to 4.00".........(**TW**) ......❽ ....$199—200

.... PRICES IN THIS GUIDE ....

We are in a period of DISCOUNTING of many items in our society. "M.I. Hummel" figurines are no exception. The prices in this guide give the relative values in relationship to new or current prices of (TM 8) trademark items. If the new figurines are discounted, the older models will likely be discounted, too, but possibly in a lesser degree. This guide reduces all items to one common denominator.

170/III (TM 5)   *170/I (TM 4)*

HUM 170 — School Boys

First modeled by master sculptor Reinhold Unger in 1943 and later remodeled by master sculptor Gerhard Skrobek in 1961. Originally produced in one size with incised number 170 only. Small size first produced in the early 1960s and has an incised 1961 copyright date. Old name: "Difficult Problems." Some color variations on older models —middle boy with green rather than maroon trousers. Large size was again restyled in the early 1970s with the new textured finish and 1972 copyright date. In the spring of 1982 the large size (170/III) was withdrawn from production by Goebel and then made in a (LE) Limited Edition of 100 in (TM 8). The small size 170/I is still in current production. HUM 460 "Authorized Retailer Plaque" was issued in 1986 utilizing the middle boy as part of the plaque motif. Issued in eight different languages. See: HUM 460.

☐ 170/I ....7.25 to 7.50" ....(CE) ...... ❸ ...... $1800—1900
☐ 170/I ....7.25 to 7.50" ....(CE) ...... ❹ ...... $1700—1800
☐ 170/I ....7.25 to 7.50" ....(CE) ...... ❺ ...... $1600—1700
☐ 170/I ....7.25 to 7.50" ....(CE) ...... ❻ ...... $1500—1600
☐ 170/I ....7.25 to 7.50" ....(CE) ...... ❼ ...... $1480—1500
☐ 170/I ....7.25 to 7.50" ....(**OE**) ...... ❽ $1480
☐ 170 ....10.00 to 10.25" .....(CE) ...... ❶ ...... $4500—5000
☐ 170 ....10.00 to 10.25" .....(CE) ...... ❷ ...... $3500—4000
☐ 170 ....10.00 to 10.25" .....(CE) ...... ❸ ...... $3200—3300
☐ 170/III ....10.00 to 10.25" .....(CE) ...... ❸ ...... $3000—3100
☐ 170/III ....10.00 to 10.25" .....(CE) ...... ❹ ...... $2900—3000
☐ 170/III ....10.00 to 10.25" .....(CE) ...... ❺ ...... $2800—2850
☐ 170/III ....10.00 to 10.25" .....(CE) ...... ❻ ...... $2600—2800
☐ 170/III ....9.50 to 9.75" ....(**LE**) ...... ❽ $3200

Old style (TM 1)   *New style (TM 6)*

HUM 171 — Little Sweeper

This figurine was first modeled by master sculptor Reinhold Unger in 1944. Very little change between older and newer models. Old name: "Mother's Helper." Restyled in 1981 by master sculptor Gerhard Skrobek. The current production now has the new textured finish and is slightly larger. A new miniature size figurine was issued in 1988 with a suggested retail price of $45 to match a new miniature plate series called the "Little Homemakers"—one each year for four years. This is the first in the series. The miniature size figurine has an incised 1986 copyright date. The normal size will be renumbered 171/0 and the old number 171 is now classified as a (CE) Closed Edition because of this change. The miniature size (171 4/0) was (TW) "Temporarily Withdrawn" from production on 31 December 1997. Permanently retired in 2006.

☐ 171 4/0	3.00"	(CE)	❻	$125—140
☐ 171 4/0	3.00"	**(TW)**	❼	$115—120
☐ 171	4.25"	(CE)	❶	$450—500
☐ 171	4.25"	(CE)	❷	$275—325
☐ 171	4.25"	(CE)	❸	$240—250
☐ 171	4.25"	(CE)	❹	$210—240
☐ 171	4.25"	(CE)	❺	$200—205
☐ 171	4.25"	(CE)	❻	$190—195
☐ 171/0	4.25"	(CE)	❻	$190—195
☐ 171/0	4.25 to 4.50"	(CE)	❼	$185—190
☐ 171/0	4.25 to 4.50"	(CE)	❽	$179

FINAL ISSUE
2006

| Crown (TM 1) | Full Bee (TM 2) | Stylized (TM 3) | 172/0 (TM 3) |

HUM 172 — Festival Harmony (Mandolin)

Originally modeled in 1947 by master sculptor Reinhold Unger in the large size only with incised number 172. Old crown mark and some full bee examples have the bird resting on flowers in front of angel (rare). Restyled in the early 1950s with bird resting on mandolin and one flower at hem of angel's gown. Restyled again in the late 1960s with the new textured finish and flowers placed at angel's feet. There are variations in color of gown and color of birds. The small size (172/0) was modeled by master sculptor Theo R. Menzenbach in 1961 and can be found in one style only. The large size (172/II) was (TW) "Temporarily Withdrawn" from production on 31 December 1984, but may be reinstated at some future date. A new miniature size figurine, 172 4/0 in a matte finish was put on the market in 1994 with a suggested retail price of $95 and an incised 1991 copyright date and a "First Issue 1994" decal on the bottom. Both sizes (172 4/0) and (172/0) were listed as (TW) "Temporarily Withdrawn" in January 1999.

- ☐ 172 4/0 ....3.125" ....(**TW**) ...... ❼ ....$130—135
- ☐ 172/0 ....8.00" ....(CE)...... ❸ ....$500—650
- ☐ 172/0 ....8.00" ....(CE)...... ❹ ....$400—475
- ☐ 172/0 ....8.00" ....(CE)...... ❺ ....$380—400
- ☐ 172/0 ....8.00" ....(CE)...... ❻ ....$360—380
- ☐ 172/0 ....8.00" ....(**TW**) ...... ❼ ....$350—360
- ☐ 172/II ....10.25 to 10.75" .....(CE)...... ❸ ....$650—800
- ☐ 172/II ....10.25 to 10.75" .....(CE)...... ❹ ....$550—600
- ☐ 172/II ....10.25 to 10.75" .....(CE)...... ❺ ....$475—500
- ☐ 172/II ....10.25 to 10.75" .....(**TW**) ...... ❻ ....$450—475
- ☐ 172 ....10.75" ....(CE)...... ❶ ....$3000—3500 (Bird in front)
- ☐ 172 ....10.75" ....(CE)...... ❷ ....$2500—3000 (Bird in front)
- ☐ 172 ....10.75" ....(CE)...... ❷ ....$1250—1500 (Flower at hem)
- ☐ 172 ....10.75" ....(CE)...... ❸ ....$1000—1250 (Flower at hem)

Crown (TM 1)   *Full Bee (TM 2)*   *Stylized (TM 3)*   *173/0 (TM 4)*

HUM 173 — Festival Harmony (Flute)

Originally modeled in 1947 by master sculptor Reinhold Unger in the large size only with incised number 173. Old crown mark and some full bee examples have a much larger bird and flower in front of angel (rare). Restyled in the early 1950s with smaller bird and one flower at hem of angel's gown. Restyled again in the late 1960s with the new textured finish and flowers placed at angel's feet. There are variations in color of gown and color of birds. The small size (173/0) was modeled by master sculptor Theo R. Menzenbach in 1961 and can be found in one style only. The large size (173/II) was (TW) "Temporarily Withdrawn" from production on 31 December 1984, but may be reinstated at some future date. A new miniature size figurine, 173 4/0 in a matte finish was put on the market in 1995 with a suggested retail price of $95 and an incised 1991 copyright date and a "First Issue 1995" decal on the bottom. Both sizes (173 4/0) and (173/0) were listed as (TW) "Temporarily Withdrawn" in January 1999.

☐	173 4/0 ..3.125"	(TW)	❼	$130—135	
☐	173/0 ....8.00"	(CE)	❸	$500—650	
☐	173/0 ....8.00"	(CE)	❹	$400—475	
☐	173/0 ....8.00"	(CE)	❺	$380—400	
☐	173/0 ....8.00"	(CE)	❻	$360—380	
☐	173/0 ....8.00"	(TW)	❼	$350—360	
☐	173/II ....10.25 to 11.00"	(CE)	❸	$650—800	
☐	173/II ....10.25 to 11.00"	(CE)	❹	$550—600	
☐	173/II ....10.25 to 11.00"	(CE)	❺	$475—500	
☐	173/II ....10.25 to 11.00"	(TW)	❻	$450—475	
☐	173 ....11.00"	(CE)	❶	$3000—3500	(Flowers up front of dress)
☐	173 ....11.00"	(CE)	❷	$2500—3000	(Flowers up front of dress)
☐	173 ....11.00"	(CE)	❷	$1250—1500	(Flower at hem)
☐	173 ....11.00"	(CE)	❸	$1000—1250	(Flower at hem)

TM 1   *TM 2*   *TM 5*

HUM 174 — She Loves Me, She Loves Me Not!

Originally modeled by master sculptor Arthur Moeller in 1945. Has been restyled several times. Early crown mark pieces have smaller feather in boy's hat, no flower on left fence post and eyes are open. The 2, 3 and 4 trademark period pieces have a flower on left fence post and eyes are open. Current production pieces have no flower on left fence post (same as crown mark piece) but with eyes looking down. Newer models have an incised 1955 copyright date. Some (TM 1) crown examples have the flower on the fence post, as well as TM 2, 3 & 4 trademark periods.

- ☐ 174 ....4.25 to 4.50" ....(CE)....... ❶ ......$600—700
- ☐ 174 ....4.25 to 4.50" ....(CE)....... ❷ ......$400—450
- ☐ 174 ....4.25 to 4.50" ....(CE)....... ❸ ......$300—325
- ☐ 174 ....4.25 to 4.50" ....(CE)....... ❹ ......$275—300
- ☐ 174 ....4.25 to 4.50"" ....(CE)....... ❺ ......$270—275
- ☐ 174 ....4.25 to 4.50" ....(CE)....... ❻ ......$265—270
- ☐ 174 ....4.25 to 4.50" ....(CE)....... ❼ ......$260—265
- ☐ 174 ....4.25" ....(**OE**)....... ❽ $259

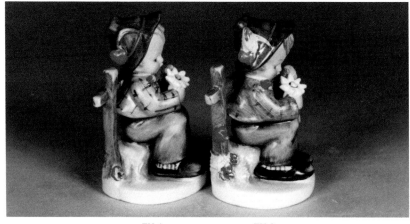

TM 1   *TM 2*

Old style (TM 1)　　　　　*New style (TM 3)*

HUM 175 — Mother's Darling
Older models have pink and green-colored kerchiefs (bags) while newer models have blue ones. Trademark (TM 3) can be found in both color variations. Older models do not have polka dots on head scarf. Old name: "Happy Harriet." First modeled by master sculptor Arthur Moeller in 1945, and has been restyled several times since then. "Mother's Darling" was permanently retired by Goebel on 31 December 1997 and will not be produced again. It has a "Final Issue 1997" backstamp and small gold "Final Issue" modallion

- ☐ 175............5.50"......................(CE).......❶ ....$600—800 (pink & green)
- ☐ 175............5.50"......................(CE).......❷ ....$400—525 (pink & green)
- ☐ 175............5.50"......................(CE).......❸ ....$325—375 (both ways)
- ☐ 175............5.50"......................(CE).......❹ ....$285—325
- ☐ 175............5.50"......................(CE).......❺ ....$260—285
- ☐ 175............5.50"......................(CE).......❻ ....$250—260
- ☐ 175............5.50"......................(CE).......❼ ....$240—250

FINAL ISSUE
1997

176/I New (TM 6)   *176 Old (TM 1)*

HUM 176 — Happy Birthday

When first modeled in 1945 by master sculptor Arthur Moeller this figurine was produced in one size only with the incised number 176. A smaller size was issued in the mid-1950s with the incised number 176/0 and an oval base. At the same time, the large size was changed to 176/I. The large size figurine has always had a round base until it was completely restyled in 1979 and now has an oval base, also. The large size (176/I) was listed as (TW) "Temporarily Withdrawn" in January 1999, but may be reinstated at some future date.

☐ 176/0	5.00"	(CE)	❷	$450—500
☐ 176/0	5.00"	(CE)	❸	$350—375
☐ 176/0	5.00"	(CE)	❹	$300—350
☐ 176/0	5.00"	(CE)	❺	$290—295
☐ 176/0	5.00"	(CE)	❻	$285—290
☐ 176/0	5.00"	(CE)	❼	$280—285
☐ 176/0	5.00"	(**OE**)	❽	$279
☐ 176/I	5.50"	(CE)	❶	$800—1100
☐ 176/I	5.50"	(CE)	❷	$550—700
☐ 176/I	5.50"	(CE)	❸	$450—525
☐ 176/I	5.50"	(CE)	❹	$390—450
☐ 176/I	5.50"	(CE)	❺	$360—390
☐ 176/I	5.50"	(CE)	❻	$340—360
☐ 176/I	5.50"	(**TW**)	❼	$330—340
☐ 176	5.50"	(CE)	❶	$850—1150
☐ 176	5.50"	(CE)	❷	$600—750

m ine 7 1/2"   **177 (TM 2)**   **177/I (TM 4)**

HUM 177 — School Girls

First modeled by master sculptor Reinhold Unger in 1946 and later remodeled by master sculptor Theo R. Menzenbach in 1961. Originally produced in one size with incised number 177 only. Small size first produced in the early 1960s and has an incised 1961 copyright date. Old name. "Mootor Piece." Some slight color variations on older models, particularly the shoes. Large size again restyled in the early 1970s with the new textured finish and a 1972 incised copyright date. In the spring of 1982 the large size (177/III) was withdrawn from production by Goebel and then made in a (LE) Limited Edition of 100 in (TM 8). The small size (177/I) is still in current production. See HUM 255 "Stitch in Time" and HUM 256 "Knitting Lesson" for interesting comparison.

☐ 177/I	7.50"	(CE)	❸	$1800—1900
☐ 177/I	7.50"	(CE)	❹	$1700—1800
☐ 177/I	7.50"	(CE)	❺	$1600—1700
☐ 177/I	7.50"	(CE)	❻	$1500—1600
☐ 177/I	7.50"	(CE)	❼	$1480—1500
☐ 177/I	7.50"	(OE)	❽	$1480
☐ 177	9.50"	(CE)	❶	$4500—5000
☐ 177	9.50"	(CE)	❷	$3500—4000
☐ 177	9.50"	(CE)	❸	$3200—3300
☐ 177/III	9.50"	(CE)	❸	$3000—3100
☐ 177/III	9.50"	(CE)	❹	$2900—3000
☐ 177/III	9.50"	(CE)	❺	$2800—2850
☐ 177/III	9.50"	(CE)	❻	$2600—2800
☐ 177/III	9.50"	(LE)	❽	$3200

HUM 178 — Photographer, The
Originally modeled by master sculptor Reinhold Unger in 1948 and has been restyled several times through the years. There are many size variations with the older model being larger. Some color variations on dog and camera. Newer models have a 1948 copyright date.

Old style (TM 2)   *New style (TM 4)*

☐ 178 ....4.75 to 5.25".........(CE)......❶ ....$900—1100
☐ 178 ....4.75 to 5.25".........(CE)......❷ ....$550—650
☐ 178 ....4.75 to 5.25".........(CE)......❸ ....$450—500
☐ 178 ....4.75 to 5.25".........(CE)......❹ ....$390—450
☐ 178 ....4.75 to 5.25".........(CE)......❺ ....$380—390
☐ 178 ....4.75 to 5.25".........(CE)......❻ ....$375—380
☐ 178 ....4.75 to 5.25".........(CE)......❼ ....$370—375
☐ 178 ....4.75 to 5.25".........(**OE**)......❽ $369

HUM 179 — Coquettes
Modeled originally by master sculptor Arthur Moeller in 1948 and has been restyled in recent years. Older examples are usually slightly larger in size. Minor color variations can be found in older models. Listed as (TW) "Temporarily With-

Old style (TM 1)   *New style (TM 3)*

drawn" in January 1999, but may be reinstated at some future date.

☐ 179 ....5.00 to 5.50".........(CE)......❶ ....$900—1100
☐ 179 ....5.00 to 5.25".........(CE)......❷ ....$550—650
☐ 179 ....5.00 to 5.25".........(CE)......❸ ....$450—500
☐ 179 ....5.00 to 5.25".........(CE)......❹ ....$370—450
☐ 179 ....5.00 to 5.25".........(CE)......❺ ....$350—370
☐ 179 ....5.00 to 5.25".........(CE)......❻ ....$335—350
☐ 179 ....5.00 to 5.25".........(**TW**)......❼ ....$325—335

New style (TM 6)   *Old style (TM 6)*

HUM 180 — Tuneful Goodnight, Wall Plaque

Modeled by master sculptor Arthur Moeller in 1946. Restyled in 1981 by master sculptor Rudolf Wittman, a twenty-five-year veteran of the Goebel factory. In the restyled version, the position of the girl's head and hairstyle have been changed, as well as the position of the horn which is no longer attached to the heart-shaped back. Old name: "Happy Bugler" plaque. Had been considered rare and was difficult to find, but is readily available with (TM 5) and (TM 6) trademarks. "Tuneful Goodnight" wall plaque was (TW) "Temporarily Withdrawn" from production on 31 December 1989 for a time. Early "crown" (TM 1) also found made of porcelain instead of normal ceramic material, usually smaller in size. "Tuneful Goodnight" was released in 2000 in (TM 8) trademark in a combination with Hummelscape "Heart of Hearts" (Mark #1024-D), retail price $305 in 2000. Sold in European market in (TM 7) and (TM 8). Not on current U.S. price list.

☐ 180........   4.50 x 4.25"..........(CE).......❶ ......$900—1200 (Porcelain)
☐ 180.............5.00 x 4.75"..........(CE).......❶ $600   800
☐ 180.............5.00 x 4.75"..........(CE).......❷ ......$400—550
☐ 180.............5.00 x 4.75"..........(CE).......❸ ......$350—400
☐ 180.............5.00 x 4.75"..........(CE).......❹ ......$310—350
☐ 180.............5.00 x 4.75"..........(CE).......❺ ......$300—310
☐ 180.............5.00 x 4.75"..........(CE).......❻ ......$290—300
☐ 180.............5.00 x 4.75"..........(CE).......❼ ......$280—290
☐ 180.............5.00 x 4.75"..........(CE).......❽ ......$275—280

(TM 3)   *(TM 1)*   *(Mark #1024-D)*

Incised "M.I. Hummel"

Old Postcard Drawing

HUM 181 — Old Man Reading Newspaper (CN)

This unusual piece was made as a sample only in 1948 by master sculptor Arthur Moeller and was not approved by the Siessen Convent for production. It was not considered typical of Sister M.I. Hummel's work, although it is an exact reproduction of one of her early sketches. This early sample does have the familiar "M.I. Hummel" signature and is part of the Robert L. Miller collection. Listed as a (CN) Closed Number on 18 February 1948 and will not be produced again. Often referred to as one of the "Mamas" and the "Papas." Also produced as a lamp base; see HUM 202. Several other examples have been found in recent years.

☐ 181 ....6.75" ....(CN)................$15,000—20,000

.... **HUM TERM** ....

RARE: (Webster) marked by unusual quality, merit, or appeal. Distinctive, superlative or extreme of its kind, seldom occurring or found, uncommon.

New style (TM 5)   *Old style (TM 1)*

HUM 182 — Good Friends

Originally modeled by master sculptor Arthur Moeller in 1946 and later restyled by master sculptor Gerhard Skrobek in 1976. The current model is slightly larger and has the new textured finish. Called "Friends" in old catalogues.

- ☐ 182 ....4.00 to 4.25" ....(CF) ..,,,,, ❶ ....$650—750
- ☐ 182 ....4.00 to 4.25" ....(CE) ...... ❷ ......$400—500
- ☐ 182 ....4.00 to 4.25" ....(CE) ...... ❸ ......$325—350
- ☐ 182 ....4.00 to 4.25" ....(CE) ...... ❹ ......$300—325
- ☐ 182 ....4.00 to 4.25" ....(CE) ...... ❺ ......$270—285
- ☐ 182 ....4.00 to 4.25" ....(CE) ...... ❻ ......$265—270
- ☐ 182 ....4.00 to 4.25" ....(CE) ...... ❼ ......$260—265
- ☐ 182 ....4.00 to 4.25" ....(TW) ...... ❽ $259

.... HUM TERM ....

MOLD GROWTH: In the earlier days of figurine production the working molds were made of plaster of paris. As these molds were used, the various molded parts became larger due to the repeated usage. With modern technology at the Goebel factory and the use of acrylic resin molds, this problem has been eliminated and today the collector finds very few size differences within a given size designation.

Old style (TM 1)   *New style (TM 6)*

HUM 183 — Forest Shrine

First modeled in 1946 by master sculptor Reinhold Unger and can be found with all trademarks except trademark 4. Had been considered rare but was put back into production in 1977 and can be found with 5, 6, 7 and 8 trademarks. Older models have a shiny finish on the deer while newer models have a dull finish. Old name: "Doe at Shrine." This figurine has recently been restyled with a more lifelike finish on the deer. Listed as (TW) "Temporarily Withdrawn" in January 1999, but re-released in (TM 8).

☐ 183 .....9.00"....(CE) ....❶ ....$1500—1900
☐ 183 .....9.00"....(CE) ....❷ ....$1000—1300
☐ 183 .....9.00"....(CE) ....❸ ....$700—950
☐ 183 .....9.00"....(CE) ....❺ ....$660—700
☐ 183 .....9.00"....(CE) ....❻ ....$650—660
☐ 183 .....9.00"....(CE) ....❼ ....$640—650
☐ 183 .....9.00"....(**TW**).......❽ ....$630—640

Japanese Copy

151

| Old style (TM 1) | New style (TM 3) | New style (TM 6) |

HUM 184 — Latest News

First modeled by master sculptor Arthur Moeller in 1946. Older models were made with square base and boy's eyes open. Restyled in the mid-1960s and changed to round base and boy's eyes looking down at paper. At one time the newspaper was produced without any name so that visitors to the factory could have the name of their choice put on. An endless variety of names can be found. Most common names are: "Das Allerneueste," "Munchener Presse" and "Latest News." Some collectors specialize in collecting the different names on the newspaper and will pay from $500 to $1000 for some names. Some catalogues list as 184/O.S. which means: Ohne Schrift (without lettering). Early "crown" (TM 1) also found made of porcelain instead of normal ceramic material, usually smaller in size. "Latest News" is now part of the "Personal Touch Personalization" program and can be personalized with a name and date by a Goebel artist. In recent years countless special inscriptions have been produced for various dealers and various occasions, such as: "Cayman News," "Island News," "Bermuda News," "Stars & Stripes," "Milwaukee Journal-Sentinel," "The Chancellor's Visit," "The Hummel Museum," "Leipzig Fair – 70th Anniversary" etc.

☐ 184 ....4.25 to 4.50" ....(CE)....... ❶ ....$1500—2000 (Porcelain)
☐ 184 ....5.00 to 5.25" ....(CE)....... ❶ ....$900—1100
☐ 184 ....5.00 to 5.25" ....(CE)....... ❷ ....$600—700
☐ 184 ....5.00 to 5.25" ....(CE)....... ❸ ....$450—525
☐ 184 ....5.00 to 5.25" ....(CE)....... ❹ ....$400—450
☐ 184 ....5.00 to 5.25" ....(CE)....... ❺ ....$370—375
☐ 184 ....5.00" ....(CE)....... ❻ ....$365—370
☐ 184 ....5.00" ....(CE)....... ❼ ....$360—365
☐ 184 ....5.00" ....(OE)....... ❽ $359
☐ 184 ....5.00" ....(LE) .... ❽ ....$429   (70th Anniversary)

(TM 7) left
(TM 1) right

HUM 185 — Accordion Boy

First modeled by master sculptor Reinhold Unger in 1947, this figurine has never had a major restyling although there are many size variations due mainly to "mold growth." In the early years, the molds were made of plaster of paris and had a tendency to "wash out" or erode with use, thereby producing figurines each being slightly larger than the last. Since 1954, the use of acrylic resin for molds has led to greater uniformity in the figurines themselves. There are some slight color variations on the accordion. Old name: "On the Alpine Pasture." One of several figurines that make up the Hummel orchestra. "Accordian Boy" was permanently retired

New   Old

at the end of 1994 and will not be produced again. The 1994 production bears a special "Final Issue" backstamp and a small gold "Final Issue" commemorative tag.

☐ 185 ....5.00 to 6.00".........(CE)......❶ ....$550—750
☐ 185 ....5.00 to 6.00".........(CE)......❷ ....$375—450
☐ 185 ....5.00 to 6.00".........(CE)......❸ ....$300—325
☐ 185 ....5.00" ....(CE)......❹ ....$270—300
☐ 185 ....5.00" ....(CE)......❺ ....$240—270
☐ 185 ....5.00" ....(CE)......❻ ....$225—240
☐ 185 ....5.00" ....(CE)......❼ ....$200—225

FINAL ISSUE
1994

HUM 186 — Sweet Music

Originally modeled in 1947 by master sculptor Reinhold Unger. Many size variations. Was restyled slightly in the mid-1960s. Some old crown mark pieces have white slippers with blue-green stripes instead of the normal brownish color. This variation will usually sell for $1000 to $1500. Old name: "Playing To The Dance." One of several figurines that make up the Hummel orchestra. Retired in size 186 in July 2006 (CE) Closed Edition.

New   Old

☐ 186 ....5.00 to 5.50".........(CE)......❶ ....$1000—1500 (with striped slippers)
☐ 186 ....5.00 to 5.50".........(CE)......❶ ....$600—750
☐ 186 ....5.00 to 5.50".........(CE)......❷ ....$400—450
☐ 186 ....5.00 to 5.50".........(CE)......❸ ....$325—350
☐ 186 ....5.00" ....(CE)......❹ ....$300—325
☐ 186 ....5.00" ....(CE)......❺ ....$270—275
☐ 186 ....5.00" ....(CE)......❻ ....$265—270
☐ 186 ....5.00" ....(CE)......❼ ....$260—265
☐ 186 ....5.00" ....(CE)......❽ ....$259 (Closed Edition)
☐ 186/III ....13.00" ....(OE)......❽ $1550

☐ *All Black Lettering*

☐ *Dotted "i"s No Quotations*

☐ *Note Quotation Marks*

☐ *"Moon" Style*

☐ *Factory sample*

☐ *"Moon" Style*

☐ *"Moon" Style*

☐ *Rare factory sample*

HUM 187 — M.I. Hummel Plaques (In English)

There seems to have been an endless variety of plaques throughout the years, some for dealers and some for collectors. Originally modeled by master sculptor Reinhold Unger in 1947 and later restyled by Gerhard Skrobek in 1962. Two incised copyright dates have been used, 1947 and 1976. Current display plaques for collectors are

□ □ *Australian Dealer*

□ □

□ □

incised 187 A. At one time in recent years, dealers' names were printed on the plaques for Australian dealers only. Pictured here is only a small portion of the many variations issued. 187 (with 1947 copyright date) and 187 A (with 1976 copyright date) can both be found with TM 5. Retired from production in 1986, but put back into service in 1990 with new graphics, now listed as (CE) Closed Edition.

□ 187	5.50 x 4.00"	(CE)	❶	$1250—1600
□ 187	5.50 x 4.00"	(CE)	❷	$750—900
□ 187	5.50 x 4.00"	(CE)	❸	$500—600
□ 187	5.50 x 4.00"	(CE)	❹	$450—500
□ 187	5.50 x 4.00"	(CE)	❺	$175—225
□ 187A	5.50 x 4.00"	(CE)	❺	$175—225
□ 187A	5.50 x 4.00"	(CE)	❻	$150—175
□ 187A	5.50 x 4.00"	(CE)	❻	$115—120
□ 187A	5.50 x 4.00"	(CE)	❼	$110—115
□ 187A	5.50 x 4.00"	(CE)	❽	$100—115

HUM 187 (SPECIAL) — W.G.P. "Service" Plaque
This service plaque was first introduced in the late 1950s and has become a Goebel tradition. Each employee of W. Goebel Porzellanfabrik, regardless of his/her position or the department he/she is working in receives such a special plaque on the occasion of his/her 25th, 40th or 50th anniversary with Goebel. These special plaques normally sell for $1000–$2000 depending on the age, style, and condition of the plaque.

Special personalized plaques were made available to Goebel Collectors' Club local chapter members in 1984 for a limited time. It was necessary to belong to an officially authorized "local chapter" of the GCC. The plaque sold for $50. HUM 187 was also used for many other special occasions, such as Festivals, Expos, shows, conventions, etc. This 20th Anniversary plaque, to the right, sold for $125 in 1997.

188/I (TM 2)　　　　*188/0 (TM 6)*　　　　*188 4/0 (TM 7)*

HUM 188 — Celestial Musician

Originally molded by master sculptor Reinhold Unger in 1948, this figurine has never had a major restyling. Older models are slightly larger, have a bluish-green gown and an open quartered base. Newer models are slightly smaller, have a green gown and a closed flat base, and some have 1948 incised copyright date. According to factory information, this figurine was also sold in white overglaze finish at one time, but would now be considered extremely rare in that finish. A new smaller size was first released in 1983. Designed by master sculptor Gerhard Skrobek and Maria Mueller in 1982, this new size measures 5.50" and is incised 188/0 on the bottom. Original issue price was $80 in 1983. The older large size has been renumbered 188/1. A new miniature size figurine, 188 4/0 in a matte finish was put on the market in 1993 with suggested retail price of $90, an incised 1991 copyright date and a "First Issue 1993" decal. Large size (188/I) was (TW) "Temporarily Withdrawn" in January 1999. 188 4/0 was listed as (TW) "Temporarily Withdrawn" in June 2002.

☐ 188 4/0	3.125"	(CE)	❼	$135—140
☐ 188 4/0	3.125"	(**TW**)	❽	$130—135
☐ 188/0	5.50"	(CE)	❻	$285—290
☐ 188/0	5.50"	(CE)	❼	$280—285
☐ 188/0	5.50"	(**OE**)	❽	$279
☐ 188	7.00"	(CE)	❶	$1800—2000
☐ 188	7.00"	(CE)	❷	$900—1100
☐ 188	7.00"	(CE)	❸	$450—500
☐ 188	7.00"	(CE)	❹	$400—450
☐ 188	7.00"	(CE)	❺	$350—375
☐ 188	7.00"	(CE)	❻	$325—350
☐ 188/I	7.00"	(CE)	❻	$325—350
☐ 188/I	7.00"	(CE)	❼	$310—325
☐ 188/I	7.00"	(**CE**)	❽	$300—310

Incised "M.I. Hummel"

HUM 189 — Old Woman Knitting (CN)

This unusual piece was made as a sample only in 1948 by master sculptor Arthur Moeller and was not approved by the Siessen Convent for production. It was not considered typical of Sister M.I. Hummel's work, although it is an exact replica of one of her early sketches. This early sample does have the familiar "M.I. Hummel" signature and is part of the Robert L. Miller collection. Listed as a (CN) Closed Number on 18 February 1948 and will not be produced again. Often referred to as one of the "Mamas" and the "Papas." Several other examples have been found in recent years.

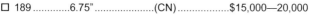

☐ 189 ....6.75" ....(CN) ....$15,000—20,000

Incised "M.I. Hummel"

HUM 190 — Old Woman Walking to Market (CN)

This unusual piece was made as a sample only in 1948 by master sculptor Arthur Moeller and was not approved by the Siessen Convent for production. It was not considered typical of Sister M.I. Hummel's work, although it is an exact replica of one of her early sketches. This early sample does have the familiar "M.I. Hummel" signature and is part of the Robert L. Miller collection. Listed as a (CN) Closed Number on 18 February 1948 and will not be produced again. Often referred to as one of the "Mamas" and the "Papas." Several other examples have been found in recent years.

☐ 190 ....6.75" ....(CN) ....$15,000—20,000

Old Postcard Drawing

Incised "M.I. Hummel"

HUM 191 — Old Man Walking to Market (CN)

This unusual piece was made as a sample only in 1948 by master sculptor Arthur Moeller and was not approved by the Siessen Convent for production. It was not considered typical of Sister M.I. Hummel's work, although it is an exact replica of one of her early sketches. This early sample does have the familiar "M.I. Hummel" signature and is part of the Robert L. Miller collection. Listed as a (CN) Closed Number on 18 February 1948 and will not be produced again. Often referred to as one of the "Mamas" and the "Papas." Several other examples have been found in recent years. The original drawing appeared on old German post card.

☐ 191 ....6.75" ....(CN) ....$15,000—20,000

.... HUM TERM ....

TERRA COTTA: A reddish clay used in an experimental fashion by artisans at the W. Goebel Porzellanfabrik. There are a few sample pieces of "M.I. Hummel" figurines that were produced with the terra cotta material. These terra cotta pieces have the look of the reddish-brown clay and were not painted.

Old style (TM 2)   New style (TM 3)

New   *Old*

HUM 192 — Candlelight, Candleholder

Originally modeled by master sculptor Reinhold Unger in 1948 with a long red ceramic candle. Later restyled by master sculptor Theo R. Menzenbach in 1958 with a short candleholder ending in angels hands. Both models have a receptical for holding a wax candle. Older models are slightly larger. Old name: "Carrier of Light." The incised copyright date on both models is 1948. Both long and short candle variations can be found with (TM 3) "stylized" trademarks. Listed as (TW) "Temporarily Withdrawn" in January 1999, but may be reinstated at some future date.

☐ 192....6.75 to 7.00" ...(CE)..... ❶ ...$1350—1800
☐ 192....6.75 to 7.00" ...(CE)..... ❷ ...$800—1000
☐ 192....6.75 to 7.00" ...(CE)..... ❸ ...$600—700
(Long candle)
☐ 192....6.75 to 7.00" ...(CE)..... ❸ ...$350—375
(Short candle)
☐ 192....6.75 to 7.00" ...(CE)..... ❹ ...$315—350
☐ 192....6.75 to 7.00" ...(CE)..... ❺ ...$290—315
☐ 192....6.75 to 7.00" ...(CE)..... ❻ ...$275—290
☐ 192....6.75 to 7.00" ...(**TW**)....❼ ...$270—275

HUM 193 — Angel Duet, Candleholder

First modeled by master sculptor Reinhold Unger in 1948 and later restyled by master sculptor Theo R. Menzenbach in 1958. Notice the position of angel's arm in rear view—this was changed by Menzenbach because he thought it would be easier for artists to paint—looks better and is a more natural position. Menzenbach began working at the Goebel factory in October 1948, at the age of 18. He left the factory in October 1961 to start his own business as a commercial artist. He is still living and resides in Germany, near Coburg. According to factory information, this figurine was also sold in white overglaze finish at one time—extremely rare. Also produced without holder for candle—see HUM 261. Listed as (TW) "Temporarily Withdrawn" in January 1999, but may be reinstated at some future date.

☐ 193.........5.00" ......(CE) ...... ❶ .....$1350—1800
☐ 193.........5.00" ......(CE) ...... ❷ .....$600—700
☐ 193.........5.00" ......(CE) ...... ❸ .....$325—400
☐ 193.........5.00" ......(CE) ...... ❹ .....$290—325
☐ 193.........5.00" ......(CE) ...... ❺ .....$265—290
☐ 193.........5.00" ......(CE) ...... ❻ .....$255—265
☐ 193.........5.00" ......(**TW**)...... ❼ .....$250—255

HUM 194 — Watchful Angel

Originally modeled by master sculptor Reinhold Unger in 1948 and later restyled by master sculptor Gerhard Skrobek in 1959. Older models are usually larger. Most models have an incised 1948 copyright date. Old name: "Angelic Care" or "Guardian Angel."

- ☐ 194...6.25 to 6.75" ..(CE)..❶ ..$1800—2100
- ☐ 194...6.25 to 6.75" ..(CE)..❷ ..$700—800
- ☐ 194...6.25 to 6.75" ..(CE)..❸ ..$500—600
- ☐ 194...6.25"..............(CE)..❹ .$425—500
- ☐ 194...6.25"..............(CE)..❺ .$415—425
- ☐ 194...6.25"..............(CE)..❻ .$410—415
- ☐ 194...6.25"..............(CE)..❼ .$400—410
- ☐ 194...6.25"..............(OE)..❽ ..$399

Full Bee (TM 2)   Three Line (TM 4)

HUM 195 — Barnyard Hero

First modeled by master sculptor Reinhold Unger in 1948. Originally made in one size only with the incised number 195. A smaller size was produced in the mid-1950s with the incised number 195 2/0. Both sizes have been restyled in recent years. Many size variations as well as variation in position of boy's hands in small size only: old model has one hand on each side of fence; new model, one hand on top of the other one. Most

195/I (TM 2)   195 2/0 (TM 4)

models have an incised 1948 copyright date. Large size (195/I) was listed as (TW) "Temporarily Withdrawn" in January 1999, but may be reinstated at some future date.

- ☐ 195 2/0 ....3.75 to 4.00".........(CE)......❷ ....$400—450
- ☐ 195 2/0 ....3.75 to 4.00".........(CE)......❸ ....$300—325
- ☐ 195 2/0 ....3.75 to 4.00".........(CE)......❹ ....$250—300
- ☐ 195 2/0 ....3.75 to 4.00".........(CE)......❺ ....$230—250
- ☐ 195 2/0 ....3.75 to 4.00".........(CE)......❻ ....$225—230
- ☐ 195 2/0 ....3.75 to 4.00".........(CE)......❼ ....$220—225
- ☐ 195 2/0 ....3.75 to 4.00".........(OE)......❽ $219
- ☐ 195/I ....5.50"...................(CE)......❷ .....$600—700
- ☐ 195/I ....5.50"...................(CE)......❸ .....$475—525
- ☐ 195/I ....5.50"...................(CE)......❹ .....$420—475
- ☐ 195/I ....5.50"...................(CE)......❺ .....$375—420
- ☐ 195/I ....5.50"...................(CE)......❻ .....$360—375
- ☐ 195/I ....5.50"...................(TW) .....❼ ....$350—360
- ☐ 195 ....5.75 to 6.00".........(CE)......❶ .....$1000—1200
- ☐ 195 ....5.75 to 6.00".........(CE)......❷ .....$650—750

196/I (TM 3)   *196/0 (TM 2)*

HUM 196 — Telling Her Secret

When first modeled in 1948 by master sculptor Reinhold Unger this figurine was produced in one size only with the incised number 196. A smaller size was issued in the mid-1950s with the incised number 196/0. Some older models have "0" size designator directly under the 196 rather than 196/0. At the same time, the large size was changed to 196/I. Slightly restyled in recent years. Most models have an incised 1948 copyright date. Old name: "The Secret." The girl on the right is the same as HUM 258. "Which Hand?" HUM 196/I (large size only) was (TW) "Temporarily Withdrawn" from production on 31 December 1984, but may be reinstated at some future date.

☐ 196/0	.........5.00 to 5.50"	.........(CE)	...... ❷	.......$650—750
☐ 196/0	.........5.00 to 5.50"	.........(CE)	...... ❸	.......$475—525
☐ 196/0	.........5.00 to 5.50"	.........(CE)	...... ❹	.......$425—475
☐ 196/0	.........5.00 to 5.50"	.........(CE)	...... ❺	.......$415—425
☐ 196/0	.........5.00 to 5.50"	.........(CE)	...... ❻	.......$410—415
☐ 196/0	.........5.00 to 5.50"	.........(CE)	...... ❼	.......$400—410
☐ 196/0	.........5.00 to 5.50"	.........(OE)	...... ❽	.......$399
☐ 196/I	.........6.50 to 6.75"	.........(CE)	...... ❷	.......$750—950
☐ 196/I	.........6.50 to 6.75"	.........(CE)	...... ❸	.....$500—550
☐ 196/I	.........6.50 to 6.75"	.........(CE)	...... ❹	.....$450—500
☐ 196/I	.........6.50 to 6.75"	.........(CE)	...... ❺	.......$425—450
☐ 196/I	.........6.50 to 6.75"	.........(TW)	...... ❻	.......$400—425
☐ 196	.............6.75"	.................(CE)	...... ❶	.......$1200—1500
☐ 196	.............6.75"	.................(CE)	...... ❷	.......$800—1000

197/I (TM 4)   *197 2/0 (TM 6)*

HUM 197 — Be Patient

When first modeled in 1948 by master sculptor Reinhold Unger this figurine was produced in one size only with the incised number 197. A smaller size was issued in the mid-1950s with the incised number 197 2/0. At the same time, the large size was changed to 197/I. Both sizes have been restyled with the new textured finish and usually have an incised 1948 copyright date. Old name: "Mother of Ducks." The large size 197/I was (TW) "Temporarily Withdrawn" from production in January 1999. New 3.25" size in 2005.

☐ 197 4/0	.......3.25"	....................(OE)	...... ❽	.......$109
☐ 197 2/0	.......4.25 to 4.50"	.........(CE)	...... ❷	.......$450—550
☐ 197 2/0	.......4.25 to 4.50"	.........(CE)	...... ❸	.......$325—375
☐ 197 2/0	.......4.25 to 4.50"	.........(CE)	...... ❹	.......$275—310

(prices continued on next page)

☐ 197 2/0 ......4.25 to 4.50" ....(CE)...... ❺ ...... $270—275
☐ 197 2/0 ......4.25 to 4.50" ....(CE)...... ❻ ...... $265—270
☐ 197 2/0 ......4.25 to 4.50" ....(CE)...... ❼ ...... $260—265
☐ 197 2/0 ......4.25 to 4.50" ....(**OE**)...... ❽ $259
☐ 197/I ....6.00 to 6.25" ....(CE)...... ❷ ...... $500—650
☐ 197/I ....6.00 to 6.25" ....(CE)...... ❸ ...... $425—475
☐ 197/I ....6.00 to 6.25" ....(CE)...... ❹ ...... $360—425
☐ 197/I ....6.00 to 6.25" ....(CE)...... ❺ ...... $350—360
☐ 197/I ....6.00 to 6.25" ....(CE)...... ❻ ...... $340—350
☐ 197/I ....6.00 to 6.25" ....(**TW**) ...... ❼ ...... $330—340
☐ 197 ....6.25" ....(CE)...... ❶ ...... $800—1000
☐ 197 ....6.25" ....(CE)...... ❷ ...... $550—700

HUM 198 — Home From Market

When first modeled in 1948 by master sculptor Arthur Moeller this figurine was produced in one size only with the incised number 198. A smaller size was issued in the mid-1950s with the incised number 198 2/0. At the same time, the large size was changed to 198/I. Many size variations with older models slightly larger

(TM 2)   198/I   (TM 3)   (TM 4)   198 2/0   (TM 7)

than new. Both sizes have been restyled and now have an incised 1948 copyright date. The small size 198 2/0 has been slightly restyled in recent years, with new hair style and smaller tie. A small size 4.50" has also been found with incised number 198 only (no size designator). The large size (198/I) was listed as (TW) "Temporarily Withdrawn" in January 1999, but may be reinstated at some future date.

☐ 198 ....4.50" ....(CE)...... ❷ ...... $375—400
☐ 198 2/0 ......4.50 to 4.75" ....(CE)...... ❷ ...... $325—375
☐ 198 2/0 ......4.50 to 4.75" ....(CE)...... ❸ ...... $250—275
☐ 198 2/0 ......4.50 to 4.75" ....(CE)...... ❹ ...... $215—250
☐ 198 2/0 ......4.50 to 4.75" ....(CE)...... ❺ ...... $210—215
☐ 198 2/0 ......4.50 to 4.75" ....(CE)...... ❻ ...... $205—210
☐ 198 2/0 ......4.50 to 4.75" ....(CE)...... ❼ ...... $200—205
☐ 198 2/0 ......4.50 to 4.75" ....(**OE**)...... ❽ $199
☐ 198/I ....5.50" ....(CE)...... ❷ ...... $400—500
☐ 198/I ....5.50" ....(CE)...... ❸ ...... $325—375
☐ 198/I ....5.50" ....(CE)...... ❹ ...... $275—325
☐ 198/I ....5.50" ....(CE)...... ❺ ...... $260—275
☐ 198/I ....5.50" ....(CE)...... ❻ ...... $250—260
☐ 198/I ....5.50" ....(**TW**) ...... ❼ ...... $240—245
☐ 198 ....5.75 to 6.00" ....(CE)...... ❶ ...... $650—800
☐ 198 ....5.75 to 6.00" ....(CE)...... ❷ ...... $450—550

199 (TM 1)   Old style   (TM 3)   199/I (TM 4)   New style   (TM 4)

HUM 199 — Feeding Time

When first modeled in 1948 by master sculptor Arthur Moeller this figurine was produced in one size only with the incised number 199. A smaller size was issued in the
mid-1950s with the incised number 199/0. At the same time, the large size was changed
to 199/I. Both sizes were restyled in the mid-1960s by master sculptor Gerhard
Skrobek. The girl is blonde on older figurines—changed to dark hair and new facial features on newer ones. Note position of girl's hand under bowl in new style figurines. All
small size and the new large size figurines have an incised 1948 copyright date. Small
size (199/0) sometimes found with old style head and new style hand under bowl. Large
size (199/I) was listed as (TW) "Temporarily Withdrawn" in January 1999, but may be
reinstated at some future date.

☐	199/0	4.25 to 4.50"	(CE)	❷	$425—500
☐	199/0	4.25 to 4.50"	(CE)	❸	$325—375
☐	100/0	4.25 to 4.50"	(CE)	❹	$275—325
☐	199/0	4.25 to 4.50"	(CE)	❺	$270—275
☐	199/0	4.25 to 4.50"	(CE)	❻	$265—2760
☐	199/0	4.25 to 4.50"	(CE)	❼	$260—265
☐	199/0	4.25 to 4.50"	(OE)	❽	$259
☐	199/I	5.50 to 5.75"	(CE)	❷	$475—575
☐	199/I	5.50 to 5.75"	(CE)	❸	$425—475
☐	199/I	5.50 to 5.75"	(CE)	❹	$375—425
☐	199/I	5.50 to 5.75"	(CE)	❺	$370—375
☐	199/I	5.50 to 5.75"	(CE)	❻	$360—365
☐	199/I	5.50 to 5.75"	(CE)	❼	$360—365
☐	199/I	5.50 to 5.75"	(TW)	❽	$350—360
☐	199	5.75"	(CE)	❶	$800—1000
☐	199	5.75"	(CE)	❷	$525—625

.... HUM TERM ....

FULL BEE: The term "Full Bee" refers to the trademark used by the Goebel Co.
from 1950 to 1957. Early usage of this trademark was incised into the material.
Later versions of the "full bee" were stamped onto the material.

200/I (TM 2)   *200/0 (TM 2)*

HUM 200 — Little Goat Herder
When first modeled in 1948 by master sculptor Arthur Moeller this figurine was made in one size only with the incised number 200. A smaller size was issued in the mid-1950s with the incised number 200/0. At the same time, the large size was changed to 200/I. Both sizes have been restyled with only minor changes. Older models have a blade of grass between hind legs of the small goat. Newer models do not. Newer models have an incised 1948 copyright date. Older pieces slightly larger. Old name: "Goat Boy." Some "full bee" (TM 2) trademark examples in the small size (200/0) version have been found with a slight variation in the signature—the initials "M.I." are directly above the "Hummel."

- ☐ 200/0 ....4.50 to 4.75".........(CE)......❷ ....$425—500
- ☐ 200/0 ....4.50 to 4.75".........(CE)......❸ ....$325—350
- ☐ 200/0 ....4.50 to 4.75".........(CE)......❹ ....$280—325
- ☐ 200/0 ....4.50 to 4.75".........(CE)......❺ ....$270—280
- ☐ 200/0 ....4.50 to 4.75".........(CE)......❻ ....$265—270
- ☐ 200/0 ....4.50 to 4.75".........(CE)......❼ ....$260—265
- ☐ 200/0 ....4.50 to 4.75".........(**OE**)......❽ $259
- ☐ 200/I ....5.00 to 5.50".........(CE)......❷ ....$450—550
- ☐ 200/I ....5.00 to 5.50".........(CE)......❸ ....$350—400
- ☐ 200/I ....5.00 to 5.50".........(CE)......❹ ....$320—350
- ☐ 200/I ....5.00 to 5.50".........(CE)......❺ ....$310—320
- ☐ 200/I ....5.00 to 5.50".........(CE)......❻ ....$305—310
- ☐ 200/I ....5.00 to 5.50".........(CE)......❼ ....$300—305
- ☐ 200/I ....5.00 to 5.50".........(**TW**) .....❽ ....$290—300
- ☐ 200 ....5.50 to 5.75".........(CE)......❶ ....$650—850
- ☐ 200 ....5.50 to 5.75".........(CE)......❷ ....$500—600

201/I (TM 3)   *201 2/0 (TM 4)*

HUM 201 — Retreat To Safety

When first modeled in 1948 by master sculptor Reinhold Unger this figurine was produced in one size only with the incised number 201. A smaller size was issued in the mid-1950s with the incised number 201 2/0. At the same time, the large size was changed to 201/I. Both sizes have been restyled in recent years. Many size variations as well as variation in the position of boy's hands in small size only: old model has one hand on each side of fence; new model, one hand on top of the other one. Most models have an incised 1948 copyright date. Old name: "Afraid." Large size (201/I) was listed as (TW) "Temporarily Withdrawn" in January 1999, but may be reinstated at some future date.

☐ 201 2/0 ....3.75 to 4.00" ....(CE)...... ❷ ....$400—450
☐ 201 2/0 ....3.75 to 4.00" ....(CE)...... ❸ ....$300—325
☐ 201 2/0 ....3.75 to 4.00" ....(CE)...... ❹ ....$250—300
☐ 201 2/0 ....3.75 to 4.00" ....(CE)...... ❺ ....$230—240
☐ 201 2/0 ....3.75 to 4.00" ....(CE)...... ❻ ....$225—230
☐ 201 2/0 ....3.75 to 4.00" ....(CE)...... ❼ ....$220—225
☐ 201 2/0 ....3.75 to 4.00" ....(**OE**)...... ❽ $219
☐ 201/I ....5.50 to 5.75" ....(CE)...... ❷ ....$600—700
☐ 201/I ....5.50 to 5.75" ....(CE)...... ❸ ....$475—525
☐ 201/I ....5.50 to 5.75" ....(CE)...... ❹ ....$420—475
☐ 201/I ....5.50 to 5.75" ....(CE)...... ❺ ....$375—420
☐ 201/I ....5.50 to 5.75" ....(CE)...... ❻ ....$360—375
☐ 201/I ....5.50 to 5.75" ....(**TW**)...... ❼ ....$350—360
☐ 201 ....5.75 to 6.00" ....(CE)...... ❶ ....$1000—1200
☐ 201 ....5.75 to 6.00" ....(CE)...... ❷ ....$650—750

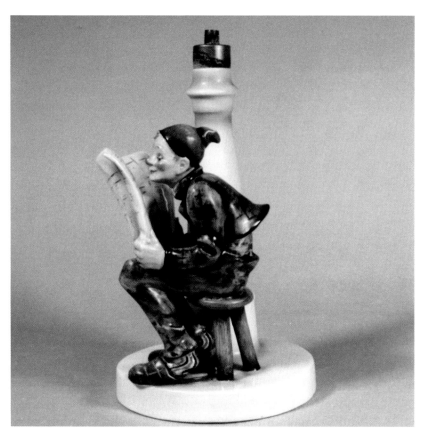

Miller collection

HUM 202 — Old Man Reading Newspaper, Table Lamp (CN)
This unusual piece was made as a sample only in 1948 by master sculptor Arthur Moeller and was not approved by the Siessen Convent for production. It was not considered typical of Sister M.I. Hummel's work, although it is an exact replica of one of her early sketches. Same figure as HUM 181 except on lamp base. Listed as a (CN) Closed Number on 18 August 1948.

☐ 202 ....8.25" ....(CN).............$15,000—20,000

.... HUM TERM ....

DOUGHNUT BASE: A term used to describe the raised circular support on the underside of a figurine. Many figurine bases with a circle inside the regular circular base gave rise to the term, but has now been used to describe many bases with the circular support on the underside.

203/I (TM 3)   *203 2/0 (One bare foot)*   *203 2/0 (Two shoes)*

HUM 203 — Signs of Spring (CE)

When first modeled in 1948 by master sculptor Arthur Moeller this figurine was produced in one size only with the incised number 203. A smaller size was issued in the mid-1950s with the incised number 203 2/0. At the same time, the large size was changed to 203/I. Many size variations. At one time, small size only, was made with the girl wearing both shoes. Full bee trademark pieces found both with or without shoe. Newer models have an incised 1948 copyright date. Old name: "Scandal." "Two shoe" variety considered rare. Both sizes of "Signs of Spring" were permanently retired by Goebel in the fall of 1990 and will not be produced again. The 1990 retail list price was $120 for the small size and $155 for the large.

□ 203 2/0 ......4.00" ....(CE)......❷ ......$1200—1500 (with two shoes)
□ 203 2/0 ......4.00" ....(CE)......❷ ......$425—500
□ 203 2/0 ......4.00" ....(CE)......❸ ......$350—400
□ 203 2/0 ......4.00" ....(CE)......❹ ......$275—350
□ 203 2/0 ......4.00" ....(CE)......❺ ......$250—275
□ 203 2/0 ......4.00" ....(CE)......❻ ......$225—250
□ 203/I ....5.00 to 5.50" ....(CE)......❷ ......$500—600
□ 203/I ....5.00 to 5.50" ....(CE)......❸ ......$400—450
□ 203/I ....5.00 to 5.50" ....(CE)......❹ ......$350—400
□ 203/I ....5.00 to 5.50" ....(CE)......❺ ......$300—325
□ 203/I ....5.00 to 5.50" ....(CE)......❻ ......$275—300
□ 203 ....5.25" ....(CE)......❶ ......$750—1000
□ 203 ....5.25" ....(CE)......❷ ......$550—650

FINAL ISSUE
1990

NOTE: See RARE VARIATIONS in the back of book for an unusual variation of this figurine.

Old style (TM 2)   *New style (TM 5)*

HUM 204 — Weary Wanderer

Many size variations. Most models have 1949 as the incised copyright date. Old name: "Tired Little Traveler." Has been restyled with the new textured finish. The word "Lauterbach" on the back of figurine is the name of a village used in an old German song. The first model was made by master sculptor Reinhold Unger in 1949. Occasionally found with blue eyes. This variation would command a premium of $2000 to $3000, if authenticated. "Weary Wanderer" was (TW) "Temporarily Withdrawn" from production in January 1999, but may be reinstated at some future date.

☐ 204 ....5.50 to 6.00".........(CE)......❶ ......$700—900
☐ 204 ....5.50 to 6.00".........(CE)......❷ ......$500—600
☐ 204 ....5.50 to 6.00".........(CE)......❸ ......$375—425
☐ 204 ....5.50 to 6.00".........(CE)......❹ ......$325—375
☐ 204 ....5.50 to 6.00".........(CE)......❺ ......$300—325
☐ 204 ....5.50 to 6.00".........(CE)......❻ ......$295—300
☐ 204 ....5.50 to 6.00".........(**TW**) ......❼ ......$280—290

Rear view

HUM 205 —
M.I. Hummel
Dealer's Plaque
(in German) (CE)

This German dealer's plaque was first modeled by master sculptor Reinhold Unger in 1949. There are three color variations of lettering: all black lettering, black and red combination, and all black except the capital letters O, H and F in red lettering. Usually has an incised crown mark in addition to other trademarks. The all-black variety usually has a "Made in U.S. Zone, Germany" stamped on bottom. Listed in factory records as a (CE) Closed Edition on 18 June 1949 although it is found with the stylized trademark (in addition to the crown), indicating they were painted at a later date.

- ☐ 205 ....5.50 x 4.25" ....(CE).......❶ ......$1400—1700
- ☐ 205 ....5.50 x 4.25" ....(CE).......❷ ......$1000—1200
- ☐ 205 ....5.50 x 4.25" ....(CE).......❸ ......$850—1000

Crown (TM 1)   *Full Bee (TM 2)*   *Current (TM 6)*

HUM 206 — Holy Water Font, Angel Cloud

This holy water font was originally modeled by master sculptor Reinhold Unger in 1949 but has been restyled several times. At least three different variations. Early models do not have rim on back side of bowl. Also color variations on lip of water bowl. Has been considered rare in the older trademarks but was put back into current production in 1978 and can now be found with 5, 6 and 7 trademarks at more reasonable prices. Newer models have an incised 1949 copyright date. Listed as (TW) "Temporarily Withdrawn" in January 1999.

- ☐ 206 ....3.25 x 4.75" ....(CE).......❶ ......$350—500
- ☐ 206 ....3.25 x 4.75" ....(CE).......❷ ......$250—350
- ☐ 206 ....3.25 x 4.75" ....(CE).......❸ ......$200—250
- ☐ 206 ....3.25 x 4.75" ....(CE).......❹ ......$80—90
- ☐ 206 ....3.25 x 4.75" ....(CE).......❺ ......$75—80
- ☐ 206 ....3.25 x 4.75" ....(CE).......❻ ......$70—75
- ☐ 206 ....3.25 x 4.75" ....(TW).......❼ ......$60—62

HUM 207 — Holy Water Font, Heavenly Angel

This holy water font was originally modeled by master sculptor Reinhold Unger in 1949 and is the highest numbered piece with the crown trademark. Older models have a hole on the back for hanging while the newer models have a visible hole on the front. Early models do not have rim on the back side of bowl. Newer models have an incised 1949 copyright date. The "Heavenly Angel" motif was used on the First Annual Plate HUM 264 in 1971.

Newer style   *Old style*

☐	207	3.00 x 5.00"	(CE)	❶	$400—500
☐	207	3.00 x 5.00"	(CE)	❷	$150—175
☐	207	3.00 x 5.00"	(CE)	❸	$100—125
☐	207	3.00 x 5.00"	(CE)	❹	$85—90
☐	207	3.00 x 5.00"	(CE)	❺	$80—85
☐	207	3.00 x 5.00"	(CE)	❻	$75—80
☐	207	3.00 x 5.00"	(CE)	❼	$70—75
☐	207	3.00 x 5.00"	(OE)	❽	$69.50

Old style (TM 2)   *Newer style (TM 3)*

HUM 208 — M.I. Hummel Dealer's Plaque (In French) (CE)

Originally modeled in 1949 by master sculptor Reinhold Unger. Two known variations. Made with dotted "i" and without quotation marks on Hummel. Newer model has quotation marks: "HUMMEL" + "Reg. trademark."

☐	208	5.50 x 4.00"	(CE)	❷	$4000—6000
☐	208	5.50 x 4.00"	(CE)	❸	$3000—4000

171

HUM 209 — M.I. Hummel Dealer's Plaque (In Swedish) (CE)
This extremely rare plaque was first modeled in 1949 by master sculptor Reinhold Unger and was apparently issued in extremely limited quantities. Some have sold for over $7000.

☐ 209 ....5.50 x 4.00" ....(CE)......❷ ....$4000—6000

HUM 210 — M.I. Hummel Dealer's Plaque (Schmid Bros.) (CE)
Normal dealers's plaque in English with "SCHMID BROS. INC. BOSTON" embossed on side of satchel of "Merry Wanderer." This extremely rare plaque was first modeled in 1950 by master sculptor Reinhold Unger. Also made with dotted "i" and without quotation marks. Very few are known to exist. Schmid Bros. was one of the early importers of "M.I. Hummel" figurines in 1935.

☐ 210 ....5.50 x 4.00" ....(CE)......❷ ....$20,000—25,000

Unpainted sample

HUM 211 — M.I. Hummel Dealer's Plaque (in English) (CE)

This is probably the most rare of all "M.I. Hummel" dealer's plaques. The only known painted example was located in 1975 by Major Larry Spohn and his wife Anne while they were living in Germany, and is now in the Robert L. Miller collection. All the lettering on this plaque is in lower case and the word "Oeslau" is used as the location of W. Goebel Porzellanfabrik. Modeled in 1950 by master sculptor Reinhold Unger. The exact purpose or reason for designing this plaque still remains a mystery today. Note quotation marks (",") around "Hummel" on white unpainted sample.

☐ 211 ....5.50 x 4.00" ....(CE)....... ❷ ......$20,000—25,000

HUM 212 — Orchestra (CN)

Most notes from the Goebel factory state: "No information available" on this number. However, one old list indicates "Orchestra A-F" and the date "13 May 51." This is possibly a number assigned to a Hummel orchestra as a set, such as HUM 214 "Hummel Nativity Set". Another note states: "Modeled by Arthur Moeller in 1951."

☐ 212 ....(CN).....................

HUM 213 — M.I. Hummel Dealer's Plaque (in Spanish) (CE)

This Spanish dealer's plaque was first modeled in 1951 by master sculptor Reinhold Unger and apparently only a very limited number were produced. Considered extremely rare.

☐ 213 ....5.75 x 4.25" ....(CE)....... ❷ ......$8000—10,000

HUM 214 — Nativity Set with Wooden Stable

This set was modeled by master sculptor Reinhold Unger in 1951. First produced and sold in 1952. Normally sold as a set but is also available in individual pieces. At one time this set was produced and sold in white overglaze finish but is no longer sold this way. The white overglaze finish is considered rare and usually brings a premium. Early production of HUM 214 A (Virgin Mary and Infant Jesus) was made in one piece. Because of production problems, it was later produced as two separate pieces, both with the same number (214 A) incised on the bottom of each piece. The one-piece unit was sold in white overglaze finish as well as full color finish and both are considered rare today. Two different styles of lambs (HUM 214/O) have been used with the Nativity sets—note variations in photo. Some Nativity set pieces have an incised 1951 copyright date. HUM 214/C, 214/D, 214/E and 214/H are not always included in sets and are considered "optional" pieces. The wooden stable is usually sold separately. The sixteenth piece, "Flying Angel" HUM 366, was added to the set in 1963. Goebel also produces three different camels to match this set which do not have the "M.I. Hummel" signature since they were not designed by Sister Hummel. In 1985 the "Infant Jesus" (214/A) was renumbered to 214 A/K which is now incised on the bottom of this piece only. The "K" refers to the German word "Kinder" which means child in English. New productions of the HUM 214 nativity set are now being numbered with (/I) size designator: Example: 214/A now 214/A/I. This nativity set was also produced in terra cotta finish—probably experimentally only.

214/A	214/A/I	Virgin Mary and Infant Jesus (one piece-CE)
214/A	214/A/I	Virgin Mary
214/A (or 214 A/K)	214/A/K/I	Infant Jesus
214/B	214/B/I	Joseph
214/C	214/C/I	Angel standing, "Good Night"
214/D	214/D/I	Angel kneeling, "Angel Serenade"
214/E	214/E/I	We Congratulate
214/F	214/F/I	Shepherd standing with sheep
214/G	214/G/I	Shepherd kneeling
214/H	214/H/I	Shepherd Boy, kneeling with flute "Little Tooter"
214/J	214/J/I	Donkey
214/K	214/K/I	Ox (cow)
214/L	214/L/I	Moorish king, standing
214/M	214/M/I	King, kneeling on one knee
214/N	214/N/I	King, kneeling with cash-box
214/O	214/O/I	Lamb
366	366/I	Flying Angel

New Style　　　　*Rare Old Style*

Nativity set in color

Discontinued white nativity set

			COLOR	WHITE
☐ 214A..........1 PIECE 6.50" ..(CE) ......❷........☐	$2000—2500	......☐ $2500—3000
☐ 214A..........6.25 to 6.50" ....(CE) ......❷........☐	$300—400	..........☐ $395—495
☐ 214A..........6.25 to 6.50" ....(CE) ......❸........☐	$250—285	..........☐ $320—395
☐ 214A..........6.25 to 6.50" ....(CE) ......❹........☐	$230—250	..........☐ $245—320
☐ 214A..........6.25 to 6.50" ....(CE) ......❺........☐	$225—230	..........☐ $195—220
☐ 214A..........6.25 to 6.50" ....(CE) ......❻........☐	$220—225	..........☐ $195—220
☐ 214A/I........6.25 to 6.50" ....(CE) ......❼........☐	$220—225	.... —
☐ 214A/M/I....6.25 to 6.50" ......(OE) ......❽........☐	$219	.... —

					COLOR	WHITE
☐ 214A	1.50 x 3.50"	(CE)	❷	☐	$115—135	☐ $210—260
☐ 214A	1.50 x 3.50"	(CE)	❸	☐	$110—115	☐ $160—210
☐ 214A	1.50 x 3.50"	(CE)	❹	☐	$100—110	☐ $85—110
☐ 214A	1.50 x 3.50"	(CE)	❺	☐	$99—100	☐ $60—70
☐ 214A/K	1.50 x 3.50"	(CE)	❻	☐	$99—100	☐ $60—70
☐ 214A/K/I	1.50 x 3.50"	(CE)	❼	☐	$99—100	—
☐ 214A/K/I	1.50 x 3.50"	(OE)	❽	☐	$99	—
☐ 214B	7.50"	(CE)	❷	☐	$300—400	☐ $345—420
☐ 214B	7.50"	(CE)	❸	☐	$250—285	☐ $270—345
☐ 214B	7.50"	(CE)	❹	☐	$230—250	☐ $220—270
☐ 214B	7.50"	(CE)	❺	☐	$225—230	☐ $170—195
☐ 214B	7.50"	(CE)	❻	☐	$225—230	☐ $145—170
☐ 214B/I	7.50"	(CE)	❼	☐	$220—225	—
☐ 214B/I	7.50"	(OE)	❽	☐	$219	—
☐ 214C	3.50"	(CE)	❷	☐	$160—200	☐ $365—415
☐ 214C	3.50"	(CE)	❸	☐	$130—150	☐ $315—365
☐ 214C	3.50"	(CE)	❹	☐	$125—130	☐ $265—315
☐ 214C	3.50"	(CE)	❺	☐	$120—125	— —
☐ 214C	3.50"	(CE)	❻	☐	$120—125	— —
☐ 214C/I	3.50"	(CE)	❼	☐	$119—120	—
☐ 214C/I	3.50"	(OE)	❽	☐	$119	—
☐ 214D	3.00"	(CE)	❷	☐	$160—200	☐ $240—290
☐ 214D	3.00"	(CE)	❸	☐	$130—150	☐ $215—240
☐ 214D	3.00"	(CE)	❹	☐	$125—130	☐ $165—215
☐ 214D	3.00"	(CE)	❺	☐	$120—125	— —
☐ 214D	3.00"	(CE)	❻	☐	$120—125	— —
☐ 214D/I	3.00"	(CE)	❼	☐	$119—120	—
☐ 214D/I	3.00"	(OE)	❽	☐	$119	—
☐ 214E	3.75"	(CE)	❷	☐	$320—390	☐ $395—470
☐ 214E	3.75"	(CE)	❸	☐	$250—285	☐ $320—395
☐ 214E	3.75"	(CE)	❹	☐	$215—250	☐ $270—320
☐ 214E	3.75"	(CE)	❺	☐	$210—215	— —
☐ 214E	3.75"	(CE)	❻	☐	$205—210	— —
☐ 214E/I	3.75"	(CE)	❼	☐	$200—205	—
☐ 214E/I	3.75"	(OE)	❽	☐	$199	—
☐ 214F	7.00"	(CE)	❷	☐	$340—415	☐ $370—470
☐ 214F	7.00"	(CE)	❸	☐	$270—310	☐ $270—370
☐ 214F	7.00"	(CE)	❹	☐	$230—270	☐ $220—270
☐ 214F	7.00"	(CE)	❺	☐	$225—230	— —
☐ 214F	7.00"	(CE)	❻	☐	$225—230	— —
☐ 214F/I	7.00"	(CE)	❼	☐	$220—225	—
☐ 214F/I	7.00"	(OE)	❽	☐	$219	—
☐ 214G	5.00"	(CE)	❷	☐	$255—310	☐ $270—320
☐ 214G	5.00"	(CE)	❸	☐	$200—225	☐ $220—270
☐ 214G	5.00"	(CE)	❹	☐	$195—200	☐ $170—220

(prices continued on next page)

□ 214G ....5.00".................(CE) .....❺........□ $190—195 .... — —
□ 214G ....5.00".................(CE) .....❻........□ $185—190 .... — —
□ 214G/I ....5.00" ....(CE) .....❼........□ $180—185 .... —
□ 214G/I ....5.00" ....(OE) .....❽........□ $179 .... —
□ 214H ......3.75 to 4.00" ......(CE) ......❷........□ $230—280 ....□ $270—320
□ 214H ......3.75 to 4.00" ......(CE) ......❸........□ $200—230 ....□ $220—270
□ 214H ......3.75 to 4.00" .....(CE) ......❹........□ $195—200 ....□ $170—220
□ 214H ......3.75 to 4.00" ......(CE) ......❺........□ $190—195 .... — —
□ 214H ......3.75 to 4.00" ......(CE) ......❻........□ $185—190 .... — —
□ 214H/I ...3.75 to 4.00" ......(CE) ......❼........□ $180—185 .... —
□ 214H/I ...3.75 to 4.00" ......(OE) .....❽........□ $179 .... —
□ 214J.......5.00".................(CE) .....❷........□ $130—160 ....□ $180—255
□ 214J.......5.00".................(CE) .....❸........□ $115—120 ....□ $155—180
□ 214J.......5.00".................(CE) .....❹........□ $110—115 ....□ $130—155
□ 214J.......5.00".................(CE) .....❺........□ $105—110 .... — —
□ 214J.......5.00".................(CE) .....❻........□ $100—105 .... — —
□ 214J/I .....5.00".................(CE) .....❼........□ $99—100 .... —
□ 214J/I .....5.00".................(OE) .....❽........□ $99 .... —
□ 214K ......3.50 to 6.25" ....(CE) .....❷........□ $130—160 ....□ $180—255
□ 214K ......3.50 to 6.25" ....(CE) .....❸........□ $115—120 ....□ $155—180
□ 214K ......3.50 to 6.25" ....(CE) .....❹........□ $110—115 ....□ $130—155
□ 214K ......3.50 to 6.25" ....(CE) .....❺........□ $105—110 .... — —
□ 214K ......3.50 to 6.25" ....(CE) .....❻........□ $100—105 .... — —
□ 214K/I ....3.50 to 6.25" ....(CE) .....❼........□ $99—100 .... —
□ 214K/I ....3.50 to 6.25" ....(OE) .....❽........□ $99 .... —
□ 214L........8.00 to 8.25" ....(CE) .....❷........□ $340—415 ....□ $375—475
□ 214L........8.00 to 8.25" ....(CE) .....❸........□ $270—310 ....□ $275—375
□ 214L........8.00 to 8.25" ....(CE) .....❹........□ $230—270 ....□ $225—275
□ 214L........8.00 to 8.25" ......(CE) .....❺........□ $225—230 .... — —
□ 214L........8.00 to 8.25" ....(CE) .....❻........□ $225—230 .... — —
□ 214L/I.....8.00 to 8.25" ....(CE) .....❼........□ $220—225 .... —
□ 214L/I.....8.00 to 8.25" ....(OE) .....❽........□ $219 .... —
□ 214M ......5.50"..................(CE) .....❷........□ $315—415 ....□ $375—475
□ 214M ......5.50"..................(CE) .....❸........□ $265—300 ....□ $275—375
□ 214M ......5.50"..................(CE) .....❹........□ $235—265 ....□ $225—275
□ 214M ......5.50"..................(CE) .....❺........□ $230—235 .... — —
□ 214M ......5.50"..................(CE) .....❻........□ $225—230 .... — —
□ 214M/I ...5.50"..................(CE) .....❼........□ $220—225 .... —
□ 214M/I ...5.50"..................(OE) .....❽........□ $219 .... —
□ 214N ......5.50"..................(CE) .....❷........□ $315—385 ....□ $375—475
□ 214N ......5.50"..................(CE) .....❸........□ $245—280 ....□ $275—375
□ 214N ......5.50"..................(CE) .....❹........□ $235—245 ....□ $225—275
□ 214N ......5.50"..................(CE) .....❺........□ $230—235 .... — —
□ 214N ......5.50"..................(CE) .....❻........□ $225—230 .... — —
□ 214N/I ....5.50"..................(CE) .....❼........□ $220—225 .... —

(prices continued on next page)

☐ 214N/I ....5.50" ....(OE) ..... ❽ .... ☐ $219 .... —
☐ 214O ......1.75 x 2.50" ....(CE) ..... ❷ ..... ☐ $50—55 .... ☐ $105—130
☐ 214O ......1.75 x 2.50" ....(CE) ..... ❸ ..... ☐ $45—50 .... ☐ $80—105
☐ 214O ......1.75 x 2.50" ....(CE) ..... ❹ ..... ☐ $40—45 .... ☐ $55—70
☐ 214O ......1.75 x 2.50" ....(CE) ..... ❺ ..... ☐ $35—40 .... — —
☐ 214O ......1.75 x 2.50" ....(CE) ..... ❻ ..... ☐ $30—35 .... — —
☐ 214O/I ....1.75 x 2.50" ....(CE) ..... ❼ ..... ☐ $29—30 .... —
☐ 214O/I ....1.75 x 2.50" ....(OE) ..... ❽ ..... ☐ $29 .... —
☐ 366..........3.50" ....(CE) ..... ❹ ..... ☐ $225—275 .... ☐ $225—275
☐ 366..........3.50" ....(CE) ..... ❺ ..... ☐ $190—200 .... ☐ $150—175
☐ 366..........3.50" ....(CE) ..... ❻ ..... ☐ $185—190 .... ☐ $150—175
☐ 366/I.......3.50" ....(CE) ..... ❼ ..... ☐ $180—185 .... —
☐ 366/I.......3.50" ....(OE) ..... ❽ ..... ☐ $179 .... —

☐ Wooden stable, to fit 12–16 piece sets ....Current retail $225
☐ Wooden stable, to fit 3 piece sets ....Current retail $100

Old   (Color)   New

Old   (White)   New

A new small size Nativity set was first announced in 1988. Three pieces only were released—Mary, Infant Jesus and Joseph—and sold as a set for $185. In 1989 four other pieces were released—the donkey, ox, lamb and Flying Angel. In 1990 the three Kings were released. In 1991 the two "Shepherds" and "Little Tooter" were released. "Mary", "Joseph" and "Jesus" are also avaialble in this size in white. The small size "Nativity Set" was permanently retired in 2005.

FINAL ISSUE
2005

☐ 214 A/M/0 ...Mary ....5.25" ....(CE)..........❻ ....$170—175
☐ 214 A/M/0 ...Mary ....5.25" ....(CE)..........❼ ....$165—170
☐ 214 A/M/0 ...Mary ....5.25" ....(CE)..........❽ $165
☐ 214 A/K/0....Infant Jesus................2.875" .....(CE)..........❻ ....$65—70
☐ 214 A/K/0....Infant Jesus................2.875" .....(CE)..........❼ ....$60—65

(prices continued on next page)

☐ 214 A/K/0....Infant Jesus................2.875".....(OE)..........❽...........$57.50

☐ 214 B/0.......Joseph.......................6.125".....(CE)..........❻...........$170—175

☐ 214 B/0.......Joseph.......................6.125".....(CE)..........❼...........$165—170

☐ 214 B/0.......Joseph.......................6.125".....(CE)..........❽...........$165

☐ 214 D/0.......Angel Serenade.........2.875".....(CE)..........❼—❽....$95

☐ 366/0..........Flying Angel...............2.875".....(CE)..........❻...........$135—140

☐ 366/0..........Flying Angel...............2.875".....(CE)..........❼...........$130—135

☐ 366/0..........Flying Angel................................**(OE)**..........❽...........$132.50

☐ 214 J/0........Donkey.....................3.875".....(CE)..........❻...........$70—75

☐ 214 J/0........Donkey.....................3.875".....(CE)..........❼...........$65—70

☐ 214 J/0........Donkey................................(CE)..........❽...........$62.50

☐ 214 K/0.......Ox.............................2.75".......(CE)..........❻...........$70—75

☐ 214 K/0.......Ox.............................2.75".......(CE)..........❼...........$65—70

☐ 214 K/0.......Ox...(CE)..........❽...........$62.50

☐ 214 O/0.......Lamb.........................1.50".......(CE)..........❻...........$30—35

☐ 214 O/0.......Lamb.........................1.50".......(CE)..........❼...........$28—30

☐ 214 O/0.......Lamb.......................................(CE)..........❽...........$27.50

☐ 214 L/0.......King Standing.............6.25".......(CE)..........❻...........$190—195

☐ 214 L/0.......King Standing.............6.25".......(CE)..........❼...........$185—190

☐ 214 L/0.......King Standing.........................(CE)..........❽...........$185

☐ 214 M/0......King on one knee.......4.25".......(CE)..........❻...........$180—185

☐ 214 M/0......King on one knee.......4.25".......(CE)..........❼...........$175—180

☐ 214 M/0......King on one knee....................(CE)..........❽...........$175

☐ 214 N/0.......King on two knees.....4.50".......(CE)..........❻...........$175—180

☐ 214 N/0.......King on two knees.....4.50".......(CE)..........❼...........$170—175

☐ 214 N/0.......King on two knees...................(CE)..........❽...........$170

☐ 214 F/0.......Shepherd Standing.....5.75".......(CE)..........❻...........$190—195

☐ 214 F/0.......Shepherd Standing.....5.75".......(CE)..........❼...........$185—190

☐ 214 F/0.......Shepherd Standing...................(CE)..........❽...........$185

☐ 214 G/0......Shepherd Kneeling.....4.00".......(CE)..........❻...........$155—160

☐ 214 G/0......Shepherd Kneeling.....4.00".......(CE)..........❼...........$150—155

☐ 214 G/0......Shepherd Kneeling...................(CE)..........❽...........$150

☐ 214 H/0.......Little Tooter................3.25".......(CE)..........❻...........$125—130

☐ 214 H/0.......Little Tooter................3.25".......(CE)..........❼...........$123—125

☐ 214 H/0.......Little Tooter.............................(CE)..........❽...........$122.50

HUM 215 (CN)
Factory records indicate: A child Jesus standing with lamb in arms. Listed as a (CE) Closed Number on 16 August 1951. No known examples.

☐ 215..(CN)..........................

HUM 216 (CN)
Factory records indicate: Joyful, ashtray without rest for cigarette. Listed as a (CE) Closed Number on 10 September 1951. No known examples.

☐ 216..(CN)..........................

HUM 217 — Boy With Toothache

First modeled by master sculptor Arthur Moeller in 1951. Older figurines are slightly larger. Older models have "© WG" after the "M.I. Hummel" signature. Old name: "At the Dentist" or "Toothache." Newer models have an incised 1951 copyright date. Some slight variations in color are found, but would not affect value. (TW) "Temporarily Withdrawn" in March 2005.

TM 2   *TM 4*

☐ 217	...........5.25 to 5.50"	.........(CE)	.... ❷	....	$425—525
☐ 217	...........5.25 to 5.50"	.........(CE)	.... ❸	....	$325—375
☐ 217	...........5.25 to 5.50"	.........(CE)	.... ❹	....	$270—325
☐ 217	...........5.25 to 5.50"	.........(CE)	.... ❺	....	$260—265
☐ 217	...........5.25 to 5.50"	.........(CE)	.... ❻	....	$255—260
☐ 217	...........5.25 to 5.50"	.........(CE)	.... ❼	....	$250—255
☐ 217	...........5.25 to 5.50"	.........(TW)	.... ❽	....	$250—255

New style (OE)   *Old style (CE)*

HUM 218 — Birthday Serenade

First modeled by master sculptor Reinhold Unger in 1952. Early models bearing an incised 1952 copyright date have boy playing horn, girl playing accordion. Remodeled in 1964 by master sculptor Gerhard Skrobek. Newer models bearing an incised 1965 copyright date have boy playing accordion, girl playing horn. This change was made at the request of the convent. The large size (HUM 218/0) had been considered rare but is again back in production with current trademark with boy playing accordion and girl playing horn with an incised 1952 copyright date. This was an error as it should have been 1965. Note that a tie has been added to the boy when he plays the accordion. Both styles can be found with TM 3 or TM 4 trademark. Large size (218/0) was listed as (TW) "Temporarily Withdrawn" in January 1999, but may be reinstated at some future date.

Small size (218 2/0) was listed as (TW) "Temporarily Withdrawn" in March of 2005.

- ☐ 218 2/0 ......4.25 to 4.50" ....(CE)....... ❷ ....$650—700
- ☐ 218 2/0 ......4.25 to 4.50" ....(CE)....... ❸ ....$600—650 (Old style)
- ☐ 218 2/0 ......4.25 to 4.50" ....(CE)....... ❸ ....$275—300 (New Style)
- ☐ 218 2/0 ......4.25 to 4.50" ....(CE)....... ❹ ....$475—550 (Old Style)
- ☐ 218 2/0 ......4.25 to 4.50" ....(CE)....... ❹ ....$250—275 (New Style)
- ☐ 218 2/0 ......4.25 to 4.50" ....(CE)....... ❺ ....$220—225
- ☐ 218 2/0 ......4.25 to 4.50" ....(CE)....... ❻ ....$220—225
- ☐ 218 2/0 ......4.25 to 4.50" ....(CE)....... ❼ ....$219—220
- ☐ 218 2/0 ......4.25 to 4.50" ....(**TW**) ...... ❽ $219
- ☐ 218/0 ....5.25" ....(CE)....... ❷ ....$875—975
- ☐ 218/0 ....5.25" ....(CE)....... ❸ ....$775—875 (Old Style)
- ☐ 218/0 ....5.25" ....(CE)....... ❸ ....$450—500 (New Style)
- ☐ 218/0 ....5.25" ....(CE)....... ❹ ....$725—825 (Old Style)
- ☐ 218/0 ....5.25" ....(CE)....... ❹ ....$370—450 (New Style)
- ☐ 218/0 ....5.25" ....(CE)....... ❺ ....$350—370
- ☐ 218/0 ....5.25" ....(CE)....... ❻ ....$340—350
- ☐ 218/0 ....5.25" ....(**TW**) ...... ❼ ....$330—340
- ☐ 218 ....5.25" ....(CE)....... ❷ ....$900—1000
- ☐ 218/I ....5.25" ....(CE)....... ❷ ....$1000—1500

(218/I possible factory error)

HUM 219 — Little Velma (CN)
This figurine was designed in 1952 by master sculptor Reinhold Unger. According to factory records this figurine was produced in very limited numbers (possibly less than 100 pieces) because of its similarity to other models. The name "Little Velma" was affectionately assigned to this piece in honor of the lady who first brought it to the attention of, and sold it to, this author. Most of these figurines must have been shipped to Canada as most known examples can be traced to that country.

"Little Velma"

- ☐ 219 2/0 ....4.00" ....(CN)....... ❷ ....$4000—6000

220 2/0 (TM 2)   *260F (TM 4)*   *214E (TM 2)*

HUM 220 — We Congratulate (with base)

First modeled by master sculptor Arthur Moeller in 1952. Early production pieces have
the incised number 220 2/0. Later production dropped the 2/0 size designator and added
the 1952 incised copyright date. This figurine is the same as HUM 214/E and HUM 260/F
in the Nativity Sets, except with base and no flowers in girl's hair. Also note lederhosen
strap added to boy. The 220 size was retired in April 2006 (CE) Closed Edition.

☐ 220 ....3.75 to 4.00”.........(CE).......❷ ......$350—400
☐ 220 ....3.75 to 4.00”.........(CE).......❸ ......$250—300
☐ 220 ....3.75 to 4.00”.........(CE).......❹ ......$215—260
☐ 220 ....3.75 to 4.00”.........(CE).......❺ ......$210—215
☐ 220 ....3.75 to 4.00”.........(CE).......❻ ......$205—210
☐ 220 ....3.75 to 4.00”.........(CE).......❼ ......$200—205
☐ 220 ....3.75 to 4.00”.........(CE).......❽ ......$199 (Closed Edition)
☐ 220 2/0 ....4.00” ....(CE).......❷ ......$475—575

Incised signature (HUM 214 E)   *Painted signature*

182

(Factory sample)

HUM 221 — Happy Pastime, Candy Jar (CN)

This candy jar was made as a sample only and was never produced for sale. First modeled by master sculptor Arthur Moeller in 1952. To my knowledge, there are no examples in private collections.

☐ 221..(CN)..................$5000—10,000

Two variations

HUM 222 — Madonna Plaque (with metal frame) (CE)

Originally modeled by master sculptor Reinhold Unger in 1952. There are basically two dif-ferent styles of metal frames—both pictured here. Found without frame with full bee trademark but unconfirmed if actually sold that way. Similar in design to HUM 48 "Madonna Plaque." Usually found with gray or tan felt backing, which would have to be removed to see the incised number. The number 222 is normally found upside down!

☐ 222.............4.00 x 5.00"..........(CE)....... ❷ ....$750—1250
☐ 222.............4.00 x 5.00"..........(CE)....... ❸ ....$750—1000

223 (TM 2)   *101 (TM 3)*

HUM 223 — To Market, Table Lamp

This lamp was originally modeled by master sculptor Arthur Moeller in 1937 as HUM 101 and later restyled by him in 1952. It is similar to the original model with the exception of the size and a flower added to branch of tree trunk. Measures 5.25" across the base. Called "Surprise" in old catalogue and sold for $25 in 1955. "To Market" table lamp was "Temporarily Withdrawn" from production on 31 December 1989, but may be reinstated at some future date. For a limited time, it was sold through Danbury Mint at $495 (10 monthly payments of $49.50 each. Plus sales tax.)—but is no longer available from them. We list as (OE) "Open Edition" since they are available in Germany and other markets, but are NOT currently available in the U.S. market.

☐ 223 ....9.50" ....(CE)......❷ ......$700—850
☐ 223 ....9.50" ....(CE)......❸ ......$650—700
☐ 223 ....9.50" ....(CE)......❹ ......$575—650
☐ 223 ....9.50" ....(CE)......❺ ......$540—575
☐ 223 ....9.50" ....(CE)......❻ ......$525—540
☐ 223 ....9.50" ....(CE)......❼ ......$495—500
☐ 223 ....9.50" ....(**OE**)......❽ ......$495—500 (Estimated Price)

224/II (TM 2)   *224/I (TM 2)*

HUM 224 — Wayside Harmony, Table Lamp

This lamp was modeled by master sculptor Reinhold Unger in 1952 and is actually a restyling of HUM II/111 "Wayside Harmony" lamp made in 1938. Large size same as small with the exception of a flower on branch of tree trunk. Small size measures 4.25" across base. Large size measures 6.25" across base. Early examples of the large (9.50") size usually found without size designator, incised 224 only and usually have a switch on the base. Both sizes of "Wayside Harmony" table lamps were (TW) "Temporarily Withdrawn" from production on 31 December 1989, but may be reinstated at some future date. We list as (OE) "Open Edition" since they are available in Germany and other markets, but are NOT currently available in the U.S. market.

☐ 224/I	7.50"	(CE)	❷	$550–600	
☐ 224/I	7.50"	(CE)	❸	$450–475	
☐ 224/I	7.50"	(CE)	❹	$425–450	
☐ 224/I	7.50"	(CE)	❺	$400–425	
☐ 224/I	7.50"	(CE)	❻	$350–400	
☐ 224/I	7.50"	(CE)	❼	$350–400	(Estimated Price)
☐ 224/I	7.50"	(**OE**)	❽	$350–400	(Estimated Price)
☐ 224/II	9.50"	(CE)	❷	$650–800	
☐ 224/II	9.50"	(CE)	❸	$500–600	
☐ 224/II	9.50"	(CE)	❹	$475–500	
☐ 224/II	9.50"	(CE)	❺	$450–475	
☐ 224/II	9.50"	(CE)	❻	$400–450	
☐ 224/II	9.50"	(CE)	❼	$400–450	(Estimated Price)
☐ 224/II	9.50"	(**OE**)	❽	$400–450	(Estimated Price)
☐ 224	9.50"	(CE)	❷	$650–800	
☐ 224	9.50"	(CE)	❸	$500–600	

225/II (TM 2)   225/I (TM 5)

HUM 225 — Just Resting, Table Lamp

This lamp was modeled by master sculptor Reinhold Unger in 1952 and is actually a restyling of HUM II/112 "Just Resting" lamp made in 1938. Large size same as small with the exception of a flower on branch of tree trunk. Small size measures 4.25" across base. Large size measures 6.25" across base. Early examples of the large (9.50") size usually found without size designator, incised 225 only and usually have a switch on the base. Both sizes of "Just Resting" table lamps were (TW) "Temporarily Withdrawn" from production on 31 December 1989, but may be reinstated at some future date. See: "Just Resting, Table Lamp" HUM 11/112. We list as (OE) "Open Edition" since they are available in Germany and other markets, but are NOT currently available in the U.S. market.

☐ 225/I ....7.50" ....(CE).......❷ $550–600
☐ 225/I ....7.50" ....(CE).......❸ $450–475
☐ 225/I ....7.50" ....(CE).......❹ $425–450
☐ 225/I ....7.50" ....(CE).......❺ $400–425
☐ 225/I ....7.50" ....(CE).......❻ $350–400
☐ 225/I ....7.50" ....(CE).......❼ ......$350–400   (Estimated Price)
☐ 225/I ....7.50" ....(OE).......❽ ......$350–400   (Estimated Price)
☐ 225/II ....9.50" ....(CE).......❷ $650–800
☐ 225/II ....9.50" ....(CE).......❸ $500–600
☐ 225/II ....9.50" ....(CE).......❹ $475–500
☐ 225/II ....9.50" ....(CE).......❺ $450–475
☐ 225/II ....9.50" ....(CE).......❻ $400–450
☐ 225/II ....9.50" ....(CE).......❼ ......$400–450   (Estimated Price)
☐ 225/II ....9.50" ....(OE).......❽ ......$400–450   (Estimated Price)
☐ 225 ....9.50" ....(CE).......❷ $650–800
☐ 225 ....9.50" ....(CE).......❸ $500–600

HUM 226 — Mail Is Here, The

Originally modeled by master sculptor Arthur Moeller in 1952. Older pieces are slightly larger in size. Also called "Mail Coach." Usually has an incised 1952 copyright date. Some older examples have a very faint "M. I. Hummel" signature while others have the signature painted on because of this light impression. Refer to HUM 140 "Mail is Here" plaque for another version of this same motif.

☐ 226 ....4.50 x 6.25" ....(CE)....... ❷ ....$1150—1350
☐ 226 ....4.25 x 6.00" ....(CE)....... ❸ ....$900—1100
☐ 226 ....4.25 x 6.00" ....(CE)....... ❹ ....$800—850
☐ 226 ....4.25 x 6.00" ....(CE)....... ❺ ....$750—800
☐ 226 ....4.25 x 6.00" ....(CE)....... ❻ ....$725—750
☐ 226 ....4.25 x 6.00" ....(CE)....... ❼ ....$720—725
☐ 226 ....4.25 x 6.00" ....(OE)...... ❽ $719

.... HUM TERM ....

MEL: A Goebel-produced figurine with the letters "MEL" incised somewhere on the base of the piece. These pieces were designed from original drawings by Sister M.I. Hummel, but for some undetermined reasons were not approved by the Siessen Convent for inclusion in the "M.I. Hummel" line of figurines.

HUM 227 — She Loves Me, She Loves Me Not, Table Lamp

This lamp was first modeled in 1953 by master sculptor Arthur Moeller and has been restyled several times. On the older lamps the figure is much larger and the boy's eyes are open. On the newer models the eyes are looking down. Same motif as HUM 174 of the same name. Measures 4.00" across the base. Refer to HUM 251 for matching bookends. "She Loves Me, She Loves Me Not" table lamp was (TW) "Temporarily Withdrawn" from the North American market on 31 December 1989, but may be reinstated at some future date. Still available on European market.

☐	227	7.50"	(CE)	❷	$650—850
☐	227	7.50"	(CE)	❸	$475—525
☐	227	7.50"	(CE)	❹	$425—475
☐	227	7.50"	(CE)	❺	$400—425
☐	227	7.50"	(TW)	❻	$375—400

HUM 228 — Good Friends, Table Lamp

This lamp was first modeled in 1953 by master sculptor Arthur Moeller and has been restyled several times. On the older lamps the figure is much larger and the tree trunk post has a smoother finish. Same motif as HUM 182 of the same name. Measures 4.25" across the base. Refer to HUM 251 for matching bookends. "Good Friends" table lamp was (TW) "Temporarily Withdrawn" from the North American market on 31 December 1989, but may be reinstated at some future date. Still available on European market.

☐	228	7.50"	(CE)	❷	$650—850
☐	228	7.50"	(CE)	❸	$475—525
☐	228	7.50"	(CE)	❹	$425—475
☐	228	7.50"	(CE)	❺	$400—425
☐	228	7.50"	(TW)	❻	$375—400

HUM 229 (TM 5)   HUM 230 (TM 5)

HUM 229 — Apple Tree Girl, Table Lamp

This lamp was first modeled in 1953 by master sculptor Arthur Moeller and has been restyled several times. On the older lamps the figure is much larger but the post still measures only 7.50 inches. Measures 4.25" across base. Old name: "Spring" or "Springtime." Refer to HUM 252 for matching bookends. "Apple Tree Girl" table lamp was (TW) "Temporarily Withdrawn" from the North American market on 31 December 1989, but may be reinstated at some future date. Still available on European market.

- ☐ 229 ....7.50" ....(CE)...... ❷ ....$900—1000
- ☐ 229 ....7.50" ....(CE)....... ❸ ....$475—525
- ☐ 229 ....7.50" ....(CE)....... ❹ ....$425—475
- ☐ 229 ....7.50" ....(CE)....... ❺ ....$400—425
- ☐ 229 ....7.50" ....(**TW**) ...... ❻ ....$375—400

HUM 230 — Apple Tree Boy, Table Lamp

This lamp was first modeled in 1953 by master sculptor Arthur Moeller and has been restyled several times. On the older lamps the figure is much larger but the post still measures only 7½ inches. Measures 4.25" across base. Old name: "Autumn" or "Fall" table lamp. Refer to HUM 252 for matching bookends. "Apple Tree Boy" table lamp was (TW) "Temporarily Withdrawn" from the North American market on 31 December 1989, but may be reinstated at some future date. Still available on European market.

- ☐ 230 ....7.50" ....(CE)...... ❷ ....$900—1000
- ☐ 230 ....7.50" ....(CE)....... ❸ ....$475—525
- ☐ 230 ....7.50" ....(CE)....... ❹ ....$425—475
- ☐ 230 ....7.50" ....(CE)....... ❺ ....$400—425
- ☐ 230 ....7.50" ....(**TW**) ...... ❻ ....$375—400

| 231 | New style | 234 | | 231 | Old style | 234 |

HUM 231 — Birthday Serenade, Table Lamp

This lamp was first modeled by master sculptor Reinhold Unger and was restyled in 1976 by master sculptor Rudolf Wittman. The early model measures 6.00" across the base and has a hole for electrical switch on top of the base. Had been considered rare but was put back into production with 5 and 6 trademarks. Early models have an incised 1954 copyright date. The musical instruments have been reversed on the current production models. Refer to HUM 218 "Birthday Serenade" figurine for more details. Both sizes of "Birthday Serenade" table lamps were (TW) "Temporarily Withdrawn" from production on 31 December 1989, but may be reinstated at some future date.

- ☐ 231 ....9.75" ....(CE)...... ❷ ....$2000—3000
- ☐ 231 ....9.75" ....(CE)...... ❺ ....$550—600
- ☐ 231 ....9.75" ....(TW) ...... ❻ ....$500—550

HUM 234 — Birthday Serenade, Table Lamp

This smaller size lamp was also modeled in 1954 by master sculptor Reinhold Unger and the first sample was painted in October 1954 by artist Georg Mechtold (initials "GM"). Similar to HUM 231 with the exception of having no flower on branch of tree trunk. Older models have an incised 1954 copyright date. Restyled in 1976 by master sculptor Rudolf Wittmann with the musical instruments in the reverse position. Had been considered rare but was put back into production with 5 and 6 trademarks. Trademark 4 examples can be found in either style. Both sizes of "Birthday Serenade" table lamps were (TW) "Temporarily Withdrawn" from production on 31 December 1989, but may be reinstated at some future date.

- ☐ 234 ....7.75" ....(CE)...... ❷ ....$1600—2100
- ☐ 234 ....7.75" ....(CE)...... ❸ ....$1100—1600
- ☐ 234 ....7.75" ....(CE)...... ❹ ....$500—1100
- ☐ 234 ....7.75" ....(CE)...... ❺ ....$450—500
- ☐ 234 ....7.75" ....(TW) ...... ❻ ....$425—450

HUM 232 — Happy Days, Table Lamp
This lamp was first modeled in 1954 by master sculptor Reinhold Unger and was restyled in 1976. The early model measures 6.00" across the base and has a hole for electrical switch at top of

Hum 232 (Old style)   *HUM 235 (Old style)*

base. Had been considered rare but was again put back into production with 5 and 6 trademarks. Early models have an incised 1954 copyright date. Both sizes of "Happy Days" table lamps were (TW) "Temporarily Withdrawn" from production on 31 December 1989, but may be reinstated at some future date.

☐ 232 ....9.75" ....(CE)....... ❷ ....$1200—1700
☐ 232 ....9.75" ....(CE)....... ❺ ....$525—550
☐ 232 ....9.75" ....(TW) ...... ❻ ....$500—525

HUM 233 (CN)
Factory records indicate a sample of a "boy feeding birds." Listed as a (CN) Closed Number on 7 September 1954. No known examples. Gerhard Skrobek, master modeler at the factory, stated that this was the first figure he modeled after starting to work at W. Goebel Porzellanfabrik in 1954. Skrobek later restyled this figurine which now appears as HUM 300 "Bird Watcher," issued in 1979.

HUM 235 — Happy Days, Table Lamp
This smaller size lamp was also modeled in 1954 by master sculptor Reinhold Unger and the first sample was painted in October 1954 by artist Georg Mechtold (initials "GM"). Similar to HUM 232 with the exception of having no flower on branch of tree trunk. Older models have an incised 1954 copyright date. Restyled in 1976 and again put back into production until 1989 when both sizes of "Happy Days" table lamps were (TW) "Temporarily Withdrawn" from production on 31 December 1989, but may be reinstated at some future date.

☐ 235 ....7.75" ....(CE)....... ❷ ....$900—1100
☐ 235 ....7.75" ....(CE)....... ❸ ....$625—850
☐ 235 ....7.75" ....(CE)....... ❹ ....$500—625
☐ 235 ....7.75" ....(CE)....... ❺ ....$475—500
☐ 235 ....7.75" ....(TW) ...... ❻ ....$450—475

236 A   238 B

HUM 236 A & B (CN)

Original research revealed no information about this number, so it was listed as an (ON) Open Number in our previous price guide. Sample models were located at the Goebel factory in 1984 and were put on display at the Goebel Collectors' Club in Tarrytown, N.Y. Designed in 1954 by master sculptor Arthur Moeller but for some unknown reason they were not approved by the Siessen Convent for production.

☐ 236 A   ,,,,,6.50" ....(CN).......❷ ....\$10,000—15,000
☐ 236 B ....6.50" ....(CN).......❷ \$10,000 15,000

HUM 237 — Star Gazer, Wall Plaque (CN)

This plaque was made as a sample only and not produced for sale as an (OE) Open Edition. This white overglaze (unpainted) example was located at the Goebel factory. Was designed in 1954 and apparently rejected by Siessen Convent for production. Note the "M.I. Hummel" signature in the left hand corner. I have not been able to confirm the name of the original modeler of this rare item. Now part of the Robert L. Miller collection.

☐ 237 ....4.75 x 5.00" ....(CN).......❷ ....\$10,000—15,000

HUM 238 A — Angel With Lute

One of a set of three small angel figures known as the "Angel Trio." Similar to HUM 38 except without holder for candle. Modeled by master sculptor Gerhard Skrobek in 1967. Has a 1967 incised copyright date. Occasionally found in (TM 3). (TW) "Temporarily Withdrawn"January 2004.

☐ 238 A.......2.00 to 2.50".......(CE).....❸.....$100—125
☐ 238 A.......2.00 to 2.50".......(CE).....❹.....$85—100
☐ 238 A.......2.00 to 2.50".......(CE).....❺.....$80—85
☐ 238 A.......2.00 to 2.50".......(CE).....❻.....$75—80
☐ 238 A.......2.00 to 2.50".......(CE).....❼.....$73—75
☐ 238 A.......2.00 to 2.50".......(**TW**) .....❽......$72 —73

238 A

HUM 238 B — Angel With Accordion

One of a set of three small angel figures known as the "Angel Trio." Similar to HUM 39 except without holder for candle. Modeled by master sculptor Gerhard Skrobek in 1967. Has a 1967 incised copyright date. Occasionally found in (TM 3). (TW) "Temporarily Withdrawn"January 2004.

☐ 238 B ......2.00 to 2.50".......(CE).....❸......$100—125
☐ 238 B ......2.00 to 2.50".......(CE).....❹.....$85—100
☐ 238 B ......2.00 to 2.50".......(CE).....❺.....$80—85
☐ 238 B ......2.00 to 2.50".......(CE).....❻......$75—80
☐ 238 B ......2.00 to 2.50".......(CE).....❼.....$73—75
☐ 238 B ......2.00 to 2.50".......(**TW**) .....❽.....$72 —73

238 B

HUM 238 C — Angel With Trumpet

One of a set of three small angel figures known as the "Angel Trio." Similar to HUM 40 except without holder for candle. Modeled by master sculptor Gerhard Skrobek in 1967. Has a 1967 incised copyright date. Occasionally found in (TM 3). (TW) "Temporarily Withdrawn"January 2004.

☐ 238 C ......2.00 to 2.50".......(CE).....❸ .....$100—125
☐ 238 C ......2.00 to 2.50".......(CE).....❹.....$85—100
☐ 238 C ......2.00 to 2.50".......(CE).....❺.....$80—85
☐ 238 C ......2.00 to 2.50".......(CE).....❻.....$75—80
☐ 238 C ......2.00 to 2.50".......(CE).....❼.....$73—75
☐ 238 C ......2.00 to 2.50".......(**TW**) .....❽.....$72 —73

238 C

| *239 A* | *239 B* | *239 C* | *239 D* |

This set of three small children figurines is known as the "Children Trio." Similar to HUM 115, 116 and 117 but without holder for candle. Modeled by master sculptor Gerhard Skrobek in 1967. Have a 1967 incised copyright date. Occasionally found in TM 3. Two new figurines were added in 2003—both with the same model number—239 E. "Little Flag Bearer" has decal "First Issue 2003" and an incised 2002 copyright date, plus a small U.S. Flag on the bottom. "Carnival Fun" has only "First Issue 2003" and (TM 8) trademark.

HUM 239 A — Girl With Nosegay
☐ 239 A..........3.50"......................(CE).......❸ ......$150—200
☐ 239 A..........3.50"......................(CE).......❹ ......$85—100
☐ 239 A..........3.50".......... .....,,(CE).......❺ ......$80—85
☐ 239 A..........3.50"......................(CE).......❻ ......$75—80
☐ 239 A..........3.50"......................(CE).......❼ ......$73—75
☐ 239 A..........3.50"......................(TW) ......❽ $69.50

HUM 239 B — Girl With Doll
☐ 239 B..........3.50"......................(CE).......❸ ......$150—200
☐ 239 B..........3.50"......................(CE).......❹ ......$85—100
☐ 239 B..........3.50"......................(CE).......❺ ......$80—85
☐ 239 B..........3.50"......................(CE).......❻ ......$75—80
☐ 239 B..........3.50"......................(CE).......❼ ......$73—75
☐ 239 B..........3.50"......................(TW) ......❽ $69.50

HUM 239 C — Boy With Horse
☐ 239 C ....3.50"......................(CE).......❸ ......$150—200
☐ 239 C ....3.50"......................(CE).......❹ ......$85—100
☐ 239 C ....3.50"......................(CE).......❺ ......$80—85
☐ 239 C ....3.50"......................(CE).......❻ ......$75—80
☐ 239 C ....3.50"......................(CE).......❼ ......$73—75
☐ 239 C ....3.50"......................(TW) ......❽ $69.50

HUM 239 D — Girl With Fir Tree

In the fall of 1997, a 4th figurine was added to this set; HUM 239 D "Girl with Fir Tree," similar to HUM 116 candleholder.

☐ 239 D ....3.50".....................(CE).......❼ ......$73—75
☐ 239 D ....3.50".....................(TW) ......❽ $69.50

HUM 239 E — Carnival Fun
aka Little Flag Bearer

☐ 239 E..........3.50".....................(OE).......❽ $69.50
☐ 239 E..........3.50".....................(OE).......❽ $69.50

239 E

239 E

| *239 A/0* | *239 B/0* | *239 C/0* | *239 D/0* |
| Girl with Nosegay | Glrl with Doll | Boy with Horse | Girl with Fur Tree |

HUM 239 Ornaments

This set of four small children ornaments was issued in the fall of 1997. They are the same as HUM 239 A, B, C, and D figurines, but are without bases; are made as hanging ornaments, with a brass ring in each head. The model number and trademark are stamped on the feet of each ornament. Also sold in European market without brass ring in head and <u>no</u> base.

(with ring)   (with<u>out</u> ring)
☐ 239 A/0 ......☐ 239 A/X ....3.00"..........(OE) ......❼—❽ $69.50
☐ 239 B/0 ......☐ 239 B/X ....3.00"..........(OE) ......❼—❽ $69.50
☐ 239 C/0 ......☐ 239 C/X ....3.00"..........(OE) ......❼—❽ $69.50
☐ 239 D/0 ......☐ 239 D/X ....3.00"..........(OE) ......❼—❽ $69.50

TM 2 **TM 4**

HUM 240 — Little Drummer
First modeled by master sculptor Reinhold Unger in 1955. Older pieces are usually slightly larger. Has an incised 1955 copyright date. Sometimes listed as "Drummer" even in recent price lists and catalogues. Similar to boy in HUM 50 "Volunteers." (TW) "Temporarily Withdrawn" from production in March 2005.

☐ 240 ..4.00 to 4.25" ..(CE)....❷ ....$325—400
☐ 240 ..4.00 to 4.25" ..(CE)....❸ ....$250—275
☐ 240 ..4.00 to 4.25" ..(CE)....❹ ....$200—250
☐ 240 ..4.00 to 4.25" ..(CE)....❺ ....$195—200
☐ 240 ..4.00 to 4.25" ..(CE)....❻ ....$190—195
☐ 240 ..4.00 to 4.25" ..(CE)....❼ ....$185—190
☐ 240 ..4.00 to 4.25" ..(TW) ..❽ ....$179—185

HUM 241 — Angel Lights, Candleholder
First released in the U.S. market in 1978 with a suggested retail price of $100. This number was assigned to this newly designed piece in error. Sometimes referred to as "Angel Bridge." Originally modeled by master sculptor Gerhard Skrobek in 1976, this is an adaptation of HUM 21 "Heavenly Angel." Usually sold with a round plate which this piece is designed to fit. Found with trademarks 5 and 6 only. Sometimes listed as "241 B" but only the number 241 is incised on this item. "Angel Lights" candleholder was (TW) "Temporarily Withdrawn" from production on 31 December 1989, but may be reinstated at some future date.

☐ 241 ..10.33 x 8.33"..(CE)....❺ ....$400—500
☐ 241 ..10.33 x 8.33"..(TW) ..❻ ....$300—350

HUM 241 — Holy Water Font, Angel Joyous News With Lute (CN)
This font was first modeled by master sculptor Reinhold Unger in 1955. Has a stamped 1955 copyright date. Made as a sample only and not produced for sale as an open edition. Listed as a Closed Number on 6 April 1955. Several examples of this font are now in private collections including the Robert L. Miller collection.

☐ 241 ..3.00 x 4.50"....(CN)....❷ ..$1500—2000

HUM 242 — Holy Water Font, Angel Joyous News With Trumpet (CN)

This font was first modeled by master sculptor Reinhold Unger in 1955. Has a stamped 1955 copyright date. Made as a sample only and not produced for sale as an (OE) Open Edition. Listed as a (CN) Closed Number on 6 April 1955. Several examples of this font are now in private collections including the Robert L. Miller collection.

☐ 242 ..3.00 x 4.50" ....(CN) ....❷....$1500—2000

HUM 243 — Holy Water Font, Madonna And Child

This font was first modeled by master sculptor Reinhold Unger in 1955. Has an incised 1955 copyright date. Apparently not put on the market until the mid-1960s. Earliest catalogue listing found is 1967. No known variations have been recorded. (TW) "Temporarily Withdrawn in March 2005.

☐ 243 ....3.125 x 4.00" ......(CE) ..❷ ....$250—300
☐ 243 ....3.125 x 4.00" ......(CE) ..❸ ....$100—125
☐ 243 ....3.125 x 4.00" ......(CE) ..❹ ....$85—100
☐ 243 ....3.125 x 4.00" ......(CE) ..❺ ....$80—85
☐ 243 ....3.125 x 4.00" ......(CE) ..❻ ....$75—80
☐ 243 ....3.125 x 4.00" ......(CE) ..❼ ....$70—75
☐ 243 ....3.125 x 4.00" ......(**TW**) ..❽ $69.50

HUM 244–245 — (ON) OPEN NUMBERS

Factory records contain no information at all regarding these numbers. They have therefore been listed as an (ON) Open Numbers and may be assigned to a future items.

HUM 246 — Holy Water Font, Holy Family

Master sculptor Theo R. Menzenbach modeled this font in 1955. Earliest catalogue listing is in 1955 Second Edition Schmid Brothers. Has an incised 1955 copyright date. No known variations have been recorded.

☐ 246 ....3.125 x 4.50" ......(CE) ..❷ ....$250—300
☐ 246 ....3.125 x 4.50" ......(CE) ..❸ ....$100—150
☐ 246 ....3.125 x 4.50" ......(CE) ..❹ ....$85—100
☐ 246 ....3.125 x 4.50" ......(CE) ..❺ ....$80—85
☐ 246 ....3.125 x 4.50" ......(CE) ..❻ ....$75—80
☐ 246 ....3.125 x 4.50" ......(CE) ..❼ ....$70—75
☐ 246 ....3.125 x 4.50" ......(**OE**) ..❽ $69.50

HUM 247 — Standing Madonna With Child (CN)

This beautiful Madonna with Child was originally modeled by master sculptor Reinhold Unger in 1955. Restyled in a slightly smaller version by master sculptor Theo R. Menzenbach in 1961. Both versions were rejected by the Siessen Convent for some unknown reason and were never produced as an open edition. Factory samples only, none known to be in private collections.

☐ 247 ..11.50" ......(CN) ....$10,000—15,000
☐ 247 ..13.00" ......(CN) ....$10,000—15,000

HUM 248 — Holy Water Font, Guardian Angel

This font was first modeled by master sculptor Gerhard Skrobek in 1958. Most models have an incised 1959 copyright date. This is a restyled version of HUM 29 which was discontinued at the time HUM 248 was introduced. This font was originally modeled in two sizes (248/0 and 248/I) but to my knowledge the large size was never put on the market. Factory information reveals that in the future it will be made in only the smaller size and "0" size designator will eventually disappear—so far this has not happened. Small size (248/0) was listed as (TW) "Temporarily Withdrawn" in January 1999.

248/0   248/I

☐ 248/0 ..2.375 x 5.375" ..(CE) .. ❸ ..$200—250
☐ 248/0 ..2.376 x 5.375" ,,(CE) .. ❹ ..$85—100
☐ 248/0 ..2.375 x 5.375" ..(CE) .. ❺ ..$80—85
☐ 248/0 ..2.25 x 5.50" ......(CE) .. ❻ ..$75—80
☐ 248/0 ..2.25 x 5.50" ......(TW).. ❼ ..$70—75
☐ 248/I ..2.75 x 6.25" ......(CE) .. ❽ ..$1000—1500

HUM 249 — Madonna and Child (in relief) Wall Plaque (CN)

This wall plaque was made as a sample only and not produced for sale as an (ON) Open Edition. Similar to HUM 48/V except without background or frame. Actually, the piece that I saw and is pictured here was simply a cut-out of HUM 48/V in an unfinished state, with no number or signature on the back—apparently an idea that was rejected or stopped before it was even completed. Possibly the work of master sculptor Reinhold Unger who modeled the first HUM 48 in 1936.

☐ 249 ..6.75 x 8.75" .....(CN).....$10,000—15,000

250 A & B (priced as set)

HUM 250 A — Little Goat Herder, Bookend
HUM 250 B — Feeding Time, Bookend
Factory records indicate these bookends were designed by a team of modelers in 1960. First sold in the U.S in 1964. The bookends are simply normal figurines affixed to a wooden base. Refer to HUM 199 and HUM 200 for more information. Current models have current figurines. This pair of bookends was (TW) "Temporarily Withdrawn" from production on 31 December 1989, but may be reinstated at some future date.

☐ 250 A&B ....5.50"..........(CE) ....❷ ....$550—750
☐ 250 A&B ....5.50"..........(CE) ....❸ ....$375—425
☐ 250 A&B ....5.50"..........(CE) ....❺ ....$325—350
☐ 250 A&B ....5.50"..........**(TW)**..........❻ ....$300—325

.... HUM TERM ....
TEMPORARILY WITHDRAWN: A designation assigned by the W. Goebel Porzellanfabrik to indicate that a particular item is being withdrawn from production for some time, but may be reinstated at a future date.

251 A & B (priced as set)

HUM 251 A — Good Friends, Bookend
HUM 251 B — She Loves Me, She Loves Me Not! Bookend
Factory records indicate these bookends were designed by a team of modelers in 1960. First sold in the U.S. in 1964. The bookends are simply normal figurines affixed to a wooden base. Refer to HUM 174 and HUM 182 for more information. Current models have current figurines. This pair of bookends was (TW) "Temporarily Withdrawn" from production on 31 December 1989, but may be reinstated at some future date.

☐ 251 A&B ....5.00".........(CE) ....❷ ....$550—750
☐ 251 A&B ....5.00".........(CE) ....❸ ....$375—425
☐ 251 A&B ....5.00".........(CE) ....❺ ....$325—350
☐ 251 A&B ....5.00".........(TW).........❻ ....$300—325

.... **HUM TERM** ....
HOLLOW MOLD: The term used by "M. I. Hummel" collectors to describe a figurine that is open on the underside of the base. With these particular bases the collector can visually see into the cavity of the figurine.

251 A & B (priced as set)

HUM 252 A — Apple Tree Girl, Bookend
HUM 252 B — Apple Tree Boy, Bookend
Factory records indicate these bookends were designed by a team of modelers in 1962. First sold in the U.S. in 1964. The bookends are simply normal figurines affixed to a wooden base. Refer to HUM 141 and HUM 142 for more information. Current models have current figurine. "Apple Tree Girl and Boy" bookends were (TW) "Temporarily Withdrawn" from production on 31 December 1989, but may be reinstated at some future date.

☐ 252 A&B ....5.00" ....(CE) .... ❸ ....$375—425
☐ 252 A&B ....5.00" ....(CE) .... ❺ ....$325—350
☐ 252 A&B ....5.00" ....(TW) .... ❻ ....$300—325

HUM 253 (CN)
Factory records indicate a girl with basket similar to the one in HUM 52 "Going to Grandma's." No known examples.

☐ 253 ....4.50" ....(CN).......

HUM 254 — Girl With Mandolin (CN)

Modeled by a combination of sculptors in 1962, this figurine depicts a girl playing a mandolin, similar to girl in HUM 150 "Happy Days." Factory archives samples only, (however, an example recently turned up in the U.S. with an asking price of $12,000.) Refer to HUM 557 "Strum Along" for a slightly smaller version of this figurine issued in 1995.

☐ 254......4.25"............(CN)......❸ ....$5000—10,000

HUM 255 — Stitch in Time

First modeled by a combination of sculptors in 1962. Has an incised 1963 copyright date. First sold in the U.S. in 1964. Similar to one of the girls used in HUM 256 "Knitting Lesson" and HUM 177 "School Girls." No unusual variations have been recorded. A new miniature size figurine was issued in 1990 with a suggested retail price of $65 to match a new miniature plate series called the "Little Homemakers"—one each year for four years. This is the third in the series. The normal size will be renumbered 255/I and the old number 255 is now classified as a (CE) Closed Edition because of this change. The miniature size HUM 255 4/0 was (TW) "Temporarily Withdrawn" from production on 31 December 1997 and the large size (255/I) in January 1999.

☐ 255 4/0 ....3.00" ....(CE) .....❻ ....$125—140
☐ 255 4/0 ....3.00" ....(CE) ....❼ ,,,$115—120
☐ 255 ....6.50 to 6.75"....(CE) ....❸ ....$550—800
☐ 255 ....6.50 to 6.75"....(CE) ....❹ ....$375—425
☐ 255 ....6.50 to 6.75"....(CE) ....❺ ....$350—375
☐ 255 ....6.50 to 6.75"....(CE) ....❻ ....$340—350
☐ 255/I ....6.50 to 6.75"....(TW) ....❼ ....$325—335

HUM 256 — Knitting Lesson

First modeled by a combination of sculptors in 1962. Has an incised 1963 copyright date. First sold in the U.S. in 1964. Similar to two girls used in HUM 177 "School Girls." No unusual variations have been recorded. Listed as (TW) "Temporarily Withdrawn" in January 1999.

☐ 256 ....7.50" ....(CE) ....❸ ....$875—1150
☐ 256 ....7.50" ....(CE) ....❹ ....$625—750
☐ 256 ....7.50" ....(CE) ....❺ ....$550—575
☐ 256 ....7.50" ....(CE) ....❻ ....$540—550
☐ 256 ....7.50" ....(TW) ....❼ ....$525—535

| 257 (TM 5) | 257 2/0 (TM 6) | With HummelScape |

HUM 257 — For Mother

First modeled by a combination of sculptors in 1962. Has an incised 1963 copyright date. First sold in the U.S. in 1964. No unusual variations have been recorded. A new small size HUM 257 2/0 was issued in 1985 at a suggested retail price of $50. This new small size figurine has an incised 1984 copyright date. The large size has now been renumbered 257/0. In 1996 a 2.75" size (3.25" with base) with incised model number 257 5/0 was produced as part of the "Pen Pals" series of personalized name card table decorations. The original issue price was $55. The small size HUM 257 2/0 was released with a musical Hummelscape combination price of $165 in 1999. The large size HUM 257/0 was listed as (TW) "Temporarily Withdrawn" from production in June 2002, but may be reinstated at some future date.

- ☐ 257 5/0 ......2.75" ....(CE)...... ❼ ......$55—60
- ☐ 257 2/0 ......4.00" ....(CE)...... ❻ ......$160—165
- ☐ 257 2/0 ......4.00" ....(CE)...... ❼ ......$155—160
- ☐ 257 2/0 ......4.00" ....(**OE**)...... ❽ $149
- ☐ 257 ....5.00 to 5.25" ....(CE)...... ❸ ......$625—825
- ☐ 257 ....5.00 to 5.25" ....(CE)...... ❹ ......$280—325
- ☐ 257 ....5.00 to 5.25" ....(CE)...... ❺ ......$265—270
- ☐ 257 ....5.00 to 5.25" ....(CE)...... ❻ ......$260—265
- ☐ 257/0 ....5.00 to 5.25" ....(CE)...... ❻ ......$255—260
- ☐ 257/0 ....5.00 to 5.25" ....(CE)...... ❼ ......$250—255
- ☐ 257/0 ....5.00 to 5.25" ....(**TW**) ...... ❽ ......$250—255

HUM 258 — Which Hand?

First modeled by a combination of sculptors in 1962. Has an incised 1963 copyright date. First sold in the U.S. in 1964. Similar to girl used in HUM 196 "Telling Her Secret." No unusual variations have been recorded. "Which Hand?" last appeared on the January 2000 price list and has NOT been listed since. Therefore, I am listing it as (TW) "Temporarily Withdrawn." In 2004 the "Which Hand" Progression Set was released, a sequentially numbered (LE) Limited Edition of 1000, priced $450.

☐ 258	5.25 to 5.50"	(CE)	❸	$625—825	
☐ 258	5.25 to 5.50"	(CE)	❹	$265—300	
☐ 258	5.25 to 5.50"	(CE)	❺	$245—265	
☐ 258	5.25 to 5.50"	(CE)	❻	$240—245	
☐ 258	5.25 to 5.50"	(CE)	❼	$235—240	
☐ 258	5.25 to 5.50"	(TW)	❽	$235—240	
☐ 258	5.25"	(LE)	❽	$450	(Progression Set)

(Factory sample)

HUM 259 — Girl With Accordion (CN)

Modeled by a combination of sculptors in 1962, this figurine depicts a girl playing an accordion as in HUM 218 "Birthday Serenade." This piece was made as a sample only and not produced for sale as an open edition. Listed as a (CN) Closed Number on factory records of 8 November 1962. An example of this figurine was found in 2001 with (TM 4) trademark and a painting date of: O.B. TR/63. Now in a private collection here in the U.S. Sorry, NOT mine!

☐ 259	4.00"	(CN)	❸	$5000—10,000
☐ 259	4.00"	(CN)	❹	$5000—10,000

Large size nativity set

HUM 260 — Large Nativity Set (with wooden stable)

This large size Nativity Set was first modeled in 1968 by master sculptor Gerhard Skrobek. First sold in the U.S. in the early 1970s. Various styles of wooden stables have been produced through the years. The stable is priced at $480 currently, although it is usually included in the price of the set. This set consists of sixteen pieces, larger and more detailed than the small Nativity set HUM 214. Individual pieces can be purchased separately but are normally sold as a set. This large size Nativity Set was (TW) "Temporarily Withdrawn" from the North American market on 31 December 1989, but may be reinstated at some future date. Still available in (TM 7) and (TM 8) in European market.

260 A	Madonna	260 J	Shepherd Boy, kneeling
260 B	Saint Joseph	260 K	Little Tooter
260 C	Infant Jesus	260 L	Donkey, standing
260 D	Good Night	260 M	Cow, lying
260 E	Angel Serenade	260 N	Moorish King, standing
260 F	We Congratulate	260 O	King, standing
260 G	Shepherd, standing	260 P	King, kneeling
260 H	Sheep, standing with lamb	260 R	One Sheep, lying

☐ 260 ....SET 16 PIECES ......(CE) ....❹ ....$6050—6305 (Includes Stable)
☐ 260 ....SET 16 PIECES ......(CE) ....❺ ....$5890—6050 (Includes Stable)
☐ 260 ....SET 16 PIECES ......(TW) ....❻ ....$5745—5890 (Includes Stable)
☐ 260A ......9.75" ....(CE) ....❹ ....$625—650
☐ 260A ......9.75" ....(CE) ....❺ ....$600—625

(prices continued on next page)

205

☐ 260A ......9.75" ....(TW) ....❻ ....$575—600
☐ 260B ......11.75" ....(CE) ....❹ ....$625—650
☐ 260B ......11.75" ....(CE) ....❺ ....$600—625
☐ 260B ......11.75" ....(TW) ....❻ ....$575—600
☐ 260C ......5.75" ....(CE) ....❹ ....$140—150
☐ 260C ......5.75" ....(CE) ....❺ ....$135—140
☐ 260C ......5.75" ....(TW) ....❻ ....$130—135
☐ 260D ......5.25" ....(CE) ....❹ ....$170—180
☐ 260D ......5.25" ....(CE) ....❺ ....$165—170
☐ 260D ......5.25" ....(TW) ....❻ ....$160—165
☐ 260E ......4.25" ....(CE) ....❹ ....$165—170
☐ 260E ......4.25" ....(CE) ....❺ ....$160—165
☐ 260E ......4.25" ....(TW) ....❻ ....$155—160
☐ 260F ......6.25" ....(CE) ....❹ ....$435—460
☐ 260F ......6.25" ....(CE) ....❺ ....$425—435
☐ 260F ......6.25" ....(TW) ....❻ ....$415—425
☐ 260G ......11.75" ....(CE) ....❹ ....$620—650
☐ 260G ......11.75" ....(CE) ....❺ ....$600—620
☐ 260G ......11.75" ....(TW) ....❻ ....$590—600
☐ 260H ......3.75" ....(CE) ....❹ ....$120—125
☐ 260H ......3.75" ....(CE) ....❺ ....$115—120
☐ 260H ......3.75" ....(TW) ....❻ ....$110—115
☐ 260J.......7.00" ....(CE) ....❹ ....$355—370
☐ 260J.......7.00" ....(CE) ....❺ ....$345—355
☐ 260J.......7.00" ....(TW) ....❻ ....$340—345
☐ 260K ......5.125" ....(CE) ....❹ ....$205—220
☐ 260K ......5.125" ....(CE) ....❺ ....$200—205
☐ 260K ......5.125" ....(TW) ....❻ ....$195—200
☐ 260L ......7.50" ....(CE) ....❹ ....$165—170
☐ 260L ......7.50" ....(CE) ....❺ ....$160—165
☐ 260L ......7.50" ....(TW) ....❻ ....$155—160
☐ 260M ......6.00 x 11.00"............(CE) ....❹ ....$180—190
☐ 260M ......6.00 x 11.00"............(CE) ....❺ ....$175—180
☐ 260M ......6.00 x 11.00"............(TW) ....❻ ....$170—175
☐ 260N ......12.75" ....(CE) ....❹ ....$585—615
☐ 260N ......12.75" ....(CE) ....❺ ....$575—585
☐ 260N ......12.75" ....(TW) ....❻ ....$565—575
☐ 260O ......12.00" ....(CE) ....❹ ....$585—615
☐ 260O ......12.00" ....(CE) ....❺ ....$575—585
☐ 260O ......12.00" ....(TW) ....❻ ....$565—575
☐ 260P ......9.00" ....(CE) ....❹ ....$560—570
☐ 260P ......9.00" ....(CE) ....❺ ....$550—560
☐ 260P ......9.00" ....(TW) ....❻ ....$540—550
☐ 260R ......3.25 x 4.00" ....(CE) ....❹ ....$75—80
☐ 260R ......3.25 x 4.00" ....(CE) ....❺ ....$70—75
☐ 260R ......3.25 x 4.00" ....(TW) ....❻ ....$65—70
☐ 260S ......STABLE ....(OE) ....— $480

HUM 261 — Angel Duet

Same name and same design as HUM 193 but without holder for candle. Modeled by master sculptor Gerhard Skrobek in 1968. Has an incised copyright date of 1968 on the bottom of each piece. Notice position of angel's arm in rear view. HUM 193 candleholder can be found with arms in either position while HUM 261 is found with arm in lower position only. Difficult to find with "three line" (TM 4) trademark.

☐ 261	5.00"	(CE)	❹	$750—850
☐ 261	5.00"	(CE)	❺	$280—300
☐ 261	5.00"	(CE)	❻	$275—280
☐ 261	5.00"	(CE)	❼	$270—275
☐ 261	5.00"	(TW)	❽	$270

261 (TM 4)   *193 (TM 2)*

.... HUM TERM ....

LIMITED EDITION: A figurine that is produced for a specific time period or in a limited quantity.

HUM 262 — Heavenly Lullaby
This is the same design as HUM 24/I "Lullaby" without the hole for candle. Modeled by master sculptor Gerhard Skrobek in 1968. Has an incised copyright date of 1968 on the bottom of each piece. Difficult to find with "three line" (TM 4) trademark. Listed as (TW) "Temporarily Withdrawn" in January 1999.

☐ 262	3.50 x 5.00"	(CE)	❹	$750—850
☐ 262	3.50 x 5.00"	(CE)	❺	$280—300
☐ 262	3.50 x 5.00"	(CE)	❻	$275—280
☐ 262	3.50 x 5.00"	(TW)	❼	$270—275

HUM 263 (CN) — Merry Wanderer, Wall Plaque (in relief)
This unique wall plaque, modeled by master sculptor Gerhard Skrobek in 1968, was made as a sample model only and not produced for sale as an open edition. It is simply a "Merry Wanderer" figurine made without a base, slightly flattened on the back side with a hole provided for hanging. The example in our collection has the incised number 263 and the "three line" (TM 4) trademark as well as the incised "M.I. Hummel" signature. The front view photo does not give the appearance of depth that can be shown in the rear view. It looks like it would be possible for a collector to make such a plaque by taking HUM 7/0, "Merry Wanderer," removing the base and grinding the back so that it would hang flat against the wall. But then, of course, you would not have the incised number or signature, nor the "three line" trademark!

☐ 263	4.00 x 5.375"	(CN)	❹	$10,000—15,000

Special Worker's Plate Inscription

HUM 264 — Annual Plate, 1971
Heavenly Angel (CE)

1971 was the 100th anniversary of W. Goebel Porzellanfabrik. The annual plate was issued in commemoration of that occasion. Each employee of the company was presented with a 1971 Annual Plate bearing a special inscription on the back. These plates with the special inscription have become a highly sought-after collector's item because of the very limited production. Produced with the "three line" (TM 4) trademark only. The original issue price was $25.

☐ 264 ....7.50" ....(CE) ....❹ ....$500—600
☐ 264 ....7.50" ....(CE) ....❹ ....$1200—1500 (Worker's Plate)

Rare factory sample of 1948 Christmas plate. Never issued or sold on the market.

Note: There were some 1971 Hummel plates made without the two holes on the back, which were normally placed there so that cord or wire could be put through them for hanging purposes. These plates were purposely made without the holes and were shipped to the British Isles in order to qualify for a lower rate of duty. With the hanging holes made in the plates, British Customs Department would charge a higher rate of duty since the plate would be classified as a decorative or luxury item rather than the more practical dinner plate classification. In my opinion, the missing holes will not affect the value of your plate one way or the other. In fact, some collectors may prefer the more rare one without the holes!

HUM 265 — Annual Plate, 1972
Hear Ye, Hear Ye (CE)
Produced with TM 4 and TM 5 trademarks. Change was made in mid-production year. The original issue price was $30.

☐ 265 ......7.50" ....(CE) ......❹ .... $50—75
☐ 265 ......7.50" ....(CE) ......❺ .... $50—75

HUM 266 — Annual Plate, 1973
Globe Trotter (CE)
The original issue price was $32.50. "Hummel" trivia: This is the only plate in this series that has only 32 stars around the border—all the rest have 33!

☐ 266 ......7.50" ....(CE) ......❺ .... $100—150

HUM 267 — Annual Plate, 1974
Goose Girl (CE)
The original issue price was $40.

☐ 267 ......7.50" ....(CE) ......❺ .... $50—75

"Winner"

HUM 268 — Annual Plate, 1975
Ride Into Christmas (CE)
Two different samples were produced for the 1975 plate. The winning design was "Ride Into Christmas." The losing design was the "Little Fiddler" plate pictured here. There were only two or three of these samples produced—so actually it is a "winner" as far as value is concerned! Value: $5,000 +. The original issue price was $50.

☐ 268 ......7.50" ....(CE) ......❺ .... $50—75

"Loser"

HUM 269 — Annual Plate, 1976
Apple Tree Girl (CE)
The original issue price was $50.

☐ 269 ......7.50".........(CE) ......❺..........$50—75

HUM 270 — Annual Plate, 1977
Apple Tree Boy (CE)
Note the picture on the 1977 plate. The one shown here on the top is an early sample piece. Before production commenced, the boy's shoes were changed to a slightly different angle and the boy's stockings were reversed (his right one is higher than the left in most known examples). If your plate is exactly like this picture, you have a rare plate! The original issue price was $52.50.

☐ 270 ......7.50".........(CE) ......❺..........$5000 +
(Early Sample)
☐ 270 ......7.50".........(CE) ......❺..........$50—75

Early sample

Restyled version

HUM 271 — Annual Plate, 1978
Happy Pastime (CE)
The original issue price was $65.

☐ 271 ......7.50".........(CE) ......❺..........$50—75

HUM 272 — Annual Plate, 1979
Singing Lesson (CE)
The original issue price was $90.

☐ 272 ......7.50".........(CE) ......❺..........$40—60

HUM 273 — Annual Plate, 1980
School Girl (CE)
The original issue price was $100.

☐ 273 ......7.50" ....(CE) ......❻ ....$50—75

HUM 274 — Annual Plate, 1981
Umbrella Boy (CE)
The original issue price was $100.

☐ 274 ......7.50" ....(CE) ......❻ ....$40—60

HUM 275 — Annual Plate, 1982
Umbrella Girl (CE)
The original issue price was $100.

☐ 275 ......7.50" ....(CE) ......❻ ....$100—125

HUM 276 — Annual Plate, 1983
Postman (CE)
The original issue price was $108.

☐ 276 ......7.50" ....(CE) ......❻ $150–200

HUM 277 — Annual Plate, 1984
Little Helper (CE)
The original issue price was $108.

☐ 277 ......7.50" ....(CE) ......❻ ....$50—75

HUM 278 — Annual Plate, 1985
Chick Girl (CE)
The original issue price was $110.

☐ 278 ......7.50".......(CE) ...... ❻ ....$50—75

HUM 279 — Annual Plate, 1986
Playmates (CE)
The original issue price was $125.

☐ 279 ......7.50".......(CE) ...... ❻ ....$200—250

HUM 280 — Anniversary Plate, 1975
Stormy Weather (CE)
First edition of a series of plates issued at five year intervals. The inscription on the back applied by blue decal reads: "First edition M.I. Hummel Anniversary Plate 'Stormy Weather' 1975 hand painted." The original issue price was $100.

☐ 280 ......10.00"......(CE) ...... ❺ ....$100—150

HUM 281 — Anniversary Plate, 1980
Ring Around The Rosie (two girls only) (CE)
Second edition of a series of plates issued at five year intervals. The inscription on the back reads: "Second edition M.I. Hummel Anniversary Plate 1980 "Spring Dance" hand-painted." Trademark: (TM 6) 1978. Labeled "Spring Dance" in error. See HUM 353 "Spring Dance" and HUM 348 "Ring Around the Rosie." The original issue price was $225.

☐ 281 ......10.00"......(CE) ...... ❻ ....$100—150

HUM 282 — Anniversary Plate, 1985
Auf Wiedersehen (CE)
Third and last of a series of plates issued at five year intervals. The inscription on the back reads: "Third and final edition M.I. Hummel Anniversary Plate 1985 hand painted." A small round decal reads: "50 Jahre 1935—1985 M.I. Hummel Figuren." Trademark (TM 6) 1980. The original issue price was $225.

☐ 282 ......10.00"......(CE) ...... ❻ ....$150—200

HUM 283 — Annual Plate, 1987
Feeding Time (CE)
Designed by master sculptor Gerhard Skrobek in 1983. The original issue price was $135.

☐ 283 ......7.50" ....(CE) ......❻ ....$200—290

HUM 284 — Annual Plate, 1988
Little Goat Herder (CE)
Designed by master sculptor Gerhard Skrobek in 1983. The original issue price was $145.

☐ 284 ......7.50" ....(CE) ......❻ ....$125—150

HUM 285 — Annual Plate, 1989
Farm Boy (CE)
Designed by master sculptor Gerhard Skrobek in 1983. The original issue price was $160.

☐ 285 ......7.50" ....(CE) ......❻ ....$125—150

HUM 286 — Annual Plate, 1990
Shepherd's Boy (CE)
Designed by master sculptor Gerhard Skrobek in 1983. The original issue price was $170.

☐ 286 ......7.50" ....(CE) ......❻ ....$150—200

HUM 287 — Annual Plate, 1991
Just Resting (CE)
Designed by master sculptor Gerhard Skrobek in 1983. The original issue price was $196.

☐ 287 ......7.50" ....(CE) ......❻ ....$150—200
☐ 287 ......7.50" ....(CE) ......❼ ....$150—200

HUM 288 — Annual Plate, 1992
Wayside Harmony (CE)
Designed by master sculptor Gerhard Skrobek in 1983.
22nd in a series of 25. The original issue price was
$210.

☐ 288 ......7.50" ....(CE) ......❼ ....$150—200

HUM 289 — Annual Plate, 1993
Doll Bath (CE)
Designed by master sculptor Gerhard Skrobek in 1983.
23rd in a series of 25. The original issue price was
$210.

☐ 289 ......7.50" ....(CE) ......❼ ....$150—200

HUM 290 — Annual Plate, 1994
Doctor (CE)
Designed by master sculptor Gerhard Skrobek in 1983.
24th in a series of 25. The original issue price was
$210.

☐ 290 ......7.50" ....(CE) ......❼ ....$150—200

HUM 291 — Annual Plate, 1995
Come Back Soon
Designed by master sculptor Gerhard Skrobek in 1983.
25th and final plate in a series of 25. The original issue
price was $250.

☐ 291 ......7.50" ....(CE) ......❼ ....$175—250

FINAL EDITION
In 25 Year Series

HUM 292 — Meditation Plate
First released in the U.S. market in 1992, the first in the
Annual Series of four plates called "Friends Forever."
Modeled by master sculptor Gerhard Skrobeck in 1991. It
has the 1989 copyright date along with the (TM 7) trademark applied by blue decal on the back of plate. The original issue price was $180 in 1992.

☐ 292 ......7.125" ......(CE) ......❼ ....$100—150

HUM 293 — For Father Plate

First released in the U.S. market in 1993, the second in the Annual Series of four plates called "Friends Forever." Modeled by master sculptor Gerhard Skrobek in 1991. It has the 1991 copyright date along with the (TM 7) trademark applied by blue decal on the back of the plate. The original issue price was $195 in 1993.

☐ 293 ......7.125" ....(CE)......❼ ......$100—150

HUM 294 — Sweet Greetings Plate

First released in the U.S. market in 1994, the third in the Annual Series of four plates called "Friends Forever." Modeled by master sculptor Gerhard Skrobek in 1991. It has the 1991 copyright date along with the (TM 7) trademark applied by blue decal on the back of the plate. The original issue price was $205 in 1994.

☐ 294 ......7.125" ....(CE)......❼ ......$100—150

HUM 295 — Surprise Plate

First released in the U.S. market in 1995, the fourth and final edition plate in the Annual Series called "Friends Forever." Modeled by master sculptor Gerhard Skrobek in 1991. It has the 1991 copyright date along with the (TM 7) trademark applied by blue decal on the back of plate. The original issue price was $210 in 1995.

☐ 295 ......7.125" ....(CE)......❼ ......$100—150

HUM 296 — Winter Melody Plate

First released in the U.S. market in 1996, the first in an Annual Series of four plates entitled "Four Seasons." "WINTER" modeled by master sculptor Helmut Fischer in 1995. It has the 1995 copyright date along with the (TM 7) trademark applied by blue decal on the back of the plate. It features original artwork by Sister Maria Innocentia Hummel, combined with a three dimensional, sculptural relief of HUM 457 "Sound the Trumpet". The original issue price was $195 in 1996.

☐ 296 ......7.50" ......(CE)......❼ ......$195—200

HUM 297 — Springtime Serenade Plate
First released in the U.S. market in 1997, the second in an Annual Series of four plates entitled "Four Seasons." "SPRING" modeled by master sculptor Helmut Fischer in 1995. It has the 1995 copyright date along with the (TM 7) trademark applied by blue decal on the back of the plate. It features original artwork by Sister Maria Innocentia Hummel, combined with a three dimensional, sculptural relief of HUM 414 "In Tune". The original issue price was $195 in 1997.

☐ 297 ......7.50" ....(CE)...❼ ..$195—200

HUM 298 — Summertime Stroll Plate
First released in the U.S. market in 1998, the third in an Annual Series of four plates entitled "Four Seasons." "SUMMER" modeled by master sculptor Helmut Fischer in 1995. It has the 1995 copyright date along with the (TM 7) trademark applied by blue decal on the back of the plate. It features original artwork by Sister Maria Innocentia Hummel, combined with a three dimensional, sculptural relief of HUM 327 "The Run-A-Way". The original issue price was $195 in 1998.

☐ 298 ......7.50" ....(CE)...❼ ..$195—200

HUM 299 — Autumn Glory Plate
First released in the U.S. market in 1999, the fourth in an Annual Series of four plates entitled "Four Seasons." "FALL" modeled by master sculptor Helmut Fischer in 1995. It has the 1995 copyright date along with the (TM 7) trademark applied by blue decal on the back of the plate. It features original artwork by Sister Maria Innocentia Hummel, combined with a three dimensional, sculptural relief of HUM 426 "Pay Attention." The original issue price was $195 in 1999.

☐ 299 ......7.50" ....(CE)...❼ ..$195—200

(TM 2)   *(TM 5)*

HUM 300 — Bird Watcher
First sold in the U.S. in 1979. The original issue price was $80. At one time called "Tenderness." Has an incised 1956 copyright date. An early sample of this figure was modeled in 1954 by Gerhard Skrobek and was assigned the number HUM 233 (CN). Skrobek stated that this was the first figure he modeled after starting to work at the Goebel factory in 1954. An early sample model with the full bee trademark, incised 1954 date, is in the Robert L. Miller collection. (TW) "Temporarily Withdrawn" from production in December 2004.

☐ 300	........5.00"	..................(CE)	............❷	........$4000—5000	(Early Sample)
☐ 300	........5.00"	..................(CE)	............❸	........$2000—2500	(Early Sample)
☐ 300	........5.00"	..................(CE)	............❹	........$1500—2000	(Early Sample)
☐ 300	........5.00"	..................(CE)	............❺	........$280—300	
☐ 300	........5.00"	..................(CE)	............❻	........$275—280	
☐ 300	........5.00"	..................(CE)	............❼	........$270—275	
☐ 300	........5.00"	..................**(TW)**	............❽	........$270—275	

Early sample (TM 3)   *New style (TM 6)*

HUM 301 — Christmas Angel
First released in the U.S. market in 1989. Originally called: "Delivery Angel." An early sample model of this figure was modeled by Theo R. Menzenbach in 1957. Menzenbach stated that it was not approved by the Siessen Convent for production. The sample model in our collection has an early stylized (TM 3) trademark and 1957 incised copyright date. Original issue price was $160 in 1989. Was restyled by master sculptor Gerhard Skrobek in the late 1980s but still has the 1957 copyright date. A new small size (301 2/0) was released in 2003 with a 2002 copyright date. Has "Hummel" only on the back of base.

☐ 301 2/0	..4.00"	..................**(OE)**	............❽	........$179	
☐ 301	........6.25"	..................(CE)	............❸	........$4000—5000	(Early Sample)
☐ 301	........6.00"	..................(CE)	............❻	........$325—330	
☐ 301	........6.00"	..................(CE)	............❼	........$320—325	
☐ 301	........6.00"	..................**(OE)**	............❽	........$319	

HUM 302 — Concentration (PFE)

First modeled by master sculptor Arthur Moeller in 1955. Originally called "Knit One, Purl Two." Girl is similar to HUM 255 "Stitch in Time." Listed on factory records as a (PFE) Possible Future Edition and may be released at some future date, subject to possible minor changes.

☐ 302 ......5.00" ....(CE) ....❷ ....$4000—5000
   (Early Sample)
☐ 302 ......5.00" ....(**PFE**) ....

HUM 303 — Arithmetic Lesson (PFE)

Originally called "School Lesson." Modeled by master sculptor Arthur Moeller in 1955. Notice similarity to middle boy in HUM 170 "School Boys" and girl from HUM 177 "School Girls." Listed on factory records as a (PFE) Possible Future Edition and may be released at some future date, subject to possible minor changes.

☐ 303 ......5.25" ....(CE) ....❷ ....$4000—5000
   (Early Sample)
☐ 303 ......5.25" ....(**PFE**) ....

HUM 304 — Artist, The

Originally modeled by master sculptor Karl Wagner in 1955 and later restyled by master sculptor Gerhard Skrobek in 1970. First introduced in the U.S. market in 1971. Has an incised 1955 copyright date. Could possibly be found in (TM 2) and (TM 3) trademarks, but would be considered extremely rare. Had (TM 4) trademark when first issued in quantity in 1971. Note: Artist Karl Wagner is no longer living. The original issue price in 1971 was $18. Known variation on (TM 2) "full bee" example has a small drop of paint shown on base. The Artist motif was used for a new plaque issued in 1993 for the grand opening of the M.I. Hummel Museum in New Braunfels, Texas. See HUM 756 for photo.

☐ 304 ......5.50" ....(CE) ....❷ ....$4000—5000
   (Early Sample)
☐ 304 ......5.50" ....(CE) ....❸ ....$2000—3000
   (Early Sample)
☐ 304 ......5.50" ....(CE) ....❹ ....$1000—1500
☐ 304 ......5.50" ....(CE) ....❺ ....$340—375
☐ 304 ......5.50" ....(CE) ....❻ ....$335—340
☐ 304 ......5.50" ....(CE) ....❼ ....$330—335
☐ 304 ......5.50" ....(**OE**) ....❽ $329

HUM 305 — Builder, The

First introduced in the U.S. market in 1963, this figurine was originally modeled in 1955 by master sculptor Gerhard Skrobek. Has an incised 1955 copyright date. An example with (TM 2) trademark would be considered rare. Listed as (TW) "Temporarily Withdrawn" from production in June 2002.

☐ 305........5.50".........(CE)........❷ ....$4000—5000   (Early Sample)
☐ 305........5.50".........(CE)........❸ ....$1000—1500
☐ 305........5.50".........(CE)........❹ ....$350—400
☐ 305........5.50".........(CE)........❺ ....$315—350
☐ 305........5.50".........(CE)........❻ ....$310—315
☐ 305........5.50".........(CE)........❼ ....$305—310
☐ 305........5.50".........(**TW**) ......❽ $305

HUM 306 — Little Bookkeeper

First introduced in the U.S. market in 1962, this figurine was originally modeled in 1955 by master sculptor Arthur Moeller. Has an incised 1955 copyright date. A "Little Book-keeper" with a full bee, trademark 2, was recently purchased at auction in New York at a fraction of the true value. An example with (TM 2) trademark would be considered rare. Listed as (TW) "Temporarily Withdrawn" from production in June 2002.

☐ 306........4.75".........(CE)........❷ ....$4000—5000   (Early Sample)
☐ 306........4.75".........(CE)........❸ ....$1000—1500
☐ 306........4.75".........(CE)........❹ ....$400—450
☐ 306........4.75".........(CE)........❺ ....$365—390
☐ 306........4.75".........(CE)........❻ ....$360—365
☐ 306........4.75".........(CE)........❼ ....$355—360
☐ 306........4.75".........(**TW**) ......❽ $355

HUM 307 — Good Hunting

First introduced in the U.S. market in 1962, this figurine was originally modeled by master sculptor Reinhold Unger and sculptor Helmut Wehlte in 1955. Has an incised 1955 copyright date. Hat, brush, collar, hair and position of binoculars have some variations. An example with (TM 2) trademark would be considered rare. The word "musterzimmer" means "painter's sample" and should not have been removed from factory. Possibly shipped out by accident. (TW) "Temporarily Withdrawn" on December 31, 2005.

New style (TM 4)   *Old style (TM 2)*

☐ 307	........5.00"	................(CE)	...........❷	.........$4000—5000	(Early Sample)
☐ 307	........5.00"	................(CE)	...........❸	.........$1000—1500	
☐ 307	........5.00"	................(CE)	...........❹	.........$400—450	
☐ 307	........5.00"	................(CE)	...........❺	.........$330—350	
☐ 307	........5.00"	................(CE)	...........❻	.........$325—330	
☐ 307	........5.00"	................(CE)	...........❼	.........$320—325	
☐ 307	........5.00"	................(TW)	...........❽	.........$319	

HUM 308 — Little Tailor

First introduced in the U.S. market in 1972. Originally modeled by master sculptor Horst Ashermann in 1955. Later restyled by master sculptor Gerhard Skrobek in 1972. Early model on the right has an incised 1955 copyright date while the restyled version on the left has an incised 1972 copyright date. Both styles can be found in (TM 5) trademark. The original issue price was $24 in 1972. (TW) "Temporarily Withdrawn" on December 31, 2003.

New style (TM 5)   *Old style (TM 2)*

☐ 308	........5.25 to 5.75"	......(CE)	...........❷	.........$4000—5000	(Early Sample)
☐ 308	........5.25 to 5.75"	......(CE)	...........❸	.........$2000—3000	(Early Sample)
☐ 308	........5.25 to 5.75"	......(CE)	...........❹	.........$1200—1500	(Difficult to find)
☐ 308	........5.25 to 5.75"	......(CE)	...........❺	.........$800—900	(Old Style)
☐ 308	........5.25 to 5.75"	......(CE)	...........❺	.........$325—350	(New Style)
☐ 308	........5.25 to 5.75"	......(CE)	...........❻	.........$310—315	
☐ 308	........5.25 to 5.75"	......(CE)	...........❼	.........$305—310	
☐ 308	........5.25 to 5.75"	......(TW)	...........❽	.........$305—310	

Current production   *Early sample*

HUM 309 — With Loving Greetings

First released in the U.S. market in 1983. Modeled in 1955 by master sculptor Karl Wagner. Originally called "Greetings From" on old factory records, but later changed to "With Loving Greetings." The original issue price was $80 in 1983. Notice the ink stopper beside the ink bottle and an extra paint brush under the boy's left arm. This is an early sample model and these two items were eliminated for production reasons. When originally introduced in 1983, the ink bottle was blue and the message was a deep turquoise. In 1987 this was changed to a brown ink bottle and the message to a periwinkle blue. Listed as (TW) "Temporarily Withdrawn".

☐ 309	3.50"	(CE)	❷	$4000—5000	(Early Sample)
☐ 309	3.25 to 3.50"	(CE)	❸	$3000—4000	(Early Sample)
☐ 309	3.25 to 3.50"	(CE)	❹	$2000—3000	(Early Sample)
☐ 309	3.25 to 3.50"	(CE)	❺	$1000—2000	(Early Sample)
☐ 309	3.25 to 3.50"	(CE)	❻	$250—300	(Blue)
☐ 309	3.25 to 3.50"	(CE)	❻	$230—240	(Brown)
☐ 309	3.25 to 3.50"	(CE)	❼	$220—225	
☐ 309	3.25 to 3.50"	(TW)	❽	$210—220	

HUM 310 — Searching Angel, Wall Plaque

First introduced in the U.S. market in 1979 along with two other "M.I. Hummol" items. This plaque was originally called "Angelic Concern" on factory records, but later changed to above name. Has an incised 1955 copyright date and was modeled by master sculptor Gerhard Skrobek in 1955. Very limited production in "Goebel Bee" (TM 5) trademark. Some catalogues list this piece as number 310 A in error; the incised number is 310 only. The original issue price was $55 in 1979. Listed as (TW) "Temporarily Withdrawn" in January 1999.

☐ 310	4.25 to 3.25"	(CE)	❷	$2000—3000	(Early Sample)
☐ 310	4.25 to 3.25"	(CE)	❸	$1200—1700	(Early Sample)
☐ 310	4.25 to 3.25"	(CE)	❹	$1000—1500	(Early Sample)
☐ 310	4.25 to 3.25"	(CE)	❺	$300—500	
☐ 310	4.25 to 3.25"	(CE)	❻	$135—140	
☐ 310	4.25 to 3.25"	(TW)	❼	$135—140	

HUM 311 — Kiss Me

First introduced in the U.S. market in 1961. Originally modeled by master sculptor Reinhold Unger in 1955. Later restyled in 1963 by master sculptor Gerhard Skrobek at the request of the Convent. The doll was redesigned to look more like a doll instead of a child. Has an incised 1955 copyright date. Both styles can be found with (TM 3) and (TM 4) trademarks. An example with a "full bee" (TM 2) trademark would be considered rare.

New style (TM 4)   *Old style (TM 2)*

☐ 311..........6.00 to 6.25".......(CE) ....❷ ....$4000—5000 (Early Sample)
☐ 311..........6.00 to 6.25".......(CE) ....❸ ....$900—1100 (Old Style)
☐ 311..........6.00 to 6.25".......(CE) ....❸ ....$500—550 (New Style)
☐ 311..........6.00 to 6.25".......(CE) ....❹ ....$700—950 (Old Style)
☐ 311..........6.00 to 6.25".......(CE) ....❹ ....$400—450 (New Style)
☐ 311..........6.00 to 6.25".......(CE) ....❺ ....$370—395
☐ 311..........6.00 to 6.25".......(CE) ....❻ ....$365—370
☐ 311..........6.00 to 6.25".......(CE) ....❼ ....$360—365
☐ 311..........6.00 to 6.25".......(**OE**) ....❽ $359

HUM 312 — Honey Lover (EE)

First modeled by master sculptor Helmut Wehlte in 1955. This figurine was originally called "In the Jam Pot" on factory records, but later changed to the above name. This early sample model pictured here has a "full bee" (TM 2) trademark and is part of the Robert L. Miller collection. Announced in 1991, "Honey Lover" will be an Exclusive Edition available to "M.I. Hummel Club" members only, who have belonged to the Club continuously for 15

Early sample (TM 2)   *(TM 7)*

years. The original issue price was $190. This figurine can be found on the secondary market.

☐ 312 ....4.00".................(CE) ....❷ ....$4000—5000 (Early Sample)
☐ 312/1 ......3.75".................(CE) ....❻ ....$400—500
☐ 312/1 ......3.75".................(CE) ....❼ ....$275—300
☐ 312/1 ......3.75".................(**EE**)..............❽ $275

HUM 313 — Sunny Morning

This figurine was originally called "Slumber Serenade" on factory records, but later changed to "Sunny Morning." Modeled in 1955 by master sculptor Arthur Moeller. This early sample model pictured here has a "full bee" (TM 2) trademark and is part of the Robert L. Miller collection. First released in fall 2002 with "First Issue 2003" backstamp, for the official issue price of $300.

☐ 313 ....4.25"..................(CE) ....❷ ....$4000—5000   (Early Sample)
☐ 313 ....4.25"..................(OE) ....❽ $319

Old style (TM 2)   Early sample (TM 2)   New style (TM 5)

HUM 314 — Confidentially

First introduced in the U.S. market in 1972. Originally modeled by master sculptor Horst Ashermann in 1955. Later restyled by master sculptor Gerhard Skrobek in 1972. Skrobek completely restyled it by changing the stand, adding a tie to the boy and giving it the new textured finish. The early models have an incised 1955 copyright date while the restyled version has an incised 1972 copyright date. When first put on the market in 1972 it was in the old style and had the (TM 4) trademark. Older trademarks such as (TM 2) and (TM 3) would be considered rare. The original issue price in 1972 was $22.50. Listed as (TW) "Temporarily Withdrawn" in January 1999, but may be reinstated at some future date.

☐ 314 ....5.25 to 5.75"......(CE) ....❷ ....$4000—5000   (Early Sample)
☐ 314 ....5.25 to 5.75"......(CE) ....❸ ....$2000—3000   (Early Sample)
☐ 314 ....5.25 to 5.75"......(CE) ....❹ ....$1000—1200
☐ 314 ....5.25 to 5.75"......(CE) ....❺ ....$800—950   (Old Style)
☐ 314 ....5.25 to 5.75"......(CE) ....❺ ....$350—390   (New Style)
☐ 314 ....5.25 to 5.75"......(CE) ....❻ ....$340—350
☐ 314 ....5.25 to 5.75"......(TW) ....❼ ....$325—335

HUM 315 — Mountaineer
First introduced in the U.S. market at the N.Y. World's Fair in 1964. Has an incised 1955 copyright date. Originally modeled by master sculptor Gerhard Skrobek in 1955. Older models are slightly smaller and have a green stick rather than the dark gray stick found on the newer models. If found with (TM 2) trademark would be considered rare. Approximately <u>850</u> pieces made with "1977 M. I. Hummel Club Convention" in green lettering on front of base. — Value $325.

☐ 315	.......5.25"	..................(CE)	............❷	.........$4000—5000	(Early Sample)
☐ 315	.......5.25"	..................(CE)	............❸	.........$800—1000	
☐ 315	.......5.25"	..................(CE)	............❹	.........$295—400	
☐ 315	.......5.25"	..................(CE)	............❺	.........$290—295	
☐ 315	.......5.25"	..................(CE)	............❻	.........$285—290	
☐ 315	.......5.25"	..................(CE)	............❼	.........$280—285	
☐ 315	.......5.25"	..................(**OE**)	............❽	.........$279	

HUM 316 — Relaxation (EE)
This figurine was originally called "Nightly Ritual" on factory records, but later changed to "Relaxation." Modeled by master sculptor Karl Wagner in 1955. An Exclusive Edition available to "M.I. Hummel Club" members only, who have belonged to the Club continuously for 25 years.

☐ 316	.......4.00"	..................(CE)	............❷	.........$4000—5000	(Early Sample)
☐ 316	.......4.00"	..................(**EE**)	............❽	.........$390	

HUM 317 — Not For You!

First introduced in the U.S. market in 1961. Has an incised 1955 copyright date. Originally modeled by master sculptor Arthur Moeller in 1955. Some catalogues and price lists incorrectly show size as 6.00". The collector should not rely on the measurements in price lists and catalogues as being absolutely accurate, as there have been many typographical errors in them throughout the years. In this book, we used the "bracket" system and show the smallest to the largest size known, verified by actual measurement. If found with (TM 2) trademark would be considered rare. (TW) "Temporarily Withdrawn" in December 2004.

☐ 317 ....5.50"..................(CE) ....❷ ....$4000—5000   (Early Sample)
☐ 317 ....5.50"..................(CE) ....❸ ....$800—1000
☐ 317 ....5.50"..................(CE) ....❹ ....$350—450
☐ 317 ....5.50"..................(CE) ....❺ ....$310—325
☐ 317 ....5.50"..................(CE) ....❻ ....$305—310
☐ 317 ....5.50"..................(CE) ....❼ ....$300—305
☐ 317 ....5.50"..................(TW) ....❽ ....$300—305

Early sample (TM 2)　　　　*(TM 7)*

HUM 318 — Art Critic

First modeled by master sculptor Horst Ashermann in 1955. Has an incised 1955 copyright date. First released in the U.S. Market in 1991 with a "First Issue 1991" backstamp. The original issue price was $230. Listed as (TW) "Temporarily Withdrawn" in January 1999.

☐ 318 ....5.75"..................(CE) ....❷ ....$4000—5000 (Early Sample)
☐ 318 ....5.75"..................(CE) ....❻ ....$330—340
☐ 318 ....5.75"..................(TW) ....❼ ....$315—325

HUM 319 — Doll Bath

First introduced in the U.S. market in 1962. Has an incised 1956 copyright date. Originally modeled by master sculptor Gerhard Skrobek in 1956 and was restyled with the new textured finish in the early 1970s. If found with (TM 2) trademark would be considered rare.

☐ 319	5.00"	(CE)	❷	$4000—5000 (Early Sample)
☐ 319	5.00"	(CE)	❸	$800—1000
☐ 319	5.00"	(CE)	❹	$400—450
☐ 319	5.00"	(CE)	❺	$365—390
☐ 319	5.00"	(CE)	❻	$360—365
☐ 319	5.00"	(CE)	❼	$355—360
☐ 319	5.00"	(OE)	❽	$359

Early sample (TM 2)   Current production (TM 7)   *(Rear veiws)*

HUM 320 — Professor, The

Originally modeled in 1955 by master sculptor Gerhard Skrobek. First released in the U.S. market in the fall of 1991 with an incised 1989 copyright date, and "First Issue 1992" backstamp. The original issue price was $180 in 1991. Listed as (TW) "Temporarily Withdrawn" in January 2002.

☐ 320	5.50 to 5.75"	(CE)	❷	$4000—5000 (Early Sample)
☐ 320/0	4.875"	(CE)	❼	$260—275
☐ 320/0	4.875"	(TW)	❽	$260—275

Early sample (TM 2)   *Current style (TM 5)*

HUM 321 — Wash Day

First introduced in the U.S. market in 1963. Has an incised 1957 copyright date. Originally modeled in 1955 by master sculptor Reinhold Unger and Helmut Wehlte. Notice early sample model pictured here. Older pieces are usually slightly larger in size. If found with trademark 2 would be considered rare. A new miniature size figurine was issued in 1989 with a suggested retail price of $60 to match a new miniature plate series called the "Little Homemakers"—one each year for four years. This is the second in the series. The miniature size figurine has an incised 1987 copyright date. The original size will be renumbered 321/1 and the old number 321 is now classified as a (CE) Closed Edition because of this change. The miniature size (321 4/0) was (TW) "Temporarily Withdrawn" from production on 31 December 1997.

- ☐ 321 4/0 ....3.00".....................(CE) ....❻ ....$130—140
- ☐ 321 4/0 ....3.00".....................(TW).........❼ ....$125—130
- ☐ 321 ....5.50 to 6.00" ......(CE) ....❷ ....$4000—5000 (Early Sample)
- ☐ 321 ....5.50 to 6.00" ......(CE) ....❸ ....$800—1000
- ☐ 321 ....5.50 to 6.00" ......(CE) ....❹ ....$440—475
- ☐ 321 ....5.50 to 6.00" ......(CE) ....❺ ....$430—440
- ☐ 321 ....5.50 to 6.00" ......(CE) ....❻ ....$420—430
- ☐ 321/1........5.50 to 6.00" ......(CE) ....❻ ....$410—420
- ☐ 321/1........5.50 to 6.00" ......(CE) ....❼ ....$400—410
- ☐ 321/1........5.50 to 6.00" ......(OE).........❽ $399

321 4/0 (TM 6)

228

HUM 322 — Little Pharmacist

First introduced in the U.S. market in 1962. Originally modeled by master sculptor Karl Wagner in 1955. Most examples have an incised 1955 copyright date. Older models are slightly larger in size. Several variations on label of bottle; "Rizinusol" (German for Castor Oil) and "Vit-

German   Spanish   English

amins" are most common. Also found with "Castor bil" (Spanish for Castor Oil). If found with (TM 2) trademark would be considered rare. On 31 December 1984 the German language variation was (TW) "Temporarily Withdrawn" from production but may be reinstated at some future date. This variation now commands a premium of $100 to 200 more than "Vitamins" when found. "Little Pharmacist" was restyled in the fall of 1987. The figurine has a new base with a smoother surface and rounded corners and edges. It is slightly smaller in size, the eyeglass stems disappear into the hair and his bowtie has been straightened. On his coat the button tape now runs along a curve rather than straight up and down, and a breast pocket has been added. Also, on the back there is a wider coat strap with two buttons instead of one. In 1990 a few pieces of the "Little Pharmacist" were accidentally produced in the new style with the German "Rizinusol" decal on the bottle and the English "Recipe" on the paper boy is holding. Only a few of these rare pieces have been found and would have a value of $1000 to $1500. Retired in 2006 (CE) Closed Edition.

☐ 322 ....5.75 to 6.00".......(CE) ....❷ ....$4000—5000 (Early Sample)
☐ 322 ....5.75 to 6.00".......(CE) ....❸ ....$800—1000
☐ 322 ....5.75 to 6.00".......(CE) ....❹ ....$350—400
☐ 322 ....5.75 to 6.00".......(CE) ....❹ ....$2000—3000 (Castor Bil)
☐ 322 ....5.75 to 6.00".......(CE) ....❺ ....$340—350
☐ 322 ....5.75 to 6.00".......(CE) ....❻ ....$330—340
☐ 322 ....5.75 to 6.00".......(CE) ....❼ ....$320—330
☐ 322 ....5.75 to 6.00".......(CE) ....❽ ....$319 (Closed Edition)

Back view   Old style   Old style   New style

HUM 323 — Merry Christmas, Wall Plaque

First introduced in the U.S. market in 1979 along with two other "M.I. Hummel" items, HUM 310 "Searching Angel" plaque and HUM 300 "Bird Watcher." Has an incised 1955 copyright date. Originally modeled by master sculptor Gerhard Skrobek in 1955. The original issue price in 1979 was $55. Very limited production in "Goebel bee" (TM 5) trademark. Listed as (TW) "Temporarily Withdrawn" in January 1999.

☐ 323 ....5.25 x 3.50" ......(CE) ....❷ ....$2000—3000 (Early Sample)
☐ 323 ....5.25 x 3.50" ......(CE) ....❸ ....$1200—1700 (Early Sample)
☐ 323 ....5.25 x 3.50" ......(CE) ....❹ ....$1000—1200 (Early Sample)
☐ 323 ....5.25 x 3.50" ......(CE) ....❺ ....$350—500
☐ 323 ....5.25 x 3.50" ......(CE) ....❻ ....$150—175
☐ 323 ....5.25 x 3.50" ......(TW) ....❼ ....$140—150

Early sample (TM 2)

HUM 324 — At The Fence (PFE)

Originally called "The Other Side of the Fence" on factory records, but later changed to "At The Fence." Modeled in 1955 by master sculptor Arthur Moeller. This early sample model pictured here has a "full bee" (TM 2) trademark and is part of the Robert L. Miller collection. Listed on factory records as a (PFE) Possible Future Edition and may be released at some future date, subject to possible minor changes.

☐ 324 ....4.75" ....(CE) ....❷ ....$4000—5000 (Early Sample)
☐ 324 ....4.75" ....(PFE)...........................

HUM 325 — Helping Mother (PFE)
This figurine was originally modeled by master sculptor Arthur Moeller in August 1955 and the first sample was painted in July 1956 by artist "F/K"—the initials used by Franz Kirchner. Originally called "Mother's Aid" on old factory records but later changed to "Helping Mother." Similar in design to HUM 133 "Mother's Helper". This early sample model pictured here has the "full bee" (TM 2) trademark and is in the Robert L. Miller collection. Note resemblance to girl in HUM 753 "Togetherness".

☐ 325 ....5.00" ....(CE) ....❷ ....$4000—5000 (Early Sample)
☐ 325 ....5.00" ....(**PFE**).........................

HUM 326 (TM 2) (PFE)   *HUM 794 (PFE)*

HUM 326 — Being Punished, Wall Plaque (PFE)
This figurine was originally modeled by master sculptor Gerhard Skrobek in early 1955 and the first sample was painted by artist Harald Sommer in November 1955. Originally called "Naughty Boy" on old factory records but later changed to "Being Punished." This piece has a hole on the back for hanging as a plaque or will sit upright on base. Has an incised 1955 copyright date on back. This early sample model pictured here has the "full bee" (TM 2) trademark and is part of the Robert L. Miller collection. See HUM 794 "Best Buddies" (PFE) Possible Future Edition.

☐ 326 ....4.00 x 5.00" ......(CE) ....❷ ....$4000—5000 (Early Sample)
☐ 326 ....4.00 x 5.00" ......(**PFE**).........................

New style (TM 5)   *Old style (TM 5)*

HUM 327 — Run-A-Way, The

First introduced in the U.S. market in 1972. Originally modeled by master sculptor Helmut Wehlte in 1955 and later restyled by master sculptor Gerhard Skrobek in 1972. Skrobek completely restyled this figure with the new textured finish and variations in the location of basket, hat and shoes. Slight color variations also. The early models have an incised 1955 copyright date while the restyled version has an incised 1972 copyright date. When first put on the market in 1972 it was in the old style and had the "three line" (TM 4) trademark. Older trademarks such as (TM 2) and (TM 3) would be considered rare. The original issue price in 1972 was $28.50. This motif was used for HUM 298 "Summertime Stroll" plate issued in 1998. (TW) "Temporarily Withdrawn" from production in 2002.

☐ 327	5.25"	(CE)	❷	$4000—5000	(Early Sample)
☐ 327	5.25"	(CE)	❸	$2000—3000	(Early Sample)
☐ 327	5.25"	(CE)	❹	$1000—1200	
☐ 327	5.25"	(CE)	❺	$900—1000	(Old Style)
☐ 327	5.25"	(CE)	❺	$320—325	(New Style)
☐ 327	5.25"	(CE)	❻	$315—320	
☐ 327	5.25"	(CE)	❼	$315—320	
☐ 327	5.25"	(TW)	❽	$315—320	

Early sample (TM 2)   *(TM 4)*

HUM 328 — Carnival

First introduced in the U.S. market in 1963. Originally modeled by master sculptors Reinhold Unger and Helmut Wehlte in 1955. Early sample model with "full bee" (TM 2) trademark has a 1955 incised copyright date. Later models have a 1957 incised copyright date. Older examples are slightly larger with only minor variations. The object under the child's arm is a noise maker or "slapstick," a device generally made of wood and paper or cloth—popular with stage comedians. Note difference in size and position of pom-poms on early sample model. This early sample model was purchased from a German lady in New York and is now part of the Robert L. Miller collection. Confirmed as (TW) "Temporarily Withdrawn" in November 1999, and permanently retired in 2000 with "Final Issue" or "Retirement Exclusive" backstamp.

☐ 328	5.75 to 6.00"	(CE)	❷	$4000—5000	(Early Sample)
☐ 328	5.75 to 6.00"	(CE)	❸	$800—1200	
☐ 328	5.75 to 6.00"	(CE)	❹	$300—350	
☐ 328	5.75 to 6.00"	(CE)	❺	$270—290	
☐ 328	5.75 to 6.00"	(CE)	❻	$260—270	
☐ 328	5.75 to 6.00"	(CE)	❼	$250—260	
☐ 328	5.25"	(CE)	❽	$250—260	

FINAL ISSUE
2000

HUM 329 — Off To School (PFE)
Originally called "Kindergarten Romance" on factory records, but later changed to "Off To School." Modeled by master sculptor Arthur Moeller in 1955. It has an incised 1955 copyright date. The boy is quite similar to HUM 82 "School Boy" while the girl is completely new. Listed on factory records as a (PFE) Possible Future Edition and may be released at some future date, subject to possible minor changes.

☐ 329 ....5.00" ....(CE) ....❷ ....$4000—5000 (Early Sample)
☐ 329 ....5.00" ....(PFE).........................

Early sample (TM 2)   *(TM 6)*

HUM 330 — Baking Day
First introduced to the U.S. market in 1985. Originally called "Kneading Dough" on old factory records, but later changed to "Baking Day." Modeled by master sculptor Gerhard Skrobek in 1955. It has an incised 1955 copyright date. The original issue price in 1985 was $95. Listed as (TW) "Temporarily Withdrawn" in January 1999. Available in European market in (TM 8) for $360.

☐ 330 ....5.25" ....(CE) ....❷ ....$4000—5000 (Early Sample)
☐ 330 ....5.25" ....(CE) ....❸ ....$2000—2500 (Early Sample)
☐ 330 ....5.25" ....(CE) ....❹ ....$2000—2500 (Early Sample)
☐ 330 ....5.25" ....(CE) ....❺ ....$1000—1500 (Early Sample)
☐ 330 ....5.25" ....(CE) ....❻ ....$365—370
☐ 330 ....5.25" ....(**CE**) ....❼ ....$360—365
☐ 330 ....5.25" ....(**TW**) ....❽ ....$300—360

Original Style (TM 2)   *Commemorative Issue (TM 6)*

HUM 331 — Crossroads

First introduced in the U.S. market in 1972. Modeled by master sculptor Arthur Moeller in 1955. It has an incised 1955 copyright date. The original issue price in 1972 was $45.00. In the summer of 1990, Goebel announced a worldwide (LE) Limited Edition of 20,000 pieces in a uniquely altered form, to commemorate the first anniversary of the opening of the Berlin Wall. The difference between the original 1972 version and the new limited edition version is significant and symbolic. Originally, midway up the signpost was a small sign which read "HALT." Now, like so many similar signs along the East/West border, the sign lies on the ground. Original issue price of commemorative issue was $360. During the production of this special figurine, the factory changed trademarks. Consequently, approximately 15,000 pieces bear the (TM 6) trademark and the remaining 5,000 bear the (TM 7) trademark. The numbers were not consistant, so it is possible to have a piece numbered 17,000 with a (TM 6) trademark. Naturally the (TM 7) trademark pieces will usually bring a higher price on the secondary market because of the fewer number of pieces bearing this trademark. A third variation was released in 1992 and was sold only through U.S. Military base exchange stores. This edition consists of three pieces—the regular Crossroads figurine with the "HALT" sign up in the original position, but with a special colored decal of the American and the German flags on the bottom of the figurine. The second piece is a ceramic replica of the crumbled Berlin Wall. A special inscription reads: "With esteem and grateful appreciation to the United States Military Forces for the preservation of Peace and Freedom." The same inscription is on the brass plate attached to the third piece in the set, a black hardwood display base. This limited edition consists of 20,000 sets worldwide and are hand numbered on the bottom of the Berlin Wall piece. Originally military issue price was $265 in 1992. The Special Edition "Crossroads" is the first M.I. Hummel figurine to feature the American flag by decal on the bottom. The flag has blue stars and a white background in error, but later corrected.

(prices on next page)

234

☐ 331	6.75"	(CE)	❷	$4000—5000	(Early Sample)
☐ 331	6.75"	(CE)	❸	$2500—3500	(Early Sample)
☐ 331	6.75"	(CE)	❹	$800—1000	
☐ 331	6.75"	(CE)	❺	$500—550	
☐ 331	6.75"	(CE)	❻	$500—525	(Original Style)
☐ 331	6.75"	(CE)	❻	$700—900	(Commemorative)
☐ 331	6.75"	(CE)	❼	$900—1100	(Commemorative)
☐ 331	6.75"	(CE)	❼	$500—525	(Original Style)
☐ 331	6.75"	(Military Only)	❼	$600—750	(Three Piece Set)
☐ 331	6.75"	(OE)	❽	$510	(Original Style)

This early sample model has the trombone reversed. Research at the factory indicated this was probably an accident in assembling the separate clay molds and possibly this is the only one made that way. We are unaware of any others having been found. The "full bee" example in our collection has the trombone in the normal position.

Rare old sample   **Normal position**

This three piece set originally sold only through U.S. Military base exchange stores, but can now be purchased on the secondary market. Original military price was $260.

.... HUM TERM ....

RATTLE: All "M.I. Hummel" figurines are hollow on the inside. Occasionally, when the figurine is fired, a small piece of clay will drop off on the inside. This little bit of clay when dry will cause a slight rattle. Actually, it does not hurt the figurine or affect the value one way or the other. I would not even call it a flaw, as it does not detract from the appearance. Actually, it is one means of identification that might come in handy sometime!

Red (TM 2)   **Blue (TM 3)**

HUM 332 — Soldier Boy

First introduced in the U.S. market in 1963. Modeled by master sculptor Gerhard Skrobek in 1955. The early prototype model in our collection has a full bee trademark and a 1955 incised copyright date. Later models have a 1957 incised copyright date. Older pieces are slightly larger and usually have a red ornament on hat while the newer pieces have a blue one. Trademark 4 (TM 4) can be found with either red or blue ornaments. On older models the "M.I. Hummel" signature is located on the side of the base while newer models have signature on top of the base. A special commemorative edition was issued in 1994. See back of book for information. Listed as (TW) "Temporarily Withdrawn" in January 1999.

☐	332	.......5.75 to 6.00".......(CE)	........❷	......$4000—5000	(Early Sample)
☐	332	.......5.75 to 6.00".......(CE)	........❸	......$1000—1500	(Red Ornament)
☐	332	.......5.75 to 6.00".......(CE)	........❹	......$500—700	(Red Ornament)
☐	332	.......5.75 to 6.00".......(CE)	........❹	......$300—350	(Blue Ornament)
☐	332	.......5.75 to 6.00".......(CE)	........❺	......$290—300	
☐	332	.......5.75 to 6.00".......(CE)	........❻	......$280—290	
☐	332	.......5.75 to 6.00".......(TW)	........❼	......$275—280	

HUM 726 (TM 7)

HUM 333 — Blessed Event

First introduced in the U.S. market at the N.Y. World's Fair in 1964. Originally modeled by master sculptor Arthur Moeller in 1955. Found with either 1955, 1956 or 1957 incised copyright dates.

☐	333	.......5.25 to 5.50" ....(CE)	...........❷	.........$4000—5000	(Early Sample)
☐	333	.......5.25 to 5.50".......(CE)	...........❸	.........$800—1000	
☐	333	.......5.25 to 5.50".......(CE)	...........❹	.........$450—650	
☐	333	.......5.25 to 5.50".......(CE)	...........❺	.........$420—450	
☐	333	.......5.25 to 5.50".......(CE)	...........❻	.........$410—420	
☐	333	.......5.25 to 5.50".......(CE)	...........❼	.........$400—410	
☐	333	.......5.25 to 5.50".......(OE)	...........❽	.........$399	

HUM 334 — Homeward Bound

First introduced in the U.S. market in 1971 along with three other new releases: HUM 304 "Artist," HUM 340 "Letter to Santa Claus" and HUM 347 "Adventure Bound." "Homeward Bound" was originally modeled by master sculptor Arthur Moeller in 1956 and later restyled by master sculptor Gerhard Skrobek in 1974. Found with either 1955 or 1956 incised copyright dates in early models. The restyled version has the new textured finish and no support pedestal under the goat. Current model has an incised 1975 copyright date. "Homeward Bound" can be found in both "Old

Old style (TM 4)   *New style (TM 5)*

style" as well as "New style" in both (TM 4) and (TM 5) trademarks. The original issue price in 1971 was $35. Listed as (TW) "Temporarily Withdrawn" in January 1999.

☐ 334	5.25"	(CE)	❷	$4000—5000	(Early Sample)
☐ 334	5.25"	(CE)	❸	$1000—1500	
☐ 334	5.25"	(CE)	❹	$700—850	(Old style)
☐ 334	5.25"	(CE)	❹	$475—500	(New style)
☐ 334	5.25"	(CE)	❺	$450—500	(Old style)
☐ 334	5.25"	(CE)	❺	$425—450	(New style)
☐ 334	5.25"	(CE)	❻	$410—420	
☐ 334	5.25"	(TW)	❼	$400—410	

HUM 335 — Lucky Boy

Modeled by master sculptor Arthur Moeller in 1956. Restyled by master sculptor Helmut Fischer in 1989 in a smaller 4.50" size with incised model number 335/0. Originally called "Fair Prizes" on old factory records, but later changed to "Lucky Boy." First put on the market in 1995 in a limited edition of 25,000 pieces—15,000 for the U.S. market with a "60th Anniversary Goebel" commemorative backstamp. The remaining 10,000 were available for the rest of the world in 1996 with a "Goebel 125th Anniversary" backstamp. It has an incised 1989 copyright date along with the current (TM 7) trademark. The official issue price was $190 in the U.S. when released in 1995. (Was not available in Canada.) "Lucky Boy" (335/0) was retired by Goebel in 1996 and will never be produced again in that size.

335 (TM 2)   *335/0 (TM 7)*

☐ 335	5.75"	(CE)	❷	$4000—5000	(Early Sample)
☐ 335	5.75"	(CE)	❸	$3000—4000	(Early Sample)
☐ 335/0	4.50"	(CE)	❼	$220—250	

237

New (TM 4) **Old (TM 4)**

HUM 336 — Close Harmony

First introduced in the U.S. market in 1963. Found with either 1955, 1956 or 1957 copyright dates. Originally modeled in 1956 by master modeler Gerhard Skrobek and in 1962 he also restyled it. The current production has been restyled but bears the 1955 incised copyright date. Older models have variations in girl's hairstyle and position of stockings. Listed as (TW) "Temporarily Withdrawn" in June 2002.

☐	336	5.25 to 5.50"	(CE)	❷	$4000—5000	(Early Sample)
☐	336	5.25 to 5.50"	(CE)	❸	$1000—1500	
☐	336	5.25 to 5.50"	(CE)	❹	$450—550	
☐	336	5.25 to 5.50"	(CE)	❺	$395—425	
☐	336	5.25 to 5.50"	(CE)	❻	$385—395	
☐	336	5.25 to 5.50"	(CE)	❼	$375—385	
☐	336	5.25 to 5.50"	(TW)	❽	$375—385	

New (TM 5) **Old (TM 4)**

HUM 337 — Cinderella

First introduced in the U.S. market in 1972. First modeled by master sculptor Arthur Moeller in March 1956. First sample painted by artist Franz Kirchner in July 1956. Later restyled by master sculptor Gerhard Skrobek in 1972. Early models have a 1958 or 1960 incised copyright date while the restyled version has a 1972 copyright date. Completely restyled with Skrobek's new textured finish and girl's eyes looking down. The older models have eyes open. When first put on the market in 1972 it was in the old style and had the (TM 4) trademark. Older trademarks such as (TM 2) and (TM 3) would be considered rare. The original issue price in 1972 was $26.50. Also found with a fourth bird on girl's left shoulder. (TW) "Temporarily Withdrawn" in December of 2004.

☐	337	4.50"	(CE)	❷	$4000—5000	(Early Sample)
☐	337	4.50"	(CE)	❸	$3000—4000	(Early Sample)
☐	337	4.50"	(CE)	❹	$1500—1700	(Old style)
☐	337	4.50"	(CE)	❺	$1200—1500	(Old style)
☐	337	4.50"	(CE)	❺	$375—400	(New style)
☐	337	4.50"	(CE)	❻	$365—375	
☐	337	4.50"	(CE)	❼	$355—365	
☐	337	4.50"	(OE)	❽	$355—365	

HUM 338 — Birthday Cake, Candleholder

First released in the U.S. market in 1989. Has an incised 1956 copyright date. The original issue price was $95 in 1989. Originally called "A Birthday Wish" on old factory records, but later changed to "Birthday Cake." Modeled by master sculptor Gerhard Skrobek in March 1956. First sample painted by Harald Sommer in July 1956. This early sample model pictured here has the "full bee" trademark and is part of the Robert L. Miller collection. Listed as (TW) "Temporarily Withdrawn" in January 1999.

☐ 338	3.75"	(CE)	❷	$4000—5000	(Early Sample)
☐ 338	3.75"	(CE)	❸	$3000—4000	
☐ 338	3.50"	(CE)	❻	$180—185	
☐ 338	3.50"	(TW)	❼	$175—180	

HUM 339 — Behave (EE)

First modeled by master sculptor Helmut Wehlte in 1956. Originally called "Walking Her Dog" on old factory records, but later changed to "Behave!" The early (TM 3) "stylized" trademark sample model was found in a home in New York City. It had originally been on display at the New York World's Fair in 1964. It has an incised 1956 copyright date and a painting date of 5/60 with O.S. artist initials. It is now part of the Robert L. Miller collection. "Behave!" was formerly

New restyled model (TM 7) Early sample model (TM 3)

listed as a (PFE) Possible Future Edition. Restyled by master sculptor Gerhard Skrobek in 1974. Changes were made in the base, girls hair style, color and style of rag doll, no leash for dog, position of dog's ears and dog's tail attached firmly to girl's dress. Announced in 1996, "Behave" will be an (EE) Exclusive Edition available to "M.I. Hummel Club" members only, who have belonged to the Club continuously for 20 years. The restyled figurine still has an incised 1956 copyright date. The original issue price was $350 in 1996. This figurine may be found on the secondary market.

☐ 339	5.75"	(CE)	❷	$7500—10,000	(Early Sample)
☐ 339	5.75"	(CE)	❸	$4000—5000	(Early Sample)
☐ 339	5.50"	(CE)	❼	$450—500	
☐ 339	5.50"	(EE)	❽	$360	

HUM 340 — Letter to Santa Claus

First introduced in the U.S. market in 1971. Originally modeled by master sculptor Helmut Wehlte in April 1956. Early sample was painted in September 1957 by artist Guenther Neubauer (former Chief Sample Painter at Goebel). Completely restyled by master

Prototype (TM 2)	Old style (TM 2)	Old style (TM 3)	New style (TM 4)

sculptor Gerhard Skrobek in 1970. The prototype mailbox on a tree trunk apparently was rejected in favor of the wooden post style. This piece has a full bee trademark, stamped 1956 copyright date and artist initials "HS" (probably Harald Sommer) along with a June 1956 date. The current production has new textured finish and color variations on girl's hats and leggings. (TM 4), (TM 5), (TM 6) and (TM 7) trademark models have an incised 1957 copyright date. The original issue price in 1971 was $30.

☐ 340 ....6.25"................(CE) ....❷ ....$15,000—20,000 (Prototype)
☐ 340 ....7.25"................(CE) ....❷ ....$4000—5000 (Early Sample)
☐ 340 ....7.25"................(CE) ....❸ ....$3000—4000 (Early Sample)
☐ 340 ....7.25"................(CE) ....❹ ....$750—1000
☐ 340 ....7.25"................(CE) ....❺ ....$425—450
☐ 340 ....7.25"................(CE) ....❻ ....$410—425
☐ 340 ....7.25"................(CE) ....❼ ....$400—410
☐ 340 ....7.25"................(OE) ....❽ $399

HUM 341 — Birthday Present

Originally named "The Birthday Present" on old factory records, but later changed to just "Birthday Present". First modeled by master sculptor Gerhard Skrobek in 1956. The smaller version, 341 3/0, modeled by master sculptor Helmut Fischer in 1989. It has an incised 1989 copyright date. Bears the "First Issue 1994" oval decal and "Special Event" backstamp. This figurine was available at District Manager Promotions and in-store events in 1994. The figurine was re-introduced without the special backstamp. The original issue price was $140 in 1994. (TW) "Temporarily Withdrawn" in December 2005.

☐ 341 ....5.00 to 5.333" ......(CE)........❷ ....$4000—5000 (Early Sample)
☐ 341 ....5.00 to 5.333" ......(CE)........❸ ....$3000—4000 (Early Sample)
☐ 341 ....5.00 to 5.333" ......(CE)........❹ ....$2000—3000 (Early Sample)
☐ 341 3/0 ....3.75"..................(CE)........❼ ....$180—190
☐ 341 3/0 ....3.75" ....(TW) ......❽ ....$180—190

HUM 342 — Mischief Maker

First introduced in the U. S. market in 1972. Originally modeled by master sculptor Arthur Moeller in
1956. Found with either 1958 or 1960 copyright
dates. No major variations have been recorded in
size or design. Older models have a dark green
hat on boy while newer models have a blue hat.
The original issue price in 1972 was $26.50. Listed
as (TW) "Temporarily Withdrawn" in January 1999.

□ 342 ....5.00" ....(CE) ....❷ ....$4000—5000 (Early Sample)
□ 342 ....5.00" ....(CE) ....❸ ....$3000—4000 (Early Sample)
□ 342 ....5.00" ....(CE) ....❹ ....$800—1000
□ 342 ....5.00" ....(CE) ....❺ ....$360—370
□ 342 ....5.00" ....(CE) ....❻ ....$350—360
□ 342 ....5.00" ....(**TW**) ....❼ ....$325—350

HUM 343 — Christmas Song

First introduced in the U.S. market in 1981.
Originally called "Singing Angel" on old factory records, but later changed to "Christmas
Song." Modeled by master sculptor Gerhard
Skrobek in 1956. The original issue price in
1981 was $85. An early stylized (TM 3) sam-
ple model was located in the Philadelphia
area. It has a 1957 incised copyright date
and a painting date of 6/60 with O.S. artist
initials. It is now part of the Robert L. Miller
collection. A new miniature size figurine,
HUM 343 4/0 with a matte finish was
released in the U.S. market in 1996. It has
an incised 1991 copyright date. The official
issue price was $115 in 1996. The 3.50" size
in (TM 8) has a glazed, not matte, finish.

□ 343 4/0 ..3.50" ....(CE) ....❼ ....$135—140 (Matte finish)
□ 343 4/0 ..3.50" ....(**OE**) ....❽ ....$99 (Standard finish)
□ 343 ....6.50" ....(CE) ....❷ ....$4000—5000 (Early Sample)
□ 343 ....6.50" ....(CE) ....❸ ....$2000—3000 (Early Sample)
□ 343 ....6.50" ....(CE) ....❹ ....$1000—2000 (Early Sample)
□ 343 ....6.50" ....(CE) ....❺ ....$750—1000
□ 343 ....6.50" ....(CE) ....❻ ....$285—290
□ 343 ....6.50" ....(CE) ....❼ ....$280—285
□ 343/I ......6.50" ....(**OE**) ....❽ $279

HUM 344 — Feathered Friends

First introduced in the U.S. market in 1972. Modeled by master sculptor Gerhard Skrobek in 1956. Has an incised 1956 copyright date on the base. "Full bee" (TM 2) and "early stylized" (TM 3) examples have appeared on the market. The original issue price in 1972 was $27.50.

☐ 344 ....4.75" ....(CE) ....❷ ....$4000—5000 (Early Sample)
☐ 344 ....4.75" ....(CE) ....❸ ....$2000—3000 (Early Sample)
☐ 344 ....4.75" ....(CE) ....❹ ....$750—1000
☐ 344 ....4.75" ....(CE) ....❺ ....$370—380
☐ 344 ....4.75" ....(CE) ....❻ ....$365—370
☐ 344 ....4.75" ....(CE) ....❼ ....$360—365
☐ 344 ....4.75" ....(**OE**) ....❽ $359

New (TM 5)　　　　　*Old (TM 5)*

HUM 345 — A Fair Measure

First introduced in the U.S. market in 1972. Originally modeled by master sculptor Helmut Wehlte in August 1956. First sample was painted by artist "W/Ha" Werner Hausschild in August 1957. Later restyled by master sculptor Gerhard Skrobek in 1972. Early "full bee" sample (TM 2) has a stamped 1957 copyright date. Early production models have 1956 incised copyright date. Completely restyled with new textured finish, boy's eyes looking down and weights on scale reversed. Current model has a 1972 incised copyright date. Original issue price in 1972 was $27.50. Listed as (TW) "Temporarily Withdrawn" in January 1999.

☐ 345 ....5.50 to 5.75"......(CE) ....❷ ....$4000—5000 (Early Sample)
☐ 345 ....5.50 to 5.75"......(CE) ....❸ ....$2000—3000 (Early Sample)
☐ 345 ....5.50 to 5.75"......(CE) ....❹ ....$1000—1500
☐ 345 ....5.50 to 5.75"......(CE) ....❺ ....$800—1000 (Old Style)
☐ 345 ....5.50 to 5.75"......(CE) ....❺ ....$370—380 (New Style)
☐ 345 ....5.50 to 5.75"......(CE) ....❻ ....$360—370
☐ 345 ....5.50 to 5.75"......(**TW**) ....❼ ....$350—360

HUM 346 — Smart Little Sister, The

First introduced in the U. S. market in 1962. Originally modeled by master sculptor Gerhard Skrobek in 1956. Has an incised 1956 copyright date on the bottom. No unusual variations have been recorded. Girl is similar to HUM 367, "Busy Student."

☐ 346	4.75"	(CE)	❷	$4000—5000	(Early Sample)
☐ 346	4.75"	(CE)	❸	$1000—1500	
☐ 346	4.75"	(CE)	❹	$350—400	
☐ 346	4.75"	(CE)	❺	$300—310	
☐ 346	4.75"	(CE)	❻	$290—300	
☐ 346	4.75"	(CE)	❼	$280—290	
☐ 346	4.75"	(OE)	❽	$279	

HUM 347 — Adventure Bound

First introduced in the U.S. market in 1971. The original issue price in 1971 was $400. Sometimes known as the "Seven Swabians." Has an incised 1957 copyright date. The original clay model was sculpted by Theo R. Menzenbach. Menzenbach began working at the Goebel factory in October 1948, at the age of 18. He left the factory in October 1961 to start his own business as a commercial artist. He is still living and resides in Germany, near Coburg. An early prototype with "full bee" (TM 2) trademark was painted in October 1957 and is now part of the Robert L. Miller collection.

"Full Bee" (TM 2)

☐ 347	7.50 x 8.25"	(CE)	❷	$10,000—15,000	(Early Sample)
☐ 347	7.50 x 8.25"	(CE)	❸	$7000—8000	(Early Sample)
☐ 347	7.50 x 8.25"	(CE)	❹	$5000—6000	
☐ 347	7.50 x 8.25"	(CE)	❺	$4500—4600	
☐ 347	7.50 x 8.25"	(CE)	❻	$4500—4600	
☐ 347	7.50 x 8.25"	(CE)	❼	$4500—4600	
☐ 347	7.50 x 8.25"	(OE)	❽	$4900	

"Early Stylized" (TM 3)

HUM 348 — Ring Around The Rosie

The original clay model was sculpted by Gerhard Skrobek, master modeler at the factory, in 1957. First introduced in the U.S. market in 1960 for the 25th anniversary of the introduction of "M.I. Hummel" figurines. Incised on the bottom: "© by W. Goebel, Oeslau 1957." Older models are usually slightly larger. Originally sold for less than $70 when first introduced for sale.

☐	348	........6.75 to 7.00"......(CE)	...........❷	.........$10,000—12,000 (Early Sample)
☐	348	........6.75 to 7.00"......(CE)	...........❸	.........$4000—5000
☐	348	........6.75"..................(CE)	...........❹	.........$3500—4000
☐	348	........6.75"..................(CE)	...........❺	.........$3300—3400
☐	348	........6.75"..................(CE)	...........❻	.........$3250—3300
☐	348	........6.75"..................(CE)	...........❼	.........$3200—3250
☐	348	........6.75"..................(OE)	...........❽	.........$3200

HUM 349 — Florist, The

Originally called "Flower Lover" on old factory records, but later changed to "The Florist" and finally just "Florist." First modeled by master sculptor Gerhard Skrobek in 1957 and remodeled by master sculptor Helmut Fischer in a smaller size in 1989 (HUM 349/0) with an incised 1990 copyright date. The new small size (5.25") was released in the U.S. market in the fall of 2002. The original issue price was $300 in 2002. The large size has been found in (TM 4) trademark with a 4/62 painting date.

☐	349	........6.75"..................(CE)	...........❷	.........$4000—5000 (Early Sample)
☐	349	........6.75"..................(CE)	...........❸	.........$3000—4000 (Early Sample)
☐	349	........6.75"..................(CE)	...........❹	.........$2000—3000 (Early Sample)
☐	349/0	......5.25"..................(OE)	...........❽	.........$319

HUM 350 — On Holiday

First introduced in the U.S. market in 1981. Originally called "Holiday Shopper" on old factory records, but later changed to "On Holiday." Modeled by master sculptor Gerhard Skrobek in 1964. The original sample model was 5.50" in height and had a bottle in the basket, but later reduced in size, by Gerhard Skrobek in 1980. Original issue price was $85 in 1981. Has an incised 1965 copyright date. This figurine was recently found with (TM 4) trade-

Progression Set

mark, a painting date of 12/80, and artist's initials "Bo" in the small 4.25" size. The third "Work in Progress" or "Progression" set featuring three "On Holiday" figurines was released in the fall of 2002. U.S. (LE) Limited Edition of 500 sets with a sequentially numbered plaque. "On Holiday" was (TW) "Temporarily Withdrawn" in 2002.

☐ 350	5.50"	(CE)	❸	$4000—5000	(Early Sample)
☐ 350	4.25"	(CE)	❹	$2000—3000	(Early Sample)
☐ 350	4.25"	(CE)	❺	$1500—2000	
☐ 350	4.25"	(CE)	❻	$205—210	
☐ 350	4.25"	(CE)	❼	$200—205	
☐ 350	4.25"	(TW)	❽	$200—205	
☐ 350	4.25"	(**LE**)	❽	$400—500	(Progression Set)

HUM 351 — Botanist, The

First introduced in the U.S. market in the fall of 1982. Originally called "Remembering" on old factory records, but later changed to "The Botanist" and finally just "Botanist." First modeled by master sculptor Gerhard Skrobek in 1965. Has an incised 1972 copyright date on the bottom. The original issue price was $84 in 1982. Found with 1965 copyright date. A new small size 351 4/0 was issued in 2003, with incised 2003 copyright date.

351 4/0

351

☐ 351 4/0	3.00"	(**OE**)	❽	$69.50	
☐ 351	4.00 to 4.25"	(CE)	❹	$4000—5000	(Early Sample)
☐ 351	4.00 to 4.25"	(CE)	❺	$1500—2000	
☐ 351	4.00 to 4.25"	(CE)	❻	$225—230	
☐ 351	4.00 to 4.25"	(CE)	❼	$220—225	
☐ 351	4.00 to 4.25"	(**OE**)	❽	$219	

Early Sample

HUM 352 — Sweet Greetings

First released in the U.S. market in 1981. Originally called "Musical Morning" on old factory records, but later changed to "Sweet Greetings." Modeled by master sculptor Gerhard Skrobek in 1964. Has an incised 1964 copyright date on the bottom of the base. The original issue price was $85 in 1981. The "Early Sample" figurine on the left is in a private collection in Florida.

☐ 352 ......6.25".................(CE) ....❹ ....$4000—5000 (Early Sample)
☐ 352 ......4.25".................(CE) ....❺ ....$1500—2000
☐ 352 ......4.25".................(CE) ....❻ ....$225—230
☐ 352 ......4.25".................(CE) ....❼ ....$220—225
☐ 352 ......4.25".................(OE) ....❽ $219

353/I (TM 4)   *353/0 (TM 4)*

HUM 353 — Spring Dance

First introduced in the U.S. market in 1964. According to factory records, this was first modeled in 1962 by a combination of modelers. Until recently, "Spring Dance" was the highest numbered figurine made in two sizes; HUM 396 "Ride Into Christmas" now has that distinction. The small size 353/0 has been considered rare, having been produced in very limited quantities in 1964 and then not produced again until 1978. Some of the early pieces have sold for as high as $3000. It is again in current production with the (TM 5), (TM 6), (TM 7) and (TM 8) trademarks. Both sizes have an incised 1963 copyright date. In 1982 the large size 353/I was listed as (TW) "Temporarily Withdrawn" on company records, to be possibly reinstated at a future date. The "Spring Dance" design consists of two of the four girls from HUM 348 "Ring Around The Rosie."

☐ 353/0 ......5.25".................(CE) ....❸ ....$3000—5000 (Early Sample)
☐ 353/0 ......5.25".................(CE) ....❹ ....$2000—3000
☐ 353/0 ......5.25".................(CE) ....❺ ....$425—450
☐ 353/0 ......5.25".................(CE) ....❻ ....$410—420
☐ 353/0 ......5.25".................(CE) ....❼ ....$400—410
☐ 353/0 ......5.25".................(OE) ....❽ $399
☐ 353 ....6.75".................(CE) ....❸ ....$3000—5000 (Early Sample)
☐ 353/I ......6.75".................(CE) ....❸ ....$1500—2000
☐ 353/I ......6.75".................(CE) ....❹ ....$700—800
☐ 353/I ......6.75".................(CE) ....❺ ....$600—700
☐ 353/I ......6.75".................(TW) ....❻ ....$550—600

246

HUM 354 A — Holy Water Font, Angel With Lantern (CN)

This early prototype font has the incised number 354 only, on the back. According to factory information, this design was not approved by the Siessen Convent as a font. It was then restyled into a figurine and approved as HUM 357 "Guiding Angel." Now listed on factory records as a (CN) Closed Number.

☐ 354 A ......3.25 x 5.00" ......(CN) ....

HUM 354 B — Holy Water Font, Angel With Trumpet (CN)

This early prototype font has the incised number 355 only, on the back. According to factory information, this design was not approved by the Siessen Convent as a font. It was then restyled into a figurine and approved as HUM 359 "Tuneful Angel." Now listed on factory records as a (CN) Closed Number.

☐ 354 B ......3.25 x 5.00" ......(CN) ....

HUM 354 C — Holy Water Font, Angel With Bird (CN)

This early prototype font has the incised number 356 only, on the back. According to factory information, this design was not approved by the Siessen Convent as a font. It was then restyled into a figurine and approved as HUM 358 "Shining Light." Now listed on factory records as a (CN) Closed Number.

☐ 354 C ......3.25 x 5.00" ......(CN) ....

HUM 355 — Autumn Harvest

First introduced in the U.S. market in 1972. Originally modeled by master sculptor Gerhard Skrobek in 1963. Has an incised 1963 or 1964 copyright date on the bottom. No major variations have been recorded in size, color or design. The original issue price in 1972 was $22.50. "Autumn Harvest" was permanently retired from production on 31 December 2002 and will not be produced again.

- ☐ 355 ......5.00" ......(CE).... ❸ ....$2000—3000 (Early Sample)
- ☐ 355 ......5.00" ......(CE).... ❹ ....$1000—1500
- ☐ 355 ......5.00" ......(CE).... ❺ ....$270—280
- ☐ 355 ......5.00" ......(CE).... ❻ ....$260—270
- ☐ 355 ......5.00" ......(CE).... ❼ ....$250—260
- ☐ 355 ......5.00" ......(CE).... ❽ ....$250—260

FINAL ISSUE
2002

HUM 356 — Gay Adventure

Was originally called "Joyful Adventure" when first released in the U.S. market in 1972. Originally modeled by master sculptor Gerhard Skrobek in 1963. It has an incised 1971 copyright date on the bottom. Slightly restyled with the new textured finish on current models. Early models have slightly different construction on the underside of base. The original issue price in 1972 was $22.50. Listed as (TW) "Temporarily Withdrawn" in June 2002.

- ☐ 356 ......4.75" ......(CE).... ❸ ....$2000—3000 (Early Sample)
- ☐ 356 ......4.75" ......(CE).... ❹ ....$1000—1500
- ☐ 356 ......4.75" ......(CE).... ❺ ....$260—275
- ☐ 356 ......4.75" ......(CE).... ❻ ....$250—260
- ☐ 356 ......4.75" ......(CE).... ❼ ....$245—250
- ☐ 356 ......4.75" ......(**TW**) .. ❽ ....$245—250

357 (TM 4)   *358 (TM 4)*   *359 (TM 4)*

HUM 357 — Guiding Angel

First released in the U.S. market in 1972. Originally modeled by master sculptor Reinhold Unger in 1958. Has an incised 1960 copyright date. The original issue price in 1972 was $11. Usually offered, along with HUM 358 and HUM 359, as a set of three angels, although priced separately.

☐ 357 ....2.75"..................(CE) ....❹ ....$125—150
☐ 357 ....2.75"..................(CE) ....❺ ....$120—125
☐ 357 ....2.75"..................(CE) ....❻ ....$115—120
☐ 357 ....2.75"..................(CE) ....❼ ....$110—115
☐ 357 ....2.75"..................(OE) ....❽ $99

HUM 358 — Shining Light

First released in the U.S. market in 1972. Originally modeled by master sculptor Reinhold Unger in 1958. Has an incised 1960 copyright date. The original issue price in 1972 was $11. Usually offered, along with HUM 357 and HUM 359, as a set of three angels, although priced separately.

☐ 358 ....2.75"..................(CE) ....❹ ....$125—150
☐ 358 ....2.75"..................(CE) ....❺ ....$120—125
☐ 358 ....2.75"..................(CE) ....❻ ....$115—120
☐ 358 ....2.75"..................(CE) ....❼ ....$110—115
☐ 358 ....2.75"..................(OE) ....❽ $99

HUM 359 — Tuneful Angel

First released in the U.S. market in 1972. Originally modeled by master sculptor Reinhold Unger in 1958. Has an incised 1960 copyright date. Usually offered, along with HUM 357 and HUM 358, as a set of three angels, although priced separately. The original issue price in 1972 was $11.

☐ 359 ....2.75"..................(CE) ....❹ ....$125—150
☐ 359 ....2.75"..................(CE) ....❺ ....$120—125
☐ 359 ....2.75"..................(CE) ....❻ ....$115—120
☐ 359 ....2.75"..................(CE) ....❼ ....$110—115
☐ 359 ....2.75"..................(OE) ....❽ $99

HUM 360/A — Wall Vase, Boy and Girl

One of a set of three wall vases that had been considered rare but is again in current production with the (TM 5) and (TM 6) trademarks. According to factory records, this vase was modeled by master sculptor Gerhard Skrobek in 1959. Early models incised on back: "© by W. Goebel 1958." The new model reissued in 1979 has been slightly restyled and has copyright date 1958 only incised on back. (TW) "Temporarily Withdrawn" from production on 31 December 1989, but may be reinstated at some future date.

- ☐ 360/A ....4.50 x 6.00" ....(CE) ....❸ ....$600—750
- ☐ 360/A ....4.50 x 6.00" ....(CE) ....❺ ....$200—225
- ☐ 360/A ....4.50 x 6.00" ....(TW) ....❻ ....$190—200

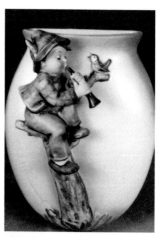

HUM 360/B — Wall Vase, Boy

One of a set of three wall vases that had been considered rare but is again in current production with the (TM 5) and (TM 6) trademarks. According to factory records, this vase was modeled by master sculptor Gerhard Skrobek in 1959. Early models incised on back: "© by W. Goebel 1958." The new model reissued in 1979 has been slightly restyled and has copyright date 1958 only incised on back. (TW) "Temporarily Withdrawn" from production on 31 December 1989, but may be reinstated at some future date.

- ☐ 360/B ....4.50 x 6.00" ....(CE) ....❸ ....$600—750
- ☐ 360/B ....4.50 x 6.00" ....(CE) ....❺ ....$200—225
- ☐ 360/B ....4.50 x 6.00" ....(TW)....❻ ....$190—200

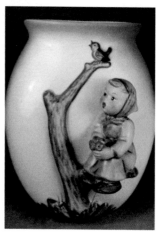

HUM 360/C — Wall Vase, Girl

One of a set of three wall vases that had been considered rare but is again in current production with the (TM 5) and (TM 6) trademarks. According to factory records, this vase was modeled by master sculptor Gerhard Skrobek in 1959. Early models incised on back: "© by W. Goebel 1958." The new model reissued in 1979 has the trunk of the tree slightly restyled and has copyright date 1958 only incised on back. (TW) "Temporarily Withdrawn" from production on 31 December 1989, but may be reinstated at some future date.

- ☐ 360/C ....4.50 x 6.00" ....(CE) ....❸ ....$600—750
- ☐ 360/C ....4.50 x 6.00" ....(CE) ....❺ ....$200—225
- ☐ 360/C ....4.50 x 6.00" ....(TW)....❻ ....$190—200

HUM 361 — Favorite Pet

First released in the U.S. market at the N.Y. World's Fair in 1964. Originally modeled by master sculptor Theo R. Menzenbach in 1959. Has an incised 1960 copyright date. No unusual variations have been recorded. Listed as (TW) "Temporarily Withdrawn" on January 2001 price list. "Permanently Retired" on QVC, March 24, 2001 with "Retirment Exclusive" backstamp. It will not be produced again.

☐ 361	4.50"	(CE)	❷	$4000—5000	(Early Sample)
☐ 361	4.50"	(CE)	❸	$1200—1700	
☐ 361	4.50"	(CE)	❹	$375—450	
☐ 361	4.50"	(CE)	❺	$345—375	
☐ 361	4.50"	(CE)	❻	$340—345	
☐ 361	4.50"	(CE)	❼	$335—340	
☐ 361	4.50"	**(CE)**	❽	$335—340	

FINAL ISSUE
2001

HUM 362 — Forget Me Not

This figurine was originally named "Thoughtful" on old factory records, but later changed to "I Forgot" and has now been changed for the third time to "Forget Me Not". Modeled by master sculptor Theo R. Menzenbach in 1959. Formerly listed as a (PFE) "Possible Future Edition" but now classified as the 30 Year Anniversary Figurine. On the left is an "Early Sample" figurine (note pig tails on sample). On the right is the current production model. The flowers in basket are a removable 30 year pin that can be worn on your lapel. This pin is free during Club Year 30 only. Figurine has the halfmoon shaped "EXCLUSIVE EDITION M.I. HUMMEL CLUB" 30 Year Membership decal on the bottom of the base.

Early Sample　　　*30th Anniversary*

☐ 362	5.50"	(CE)	❷	$4000—5000	(Early Sample)
☐ 362	5.50"	(CE)	❸	$3000—4000	(Early Sample)
☐ 362	5.50"	(CE)	❹	$2000—3000	(Early Sample)
☐ 362	5.50"	(CE)	❺	$1000—2000	
☐ 362/I	5.50"	(EE)	❽	$350	

HUM 363 — Big Housecleaning
First introduced in the U.S. market in 1972. Originally modeled by master sculptor Gerhard Skrobek in 1959. Has as incised 1960 copyright date on the bottom. No major variations have been recorded in size, color or design. The original issue price in 1972 was $28.50. Listed as (TW) "Temporarily Withdrawn" in January 1999, but may be reinstated at some future date.

☐ 363	4.00"	(CE)	❷	$4000—5000	(Early Sample)
☐ 363	4.00"	(CE)	❸	$2000—3000	
☐ 363	4.00"	(CE)	❹	$1000—1500	
☐ 363	4.00"	(CE)	❺	$355—375	
☐ 363	4.00"	(CE)	❻	$345—355	
☐ 363	4.00"	(TW)	❼	$335—345	

(TM 6)   *Unpainted sample (TM 5)*

HUM 364 — Supreme Protection (CE)
Modeled by master sculptor Gerhard Skrobek in 1963. Originally called "Blessed Madonna and Child" on old factory records but later changed to "Supreme Protection." First put on the market in 1984 and was limited to the total of that year's production and will not be produced in future years. It has an incised 1964 copyright date. The inscription on the bottom of the figurine applied by blue decal reads: "1909—1984 IN CELEBRATION OF THE 75th ANNIVERSARY OF THE BIRTH OF SISTER M.I. HUMMEL" plus the current TM 6 Goebel trademark. Early production of this figurine had an error in the decal that read "M.J. Hummel" rather that "M.I. Hummel." This was first corrected by cutting off the hook of the "J" on the decal, but still did not completely look like an "I." Ultimately corrected to read "M.I. Hummel." Of the three versions, the most difficult variation to find is the "altered J" variety. The original issue price in 1984 was $150. Originally came in a dark brown, specially designed, padded presentation case with brass fasteners. The box was inscribed: "M.I. Hummel-IN CELEBRATION OF THE 75th ANNIVERSARY OF THE BIRTH OF SISTER MARIA INNOCENTIA HUMMEL" in gold lettering. "Supreme Protection" is now listed as a (CE) Closed Edition and will not be produced again.

☐ 364	9.00 to 9.25"	(CE)	❹	$3000—4000	(Early Sample)
☐ 364	9.00 to 9.25"	(CE)	❺	$2000—3000	(Early Sample)
☐ 364	9.00 to 9.25"	(CE)	❻	$350—400	
☐ 364	9.00 to 9.25"	(CE)	❻	$400—600	("M.J." variation)
☐ 364	9.00 to 9.25"	(CE)	❻	$600—850	(Altered "J" variation)

HUM 365 — Hummele

First released in 1999 to honor the 90th Anniversary of the birth of Sister M. I. Hummel, as a special (EE) Exclusive Edition for "M. I Hummel Club" members only (with Club redemption form) for this one year only. (Retires as of 31 May 2000.) It is the first Club figurine to bear the new "Year 2000 Backstamp" and (TM 8) trademark. It has an incised 1964 copyright date. Originally called "The Wee Angel" on old factory records, but later changed to "Littlest Angel" and finally to

(TM 4)   *(TM 4) bottom view*

"Hummele." Modelled by master sculptor Gerhard Skrobek in 1963. Recently found in (TM 4) trademark with a 12/64 painting date. It has blue eyes. This piece is now in the Robert L. Miller collection. Re-released in 2005 with display and Beehive box, set priced $145.

☐ 365 ....2.75".................(CE) ....❹.........$2000—3000 (Early Sample)
☐ 365 ....2.75".................(**CE**) ....❽.........$145—175

HUM 366 — Flying Angel

First modeled by master sculptor Gerhard Skrobek in 1963, this piece was designed as an addition to the Standard size "Nativity Set", HUM 214. Makes an excellent decoration or ornament for hanging on the Christmas tree. See photo of HUM 214 "Nativity Set" for application. At one time was produced and sold in white overglaze finish. It is presently limited to full color finish only. In 1989 a new smaller size "Flying Angel" was released in the U.S. market. It

has an incised 366/0 model number and a 1987 copyright date. The issue price was $65 in 1989. The large size 366 has been renumbered 366/I.

☐ 366/0 ......3.00".................(CE) ....❻.........$135—140
☐ 366/0 ......3.00".................(CE) ....❼.........$130—135
☐ 366/0 ......3.00".................(**OE**) ....❽.........$132.50
☐ 366 ....3.50".................(CE) ....❹.........$225—275
☐ 366 ....3.50".................(CE) ....❺.........$190—200
☐ 366 ....3.50".................(CE) ....❻.........$185—190
☐ 366 ....3.50".................(CE) ....❼.........$180—185
☐ 366/I ......3.50".................(**OE**) ....❽.........$179

HUM 367 — Busy Student

First released in the U.S. market in 1964. Originally modeled in 1962 by a combination of modelers. Has an incised 1963 copyright date. Similar to the little girl in HUM 346 "Smart Little Sister." No major variations have been reported in size, color or design. The 4.25" size was retired in April 2006 (CE) Closed Edition.

☐	367	....4.25"	....(CE)	....❸	....$850—1100
☐	367	....4.25"	....(CE)	....❹	....$250—300
☐	367	....4.25"	....(CE)	....❺	....$220—230
☐	367	....4.25"	....(CE)	....❻	....$210—220
☐	367	....4.25"	....(CE)	....❼	....$200—210
☐	367	....4.25"	....**(CE)**	....❽	....$175	(Closed Edition)

HUM 368 — Lute Song (PFE)

Originally called "Lute Player" on old factory records, but later changed to "Lute Song." First modeled by master sculptor Gerhard Skrobek in July 1964. Notice the similarity between this figure and the girl in HUM 336 "Close Harmony." Now listed on factory records as a (PFE) Possible Future Edition and may be released at some future date, subject to possible minor changes. Recently found in (TM 4) trademark with a 12/65 painting date. Now in the Robert L. Miller collection.

| ☐ | 368 | ......5.00" | ....(CE) | ......❹ | ....$2000—3000 | (Early Sample) |
| ☐ | 368 | ......5.00" | ....**(PFE)** | .... |

HUM 369 — Follow The Leader
First introduced in the U.S. market in 1972. This figurine was first modeled by master sculptor Gerhard Skrobek in February 1964. It has an incised 1964 copyright date on the bottom. The original issue price in 1972 was $110. No major variations have been recorded in size, color or design. Listed as (TW) "Temporarily Withdrawn" on January 2001 price list.

☐ 369 ......7.00" ....(CE)......❸ ....$4000—5000 Early Sample)
☐ 369 ......7.00" ....(CE)......❹ ....$1700—2200
☐ 369 ......7.00" ....(CE)......❺ ....$1500—1600
☐ 369 ......7.00" ....(CE)......❻ ....$1450—1500
☐ 369 ......7.00" ....(CE)......❼ ....$1400—1450
☐ 369 ......7.00" ....(**TW**) ....❽ ....$1390—1400

HUM 370 — Companions (PFE)
Originally called "Brotherly Love" on old factory records, but later changed to "Companions." Originally modeled by master sculptor Gerhard Skrobek in May 1964. Now listed on factory records as a (PFE) Possible Future Edition and may be released at some future date, subject to possible minor changes. Recently found in (TM 5) trademark in a 9/73 painting date. Now in the Robert L. Miller collection.

☐ 370 ......5.00" ....(CE)......❹ ....$3000—4000 (Early Eample)
☐ 370 ......5.00" ....(CE)......❺ ....$2000—3000 (Early Sample)
☐ 370 ......5.00" ....(**PFE**) ....

HUM 371 — Daddy's Girls

First introduced in the U.S. market in 1989. Originally called "Sisterly Love" on old factory records, but later changed to "Daddy's Girls." Modeled by master sculptor Gerhard Skrobek in May 1964. The original issue price was $130 in 1989. It has an incised 1964 copyright date.

☐ 371 ......4.75" ....(CE)......❹ ....$3000—4000 (Early Sample)
☐ 371 ......4.75" ....(CE)......❺ ....$2000—3000 (Early Sample)
☐ 371 ......4.75" ....(CE)......❻ ....$290—310
☐ 371 ......4.75" ....(CE)......❼ ....$280—290
☐ 371 ......4.75" ....(OE)......❽ $279

HUM 372 — Blessed Mother (PFE)

Originally called "Virgin Mother and Child" on old factory records, but later changed to "Blessed Mother." Modeled by master sculptor Gerhard Skrobek in May 1964. Now listed on factory records as a (PFE) Possible Future Edition and may be released at some future date, subject to possible minor changes. Recently found in (TM 4) with a 11/73 painting date. Now in the Robert L. Miller collection.

☐ 372 ......10.25" ......(CE) ....❹ ....$3000—4000 (Early Sample)
☐ 372 ......10.25" ......(PFE)............

HUM 373 — Just Fishing
This figurine was first released in the U.S. market in 1985. Originally called "The Fisherman" on old factory records, but later changed to "Just Fishing." Modeled by master sculptor Gerhard Skrobek in 1964. It has an incised 1965 copyright date on the bottom. The original issue price was $85 in 1985. Was first listed as an ashtray on Goebel price lists but later changed to a figurine listing. Found with an old shoe on end of pole. Listed as (TW) "Temporarily Withdrawn" in January 1999, but may be reinstated at some future date. Approximately 900 pieces were made with: "1999 M.I. Hummel Club Convention" around base and fish on the end of the line and given to club members at the Baltimore Convention.

□ 373 ....4.25 to 4.50"......(CE) ....❹ ....$3000—4000 (Early Sample)
□ 373 ....4.25 to 4.50"......(CE) ....❺ ....$1000—1500
□ 373 ....4.25 to 4.50"......(CE) ....❻ ....$300—325
□ 373 ....4.25 to 4.50"......(**TW**) ....❼ ....$290—300

HUM 374 — Lost Stocking
This figurine was one of twenty-four new motifs first released in the U.S. market in 1972. Originally modeled by master sculptor Gerhard Skrobek in 1965. It has an incised 1965 copyright date. No major variations have been recorded in size, color or design. The original issue price in 1972 was $17.50. Listed as (TW) "Temporarily Withdrawn" in June 2002.

□ 374 ......4.25 to 4.50" ....(CE) ....❸....$3000—4000
  (Early Sample)
□ 374 ......4.25 to 4.50" ....(CE) ....❹....$1000—1500
□ 374 ......4.25 to 4.50" ....(CE) ....❺....$195—200
□ 374 ......4.25 to 4.50" ....(CE) ....❻....$190—195
□ 374 ......4.25 to 4.50" ....(CE) ....❼....$185—190
□ 374 ......4.25 to 4.50" ....(**TW**) ....❽....$185—190

HUM 375 — Morning Stroll

Originally called "Walking the Baby" on old factory records, but later changed to "Morning Stroll." First modeled by master sculptor Gerhard Skrobek in 1964 with an incised 1964 copyright date. The small size, HUM 375 3/0 was released in the U.S. market in 1994, modeled by master sculptor Helmut Fischer in 1991, with an incised 1991 copyright date and the "First Issue 1994" oval decal on the bottom. The official issue price was $170 in 1994. In July 2006 the 3.75" size was retired (CE) Closed Edition.

- ☐ 375 ....4.75" ....(CE).... ❹ ....$3000—4000   (Early Sample)
- ☐ 375 3/0 ....3.75" ....(CE).... ❼ ....$220—225
- ☐ 375 3/0 ....3.75" ....(CE).... ❽ ....$219   (Closed Edition)

HUM 376 — Little Nurse

This figurine was first released in the U.S. market in the fall of 1982. Originally called "First Aid" on old factory records, but later changed to "Little Nurse." Modeled by master sculptor Gerhard Skrobek in April 1965. It has an incised 1972 copyright date on the bottom. The original issue price was $95 in 1982. Recently found with (TM 5) trademark and incised 1965 copyright date. In July 2006 the 4" size was retired (CE) Closed Edition.

- ☐ 376 ......4.00" ....(CE).... ❹ ....$3000—4000 (Early Sample)
- ☐ 376 ......4.00" ....(CE).... ❺ ....$2000—3000
- ☐ 376 ......4.00" ....(CE).... ❻ ....$300—310
- ☐ 376 ......4.00" ....(CE).... ❼ ....$295—300
- ☐ 376 ......4.00" ....(CE).... ❽ ....$295 (Closed Edition)

HUM 377 — Bashful!

First released in the U.S. market in 1972. Originally modeled by master sculptor Gerhard Skrobek in January 1966. It usually was found with an incised 1966 copyright date, but occasionally found with a 1971 incised date. Models in current production have no incised date at all. No major variations have been recorded in size, color or design. The original issue price was $17.50 in 1972. Found with (TM 4) trademark and a 11/69 painting date. Now in the Robert L. Miller collection. New small size HUM 377 3/0 with "First Issue 2005" oval decal and 1998 copyright date was issued in 2005. Available in "Bashful Progression Set" a (LE) Limited Edition of 1000.

- ☐ 377 3/0 ..4.75" ....(**OE**)....❽ $165
- ☐ 377 ....4.75" ....(CE)....❹ ....$3000—4000 (Early Sample)
- ☐ 377 ....4.75" ....(CE)....❹ ....$1000—1500 (Production Model)
- ☐ 377 ....4.75" ....(CE)....❺ ....$260—275
- ☐ 377 ....4.75" ....(CE)....❻ ....$255—260
- ☐ 377 ....4.75" ....(CE)....❼ ....$250—255
- ☐ 377 ....4.75" ....(**OE**)....❽ $250

HUM 378 — Easter Greetings!

First released in the U.S. market in 1972 as one of twenty-four new motifs released that year. Originally modeled by master sculptor Gerhard Skrobek in January 1966. It has an incised 1966 or 1971 copyright date on the bottom. No major variations have been found in size, color or design. The original issue price was $24 in 1972. Listed as (TW) "Temporarily Withdrawn" in January 1999, but may be reinstated at some future date.

- ☐ 378 ....5.00 to 5.25" ..(CE)..❹ ..$3000—4000 (Early Sample)
- ☐ 378 ....5.00 to 5.25" ..(CE)..❹ ..$1000—1500 (Production Model)
- ☐ 378 ....5.00 to 5.25" ..(CE)..❺ ..$245—270
- ☐ 378 ....5.00 to 5.25" ..(CE)..❻ ..$240—245
- ☐ 378 ....5.00 to 5.25" ..(**TW**) ❼ ..$225—235

HUM 379 — Don't Be Shy (PFE)
Originally called "One For You—One For Me" on old factory records, but later changed to "Don't Be Shy." This figurine was first modeled by master sculptor Gerhard Skrobek in February 1966. It is now listed on factory records as a (PFE) Possible Future Edition and may be released at some future date, subject to possible minor changes. Recently found with (TM 3) trademark.

☐ 379 ....4.25 to 4.50" ......(CE) ......❸ ......$4000—5000 (Early Sample)
☐ 379 ....4.25 to 4.50" ......(CE) ......❹ ......$3000—4000 (Early Sample)
☐ 379 ....4.25 to 4.50" ......(PFE) ....

HUM 380 — Daisies Don't Tell (CE)
First introduced in 1981 for members of the Goebel Collector's Club only as "Special Edition No. 5." Was not sold as an open edition but can be purchased on the secondary market at premium prices. The original issue price was $80 in the U.S. and $95 in Canada. It has an incised 1972 copyright date and the (TM 6) trademark. The original name was "Does He?" on old factory records. Modeled by master sculptor Gerhard Skrobek in February 1966. Also found with incised 1966 copyright date.

☐ 380 ....5.00".................(CE) ......❹ ......$3000—4000 (Early Sample)
☐ 380 ....5.00".................(CE) ......❺ ......$1000—2000
☐ 380 ....5.00".................(CE) ......❻ ......$275—300

HUM 381 — Flower Vendor

First introduced in the U.S. market in 1972. Originally modeled by master sculptor Gerhard Skrobek in October 1966. It has an incised 1971 copyright date on the underside of the base. No major variations have been found in size, color or design. The original issue price was $24 in 1972. Also found with incised 1967 copyright date. (TW) "Temporarily Withdrawn" in December 2004.

☐ 381	....5.25"	....................(CE)	......❹	......$3000—4000 Early Sample)
☐ 381	....5.25"	....................(CE)	......❺	......$315—340
☐ 381	....5.25"	....................(CE)	......❻	......$310—315
☐ 381	....5.25"	....................(CE)	......❼	......$305—310
☐ 381	....5.25"	....................**(TW)**	......❽	......$305—310

HUM 382 — Visiting An Invalid

First released in the U.S. market in 1972. Originally modeled by master sculptor Gerhard Skrobek in October 1966. It has an incised 1971 copyright date on the underside of the base. No major variations have been noticed in size, color or design. The original issue price was $26.50 in 1972. Also found with incised 1967 copyright date. Listed as (TW) "Temporarily Withdrawn" in January 1999, but may be reinstated at some future date.

☐ 382	....5.00"	....................(CE)	......❹	......$1000—1500
☐ 382	....5.00"	....................(CE)	......❺	......$260—295
☐ 382	....5.00"	....................(CE)	......❻	......$255—260
☐ 382	....5.00"	....................**(TW)**	......❼	......$250—255

HUM 383 — Going Home

This figurine was first released in the U.S. market in the spring of 1985. Originally called "Fancy Free" on old factory records, but later changed to "Going Home." Modeled by master sculptor Gerhard Skrobek in November 1966. It has an incised 1967 or 1972 copyright date on the bottom. The original issue price in 1985 was $125. "Going Home" has now been made into two separate figurines. See HUM 561 "Grandma's Girl" and HUM 562 "Grandpa's Boy".

- ☐ 383 ....4.75 to 5.00" ....(CE)........❹ ....$3000—4000 (Early Sample)
- ☐ 383 ....4.75 to 5.00" ....(CE)........❺ ....$2000—3000
- ☐ 383 ....4.75 to 5.00" ....(CE)........❻ ....$410—425
- ☐ 383 ....4.75 to 5.00" ....(CE)........❼ ....$400—410
- ☐ 383 ....4.75 to 5.00" ....(**OE**)........❽ $399

HUM 384 — Easter Time

First introduced in the U.S. market in 1972. Originally modeled by master sculptor Gerhard Skrobek in January 1967. It has an incised 1971 copyright date on the underside of the base. No major variations have been recorded in size, color or design. The original issue price was $27.50 in 1972. Also called "Easter Playmates" in some catalogues.

- ☐ 384 ....4.00" ....(CE)........❹ ....$1000—1500
- ☐ 384 ....4.00" ....(CE)........❺ ....$325—350
- ☐ 384 ....4.00" ....(CE)........❻ ....$290—310
- ☐ 384 ....4.00" ....(CE)........❼ ....$279—290
- ☐ 384 ....4.00" ....(**OE**)........❽ $279

HUM 385 — Chicken-Licken

First introduced in the U.S. market in 1972 as one of twenty-four new motifs released that year. Originally modeled by master sculptor Gerhard Skrobek in June 1967. It has an incised 1971 copyright date on the bottom of the base. The original issue price was $28.50 in 1972. A new miniature size figurine, without the fence, was issued in 1991 with a suggested retail price of $80 to match a new miniature plate series called the "Little Homemakers"—one each year for four years. This is the fourth and last in this series. It has an incised 1987 copyright date. The miniature size (385 4/0) was (TW) "Temporarily Withdrawn" from production on 31 December 1997, and then listed as a (CE) Closed Edition in January 1999, but has been re-released.

- ☐ 385 4/0 ..3.25" ....(CE)...... ❻ ....$125—140 (Matte finish)
- ☐ 385 4/0 ..3.25" ....(CE)...... ❼ ....$115—120 (Matte finish)
- ☐ 385 4/0 ..3.25" ....**(OE)** .... ❽ ....$99 (Standard finish)
- ☐ 385 ....4.75" ....(CE)...... ❹ ....$1000—1500
- ☐ 385 ....4.75" ....(CE)...... ❺ ....$380—390
- ☐ 385 ....4.75" ....(CE)...... ❻ ....$370—380
- ☐ 385 ....4.75" ....(CE)...... ❼ ....$360—370
- ☐ 385 ....4.75" ....**(TW)** .... ❽ $359

HUM 386 — On Secret Path

First introduced in the U.S. market 1972. Originally modeled by master sculptor Gerhard Skrobek in July 1967. It has an incised 1971 copyright date on the bottom of the base. No major variations have been found in size, color or design. The original issue price was $26.50 in 1972. Listed as (TW) "Temporarily Withdrawn" in June 2002.

- ☐ 386 ......5.25" ....(CE)...... ❹ ....$1000—1500
- ☐ 386 ......5.25" ....(CE)...... ❺ ...$310—350
- ☐ 386 ......5.25" ....(CE)...... ❻ ....$305—310
- ☐ 386 ......5.25" ....(CE)...... ❼ ....$300—305
- ☐ 386 ......5.25" ....**(TW)** .... ❽ $300

(Note bird on early sample)   *(TM 4)*

HUM 387 — Valentine Gift

This figurine was first introduced in 1977 for members of the Goebel Collectors' Club only and not sold in Open Edition. Originally modeled by master sculptor Gerhard Skrobek in July 1967. It has an incised 1972 copyright date along with the (TM 5) trademark. Also bears the inscription "EXCLUSIVE SPECIAL EDITION No. 1 FOR MEMBERS OF THE GOEBEL COLLECTORS' CLUB" applied by blue decal. The original issue price was $45 in addition to the member's redemption card. Translation of message on heart: "I Love You Very Much" or "I Like You." Several examples without the special inscription but with (TM 4) trademark only have appeared on the market. Some have 1968 or 1971 copyright date and usually sell for $2000 to $3000.

☐ 387 ....5.75"..................(CE) ....❹ ....$5000—7500 (with bird)
☐ 387 ....5.75"..................(CE) ....❹ ....$2000—3000
☐ 387 ....5.75"..................**(CE)** ....❺ ....$450—600

388   *388 M*

HUM 388 — Little Band, Candleholder

This piece is a candleholder with three figurines, HUM 389, HUM 390 and HUM 391, attached to a round ceramic base. Modeled by master sculptor Gerhard Skrobek in December 1967. It has incised 1968 or 1972 copyright date. Little Band, Candleholder was (TW) "Temporarily Withdrawn" from production on 31 December 1990, but may be reinstated at some future date.

☐ 388 ....3.00 x 4.75" ......(CE) ....❹ ....$350—450
☐ 388 ....3.00 x 4.75" ......(CE) ....❺ ....$300—350
☐ 388 ....3.00 x 4.75" ......**(TW)** ....❻ ....$275—300

HUM 388 M — Little Band, Candleholder on Music Box

Same as HUM 388 but fastened on a music box. There are variations in type of music box as well as tunes played. The music box is usually Swiss-made and not produced by Goebel. This Music Box was "Temporarily Withdrawn" (TW) from production on 31 December 1990, but may be reinstated at some future date.

☐ 388 M ....3.00 x 4.75" ......(CE) ....❹ ....$475—500
☐ 388 M ....3.00 x 4.75" ......(CE) ....❺ ....$450—475
☐ 388 M ....3.00 x 4.75" ......**(TW)** ....❻ ....$400—425

389   *390*   *391*

HUM 389 — Girl With Sheet of Music
One of a set of three sometimes referred to as the "Little Band." Originally modeled by master sculptor Gerhard Skrobek in May 1968. It has an incised 1968 copyright date. Occasionally found in (TM 3).

☐ 389 ....2.50" ....(CE) ....❸ ....$225—275
☐ 389 ....2.50" ....(CE) ....❹ ....$175—225
☐ 389 ....2.50" ....(CE) ....❺ ....$120—125
☐ 389 ....2.50" ....(CE) ....❻ ....$110—120
☐ 389 ....2.50" ....(CE) ....❼ ....$100—110
☐ 389 ....2.50" ....(**OE**) ....❽ $99
☐ IV/389 ....4.75" ....(**LE**)..............❽ ....$175 (Music Box)

HUM 390 — Boy With Accordion
One of a set of three sometimes referred to as the "Little Band." Originally modeled by master sculptor Gerhard Skrobek in May 1968. It has an incised 1968 copyright date. Occasionally found in (TM 3).

☐ 390 ....2.50" ....(CE) ....❸ ....$225—275
☐ 390 ....2.50" ....(CE) ....❹ ....$175—225
☐ 390 ....2.50" ....(CE) ....❺ ....$120—125
☐ 390 ....2.50" ....(CE) ....❻ ....$110—120
☐ 390 ....2.50" ....(CE) ....❼ ....$100—110
☐ 390 ....2.50" ....(**OE**) ....❽ $99
☐ IV/390 ....4.75" ....(**LE**)..............❽ ....$175 (Music Box)

HUM 391 — Girl With Trumpet
One of a set of three sometimes referred to as the "Little Band." Originally modeled by master sculptor Gerhard Skrobek in May 1968. It has an incised 1968 copyright date. Occasionally found in (TM 3). Not on current price list.

☐ 391 ....2.50" ....(CE) ....❸ ....$225—275
☐ 391 ....2.50" ....(CE) ....❹ ....$175—225
☐ 391 ....2.50" ....(CE) ....❺ ....$120—125
☐ 391 ....2.50" ....(CE) ....❻ ....$110—120
☐ 391 ....2.50" ....(CE) ....❼ ....$100—110
☐ 391 ....2.50" ....(**TW**) ....❽ $99

HUM 392 — Little Band (on base)

Same as HUM 388 but without socket for candle. Modeled by master sculptor Gerhard Skrobek in May 1968. It has an incised 1968 or 1972 copyright date. On 31 December 1984 this figurine was listed as (TW) "Temporarily Withdrawn" from production by Goebel, but could possibly be reinstated at some future date.

☐ 392 ......3.00 x 4.75"....(CE) ....❹ ..$350—450
☐ 392 ......3.00 x 4.75"....(CE) ....❺ .$300—350
☐ 392 ......3.00 x 4.75"....(TW) ....❻ ..$275—300

HUM 392 M — Little Band on Music Box

Same as HUM 392 but fastened on a music box. There are variations in type of music box as well as in tunes played. The music box is usually Swiss-made and not produced by Goebel. This Music Box was (TW) "Temporarily Withdrawn" from production on 31 December 1990, but may be reinstated at some future date.

☐ 392 M ..3.00 x 4.75"....(CE) ....❹ ..$475—500
☐ 392 M ..3.00 x 4.75"....(CE) ....❺ .$450—475
☐ 392 M ..3.00 x 4.75"....(TW) ....❻ .$400—425

HUM 393 — Holy Water Font, Dove (PFE)

This holy water font was modeled by master sculptor Gerhard Skrobek in June 1968. The inscription reads: "Come Holy Spirit." Now listed on factory records as a (PFE) Possible Future Edition and may be released at some future date, subject to possible minor changes. Recently found with (TM 4) and a 8/69 painting date, now part of the Robert L. Miller collection.

☐ 393 ......2.75 x 4.25"....(CE) ....❹ ..$2000—3000
   (Early Sample)
☐ 393 ......2.75 x 4.25"....(PFE)..........

HUM 394 — Timid Little Sister

First released in the U.S. market in 1981 along with five other figurines. Originally modeled by master sculptor Gerhard Skrobek in February 1972. It has an incised 1972 copyright date on the underside of the base. The original issue price was $190 in 1981. The girl normally does not have eyelashes.

☐ 394	........6.75 to 7.00".......(CE)	...........**❺**	..........$3000—4000	(Early Sample)
☐ 394	........6.75 to 7.00".......(CE)	...........**❻**	..........$540—550	
☐ 394	........6.75 to 7.00".......(CE)	...........**❼**	..........$530—540	
☐ 394	........6.75 to 7.00".......(**OE**)	...........**❽**	..........$529	

HUM 395 — Shepherd Boy

Originally named "Young Shepherd" on old factory records, but later changed to "Shepherd Boy." This figurine was modeled by master sculptor Gerhard Skrobek in February 1971, with an incised 1972 copyright date. A smaller version, without the fence was released in 1996 with a combination "First Issue 1996" and "125th Anniversary Goebel" backstamp. The smaller 395/0 version was

395 Early sample (TM 5)   *395/0 (TM 7)*

modeled by master sculptor Helmut Fischer in 1989 with an incised 1989 copyright date in addition to the (TM 7) trademark. The original issue price was $295 in 1996. The Early Sample model was recently found with (TM 5) trademark and a 11/73 painting date, and is now in the Robert L. Miller collection. Listed as (TW) "Temporarily Withdrawn" in June 2002.

☐ 395	........6.75"..................(CE)	...........**❺**	..........$3000—4000	(Early Sample)
☐ 395/0	......4.875"................(CE)	...........**❼**	..........$310—315	
☐ 395/0	......4.875"................(**TW**)	...........**❽**	..........$280—300	

| 396 2/0 (TM 6) | 396/I (TM 6) | 396 /III (TM 8) |

HUM 396 — Ride Into Christmas

This design was first introduced in the U.S. market in 1972. First modeled by master sculptor Gerhard Skrobek in December 1970. It has an incised 1971 copyright date. The original issue price was $48.50 on the 1972 price list. A smaller model was released in 1982 with the incised number 396 2/0 and incised 1981 copyright date. The small version was also modeled by Gerhard Skrobek but in 1980. The original issue price was $95 in 1982. The large size has been renumbered 396/I and the old number 396 is now classified as a closed edition because of this change. This same motif is used on the 1975 Annual Plate, HUM 268. The new large size (396/III) was modeled by Gerhard Skrobek in 1991. It has an incised 1991 copyright date, and was released in 2003.

□ 396 2/0 ..4.25".................(CE) ....❻ ....$300—325
□ 396 2/0 ..4.25" ....(CE) ....❼ ....$290—300
□ 396 2/0 ..4.25".................(OE) ....❽ $279
□ 396 ....5.75".................(CE) ....❹ ....$2000—2500
□ 396 ....5.75".................(CE) ....❺ ....$575—600
□ 396 ....5.75".................(CE) ....❻ ....$550—575
□ 396/I .....5.75".................(CE) ....❻ ....$540—550
□ 396/I .....5.75".................(CE) ....❼ ....$530—540
□ 396/I .....5.75".................(OE) ....❽ $529
□ 396/III ....9.00".................(OE) ....❽ $1550

"Christmas Delivery"
HUM 2014
Released in 1997

HUM 397 — Poet, The

First released in the U.S. market in 1994. Modeled by master sculptor Gerhard Skrobek in 1973. It has an incised 1974 copyright date and the "First Issue 1994" oval decal on the bottom along with (TM 7) trademark. The issue price was $220 in 1994. A new 4.00" size (397 3/0) called "Poet at the Podium" was released in 1998 as a Member's Exclusive (PE) Preview Edition for Club year 22. Modeled by master sculptor Helmut Fischer in 1988. It has an incised 1988 copyright date along with the (TM 7) trademark. Also bears the "Club Exclusive 1998/99" backstamp. The official issue price was $150 in the U.S., in addition to member's redemption card. To be retired 31 May 2000. 397/1 (TW) "Temporarily Withdrawn" in June 2002.

- ☐ 397 ....6.00" ....(CE) ....❹ ......$3000—4000
  (Early Sample)
- ☐ 397 3/0 ..4.00" ....(CE) ....❼ ......$150—175
  (Club Exclusive)
- ☐ 397/I ......6.25" ....(CE) ....❼ ......$280—285
- ☐ 397/I ......6.25" ....(**TW**) ....❽ $280

HUM 398 — Spring Bouquet (PFE)

This figurine was first modeled by master sculptor Gerhard Skrobek in 1973. Presently listed on factory records as a (PFE) Possible Future Edition and may be released at some future date, subject to possible minor changes.

- ☐ 398 ....6.25" ....(CE) ....❺ ......$3000—4000
  (Early Sample)
- ☐ 398 ....6.25" ....(**PFE**) ....

HUM 399 — Valentine Joy (CE)

This figurine was first introduced in 1980 for members of the Goebel Collectors' Club only and not sold as an Open Edition. Originally modeled by master sculptor Gerhard Skrobek. It has an incised 1979 copyright date along with the (TM 6) trademark. Also bears the inscription "EXCLUSIVE SPECIAL EDITION No. 4 FOR MEMBERS OF THE GOEBEL COLLECTORS' CLUB" applied by blue decal. The original issue price was $95 in the U.S. and $105 in Canada, in addition to the member's redemption card. Translation of message on heart: "I Like You." The early sample of this piece is larger in size, has a rounded base showing grass and a bird at boy's feet. It has an incised 1973 copyright date along with the (TM 5) trademark.

- ☐ 399 ....6.25" ....(CE) ....❺ ......$5000—7500
  (Early Sample)
- ☐ 399 ....5.75" ....(CE) ....❻ ......$250—300

Early sample (TM 5)　　　*(TM 6)*

HUM 400 — Well Done! (PFE)

This figurine was first modeled by master sculptor Gerhard Skrobek in 1973. Presently listed on factory records as a (PFE) Possible Future Edition and may be released at some future date, subject to possible minor changes.

- ☐ 400 ......6.25" ....(CE)......❺ ....\$3000—4000
  (Early Sample)
- ☐ 400 ......6.25" ....(PFE) ....

HUM 401 — Forty Winks

First released in the Fall of 2005 with an original issue price of \$319 and a First Issue 2006 backstamp. Formerly a (PFE) Possible Future Edition. Sculpted by master sculptor Gerhard Skrobek. Has an incised 1974 copyright date and the (TM 8) trademark. In October 2005 a limited edition of 100 Arbeitsmuster Editions were made available in North America to M.I. Hummel Club members. These painters' samples bear a crimped "Arbeitsmuster Series" metal tag, are signed by chief master sample painter Frank Knoch, and have a certificate of authenticity also signed by Frank Knoch. The Arbeitsmuster Edition has an incised 1974 copyright date, "First Issue 2006" backstamp, and the (TM 8) trademark, and was priced \$319 in 2005.

- ☐ 401 ......5.25" ....(CE)......❺ ....\$3000—4000
  (Early Sample)
- ☐ 401 ......5.25" ....(OE)......❽ \$319

HUM 402 — True Friendship

First released in the U.S. market in the fall of 2001 with "First Issue 2002" oval decal backstamp. Modeled by master sculptor Gerhard Skrobek in 1973. It has an incised 1976 copyright date along with the (TM 8) trademark. The original issue price was \$365 in 2001.

- ☐ 402 ....4.75" ....(CE)..❺ ..\$3000—4000
  (Early Sample)
- ☐ 402 ....5.00 to 5.25" ....(OE)..❽ ..\$399

HUM 403 — An Apple A Day

This figurine was first modeled by master sculptor Gerhard Skrobek in 1973. First released in the U.S. Market in 1989. It has an incised 1974 copyright date. The original issue price was $195 in 1989. A new small size 403 4/0 was issued in 2003 with an incised 2003 copyright date. (TW) "Temporarily Withdrawn" from production.

- ☐ 403 4/0....3.50" ....**(OE)** ....❽ $99
- ☐ 403..........6.25" ....(CE) ....❺ ....$3000—4000
  (Early Sample)
- ☐ 403..........6.25" ....(CE) ....❻ ....$360—370
- ☐ 403..........6.25" ....(CE) ....❼ ....$350—360
- ☐ 403..........6.25" ....**(TW)** ....❽ $350

HUM 404 — Sad Song (EE)

First released in Spring of 2005 with an original issue price of $295. An (EE) Exclusive Edition for 2005/2006 Club year, for members of the M.I. Hummel Club. Includes wooden easel and ceramic postcard of original artwork. Formerly a (PFE) Possible Future Edition. The figurine is of an unhappy boy crying, with tears on his cheeks, perhaps because the sheet of music he holds behind him is torn. Has an incised 1974 copyright date along with the (TM 8) trademark and bears the Club Exclusive backstamp, (EE) Exclusive Edition 2005/2006.

- ☐ 404..........6.25" ....(CE) ....❺ ....$3000—4000
  (Early Sample)
- ☐ 404..........6.25" ....**(EE)** ....❽ $295

HUM 405 — Sing With Me

This figurine was first released in the U.S. market in 1985 along with three other new models formerly listed as (PFE) Possible Future Editions. Modeled by master sculptor Gerhard Skrobek in 1973. It has an incised 1973 or 1974 copyright date on the bottom. The original issue price was $125 in 1985. Listed as (TW) "Temporarily Withdrawn" in January 1999, and again in December 2004, but may be reinstated at some future date.

- ☐ 405..........5.00" ....(CE) ....❺ ....$3000—4000
  (Early Sample)
- ☐ 405..........5.00" ....(CE) ....❻ ....$375—385
- ☐ 405..........5.00" ....(CE) ....❼ ....$350—360
- ☐ 405..........5.00" ....**(TW)** ....❽ $325

HUM 406 — Pleasant Journey (CE)

This figurine was first released in the U.S. market in 1987 along with four other new figurines. This is the second figurine in the Century Collection and was produced for this one year only in the twentieth century. It was modeled by master sculptor Gerhard Skrobek in 1974 but has an incised 1976 copyright date. A circular inscription applied by blue decal reads: "M.I. HUMMEL CENTURY COLLECTION 1987 XX" and the name "PLEASANT JOURNEY" along with the (TM 6) trademark. The issue price was $500 in 1987.

- ☐ 406.....7.00 x 6.50".....(CE)....❺....$5000—6000 (Early Sample)
- ☐ 406.....7.00 x 6.50".....(CE)....❻....$2750—3000

HUM 407 — Flute Song (PFE)

This figurine was first modeled by master sculptor Gerhard Skrobek in 1974. Presently listed on factory records as a (PFE) Possible Future Edition and may be released at some future date, subject to possible minor changes.

- ☐ 407......6.00".............(CE).....❺.....$3000—4000 (Early Sample)
- ☐ 407......6.00".............(PFE).........

HUM 408 — Smiling Through (CE)

This figurine was first introduced in 1985 for members of the Goebel Collector's Club only and not sold as an Open Edition. Originally modeled by master sculptor Gerhard Skrobek from an original drawing by sister M.I. Hummel. It has an incised 1983 copyright date along with the (TM 6) trademark. Also bears the inscription "EXCLUSIVE SPECIAL EDITION No. 9 FOR MEMBERS OF THE GOEBEL COLLECTORS' CLUB" applied by blue decal. The original issue price was $125 in the U.S. and $165 in Canada, in addition to the member's redemption card. It is interesting to note the incised model number of 408/0, which indicates that

Early sample (TM 5)   *408/0 (TM 6)*

more than one size was produced. The club piece was designed to be smaller, more uniform in size to the other club figurines. See HUM 690 for more information.

- ☐ 408 ....5.50"..................(CE) ....❺ ....$4000—5000 (Early Sample)
- ☐ 408/0 ......4.75"..................(CE) ....❻ ....$350—375

HUM 409 — Coffee Break (CE)
This figurine was first introduced in 1984 for members of the Goebel Collector's Club only and not sold as an (OE) Open Edition. Originally modeled by master sculptor Gerhard Skrobek from an original drawing by Sister M.I. Hummel. It has an incised 1976 copyright date along with the (TM 6) trademark. Also bears the inscription "EXCLUSIVE SPECIAL EDITION No. 8 FOR MEMBERS OF THE GOEBEL COLLEC-TORS' CLUB" applied by blue decal. The original issue price was $90 in the U.S. and $110 in Canada, in addition to the member's redemption card. "Coffee Break" can now be purchased on the secondary market at premium prices.

☐ 409 ....4.00"....(CE) ....❺ ....$3000—4000 (Early Sample)
☐ 409 ....4.00"....(**CE**) ....❻ ....$300—325

HUM 410 — Little Architect, The
First released in the U.S. market in 1993. Originally called "Truant" on old factory records, but later changed to "The Little Architect". Modeled by master sculptor Gerhard Skrobek in 1978. First released with an incised 1978 copyright date and the "First Issue 1993" oval decal on the bottom along with the current (TM 7) trademark. The official issue price was $290 in 1993. (TW) "Temporarily Withdrawn" from production in December 2005. May be reinstated at some future date.

☐ 410 ....6.00"....(CE) ....❺ ....$3000—4000 (Early Sample)
☐ 410/I ......6.00"....(CE) ....❼ ....$365—375

273

Convention Commemorative

Regular issue

HUM 411 — Do I Dare?

This figurine was first modeled by master sculptor Gerhard Skrobek in 1978. First appearance was in September of 2005, as gift to attendees of the 2005 M.I. Hummel Club Convention held in Boston, MA., with "2005 - M.I. Hummel Club Convention Boston MA" written on the side of the base, and incised 1988 copyright date, "First Issue 2006" backstamp and the (TM 8) trademark. The regular issue, without the convention marking, was first released in the Fall of 2005, with an original issue price of $149 and a "First Issue 2006" backstamp. Has incised 1988 copyright date and the (TM 8) trademark. Formerly a (PFE) Possible Future Edition.

☐ 411..........6.00".....(CE).....❺.....$3000—4000 (Early Sample)
☐ 411 3/0....4.00".....(OE).....❽.....$149

HUM 412 — Bath Time

This figurine was first modeled by master sculptor Gerhard Skrobek in 1978. First introduced in the U.S. market in 1990. It has an incised 1978 copyright date. Original issue price was $300 in 1990. Listed as (TW) "Temporarily Withdrawn" in June 2002, but may be reinstated at some future date.

☐ 412 ....6.00" ....(CE).....❺......$3000—4000 (Early Sample)
☐ 412 ....6.00" ....(CE).....❻......$540—550
☐ 412 ....6.00" ....(CE).....❼......$535—540
☐ 412 ....6.00" ....(TW).....❽.....$535

HUM 413 — Whistler's Duet

This figurine was first modeled by master sculptor Gerhard Skrobek in 1979. First released in the U.S. market in the fall of 1991, the original issue price was $235. Listed as (TW) "Temporarily Withdrawn" in January 1999, and again in June 2002.

☐ 413 ....4.00 to 4.50" ..(CE) ..❺ ..$3000—4000 (Early Sample)
☐ 413 ....4.00 to 4.50" ..(CE) ..❻ ..$500—1000
☐ 413 ....4.00 to 4.50" ..(**TW**) ..❼ ..$330—350

HUM 414 — In Tune

First released in the U.S. market in 1981. Modeled by Gerhard Skrobek in 1979. This figurine was designed to match the fourth edition of the annual bell series, HUM 703 "In Tune" 1981 Annual. The figurine has an incised 1979 copyright date on the bottom of the base. The original issue price was $115 in 1981. This same motif was used on HUM 297 "Springtime Serenade" plate in 1997. Listed as (TW) "Temporarily Withdrawn" in January 1999, but was released in 2006 in 25th Anniversary Edition with 25th Anniversary backstamp.

☐ 414 ....4.00" ....(CE)....❺.....$3000—4000 (Early Sample)
☐ 414 ....4.00" ....(CE)....❻.....$330—340
☐ 414 ....4.00" ....(CE)....❼.....$310—320
☐ 414 ....4.00" ....(**OE**)....❽.....$259

HUM 415 — Thoughtful

First released in the U.S. market in 1981. Modeled by Gerhard Skrobek in 1979. This figurine was designed to match the third edition of the annual bell series, HUM 702 "Thoughtful" 1980 Annual. The figurine has an incised 1980 copyright date on the bottom of the base. The original issue price was $105 in 1981. A Special Commemorative Edition of 2,000 pieces was issued in the fall of 1996 with master sculptor Gerhard Skrobek's signature, to coincide with the release of his autobiography, "Hummel & Me, Life Stories," by Gerhard Skrobek.

- ☐ 415 ....4.50" ......(CE) ...... **❺** ....$3000—4000 (Early Sample)
- ☐ 415 ....4.50" ......(CE) ...... **❻** ...$290—295
- ☐ 415 ....4.50" ......(CE) ...... **❼** ...$285—290 (Special Edition)
- ☐ 415 ....4.50" ......(CE) ...... **❼** ....$280—285
- ☐ 415 ....4.50" ......(OE) ...... **❽** $279

HUM 416 — Jubilee (CE)

This special limited edition figurine was issued in 1985 in celebration of the Golden Anniversary of the introduction of the first "M.I. Hummel" figurines in 1935. It was modeled by master sculptor Gerhard Skrobek in 1979 and has an incised 1980 copyright date. This figurine was limited to the total of the 1985 production and will not be produced in future years. On the bottom is the special inscription which reads: "50 YEARS M.I. HUMMEL FIGURINES 1935—1985" in a circular design. Directly below is "THE LOVE LIVES ON" in addition to the current (TM 6) trademark, all applied by blue decal. Originally sold in a special white padded presentation case. The original issue price was $200 in the U.S. and $270 in Canada.

- ☐ 416 ....6.25" ......(CE) ...... **❻** ....$500—600

HUM 417 — Where Did You Get That? (PFE)

This figurine was first modeled by master sculptor Gerhard Skrobek in 1982 and has an incised 1982 copyright date. Presently listed on factory records as a (PFE) Possible Future Edition and may be released at some future date, subject to possible minor changes. This figurine has now been made into two separate figurines. See HUM 485 "Gift From A Friend" and HUM 486 "I Wonder."

- ☐ 417 ....5.25" ......(PFE) ....

HUM 418 — What's New?

First introduced in the U.S. market in 1990. This figurine was modeled by master sculptor Gerhard Skrobek in 1980. It has an incised 1980 copyright date. The original issue price was $200 in 1990. A Special Edition for members of the M.I. Hummel Club was issued for Club year 1996/1997 for seven International Clubs using the special "INSIGHTS" logo and the National flag of their individual country: ☐ U.S.A. ☐ Austria ☐ Belgian ☐ Canada ☐ Dutch ☐ German and ☐ Swiss. Many other figurines with special backstamps have been issued in recent years. (TW) "Temporaily WIthdrawn" in December 2005.

☐ 418......5.25"......(CE).....❻....$380—390
☐ 418......5.25"......(CE).....❼....$370—380
   (Special Edition)
☐ 418......5.25"......(CE).....❼....$360—370
☐ 418.....5.25"......(**TW**).....❽....$359

HUM 419 — Good Luck! (PFE)

This figurine was first modeled by master sculptor Gerhard Skrobek in 1981. Presently listed on factory records as a (PFE) Possible Future Edition and may be released at some future date, subject to possible minor changes.

☐ 419 ....6.25" ......(PFE) ....

HUM 420 — Is It Raining?

First introduced in the U.S. market in 1989. This figurine was modeled by master sculptor Gerhard Skrobek in 1981. It has an incised 1981 copyright date. Original issue price was $175 in 1989.

☐ 420.......6.00".....(CE).....❻....$375—380
☐ 420.......6.00".....(CE).....❼....$370—375
☐ 420......6.00".....(**OE**).....❽....$369

HUM 421 — It's Cold

This figurine was first introduced in 1982 for members of the Goebel Collectors' Club only and not sold as an Open Edition. Originally modeled by master sculptor Gerhard Skrobek from an original drawing by Sister M.I. Hummel. It has an incised 1981 copyright date along with the 6 trademark. Also bears the inscription "EXCLUSIVE SPECIAL EDITION No. 6 FOR MEMBERS OF THE GOEBEL COLLECTORS' CLUB" applied by blue decal. The official issue price was $80 in the U.S. and $95 in Canada, in addition to the member's redemption card. This figurine can be purchased on the secondary market at premium prices. The 3.25" size, new in 2005, is an (OE) Open Edition not an (EE) Exclusive Edition.

☐ 421 4/0 ..3.25"...............(**OE**) ..❽....$99
☐ 421 ....5.00 to 5.25" ..(**EE**) ..❻....$350—400

HUM 422 — What Now? (CE)

This figurine was first introduced in 1983 for members of the Goebel Collectors' Club only and not sold as an Open Edition. Originally modeled by master sculptor Gerhard Skrobek from an original drawing by Sister M.I. Hummel. It has an incised 1981 copyright date along with the (TM 6) trademark. Also bears the inscription "EXCLUSIVE SPECIAL EDITION No. 7 FOR MEMBERS OF THE GOEBEL COLLECTORS' CLUB" applied by blue decal. The official issue price was $80 in the U.S. and $95 in Canada, in addition to the member's redemption card. This figurine can be purchased on the secondary market at premium prices.

☐ 422 ....5.25"...............(**CE**) ..❻....$350—400

HUM 423 — Horse Trainer

First introduced in the U.S. market in 1990. This figurine was modeled by master sculptor Gerhard Skrobek in 1980. It has an incised 1981 copyright date. The original issue price was $155 in 1990. (TW) "Temporarily Withdrawn" in December 2004.

☐ 423 ....4.50"...............(CE) ..❻....$275—280
☐ 423 ....4.50"...............(CE) ..❼....$270—275
☐ 423 ....4.50"...............(**TW** ..❽....$267.50

HUM 424 — Sleep Tight

First released in the U.S. market in 1990. This figurine was modeled by master sculptor Gerhard Skrobek in 1980. It has an incised 1981 copyright date. The original issue price was $155 in 1990. (TW) "Temporarily Withdrawn" in Decembr 2004.

☐ 424 ....4.50"....(CE) ..❻ ..$275—280
☐ 424 ....4.50"....(CE) ..❼ ..$270—275
☐ 424 ....4.50"....(TW)..❽ ..$267.50

Front view

Rear view

HUM 425 — Pleasant Moment (PFE)

This figurine was first modeled by master sculptor Gerhard Skrobek in 1980. It has an incised 1981 copyright date. Presently listed on factory records as a (PFE) Possible Future Edition and may be released at some future date, subject to possible minor changes.

☐ 425 ....4.50" ....(PFE) ....

426 (Factory Sample)   **426 3/0 (TM 7)**

HUM 426 — Pay Attention

This figurine was first modeled by master sculptor Gerhard Skrobek in 1980. It has an incised 1981 copyright date. This same motif was used on HUM 299 1999 "Autumn Glory" plate. A new smaller size (426 3/0) was released in 1999 with a "First Issue 1999" decal, (TM 7) trademark and 1997 copyright date. Modeled by master sculptor Helmut Fischer in 1997. The original issue price was $175 in 1999.

☐ 426.........5.75" ....(CE)......❻ ......$1500—2000 (Early Sample)
☐ 426 3/0 ..4.25" ....(CE)......❼ ......$180—195
☐ 426 3/0 ..4.25" ....(**OE**).....❽ $179

427 (Factory Sample)   **427 3/0 (TM 7)**

HUM 427 — Where Are You?

This figurine was first modeled by master sculptor Gerhard Skrobek in 1980. It has an incised 1981 copyright date. A new smaller size (427 3/0) was released in 1999 with a "First Issue 1999" decal, (TM 7) trademark and 1997 copyright date. Modeled by master sculptor Helmut Fischer in 1997. The original issue price was $175 in 1999.

☐ 427 (427 II)....5.75" to 6.00" ..(CE) ......❻ ....$1500—2000 (Early Sample)
☐ 427 3/0 ....4.25" ....(CE) ......❼ ....$180—195
☐ 427 3/0 ....4.25" ....(**OE**) ......❽ $179

HUM 428 — Summertime Surprise
This figurine was first modeled by master sculptor Gerhard Skrobek in 1980 in the 5.75" size with an incised 1981 copyright date. It was listed as a (PFE) Possible Future Edition under the name of "I Won't Hurt You" until 1989 when master sculptor Helmut Fischer modeled it in the 3.50" size with model number 428 3/0, under the name of "Summertime Surprise." The small size was first released in the U. S. market in the fall of 1997 with a "First Issue 1998" backstamp. It has an incised 1989 copyright date and the (TM 7) trademark. The original issue price was $140 in 1997.

☐ 428 ....5.75" ......(CE) ....❻ ....$2000—3000
   (Early Sample)
☐ 428 3/0 ..3.50" ......(CE) ....❼ ....$140—150
☐ 428 3/0 ..3.50" ......(**OE**) ....❽ $139

HUM 429 — Hello World (CE)
This was first introduced in 1989 for members of the M.I. Hummel Club only and not sold as an Open Edition. Originally modeled by master sculptor Gerhard Skrobek in 1980. It has an incised 1983 copyright date along with either the (TM 6) or (TM 7) trademark. Also bears the inscription: "EXCLUSIVE EDITION 1989/90 M.I. HUMMEL CLUB" applied by blue decal. A large black flying bumble bee is located on the bottom. The official issue price was $130 in the U.S., in addition to the member's redemption card. This figurine can now be purchased on the secondary market at premium prices. Early production pieces are labeled "Goebel Collectors' Club" while later pieces have "M.I. Hummel Club" decal.

☐ 429 ....5.50" ......(CE) ....❻ ....$350—400
☐ 429 ....5.50" ......(CE) ....❼ ....$300—350

HUM 430 — In "D" Major
First released in the U.S. market in 1989. This figurine was modeled by master sculptor Gerhard Skrobek in 1980. It has an incised 1981 copyright date. The original issue price was $135 in 1989. In the rear view—the "K B" on the boundry stone the little boy is sitting on means: "Koenig-reich Bayern." English: "Kingdom of Bavaria." Listed as (TW) "Temporarily Withdrawn" in June 2002.

☐ 430 ....4.25" ......(CE) ....❻ ....$255—260
☐ 430 ....4.25" ......(CE) ....❼ ....$250—255
☐ 430 ....4.25" ......(**TW**) ....❽ $250

HUM 431 — The Surprise (CE)

This figurine was first introduced in 1988 for members of the Goebel Collectors' Club only and not sold as an Open Edition. Originally modeled by master sculptor Gerhard Skrobek in 1980. It has an incised 1981 copyright date along with the current (TM6) trademark. Also bears the inscription: "EXCLUSIVE SPECIAL EDITION No. 12 FOR MEMBERS OF THE GOEBEL COLLECTORS' CLUB" applied by blue decal. A large black flying bumble bee is located on the bottom of the base. The original price was $125 in the U.S., in addition to the member's redemption card. "The Surprise" can now be purchased on the secondary market at premium prices. There is no club inscription on Factory Sample.

☐ 431 ....4.25 to 5.50"....(CE) ....❻ ....$2000—3000
    (Early Sample)
☐ 431 ....5.50" ....(CE) ....❻ ....$300—350

(Factory Sample)

HUM 432 — Knit One, Purl One

First released in the U.S. market in 1983. Modeled by master sculptor Gerhard Skrobek in 1982. This figurine was designed especially to match the sixth edition of the annual bell series, HUM 705 "Knit One" 1983 annual. The figurine has an incised 1982 copyright date. The original issue price was $52 in the U.S. and $74 in Canada.

☐ 432 ....3.00" ....(CE) ....❻ ....$185—190
☐ 432 ....3.00" ....(CE) ....❼ ....$180—185
☐ 432 ....3.00" ....(OE) ....❽ $179

HUM 433 — Sing Along

First released in the U.S. market in 1987. Modeled by master sculptor Gerhard Skrobek in 1981. This figurine was designed especially to match the ninth edition of the annual bell series, HUM 708 "Sing Along" 1986 annual. The figurine has an incised 1982 copyright date on the bottom of the base. The original issue price was $145 in the U.S. and $200 in Canada. Listed as (TW) "Temporarily Withdrawn" in January 1999, but may be reinstated at some future date.

☐ 433 ....4.50" ....(CE) ....❻ ....$330—340
☐ 433 ....4.50" ....(TW) ....❼ ....$310—320

HUM 434 — Friend or Foe?

First released in the U.S. market in 1991 with "First Issue 1991" decal. Modeled by master sculptor Gerhard Skrobek in 1981. It has an incised 1983 copyright date. The original issue price was $190. Listed as (TW) "Temporarily Withdrawn" in June 2002, but may be reinstated at some future date.

- ☐ 434 ....3.75" ....(CE).....❻ ....$275—280
- ☐ 434 ....3.75" ....(CE).....❼ ....$270—275
- ☐ 434 ....3.75" ....(**TW**) ....❽ $267.50

HUM 435 — Delicious

This figurine was first modeled by master sculptor Gerhard Skrobek in 1981 in the 6.00" size with an incised 1982 copyright date. It was listed as a (PFE) Possible Future Edition until 1986 when master sculptor Helmut Fischer modeled it in the 3.75" size with model number 435 3/0. This small size was first released in the U. S. market in 1996 with a combination "First Issue 1996" and the "125th Anniversary Goebel" backstamp. It has an incised 1988 copyright date and the (TM 7) trademark. The original issue price was $155 in 1996. Listed as (TW) "Temporarily Withdrawn" in June 2002.

- ☐ 435 ....6.00" ....(CE) ......❻ ....$2000—3000
  (Early Sample)
- ☐ 435 3/0 ..3.75" ....(CE).....❼ ....$175—180
- ☐ 435 3/0 ..3.75" ....(**TW**) ....❽ $175

HUM 436 — An Emergency (PFE)

This figurine was first modeled by master sculptor Gerhard Skrobek in 1981. It has an incised 1983 copyright date. Presently listed on factory records as a (PFE) Possible Future Edition and may be released at some future date, subject to possible minor changes.

- ☐ 436 ....5.50" ....(PFE) ....

HUM 436 (Early Sample)

HUM 437 — Tuba Player

First released in the U.S. market in 1989. This figurine was modeled by master sculptor Gerhard Skrobek in 1982. It has an incised 1983 copyright date. The original issue price was $160 in 1989. Listed as (TW) "Temporarily WIthdrawn" in June 2002, but may be reinstated at some future date.

- ☐ 437......6.25"................(CE) ....❻....$345—350
- ☐ 437......6.25"................(CE) ....❼....$340—345
- ☐ 437......6.25"................(**TW**)....❽....$340

HUM 438 — Sounds of the Mandolin

First released in the U.S. market in 1988. This figurine was modeled by master sculptor Gerhard Skrobek in 1982. It has an incised 1984 copyright date. It was originally called "Mandolin Serenade" but later changed to "Sounds of the Mandolin" at time of release. The original issue price was $65 in 1988. Listed as (TW) "Temporarily WIthdrawn" in June 2002, but may be reinstated at some future date.

- ☐ 438......3.75"................(CE) ....❻....$165—170
- ☐ 438......3.75"................(CE) ❼ $160 165
- ☐ 438......3.75"................(**TW**)....❽....$160

HUM 439 — A Gentle Glow, Candleholder

First released in the U.S. market in 1987. Modeled by master sculptor Gerhard Skrobek in 1982. The figurine has an incised 1983 copyright date on the bottom of the base. The original issue price was $110 in the U.S. and $160 in Canada. Listed as (TW) "Temporarily Withdrawn" in January 1999, but may be reinstated at some future date.

- ☐ 439......5.25 to 5.50"....(CE) ....❻....$240—250
- ☐ 439......5.25 to 5.50"....(**TW**)....❼....$230—240

HUM 440 — Birthday Candle, Candleholder (CE)

This figurine was first introduced in 1986 for members of the Goebel Collectors' Club only and not sold as an Open Edition. Originally modeled by master sculptor Gerhard Skrobek from an original drawing by Sister M.I. Hummel. It has an incised 1983 copyright date along with the current (TM 6) trademark. Also bears the inscription "EXCLUSIVE SPECIAL EDITION No. 10 FOR MEMBERS OF THE GOEBEL COLLECTORS' CLUB" applied by blue decal. Also a circular "CELEBRATING 10 YEARS OF THE GOEBEL COLLECTORS' CLUB." The original issue price was $95 in the U.S. and $140 in Canada, in addition to the member's redemption card. "Birthday Candle" can now be purchased on the secondary market at premium prices.

☐ 440....5.50" ......(CE) ..**❻** ..$350—400

HUM 441 — Call To Worship, Clock (CE)

First released in the U.S. market in 1988. This figurine, an actual working clock, battery operated, with chimes. It was modeled by master sculptor Gerhard Skrobek in 1982. This is the third figurine in the Century Collection and was produced for only this one year in the twentieth century. It has an incised 1983 copyright date. A circular inscription applied by blue decal reads: "M.I. HUMMEL CENTURY COLLECTION 1988 XX" and the current (TM 6) trademark. The issue price was $600 in 1988.

☐ 441....13.00" ....(CE) ..**❻** ..$1400—1500

HUM 442 — Chapel Time, Clock (CE)

This figurine, an actual working clock, was first modeled by master sculptor Gerhard Skrobek in 1982. It has an incised 1983 copyright date. Released in 1986, it was produced for one year only as a limited edition and was not produced again in the twentieth century. Hand lettered XX to signify the twentieth century. The suggested retail price was $500 in the U.S. and $650 in Canada. Several variations are noted: Early production of "Chapel Time" had a closed bell tower with only painted windows. In later production, the bell tower windows were opened to allow air to escape more easily during the firing process. A third variation is in the small round window directly beneath the bell tower but above the clock. Slight variations have been noted in the base construction and color variations on the face of the clock. The clock is battery operated, using one "C" cell battery and keeps accurate time.

☐ 442	11.50"	(CE)	❻	$1750—2000	(Open windows/closed hole)
☐ 442	11.50"	(CE)	❻	$2000—2500	(Painted windows variation)
☐ 442	11.50"	(CE)	❻	$2500—3000	(Open windows/open hole)

286

(Factory Sample)

HUM 443 — Country Song, Clock (PFE)

This figurine, an actual working clock, was first modeled by master sculptor Gerhard Skrobek in 1982. It has an incised 1983 copyright date. Presently listed on factory records as a (PFE) Possible Future Edition and may be released at some future date, subject to possible minor changes.

☐ 443 ....8.00" ....(PFE) ....

HUM 444–445 — (ON) OPEN NUMBERS

HUM 446 — A Personal Message (PFE)

This figurine was first modeled by master sculptor Gerhard Skrobek in 1983. Presently listed on factory records as a (PFE) Possible Future Edition and may be released at some future date, subject to possible minor changes.

□ 446 ....3.75" ....(PFE) ....

HUM 447 — Morning Concert (CE)

This figurine was first introduced in 1987 for members of the Goebel Collectors' Club only and not sold as an (OE) Open Edition. Originally modeled by master sculptor Gerhard Skrobek from an original drawing by Sister M. I. Hummel. It has an incised 1984 copyright date along with the current (TM 6) trademark. Also bears the inscription: "EXCLUSIVE SPECIAL EDITION No. 11 FOR MEMBERS OF THE GOEBEL COLLECTORS' CLUB" applied by blue decal. The original issue price was $98 in the U.S., in addition to the member's redemption card. "Morning Concert" can now be purchased on the secondary market at premium prices.

□ 447.......5.25".....(CE).....**❻**.....$250—300

Enrich your knowledge and enjoyment of *M.I. Hummel* figurines with membership in the M.I. Hummel Club. Make new friends and share your love for *M.I. Hummel* with other *Hummel* enthusiasts.

Membership in the Club brings a world of benefits, including:

- An authentic *M.I. Hummel* figurine as a free gift of welcome, valued at over $100

- The members-only quarterly magazine, INSIGHTS

- The opportunity to purchase figurines made exclusively for Club members

- Entrance to the Club House, exclusive members-only section of the *M.I. Hummel* web site

- Official *M.I. Hummel* membership card

- Club services, such as the Research Department and Collector's Market

- Local Chapters to share information with collectors near you

- Inside information on *M.I. Hummel* figurines

For more information, contact Membership Services at 1-800-666-CLUB (2582) or log onto our web site at www.mihummel.com.

M.J. Hummel

C·L·U·B®

NEW MEMBER APPLICATION
Goebel Plaza, P.O. Box 11, Pennington, New Jersey 08534-0011

Please enroll me as a new member.
My ❑ check ❑ money order in the amount of $50, for one year, is enclosed.
We honor: ❑ AMEX ❑ MC ❑ VISA ❑ DISCOVER (US only)

_____

CREDIT CARD NUMBER   EXPIRATION DATE

_____

CREDIT CARD BILLING ADDRESS

_____

NAME AS IT APPEARS ON CARD

✔
_____

SIGNATURE   DATE

(PLEASE PRINT)

NAME, FIRST											MIDDLE INITIAL	

NAME, LAST												

STREET ADDRESS												

CITY										APT. NUMBER		

STATE		ZIP + 4										

AREA CODE		PHONE NUMBER										

E-MAIL ADDRESS												

Within 6 to 8 weeks you will send me my membership card, redemption forms, and membership package with an authentic *M.I. Hummel* figurine.

* For credit card purchases, use U.S. price. Credit card company will establish and apply the exchange rate.

MEMBERSHIP FEE IS SUBJECT TO CHANGE WITHOUT NOTICE. CURRENT FEE VALID UNTIL MAY 31, 2007. AFTER MAY 31, 2007 CALL (800) 666-CLUB (2582) FOR CURRENT MEMBERSHIP FEE.

MG10ED

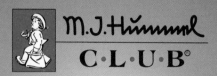

Join Now!

To experience the benefits of belonging, simply fill out
the attached registration form and send it along with
your personal check or money order payable to the
M.I. Hummel Club in the envelope provided.

One year's membership fee is $50. Price is subject to
change. Credit card orders are also welcome.
To enroll over the phone call the Club at 1-800-666-CLUB
(2582), or you can join immediately on our web site at
www.mihummel.com.

FOLD
HERE

FROM:

M.I. HUMMEL CLUB
GOEBEL PLAZA
P.O. BOX 11
PENNINGTON   NJ 08534-0011

HUM 448 — Children's Prayer (PFE)

This beautiful figurine was modeled by master sculptor Gerhard Skrobek in 1983. It has an incised 1984 copyright date. Presently listed on factory records as a (PFE) Possible Future Edition and may be released at some future date, subject to possible minor changes.

☐ 448 ....8.25" ....(PFE) ....

HUM: 448 Rear view

Original Drawing

HUM 449 — The Little Pair

This figurine was first modeled by master sculptor Gerhard Skrobek in 1984. It has an incised 1985 copyright date. Announced in 1990, "The Little Pair" will be an (EE) Exclusive Edition available to "M.I. Hummel Club" members only, who have belonged to the Club continuously for 10 years. The original issue price was $170. Retired on 31 May 2000.

☐ 449 ......5.00 to 5.25"........(CE) ......❻ .....$350—400
☐ 449 ......5.00 to 5.25"........(CE) ......❼ .....$235—240
☐ 449 ......5.00 to 5.25"........(**CE**) ......❽ .....$225—235

HUM 450 — Will It Sting?

Members' (EE) Exclusive Edition for Club year 24. This figurine was first released in 2000 for members of the M.I. Hummel Club only and <u>not</u> sold as an (OE) "Open Edition" to the general public. First modeled by master sculptor Gerhard Skrobek in 1984. Size 450/0 was modeled by master sculptor Helmut Fischer in 1990. It has an incised 1990 copyright date along with the (TM 8) trademark. Also bears the inscription: "EXCLUSIVE EDITION 2000/01 M.I. HUMMEL CLUB" applied by blue decal. A large black flying bumblebee is located on the bottom. The official issue price was $260 in 2000, in addition to the members' redemption card.

☐ 450/1 5.75" ....(CE) ......❻ ......$2000—3000 (Early Sample)
☐ 450/0 5.00" ....(**CE**) ......❽ ......$260—275

HUM 451 — Just Dozing

First released in the U.S. market in 1995. Modeled by master sculptor Gerhard Skrobek in 1984. It has an incised 1984 copyright date. The first year of issue figurines have the (TM 7) trademark and bear the "First Issue 1995" oval decal on the bottom. The official issue price was $220 in 1995.

☐ 451 ....4.25" ....(CE) ......❼ ......$280—285
☐ 451 ....4.25" ....(**OE**) ......❽ $279

HUM 452 — Flying High (CE)

Annal Ornament 1988. First released in the U.S. market in 1988 as a hanging orna-ment. Modeled by master sculptor Gerhard Skrobek in 1984. It has an incised 1984 copyright date. The original issue price was $75 in 1988. Early releases were not dated. Later pieces dated 1988 with "First Edition" decal. Third variation was dated but without "First Edition" decal. Undated pieces bring a premium.

☐ 452 ....4.50 x 2.75" ......(CE) ...... ❻ ......$250—300 (undated)
☐ 452 ....4.50 x 2.75" ......(CE) ...... ❻ ......$175—200 (dated with "First Edition")
☐ 452 ....4.50 x 2.75" ......(CE) ...... ❻ ......$175—200 (dated without "First Edition")

HUM 453 — Accompanist, The

First released in the U.S. market in 1988. Modeled by master sculptor Gerhard Skrobek in 1984. It has an incised 1984 copyright date. The original issue price was $39 in 1988.

☐ 453 ....3.25"....(CE).... ❻ ....$140—145
☐ 453 ....3.25"....(CE).... ❼ ....$135—140
☐ 453 ....3.25"....(OE) ..❽ $135

HUM 454 — Song Of Praise
First released in the U. S. market in 1988. Modeled by master sculptor Gerhard Skrobek in 1984. It has an incised 1984 copyright date. The original issue price was $39 in 1988.

☐ 454......3.00" ....(CE) .... ❻ ....$140—145
☐ 454......3.00" ....(CE) .... ❼ ....$135—140
☐ 454......3.00" ....(**OE**) .... ❽ $135

HUM 455 — Guardian, The
First released in the U.S. market in 1991. Modeled by master sculptor Gerhard Skrobek in 1984. It has an incised 1985 copyright date. The original issue price was $140. It has been noted that there are two different base constructions on this figurine. This figurine, minus the bird, can be personalized with a name or date by a Goebel artist.

☐ 455......2.75 x 3.50" ......(CE) .... ❻ ....$205—210
☐ 455......2.75 x 3.50" ......(CE) .... ❼ ....$200—205
☐ 455......2.75 x 3.50" ......(**OE**) .... ❽ $200

HUM 456 — Sleep, Little One, Sleep (PFE)

This figurine was first modeled by master sculptor Gerhard Skrobek in 1984. Presently listed on factory records as a (PFE) Possible Future Edition and may be released at some future date, subject to possible minor changes.

☐ 456......4.25" ....(PFE)..........

HUM 457 — Sound The Trumpet

First released in the U.S. market in 1988. Modeled by master sculptor Gerhard Skrobek in 1984. It has an incised 1984 copyright date. The original issue price was $45 in 1988. Listed as (TW) "Temporarily Withdrawn" in June 2002, but may be reinstated at some future date.

☐ 457....3.00"....(CE)......❻ ..$140—145
☐ 457....3.00"....(CE)......❼ ..$135—140
☐ 457....3.00"....(TW) ....❽ ..$135

HUM 458 — Storybook Time
First released in the U.S. market in
the fall of 1991. Modeled by master
sculptor Gerhard Skrobek in 1984.
It has an incised 1985 copyright
date. The original issue price was
$330. (TW) "Temporarily With-
drawn" in December 2005.   May
be reinstated at some future date.

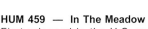

☐ 458 ....5.25" ....(CE)......❼ ....$540—580
☐ 458 ....5.25" ....(**TW**) ....❽ ....$529—530

HUM 459 — In The Meadow
First released in the U.S. market in
1987. Modeled by master sculptor Gerhard Skrobek in 1984. The figurine has
an incised 1985 copyright date. The
original issue price was $110 in the
U.S. and $160 in Canada. Listed as
(TW) "Temporarily Withdrawn" in June
2002, but may be reinstated at some
future date.

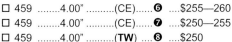

☐ 459 ....4.00" ....(CE)......❻ ....$255—260
☐ 459 ....4.00" ....(CE)......❼ ....$250—255
☐ 459 ....4.00" ....(**TW**) ....❽ $250

HUM 460 — Goebel Authorized Retailer Plaque

This authorized retailer plaque was issued to all authorized "M. I. Hummel" retailers in 1986 and became the official identification for distributors of Hummel figurines. It replaced the older HUM 187 dealers plaque with "Merry Wanderer" that has been in use, with many variations, since the late 1940s. You will notice the boy is similar to the middle boy on HUM 170 "School Boys." The new plaque has an incised "M. I. Hummel" signature on the back as well as the decal signature on the front. It has an incised 1004 copyright date along with the current (TM 0) trademark on the bottom. It is also known as "The Tally." This plaque was issued in nine decal variations for use in other countries (languages). Only the U.S. version was discontinued in December 1989, to be replaced by HUM 187A with new graphics. (See HUM 187)

☐ 460 ....5.00 x 6.00" U.S. VERSION ..(CE)....❻ ....$200—225
☐ 460 ....5.00 x 6.00" BRITISH..............(CE)....❻ ....$500—750   (CE) ..❼ ..$300—500
☐ 460 ....5.00 x 6.00" GERMAN ....(CE)....❻ ....$750—1000   (CE) ..❼ ..$300—500
☐ 460 ....5.00 x 6.00" DUTCH ....(CE)....❻ ....$900—1500   (CE) ..❼ ..$300—500
☐ 460 ....5.00 x 6.00" ITALIAN ....(CE)....❻ ....$900—1500   (CE) ..❼ ..$300—500
☐ 460 ....5.00 x 6.00" FRENCH ....(CE)....❻ ....$750—1000   (CE) ..❼ ..$300—500
☐ 460 ....5.00 x 6.00" SWEDISH ....(CE)....❻ ....$750—1000   (CE) ..❼ ..$300—500
☐ 460 ....5.00 x 6.00" SPANISH ....(CE)....❻ ....$900—1500   (CE) ..❼ ..$300—500
☐ 460 ....5.00 x 6.00" JAPANESE ....(Issued in 1996)............. (CE) ..❼ ..$500—750

.... **HUM TERM** ....

CURRENT TRADEMARK: Designates the symbol presently being used by the W. Goebel Porzellanfabrik to represent the company's trademark.

☐ *UNITED STATES*

☐ *BRITISH*

☐ *GERMAN*

☐ *DUTCH*

☐ *ITALIAN*

☐ *FRENCH*

☐ *SWEDISH*

☐ *SPANISH*

☐ *JAPANESE*

☐ *HUM 460 AS SERVICE AWARD*

HUM 461 — In The Orchard (PFE)

This figurine was first modeled by master sculptor Gerhard Skrobek in 1984. Presently listed on factory records as a (PFE) "Possible Future Edition" and may be released at some future date, subject to possible minor changes. See HUM 727 "Garden Treasures" for smaller variation of this figurine.

☐ 461.......5.50".......(PFE)...........

HUM 462 — Tit for Tat

Formerly a (PFE) "Possible Future Edition". Sculpted by master sculptor Gerhard Skrobek in 1984. First released in January of 2004, with an incised 1985 copyright date and the (TM 8) trademark. Five hundred were available through AAFES from January to June 2004 for $179, with First Issue 2004 backstamp. Available from January 2004 in a (LE) Limited Edition of 600, with "Caribbean Collection" backstamp, a band of matching flowers on side of base, and First Issue 2004 backstamp. Regular issue was first announced in the Summer, 2004 issue of *INSIGHTS* magazine, and made available at that time with "First Issue 2004" backstamp, and original issue price of $310. Priced $279 on 2005 and 2006 Goebel NA US Suggested Retail Price Lists.

☐ 462.......3.75".......(OE).....❽.....$279

Caribbean Collection

Early Sample (TM 6)   *(TM 7)*

HUM 463 — My Wish Is Small (CE)

Members' Exclusive Edition for Club Year 16. This figurine was first introduced in 1992 for members of the M.I. HUMMEL CLUB only and not sold as an (OE) Open Edition. Modeled by master sculptor Gerhard Skrobek in 1985. It has an incised 1985 copyright date along with the (TM 7) trademark. Also bears the inscription: "EXCLUSIVE EDITION 1992/93 M.I. HUMMEL CLUB" applied by blue decal. A large black flying bumble bee is located on the bottom. The original issue price was $170 in the U.S., in addition to the member's redemption card. Note: The Early Sample model has a square base, while the normal production figurine has a round base.

☐ 463......5.50"................(CE) ..❻..$2000—2500 (Early Sample)

☐ 463/0 ..5.50 to 5.75"....(CE) ..❼..$250—300

HUM 464 — Young Scholar (PFE)

This figurine was first modeled by master sculptor Gerhard Skrobek in 1985. Presently listed on factory records as a (PFE) "Possible Future Edition" and may be released at some future date, subject to possible minor changes.

☐ 464 ....5.00 to 5.25"....(PFE)..........

299

HUM 465 — Where Shall I Go? (PFE)
This figurine was first modeled by master sculptor Gerhard Skrobek in 1985 and has an incised 1985 copyright date. It is based on a portrait sketched by Sister Hummel in 1938. His name was Jochen Edinger. This figurine is presently listed on factory records as a (PFE) "Possible Future Edition" and may be released at some future date, subject to possible changes. The original drawing and this Early Sample model are owned by Mr. & Mrs. Robert L. Miller.

☐ 465 ....4.25" ....(CE) ....**❻** ..$4000—5000 (Early Sample)
☐ 465 ....4.25" ....(**PFE**)..........

HUM 466 — DoReMi (PFE)
This figurine was first modeled by master sculptor Gerhard Shrobek in 1985. Presently listed on factory records as a (PFE) "Possible Future Edition" and may be released at some future date, subject to possible minor changes.

☐ 466.......5.50".....(**PFE**)....

HUM 467 — Kindergartner, The

First released in the U.S. market in 1987. Modeled by master sculptor Gerhard Skrobek in 1985. The figurine has an incised 1985 copyright date. The original issue price was $100 in 1987. A new small size 467 4/0 was released in 2004. The 5.50" size was (TW) "Temporarily Withdrawn" in December 2004.

☐ 467 4/0 ..3.25" ......(**OE**) ......❽ $69.50
☐ 467 ....5.25" ......(CE) ......❻ ....$255—260
☐ 467 ....5.25" ......(CE) ......❼ ....$250—255
☐ 467 ....5.25" ......(**TW**) ......❽ ....$250—255

HUM 468 — Come On (PFE)

This figurine was first modeled by master sculptor Gerhard Skrobek in 1986. Presently listed on factory records as a (PFE) Possible Future Edition and may be released at some future date, subject to possible minor changes.

☐ 468 ....5.25" ......(**PFE**).............

(Factory Sample)

301

HUM 469 — Starting Young (PFE)

This figurine was first modeled by master sculptor Gerhard Skrobek in 1986. Presently listed on factory records as a (PFE) Possible Future Edition and may be released at some future date, subject to possible minor changes.

☐ 469 ....4.75" ......(PFE) ....

HUM 470 — Time Out (PFE)

This figurine was first modeled by master sculptor Gerhard Skrobek in 1986. Presently listed on factory records as a (PFE) "Possible Future Edition" and may be released at some future date, subject to possible minor changes.

☐ 470........4.50"......(PFE)........

HUM 471 — Harmony In Four Parts (CE)

This figurine was first released in the U.S. market in 1989 along with seven other new figurines. This is the fourth figurine in the Century Collection and was produced for only this one year in the twentieth century. It was modeled by master sculptor Gerhard Skrobek in 1986. It has an incised 1987 copyright date. A circular inscription applied by blue decal reads: "M.I. HUMMEL CENTURY COLLECTION 1989 XX" and the name "HARMONY IN FOUR PARTS" along with the (TM 6) trademark. The issue price was $850 in 1989.

☐ 471 ....9.75" ....(**CE**) ....**❻** ....$2000—2500

HUM 472 — On Our Way (CE)
This figurine was first released in the U.S. market in 1992 along with five other new figurines. This is the seventh figurine in the Century Collection and was produced for this
one year only in the twentieth century. It was modeled by master sculptor Gerhard
Skrobek in 1986 but has an incised 1987 copyright date. A circular inscription applied by
blue decal reads: "M.I. HUMMEL CENTURY COLLECTION 1992 XX" and the name
"ON OUR WAY" along with the current (TM 7) trademark. The issue price was $950 in
1992.

☐ 472....8.00 to 8.25" ....(CE) ..❻ ..$2000—3000 (Early Sample)
☐ 472....8.00 to 8.25" ....**(CE)** ..❼ ..$1200—1500

HUM 473 — Ruprecht (Knecht Ruprecht)

This figurine was first modeled by master sculptor Gerhard Skrobek in 1986 under the name of "Father Christmas." It has an incised 1987 copyright date. Released in the spring of 1997 in a (LE) Limited Edition of 20,000 sequentially-numbered pieces. A companion figurine of "St. Nicholas' Day," (HUM 2012) was released at the same time with matching edition numbers at a specially reduced price of $1000 (per set) for members of the "M.I. Hummel Club."

☐ 473....6.00" ....(CE) ..❻ ..$2000—3000 (Early Sample)
☐ 473....6.00 to 6.25" ....(CE) ..❼ ..$470—600

HUM 474 — Gentle Care (PFE)

This figurine was first modeled by master sculptor Gerhard Skrobek in 1986. Presently listed on factory records as a (PFE) "Possible Future Edition" and may be released at some future date, subject to possible minor changes.

☐ 474....6.00" ....(PFE)........

HUM 475 — Make A Wish

First released in the U.S. market in 1989. This figurine was modeled by master sculptor Gerhard Skrobek in 1986. It has an incised 1987 copyright date. Original issue price was $135 in 1989. This figurine was (TW) "Temporarily Withdrawn" from the U.S. market only at the end of 1997. Once again listed as (TW) "Temporarily Withdrawn" in January 1999, but may be reinstated at some future date.

☐ 475 ....4.50"....................(CE)........❻ ....$240—250
☐ 475 ....4.50"....................**(TW)** ......❼ ....$225—230

HUM 476 — Winter Song, A

First released in the U.S. market in 1988. Modeled by master sculptor Gerhard Skrobek in 1987. It has an incised 1987 copyright date. The original issue price was $45 in 1988.

☐ 476 ....4.00 to 4.25" ......(CE)........❻ ....$150—155
☐ 476 ....4.00 to 4.25" ......(CE)........❼ ....$149—150
☐ 476 ....4.00 to 4.25" ......**(OE)**........❽ $149

HUM 477 — A Budding Maestro
First released in the U.S. market in 1988. Modeled by
master sculptor Gerhard Skrobek in 1987. It has an
incised 1987 copyright date. The original issue price
was $45 in 1988. This figurine was (TW) "Temporarily
Withdrawn" from the U.S. market only at the end of
1997. Once again listed as (TW) "Temporarily Withdrawn" in January 1999, but may be reinstated at
some future date.

☐ 477 ....4.00" ....(CE) ....❻ ....$130—135
☐ 477 ....4.00" ....(**TW**) ....❼ ....$120—125

HUM 478 — I'm Here
First released in the U.S. market in 1989.
Modeled by master sculptor Gerhard Skrobek
in 1987. It has an incised 1987 copyright
date. The original issue price was $50 in
1989. Listed as (TW) "Temporarily Withdrawn"
in June 2002, but may be reinstated at some
future date.

☐ 478 ....3.00" ....(CE) ....❻ ....$145—150
☐ 478 ....3.00" ....(CE) ....❼ ....$140—145
☐ 478 ....3.00" ....(**TW**) ....❽ ....$140—145

HUM 479 — I Brought You A Gift (CE)

First released in the U.S. market in 1989 as a free gift for joining the M.I. HUMMEL CLUB (formerly Goebel Collectors' Club). Modeled by master sculptor Gerhard Skrobek in 1987. It has an incised 1987 copyright date. Early models have a special blue decal: "Goebel Collectors' Club" in addition to a black flying bumble bee, in a half circle. Later models have: "M.I. Hummel Club." Some examples have eyelashes, some do not. Six different versions exist: (TM 6) "Goebel Collectors' Club" — with eyelashes; (TM 6) "Goebel Collectors' Club — without eyelahes; (TM 6) "M.I. Hummel Club" — with eyelashes; (TM 6) "M.I. Hummel Club" — without eyelashes; (TM 7) "M.I. Hummel Club" — with eyelashes; (TM 7) "M.I. Hummel Club" — without eyelashes. This figurine was retired on 31 May 1996.

☐ 479 ......4.00" ......(CE) ....❻ ......$150—175
☐ 479 ......4.00" ......(CE) ....❼ ......$125—150

HUM 480 — Hosanna

First released in the U.S. market in 1989. Modeled by master sculptor Gerhard Skrobek in 1987. It has an incised 1987 copyright date. The original issue price was $68 in 1989. Listed as (TW) "Temporarily Withdrawn" in June 2002, but may be reinstated at some future date.

☐ 480 ......4.00" ......(CE) ....❻ ......$140—145
☐ 480 ......4.00" ......(CE) ....❼ ......$135—140
☐ 480 ......4.00" ......(TW)....❽ $135

HUM 481 — Love From Above (CE)
Annual Ornament 1989. First released in the U.S. market in 1989, the second in the annual series of ornaments. Modeled by master sculptor Gerhard Skrobek in 1987. It has an incised 1987 copyright date. The original issue price was $75 in 1989.

☐ 481............3.25" ....(**CE**) ....❻ ....$125—150

HUM 482 — One For You, One For Me
First released in the U.S. market in 1989. Modeled by master sculptor Gerhard Skrobek in 1987. It has an incised 1987 copyright date. The original issue price was $50 in 1989. In 1996 a 2.25" size (2.75" with base) with model number 482 5/0 was produced as part of the "Pen Pals" series of personalized name card table decorations. The original issue price was $55. Listed as (TW) "Temporarily Withdrawn" in June 2002, but may be reinstated at some future date.

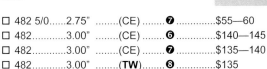

☐ 482 5/0......2.75" ....(CE) ....❼ ....$55—60
☐ 482............3.00" ....(CE) ....❻ ....$140—145
☐ 482............3.00" ....(CE) ....❼ ....$135—140
☐ 482............3.00" ....(**TW**)........❽ $135

HUM 483 — I'll Protect Him
First released in the U.S. market in 1989. Modeled by master sculptor Gerhard Skrobek in 1987. It has an incised 1987 copyright date. The original issue price was $55 in 1989. Listed as (TW) "Temporarily Withdrawn" in June 2002, but may be reinstated at some future date.

☐ 483.......3.75".......(CE).....**❻**.....$115—120
☐ 483.......3.75".......(CE).....**❼**.....$110—115
☐ 483.......3.75".......(**TW**)....**❽**.....$110

HUM 484 — Peace On Earth (CE)
Annual Ornament 1990. First released in the U.S. market in 1990, the third in the Annual Series of Ornaments. Modeled by master sculptor Gerhard Skrobek in 1987. It has an incised 1987 copyright date. The original issue price was $80.

☐ 484....3.25"...(**CE**)..**❻**...$125—150

HUM 485 — Gift From A Friend (CE)

This figurine was first introduced in 1991 for members of the M.I. Hummel Club only and not sold as an open edition. Modeled by master sculptor Gerhard Skrobek in 1988. It has an incised 1988 copyright date. Also bears the inscription: "EXCLUSIVE EDITION 1991/92 M.I. HUMMEL CLUB" applied by blue decal. A large black flying bumble bee is located on the bottom. The official issue price was $160 in 1991, in addition to the member's redemption card. Can now be purchased on the secondary market at premium prices.

☐ 485 ....5.00" ....(CE) ..❻ ....$300—350
☐ 485 ....5.00" ....**(CE)** ..❼ ....$250—300

HUM 486 — I Wonder (CE)

This figurine was first introduced in 1990 for members of the M.I. Hummel Club only and not sold as an open edition. Modeled by master sculptor Helmut Fischer in 1988. It has an incised 1988 copyright date. Also bears the inscription: "EXCLUSIVE EDITION 1990/91 M.I. HUMMEL CLUB" applied by blue decal. A large black flying bumble bee is located on the bottom. The official issue price was $140 in the U.S., in addition to the member's redemption card. Can now be purchased on the secondary market at premium prices.

☐ 486 ....5.25" ....(CE) ..❻ ....$300—350
☐ 486 ....5.25" ....**(CE)** ..❼ ....$250—300

HUM 487 — Let's Tell The World (CE)

This figurine was first released in the U.S. market in 1990. This is the fifth figurine in the Century Collection and will be produced for only this one year in the twentieth century. It was modeled by master sculptor Gerhard Skrobek in 1987. It has an incised 1988 copyright date. A circular inscription applied by blue decal reads: "M.I. HUMMEL CENTURY COLLECTION 1990 XX" and "1935-1990-55 Years of M.I. Hummel Figurines" in a straight line through the circle, along with the (TM 6) trademark. The official issue price was $875 in 1990.

☐ 487 ....10.50 x 7.00" ....**(CE)** ....❻ ....$1500—1800

HUM 488 — What's That?

Members' Exclusive *Preview* Edition for Club year 21. This figurine was first introduced in 1997 for members of the M. I. Hummel Club only and not sold as an open edition. Modeled by master sculptor Helmut Fischer in 1988. It has an incised 1988 copyright date along with (TM 7) trademark. Also bears the inscription: "EXCLUSIVE EDITION 1997/98 M. I. HUMMEL CLUB" applied by blue decal. A large black flying bumble bee is located on the bottom. The original issue price was $150 in 1997, in addition to the member's redemption card. Designed as a companion piece to HUM 555 "One, Two, Three." Goebel did reintroduce this figurine as an (OE) Open Edition, minus the special backstamp.

☐ 488 ......4.00" ....**(TW)** ....❼ ....$175—200

HUM 489 — Pretty Please
First released in the U. S. market in 1996 with "First Issue 1996" and "Goebel 125th Anniversary" backstamp. Modeled by master sculptor Helmut Fischer in 1988. It has an incised 1988 copyright date along with (TM 7) trademark. Designed as a companion piece to HUM 535 "No Thank You" as part of the "Cozy Companions" series. "Pretty Please" is similar to girl from HUM 47 "Goose Girl." The official issue price was $120 in 1996.

☐ 489 ....3.50" ....(CE)....❼ ....$135—140
☐ 489 ....3.50" ....(OE)....❽ $135

HUM 490 — Carefree
First released in the U.S. market in the fall of 1996 with "First Issue 1997" oval decal on the bottom. Modeled by master sculptor Helmut Fischer in 1988. It has an incised 1988 copyright date along with (TM 7) trademark. Designed as a companion piece to HUM 564 "Free Spirit" as part of the "Cozy Companions" series. The official price was $120 in 1996. (TW) "Temporarily Withdrawn" in December 2005.

☐ 490 ....3.50" ....(CE)....❼ ....$135—140
☐ 490 ....3.50" ....(OE)....❽ $135

HUM 491—492 — (PFE) STILL UNDER DEVELOPMENT

HUM 493 — Two Hands, One Treat (CE)

First released in the U.S. market in 1991 as a free gift for renewing membership in the M.I. HUMMEL CLUB for the 1991/92 Club year. Modeled by master sculptor Helmut Fischer in 1988. It has an incised 1988 copyright date, in addition to a special blue decal: "M.I. HUMMEL CLUB" along with a black flying bumble bee, in a half circle. Can now be purchased on the secondary market at premium prices.

☐ 493.......4.00".....(CE).....❼....$125—150

HUM 494 — (PFE) STILL UNDER DEVELOPMENT

HUM 495 — Evening Prayer

First released in the U.S. market in the fall of 1991. Modeled by master sculptor Helmut Fischer in 1988. It has an incised 1988 copyright date. The original issue price was $95 in 1991. Similar to girl on HUM 67 "Doll Mother," but with different colors. (TW) "Temporarily Withdrawn" in December 2005.

☐ 495.......3.75".....(CE).....❼...$135—140
☐ 495.......3.75".....(TW).....❽...$135

HUM 496—497 — (PFE) STILL UNDER DEVELOPMENT

HUM 498 — All Smiles

First released in the U.S. market in the spring of 1997. Modeled by master sculptor Helmut Fischer in 1988. It has an incised 1988 copyright date. Released as a (LE) Limited Edition of 25,000 sequentially-numbered pieces. (Only 15,000 were released in the U.S.) Similar to girl from HUM 196 "Telling Her Secret" but with a longer dress and no pigtails. Original issue price was $175 in 1997.

☐ 498........4.00"......(**CE**)....❼...$200—225

HUM 499 — (PFE) STILL UNDER DEVELOPMENT

HUM 500

This number was assigned to a Mother's Day plate that was never issued

HUM 501—508 DOLL HEADS

HUM 509	DOLL PARTS (arms & legs)
HUM 510	Carnival Doll
HUM 511	DOLL PARTS (arms & legs)
HUM 512	Umbrella Girl Doll (TW)
HUM 513	Little Fiddler Doll (TW)
HUM 514	Friend or Foe Doll (TW)
HUM 515	Kiss Me Doll (TW)
HUM 516	Merry Wanderer Doll (TW)
HUM 517	Goose Girl Doll (TW)
HUM 518	Umbrella Boy Doll (TW)
HUM 519	Ride Into Christmas Doll (TW)
HUM 520	(ON) STILL UNDER DEVELOPMENT
HUM 521	School Girl Doll (TW)
HUM 522	Little Scholar Doll (TW)
HUM 523	(ON) STILL UNDER DEVELOPMENT
HUM 524	Valentine Gift Doll (TW)

Valentine Gift Doll

HUM 525—529 — (ON) STILL UNDER DEVELOPMENT

HUM 530 — Land in Sight (CE)

First released in the U.S. market in the fall of 1991. Modeled by master sculptor Gerhard Skrobek in 1988. Issued as a limited production of 30,000 pieces, individually numbered, to commemorate the 500th Anniversary of Columbus's discovery of America. The inscription reads: "1492-1992—The Quincentennial of America's Discovery" applied by blue decal. It has an incised 1988 copyright date. The "M.I. Hummel" signature is located on the back side of the boat. The original issue price was $1600.

☐ 530 ....9.00 x 9.50" ......(CE) ....❼ ....$1800—2250

HUM 531—532 — (PFE) STILL UNDER DEVELOPMENT

HUM 533 — Ooh, My Tooth

First released in the U.S. market in 1995 with "First Issue 1995" oval decal and "Special Event" backstamp. Modeled by master sculptor Gerhard Skrobek in 1988. It has an incised 1988 copyright date along with the (TM7) trademark. This figurine will be available at District Manager Promotions and in-store events, then will be re-introduced as part of the regular line, but minus the special backstamp. The original issue price was $110. Listed as (TW) "Temporarily Withdrawn" in June 2002, but may be reinstated at some future date.

☐ 533 ....3.00" ......(CE) ..❼ ....$145—150
☐ 533 ....3.00" ......(TW) ..❽ $145

HUM 534 — Nap, A

First released in the U.S. market in 1991. Modeled by master sculptor Gerhard Skrobek in 1988. It has an incised 1988 copyright date. The original issue price was $95 in 1991.

☐ 534 ....2.25 to 2.50"....(CE) ....❻ ....$155—160
☐ 534 ....2.25 to 2.50"....(CE) ....❼ ....$150—155
☐ 534 ....2.25 to 2.50"....(OE) ....❽ $149

(Backs are interesting, too!)

HUM 535 — No Thank You

First released in the U.S. market in 1996 with "First Issue 1996" and "Goebel 125th Anniversary" backstamp. Modeled by master sculptor Helmut Fischer in 1988. It has an incised 1988 copyright date along with (TM 7) trademark. Designed as a companion piece to HUM 489 "Pretty Please" as part of the "Cozy Companions" series. The official issue price was $120 in 1996. Listed as (TW) "Temporarily Withdrawn" in June 2002.

☐ 535 ....3.50" ....(CE)....❼ ....$135—140
☐ 535 ....3.50" ....(TW) ..❽ $135

HUM 536 — Christmas Surprise (CE)

First released in the U.S. market in 1998. Modeled by master sculptor Helmut Fischer in 1988. It has an incised 1988 copyright date along with the (TM 7) trademark. (LE) Limited Edition of 15,000 pieces were sold exclusively on QVC starting at 12:00 AM EST on 19 November 1998 and sold out the complete edition in one day! Came with a Hummelscape "Musikfest" display Collector's Set. This figurine was introduced and retired and mold-breaking ceremony was held all on the same day! The issue price was $139.50 (plus shipping) in 1998. "Christmas Surprise, Ornament" was released in 2001. Original issue price was $80.00.

☐ 536 3/0 ....4.00" ....(CE) ......❼ ....$175—200
☐ 536 3/0/O ......3.25" ....(CE) ......❽ $69.50
☐ 536/0 ....5.25" ....(PFE) ....

HUM 537 — (PFE) STILL UNDER DEVELOPMENT

HUM 538 — School's Out

First released in the U.S. market in 1997 with "First Issue 1997" oval decal. Modeled by master sculptor Helmut Fischer in 1988. It has an incised 1988 copyright. The girl is similar to girl from HUM 329 (PFE) "Off to School." The official issue price was $170 in 1997. In April 2006 the 538 size became available bearing a (CE) Closed Edition hangtag and it was announced the figurine would never again be produced in this size. The HUM "School's Out" has effectively been retired in the 4" size.

☐ 538 ....4.00" ....(CE)......❼ ....$180—185
☐ 538 ....4.00" ....**(CE)**......❽ ....$143   (Closed Edition)

HUM 539 — Good News
First released in 1996 at the "M.I. Hummel Club" convention in Coburg, Germany for those members attending. First released in the U.S. market in 1997. Modeled by master sculptor Helmut Fischer in 1988 and has an incised 1988 copyright date. Two initials or two numbers can be permanently applied by a Goebel artist. The original issue price was $180 in 1997. (TW) "Temporarily Withdrawn" in December 2005.

☐ 539 ....4.50" ....(CE)......❼ ....$220—225
☐ 539 ....4.50" ....**(TW)** ....❽ $219

HUM 540 — Best Wishes
First released in 1996 at the "M.I. Hummel Club" convention in Coburg, Germany for those members attending. First released in the U.S. market in 1997. Modeled by master sculptor Helmut Fischer in 1988 and has an incised 1988 copyright date. Two initials or two numbers can be permanently applied by a Goebel artist. Also used as a 1997 "Special Event" figurine with a flying bumble bee decal on the area among the flowers. The original issue price was $180 in 1997.

☐ 540 ......4.75" ....(CE)......❼ ....$219—225
☐ 540 ......4.75" ....**(OE)**......❽ $219

319

HUM 541 — Sweet As Can Be

Members' Exclusive Preview Edition for Club year 17. This figurine was first introduced in 1993 for members of the M.I. Hummel Club only and not sold as an open edition. Modeled by master sculptor Helmut Fischer in 1988. It had an incised 1988 copyright date along with the (TM 7) trademark. Also bears the inscription: "EXCLUSIVE EDITION 1993/94 M.I. HUMMEL CLUB" applied by blue decal. A large black flying bumble bee is located on the bottom. The official issue price was $125 in the U.S., in addition to the member's redemption card. Goebel reintroduced this figurine as an open edition in 1998 minus the special Club backstamp as part of a "Happy Birthday" Hummelscape (Mark #925-D) gift set at $160. Similar to one girl from HUM 176 "Happy Birthday."

☐ 541 ....3.75 to 4.00" ....(CE) ....❼ ....$150—160
☐ 541 ....3.75 to 4.00" ....(OE) ....❽ $149

HUM 542 — (PFE) STILL UNDER DEVELOPMENT

HUM 543 — I'm Sorry (PFE)

This figurine was first modeled by master sculptor Gerhard Skrobek in 1988. It has an incised 1988 copyright date. Presently listed on factory records as a (PFE) Possible Future Edition and may be released at some future date, subject to possible minor changes.

☐ 543 ....4.00" ....(PFE) ....

HUM 544 — (PFE) STILL UNDER DEVELOPMENT

HUM 545 — Come Back Soon

First released in the U.S. market in 1995 with "First Issue 1995" oval decal on the bottom. The official issue price was $135 in 1995. Modeled by master sculptor Helmut Fischer in 1989. Designed as a matching figurine for the 25th and final issue of the annual plate series. It has an incised 1989 copyright date. Listed as (TW) "Temporarily Withdrawn" in June 2002, but may be reinstated at some future date.

☐ 545 ....4.25" ......(CE) ....❻ ..$300—500
☐ 545 ....4.25" ......(CE) ....❼ ..$180—185
☐ 545 ....4.25" ......(TW) ....❽ ..$180

HUM 546 — (PFE) STILL UNDER DEVELOPMENT

HUM 547 — Bunny's Mother

First made available in Fall of 2005, with Bunny backstamp in European Market in Summer Landscape: Hummel Pond, with HUM 136 4/0 "Friends", HUM 2226 "Shepherd's Apprentice", HUM 2219 "Sunflower Boy" and three Summer accessories (Wayside Cross, Fence and Bench); the set representing Summer in a "Four Seasons" Collector Series. Available on the North American Market from January 2006 as part of the "Animal Friends" Collection with an original issue price of $109. The figurine has incised 2005 copyright date, Bunny backstamp, and the (TM 8) trademark, no first issue markings. Available in Spring of 2006 for $109 in A Mother's Love Collector Set with a heart-shaped wooden base bearing a Mother's Day saying: "A mother's love offers us two lasting gifts ... one is roots ... the other is wings." Resembles one of the girls in HUM 384 "Easter Time".

☐ 547 4/0 ....2.75" ....(CE) ....❽ $109

HUM 548 — Flower Girl (CE)

Announced in 1990, "Flower Girl" was an (EE) Exclusive Edition available to "M.I. Hummel Club" members only, who belonged to the Club continuously for 5 years. Modeled by master sculptor Helmut Fischer in 1989. It has an incised 1989 copyright date. The original issue price was $105. Retired on 31 May 2000.

☐ 548 ....4.50" ....(CE) ......**❻** ....$175—225
☐ 548 ....4.50" ....(CE) ......**❼** ....$150—175
☐ 548 ....4.50" ....**(CE)** ......**❽** $150

HUM 549 — A Sweet Offering (CE)

First released in the U.S. market in 1993 as a FREE gift for renewing membership in the M.I. HUMMEL CLUB for the 1993/94 Club year. Modeled by master sculptor Helmut Fischer in 1992. It has an incised 1992 copyright date. It bears the inscription: "M.I. HUMMEL CLUB Membership Year 1993/94" in addition to be black flying bumble bee, in a half circle. It is similar to the girl from HUM 52 "Going To Grandma's." Can be purchased on the secondary market at premium prices.

☐ 549 3/0 ......3.50" ....(CE) ......**❼** ....$100—125
☐ 549/0 ....4.75" ....(PFE) ....

HUM 550–552 — (ON) OPEN NUMBERS

HUM 553 — Scamp

First released in the U.S. market in the fall of 1991. Modeled by master sculptor Helmut Fischer in 1989. It has an incised 1989 copyright date. The boy is similar to "Max" on HUM 123 "Max and Moritz." The original issue price was $95 in 1991. Designed as a companion figurine to HUM 768 "Pixie" in the "Cozy Companion" series. (TW) "Temporarily Withdrawn" in December 2005.

☐ 553 ....3.50" ....(CE) ......**❼** ....$135—140
☐ 553 ....3.50" ....**(TW)** ......**❽** $135

HUM 554 — Cheeky Fellow

Members' first Exclusive *Preview* Edition for Club year 16. This figurine was first introduced in 1992 for members of the M.I. Hummel Club only and not sold as an open edition. Modeled by master sculptor Helmut Fischer in 1989. It has an incised 1989 copyright date along with the (TM 7) trademark. Also bears the inscription: "EXCLUSIVE EDITION 1992/93 M.I. HUMMEL CLUB" applied by blue decal. A large black flying bumble bee is located on the bottom. The original issue price was $120 in the U.S., in addition to the member's redemption card. Goebel did re-introduce this figurine as an (OE) Open Edition, minus the special backstamp. The boy is similar to "Moritz" on HUM 123 "Max & Moritz." (TW) "Temporarily Withdrawn" in December 2005.

☐ 554 ....4.00" ....(CE) ....❼ ....$150—155
☐ 554 ....4.00" ....(**TW**)....❽ $149

HUM 555 — One, Two, Three

Members' Exclusive *Preview* Edition for Club year 20. First released in the U.S. market in 1996 for members of the M.I. Hummel Club only and not sold as an (OE) Open Edition. Modeled by master sculptor Helmut Fischer in 1989. It has an incised 1989 copyright date along with the (TM 7) trademark. Also bears the inscription: "EXCLUSIVE EDITION 1996/97 M. I. HUMMEL CLUB" applied by blue decal. A large black flying bumble bee is located on the bottom. The official issue price was $145 in the U.S., in addition to the member's redemption card. Goebel reserves the right to reintroduce this figurine as an (OE) Open Edition, minus the special backstamp.

☐ 555 ....4.00" ....(**TW**)....❼ ....$150—175

HUM 556 — One Plus One

First released in the U.S. market in 1993. Modeled by master sculptor Helmut Fischer in 1989. It has an incised 1989 copyright date along with the (TM 7) trademark. Also bears the "First Issue 1993" oval decal and "Special Event" backstamp. This figurine was available at District Manager Promotions and in-store events, but was re-introduced as part of the regular line, minus the special backstamps. The original issue price was $115. Listed as (TW) "Temporarily Withdrawn" in June 2002, but may be reinstated at some future date.

☐ 556 ....4.00"..(Special Event) ....❼ ....$170—200
☐ 556 ....4.00" ....(CE) ....❼ ....$165—170
☐ 556 ....4.00" ....(**TW**)....❽ ....$165—170

HUM 557 — Strum Along

Members' Exclusive *Preview* Edition for Club year 19. This figurine was first introduced in 1995 for members of the M.I. Hummel Club only and not sold as an open edition. Modeled by master sculptor Helmut Fischer in 1989. It has an incised 1989 copyright date along with the (TM 7) trademark. Also bears the inscription: "EXCLUSIVE EDITION 1995/96 M.I. HUMMEL CLUB" applied by blue decal. A large black flying bumble bee is located on the bottom. The official issue price was $135 in the U.S., in addition to the member's redemption card, Goebel did re-introduce this figurine as an (OE) Open Edition, minus the special backstamp. Girl similar to girl from HUM 150 "Happy Days." (TW) "Temporarily Withdrawn" in December 2005.

☐ 557.....4.00".........(CE).....❼.....$150—155
☐ 557.....4.00".........(TW).....❽....$149

HUM 558 — Little Troubadour

Members' Exclusive *Preview* Edition for Club year 18. This figurine was first introduced in 1994 for members of the M.I. Hummel Club only and not sold as an (OE) Open Edition. Modeled by master sculptor Helmut Fischer in 1989. It has an incised 1989 copyright date along with the (TM 7) trademark. Also bears the inscription: "EXCLUSIVE EDITION 1994/95 M.I. HUMMEL CLUB" applied by blue decal. A large black flying bumble bee is located on the bottom. The official issue price was $130 in the U.S., in addition to the member's redemption card. Goebel did re-introduce this figurine as an (OE) Open Edition, minus the special backstamp. Boy similar to boy from HUM 150 "Happy Days". (TW) "Temporarily Withdrawn" in December 2005.

☐ 558.....4.00 to 4.25"...(CE)....❼....$150—155
☐.558.....4.00 to 4.25"...(TW)....❽....$149

HUM 559 — Heart and Soul

First released in the U.S. market in 1996 with "First Issue 1996" and "Goebel 125th Anniversary" backstamp. Modeled by master sculptor Helmut Fischer in 1988. It has an incised 1989 copyright date along with the (TM 7) trademark. Designed as a companion piece to HUM 761 "From the Heart" as part of the "Cozy Companions" series. The official issue price was $120 in 1996. (TW) "Temporarily Withdrawn" in December 2005.

☐ 559 ....3.50 to 3.75" ....(CE)...... ❼ ....$135—140
☐ 559 ....3.50 to 3.75" ....(**TW**) .... ❽ ....$135—140

HUM 560 — Lucky Fellow (CE)

First released in the U.S. market in 1992 as a FREE gift for renewing membership in the M.I. HUMMEL CLUB for the 1992/93 Club year. Modeled by master sculptor Helmut Fischer in 1989. It has an incised 1989 copyright date. It bears the inscription: "M.I. HUMMEL CLUB" in addition to a black flying bumble bee, in a half circle, along with (TM 7) trademark. Not sold as an (OE) Open Edition, but can be purchased on the secondary market.

☐ 560 ....3.75" ....(**CE**) .. ❼ ....$100—120

HUM 561 — Grandma's Girl

First released in the U.S. market in the summer of 1990. Modeled by master sculptor Helmut Fischer in 1989. It has an incised 1989 copyright date. The girl is a smaller verison of the same girl on HUM 383 "Going Home." The original issue price was $100 in 1990. Approximately 825 were made with "1991 M.I. Hummel Club Convention" on base.

☐ 561.......4.00".....(CE).....❻.....$185—190
☐ 561.......4.00".....(CE).....❼.....$180—185
☐ 561.......4.00".....(OE).....❽.....$179

HUM 562 — Grandpa's Boy

First released in the U.S. market in the summer of 1990. Modeled by master sculptor Helmut Fischer in 1989. It has an incised 1989 copyright date. The boy is a smaller version of the same boy on HUM 383 "Going Home." The original issue price was $100 in 1990. Approximately 825 were made with "1991 M.I. Hummel Club Convention" on base.

☐ 562.......4.25".....(CE).....❻.....$185—190
☐ 562.......4.25".....(CE).....❼.....$180—185
☐ 562.......4.25".....(OE).....❽.....$179

HUM 563 — Little Visitor (CE)

Members' Exclusive Edition for Club year 18. This figurine was first introduced in 1994 for members of the M.I. Hummel Club only and not sold as an (OE) Open Edition. Modeled by master sculptor Helmut Fischer in 1991. It has an incised 1991 copyright date along with the (TM 7) trademark. Also bears the inscription: "EXCLUSIVE EDITION 1994/95 M.I. HUMMEL CLUB" applied by blue decal. A large black flying bumble bee is located on the bottom. The official issue price was $180 in the U.S., in addition to the member's redemption card.

☐ 563/0.......5.25".....(**CE**).....❼.....$200—225

HUM 564 — Free Spirit

First released in the U.S. market in the fall of 1996 with "First Issue 1997" oval decal on the bottom. Modeled by master sculptor Helmut Fischer in 1988. It has an incised 1989 copyright date along with the (TM 7) trademark. Designed as a companion piece to HUM 490 "Carefree" as part of the "Cozy Companions" series. The official issue price was $120 in 1996.

☐ 564.......3.50".....(**CE**).....❼.....$135—140
☐ 564.......3.50".....(**OE**).....❽.....$135

HUM 565 — (PFE) STILL UNDER DEVELOPMENT

HUM 566 — Angler, The

First released in the U.S. market in 1995 with "First Issue 1995" oval decal on the bottom. Modeled by master sculptor Gerhard Skrobek in 1989. It has an incised 1989 copyright date along with (TM 7) trademark. The official issue price was $320 in 1995. Listed as (TW) "Temporarily Withdrawn" in December 2004.

☐ 566 ....6.00"..........(CE) .....❼ ..$395—400
☐ 566 ....6.00"..........(TW).....❽ ..$395

HUM 567—568 — (PFE) STILL UNDER DEVELOPMENT

HUM 569 — A Free Flight

First released in the U.S. market in 1993 with "First Issue 1993" oval decal on the bottom. Modeled by master sculptor Gerhard Skrobek in 1989. It has an incised 1989 copyright date. The official issue price was $185 in 1993. A variation called "O Canada," sold only in Canada, was released in 1997, with special decals and backstamp. The retail price was approximately $200 (in U.S. funds). Listed as (TW) "Temporarily Withdrawn" in June 2002, but may be reinstated at some future date.

☐ 569.......4.75".......(CE).....❼.....$215—220
☐ 569.......4.75".......(TW).....❽.....$215

HUM 570 — (PFE) STILL UNDER DEVELOPMENT

HUM 571 — Angelic Guide (CE)
Annual Ornament 1991. First released in the U.S. market in 1991, the fourth in the Annual Series of ornaments. Modeled by master sculptor Gerhard Skrobek in 1989. It has an incised 1989 copyright date. The original issue price was $95 in 1991.

☐ 571 ....4.00" ....(CE) ......❻....$150—200
☐ 571 ....4.00" ....(**CE**) ......❼....$125—150

HUM 572 — Country Devotion (PFE)
This figurine was first modeled by master sculptor Gerhard Skrobek in 1989. It has an incised 1989 copyright date. Presently listed on factory records as a (PFE) Possible Future Edition and may be released at some future date, subject to possible minor changes. See HUM 903 "Adoring Children" for an interesting comparison.

☐ 572 ....11.00" ....(**PFE**) ...

HUM 573 — Will You Be Mine?
aka Loving Wishes
One figurine, two names - depending on what is in her apron: "Loving Wishes" with flowers or "Will You Be Mine?" with heart. "Will You Be Mine?" was first released in Europe in 2004 with "First Issue 2004" backstamp and 2002 incised copyright date, then first appeared on Goebel North America Retail Price List in 2005, priced $219. "Loving Wishes" was created in a numbered (LE) Limited Edition of 10,000, available with "Loving Letters" Hummelscape, for the North American market. With (SE) Special Edition and Bouquet backstamps, incised 2002 copyright date, but no first issue marking. Available beginning Spring 2003. Price of "Loving Wishes" with Hummelscape was $230 in 2005.

☐ 573 2/0 ..4.50".........(**OE**)....❽ $219

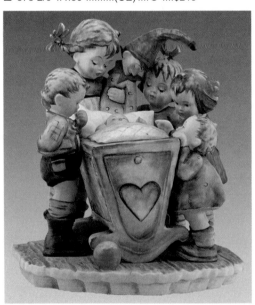

HUM 574 — Rock-A-Bye (CE)
This figurine was first introduced in the U.S. market in 1994. This is the ninth figurine in the "Century Collection" and was produced for only this one year in the twentieth century. It was modeled by master sculptor Helmut Fischer in 1991. It has an incised 1991 copyright date. A circular inscription applied by blue decal reads: "M.I. HUMMEL CENTURY COLLECTION 1994 XX" and the name "Rock-A-Bye" along with the (TM 7) trademark. The original issue price was $1150 in 1994.

☐ 574 ....7.50".........(**CE**)....❼ ....$1400—1600

HUM 575
Heavenly Angel

HUM 576
Festival Harmony
w/mandolin

HUM 577
Festival Harmony
w/flute

M.I. Hummel — ANGEL OF CHRISTMAS — ORNAMENT SERIES

First released in the U.S. market in 1990 and were sold exclusively by mail order through the Danbury Mint of Norwalk, Connecticut, at the rate of one every other month. Modeled by master sculptor Helmut Fischer in 1988. They have an incised "M.I. Hummel" signature and the Goebel (TM 6) trademark, but do NOT have an incised model number. The original issue price was $39.50 each (plus sales tax and $2.50 shipping and handling).

HUM 578
Celestial Musician

HUM 581
Prayer of Thanks

HUM 582
Gentle Song

ANGELS OF CHRISTMAS — ORNAMENT SERIES

Also produced in white overglaze with painted facial features only and gold tipped wings. Could be purchased from your local "M.I. Hummel" dealer. List price: $40. Both white and color series of the "Angels of Christmas" ornaments are (TW) "Temporarily Withdrawn".

Left: HUM 579 Song of Praise

Right: HUM 580 Angel with Lute

Left: HUM 585 Angel in Cloud

Right: HUM 586 Angel with Trumpet

				(in color)			(in white)	
☐ 575	3.00"	(CE)	❻	$50—60	(CE)	❼	$40
☐ 576	3.00"	(CE)	❻	$50—60	(CE)	❼	$40
☐ 577	3.00"	(CE)	❻	$50—60	(CE)	❼	$40
☐ 578	3.00"	(CE)	❻	$50—60	(CE)	❼	$40
☐ 579	2.50"	(CE)	❻	$50—60	(CE)	❼	$40
☐ 580	2.50"	(CE)	❻	$50—60	(CE)	❼	$40
☐ 581	3.00"	(CE)	❻	$50—60	(CE)	❼	$40
☐ 582	3.00"	(CE)	❻	$50—60	(CE)	❼	$40
☐ 583	OPEN NUMBER	(ON)					
☐ 584	OPEN NUMBER	(ON)					
☐ 585	2.50"	(CE)	❻	$50—60	(CE)	❼	$40
☐ 586	2.50"	(CE)	❻	$50—60	(CE)	❼	$40

Ornament Gift Cards: 3.25 to 3.50" ornaments created by placing a decal over formed ceramic, presented in an attractive greeting card, priced $27.50 each in 2004.

☐.575 FD	Heavenly Angel	☐.576 FD	Festival Harmony Mandolion
☐.577 FD	Festival Harmony Flute	☐.578 FD	Celestial Musician

HUM 587—595 — (ON) OPEN NUMBERS

HUM 596 — Thanksgiving Prayer
Annual Ornament 1997 (CE)

First released in the U.S. market in 1997. Modeled by master sculptor Helmut Fischer in 1995. It has NO incised copyright date that I can find, but does have a "First Issue 1997" oval cello sticker on the lower gown of the angel. "Hummel" only is incised on the back. Incised model number 596 and (TM 7) trademark, plus 1995 applied by blue decal on the bottom of this very small area. A brass ring is attached to top of head for hanging as an ornament. Original issue price was $120 in 1997. Similar to HUM 641 "Thanksgiving Prayer" but without base.

☐ 596 ....2.75 to 3.00" ..**(CE)** ..❼ ..$130—140

HUM 597 — Echoes of Joy
Annual Ornament 1998 (CE)

First released in the U.S. market in the fall of 1997. Modeled by master sculptor Helmut Fischer in 1996. It has NO incised copyright date that I can find, but does have a "First Issue 1998" oval cello sticker on the lower gown of the angel. "Hummel" only is incised on the back. Incised model number 597 and (TM 7) trademark, plus 1996 applied by blue decal on the bottom of this very small area. A brass ring is attached to top of head for hanging as an ornament. Original issue price was $120 in 1997. Similar to HUM 642 "Echoes of Joy" figurine but without base.

☐ 597 ....2.75 to 3.00"......**(CE)**......❼ ..$130—140

HUM 598 — Joyful Noise
Annual Ornament 1999 (CE)
First released in the U.S. market in the fall of 1998. Modeled by master sculptor Helmut Fischer in 1995. It has NO incised copyright date that I can find, but does have a "First Issue 1999" oval cello sticker on the lower gown of angel. "Hummel" only is incised on the back. Incised model number 598 and (TM 7) trademark, plus 1996 applied by blue decal on the bottom of this very small area. A brass ring is attached to top of head for hanging as an ornament. Original issue price was $120 in 1998. Similar to HUM 643 "Joyful Noise" figurine but without base.

☐ 598.....2.75 to 3.00".....(**CE**).....❼.....$120—125

HUM 599 — Light The Way
Annual Ornament 2000 (CE)
First released in the U.S. maket in the fall of 1999. Modeled by master sculptor Helmut Fischer in 1995. It has an incised 1995 copyright date in addition to a "First Issue 2000" oval cello sticker on the lower gown of angel. Incised "Hummel" only on back, incised model number 599 and (TM 8) trademark on the bottom. A brass ring is attached to top of head for hanging as an ornament. Original issue price was $120 in 1999. Similar to HUM 715 "Light The Way" figurine but without base.

☐ 599 ....2.75 to 3.00"......(**CE**)......❽ ..$120—125

"The Four Hummel Sisters"
Katarina   *Vicktoria*   *Berta*   *Centa*

HUM 600 — We Wish You The Best (CE)

This figurine was first released in the U.S. market in 1991. This is sixth figurine in the "Century Collection" and was produced for only this one year in the twentieth century. Modeled by master sculptor Helmut Fischer in 1989. It has an incised 1989 copyright date. A circular inscription applied by blue decal reads: "M.I. HUMMEL CENTURY COLLECTION 1991 XX" and the name "We Wish You The Best." The original issue price was $1300 in 1991.

☐ 600 ....8.25 x 9.50" ......(**CE**) ....❻ ....$1900—2100
☐ 600 ....8.25 x 9.50" ......(**CE**) ....❼ ....$1700—1900

HUM 601—607 — (ON) OPEN NUMBERS

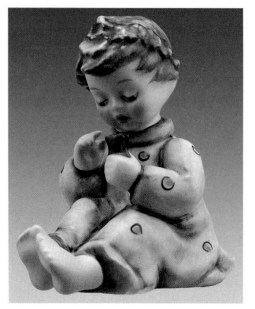

HUM 608 — Blossom Time

First released in the U.S. market in 1996 with a combination "First Issue 1996" and "Goebel 125th Anniversary" backstamp on the bottom. Modeled by master sculptor Helmut Fischer in 1989. It has an incised 1989 copyright date along with the (TM 7) trademark. The official issue price was $155 in 1996. (TW) "Temporarily Withdrawn" in December 2004.

☐ 608 ....3.25" ....(CE) ...... ❼ ...$175—180
☐ 608 ....3.25" ....(TW) ...... ❽ ...$175—180

HUM IV/608 — Blossom Time, Music Box (CE)

In 1999 a new music box was produced with model number IV/608 in a (LE) Limited Edition of only 500 pieces and sold exclusively through The Hummel Museum and Art Gallery in New Braunfels, Texas. Melody played "Edelweiss." The original issue price was $250 in 1999. It has a (TM 7) trademark and an incised 1999 copyright date.

☐ IV/608 ....5.50" ......(CE) .... ❼ ....$300—400

HUM 609 — (ON) OPEN NUMBER

HUM 610 — April Showers

First released in Spring of 2005 with an original issue price of $745 as an (EE) Exclusive Edition (EE) for 2005/2006 Club year, for members of the M.I. Hummel Club. Formerly a (PFE) "Possible Future Edition". Sculpted by master sculptor Helmut Fischer in 1990. Second in "Young Love" series. "Special April Showers" backstamp in addition to incised 1990 copyright date, the (TM 8) trademark, and "Special Edition 2005 M.I. Hummel Club" backstamp. Signed by Frank Knoch, chief master sample painter. North American Limited Edition of 2005 denoted by sequentially numbered ceramic heart crimped to figurine. A like number available for the European market. In January 2006 made available for sale to the general public.

☐ 610 ....9.50" ......(EE) ....❽ ..$745

HUM 611 — Sunny Song (PFE)

This figurine was first modeled by master sculptor Helmut Fischer in 1989. It has an incised 1990 copyright date. Presently listed on factory records as a (PFE) Possible Future Edition and may be released at some future date, subject to possible minor changes.

☐ 611..........5.25" ......(PFE) ......

HUM 612 — Lazybones

First appearance was in September of 2003, as gift to attendees of the 2003 M.I. Hummel Club Convention held in Anaheim, CA., with incised 2002 copyright date, First Issue 2004 backstamp and (TM 8) trademark. Formerly a (PFE) Possible Future Edition. The regular issue, without the convention marking, was first released in 2004, with an original issue price of $250 and a "First Issue 2004" backstamp. Has incised 2002 copyright date and the (TM 8) trademark. Companion to HUM 2105 "Miss Beehaving".

☐ 612 2/0 ..3.25" ....(OE) ....❽....$259
☐ 612 ....4.00" ....(PFE) ...

HUM 613 — What's Up (PFE)

This figurine was first modeled by master sculptor Helmut Fischer in 1989. It has an incised 1990 copyright date. Presently listed on factory records as a (PFE) Possible Future Edition and may be released at some future date, subject to possible minor changes. John Riedl was the model for this figurine in 1939, when he became the first American child to sit for Sister M. I. Hummel. He still lives in Central Ohio.

☐ 613 ....5.50" ....(**PFE**) ....(Emil Fink postcard Nr. 798)

HUM 614 — Harmonica Player (PFE)

This figurine was first modeled by master sculptor Helmut Fischer in 1989. It has an incised 1990 copyright date. Presently listed on factory records as a (PFE) Possible Future Edition and may be released at some future date, subject to possible minor changes. John Riedl was the model for this figurine in 1939, when he became the first American child to sit for Sister M. I. Hummel. He still lives in Central Ohio.

☐ 614 ....5.50" ....(**PFE**)............(Emil Fink postcard Nr. 799)

Factory Sample   *Normal Production*

Note: Base Construction

HUM 615 — Private Conversation

Members' Exclusive Edition for Club year 23. This figurine was first introduced in 1999 for members of the M. I. Hummel Club only and not sold as an (OE) Open Edition. Modeled by master sculptor Helmut Fischer in 1989. It has an incised 1990 copyright date along with the (TM 7) trademark. Also bears: "EXCLUSIVE EDITION 1999/2000 M.I. HUMMEL CLUB" club decal, plus a black flying bumble bee on the bottom. The official issue price was $260 in addition to member's redemption card. Figure will be available until 31 May 2000.

☐ 615 ....4.50".................(**CE**) ....❽ ....$260—280

HUM 616 — Parade of Lights

First released in the U.S. market in 1993 with an incised 1990 copyright date and the "First Issue 1993" oval decal on the bottom. Modeled by master sculptor Helmut Fischer in 1990. The little clown is holding a "paper" lantern, but made out of ceramics. It is a companion piece for HUM 328 "Carnival" which was released in 1963. The official issue price was $235 in 1993. (TW) "Temporarily Withdrawn" in December 2004.

☐ 616 ....6.00" ......(CE)......❼ ....$305—310
☐ 616 ....6.00" ......(**TW**) ....❽ ....$305—310

HUM 617 — (ON) OPEN NUMBER

HUM 618 — Basket of Gifts

First released in the U.S. market in the fall of 2001 with "First Issue 2002" backstamp. Modeled by master sculptor Helmut Fischer in 1990. It has an incised 1990 copyright date along with the (TM 8) trademark. The official issue price was $375 in 2002.

☐ 618 ....5.25"..................(OE) ....❽ $375

HUM 619 — Garden Gift

First released in the Fall of 2003 with an original issue price of $260 and a First Issue 2004 backstamp. Has an incised 2003 copyright date, and the (TM 8) trademark. Sculpted by master sculptor Helmut Fischer. In October 2003 a limited edition of 150 Arbeitsmuster Editions were made available in North America to M.I. Hummel Club members. These painters' samples bear a crimped metal "Arbeitsmuster Series" tag and are signed by master sample painter Frank Knoch. The Arbeitsmuster Edition has an incised 2003 copyright date, First Issue 2004 backstamp, and the (TM 8) trademark, and was priced $260 in 2003. Companion to HUM 925 Annual Plate 2004, "Garden Gift".

☐ 619 ....4.75"..................(OE) ....❽ $279

HUM 620 — A Story from Grandma (CE)

This figurine was released in the U.S. market in 1995. It was an (EE) Exclusive Edition for M.I. Hummel Club members only and was not made available to the general public. Sequentially numbered (LE) Limited Edition of 10,000 pieces worldwide. It bears a Club Exclusive backstamp, and comes with a Certificate of Authenticity. It was offered for one year only, from 1 June 1995 through 31 May 1996. Modeled by a team of artists in 1993 and has an incised 1993 copyright date. The official issue price was $1300 in 1995. Available on the secondary market only.

☐ 620 ....8.00"..........(CE) ..❼ ....$1500—1600

HUM 621 — At Grandpa's (CE)

First released in the U.S. market in the fall of 1994. It was an (EE) Exclusive Edition for M.I. Hummel Club members only and was not made available to the general public. Sequentially numbered (LE) Limited Edition of 10,000 pieces worldwide. It bears a Club Exclusive backstamp, and comes with a Certificate of Authenticity. It was offered for one year only, from 1 June 1994 through 31 May 1995. Modeled by a team of artists in 1993 and has an incised 1993 copyright date. The official issue price was $1300 in 1994. Available on the secondary market only.

☐ 621 ....9.00"..........(CE) ..❼ ....$1500—1600

HUM 622 — Light Up The Night (CE)

Annual Ornament 1992. First released in the U.S. market in 1992, the fifth in the Annual Series of Ornaments. Modeled by master sculptor Gerhard Skrobek in 1990. It has an incised 1990 copyright date. The original issue price was $95.

☐ 622......3.25"....**(CE)**...❼...$125—150

HUM 623 — Herald on High (CE)

Annual Ornament 1993. First released in the U.S. market in 1993. The sixth and final issue in the Annual Series of Ornaments. Modeled by master sculptor Gerhard Skrobek

in 1990. It has *no* incised copyright date that I can find, but does have 1993 fired on the lower end of angel's gown. "Final Issue" and (TM 7) trademark are fired on the underside of gown. The original issue price was $155 in 1993.

☐ 623 ....2.75 x 4.50" ..**(CE)**....❼ ....$175—200

HUM 624 — Fresh Blossoms

First released in July 2006 with an original issue price of $199, bearing the (TM 8) trademark, one of four Hummels in the "Heart of Hummel" Collection. Heart backstamp and heart in bouquet. Worldwide (LE) Limited Edition of 5000, sequentially numbered. Just 2500 "Heart of Hummel" Collection Sets are available with matching (LE) Limited Edition numbers on all four Hummels. The Collection Set features HUM 624 "Fresh Blossoms", HUM 908 "Gone-A-Wandering", HUM 2235 "Lucky Friend", and HUM 2237 "Sunday Stroll" in a blue rectangular collector tin: set priced $795.

☐ 624........4.50"..........(LE)....❽.....$199

HUM 625 — Goose Girl Vase

A bisque porcelain vase with "Goose Girl" in bas relief on the front. A "Sampler" was released in 1997 with HUM 47 3/0 "Goose Girl" figurine and the vase. This combination retailed for $200. The retail value of the figurine was $185 plus only $15 for the vase. The vase is a first for Goebel—it has the (TM 7) trademark with 1989 copyright date applied by blue decal on the bottom, in addition to the "M.I. Hummel" signature incised on the vase.

☐ 625 ....4.00 x 3.50" ......(CE) ....❼ ....$50—75

HUM 626 — I Didn't Do It (CE)

Members' Exclusive Edition for Club year 17. This figurine was first introduced in 1993 for members of the M.I. HUMMEL CLUB only and not sold as an (OE) Open Edition. Modeled by master sculptor Helmut Fischer in 1992. It has an incised 1992 copyright date, along with the inscription: "EXCLUSIVE EDITION 1993/94 M.I. HUMMEL CLUB" applied by blue decal. A large black flying bumble bee is located on the bottom. The official issue price was $175 in the U.S., in addition to the member's redemption card. This figurine can be purchased on the secondary market at premium prices.

☐ 626 ....5.50" ....(CE) ....❼ ....$200—225

HUM 627 — (ON) OPEN NUMBER

HUM 628 — Gentle Fellowship (CE)

First released in the U.S. market in 1995, the third and final figurine in the UNICEF series. HUM 662 "Friends Together" in 1993 and HUM 754 "We Come In Peace" in 1994. It bears a special UNICEF Commemorative "Limited Edition No. ___ of 25,000" backstamp in addition to the (TM 7) trademark. Modeled by master sculptor Helmut Fischer in 1992. It has an incised 1992 copyright date. The original issue price was $550 in 1995. A $25 contribution was made to the U.S. Committee for UNICEF as part of a co-operative fund raising effort.

☐ 628 ....5.75" ....(CE) ....❼ ....$600—625

HUM 629 — From Me To You (CE)

First released in the U.S. market in 1995 as a FREE gift for renewing membership in the M.I. HUMMEL CLUB for the 1995/96 Club year. Modeled by master sculptor Helmut Fischer in 1992. It has an incised 1992 copyright date. It bears the inscription: "M.I. HUMMEL CLUB Membership Year 1995/96" in addition to a black flying bumble bee, in a half circle. It is similar to girl from HUM 199 "Feeding Time." Can now be purchased on the secondary market at premium prices.

☐ 629.......3.50".......(**CE**).....❼.....$100—125

HUM 630 — For Keeps (CE)

First released in the U.S. market in 1994 as a FREE gift for renewing membership in the M.I. HUMMEL CLUB for the 1994/95 Club year. Modeled by master sculptor Helmut Fischer in 1992. It has an incised 1992 copyright date. It bears the inscription: "M.I. HUMMEL CLUB Membership Year 1994/95" in addition to a black flying bumble bee, in a half circle. It is similar to the boy from HUM 200 "Little Goat Herder". Can now be purchased on the secondary market at premium prices.

☐ 630.......3.50".....(**CE**).....❼.....$100—125

HUM 631 — (ON) OPEN NUMBER

HUM 632 — At Play (CE)

Members' Exclusive Edition for Club year 22. This figurine was first introduced in 1998 for members of the M. I. Hummel Club only and not sold as an (OE) Open Edition (OE). Modeled by master sculptor Helmut Fischer in 1990. It has an incised 1990 copyright date along with the (TM 7) trademark. Also bears: "EXCLUSIVE EDITION 1998/99 M.I. HUMMEL CLUB" applied by blue decal, plus a black flying bumble bee located on the bottom. The official issue price was $260 in 1998, in addition to member's redemption card.

☐ 632......3.50" ....(**CE**) ....❼....$275—300

HUM 633 — I'm Carefree

First released in the U.S. market in 1994 with an incised 1990 copyright date and the "First Issue 1994" oval decal on the bottom. Modeled by master sculptor Helmut Fischer in 1990. The official issue price was $365. The incised "M.I. HUM-MEL" signature is located on the rear of the wagon on early production figurines, but later changed to the left side of wagon (left side as boy is facing front) because of production problems. Possibly fewer than 1,000 pieces have signature on rear. Listed as (TW) "Temporarily Withdrawn" in June 2002, but may be reinstated at some future date.

☐ 633 ......4.75 x 4.25" ....(CE) ....❼......$800—1000   (signature on back)
☐ 633 ......4.75 x 4.25" ....(CE) ....❼......$440—450   (signature on side)
☐ 633 ......4.75 x 4.25" ....(**TW**) ....❽......$440   (signature on side)

HUM 634 — Sunshower

First released in the U.S. market in the fall of 1997 with a "First Issue 1997" backstamp. The original issue price was $360 in 1997. Modeled by master sculptor Helmut Fischer in 1990. It has an incised 1990 copyright date. Sold in the North American market as a (LE) Limited Edition of 10,000 pieces to celebrate the 60th Anniversary of HUM 71 "Stormy Weather" which was first issued in 1937. Designed as a companion piece to "Stormy Weather" with some minor changes.

☐ 634 2/0.......4.50".......(CE).....❼.....$360—370
☐ 634 2/0.......4.50".......(OE).....❽.....$359

HUM 635 — Welcome Spring (CE)

This figurine was first released in the U.S. market in 1993. This is the eighth figurine in the "Century Collection" and was produced for only this one year in the twentieth century. Modeled by master sculptor Helmut Fischer in 1990. It has an incised 1990 copyright date. A circular inscription applied by blue decal reads: "M.I. HUMMEL CENTURY COLLECTION 1993 XX" and the name "Welcome Spring" along with the (TM 7) trademark. The original issue price was $1085 in 1993.

☐ 635..........12.25"..........(CE).....❼.......$1500—1700

HUM 636–637 — (ON) OPEN NUMBERS

HUM 638 — The Botanist Vase

A bisque porcelain vase with bas relief figurine on the front. A special combination "Sampler" offer was released in 1998. Contained HUM 351 "The Botanist" figurine in combination with the vase with the Hummel Museum, Inc. logo on the back. This combination set was released for $210. The vase has (TM 7) trademark with a 1997 copyright date applied by blue decal on the bottom, in addition to the "M.I. Hummel" signature incised on the vase.

☐ 638.....4.00 x 3.50".....(**TW**).....❼....$50—75

HUM 639–640 — (ON) OPEN NUMBERS

HUM 641 — Thanksgiving Prayer

Both sizes were released in the U.S. market in 1997 with "First Issue 1997" oval decal. Modeled by master sculptor Helmut Fischer in 1991 and 1995. The large size has an incised 1991 copyright date, while the small size has an incised 1995 copyright date. The small size has a matte finish while the large size has the normal glazed finish. The original issue price was $180 for the large (641/0) while the small (641 4/0) was $120 in 1997. Listed as (TW) "Temporarily Withdrawn" in June 2002.

☐ 641 4/0 ....3.25" ....(CE)............❼ ....$130—135
☐ 641 4/0 ....3.25" ....(**TW**) ....❽ ....$130—135
☐ 641/0........5.00" ....(CE)............❼ ....$200—205
☐ 641/0........5.00" ....(**TW**) ....❽ ....$200—205

642 4/0

HUM 642 — Echoes of Joy

Both sizes were released in the U.S. market in 1997 with "First Issue 1998" oval decal. Modeled by master sculptor Helmut Fischer in 1991 and 1995. The large size has an incised 1991 copyright date, while the small size has an incised 1995 copyright date. The small size has a matte finish while the large size has the normal glazed finish. The original issue price was $180 for the large (642/0) while the small (642 4/0) was $120 in 1997. Listed as (TW) "Temporarily Withdrawn" in June 2002.

☐ 642 4/0 ..3.00" ......(CE)....**❼** ....$130—135
☐ 642 4/0 ..3.00" ......**(TW)** ..**❽** ....$130—135
☐ 642/0 ......5.00" ......(CE)....**❼** ....$200—205
☐ 642/0 ......5.00" ......**(TW)** ..**❽** ....$200—205

642/0

HUM 643 — Joyful Noise

Both sizes were released in the U.S. market in 1999 with "First Issue 1999" oval decal. Modeled by master sculptor Helmut Fischer in 1991 and 1996. The large size has an incised 1991 copyright date, while the small size has an incised 1996 copyright date. The small size has a matte finish while the large size has the normal glazed finish. The original issue price was $180 for the large (643/0) while the small (643 4/0) was $120 in 1999. Listed as (TW) "Temporarily Withdrawn" in June 2002.

☐ 643 4/0 ..3.00" ......(CE)....**❼** ....$130—135
☐ 643 4/0 ..3.00" ......**(TW)** ..**❽** ....$130—135
☐ 643/0 ......5.00" ......(CE)....**❼** ....$195—200
☐ 643/0 ......5.00" ......**(TW)** ..**❽** ....$195—205

HUM 644 — (ON) OPEN NUMBER

HUM 645 — Christmas Song
Annual Ornament 1996 (CE)
First released in the U.S. market in 1996.
Modeled by master sculptor Helmet Fischer
in 1991. It has no incised copyright date that
I can find, but does have a "First Issue 1996"
round cello sticker, with "125th Anniversary
Goebel" on the lower gown of the angel.
"Hummel" only is incised on the back. The
incised model number 645 and (TM 7) trademark, plus 1991 copyright date applied by
blue decal on the bottom of this very small
area. A brass ring is attached to top of head
for hanging as an ornament. Original issue
price was $115 in 1996. Similar to HUM 343
4/0 "Christmas Song" but without base.

☐ 645 ......3.25" ......(CE) ....❼ ....$130—135

HUM 646 — Celestial Musician
Annual Ornament 1993 (CE)
First released in the U.S. market in 1993.
Modeled by master sculptor Gerhard Skrobek
in 1991. It has no incised copyright date that
I can find, but does have a "First Issue 1993"
oval cello sticker on the lower gown of the
angel. "Hummel" only incised on the back.
Incised model number 646 and (TM 7) trademark, plus 1991 applied by blue decal on the
bottom of this very small area. A brass ring is
attached to top of head for hanging as an
ornament. Original issue price was $90 in
1993. Similar to HUM 188 "Celestial Musician" but without base.

☐ 646 ......3.00" ......(CE) ....❼ ....$130—135

HUM 647 — Festival Harmony with Mandolin Annual Ornament 1994 (CE)

First released in the U.S. market in 1994. Modeled by master sculptor Helmut Fischer in 1991. It has no incised copyright date that I can find, but does have a "First Issue 1994" oval cello sticker on the lower gown of the angel. "Hummel" only incised on the back. Incised model number 647 and (TM 7) trademark, plus 1991 applied by blue decal on the bottom of this very small area. A brass ring is attached to top of head for hanging as an ornament. Original issue price was $95 in 1994. Similar to HUM 172 "Festival Harmony (mandolin)" but without base.

☐ 647.......2.75".......(CE).....❼.....$130—135

HUM 648 — Festival Harmony with Flute Annual Ornament 1995 (CE)

First released in the U.S. market in 1995. Modeled by master sculptor Gerhard Skrobek in 1991. It has no incised copyright date that I can find, but does have a "First Issue 1995" oval cello sticker on the lower gown of the angel. "Hummel" only incised on the back. Incised model number 648 and (TM 7) trademark, plus 1991 applied by blue decal on the bottom of this very small area. A brass ring is attached to top of head for hanging as an ornament. Original issue price was $100 in 1995. Similar to HUM 173 "Festival Harmony (flute)" but without base.

☐ 648.......2.75".......(CE).....❼.....$130—135

HUM 649 — Fascination (PFE)

First released in the U.S. market on October 5, 1996 at Goebel's National Open House promotions by participating retailers honoring Goebel's 125th Anniversary. Modeled by master sculptor Helmut Fischer in 1990. It has an incised 1991 copyright date along with (TM 7) trademark. Produced in a worldwide (LE) Limited Edition of 25,000 sequentially-numbered pieces with only 15,000 available in the U.S. The original issue price was $190 in 1996.

☐ 649/0 ......4.75" ....(CE) ......❼......$200—210
☐ 649/1 ......5.50" ....(PFE) ....

HUM 650–657 — (ON) OPEN NUMBERS

HUM 658 — Playful Blessing (CE)

Members' Exclusive Edition (EE) for Club year 21. This figurine was first introduced in 1997 for members of the M.I. Hummel Club only and not sold as an (OE) Open Edition. Modeled by master sculptor Helmut Fischer in 1992. It has an incised 1992 copyright date along with the (TM 7) trademark. Also bears the inscription: "EXCLUSIVE EDITION 1997/98 M.I. HUMMEL CLUB" applied by blue decal. A large black flying bumble bee is located on the bottom.

The official issue price was $260 in 1997, in addition to the member's redemption card.

☐ 658 ....3.50".......(CE).....❼......$280—300

HUM 659 — (ON) OPEN NUMBER

HUM 660 — Fond Goodbye (CE)

This figurine was first released in the U.S. market in 1997. This is the 12th figurine in the "Century Collection" and was produced for only this one year in the twentieth century. It was modeled by master sculptor Helmut Fischer in 1991. It has an incised 1992 copyright date. A circular inscription applied by blue decal reads: "M.I. Hummel CENTURY COLLECTION 1997 XX" and the name "Fond Goodbye" along with the (TM 7) trademark. The original issue price was $1450 in 1997.

☐ 660.......6.876 x 11 00"........(CE).....❼.....$1600—1800

HUM 661 — My Little Lamb

First made available in Fall of 2005, with Standing Lamb backstamp in European Market in Spring Landscape: Hummel Source, with HUM 2227 "Morning Call", HUM 2218 "Springtime Friends", HUM 197 4/0 "Be Patient" and three Spring accessories (Fountain, Wagon and Spring Tree); the set representing "Spring in a Four Seasons" Collector Series. Available on the North American Market from January 2006 as part of the "Animal Friends" Collection with an original issue price of $109. The figurine has incised 2005 copyright date, "Standing Lamb" backstamp, and the (TM 8) trademark, no first issue markings.

☐ 661.........3.25".........(OE).....❽......$109

HUM 662 — Friends Together

First released in the U.S. market in 1993 in both sizes. The small size, HUM 662/0 as an Open Edition (OE) and will become part of the regular line. It bears a special Commemorative UNICEF backstamp along with (TM 7) trademark. The large size, HUM 662/I is the first in a series in co-operation with the United Nations UNICEF Committee. It is a limited edition of 25,000 pieces, each sequentially numbered, and bears a special UNICEF Limited Edition backstamp, in addition to No. ____ of 25,000 along with the (TM 7) trademark. Both sizes were modeled by master sculptor Helmut Fischer in 1990 and both have an incised 1992 copyright date. The original issue price was $260 and $475 respectively. A $25 contribution was made to the U.S. Committee for UNICEF as part of a co-operative fund raising effort.

□ 662/0 ......4.25”..........(CE) ......❼ ....$300—350 (Commemorative Edition)
□ 662/I ......6.00”..........(**CE**) ......❼ ....$550—600 (Limited to 25,000)

HUM 663–666 — (ON) OPEN NUMBERS

HUM 667 — Pretty As A Picture (PFE)

This figurine was first modeled by master sculptor Gerhard Skrobek in 1992. It has an incised 1992 copyright date. Presently listed on factory records as a (PFE) Possible Future Edition and may be released at some future date, subject to possible minor changes. Resembles HUM 2132 “Camera Ready” and HUM 2100 “Picture Perfect”.

□ 667 ....7.00”..........(**PFE**) ....

HUM 668 — Strike Up the Band (CE)

This figurine was first released in the U.S. market in 1995. This is the tenth figurine in the "Century Collection" and was produced for only this one year in the twentieth century. It was modeled by master sculptor Helmut Fischer in 1993. It has an incised 1993 copyright date. A circular inscription applied by blue decal reads: "M.I. HUMMEL CENTURY COLLECTION 1995 XX" and the name "Strike Up the Band" along with the (TM 7) trademark. The original issue price was $1,200 in 1995.

☐ 668 ....7.25"..................(**CE**) ....❼ ....$1400—1600

M.I. Hummel
KITCHEN MOULD COLLECTION (CE)
First released in the U.S. market in 1991 and were sold exclusively by mail order at the rate of one every three months. They have an incised "M.I. Hummel" signature and the Goebel (TM 6 or TM 7) trademark, but do NOT have an incised model number. Modeled by master sculptor Helmut Fischer in 1989. The original issue price was $99 each (plus sales tax and $4.50 shipping and handling).

HUM 669
Baking Day

HUM 670
A Fair Measure

HUM 671
Sweet As Can Be or
Happy Birthday

HUM 672
For Father

HUM 673
Supper's Coming or
Going to Grandma's

HUM 674
Baker

☐ 669 ....7.50" ....(**TW**) ....❻ – ❼ ......$170—190
☐ 670 ....7.50" ....(**TW**) ....❻ – ❼ ......$170—190
☐ 671 ....7.50" ....(**TW**) ....❻ – ❼ ......$170—190 Found with either
☐ 672 ....8.00" ....(**TW**) ....❻ – ❼ ......$170—190 trademark ❻ or ❼.
☐ 673 ....8.00" ....(**TW**) ....❻ – ❼ ......$170—190
☐ 674 ....8.00" ....(**TW**) ....❻ – ❼ ......$170—190

HUM 675 — (ON) OPEN NUMBER

HUM 676—677 — Apple Tree Girl/Apple Tree Boy, Candle Stick Holders (CE)
First released in the U.S. market in 1989 and were sold exclusively by mail order at the rate of one every three months. Modeled by master sculptor Helmut Fischer in 1989. They have an incised 1988 copyright date. The original issue price was $142.50 each (plus sales tax and $3.00 shipping and handling).

☐ 676 ....6.50".................(TW) ....❻ or ❼ ....$200—250
☐ 677 ....6.50".................(TW) ....❻ ....$200—250

.... HUM TERM ....

ASSEMBLERS NUMBER: The small incised number (usually two digits) on the bottom of the figurine identifies the person who assembled the individual soft clay parts of the figurine. Smaller than the incised model number or the copyright date. Has no real meaning to the collector, only for Goebel production control.

HUM 678—679 — She Loves Me, She Loves Me Not/Good Friends Candle Stick Holders (CE)

First released in the U.S. market in 1990 and were sold exclusively by mail order through at the rate of one every three months. Modeled by master sculptor Helmut Fischer in 1989. They have an incised 1989 copyright date. The original issue price was $142.50 each (plus sales tax and $3.00 shipping and handling).

☐ 678 ....6.50" ....(**TW**) ....❻ or ❼ ....$200—250
☐ 679 ....6.50" ....(**TW**) ....❻ ....$200—250

HUM 680–683 — (ON) OPEN NUMBERS

HUM 684 —
Thoughtful Trinket Box
The original issue price was $50.

HUM 685 —
Bookworm Trinket Box
The original issue price was $50.

☐ 684 ....3.75 x 2.00" ......(**OE**) ....❽ $50
☐ 685 ....3.75 x 2.00" ......(**OE**) ....❽ $50

HUM 686 —
Sweet Greetings Trinket Box
The original issue price was $50.

HUM 687 —
She Loves Me Trinket Box
The original issue price was $50.

☐ 686 ....3.75 x 1.75" ......(**OE**) ....❽ $50
☐ 687 ....3.75 x 1.75" ......(**OE**) ....❽ $50

HUM 688 —
Umbrella Boy Trinket Box
The original issue price was $60.

HUM 689 —
Umbrella Girl Trinket Box
The original issue price was $60.

☐ 688 ....5.00 x 2.00" ......(**OE**) ....❽ $60
☐ 689 ....5.00 x 2.00" ......(**OE**) ....❽ $60

HUM 690 — Smiling Through, Plaque (CE)

This round plaque was first issued in 1978 for members of the Goebel Collector's Club only and not sold as an (OE) Open Edition. Originally modeled by master sculptor Gerhard Skrobek from an original drawing by Sister M.I. Hummel. There is nothing incised on the back but the inscription "EXCLUSIVE SPECIAL EDITION No. 2 HUM 690 FOR MEMBERS OF THE GOEBEL COLLECTORS' CLUB" is applied by blue decal. Also has (TM 5) trademark and W. Germany 1978. No holes are provided for hanging. The original issue price was $50 in the U.S. and $55 in Canada, in addition to the member's redemption card. This plaque can be purchased on the secondary market at premium prices. This same motif of "Smiling Through" was made into a figurine and released in 1985 as "EXCLUSIVE SPECIAL EDITION No. 9" for members of the Goebel Collectors' Club. See HUM 408.

☐ 690 ....5.75" ....(CE) ....**❺** ....$50—75

HUM 691 — (ON) OPEN NUMBER

HUM 692 — Christmas Song
Christmas Plate 1996 (CE)

Second issue in the Annual Christmas Plate series. Modeled by master sculptor Helmut Fischer in 1994. It bears a special "125th Anniversary Goebel" backstamp, plus (TM 7) trademark and 1994 copyright date applied by blue decal. Also has an incised "M.I. Hummel" signature on the front plus a decal signature on the back. The original issue price was $130 in 1996

☐ 692 ....6.00" ....(**CE**) ....**❼** ....$50—75

HUM 693 — Festival Harmony with Flute
Christmas Plate 1995 (CE)

First issue in new series of Annual Christmas plates. Modeled by master sculptor Helmut Fischer in 1994. It bears a special backstamp which reads: "M.I. Hummel Annual Christmas Plate, W. Goebel Porzellanfabrik, Rödental." Also has an incised "M.I. Hummel" signature in addition to HUM 693 (TM 7) trademark and 1994 copyright date applied by blue decal. The original issue price was $125 in 1995.

☐ 693 ....6.00" ....(**CE**) ....**❼** ....$50—75

HUM 694 — Thanksgiving Prayer
Christmas Plate 1997 (CE)

Third issue in the Annual Christmas plate series. Modeled by master sculptor Helmut Fischer in 1994. It bears an "M.I. Hummel Annual Christmas Plate 1997 Rödental, Germany" backstamp, plus (TM 7) trademark and 1995 copyright date applied by blue decal. Also has an incised "M.I. Hummel" signature on the front. The original issue price was $140 in 1997.

☐ 694 ......6.00"..........(**CE**)......❼ ....$50—75

HUM 695 — Echoes of Joy
Christmas Plate 1998 (CE)

Fourth issue in the Annual Christmas plate series. Modeled by master sculptor Helmut Fischer in 1996. It bears an "M.I. Hummel Annual Christmas Plate 1998 Rödental, Germany" backstamp, plus (TM 7) trademark and 1996 copyright date applied by blue decal. Also has an incised "M.I. Hummel" signature on the front. The original issue price was $145 in 1997.

☐ 695 ......6.00"..........(**CE**)......❼ ....$75—100

HUM 696 — Joyful Noise
Christmas Plate 1999 (CE)

Fifth issue in the Annual Christmas plate series. Modeled by master sculptor Helmut Fischer in 1995. It bears an "M.I. Hummel Annual Christmas Plate 1999 Rödental, Germany" backstamp, plus (TM 7) trademark and 1996 copyright date applied by blue decal. Also has an incised "M.I. Hummel" signature on the front. The original issue price was $145 in 1998.

☐ 696 ......6.00"..........(**CE**)......❼ ....$75—100

HUM 697 — Light The Way
Christmas Plate 2000

Sixth issue in the Annual Christmas plate series. Modeled by master sculptor Helmut Fischer in 1995. It bears an "M.I. Hummel Annual Christmas Plate 2000 Rödental, Germany" backstamp, plus (TM 8) trademark and 1996 copyright date applied by blue decal. Also has an incised "M.I. Hummel" signature on the front. The original issue price was $145 in 1999.

☐ 697 ......6.00"..........(**CE**)......❽ ....$75—100

HUM 698 — Heart's Delight

First released in the U.S. market in the fall of 1997 with "First Issue 1998" oval decal on the bottom. Modeled by master sculptor Helmut Fischer in 1996. It has an incised 1996 copyright date along with (TM 7) trademark. It comes with a separate red wooden chair. The official issue price was $220 in 1997 with chair included.

☐ 698 ....4.25" (5.00" w/chair) ....(CE) ......❼ ....$220—230
☐ 698 ....4.25" (5.00" w/chair) ....**(TW)**......❽ $219

HUM 699 — Love In Bloom

First released in the U.S. market in the fall of 1997 with "First Issue 1998" oval decal on the bottom. Modeled by master sculptor Helmut Fischer in 1996. It has an incised 1996 copyright date along with (TM 7) trademark. Incised "Hummel" only on back of figurine. It comes with a natural finish wooden wagon. The official issue price was $220 in 1997 with wagon included. (TW) "Temporarily Withdrawn" in December 2005.

☐ 699 ....4.25" (5.00" w/wagon) ....(CE) ......❼ ....$245—250
☐ 699 ....4.25" (5.00" w/wagon) ....**(TW)**......❽ $245

HUM 700 — Annual Bell 1978, Let's Sing (CE)
First edition in a series of annual bells. The motif of
HUM 110 "Let's Sing" is in bas-relief on the front, and
1978 is embossed in red on the reverse side along
with the "M.I. Hummel" signature. "HUM 700" is affixed by blue decal along with the (TM 5) trademark
on the inside of the bell. The original issue price was
$50 in 1978.

☐ 700........6.00"..........(**CE**)..........❺........$25—50

HUM 701 — Annual Bell 1979, Farewell (CE)
Second edition in a series of annual bells. The motif
of HUM 65 "Farewell" is in bas-relief on the front,
and 1979 is embossed in red on the reverse side
along with the "M.I. Hummel" signature. "HUM 701"
is affixed by blue decal along with the (TM 5) trademark on the inside of bell. The original issue price
was $70 in 1979.

☐ 701........6.00"..........(**CE**)..........❺........$20—30

HUM 702 — Annual Bell 1980, Thoughtful (CE)
Third edition in a series of annual bells. The motif of
HUM 415 "Thoughtful" is in bas-relief on the front, and
1980 is embossed in red on the reverse side along
with the "M.I. Hummel" signature. "HUM 702" is affixed
by blue decal along with the (TM 6) trademark on the
inside of bell. The original issue price was $85 in 1980.

☐ 702........6.00"..........(**CE**)..........❻........$20—30

HUM 703 — Annual Bell 1981, In Tune (CE)
Fourth edition of the annual bell series. The motif of
HUM 414 "In Tune" is in bas-relief on the front, and
1981 is embossed in red on the reverse side along
with the "M.I. Hummel" signature. "HUM 703" is
affixed by blue decal along with the (TM 6) trademark on the inside of bell. The original issue price
was $85 in 1981.

☐ 703........6.00"..........(**CE**)..........❻........$25—50

HUM 704 — Annual Bell 1982, She Loves Me (CE)
Fifth edition of the annual bell series. The motif of HUM 174 "She Loves Me, She Loves Me Not!" is in bas-relief on the front, and 1982 is embossed in red on the reverse side along with the "M.I. Hummel" signature. "HUM 704" is affixed by blue decal along with the (TM 6) trademark on the inside of bell. The original issue price was $85 in 1982.

☐ 704........6.00"..........(**CE**)..........❻........$30—40

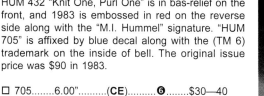

HUM 705 — Annual Bell 1983, Knit One (CE)
Sixth edition of the annual bell series. The motif of HUM 432 "Knit One, Purl One" is in bas-relief on the front, and 1983 is embossed in red on the reverse side along with the "M.I. Hummel" signature. "HUM 705" is affixed by blue decal along with the (TM 6) trademark on the inside of bell. The original issue price was $90 in 1983.

☐ 705........6.00"..........(**CE**)..........❻........$30—40

HUM 706 — Annual Bell 1984, Mountaineer (CE)
Seventh edition of the annual bell series. The motif of HUM 315 "Mountaineer" is in bas-relief on the front, and 1984 is embossed in red on the reverse side along with the "M.I. Hummel" signature. "HUM 706" is affixed by blue decal along with the (TM 6) trademark on the inside of bell. The original issue price was $90 in 1984.

☐ 706........6.00"..........(**CE**)..........❻........$30—40

HUM 707 — Annual Bell 1985, Sweet Song (CE)
Eighth edition of the annual bell series. The motif of HUM 389 "Girl with Sheet of Music" is in bas-relief on the front, and 1985 is embossed in red on the reverse side along with the "M.I. Hummel" signature. "HUM 707" is affixed by blue decal along with the (TM 6) trademark on the inside of bell. The original issue price was $90 in 1985. Also has small round decal "1935-1985 50 Years M.I. Hummel."

☐ 707........6.00"..........(**CE**)..........❻........$30—40

HUM 708 — Annual Bell 1986, Sing Along (CE)
Ninth edition of the annual bell series. The motif of
HUM 433 "Sing Along" was released in 1987, is in
bas-relief on the front, and 1986 is embossed in red
on the reverse side along with the "M.I. Hummel"
signature. "HUM 708" is affixed by blue decal along
with the (TM 6) trademark on the inside of bell. The
original issue price was $100 in 1986.

☐ 708........6.00"..........(CE)..........❻........$40—75

**HUM 709 — Annual Bell 1987, With Loving
Greetings (CE)**
Tenth edition of the annual bell series. The motif of
HUM 309 "With Loving Greetings" is in bas-relief on
the front, and 1987 is embossed in red on the
reverse side along with the "M.I. Hummel" signature.
"HUM 709" is affixed by blue decal along with the
(TM 6) trademark on the inside of bell. The original
issue price was $110 in 1987.

☐ 709........6.00"..........(CE)..........❻........$40—75

HUM 710 — Annual Bell 1988, Busy Student (CE)
Eleventh edition of the annual bell series. The motif
of HUM 367 "Busy Student" is in bas-relief on the
front, and 1988 in red on the reverse side along with
the "M.I. Hummel" signature. "HUM 710" is affixed by
blue decal along with the (TM 6) trademark on the
inside of bell. The original issue price was $120 in
1988.

☐ 710........6.00"..........(CE)..........❻........$40—75

HUM 711 — Annual Bell 1989, Latest News (CE)
Twelfth edition of the annual bell series. The motif of
HUM 184 "Latest News" is in bas-relief on the front,
and 1989 in red on the reverse side along with the
"M.I. Hummel" signature. "HUM 711" is affixed by
blue decal along with the (TM 6) trademark on the
inside of bell. The original issue price was $135 in
1989.

☐ 711........6.00"..........(CE)..........❻........$40—75

HUM 712 — Annual Bell 1990, What's New? (CE)
Thirteenth edition of the annual bell series. The motif of HUM 418 "What's New?" is in bas-relief on the front, and 1990 in red on the reverse side along with the "M.I. Hummel" signature. "HUM 712" is affixed by blue decal along with the (TM 6) trademark on the inside of bell. The original issue price was $140 in 1990.

☐ 712........6.00".........(**CE**).........**❻**........$40—75

HUM 713 — Annual Bell 1991, Favorite Pet (CE)
Fourteenth edition of the annual bell series. The motif of HUM 361 "Favorite Pet" is in bas-relief on the front, and 1991 in red on the reverse side along with the "M.I. Hummel" signature. "HUM 713" is affixed by blue decal along with the (TM 6) or (TM 7) trademark on the inside of the bell. The original issue price was $150 in 1991.

☐ 713........6.00".........(**CE**).........**❻**........$40—75
☐ 713........6.00".........(**CE**).........**❼**........$40—75

HUM 714 — Annual Bell 1992, Whistler's Duet (CE)
Fifteenth and final edition of the annual bell series. The motif of HUM 413 "Whistler's Duet" is in bas-relief on the front, and 1992 in red on the reverse side along with the "M.I. Hummel" signature. "HUM 714" is affixed by blue decal along with the (TM 7) trademark on the inside of the bell. The original issue price was $160 in 1992.

☐ 714........6.00".........(**CE**).........**❼**........$40—75

FINAL EDITION
1992

Hundreds and hundreds of hours have gone into this 10th edition of the "No. 1 Price Guide to M.I. Hummel Figurines." We have checked, rechecked and even double checked all information, prices etc. We sincerely want this to be the most accurate, complete and up to date guide to "M.I. Hummel" figurine collecting on the market today. We want it to be your '"bible"! — as some of you have said. We apologize if we have omitted any pertinent information, missed any typographical errors, or "goofed" in any way. We have tried our best! If you have any questions, suggestions, opinions or criticisms — please call or write. Our address and phone number is in the front of this book.

Sincerely,

Robert L. Miller

HUM 715 — Light The Way

Both sizes were released in the U.S. market in the fall of 1999 with First Issue 2000" backstamp. Modeled by master sculptor Helmut Fischer in 1995. "The large size has an incised 1995 copyright date, while the small size has an incised 1996 copyright date. The small size has a matte finish, while the large size has the normal glazed finish. The original issue price was $180 for the large (715/0) while the small (715 4/0) was $120 in 1999. Listed as (TW) "Temporarily Withdrawn" in June 2002, but may be reinstated at some future date.

☐ 715 4/0 ......3.00" ......(TW) ....❽ ....$120—130
☐ 715/0 ....5.00" ......(TW) ....❽ ...$180—190

HUM 716 — (ON) OPEN NUMBER

HUM 717 — Valentine Gift Plaque (CE)

To celebrate the 20th anniversary of the M.I. HUMMEL CLUB, this special plaque was issued in 1996 for Club members only. It was available to all Club members from 1 March 1996 through 31 December 1996 with special redemption form. It has an incised 1995 copyright date along with (TM 7) trademark. It has an incised "M.I. Hummel" signature diagonally on the back. The issue price was $250 plus $20 personalization fee in 1996.

☐ 717 ....5.25 x 6.50" ......(CE) ....❼ ....$300—350

718 A
Let It Shine

718 B
Hush-A-Bye

718 C
Holy Offering

718 D
Join In Song

718 E
Peaceful Sounds

214/D/0
Angel Serenade

HUM 718 — M. I. Hummel Heavenly Angels

First released in the U.S. market in 1999. Modeled by master sculptor Helmut Fischer in 1996. They have an incised "M.I. Hummel" signature. The original issue price was $90 each.

☐ 718/A..........Let It Shine ....(**TW**) ....**❼❽** $90
☐ 718/B..........Hush-A-Bye ....(**TW**) ....**❼❽** $90
☐ 718/C ....Holy Offering ....(**TW**) ....**❼❽** $90
☐ 718/D ....Join In Song ....(**TW**) ....**❼❽** $90
☐ 718/E..........Peaceful Sounds ......(**TW**) ....**❼❽** $90
☐ 214/D/0 ......Angel Serenade ....(**CE**) ....**❼❽** $90

HUM 719 — (ON) OPEN NUMBER

HUM 720 — On Parade

First released for sale to Military Post Exchanges in January 1998 and to  local U.S. retailers in mid-1998. Modeled by master sculptor Helmut Fischer in 1994. It has an incised 1995 copyright date along with the (TM 7) trademark. Also bears "First Issue 1998" oval decal back-stamp. The original issue price was $165 in 1998. Boy is similar to boy from HUM 50 "Volunteers." (TW) "Temporarily Withdrawn" in December 2004, but returned to production with a round base instead of a square base.

☐ 720 ....4.75" ....(CE)......❼ ....$180—185
☐ 720 ....4.75" ....(**OE**)......❽ $180

HUM 721 — Trio of Wishes (CE)

First released in the U.S. market in 1997, the second in the series called the "Trio Collection." Produced in a worldwide (LE) Limited Edition of 20,000 sequentially-numbered pieces. It comes with an oval hardwood base for display. It was mod-eled by master sculptor Helmut Fischer in 1995 and has an incised 1995 copyright date along with (TM 7) trademark. The official issue price was $475 in 1997.

☐ 721........4.50" ....(CE).....❼.....$550—600

HUM 722 — Little Visitor Plaque

Beginning in January 1996, Goebel designed this special plaque for those visiting the factory in Rödental, Germany. Modeled by master sculptor Helmut Fischer in 1995. It has an incised 1995 copyright date. It can be purchased at the Information Center for approximately U.S. $150. The plaque can be personalized while you wait, but you must take the plaque with you, as the factory will not ship.

☐ 722.....4.75 x 5.00" ....(CE) ....❼ ....$150—155
☐ 722.....4.75 x 5.00"............(OE) ....❽ $150

HUM 723 — Silent Vigil (PFE)

This figurine was first modeled by master sculptor Helmut Fischer in 1995. It has an incised 1995 copyright date. Presently listed on factory records as a (PFE) Possible Future Edition and may be released at some future date, subject to possible minor changes.

☐ 723......6.75" ....(PFE)........

HUM 724—725 — (ON) OPEN NUMBERS

HUM 726 — Soldier Boy Plaque
First released in 1996, this special plaque was sold exclusively by the U.S. Military post exchanges at a cost of $140 plus shipping charges. It was a (LE) Limited Edition of 7500 pieces. It bears the (TM 7) trademark and has an incised "M.I. Hummel" signature diagonally on the back. Modeled by master sculptor Helmut Fischer in 1996. It has an incised 1996 copyright date.

☐ 726 ....5.50 x 6.75".......(**CE**)....❼ ....$200—250

HUM 727 — Garden Treasures
First released in the U.S. market in 1998 as a FREE gift for renewing membership in M.I. HUMMEL CLUB for the 1998/99 club year (year 22). Modeled by master sculptor Helmut Fischer in 1996. It bears the inscription: "M.I. HUMMEL CLUB Membership Year 1998/99" in addition to a black flying bumble bee, in a half circle. It is similar to HUM 461 "In The Orchard" (PFE) Possible Future Edition.

☐ 727 ....3.50" ....(**CE**)....❼ ....$90—100

HUM 728 — (ON) OPEN NUMBER

HUM 729 — Nature's Gift
First released in the U.S. market in 1997 as a FREE gift for renewing membership in the M.I. HUMMEL CLUB for the 1997/ 98 club year. Modeled by master sculptor Helmut Fischer in 1996. It has an incised 1996 copyright date. It bears the inscription: "M.I. HUMMEL CLUB Membership Year 1997-1998" in addition to a black flying bumble bee, in a half circle. It is similar to HUM 74 "Little Gardener."

☐ 729.....3.75".......(**CE**).....❼.....$90—100

HUM 730 — Anniversary Bell 1985, Just Resting (CN)
This bell was designed by master sculptor Gerhard Skrobek in 1978 for release in 1985 but for some unknown reason it was NEVER ISSUED. Several examples are known to exist in private collections—both in color and white overglaze (unpainted).

☐ 730 ....7.128 x 4.00" ....(CN) ....❻ ....$1500—2000

373

HUM 731 — Best Friends

First released in Fall of 2005, with original issue price of $399 and "First Issue 2006" backstamp. Has an incised 1992 copyright date and the (TM 8) trademark. Formerly a (PFE) Possible Future Edition. Sculpted by master sculptor Helmut Fischer. The figurine has one girl with her eyes closed, a change from original artwork and previously pictured PFE showing her eyes open. In October 2005 a (LE) Limited Edition of 100 Arbeitsmuster Editions were made available in North America to M.I. Hummel Club members. These painters' samples bear a crimped metal "Arbeitsmuster Series" tag, are signed by master sample painter Frank Knoch, and have a certificate of authenticity signed by Frank Knoch. The Arbeitsmuster Edition has an incised 1992 copyright date, "First Issue 2006" backstamp, and the (TM 8) trademark, and was priced $399 in 2005.

☐ 731.....5.50".........(OE)....❽....$399

HUM 732 — For My Sweetheart (PFE)

This figurine was first modeled by master sculptor Helmut Fischer in 1992. It has an incised 1993 copyright date. Presently listed on factory records as a (PFE) Possible Future Edition and may be released at some future date, subject to possible minor changes.

☐ 732/I.....5.75".........(PFE).....

HUM 733—734 — (ON) OPEN NUMBERS

HUM 735 (1989)
It's Cold

HUM 736 (1988)
Daisies Don't Tell

HUM 737 (1987)
Valentine Joy

HUM 738 (1986)
Valentine Gift

HUM 735—738 — Celebration Plate Series (CE)

To celebrate the tenth anniversary of The Goebel Collectors' Club, a special series of four plates was issued for members of the Goebel Collectors' Club only. Each plate features a former club figurine in bas-relief. Issued one per year starting in 1986. Not sold as an (OE) Open Edition, but available with a redemption card only. The first edition in the series is "Valentine Gift" HUM 738. In the subsequent three years, the motif was "Valentine Joy" HUM 737, "Daisies Don't Tell" HUM 736 and "It's Cold" HUM 735. This series was designed by master sculptor Gerhard Skrobek in 1985. Each plate measures 6.25" in diameter, has the incised "M.I. Hummel" signature, and has the special inscription on the back: "EXCLUSIVELY FOR MEMBERS OF THE GOEBEL COLLECTORS' CLUB" affixed by blue decal.

☐ 735 ....6.25" ....(CE) ....❻ ....$40—50
☐ 736 ....6.25" ....(CE) ....❻ ....$40—50
☐ 737 ....6.25" ....(CE) ....❻ ....$40—50
☐ 738 ....6.25" ....(CE) ....❻ ....$40—50

HUM 739 — Call To Glory

First released in the U.S. market in 1994. Modeled by master sculptor Helmut Fischer in 1992. It has an incised 1992 copyright date and the "First Issue 1994" oval decal on the bottom. This figurine comes with three authentic flags of the U.S., Germany and Europe. (Only one flag at a time can be displayed.) I made a small plastic base with two holes to display the other flags. The issue price was $250. Approximately 900 pieces were made as gifts for the Orlando Convention. It as made with one blue flag with white lettering, reading "M. I. Hummel Club 1995 Convention". Also has "1994 M. I. Hummel Club Convention" on front of base in blue lettering. A new large sized version was introduced in 2004 for $550 with "God Bless America" and "U.S. Flag" backstamp, includes one flag (American) and a round musical wooden display that plays "American the Beauiful".

☐ 739/I ......5.75" ......(CE) ..❼....$280—290
☐ 739/I ......5.75" ......(OE) ..❽....$279
☐ 739/II ......8.00" ......(OE) ..❽....$529

739/II

HUM 740 — (ON) OPEN NUMBER

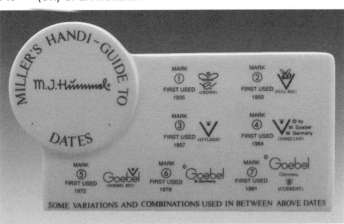

GOEBEL WZ4 or 004 Plaque

This is a universal porcelain standard stock plaque made in blank, that can be used for various advertising purposes simply by adding a message by decal, then fired. It measures 3.00 x 5.125", has an incised 1966 copyright date, an incised WZ 4 or 004 model number, and the GOEBEL trademark (NOT to be confused with "M.I. Hummel" TM 7 trademark). Normally sells for approximately $25—30.

HUM 741 (1985)
Serenade

HUM 742 (1987)
Band Leader

HUM 743 (1986)
Soloist

HUM 744 (1984)
Little Fiddler

HUM 741—744 — Little Music Maker Series (CE)

This series was first issued in 1984 as a four part bisque-porcelain "M.I. Hummel" minia-ture plate series called the "Little Music Makers." Each was a limited production plate which was produced for one year only. Modeled by master sculptor Gerhard Skrobek in 1982. A matching miniature figurine was released each year as an (OE) Open Edition to coincide with each plate. The original plate issue price was $30 in 1984, $30 in 1985, $35 in 1986 and $40 in 1987.

☐ 741 ....4.00"..................(CE) ....❻ ....$25—30
☐ 742 ....4.00"..................(CE) ....❻ ....$25—30
☐ 743 ....4.00"..................(CE) ....❻ ....$25—30
☐ 744 ....4.00"..................(CE) ....❻ ....$25—30

HUM 745 (1988)
Little Sweeper

HUM 746 (1989)
Wash Day

HUM 747 (1990)
Stitch In Time

HUM 748 (1991)
Chicken Licken

HUM 745—748 — Little Homemakers (CE)

This series was first issued in 1988 as a four part bisque-porcelain "M.I. Hummel" minia-ture plate series called the "Little Homemakers." Each is a limited production plate being produced for one year only. Modeled by master sculptor Gerhard Skrobek in 1986. A matching figurine is released each year as an (OE) Open Edition to coincide with each plate. The original issue price was $45 in 1988, $50 in 1989, $50 in 1990, $70 in 1991.

☐ 745 ....4.00"..................(CE) ....❻ ....$25—30
☐ 746 ....4.00"..................(CE) ....❻ ....$25—30
☐ 747 ....4.00"..................(CE) ....❻ ....$25—30
☐ 748 ....4.00"..................(CE) ....❻ ....$25—30
☐ 748 ....4.00"..................(CE) ....❼ ....$25—30

HUM 749 — (ON) OPEN NUMBER

HUM 750 — M.I. Hummel Anniversary Clock Goose Girl

First released in the U.S. market in 1995. The ceramic clock face modeled by master sculptor Helmut Fischer in 1993. It has an incised "M.I. Hummel" signature on the clock face in the lower right-hand corner. (TM 7) trademark is on back of the ceramic face. The entire clock is made in Germany. The official issue price was $200 in 1995. Listed as (TW) "Temporarily Withdrawn" in June 2002.

☐ 750 ....12.00" ....(CE) ....❼ ....$225—230
☐ 750 ....12.00" ....(**TW**)..........❽ ....$225—230

HUM 751 — Love's Bounty

First released in the U.S. market in 1996. This is the 11th figurine in the Century Collection and was produced for only this one year in the twentieth century. It was modeled by master sculptor Helmut Fischer in 1993. It has an incised 1993 copyright date, a combination circular "First Issue 1996" and "125th Anniversary Goebel" backstamp. Inscription reads: "M.I. Hummel CENTURY COLLECTION 1996 XX" plus "1871 W. Goebel Porzellanfabrik 1996" and the name "Love's Bounty" along with the (TM 7) trademark. It comes with an oval wood base with anniver-

sary information on the bottom in addition to a brass plate inscribed: 1871-1996—125 W. Goebel Porzellanfabrik. Early production has an incised "125" in the bouquet of flowers the boy is holding, while on later production, the "125" is applied by decal. The official issue price was $1200 in 1996.

☐ 751 ....6.50 x 8.50" ....(**CE**) ....❼ ....$1600—1800

HUM 752 — (ON) OPEN NUMBER

HUM 753 —
Togetherness
First released in Spring of 2006 with an original issue price of $745. An (EE) "Exclusive Edition" for the 2006/2007 Club Year, for members of the M.I. Hummel Club. Formerly a (PFE) Possible Future Edition, designed and approved in 1993. Resembles a blend of HUM 325 Helping Mother and HUM 306 "Little Bookkeeper". The boy is reading a love poem to the girl. Third and final in "Young Love" Series. "Special Togetherness" backstamp in addition to incised 1994 copyright date, the (TM 8) trademark, and Special Edition 2006 M.I. Hummel Club backstamp. North American (LE) Limited Edition of 1003 denoted by sequentially numbered ceramic heart crimped to figurine. A like number available for the European market, for a total of 2006 worldwide.

☐ 753........5.75 x 6.00"........(**EE**).....**❽**.....$745

HUM 754 — We Come In Peace (CE)
First released in the U.S. market in the fall of 1994. Similar to HUM 31 "Silent Night Candleholder" which was originally modeled in 1935 by Arthur Moeller. It is the second in a series in co-operation with the United Nation's UNICEF Committee. It bears a special "UNICEF Commemorative Edition" backstamp. Restyled and resculpted by master sculptor Helmut Fischer in 1993 and subsequently renamed. It has an incised 1993 copyright date. The original issue price was $350 in 1994. A $25 contribution was made to the U.S. Committee for UNICEF as part of a co-operative fund raising effort.

☐ 754.......3.50 x 5.00".......(**CE**).....**❼**.....$385—400

HUM 755 — Heavenly Angel Tree Topper

First released in the U.S. market in 1994. This is the first "M.I. Hummel" tree topper ever created. Modeled by master sculptor Helmut Fischer in 1992. It has an incised 1992 copyright date and the "First Issue 1994" oval decal on the bottom along with the (TM 7) trademark. Same basic design as HUM 21 "Heavenly Angel," except it has no feet or ceramic base. The color is a rose/salmon rather than the green of HUM 21. A wooden display stand is provided for normal display. The official issue price was $450 in 1994. The 7.75" size was listed as (TW) "Temporarily Withdrawn" in January 1999, but may be reinstated at some future date. HUM 755/0 "Heavenly Angel" with base is a (LE) Limited Edition of 5000, and is not a tree topper.

- ☐ 755/0 3.75"................(TW). ....❼ $149
- ☐ 755/0 3.75"................(TW). ....❽ ....$149   (Not tree topper, green gown)
- ☐ 755 ....7.75 to 8.00"....(TW). ....❼ ....$475—500

HUM 756 — The Artist Plaque

First released in the U.S. market in 1993 for the Grand Opening of the M.I. Hummel Museum in New Braunfels, Texas. Modeled by master sculptor Helmut Fischer in 1993. It has an incised 1993 copyright date along with (TM 7) trademark. The M.I. Hummel signature is also incised diagonally on the back as well as the decal signature on the front. This plaque was reissued without the Grand Opening designation. The original issue price was $260 in 1993. Also made for "Local Chapter Convention 1996".

- ☐ 756 ....5.00 x 6.75" ....(CE)......❼ ....$400—500

HUM 757 — A Tuneful Trio (CE)

First released in the U.S. market in 1996, the first in a new series called the "Trio Collection." Produced in a worldwide (LE) Limited Edition of 20,000 sequentially-numbered pieces. It comes with a hardwood base for display. Modeled by master sculptor Helmut Fischer in 1993 and has an incised 1993 copyright date, special "First Issue 1996" decal in combination with the Goebel "125th Anniversary" backstamp. To avoid breakage, the lamp post is made of wood, not ceramic. The official issue price was $450 in 1996.

□ 757 ......5.00".............(CE) ....❼ ......$475—500

HUM 758 — Nimble Fingers

First released in the U.S. market in 1996 with a special round "First Issue 1996" decal in combination with "Goebel 125th Anniversary" backstamp. Modeled by master sculptor Helmut Fischer in 1993. It has an incised 1993 copyright date along with (TM 7) trademark. Designed as a companion piece to HUM 759 "To Keep You Warm". Accompanied by a wooden bench large enough to hold both pieces. The original issue price was $225 in 1996. (TW) "Temporarily Withdrawn" in December 2005.

□ 758 ......4.50".............(CE) ....❼ ......$260—270
□ 758 ......4.50".............(TW) ....❽ $259

HUM 759 — To Keep You Warm

First released in the U.S. market in 1995 with "First Issue 1995" oval decal on the bottom. Modeled by master sculptor Helmut Fischer in 1993. It has an incised 1993 copyright date along with (TM 7) trademark. The official issue price was $195 in 1995. It comes with a separate wooden chair. (TW) "Temporarily Withdrawn" in December 2006.

□ 759 ......5.00".............(CE) ....❼ ......$260—265
□ 759 ......5.00".............(TW) ....❽ ......$259—260

HUM 760 — Country Suitor

Members' Exclusive Edition for Club year 19. This figurine was first introduced in 1995 for members of the M.I. HUMMEL CLUB only and not sold as an (OE) Open Edition. Modeled by master sculptor Helmut Fischer in 1993. It has an incised 1993 copyright date along with the (TM 7) trademark. Also bears the inscription: EXCLUSIVE EDITION 1995/96 M.I. HUMMEL CLUB applied by blue decal. A large black flying bumble bee is located on the bottom. The official issue price was $195 in the U.S., in addition to the member's redemption card. This figurine can be purchased on the secondary market at premium prices.

□ 760 ......5.50".............(CE) ....❼ ......$200—225

HUM 761 — From the Heart

First released in the U.S. market in 1996 with "First Issue 1996" and "Goebel 125th Anniversary" backstamp. Modeled by master sculptor Helmut Fischer in 1993. It has an incised 1993 copyright date along with the (TM 7) trademark. Designed as a companion piece to HUM 559 "Heart and Soul" as part of the "Cozy Companions" series. The official issue price was $120 in 1996. (TW) Temporarily Withdrawn" in December 2005.

□ 761 ......3.50".............(CE) ....❼ ......$135—140
□ 761 ......3.50".............(TW) ....❽ $135

HUM 762 — Roses Are Red

First released in the U.S. market in the fall of 1997 with the "First Issue 1998" oval decal back-stamp on the bottom. Modeled by master sculptor Helmut Fischer in 1993. It has an incised 1993 copyright date along with the (TM 7) trademark. The official issue price was $120 in 1997. (TW) Temporarily Withdrawn" in December 2005.

☐ 762 ....3.875" ......(CE)......❼....$135—140
☐ 762 ....3.875" ......(TW) ....❽....$135

HUM 763 — Happy Returns (PFE)

This figurine was first modeled by master sculptor Gerhard Skrobek in 1993. It has an incised 1994 copyright date. Presently listed on factory records as a (PFE) Possible Future Edition and may be released at some future date, subject to possible minor changes. It is a combination similar to HUM 17 "Congratulations" and HUM 9 "Begging His Share", but with a different dog!

☐ 763 ,.......7.125" ......(PFE)....

HUM 764 — Mission Madonna (PFE)

Modeled by master sculptor Helmut Fischer in 1993. The first example of this figurine was presented to His Eminence John Cardinal O'Connor of New York in 1996. Presently listed on factory records as a (PFE) Possible Future Edition and may be released at some future date, subject to possible minor changes.

☐ 764 ....10.50" ......(PFE).....❼ ..

HUM 765 — First Love

First released in Spring of 2004 with an original issue price of $945 as an (EE) "Exclusive Edition" for the 2004/2005 Club year, for members of the M.I. Hummel Club. Available to the general public with a free Club membership so upon purchase they could become instant Club members. Formerly a (PFE) Possible Future Edition. Sculpted by master sculptor Helmut Fischer in 1993. First in "Young Love" series. Special "First Love" backstamp in addition to incised 1994 copyright date, the (TM 8) trademark, and "Special Edition 2004 M.I. Hummel Club" backstamp. Signed by Frank Knoch, chief master sample painter. North American (LE) Limited Edition of 2004 pieces, denoted by sequentially numbered ceramic heart crimped to figurine. A like number available for the European market.

◻ 765......6.50 to 6.75"......(EE)....❽.....$945

HUM 766 — Here's My Heart

First released in the U.S. market in the fall of 1997. This is the 13th figurine in the "Century Collection" and will only be produced for the year of 1998 in the twentieth century. It was modeled by master sculptor Helmut Fischer in 1994. It has an incised 1994 copyright date. A circular inscription applied by blue decal reads: "M.I. HUMMEL CENTURY COLLECTION 1998 XX" and the name "Here's My Heart" along with the (TM 7) trademark. The original issue price was $1375 in 1997.

☐ 766 ....10.75" ....(CE)...... ❼....$1500—1600

HUM 767 — Puppy Love, Display Plaque

First released in the U.S. market in 1995. Modeled by master sculptor Helmut Fischer in 1993. It has an incised 1993 copyright date along with the (TM 7) trademark. Also bears a special backstamp: "Special Edition 1995" in German and English. The official issue price was $240 in 1995.

☐ 767 ....4.50 x 7.25" ..(CE)...... ❼.....$300—350

HUM 768 — Pixie

First released in the U.S. market in 1995 with "First Issue 1995" oval decal on the bottom. Modeled by master sculptor Helmut Fischer in 1994. It has an incised 1994 copyright date along with (TM 7) trademark. Designed as a companion piece to HUM 553 "Scamp" as part of the "Cozy Companions" series. The official issue price was $105 in 1995. A new TRINKET BOX was released in the U.S. market in 2002, retailing for $50. (See HUM 997).

☐ 768 ....3.50" ......(CE) ....❼ ....$140—145
☐ 768 ....3.50" ......(OE) ....❽ $140

HUM 769–770 — (ON) OPEN NUMBERS

HUM 771 — Practice Makes Perfect (Boy)

First released in the U.S. market in the fall of 1996 with an incised 1994 copyright date and the "First Issue 1997" oval decal backstamp. Modeled by master sculptor Helmut Fischer in 1994. Incised "Hummel" only on back of boy. It comes with a separate wooden rocking chair. The official issue price was $250 in 1997. Listed as (TW) "Temporarily Withdrawn" in June 2002. A small metal plaque is attached to back of rocking chair in variation given as a gift for "2001 M. I. Hummel Club" Convention, Nashville, Tennessee — 25th Anniversary Club. New small 3.25" size released in July 2005 includes black wooden base rather than rocking chair. Compantion to HUM 2223 "Practice Makes Perfect, Girl", and suitable for display with Kinder Choir.

☐ 771 2/0 ....3.25" ....(OE)......❽......$139
☐ 771 ....4.75" ....(CE)......❼......$310—325
☐ 771 ....4.75" ....(TW)......❽.......$300—310

HUM 772–774 — (ON) OPEN NUMBERS

HUM 775
1989
(Ride into Christmas)

HUM 776
1990
(Letter to Santa Claus)

HUM 777
1991
(Hear Ye, Hear Ye)

HUM 778
1992
(Harmony in Four Parts)

HUM 775–778 — Christmas Bells (CE)

This series was first issued in 1989 as a four part bisque-porcelain bell series. Each is a limited production item being produced for one year only. Modeled by master sculptor Helmut Fischer in 1987-1988. The original issue price was $35 in 1989, $37.50 in 1990, $39.50 in 1991 and $45 in 1992.

☐ 775 ....3.25”..................(CE) ....❻ ....$25—30
☐ 776 ....3.25”..................(CE) ....❻ ....$25—30
☐ 777 ....3.25”..................(CE) ....❼ ....$25—30
☐ 778 ....3.25”..................**(CE)** ....❼ ....$25—30

HUM 779
1993
(Celestial Musician)

HUM 780
1994
**(Festival Harmony
Mandolin)**

HUM 781
1995
(Festival Harmony Flute)

HUM 782
1996
(Christmas Song)

HUM 779—782 — Christmas Bells (CE)

This series of Christmas Bells was first issued in 1993 as a four part bisque-porcelain bell series. Each is a limited production item being produced for one year only. Modeled by master sculptor Helmut Fischer in 1991-1992. The original issue price was $50 in 1993, $50 in 1994, $55 in 1995, and $65 in 1996.

☐ 779 ....3.25"................(CE) ....❼ ....$25—30
☐ 780 ....3.25"................(CE) ....❼ ....$25—30
☐ 781 ....3.25"................(CE) ....❼ ....$25—30
☐ 782 ....3.25"................(CE) ....❼ ....$25—30

HUM 783
1997
(Thanksgiving Prayer)

HUM 784
1998
(Echoes of Joy)

HUM 785
1999
(Joyful Noise)

HUM 786
2000
(Light the Way)

HUM 783—786 — Christmas Bells

This series of Christmas Bells was first issued in 1997 as a four part bisque-porcelain bell series III. Each is a limited production item being produced for one year only. Modeled by master sculptor Helmut Fischer in 1995-1996. The original issue price was $68 in 1997, and $70 in 1998, 1989 and 2000.

☐ 783 ....3.25"..................(CE) ....❼ ....$25—30
☐ 784 ....3.25"..................(CE) ....❼ ....$25—30
☐ 785 ....3.25"..................(CE) ....❼ ....$25—30
☐ 786 ....3.25"..................(**CE**) ....❽ ....$25—30

HUM 787 — Traveling Trio (CE)
First released in the U.S. market in the fall of 1997, the third and final figurine in the "Trio Collection" series. Produced in a worldwide (LE) Limited Edition of 20,000 sequentially-numbered pieces. Modeled by master sculptor Helmut Fischer in 1995 and has an incised 1995 copyright date along with (TM 7) trademark. It comes with a hard wood base for display. The official issue price was $490 in 1997. Similar to HUM 331 "Crossroads."

☐ 787 ....5.25".................(**CE**) ....❼ ....$500—550

HUM 788 — Perpetual Calendar (Hello)

First released in the U.S. market in the fall of 1995. Modeled by master sculptor Helmut Fischer in 1995. It has an incised 1995 copyright date along with (TM 7) trademark. Has wood holder for calendar cards—months are both in English and German—dates are perpetual. Has an incised "M.I. Hummel" signature on the base just behind the figurine. The original issue price was $295 in 1995.

HUM 124 "Hello" was originally modeled by master sculptor Arthur Moeller in 1939 but has been restyled several times through the years. Listed as (TW) "Temporarily Withdrawn" in January 1999.

☐ 788/A (Hello) ....7.50 x 6.128".......(TW) ......❼.......$300—350

HUM 788 — Perpetual Calendar (Sister)

First released in the U.S. market in the fall of 1995. Modeled by master sculptor Helmut Fischer in 1995. It has an incised 1995 copyright date along with (TM 7) trademark. Has wood holder for calendar cards—months are both in English and German—dates are perpetual. Has an incised "M.I. Hummel" signature on the base just behind the figurine. The original issue price was $295 in 1995.

HUM 98 "Sister" was originally modeled by master sculptor Arthur Moeller in 1938 and has changed very little through the years. Listed as (TW) "Temporarily Withdrawn" in January 1999.

☐ 788/B (Sister) ....7.50 x 5.625".......(TW) ......❼.......$300—350

HUM 789 — (ON) OPEN NUMBER

HUM 790 — Celebrate With Song (CE)

Members' Exclusive Edition for Club year 20. This figurine was first introduced in 1996 for members of the M.I. Hummel Club only and not sold as an open edition. Modeled by master sculptor Helmut Fischer in 1994. It has an incised 1994 copyright date along with the (TM 7) trademark. Also bears the inscription: "EXCLUSIVE EDITION 1996/97 M.I. HUMMEL CLUB 1977 (20) 1997" applied by blue decal. A black flying bumble bee is located within a semi-circle on the bottom. The official issue price was $295 in the U.S., in addition to the member's redemption card, valid until 31 May 1998.

☐ 790 ....6.00" ....(**CE**)...... ❼ ....$300—325

HUM 791 — May Dance

First released in the U.S. market in the spring of 2000 as a "Special Event" figurine, available in North America this one year only at "Mai Fest" Celebrations, M.I. Hummel Artist and Goebel Sales Representative Events occurring from 1 April through 31 December 2000. Modeled by master sculptor Helmut Fischer in 1994. It has the (TM 8) trademark and a "Special Event" decal on the bottom. The official issue price was $199 in 2000. Other variations available.

☐ 791 ....7.00" ....(**CE**)...... ❽ $199

HUM 792 — (ON) OPEN NUMBER

HUM 793 — Forever Yours

First released in the U.S. market in 1996 as a FREE gift for renewing membership in the M.I. HUMMEL CLUB for the 1996/ 97 Club year. Modeled by master sculptor Helmut Fischer in 1994. It has an incised 1994 copyright date. It bears the inscription: "M.I. HUMMEL CLUB" in addition to a black flying bumble bee, in a half circle, plus the (TM 7) trademark. It comes with a gold medallion that reads "First Issue 1996/97." Can now be purchased on the secondary market at premium prices.

☐ 793 ....4.00" ....(CE)......❼ ....$75—100

HUM 794 "Best Buddies"

HUM 326

HUM 794 — Best Buddies (PFE)

This figurine was first modeled by master sculptor Helmut Fischer in 1995. It has an incised 1996 copyright date. Presently listed on factory records as a (PFE) Possible Future Edition and may be released at some future date, subject to possible minor changes. See HUM 326 (PFE) "Being Punished, Wall Plaque", for comparison.

☐ 794 ....3.50" ....(PFE) ....

HUM 795 — From My Garden

First released in the U.S. market in 1997 with "First Issue 1997" oval decal on the bottom. Modeled by master sculptor Helmut Fischer in 1994. It has an incised 1994 copyright date along with the (TM 7) trademark. The official issue price was $180 in 1997. A larger size (795/1) 5.50" was modeled by master sculptor Helmut Fischer in 1996 for possible release at some future date. The small size 795/0 was listed as (TW) "Temporarily Withdrawn" in December 2004.

☐ 795/0 ......4.75" ....(CE) ......❼ ....$200—205
☐ 795/0 ......4.75" ....(TW)......❽ ....$200—205
☐ 795/1 ......5.50" ....(PFE) ....

HUM 796 — Brave Voyager (PFE)

This figurine was first modeled by master sculptor Helmut Fischer in 1994. It has an incised 1994 copyright date. Presently listed on factory records as a (PFE) Possible Future Edition and may be released at some future date, subject to possible minor changes.

☐ 796 ....4.00" ....(PFE) ....

HUM 797 — Rainy Day Bouquet (PFE)

This figurine was first modeled by master sculptor Helmut Fischer in 1994. It has an incised 1995 copyright date. Presently listed on factory records as a (PFE) Possible Future Edition and may be released at some future date, subject to possible minor changes.

☐ 797 ....5.00"................(**PFE**) ....

HUM 798 — (ON) OPEN NUMBER

HUM 799 — Vagabond (PFE)

This figurine was first modeled by master sculptor Helmut Fischer in 1994. It has an incised 1995 copyright date. Presently listed on factory records as a (PFE) Possible Future Edition and may be released at some future date, subject to possible minor changes.

☐ 799 ....6.00"................(**PFE**) ......

HUM 800 — Proud Moments
Modeled by master sculptor Helmut Fischer in 1998. First released in the U.S. market in the fall of 1999 with an incised 1998 copyright date in addition to a "First Issue 2000 MILLEN-NIUM" oval decal and the (TM 8) trademark. The original issue price was $300 in 1999. Variations show differences in what is on the pages of her book.

☐ 800.......3.50".......**(OE)**......❽......$279

HUM 801 — (ON) OPEN NUMBER

HUM 802 — Brave Soldier (PFE) / (LE)
This figurine was first modeled by master sculptor Helmut Fischer in 1996. It has an incised 1997 copyright date. Recently released in a large 8.00" size with incised model number 802/II. It is being sold exclusively through the AAFES catalog and at U.S. Military Post Exchanges in a (LE) Limited Edition of 3000 pieces. Each piece is sequentially numbered and bears a red, white and blue flying eagle on the bottom, with the inscription "Ambassadors of Freedom" plus the TM 8 trademark. Each figurine comes with a one-inch wooden base with a brass plate that reads: "Brave Soldier" and "Ambassadors of Freedom." The military price was $228 plus shipping. This is the first of a series.

☐ 802 ....5.25" ......(PFE) .....
☐ 802/II ....8.00" ......(LE) .❽ $300—400

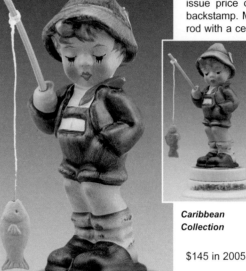

HUM 803 — Little Fisherman

First released in Fall of 2003, with original issue price of $59.50 and First Issue 2004 backstamp. Mixed media - boy holds wooden rod with a ceramic fish dangling on the string. Has incised 1997 copyright date and the (TM 8) trademark. Part of "Create-A-Gift" Collection when paired with a Sentiment Occasion base. Available in collector set with Barnegat Lighthouse Hummelscape. Available in (LE) Limited Edition of 500 with "Caribbean Collection" backstamp and matching decorated ceramic base to elevate the figurine. Available in collector set with Lighthouse Plaque and wooden stand, set priced $145 in 2005.

Caribbean Collection

☐ 803....3.50" ....(OE) ... ❽ $69.50

HUM 804 — Love Petals

First released in January 2003 with original issue price of $100 and "First Issue 2003" backstamp. Shortly thereafter, when incorporating "Love Petals" into the "Create-A-Gift" Collection, Goebel NA reduced the suggested retail price to $59.50. Part of the "Create-A-Gift" Collection when paired with a Sentiment Occasion base. Has an incised 1997 copyright date and the (TM 8) trademark. The girl holds a flower.

☐ 804.............3.50".........(OE).... ❽ ...$69.50

Shown with Happy Anniversary Sentiment Occasion base

HUM 805 — Little Toddler (PFE)

This figurine was first modeled by master sculptor Helmut Fischer in 1996. It has an incised 1997 copyright date. Presently listed on factory records as a (PFE) Possible Future Edition and may be released at some future date, subject to possible minor changes.

☐ 805.............2.75".........(PFE)...

HUM 806–813 — SEE: INTERNATIONAL SECTION

HUM 814 — Peaceful Blessing

First released in the U.S. market in the fall of 1998 with "First Issue 1999" oval decal backstamp. The official issue price was $180 in 1999. Modeled by master sculptor Helmut Fischer in 1997. It has an incised 1997 copyright date along with the (TM 7) trademark. (TW) "Temporarily Withdrawn" in December 2003.

☐ 814.............4.50".........(CE)....❼ ...$195—200
☐ 814.............4.50".........(TW)...❽ ...$195—200

399

HUM 815 — Heavenly Prayer

First released in the U.S. market in the fall of 1998 with "First Issue 1999" oval decal backstamp. Modeled by master sculptor Helmut Fischer in 1997. It has an incised 1997 copyright date along with the (TM 7) trademark. The official issue price was $180 in 1999. (TW) "Temporarily Withdrawn" in December 2003.

☐ 815 ....5.00"................(CE) ....❼ ....$195—200
☐ 815 ....5.00"................(TW) ....❽ ....$195—200

HUM 816–819 — (ON) OPEN NUMBERS

HUM 820 — Caribbean Collection Plaque

Modeled by master sculptor Helmut Fischer in 1997. It has an incised 1997 copyright date. First released in the Cayman Islands B.W.I., (British West Indies) in 1999 and sold exclusively by Kirk Freeport Plaza, Ltd. along with 10 other models of M.I. Hummel figurines with a special floral backstamp and the words "CARIBBEAN COLLECTION." The original issue price was $127 plus shipping and handling. (My total was $157.70 which included next day air charges.) Limited to approximately 300 pieces, but later reissued. Variation produced in 2004 at the Reading, PA Local Chapter Conference reading "Hummel Goebel Collector's Anchored To The Past, Welcoming The New Millennium" — Retail price $140.

☐ 820.........3.75 by 6.00".....(TW).....❼.....$200—225
☐ 820.........3.75 by 6.00".....(OE).....❽.....$140—190

HUM 821 — (ON) OPEN NUMBER

HUM 822 — Hummelnest

First released in Rödental, Germany in the fall of 1997 as a new Visitors Plaque for those visiting the Goebel Factory. It can be personalized while you wait. Modeled by master sculptor Helmut Fischer in 1997. It has an incised 1997 copyright date and measures 5.25" W x 4.375" H. The original issue price was DM 195 (approximately U.S. $100) in 1999. (Still available at factory in 2006.) Available in several variations in both (TM 7) and (TM 8). Released in 2004 in a (SE) Special Edition for Local Chapter Members only for the 25th Anniversary of the M.I. Hummel Club.

☐ 822 ....5.25 x 4.25" ....(CE) ....❼ ....$110—200
☐ 822 ....5.25 x 4.25" ....(OE) ....❽ ....$100—190

HUM 823 — (ON) OPEN NUMBER
HUM 824—825 — SEE: <u>INTERNATIONAL</u> SECTION

HUM 826 — Little Maestro

First released in the U.S. market in the fall of 1999. Modeled by master sculptor Helmut Fischer in 1997. It has an incised 1997 copyright date along with the (TM 8) trademark and the "First Issue 2000 MILLENNIUM" oval decal backstamp. Produced in a (LE) Limited Edition of 20,000 pieces worldwide. Sold in a collector's set with a FREE jointed, mohair, Steiff Teddy Bear and a porcelain medallion. The official issue price was $425 in 1999 for the set. Figurine available separately as of 2004, priced $320. A small size (826 2/0) 3.50" was modeled by master sculptor Helmut Fischer in 1997 for possible release at some future date.

☐ 826 2/0........3.50"........(PFE).......
☐ 826/I............5.50"........(CE).......❽.......$320—325

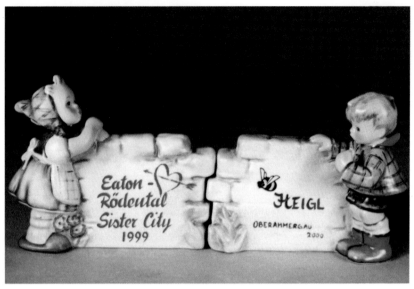

HUM 827   HUM 828

HUM 827 — Daydreamer Plaque

Modeled by master sculptor Helmut Fischer in 1998. First released in Rodental, Germany in the fall of 1999 with incised 1998 copyright date, the (TM 7) trademark, and the "First Issue 2000 Millennium" oval decal backstamp. The official issue price was $140 in 1999. As the new Visitors plaque for those visiting the Goebel factory, it could be personalized while you waited. Later available through Hummel retailers as a standard production piece, ready for personalization. Priced $150 on 2004 Goebel NA Suggested Price List. Similar to girl from HUM 196 "Telling Her Secret." Companion to HUM 828 "Over the Horizon."

☐ 827 ....3.50 x 4.50" ......(CE) ....❼ ....$140—150
☐ 827 ....3.50 x 4.50" ......(OE) ....❽ $139

HUM 828 — Over The Horizon

A plaque similar to HUM 827 "Daydreamer" with boy on right side, was released in the U.S. market in mid-2000. Has (TM 8) and sold for $140 in 2000. May be personalized.

☐ 828 ....3.25 x 4.25" ......(OE) ....❽ $139

HUM 829 — Where To Go?

First released in a four piece set: Special Edition "ENDURING GLOW OF FREEDOM" for the U.S. Military in 1999 consisting of HUM 829 "Where To Go?" and HUM 109 "Happy Traveler" (109/0), a wooden base with brass plate, and a plastic "rainbow." Issued in a (LE) Limited Edition of 5000 numbered pieces worldwide. Each figurine has a special decal of both German and U.S. flags on the bottom. "Where To Go" is similar to HUM 331 "Crossroads" but has only one boy in place of two. Modeled by master sculptor Helmut Fischer in 1999 to celebrate the 10th Anniversary of the fall of the Berlin Wall. The retail price to Military was $358 plus shipping & handling, and custom charges.

☐ 829 ....6.50" ....(CE) ...... ❽ ......$400—450

HUM 830—834 — (ON) OPEN NUMBERS

HUM 835 — Garden Splendor

First released in the European market in the fall of 1999. Modeled by master sculptor Helmut Fischer in 1999 to match the 2000 Annual Plate. Released in the U.S. market in spring of 2000 with a "First Issue MILLENNIUM 2000" oval decal backstamp, plus the (TM 8) trademark and the incised 1999 copyright date. The original issue price was $185 in 2000.

☐ 835........3.25".......(OE).....❽.....$199

HUM 836 — Afternoon Nap

This figurine matches the 2001 Annual plate. Modeled by master sculptor Helmut Fischer in 1999. First released in the U.S. market in the fall of 2000. with a "First Issue 2001" oval decal, plus (TM 8) trademark and the incised 2000 copyright date. The original issue price was $215 in 2001.

☐ 836..........3.50" ....(OE)......❽ $219

HUM 837 — Bumblebee Friend
This figurine matches the 2002 Annual plate. Modeled by master sculptor Helmut Fischer in 1999. First released in the U.S. market in the fall of 2001 with "First Issue 2002" oval decal, plus (TM 8) trademark and the incised 2000 copyright date. The original issue price was $260 in 2001. Similar to HUM 398 "Spring Bouquet" (PFE) Possible Future Edition which was modeled by master sculptor Gerhard Skrobek in 1973.

□ 837 ....5.25".............(OE) ....❽ $279

HUM 838 — Christmas By Candlelight
First released in the U.S. market in the fall of 2001. Available only at M.I. Hummel Artist and Sales Representative Special Events. It has a special decal "HOLIDAY EXCLUSIVE" on the bottom of the base and a yellow star with 2001 on the top. The figurine has an incised 2000 copyright date along with (TM 8) trademark. The original issue price was $215 in 2001. Released in 2001 in European market with "First Issue" backstamp and no marking in the star. Available in 2003 in a gift set with a wooden base and brass plaque reading "Christmas By Candlelight 2003 Special Edition", with 2003 in the star, the (TM 8) trademark and incised 2000 copyright date.

□ 838 ....7.50".............(OE) ....❽ $215

HUM 839—844 — (ON) OPEN NUMBERS

HUM 845 — Too Shy To Sing

First released in Spring of 2003, as a free gift for membership in the M.I. Hummel Club for the 2003/2004 Club year. Has incised 2002 copyright date, the (TM 8) trademark, and the "Club Exclusive" backstamp, (EE) Exclusive Edition 2003-2004. Sculpted by master sculptor Helmut Fischer. Resembles HUM 471 "Harmony in Four Parts". Part of First Year of Kinder Choir. Companion to HUM 2182 "First Solo" with wooden base. Currently available for $50 from Goebel NA for a limited time to permit M.I. Hummel Club members to complete their Kinder Choir. A $90 value.

☐ 845 ....4.00" ....(EE) ....❽ $90

HUM 846 — Hitting the High Note

First released in Spring of 2004, as an (EE) Exclusive Edition for the 2004/2005 Club year, for members of the M.I. Hummel Club. Includes ceramic and wooden lamppost, meant to be displayed in wooden base that comes with HUM 2182 "First Solo". Has incised 2002 copyright date, the (TM 8) trademark, and the "Club Exclusive" backstamp, (EE) Exclusive Edition 2004-2005. Sculpted by master sculptor Helmut Fischer. Resembles HUM 471 "Harmony in Four Parts" and HUM 757 "A Tuneful Trio". Part of Second Year of Kinder Choir. Companion to HUM 2181 "Clear as a Bell". Official issue price in 2004 was $110.

☐ 846 ....4.00" ....(EE) ....❽ $110

HUM 847 — Lamplight Caroler

First released in Spring of 2006, as an (EE) Exclusive Edition for the 2006/2007 Club year, for members of the M.I. Hummel Club. Has incised 2002 copyright date, the (TM 8) trademark, and the "Club Exclusive" backstamp, (EE) Exclusive Edition 2006-2007. Sculpted by master sculptor Helmut Fischer. Resembles HUM 471 "Harmony in Four Parts". Part of (final) Fourth Year of Kinder Choir. Companion to HUM 2183 "Keeping Time". Official issue price in 2006 was $110.

☐ 847 ....3.75"............(EE) ....❽ $110

HUM 848 — Steadfast Soprano

First released in Spring of 2005, as a free gift for membership in the M.I. Hummel Club for the 2005-2006 Club year. Has incised 2002 copyright date, the (TM 8) trademark, and the "Club Exclusive" backstamp, (EE) Exclusive Edition 2005-2006. Sculpted by master sculptor Helmut Fischer. Resembles HUM 471 "Harmony in Four Parts" and HUM 757 A "Tuneful Trio". Part of Third Year of Kinder Choir. Companion to HUM 2184 "First Violin" with wooden base. Currrently available at $50 from Goebel NA for a limited time to permit M.I. Hummel Club members to complete their Kinder Choir. A $100 value.

☐ 848 ....4.00"............(EE) ....❽ $100

HUM 849—854 — (ON) OPEN NUMBERS

HUM 855 — Millennium Madonna (LE)
Released during the millennium year 2000 in a (LE) Limited Edition of 7500 numbered pieces worldwide. Came in a special hinged, velvet-lined case for safe storage. Modeled by master sculptor Helmut Fischer in 2000. It has a round decal on the bottom with "MILLENNIUM MADONNA" and "In Celebration of Holy Year 2000," an incised 2000 copyright date along with (TM 8) trademark. The original issue price was $495 in 2000. Similar to HUM 764 "Mission Madonna" (PFE) Possible Future Edition which was modeled by Helmut Fischer in 1993.

☐ 855 ....10.25" ....(CE).... ❽ $495

HUM 856 — A Heartfelt Gift
First released in Fall of 2003 with an original issue price of $275. A sequentially numbered worldwide (LE) Limited Edition of 7500 (2,750 for North America). Has incised 2003 copyright date, the (TM 8) trademark and "Limited Edition" backstamp. With matching heart-shaped presentation tin. Resembles HUM 352 "Sweet Greetings". Crystal heart said to be detachable. First of mixed media pieces with Swarovski crystal – features a Swarovski crystal heart. Also see HUM 902 "Sunflowers, My Love," HUM 2222 "A Star for You" and HUM 2248 "Special Delivery".

☐ 856 ....5.50" ....(LE) .... ❽ $275

HUM 857 — Accordion Ballad

First released in 2004, with incised 2003 copyright date and the (TM 8) trademark, but no first issue marking. In North American market, part of "Create- A-Gift" Collection when paired with a Sentiment Occasion base. Original issue price in 2004 was $59.50. In European market, bearing "Music" backstamp, part of "Hummel Figurines Through the Year" Collection, with available wooden showcase and ceramic month plaques for making a figural calendar.

☐ 857 ....3.50" ....(OE)....❽ $69.50

Accordion Ballad

Shown with Happy St. Patrick's Day Sentiment Occasion base.

HUM 858/A — Favorite Pet Easter Egg

First released in 2001, with inscribed MI Hummel signature, and blue ink decal "Special Edition 2001" across back of egg. Has the (TM 8) trademark and 858/A under base of egg. With wooden stand. Features a depiction of HUM 361 "Favorite Pet "applied by decal to the front of the egg. The only Easter egg featuring a Hummel motif to date.

☐ 858/A.......3.25".......(TW).....❽.....$56

HUM 859 — (ON) OPEN NUMBERS

HUM 860—874 —
Miniature Bells

Fifteen miniature bells were released over 2000 and 2001 for sale first in the European market. The bells have had limited marketing exposure in the North American market. The original issue price was DM49, at that time approximately $30 in U.S. currency. They DO have HUM numbers 860 through 874 corresponding to the "Annual Bell Series" from 1978 to 1992. Each 3.75" bell has the M.I. Hummel signature incised on the back of the bell, and the (TM 8) trademark, the name of the bell and 1999 copyright date applied by blue decal on the inside. The bells are individually boxed. A wooden display is available for displaying the fifteen mini bells.

HUM 875 — (ON) OPEN NUMBER

HUM 876 — Heavenly Angel Ornament
This bell-shaped ornament was first released in the European market in 1999, then in the U.S. market in 2000. It has a decal "M.I. Hummel" signature, a decal trademark but NO copyright date. Both sides of ornament are identical. The original issue price was $20 in 2000. Found in both (TM 7 & TM 8).

☐ 876/A ......3.25" ....(OE)....❼ $20
☐ 876/A ......3.25" ....(OE)....❽ $20

HUM 877 — Ride Into Christmas Ornament
This Christmas Tree-shaped ornament was first released in the European market in 1999, then in the U.S. market in 2000. It has a decal "M.I. Hummel" signature, a decal trademark but NO copyright date. Both sides of ornament are identical. The original issue price was $20 in 2000. Found in both (TM 7 & TM 8).

☐ 877/A ......4.25" ....(OE)....❼ $20
☐ 877/A ......4.25" ....(OE)....❽ $20

HUM 878 — Sleep Tight Ornament
This ball-shaped Christmas ornament was first issued in the European market in 1999, then in the U.S. market in 2000. It has a decal "M.I. Hummel" signature, a (TM 8) trademark, and a 2000 copyright date. Both sides of ornament are identical. The original issue price was $20 in 2000.

☐ 878/A ......3.50"............(OE) ......❽.....$20

HUM 879 — Christmas Song Ornament
This candlestick-shaped Christmas ornament was first released in the U.S. market in the fall of 2000. It has a decal "M. I. Hummel" signature, a (TM 8) trademark and a 2001 copyright date. Both sides of the ornament are identical. The original issue price was $20 in 2000.

☐ 879/A ......3.50"............(OE) ......❽.....$20

HUM 880 — Hear Ye, Hear Ye Ornament
This lantern-shaped Christmas ornament was first released in the U.S. market in the fall of 2000. It has a decal "M. I. Hummel" signature, a (TM 8) trademark and a 2001 copyright date. Both sides of ornament are identical. The original issue price was $20 in 2000.

☐ 880/A ......4.25"............(OE) ......❽.....$20

HUM 881/A — The Guardian Christmas Ornament
First released in 2003, with an original issue price of $22.50. A star-shaped ornament of tan color shaded to darker brown edges, with light blue ribbon for hanging. Has a decal M.I. Hummel signature, the (TM 8) trademark, and a 2002 copyright date decal. Features a depiction of HUM 455 "The Guardian" applied by decal over raised detail. Both sides of the ornament are identical. Available in "The Guardian Gift Set" (Large), in presentation box, with HUM 882/A "The Guardian Framed Picture", HUM 883/A "The Guardian Birth Certificate", and HUM 884 "The Guardian Trinket Box"; set priced $197.50 in 2003.

☐ 881/A........3.50".........**(TW)**.....❽.....$25

HUM 882/A — The Guardian Framed Picture
First released in 2003 with an original issue price of $75. A ceramic 4 x 6" plaque in wooden 5.50" x 7.25" frame with loop for hanging. Features a depiction of HUM 455 "The Guardian" applied by decal over raised detail. Has a decal M.I. Hummel signature on front of framed picture. Has HUM name, number, the (TM 8) trademark, and 2002 copyright date printed in blue ink on felt backing of plaque. Available in "The Guardian Gift Set" (Large), in presentation box, with HUM 881/A "The Guardian Christmas Ornament", HUM 883/A "The Guardian Birth Certificate", and HUM 884 "The Guardian Trinket Box"; set priced $197.50 in 2003.

☐ 882/A......5.50"............**(OE)**......❽..$75

HUM 883/A — The Guardian Birth Certificate

First released in 2003 with an original issue price of $50. A book-shaped plaque, able to stand on its own. With clear film over right-hand page, suggesting how to personalize it. Film is removable so plaque may be personalized. Features a depiction of HUM 455 "The Guardian" applied by decal over raised detail. Has a decal M.I. Hummel signature, the (TM 8) trademark, and a 2002 copyright date decal. Available in "The Guardian" Gift Set (Large), in presentation box, with HUM 881/A "The Guardian Christmas Ornament", HUM 882/A "The Guardian Framed Picture", and HUM 884 "The Guardian Trinket Box"; set priced $197.50 in 2003.

☐ 883/A......3.00 x 5.50".......(OE) ......❽ $50

HUM 884 — The Guardian Trinket Box

First released in 2003, with an original issue price of $50. A ceramic
oval-shaped treasures box. Features
a depiction of HUM 455 "The
Guardian" on the cover applied by
decal over raised detail. Has a decal
M.I. Hummel signature, the (TM 8)
trademark, and a 2002 copyright
date decal. Available in "The
Guardian Gift Set" (Large), in presen-
tation box, with HUM 881/A "The
Guardian Christmas Ornament",
HUM 882/A "The Guardian Framed
Picture", and HUM 883/A "The
Guardian Birth Certificate"; set priced
$197.50 in 2003. Available in "The
Guardian Gift Set" (Small), in presen-
tation box, with HUM 455 "The
Guardian" figurine (personalizable); set priced $250 in 2003.

☐ 884 ....1.75 x 4.00" ....(OE) ......❽ ..$$50

By The Sea Collector Set

Fishing Adventure

HUM 885 — Fishing Adventure

First released in 2004 as part of collector set with "By the Sea" Hummelscape, set priced $250. Scape is (LE) Limited Edition of 5000, depicts the Assateague Island lighthouse, and features light and sea sounds (Mark #1088-D). Figurine first became available separately in 2005, priced $250 (priced the same as the set). Figurine resembles HUM 566 "The Angler". Has incised 2003 copyright date and the (TM 8) trademark, but no first issue marking. Mixed media figurine – boy holds wooden pole with ceramic fish dangling from the string.

☐ 885 ....5.00" ....(**TW**)...... ❽ ..$250

Century Collection Mini Plates

A Series of Mini-Plates to Match the Acclaimed *M.I. Hummel* Century Collection

During the final 14 years of the 20th Century, we all enjoyed an exquisite series of (LE) Limited Edition M.I. Hummel figurines available for one year only. The "Century Collection" showcases each piece in ample size, rich in detail, and among the finest work ever produced by Goebel.

Now that the century has ended, the "Century Collection" has, too. "Fanfare" (HUM 1999) is the (FE) Final Edition in the century collection.

To honor this collection, Goebel has introduced the "Century Collection Mini Plate" Series. Fourteen small plates feature the "Century Collection" motifs in miniature, using a special decal-on-relief technique. Each plate is 4 inches in diameter and affordably priced at just $30 each original issue price.

An attractive wall display has been specially designed, making it easy to exhibit your mini-plate collection. Crafted in fine walnut, the display retails approximately-for $100. The "Century Collection Mini Plates" were priced $31.50 each on the 2004 Goebel NA suggested retail price list. Now these are (CE) Closed Editions.

☐ 886 Chapel Time	1986	☐ 893 Welcome Spring	1993
☐ 887 Pleasant Journey	1987	☐ 894 Rock-A-Bye	1994
☐ 888 Call to Worship	1988	☐ 895 Strike Up the Band	1995
☐ 889 Harmony in Four Parts	1989	☐ 896 Love's Bounty	1996
☐ 890 Let's Tell the World	1990	☐ 897 Fond Goodbye	1997
☐ 891 We Wish You the Best	1991	☐ 898 Here's My Heart	1998
☐ 892 On Our Way	1992	☐ 899 Fanfare	1999

HUM 900 — Merry Wanderer Plaque (with bumblebee)

First released in the U.S. market in the fall of 1999, as a special (EE) Exclusive Edition for M.I. Hummel Club members only. Modeled by master sculptor Helmut Fischer in 1998. It has an incised 1998 copyright date along with the (TM 8) trademark. Incised on the back of the Collectors Club plaque only: "Original Goebel archival plaque ca. 1947." The official issue price was $195 in 1999, with the member's redemption card. Both the Collectors plaque and the Authorized Retailer plaque have "Goebel Rödental Germany" embossed on the satchel.

☐ 900 ....4.00 x 5.75" ......(CE) ....❽ ....$200 (Retailers)
☐ 900 ....4.00 x 5.75" ......**(CE)** ....❽ ....$200 (Collectors)
☐ 900 ....4.00 x 5.75" ......**(OE)** ....❽ ....

((OE) Open Edition for Retailers in their country only)

HUM 900 — Authorized Retailer Plaque

This plaque was issued in nine decal variations for use in other countries (languages). Modeled by master sculptor Helmut Fischer in 1998. Has an incised 1998 copyright date along with the (TM 8) trademark.

☐ *BRITISH*

☐ *GERMAN*

☐ *DUTCH*

☐ *ITALIAN*

☐ *FRENCH*

☐ *SWEDISH*

☐ *SPANISH*

☐ *JAPANESE*

☐ *UNITED STATES*

HUM 901 — (ON) OPEN NUMBER

HUM 902 — Sunflowers, My Love?

First released in Fall of 2004 with an original issue price of $275. A sequentially numbered worldwide (LE) Limited Edition of 7500. Has incised 2004 copyright date, the (TM 8) trademark and "Limited Edition" backstamp. With matching round presentation tin. Resembles HUM 569 "A Free Flight." Second of mixed media pieces with Swarovski crystal – features a Swarovski crystal in the flower he holds. See also HUM 856 "A Heartfelt Gift", HUM 2222 "A Star for You" and HUM 2248 "Special Delivery".

☐ 902 ....5.50" ....(**LE**) ....❽ $275

HUM 903 — Adoring Children

First spotted in Spring 2006 in the AAFES Online Catalog Resembles the children in PFE 572. Midyear introduction in 2006 with original issue price of $259. Described as addition to "Children's Nativity Set". Notice that the children are standing on their feet and the figurine does not have a base. The figurine has the (TM 8) trademark.

□ 903.......4.50".......(**OE**).....❽....$259

HUM 904—907 — (ON) OPEN NUMBERS

HUM 908 — Gone A-Wandering

First released in July 2006 with an original issue price of $199, bearing the (TM 8) trademark, one of four Hummels in the "Heart of Hummel" Collection. "Heart" backstamp and heart on his hat. Worldwide (LE) Limited Edition of 5000, sequentially numbered. Just 2500 "Heart of Hummel" Collection Sets are available with matching (LE) Limited Edition numbers on all four Hummels. The Collection Set features HUM 624 "Fresh Blossoms", HUM 908 "Gone-A-Wandering", HUM 2235 "Lucky Friend", and HUM 2237 "Sunday Stroll" in a blue rectangular collector tin: set priced $795. "Gone A-Wandering" is a suitable companion to HUM 356 "Gay Adventure".

□ 908.......4.50".......(**LE**).....❽....$199

418

HUM 909 — Gifts of Love

First released in Spring of 2006 with an original issue price of $350. An (EE) Exclusive Edition for the 2006/2007 Club year, for members of the M.I. Hummel Club. Resembles HUM 387 "Valentine Gift" and HUM 399 "Valentine Joy", the first and fourth club exclusives respectively, for the Goebel Collectors' Club, now the M.I. Hummel Club. Has incised 2005 copyright date, the (TM 8) trademark, and the "Club Exclusive" Backstamp, (EE) Exclusive Edition 2006-2007. Marking Club Year 30.

☐ 909.......5.25".......(**EE**).....❽.....$350

HUM 910—919 — (ON) OPEN NUMBERS

HUM 920 — Star Gazer Plate

This Special MILLENNIUM Edition plate bears a special "60th Anniversary" backstamp honoring HUM 132 "Star Gazer" figurine which was first created in 1939 by master sculptor Arthur Moeller and restyled in 1980 by master sculptor Gerhard Skrobek. "Star Gazer" plate was modeled by master sculptor Helmut Fischer in 1999. It has an incised 1999 copyright date along with the (TM 8) trademark. The official issue price was $198 in 2000. This plate's 7.50" size matches the size of the first "Annual Plates" Series from 1971-1995.

☐ 920.......7.50".....(**CE**).....❽.....$175—200

HUM 921 — Annual Plate, 2000
Garden Splendor (CE)

The original issue price was $198.

☐ 921.......7.00".....(**CE**).....❽.....$175—200

HUM 922 — Annual Plate, 2001
Afternon Nap (CE)
The original issue price was $198.

☐ 922 ....7.00" ....(CE).....❽ ....$175—200

HUM 923 — Annual Plate, 2002
Bumblebee Friend (CE)
The original issue price was $198.

☐ 923 ....7.00" ....(CE).....❽ ....$198—200

HUM 924 — Annual Plate, 2003
The Florist (OE)
The original issue price was $215.

☐ 924 ....7.00" ....(CE).....❽ $215

HUM 925 — Annual Plate, 2004
Garden Gift
First released in Fall 2003, with an original issue price of $215. The fifth and final in this annual plates series which began in 2000. Hummel design done in bas relief. Has incised M.I. Hummel signature, incised 2003 copyright date and the (TM 8) trademark. Matches Hummel 619 Garden Gift.

☐ 925 ....7.00" ....(CE).....❽ $215

HUM 926—968 — (ON) OPEN NUMBERS

HUM 969 — Puppy Love Wooden Case Clock

First released in 2005 with an original issue price of $250. The clock case is made of alder wood and glass, finished with gold-toned handle and feet. Handle folds down. Requires two batteries: one for clock and one for pendulum. Measures 10.25" tall, 9" wide, 6.00" deep. A brass plaque on back of the clock case notes that the clock commemorates the 70th Anniversary of Hummel figurines in 2005. Production limited in 2005, not sequentially numbered. Ceramic hand-painted clock face, 4" diameter, depicts HUM 1 "Puppy Love" in bas relief. A raised dot at the quarter hours takes the place of clock numerals. Gold-tone anniversary movement.

☐ 969 ....10.25" ....**(CE)** .... ❽ $250

HUM 156456 — Goose Girl Wooden Case Clock (Not Pictured)

First released in July 2003 in the North American Market in a (LE) Limited Edition of 500, with an original issue price of $180. With hardwood and glass case and ceramic clock face featuring a depiction of HUM 47 "Goose Girl", hand painted in bas relief. Requires one AA battery. Measures 9.25" x 5.25" x 13" and features a dark brown/cherry finish and a gold-tone pendulum.

☐ 156456.....13.00" ......**(LE)** .... ❽ $180

HUM 970 — In Tune Wooden Case Clock

First released in 2005 with an original issue price of $250. The clock case is made of alder wood and glass, finished with gold-toned handle, feet and decorative screening in side panels. Handle does not fold down. Requires two batteries: one for clock and one for anniversary movement. Measures 11.5" tall, 7.75" wide, and 4.75" deep. Ceramic hand-painted clock face, 4.00" diameter, depicts HUM 414 "In Tune" in bas relief. A raised dot at the quarter hours takes the place of clock numerals. Gold-tone anniversary movement.

☐ 970.......11.50".......**(OE)**..... ❽ $250

MINIATURE ANNUAL PLATE SERIES
HUM 971—995

P roduced in 1995 for sale first in the European market. They were originally released for sale at the rate of four plates at a time, but are all now readily available. The original issue price was approximately $20 in U.S. currency. They DO have HUM numbers 971 through 1995 corresponding to the "Annual Plate" Series from 1971 to 1995. Each 3.25" plate has the trademark and a 1995 copyright date applied by blue decal on the back. They are individually boxed, can be found in both TM 7 and TM 8, and were priced $25 each on the 2004 Goebel NA Suggested Retail Price List. Wooden displays are available for the plates. All are (OE) Open Editions.

HUM 996 — Scamp Trinket Box
HUM 997 — Pixie Trinket Box
Released in the U.S. market in mid-2002. Modeled by master sculptor Helmut Fischer. The original issue price was $50 each in 2002.

☐ 996 ....4.00 x 3.00" ......(OE) ....❽ $50
☐ 997 ....4.00 x 3.00" ......(OE) ....❽ $50

RETIREMENT MOTIF MINI-PLATES
HUM 1/T—355/T

A series of mini-plates depicting retired Hummel motifs. Offered for sale beginning in 2002 in the European market, so far they have not been sold by Goebel NA in the North American market. Each plate is 3.25" in diameter, and has a Hummel number, a decal M.I. Hummel signature, and the (TM 8) trademark. Design applied by decal over raised detail. Priced at approximately $25 US dollars each.

HUM 1/T — Puppy Love — Retirement Plate Motif 1988
Originally released with plain background, then redesigned in 2004 with subtle background.

Not available with plain background

HUM 4/T — Little Fiddler — Retirement Plate Motif 2003
Originally released with subtle background, not available with plain background. Has 2003 copyright decal.

HUM 5/T — Strolling Along — Retirement Plate Motif 1989

Originally released with plain background, then redesigned in 2004 with subtle background. A commemorative version was given to participants on a trip to Germany in 2006 with Robert and Ruth Miller, with the wording "'Strolling Along on the 2006 Miller Hummel Tour" on the front of the plate. Redsigned plate has 2002 copyright date decal.

HUM 16/T — Little Hiker — Retirement Plate Motif 2002

Not available with plain background

Originally released with subtle background, not available with plain background

HUM 17/T — Congratulations — Retirement Plate Motif 1999

Originally released with plain background, then redesigned in 2004 with subtle background.

HUM 65/T — Farewell — Retirement Plate Motif 1993

Originally released with plain background, then redesigned in 2004 with subtle background.

HUM 68/T — Lost Sheep — Retirement Plate Motif 1992

Originally released with plain background, then redesigned in 2004 with subtle background. Redesigned plate has 2002 copyright date decal.

HUM 69/T — Happy Pastime — Retirement Plate Motif 1996

Originally released with plain background, then redesigned in 2004 with subtle background.

HUM 79/T — Globe Trotter — Retirement Plate Motif 1991

Originally released
with plain background,
then redesigned in
2004 with subtle back-
ground.

HUM 124/T — Hello — Retirement Plate Motif 2001

Not available with plain
background

Originally released
with subtle back-
ground, not available
with plain background.

HUM 130/T — Duet — Retirement Plate Motif 1995

Originally released
with plain background,
then redesigned in
2004 with subtle back-
ground.

HUM 143/T — Boots — Retirement Plate Motif 1998

Originally released with plain background, then redesigned in 2004 with subtle background.

HUM 153/T — Auf Wiedersehen — Retirement Plate Motif 2000

Not available with plain background

Originally released with subtle background, not available with plain background. Has 2003 copyright decal.

HUM 175/T — Mother's Darling — Retirement Plate Motif 1997

Originally released with plain background, then redesigned in 2004 with subtle background. Redesigned plate has 2002 copyright date decal.

HUM 185/T — Accordion Boy — Retirement Plate Motif 1994

Originally released with plain background, then redesigned in 2004 with subtle background.

HUM 203/T — Signs of Spring — Retirement Plate Motif 1990

Originally released with plain background, then redesigned in 2004 with subtle background.

HUM 328/T — Carnival — Retirement Plate Motif 2000

Not available with plain background

Originally released with subtle background, not available with plain background.

HUM 355/T — Autumn Harvest — Retirement Plate Motif 2002

Not available with plain background

Originally released with subtle background, not available with plain background.

HUM 806—968
International
"M.I. Hummel" Figurines

The following eight "M.I. Hummel" figurines are the original "Hungarian" figurines discovered in 1976 by a man in Vienna, Austria. He had acquired them from a lady in Budapest, who had purchased them at the weekly flea market—one at a time, over a six-month period. He in turn sold them to (this author) collector Robert L. Miller, a supermarket owner in Eaton, Ohio, as a gift for his wife, Ruth.

"M.I. Hummel" figurines have always been typically German, with German-style dress or costumes; in 1940 the W. Goebel company decided to produce a line of "M.I. Hummel" figurines in the national dress of other countries. Sister M.I. Hummel made many sketches of children in their native costumes. Master modelers Reinhold Unger and Arthur Moeller then turned the sketches into the adorable figurines you see on the following pages. Due to the events of World War II, pro-

duction of the International Figurines series was not started. After the discovery in 1976 of the "Hungarian" figurines, a thorough search of the factory was conducted, including the checking and rechecking of old records. Twenty-four prototypes were found and are pictured here. Most of the people involved in the original project are no longer living; therefore the information contained here may not be absolutely accurate or complete. Since 1976, several duplicates of some models and new variations of others have been found, usually selling in the $10,000 to $15,000 price range, depending on condition. Several models have also been found without the "M.I. Hummel" signature; these would have much less value to most collectors. Author/collector Miller says, "I feel certain that there are still more rare finds to be made in the future, maybe even some Russian models! Happy Hunting!"

The following eight "M.I. Hummel" figurines were purchased by Robert L. Miller for a little less than $500 total (not each) in 1976.

| HUM 809 | HUM 807 | HUM 854 | HUM 832 (A) |

HUM 904   HUM 806   HUM 841   HUM 851

Note: All International figurines were modeled by master sculptors Arthur Moeller or Reinhold Unger in 1940.

The following thirty International "M.I. Hummel" figurines are a combination of the Robert L. Miller Collection as well as the Goebel Archives Collection.

☐ *HUM 806 Bulgarian A. Moeller* ☐ *HUM 807 Bulgarian A. Moeller* ☐ *HUM 808 Bulgarian A. Moeller*

☐ *HUM 809 Bulgarian A. Moeller*

☐ *HUM 810(A) Bulgarian R. Unger*

☐ *HUM 810(B) Bulgarian R. Unger*

☐ *HUM 811 Bulgarian R. Unger*

☐ *HUM 812(A) Serbian R. Unger*

☐ *HUM 812(B) Serbian R. Unger*

☐ *HUM 813 Serbian R. Unger*

☐ *HUM 824(A) Swedish A. Moeller*

☐ *HUM 824(B) Swedish A. Moeller*

☐ *HUM 825(A) Swedish A. Moeller*

☐ *HUM 825(B) Swedish A. Moeller*

☐ *HUM 831 Slovak   R. Unger*

☐ *HUM 832(B) Slovak   R. Unger*

☐ *HUM 833 Slovak   R. Unger*

☐ *HUM 841   Czech R. Unger*

☐ *HUM 842(A)   Czech   R. Unger*

☐ *HUM 842(B)   Czech   R. Unger*

☐ *HUM 851 Hungarian A. Moeller*

☐ *HUM 852(A) Hungarian A. Moeller*   ☐ *HUM 852(B) Hungarian A. Moeller*   ☐ *HUM 853(A) Hungarian A. Moeller*

☐ *HUM 853(B) Hungarian A. Moeller*   ☐ *HUM 854 Hungarian A. Moeller*   ☐ *HUM 904   Serbian   R. Unger*

☐ *HUM 913   Serbian   R. Unger*   ☐ *HUM 947   Serbian   A. Moeller*   ☐ *HUM 968   Serbian   R. Unger*

433

HUM 834 ???
Little Fiddler "Slovak International"???

HUM 834   "Slovak"   ???   *HUM 904   Serbian   R. Unger, 1940*

A figurine was found in Eastern Europe several years ago, in a badly damaged condition. It had NO Goebel trademark, NO incised model number (only a paper sticker with 834 written in pencil), NO incised "M. I. Hummel" signature, but it did have the "appearance" of being genuine! Could this figurino possibly be an "International" design? It is now in a private collection in the United States; sorry, not mine!

A second figurine (photo above, left) fitting this same description has reportedly been found in Hungary, also with some damage. I have not examined this figurine in person, but according to Goebel factory records, they did indeed produce a "Little Fiddler" figurine with "Slovak" costume in 1940, but are not sure who the sculptor was! According to their product-book, the sculptor was Arthur Moeller. According to their sculpting diary, the sculptor was Reinhold Unger. Whether Moeller or Unger, it would seem safe to conclude that Goebel may have produced these two "Little Fiddler" figurines. The design is quite similar to HUM 904 Serbian "Little Fiddler" also pictured above for comparison.

Possibly, as time goes by, we may find some better examples; with the "M. I. Hummel" signature, with the Goebel "crown" trademark, and the incised model number 834. Until then—the search goes on!

434

HUM 1999 — Fanfare (CE)
First released in the U.S. market in the fall of 1998. This is the 14th and final figurine in the "Century Collection" and was produced for only this one year (1999) in the twentieth century. It was modeled by master sculptors Helmut Fischer and Marion Huschka in 1993. It has an incised 1993 copyright date. A circular inscription applied by blue decal reads: "M.I. Hummel 1999 XX FINAL EDITION–CENTURY COLLECTION" and the name "Fanfare" along with the (TM 7) trademark. Came with a hardwood base with brass plaque: "CENTURY COLLECTION 1999/LETZTE AUSGABE - FINAL EDITION." The official issue price was $1275 in 1999. The incised "M.I. Hummel" signature is perpendicular on the back of the figurine.

☐ 1999 ......11.00" ....(**CE**) ....❼ ....$1275—1300

HUM 2000 — Worldwide Wanderers (CE)
First released in the U.S. market in the fall of 1999 in a sequentially-numbered (LE) Limited Edition of 2000 pieces worldwide (plus 200 Artist Proofs). Modeled by master sculptors Helmut Fischer and Tamara Fuchs in 1998. It has an incised 1998 copyright date, a special "Year 2000 Millennium" backstamp along with the (TM 8) trademark. It comes with a black hardwood, velvet-covered base and a porcelain Certificate of Authenticity. The official issue price was $4500 in 1999.

☐ 2000 ....9.50 x 17.25 x 8.50"........(CE)   ..,❽.......$4500

HUM 2001 — (ON) OPEN NUMBER

HUM 2002 — Making New Friends
Modeled by master sculptor Helmut Fischer in 1996. First released in the U.S. market in the fall of 1996 with the (TM 7) trademark, incised 1996 copyright date, and a combination "First Issue 1996" and "125th Anniversary 1871 - 1996 Goebel" backstamp applied by blue decal on the bottom. The official issue price was $595 in 1996. The boy with sled is an "interpretation" of HUM 396 "Ride Into Christmas" figurine. Available midyear in 2006 in "10th Anniversary Edition" marking the Hummel's 10th anniversary, 1996-2006, with "10th Anniversary" backstamp and the (TM 8) trademark, priced $579.

☐ 2002....6.50 - 6.75"........(CE)...❼ ..$530—550
☐ 2002....6.50" ....(OE)...❽ ..$529—579

HUM 2003 — Dearly Beloved

First released in the U.S. market in 1998. Modeled by master sculptor Helmut Fischer in 1997. It has an incised 1997 copyright date along with the (TM 7) trademark. It comes with a black hardwood base and a brass plate for engraving name or message. A new work of art, approved by the Convent of Siessen, based upon an interpretation of Sister M.I. Hummel's original art. The official issue price was $450 in 1998. Released in Fall 2002 in a new small size with "First Issue 2003" backstamp, incised 2002 copyright date, and the (TM 8) trademark, for the original issue price of $200, packaged without a wooden base and brass plaque. Subsequently a wooden base and brass plaque have been made available for the 2003 2/0 size at an additional cost. The brass plaque may be engraved.

2003

□ 2003 ....6.50" ......(CE)....❼ ....$530—540
□ 2003 ....6.50" ......(OE) ..❽ $529
□ 2003 2/0 ..4.25" ......(OE) ..❽ $219

2003 2/0

HUM 2004 — Pretzel Girl

Modeled by master sculptor Helmut Fischer in 1996. First released in the U.S. market in the fall of 1998 with an incised 1996 copyright date along with the (TM 7) trademark and the "First Issue 1999" oval decal backstamp. Available in a Special Event Collector's Set with a FREE Oktoberfest Hummelscape (Mark #1000–D) at participating retailers. The official issue price was $185 for the set in 1998. "Pretzel Girl" is now listed as a (CE) Closed Edition in the U.S. market, but is still available in other markets worldwide.

**Pretzel Girl
Collector Set**

□ 2004 ....4.00" ......(CE)....❼ ....$185—200
□ 2004 ....4.00" ......(OE) ..❽ $185

HUM 2005–2006 — (ON) OPEN NUMBERS

HUM 2007 — Tender Love (CE)

First released in the U.S. market in the spring of 1998 for the Spring Open House event at participating retailers in the U.S. Modeled by master sculptor Helmut Fischer in 1996. It has an incised 1996 copyright date along with the (TM 7) trademark. Produced in a sequentially-numbered (LE) Limited Edition of 25,000 pieces worldwide (15,000 in the U.S.) The official issue price was $198 in 1998. Companion for HUM 2008 "Frisky Friends." Available with Kinderpark Hummelscape (Mark #921-D) wIth room on the Hummelscape also for HUM 2008 "Frisky Friends."

☐ 2007.......4.25".......(CE).....❼.....$198

HUM 2008 — Frisky Friends (CE)

First released in the U.S. market in the fall of 1997 for the "Fall Open House" event on 25 October 1997 at participating retailers. Modeled by master sculptor Helmut Fischer in 1996. It has an incised 1996 copyright date along with the (TM 7) trademark. Produced in a sequentially-numbered (LE) Limited Edition of 25,000 pieces worldwide (15,000 in the U.S.) The official issue price was $198 in 1997. Companion to HUM 2007 "Tender Love." Fits on Kinderpark Hummelscape (Mark #921-D) wilth HUM 2007 "Tender Love."

☐ 2008......4.25"......(CE)...❼...$198

HUM 2009–2010 — (ON) OPEN NUMBERS

HUM 2011 — Little Landscaper
Modeled by master sculptor Helmut Fischer in 1996. First released in the U.S. market in fall 2001 with incised 1996 copyright date, the (TM 8) trademark and "First Issue 2002" backstamp. Available in a collector set with a "Bountiful Garden" Hummelscape (Mark #1071-D), a $75 value. The original issue price of the collector set was $250 in 2002. The "Little Landscaper "with Hibiscus was released in January 2005 in a limited edition of 500 with numbered certificate as part of the "Caribbean Collection", distinguished by a load of red hibiscus flowers in the wheelbarrow, "Caribbean Collection" backstamp and "First Issue 2002" backstamp. The "Little Landscaper" with Bananas was released in January 2006 in a (LE) Limited Edition of 499 with numbered certificate as part of the "Caribbean Collection", distinguished by a load of yellow bananas in the wheelbarrow and the "Caribbean Collection" backstamp. A variation with an orange pumpkin in the wheelbarrow, a "Pumpkin Special Edition" backstamp, and new paint colors was released for Artist Events in Fall 2005, with the (TM 8) trademark and incised 1996 copyright date, priced $259. A ceramic display called "In the Garden" (Mark #1121-D) was free at Artist Events in Fall 2005 with purchase of "Little Landscaper with Pumpkin". The display for "Little Landscaper with Pumpkin" has a place for another Hummel, suggested to be HUM 74 "Little Gardener" – "Final Issue 2006" or HUM 2175/0 "From the Pumpkin Patch".

□ 2011........4.25" ....(OE) ....❽ $259

Bountiful Garden Collector Set

HUM 2012 — St. Nicholas' Day (CE)
First released in the U.S. market in the fall of 1997. Modeled by master sculptor Helmut Fischer in 1996. It has an incised 1996 copyright date along with the (TM 7) trademark. Produced in a sequentially numbered (LE) Limited Edition of 20,000 pieces worldwide (only 10,000 for the U.S.). A companion piece to HUM 473 "Ruprecht" (formerly "Father Christmas") also a (LE) Limited Edition of 20,000 pieces. The little child is based on HUM 476 "Winter Song." The official issue price was $650 in 1997, but was sold as a matching-numbered set with "Ruprecht" ($450 official issue price) for the combination price of $1000. The January 1, 2000 price list shows $1100 for the pair.

□ 2012 ......6.75" ....(CE) ....❼ ......$650—700

HUM 2013 — Surprise Visit

First released in the U.S. market in the summer of 2002 with a "First Issue 2003" oval decal. Modeled by master sculptor Helmut Fischer. It has an incised 2001 copyright date along with the (TM 8) trademark. Available in a collectors set with a musical "Bee Happy " Display that plays "In The Good Old Summer Time." The official issue price for the set was $225 in 2002. Figurine also available separately.

☐ 2013.......4.00".......(OE).....❽.....$219

*Surprise Visit
Collector Set*

HUM 2014 — Christmas Delivery

First released in the U.S. market in 1997. Modeled by master sculptor Helmut Fischer in 1996. It has an incised 1996 copyright date along with the (TM 7) trademark. A new work of art, approved by the Convent of Siessen based on an interpretation of HUM 424 "Sleep Tight" and HUM 396 "Ride Into Christmas." The official issue price was $485 in 1997. A new smaller size (4.25") was released in 2000. It has an incised 1997 copyright date along with (TM 8) trademark, plus the "First Issue Millennium 2000" oval decal during the first year of issue. The official issue price was $275 in 2000. Released in a new jumbo size in 2004, with First Issue 2004 backstamp, incised 2002 copyright date and the (TM 8) trademark, priced $1500 in 2004. In Spring 2004 a variation of the 2014 2/0 size in new colors became available, priced $279. The color changes are especially apparent in the girl's outfit, for example: from blue to orange hair bow, dark to light stockings, and from red/orange hat and scarf to blue/gray hat and scarf.

☐ 2014 2/0 ....4.25" ....(OE)......❽.....$279
☐ 2014/I ....5.75" ....(CE)......❼.....$530—550
☐ 2014/I ....5.75" ....(OE)...,..❽.....$529
☐ 2014/III ......8.50" ....(OE)......❽.....$1550

HUM 2015 — Wonder of Christmas (CE)

First released in the U.S. market in the fall of 1998. Modeled by master sculptor Helmut Fischer in 1996. It has an incised 1996 copyright date along with the (TM 7) trademark. Sold in a (LE) Limited Edition (20,000 pieces) Collectors Set with a FREE Limited Edition Steiff Teddy Bear with matching Porcelain Medallion.

The official issue price was $575 for the two-piece set in 1998. Figurine available in (TM 8) with a KWO backstamp in a collectors set with a KWO Smoker and a tiered wooden display stand.

☐ 2015 ....7.00" ....(**CE**)....**❼**.....$575
☐ 2015 ....7.00" ....(**CE**)....**❽**.....$575

HUM 2016–2017 — (ON) OPEN NUMBERS

HUM 2018 — Toyland Express

Modeled by master sculptor Helmut Fischer in 1998. A mixed media figurine with a wooden train pull toy. Companion to HUM 2019 "My Favorite Pony". First released in the U.S. market in 2002. The Special Event piece available during Special Toyland Events in Fall 2002, including a Beehive porcelain pin free while supplies lasted. The Special Event piece has an incised 1998 copyright date, the (TM 8) trademark, "First Issue 2002" backstamp, as well as "Toy Train" and "Special Event Figurine" backstamps. The original issue price was $225 in 2002. Figurine also available with "First Issue 2002" backstamp, without the Special Event markings, in the European market.

☐ 2018.......4.25"......(**OE**)....**❽**.....$219

HUM 2019 — My Favorite Pony aka Darling Duckling
Modeled by master sculptor Helmut Fischer in 1998. A mixed media figurine with a wooden pony pull toy. Companion to HUM 2018 "Toyland Express". First released in the U.S. market in the spring of 2002 as the Special Event piece available during special artist and salesmen events by participating retailers from 1 March - 30 June 2002. A Basket of Flowers porcelain pin was included free while supplies lasted. The Special Event piece has an incised 1998 copyright date, the (TM 8) trademark, "First Issue 2002" backstamp, as well as "Pony" and "Special Event Figurine" backstamps. The original issue price was $225 in 2002. Figurine also available with "First Issue 2002" backstamp, without the Special Event markings, in the European market. A variation called "Darling Duckling" became available in 2002 with a wooden duck pull toy in place of the wooden pony pull toy.

☐ 2019 ....4.25" ....(OE).... ❽ $219

HUM 2020 — Riding Lesson
First released in the U.S. market in the fall of 2000 with "First Issue 2001" oval backstamp. Modeled by master sculptor Helmut Fischer in 1996. It has an incised 1998 copyright date along with the (TM 8) trademark. The official issue price was $195 in 2000. Companion to HUM 2021 "Cowboy Corral".

☐ 2020.....4.50".......(OE).... ❽ $219

HUM 2021 — Cowboy Corral

First released in the U.S. market in the fall of 2000 with "First Issue 2001" oval backstamp. Modeled by master sculptor Helmut Fischer in 1996. It has an incised 1998 copyright date along with the (TM 8) trademark. The official issue price was $195 in 2000. Companion to HUM 2020 "Riding Lesson".

☐ 2021 ....4.25" ......(OE) .... ❽ $219

HUM 2022–2024 — (ON) OPEN NUMBERS

HUM 2025/A — Wishes Come True

First Edition of the "Wonder of Childhood" series, released in the spring of 2000 as an Exclusive Edition for members of the M.I. HUMMEL CLUB only and not sold as an (OE) Open Edition to the general public. Modeled by master sculptor Helmut Fischer in 1997. It has an incised 1997 copyright date along with the (TM 8) trademark and bears the "Club Exclusive" backstamp with "Exclusive Edition 2000/2001" decal. Comes with a wooden base with an engraved brass plaque. The official issue price was $695 in 2000, plus the member's redemption card.

GESUCHT, GEFUNDEN
WISHES COME TRUE

☐ 2025/A ....6.75" ......(CE) .... ❽ $695

Good Tidings

HUM 2026 — Good Tidings

First released in Fall of 2003 as part of collector set with "Tidings of Joy" Hummelscape. Scape is (LE) Limited Edition of 12,000 and features motion, light and music, playing "Jingle Bells" (Mark #1083-D). Figurine in set has (EE) Exclusive Edition and Christmas Tree backstamps, an incised 2003 copyright date, and the (TM 8) trademark, but no first issue marking. Set lists for $300 on 2006 Goebel NA Suggested Retail Price List. Figurine first appeared separately on Goebel NA Suggested Retail Price List in 2005, priced $199. Mixed media figurine – hand-painted wooden sled and packages. Companion to HUM 2047 "Winter Sleigh Ride". Figurine now available without special backstamps, with incised 2003 copyright date, and the (TM 8) trademark.

☐ 2026 ....4.25" ....(**OE**) ....**❽**........$199

Tidings of Joy Collector Set

HUM 2027 — Easter's Coming

First released in the U.S. market in the spring of 2002 for a preview period without a "First Issue" backstamp, with a "Joys of Spring" Hummelscape (Mark #1026-D) in a (LE) Limited Edition of 5000 worldwide. Official issue price was $230 for the set. A second "Easter Basket" Gift Set was issued priced at $240 retail with the same "Easter's Coming" figurine with a "First Issue 2001" backstamp. Figurine available separately. (TW) "Temporarily Withdrawn.

☐ 2027 ....4.00" ....(**TW**) ....**❽**........$219

Collectors Sets

HUM 2028 — Winter Adventure

First released in the U.S. market in the fall of 2000 with "First Issue 2001" oval backstamp. Modeled by master sculptor Helmut Fischer in 1996. It has an incised 1997 copyright date along with the (TM 8) trademark. Available in collectors set with a FREE "Slalom Slopes" Hummelscape, (Mark #1053-D), a $75 value. The official issue price was $225 in 2000 for the set.

☐ 2028.......4.75".......(**OE**).....❽.....$230

HUM 2029 — (ON) OPEN NUMBER

Slalom Slopes Collector Set

NYFD

HUM 2030 — Fire Fighter

First released in the U.S. market in the fall of 1999 with "First Issue 2000 MILLENIUM" oval decal backstamp. Modeled by master sculptor Helmut Fischer in 1997. It has an incised 1997 copyright date along with the (TM 8) trademark. Available in collectors set with FREE "To The Rescue" Hummelscape (Mark #1020-D), a $75 value. The official issue price was $205 in 1999 for the set. (TW) "Temporarily Withdrawn" in December 2005. Available in 2003 for $245 in a sequentially numbered (LE) Limited Edition of 7500 to commemorate the bravery of the New York Fire Department on 9/11. Commemorative edition features the figurine dressed in the yellow and black uniform of the NYFD and includes a round wooden base with the NYFD seal and white lettering "A Salute to Our American Heroes."

☐ 2030.......4.25".......(**TW**).....❽.....$205

Fire Fighter Collector Set

HUM 2031 — Catch of The Day

First released in the U.S. market in the fall of 2000 with "First Issue 2000 MILLENNIUM" backstamp. Part of the "Off to Work Series," was modeled by sculptor Helmut Fischer in 1997. It has an incised 1997 copyright date along with the (TM 8) trademark. Available in collectors set with a FREE "Fisherman's Feast" Hummelscape, (Mark #1029-D) a $100 value. The official issue price was $250 in 2000 for the set.

☐ 2031 ......4.25" ......(TW) ..❽ ..$205

Catch of the Day Collector Set

HUM 2032 — Puppy Pause

First released in the U.S. market as a "Special Limited Edition" for Walt Disney World in 2000, with a special decal on the bottom and a gold metal tag with: "A Goebel Celebration L.E. 140." Puppy Pause was released to retailers in early 2002 with a "First Issue 2001" backstamp, in error. These were recalled, but most had been sold. They were replaced with figurines with "First Issue 2002" backstamps. Has an incised 1997 copyright date along with the (TM 8) trademark. The official issue price was $195 in 2000. Companion to HUM 2033 "Kitty Kisses".

☐ 2032 ......4.25" ......(CE)....❽ ..$220—225
(Disney Decal)
☐ 2032 ......4.25" ......(CE)....❽ ..$220—225
(First Issue 2001)
☐ 2032 ......4.25" ......(CE)....❽ ..$219
(First Issue 2002)
☐ 2032 ......4.25" ......(OE)....❽ ..$219

HUM 2033 — Kitty Kisses
First released in the U.S. market in the fall of 2001 with "First Issue 2002" oval decal back-stamp. Modeled by master sculptor Marion Huschka in 1997. It has an incised 1997 copyright date along with the (TM 8) trademark. The official issue price was $195 in 2001. Companion to HUM 2032 "Puppy Pause".

☐ 2033 ....4.25" ....**(OE)** ....❽ ..$219

HUM 2034 — Good Luck Charm
First released in the U.S. market in the fall of 2001 with "First Issue 2002" oval decal back-stamp. Modeled by master sculptor Marion Huschka in 1998. It has an incised 1998 copyright date along with the (TM 8) trademark. The official issue price was $190 in 2001.

☐ 2034 ....4.50" ....**(OE)** ....❽ ..$179

Frosty Friends Collector Set

HUM 2035 — First Snow

Modeled by master sculptor Helmut Fischer in 1997. First released in the U.S. market in the Fall of 1999 with an incised 1997 copyright date, the (TM 7) trademark and "First Issue 1999" backstamp. Available in the "Frosty Friends" Collector Set with HUM 2036 "Let It Snow" and a (LE) Limited Edition white Steiff mohair Snowman. The collector set is a (LE) Limited Edition of 20,000 sets worldwide, with an original issue price of $598 in 1999. New small size was first made available with "Snowflake" backstamp in Fall of 2005 in European market in Winter Landscape: "Hummel Hill", with HUM 421 4/0 "It's Cold", HUM 2236 "Sleigh Ride", HUM 59 4/0 "Skier" and three Winter accessories (Winter Tree, Snowman and Birdhouse); the set representing "Winter in a Four Seasons" Collector Series. Available on the North American market from June 2006 as part of the "Wintertime Wonders" Series with an original issue price of $149. The figurine has incised 2005 copyright date, Snowflake backstamp, and the (TM 8) trademark, no first issue markings. Companion to HUM 2036 4/0 "Let It Snow".

- ☐ 2035 4/0 ....3.25" ....(OE) ....❽.....$149
- ☐ 2035 ....5.50" ....(CE) ....❼.....$360—370
- ☐ 2035 ....5.50" ....(OE) ....❽.....$359

HUM 2036 — Let It Snow

Modeled by master sculptor Helmut Fischer in 1997. First released in the U.S. market in the Fall of 1999 with an incised 1997 copyright date, the (TM 7) trademark and "First Issue 1999" backstamp. Available in the "Frosty Friends" Collector Set with HUM 2035 "First Snow" and a (LE) Limited Edition white Steiff mohair Snowman. The collector set is a (LE) Limited Edition of 20,000 sets worldwide, with an original issue price of $598 in 1999. New small size was introduced in July 2006, with "Snowflake" backstamp, the (TM 8) trademark and no first issue markings, with an original issue price of $139. The new small size is part of the "Wintertime Wonders" Series and companion to HUM 2035 4/0 "First Snow".

- ☐ 2036 4/0.....3.50".....(OE).....❽.....$139
- ☐ 2036...........5.00".....(CE).....❼.....$280
- ☐ 2036...........5.00".....(OE).....❽.....$259

HUM 2037 — Star Light, Star Bright

First released in 2005, with original issue price of $305 and First Issue 2005 backstamp. Has removable leash and metal tag, suitable for engraving. Mixed media piece. Has incised 1998 copyright date and the (TM 8) trademark. There are snowballs at the girl's feet. A suitable companion for HUM 2185 "Winter's Here".

☐ 2037...5.25"....(OE)....❽...$305

HUM 2038 — In The Kitchen

Modeled by master sculptor Helmut Fischer in 1997. First released in the U.S. market in the fall of 1999 with an incised 1998 copyright date along with the (TM 8) trademark and the "First Issue 2000 MILLENNIUM" oval decal bookstamp. Available in a collectors set with a FREE "Kozy Kitchen" Hummelscape (Mark #1009–D), a $75 value. The official issue price was $250 in 1999 for the set. (TW) Temporarily Withdrawn" in December 2004.

☐ 2038 ......4.50"........(CE)..❼ ..$205—210
☐ 2038 ......4.50"........(**TW**) ❽ ..$205

*In The Kitchen
Collector Set*

HUM 2039 — Halt!

Modeled by master sculptor Helmut Fischer in 1997. First released in the U.S. market in the fall of 1999 with "First Issue 2002 MILLENNIUM" oval decal backstamp and incised 1998 copyright date along with the (TM 8) trademark. Available in collectors set with a FREE "Duck Crossing" HummelScape (Mark #1028-D), a $75 value. The official issue price was $250 in 1999 for the set. (TW) Temporarily Withdrawn" in December 2004.

Halt Collector Set

Available in 2003 for $245 in a sequentially numbered (LE) Limited Edition of 5000 to commemorate the bravery of the New York Police Department on 9/11. Commemorative edition features the figurine dressed in the blue uniform of the NYPD with the NYPD seal on the paper he holds and includes a round wooden base with white lettering "A Salute to Our American Heroes."

☐ 2039 ....4.75" ....(TW)....... ❽ $205

HUM 2040 — One Coat or Two?

Modeled by master sculptor Helmut Fischer in 1998. First released in the U.S. market in the fall of 1999 with "First Issue 2000 MILLENNIUM" oval decal backstamp. It has an incised 1998 copyright date along with the (TM 8) trademark. Available in a collectors set with a FREE "Painting Pals" Hummelscape (Mark #1019–D), a $75 value. The official issue price was $250 in 1999 for the set. (TW) Temporarily Withdrawn" in December 2004.

One Coat or Two Collector Set

☐ 2040.......4.50".......(TW).....❽.....$205

HUM 2041–2043 — (ON) OPEN NUMBERS

HUM 2044 — All Aboard

First released in the U.S. market in the fall of 2000 with "First Issue 2001" oval decal backstamp. Modeled by master sculptor Helmut Fischer in 1996. It has an incised 1997 copyright date along with the (TM 8) trademark. Available in collectors set with "To The Rescue" Hummelscape (Mark #1020-D), a $75 value. The official issue price was $250 in 1999 for the set. (TW) "Temporarily Withdrawn".

☐ 2044.....5.00".....**(TW)**..... ❽....$205—210

HUM 2045–2046 — (ON) OPEN NUMBERS

HUM 2047 — Winter Sleigh Ride

First released in Fall of 2002 as part of collector set with "Home for the Holidays" Hummelscape. Scape is a (LE) Limited Edition of 12,000 and features light and music, playing, "It Came Upon A Midnight Clear" (Mark #1075-D). Suggested retail price for the set was $310 in 2004. Figurine in set has (EE) Exclusive Edition backstamp, incised 1998 copyright date, and the (TM 8) trademark, but no first issue marking. Mixed media figurine – wooden sled and twine rope. Figurine available from Europe with addition of hand-painted wooden packages on sled, without Exclusive Edition backstamp. Companion to HUM 2026 2/0 "Good Tidings".

☐ 2047.......4.00".....**(OE)**..... ❽.....$225

*All Aboard
Collectors Set*

*Home for the Holidays
Collector Set*

*Hand-painted
Wooden Packages*

Exclusive Edition Backstamp

HUM 2048 — Little Patriot

Second in the "Ambassadors of Freedom" series issued for the U.S. Military only in a (LE) Limited Edition of 3000 pieces, released in the fall of 2002. The military price was $228 plus ($6) shipping, the same price as HUM 802 "Brave Soldier" (first in the series) and approximately the same size.

☐ 2048/II....8.00"....(LE)....❽....$500—550

HUM 2049/A — Cuddles
aka Spirit of Liberty

Modeled by master sculptor Helmut Fischer in 1997. First released in the U.S. market in the fall of 1998 with an incised 1997 copyright date along with the (TM 7) trademark and the "First Issue 1998" oval decal backstamp. The official issue price was $80 in 1998. In 2000 an ornament (2049/A/0) was added to the line. It was available only in the U.S. market. The official issue price was $80 in 2000. Available in variation called "Spirit of Liberty", with girl's teddy bear holding an American flag. "Spirit of Liberty" has incised 1997 copyright date, the (TM 8) trademark, and Special Edition and US flag backstamps, and was priced $59.50 in 2004. Figurine stands 3.5", 5.25" tall with flag. Sculpted by master sculptor Helmut Fischer.

☐ 2049/A/0 ..3.00" ....(OE)..❽....$69.50
☐ 2049/A......3.50" ....(CE)..❼....$70—75
☐ 2049/A......3.50" ....(OE)..❽....$69.50

HUM 2049/B — My Best Friend

Modeled by master sculptor Helmut Fischer in 1997. First released in the U.S. market in the fall of 1998 with an incised 1997 copyright date along with the (TM 7) trademark and the "First Issue 1998" oval decal backstamp. The official issue price was $80 in 1998. Introduced as a 3" ornament in 2004 with original issue price $59.50, part of the "Tree Trimmers Ornament" Series.

☐ 2049/B....3.00" ....(TW) ....❽ $69.50
☐ 2049/B....3.50" ....(CE)......❼ ......$70—75
☐ 2049/B....3.50" ....(**OE**)......❽ $69.50

HUM 2050/A — Messages of Love

Modeled by master sculptor Helmut Fischer in 1999. First released in the U.S. Market in the spring of 1999 with incised 1997 copyright date, the (TM 7) trademark, and "First Issue 1999" backstamp. The original issue price was $85 in 1999. This figurine was used as a promotional piece for "Miller's Hummel Expo '99" with a black bumblebee on her letter and "Miller's Expo '99" on the side of the base. The Miller's Expo figurine is distinguished by the girl's outfit: a dusky orange dress, blue apron, and dark gray socks. This is the same outfit worn by the "Messages of Love" figurine found in the "Swiss" Collection, in a (LE) Limited Edition of 1200 with a decorated base to elevate the figurine. Note: The regular production "Messages of Love" wears a very different outfit: a blue dress, rosy pink apron and cream colored socks.

Miller's Expo

☐ 2050/A....3.50" ....(CE)......❼ ......$70—75
☐ 2050/A....3.50" ....(**OE**)......❽ $69.50

453

HUM 2050/B — Be Mine

Modeled by master sculptor Helmut Fischer in 1997. First released in the U.S. market in the spring of 1999 with an incised 1997 copyright date along with the (TM 7) trademark and "First Issue 1999" oval decal backstamp. The official issue price was $85 in 1999. Found in the Swiss Collection in a (LE) Limited Edition of 1200 with a decorated base to elevate the figurine.

☐ 2050/B....3.50" ....(CE)......❼ ......$70—75
☐ 2050/B....3.50" ....(**OE**)......❽ $69.50

Swiss Collection

HUM 2051/A — Once Upon A Time

Modeled by master sculptor Helmut Fischer in 1997. First released in the U.S. market in June of 1998 with an incised 1997 copyright date along with the (TM 7) trademark and the "First Issue 1998" oval decal backstamp. This figurine was used as a promotional piece for "Miller's EXPO '98" with a black bumblebee on the book (200 pieces only). The official issue price was $80 in 1998.

☐ 2051/A ....3.50" ....(CE)....❼ ....$70—75
☐ 2051/A ....3.50" ....(**OE**)....❽ $69.50

HUM 2051/B — Let's Play
Modeled by master sculptor Helmut Fischer in 1997. First released in the U.S. market in the fall of 1998 with an incised 1997 copyright date along with the (TM 7) trademark and the "First Issue 1998" oval decal backstamp. The official issue price was $80 in 1998.

□ 2051/B........3.50"..........(CE)....❼ ....$70—75
□ 2051/B........3.50"..........(**OE**)....❽ $69.50

HUM 2052 — Pigtails
First released in the U.S. market in 1999 as a FREE gift for renewing membership in the M.I. HUMMEL CLUB for 1999/00 club year. Modeled by master sculptor Helmut Fischer in 1998. It has an incised 1998 copyright date. It bears the inscription: "M.I. HUMMEL CLUB Membership Year 1999/2000" in addition to a black bumblebee in a half circle. It is a companion piece to HUM 2071 "Lucky Charmer."

□ 2052 ....3.25"..........(**CE**)....❼ ....$90—100

*Autumn
Frolic
Collector
Set*

HUM 2053 — Playful Pals
First released in the U.S. market in the fall of 1998. Modeled by master sculptor Helmut Fischer in 1997. It has an incised 1997 copyright date along with the (TM 7) trademark. It has <u>NO</u> "First Issue" backstamp. Produced in a sequentially numbered (LE) Limited Edition of 25,000 pieces worldwide. Available with FREE Hummelscape: "Autumn Frolic" (Mark #1001–D).

☐ 2053....3.50"....**(CE)**......❼.......$198—210

HUM 2054–2057 — (ON) OPEN NUMBERS

HUM 2058/A — Skating Lesson
First released in the U.S. market in the fall of 1999 with "First Issue 2000 MILLENNIUM" backstamp. Modeled by master sculptor Helmut Fischer in 1998. It has a decal 1998 copyright date along with the (TM 8) trademark. Available with HUM 2058/B "Skate in Stride" in collectors set with "Icy Adventure" Hummelscape (Mark #1039-D), a $100 value. The official issue price was $375 for the set in 1999.

☐ 2058/A....3.25"...**(OE)**....❽....$149

*Icy Adventure
Collector Set*

HUM 2058/B — Skate In Stride

First released in the U.S. market in the fall of 1999 with "First Issue 2000 MILLEN-NIUM" backstamp. Modeled by master sculptor Helmut Fischer in 1998. It has an incised 1998 copyright date along with the (TM 8) trademark. The companion piece to HUM 2058/A "Skating Lesson". Available with HUM 2058/A "Skating Lesson" in collectors set with "Icy Adventure" Hummelscape (Mark #1039-D).

□ 2058/B ....3.00"..........(**OE**) .... **❽**....$149

Icy Adventure
Collector Set

HUM 2059 — Merry Wandress

First released in Fall of 2004 with an original issue price of $180. A companion to HUM 11 2/0 "Merry Wanderer". Available in the North American market with "North American Limited Edition" backstamp, "First Issue 2005" backstamp, and incised 2004 copyright date. Size of (LE) Limited Edition undisclosed, not sequentially numbered. Available from Europe with "First Issue 2005" backstamp and incised 2004 copyright date. Available in sequentially numbered (LE) Limited Edition of 200 in 2004 with "Sea World" markings.

□ 2059 ....4.25" ......(**OE**) .. **❽** ..$180

First Issue

North American
Limited Edition

HUM 2060 — European Wanderer

This three-piece set was first released in the U.S. market in 1999. Modeled by master sculptors Helmut Fischer and Tamara Fuchs in 1998. It has an incised 1998 copyright date along with the (TM 8) trademark and the "First Issue 2000 MILLENNIUM" oval decal backstamp. Comes with a creamic globe and a hardwood base. The official issue price was $250 in 1999.

☐ 2060 ....4.25" ......**(TW)**...❽...$250—275

HUM 2061 — American Wanderer

This three-piece set was first released in the U.S. market in 1999. Modeled by master sculptors Helmut Fischer and Tamara Fuchs in 1998. It has an incised 1998 copyright date along with the (TM 8) trademark and "First Issue 2000 MILLENNIUM" oval decal backstamp. Comes with a ceramic globe and a hardwood base. The official issue price was $250 in 1999.

☐ 2061 ....5.00" ......**(TW)**...❽...$250—275

HUM 2062 — African Wanderer

This three-piece set was first released in the U.S. market in 1999. Modeled by master sculptors Helmut Fischer and Tamara Fuchs in 1998. It has an incised 1998 copyright date along with the (TM 8) trademark and "First Issue 2000 MILLENNIUM" oval decal backstamp. Comes with a ceramic globe and a hardwood base. The official issue price was $250 in 1999.

☐ 2062 ....4.25" ....**(TW)**...❽...$250—275

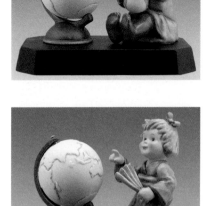

HUM 2063 — Asian Wanderer

This three-piece set was first released in the U.S. market in 1999. Modeled by master sculptors Helmut Fischer and Tamara Fuchs in 1998. It has an incised 1998 copyright date along with the (TM 8) trademark and "First Issue 2000 MILLENNIUM" oval decal backstamp. Comes with a ceramic globe and a hardwood base. The official issue price was $250 in 1999.

☐ 2063 ....4.50" ....**(TW)**...❽...$250—275

HUM 2064 — Australian Wanderer

This three-piece set was first released in the U.S. market in 1999. Modeled by master sculptors Helmut Fischer and Tamara Fuchs in 1998. It has an incised 1998 copyright date along with the (TM 8) trademark and "First Issue 2000 MILLENNIUM" oval decal backstamp. Comes with a ceramic globe and a hardwood base. The official issue price was $250 in 1999.

□ 2064 ....4.50" ....(TW)...❽...$250—275

The Wanderers (LE)

Released in the fall of 1999, this set includes five figurines representing the continents on a tiered wooden display surrounding a German, full-lead crystal globe. (LE) Limited Edition of 2000 sets created exclusively for North America. The official issue price was $1250 in 1999. Measures 8.50" H x 10.75" L x 9.50" W. Other versions on the same theme were created for other markets.

HUM 2065 — (ON) OPEN NUMBER

North American Version

HUM 2066 — Peaceful Offering

First released in the U.S. market in the spring of 1999. Modeled by master sculptor Helmut Fischer in 1998. It has an incised 1998 copyright date along with the (TM 7) trademark. It has NO "First Issue" backstamp. Produced in a sequentially numbered (LE) Limited Edition of 25,000 pieces worldwide. Came with FREE Collector's Set Hummelscape: "Friendship in Bloom" (Mark #1004–D).

□ 2066 ....6.00" ....(CE) ....❼ ..$200—225

Peaceful
Offering
Collector
Set

HUM 2067/A — Sweet Treats
aka Sweet Freedom

Both figurines and ornament were released in the fall of 1999. Modeled by master sculptor Helmut Fischer in 1998. The ornament has a stamped trademark and 1998 copyright date stamped on the feet and a small brass hook on the head for hanging as an ornament. The original issue price was $75 or FREE with $150 purchase of M.I. Hummel products by members of the "M.I. Hummel Club" with redemption card. "Sweet

2067/A   *2067/A/O*

Treats" figurine has an incised 1998 copyright date and (TM 8) trademark. The original issue price was $90. A "Holiday Baking Set Cookie Press" that formed a bumble bee cookie sold for $99. The ornament was only available in the U.S. market. Variation called "Sweet Freedom" was released in June 2004, with girl holding an American Flag. "Sweet Freedom" has the (TM 8) trademark, and Special Edition and US flag backstamps, and was priced $59.50 in 2004. Sculpted by master sculptor Helmut Fischer and Tamara Fuchs.

Gingerbread Lane Collector Set

☐ 2067/A	......3.25"	......(OE)	....❽	....$69.50
☐ 2067/A/O	..3.00"	......(CE)	....❼	....$70—75
☐ 2067/A/O	..3.00"	......(OE)	....❽	....$69.50

HUM 2067/B — For Me

First released in the U.S. market in the fall of 1999. Modeled by master sculptor Helmut Fischer in 1998. Has an incised 1998 copyright date along with (TM 8) trademark an a "First Issue 2000 MILLENNIUM" oval decal. The original issue price was $90 in 1999. The ornament was only available in the U.S. Has a stamped 1998 copyright date and signature applied by decal on the bottom of the feet. A "Gingerbread Lane" Hummelscape Collector's Set, Mark #1040-D with both 2067/A and 2067/B sold for $240.

2067/B   *2067/B/O*

☐ 2067/B	......3.50"	......(OE)	....❽	....$69.50
☐2067/B/O	..3.00"	......(OE)	....❽	....$69.50

HUM 2068/A — Bumblebee Blossom

First released in 2003 with original issue price of $59.50 and "First Issue 2004" backstamp. Has incised 1999 copyright date and the (TM 8) trademark. A bumblebee sits on her hand. Available in (LE) Limited Edition of 500 with "Caribbean Collection" backstamp and matching decorated ceramic base to elevate the figurine. Available in (LE) Limited Edition of 600 with "Swiss Collection" backstamp and matching decorated ceramic base to elevate the figurine. Part of "Create-A-Gift" collection when paired with a Sentiment Occasion base.

☐ 2068/A ......3.25" ......(**OE**)....❽ $69.50

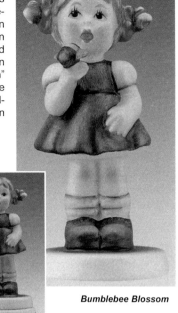

Bumblebee Blossom

Swiss Collection

HUM 2068/B — A Four Leaf Clover
aka Pledge to America

First released in 2003 with original issue price of $100 and "First Issue 2003" backstamp. Shortly thereafter, when incorporating A Four Leaf Clover into the "Create-A-Gift" Collection, Goebel reduced the suggested retail price to $59.50. Part of "Create-A-Gift" collection when paired with a Sentiment Occasion base. Has incised 1999 copyright date and the (TM 8) trademark. He holds a four leaf clover. Available in (LE) Limited Edition of 600 with *Pledge to America* "Swiss" Collection backstamp and matching decorated ceramic base to elevate the figurine. Available in variation called "Pledge to America", with boy holding an American Flag in place of his four leaf clover. "Pledge to America" has incised 1999 copyright date, the (TM 8) trademark, and "Special Edition" and "US flag" backstamps, and was priced $59.50 when it was released in June 2004. Sculpted by master sculptor Helmut Fischer.

☐ 2068/B ......3.50" ......(**OE**)....❽ $69.50

A Four Leaf Clover

Freedom Day

HUM 2069/A —
Monkey Business
aka Freedom Day
First released in 2003 with original issue price of $59.50 and "First Issue 2003" backstamp. Part of "Create-A-Gift" collection when paired with a Sentiment Occasion base. Has incised copyright date and the (TM 8) trademark. She holds a toy monkey. Available in variation called "Freedom Day", with American Flag in the hand of her toy monkey. "Freedom Day" has incised 1998 copyright date, the (TM 8) trademark, and "Special Edition" and "US flag" backstamps. "Freedom Day" was released in January 2005, priced $69.50. Sculpted by master sculptor Helmut Fischer.

Monkey Business

☐ 2069/A ......3.50" ......(OE).... ❽ $69.50

HUM 2070 —
Scooter Time (CE)
Second Edition in the "Wonder of Childhood" series. Members' Exclusive for year 25 of the M.I. Hummel Club. Modeled by master sculptor Helmut Fischer in 1999. It has an incised 2000 copyright date along with the (TM 8) trademark. Comes with a wooden base and an engraved brass plaque It has a M.I. Hummel Club Exclusive Edition 2001-2002 "Wonder of Childhood" backstamp. The original issue price was $695 in 2000.

☐ 2070 ....6.75" ....(CE) .. ❽ ....$695—750

HUM 2071 — Lucky Charmer (CE)
First released in the U.S. market in 1999 as a
companion piece to HUM 2052 "Pigtails." Formerly called a "Preview Edition" for Club
members only and not available from Goebel
to the general public. Modeled by master
sculptor Helmut Fischer in 1999. It has an
incised 1998 copyright date. It bears the
inscription: "M.I. HUMMEL CLUB Membership
Year 1999/2000" in addition to a black bumblebee in a half circle. The official issue price
was $90 in 1999 with redemption card. It was
retired as of 31 May 2000.

☐ 2071 ....3.50" ....(CE).... ❼....$90—100

HUM 2072 — Winter Days
First released in 2004 with an original issue
price of $550 and "First Issue 2004" back-
stamp. Price on Goebel NA Suggested Retail
Price List was $529 in 2005. Has incised
1999 copyright date and the (TM 8) trademark. Companion to HUM 396/I "Ride Into
Christmas" and HUM 2014/I "Christmas Delivery". Resembles HUM 2236 "Sleigh Ride".
Available in collector set with "Winter
Days" Base with Fenton Glass Evergreens (Mark #1105-D), marking the
"100th Anniversary" of Fenton. Light
glows from within the evergreens. Price
for the set on Goebel NA Suggested
Retail Price List was $599 in 2005.

☐ 2072 ....6.25" ....(OE) .. ❽ $529

Winter Days

Winter Days Collector Set with
Fenton Glass Evergreens

463

HUM 2073/A — Ring In The Season
First released in the U.S. market in mid 2001 with "First Issue 2001" backstamp. Modeled by master sculptor Helmut Fischer in 1999. It has an incised 2000 copyright date along with the (TM 8) trademark. The original issue price was $140 in 2001. Introduced as an 3.50" ornament in Fall 2005 with the (TM 8) trademark, original issue price $69.50, part of the "Tree Trimmers Ornament" Series. The "Ring in the Season" ornament is wearing clothes and accessories in different colors from the colors used on the figurine.

☐ 2073/A/O ....3.50".......(**OE**).... ❽....$69.50
☐ 2073/A ....4.00" ....(**OE**).... ❽....$139

HUM 2073/B — Christmas Carol
First released in the U.S. market in mid 2001 with "First Issue 2001" backstamp. Modeled by master sculptor Helmut Fischer in 1999. It has an incised 2000 copyright date along with the (TM 8) trademark. The original issue price was $140 in 2001.

☐ 2073/B ....4.00" ....(**OE**).... ❽....$139

**HUM 2074 — Christmas Gift
aka A Salute To The U.S.A.**
First released in the U.S. market in
1998 as a FREE ornament with the
purchase of $150 or more of M.I.
Hummel merchandise between 1
November and 31 December 1998
at participating retailers or while
supplies last. Released as a figurine with normal base in early
1999. Modeled by master sculptor
Helmut Fischer in 1998. It has an
incised 1998 copyright date along
with the (TM 7) trademark. It has
NO "First Issue" backstamp. The
official issue price was $90 in 1999.
HUM 2074 "Christmas Gift" is available in variation called "A Salute to
the U.S.A.", with boy's teddy bear

holding an American flag. The figurine stands 3.50",
5.25" with flag. "A Salute to the U.S.A." has incised
1998 copyright date, the (TM 8) trademark, and
"Special Edition" and "US flag" backstamps, priced
$69.50 in 2006. Sculpted by master sculptor Hel-
mut Fischer.

☐ 2074/A/O..3.25" ....(CE)....❼....$69.50
☐ 2074/A ....3.50" ....(CE)....❼....$70—75
☐ 2074/A ....3.50" ....(**OE**)....❽....$69.50

Comfort and Care Collector Set

HUM 2075 — Comfort And Care
First released in the U.S. market in the fall of 1999
with "First Issue 2000 MILLENNIUM" backstamp.
Modeled by master sculptor Helmut Fischer in
1998. It has an incised 1998 copyright date along
with the (TM 8) trademark. Available in a collectors
set with a FREE "Healing Hands" Hummelscape
(Mark #1027-D). The official price of the collector
set was $250 in 1999. (TW) "Temporarily With-
drawn" in December 2004.

☐ 2075 ....4.25" ......(**TW**)....❽....$205

HUM 2076 — (ON) OPEN NUMBER

465

2077/A   **2077/A/O**

HUM 2077/A — First Bloom
aka Miss Patriot

Released in the U.S. Market in the Fall of 1999 with the "First Issue 2000 MILLENNIUM" backstamp for the original issue price of $85. Modeled by master sculptor Helmut Fischer in 1998. Has incised 1999 copyright date along with the (TM 8) trademark. The matching Christmas ornament, numbered 2077/A/O, has the Hummel number, M.I. Hummel signature, and 1998 copyright date applied by decal to the bottom of the feet. The original issue price was $80 in 1999. HUM 2077/A "First Bloom" was released in November 2003 in a variation called "Miss Patriot", with the girl holding an American Flag in place of her flower. The "Miss Patriot" figurine stands 3.25", 5.75" tall with flag. "Miss Patrio"t has incised 1999 copyright date, the (TM 8) trademark, and "Special Edition" and "US flag" backstamps, and was priced $69.50 in 2006. Sculpted by master sculptors Helmut Fischer and Tamara Fuchs.

☐ 2077/A ....3.25"..........(**OE**)........❽......$69.50
☐ 2077/A/O ....3.00"..........(**OE**)........❽......$69.50

2077/B   **2077/B/O**

HUM 2077/B — A Flower For You
aka Flag Day

Released in the U.S. Market in the Fall of 1999 with the First Issue 2000 MILLENNIUM backstamp for the original issue price of $85. Modeled by master sculptor Helmut Fischer in 1998. Has incised 1999 copyright date along with the (TM 8) trademark. The matching Christmas ornament, numbered 2077/B/O, has the Hummel number, M.I. Hummel signature, and 1998 copyright date applied by decal to the bottom of the feet. The original issue price was $80 in 1999. HUM 2077/B "A Flower for You" was released in June 2004 in a variation called "Flag Day", with the boy holding an American Flag in place of his flower. The "Flag Day" figurine stands 3.25", 6.00" tall with flag. "Flag Day" has incised 1999 copyright date, the (TM 8) trademark, and "Special Edition" and "US flag" backstamps, and was priced $59.50 in 2004. Sculpted by master sculptor Helmut Fischer.

☐ 2077/B ....3.25"..........(**OE**) ....❽.....$69.50
☐ 2077/B/O ....3.00"..........(**OE**) ....❽.....$69.50

HUM 2078 — My Toy Train

First released in 2003 with an original issue price of $59.50 and "First Issue 2003" backstamp. Part of "Create-A-Gift" Collection when paired with a Sentiment Occasion base. Has incised 1999 copyright date and the (TM 8) trademark. The boy holds a black train locomotive.

☐ 2078 ....3.50" ......(OE)....❽ $69.50

*Shown with
Happy Father's
Day Sentiment
Occasion base*

My Toy Train

HUM 2079 — All By Myself (2079/A)
Windy Wishes (2079/B)

Both figurines were first released in the fall of 2002 with "First Issue 2003" backstamp. Modeled by master sculptor Helmut Fischer in 1999. They both have an incised 2000 copyright date along with the (TM 8) trademark. The original issue price was $140 each in 2002. HUM 2079/A "All By Myself" is available in a collector set with Cape Hatteras Lighthouse Hummelscape (Mark #1079-D), featuring light from the lighthouse: set priced $175 in 2003.

☐ 2079/A ....3.75" ......(OE)....❽......$140
☐ 2079/B ....4.00" ......(OE)....❽......$140

HUM 2080–2083 — (ON) OPEN NUMBERS

Jump For Joy

HUM 2084/A — Jump For Joy

First released in Fall of 2004 with an original issue price of $305 and "First Issue 2005" backstamp. Has 2001 incised copyright date and (TM 8) trademark.

Jump for Joy with Decorated Base

Sculpted by master sculptor Helmut Fischer. The first 2500 released in the North American market in Fall 2004 have Goebel artist signature, "First Issue 2005" backstamp, 2001 incised copyright date and (TM 8) trademark, and a display base decorated with teddy bears, priced $305. In October 2004 a (LE) Limited Edition of 100 Arbeitsmuster Editions were made available in North America to M.I. Hummel Club members. These painters' samples bear a crimped metal Arbeitsmuster Series tag, are signed by master sample painter Frank Knoch, and have a certificate of authenticity signed by Frank Knoch. The Arbeitsmuster Edition has an incised 2001 copyright date, "First Issue 2005" backstamp, and the (TM 8) trademark, and was priced $305 in 2004.

☐ 2084/A........5.25" ......(OE)....❽ $305

HUM 2084/B — Count Me In

First released in Fall of 2004 with an original issue price of $305 and "First Issue 2005" backstamp. Has 2001 incised copyright date and (TM 8) trademark. Sculpted by master sculptor Helmut Fischer. The

Count Me In with Decorated Base

first 2500 released in the North American market in Fall 2004 have Goebel artist signature, "First Issue 2005" backstamp, 2001 incised copyright date and (TM 8) trademark, and a display base decorated with train locomotives, priced $305. In October 2004 a (LE) Limited Edition of 100 Arbeitsmuster Editions were made available in North America to M.I. Hummel Club members. These painters' samples bear a crimped metal Arbeitsmuster Series tag, are signed by master sample painter Frank Knoch, and have a certificate of authenticity signed by Frank Knoch. The Arbeitsmuster Edition has an incised 2001 copyright date, "First Issue 2005" backstamp, and the (TM 8) trademark, and was priced $305 in 2004.

Count Me In

☐ 2084/B........5.25" ......(OE)....❽ $305

HUM 2085 — Little Farm Hand (CE)

First released in the U.S. market in the fall of 1999. Modeled by master sculptor Helmut Fischer in 1999. It has an incised 1999 copyright date along with the (TM 8) trademark. It has <u>NO</u> "First Issue" backstamp. Produced in a sequentially numbered (LE) Limited Edition of 25,000 pieces worldwide. Available in a collectors set with a FREE "Millennium Harvest" Hummelscape (Mark #1013-D), a $75 value. The official issue price of the collectors set was $198 in 1999. Companion piece to HUM 2086 "Spring Sowing".

☐ 2085.......4.50".....(**CE**)..... ❽.....$225—250

Millennium Harvest Collector Set

Spring Sowing Collector Set

HUM 2086 — Spring Sowing

First released in the U.S. market in the spring of 2000. Modeled by master sculptor Helmut Fischer in 1999. It has an incised 1999 copyright date along with the (TM 8) trademark. Produced in a sequentially numbered (LE) Limited Edition of 25,000 pieces worldwide. Available in a collectors set with a FREE "Seeds of Friendship" Hummelscape (Mark #1014–D), a $75 value. The official issue price of the collectors set was $198 in 2000. Companion piece to HUM 2085 "Millennium Harvest" (Little Farm Hand).

☐ 2086.......3.50".....(**CE**).....❽.....$198—200

HUM 2087/A — Sharpest Student

First released in the U.S. market in the spring of 2000 as an Exclusive Edition for members of the M.I. Hummel Club only and not sold as an (OE) Open Edition to the general public. Modeled by master sculptor Helmut Fischer in 1999. It has as incised 1999 copyright date along with the (TM 8) trademark and bears the Club exclusive backstamp. The official issue price was $95 in 2000, plus the members redemption card.

☐ 2087/A ....4.00" ....(CE) ...... ❽ ....$95—100

HUM 2087/B — Honor Student

First released in the U.S. market in the spring of 2000 as a FREE gift for renewing membership in the M.I. HUMMEL Club for the 2000/01 club year. Modeled by master sculptor Helmut Fischer in 1999. It has an incised 1999 copyright date along with the (TM 8) trademark and bears the "Club Exclusive" backstamp. Available in the "Back to School" Collectors Set, with an original issue price of $115 for the set when made available midyear in 2006. This represents an instance of a club (EE) Exclusive Edition figurine now offered for sale on the primary market to the general public as an (OE) Open Edition.

☐ 2087/B ....3.75" ....(CE) ...... ❽ ....$85—100

HUM 2088/A — Playing Around

Third in "Clowning Around" Series with HUM 2088/B "Rolling Around", HUM 2089/A "Looking Around", and HUM 2089/B "Waiting Around". Has decal 1999 copyright date, the (TM 8) trademark, and the "Club Exclusive" backstamp, (EE) Exclusive Edition 2003-2004. Marking Club Year 27. First released in Spring of 2003 with an original issue price of $230 as an (EE) Exclusive Edition for the 2003/2004 Club year, for members of the M.I. Hummel Club. Then made available for sale by authorized Hummel dealers to the general public in 2006. Available in a set with a wooden base and HUM 2088/B "Rolling Around", and HUM 2089/A "Looking Around" (no Waiting Around, HUM 2089/B).

☐ 2088/A Club Year 27...4.00"...(EE)... ❽ ...$230

HUM 2088/B — Rolling Around

Second in "Clowning Around" Series with HUM 2088/A "Playing Around", HUM 2089/A "Looking Around", and HUM 2089/B "Waiting Around". Has incised 1999 copyright date, the (TM 8) trademark, and the "Club Exclusive" backstamp, (EE) Exclusive Edition 2002-2003. Marking Club Year 26. First released in Spring of 2002 with an original issue price of $230 as an (EE) Exclusive Edition for the 2002/2003 Club year, for members of the M.I. Hummel Club. Then made available for sale by authorized Hummel dealers to the general public in 2006. Available in a set with a wooden base and HUM 2088/A "Playing Around", and HUM 2089/A "Looking Around" (no Waiting Around, HUM 2089/B).

☐ 2088/B Club Year 26......3.25"...(**EE**)..❽..$230

HUM 2089/A — Looking Around

First in "Clowning Around" Series with HUM 2088/A "Playing Around", HUM 2088/B "Rolling Around", and HUM 2089/B "Waiting Around". Has incised 1999 copyright date, the (TM 8) trademark, and the "Club Exclusive" backstamp, (EE) Exclusive Edition 2001-2002. Marking Club Year 25. First released in Spring of 2001 with an original issue price of $230 as an (EE) Exclusive Edition for the 2001/2002 Club year, for members of the M.I. Hummel Club. Then made available for sale by authorized Hummel dealers to the general public in 2006. Available in a set with a wooden base and HUM 2088/B "Rolling Around", and HUM 2088/A "Playing Around" (no "Waiting Around", HUM 2089/B).

☐ 2089/A Club Year 25.....4.25"...(**EE**)..❽..$230

HUM 2089/B — Waiting Around

Fourth and final in "Clowning Around" Series with HUM 2088/B "Rolling Around", HUM 2089/A "Looking Around", and HUM 2088/A "Playing Around". Has incised 1999 copyright date, the (TM 8) trademark, and the "Club Exclusive" backstamp, (EE) Exclusive Edition 2004-2005. Marking Club Year 28. First released with an original issue price of $230 in Spring of 2004 as an (EE) Exclusive Edition for the 2004/2005 Club year, for members of the M.I. Hummel Club. A mixed media figurine — his balloon is glass, held on a metal "string". Made available for sale by authorized Hummel retailers as an (OE) Open Edition to the general public in 2006.

☐ 2089/B Club Year 28...4.75"...(**EE**)...❽...$230

HUM 2090 — (ON) OPEN NUMBER

HUM 2091 — Maid To Order

First released in the U.S. market in the fall of 2000 with "First Issue 2001" backstamp. Modeled by master sculptor Helmut Fischer in 1999. It has an incised 1999 copyright date along with the (TM 8) trademark. Part of "Maid to Order" Collector's Set with "Strudel Haus Hummelscape" (Mark #1043-D). The original issue price of the collectors set was $250 in 1999. (TW) "Temporarily Withdrawn" in December 2004.

☐ 2091 ....4.25" ....(**TW**) ....❽ $205

Maid to Order Collector Set

HUM 2092 — Make Me Pretty

First released in the U.S. market in the fall of 2000 with "First Issue 2001" backstamp. Modeled by master sculptor Helmut Fischer in 1999. It has an incised 1999 copyright date along with the (TM 8) trademark. Part of "Make Me Pretty" Collector's Set with "Day of Beauty" Hummelscape (Mark #1045-D). The original issue price of the collectors set was $250 in 1999. (TW) "Temporarily Withdrawn" in December 2004.

☐ 2092 ....4.25" ....(**TW**) ....❽ $205

Make Me Pretty Collector Set

HUM 2093 — Pretzel Boy

First released in the U.S. market in the fall of 1999 as a companion piece to HUM 2004 "Pretzel Girl." Modeled by master sculptor Helmut Fischer in 1999. It has an incised 1999 copyright date along with the (TM 8) trademark. Figurines released in the first year bear the "First Issue 2000 Millennium" backstamp. Available in Special Event Collector's Set with a FREE "Bavarian Bier Garten" Hummelscape (Mark #1016–D), a $75 value. The official issue price was $185 in 1999.

☐ 2093 ....4.00" ....(**OE**) .... **❽** $199

*Pretzel Boy
Collector Set*

*Christmas
Wish
Collector
Set*

HUM 2094 — Christmas Wish

First released in the U.S. market in 1999. Modeled by master sculptor Helmut Fischer in 1999. It has an incised 1999 copyright date along with the (TM 8) trademark and an "Exclusive Edition" backstamp on the bottom. A (LE) Limited Edition of 20,000 pieces were sold exclusively on QVC starting at 12:00 AM EST on 17 November 1999 and sold out the complete edition in only one day! Came with a "Christmas Wish" Collector's Set (Musikfest Display)

2094   *2094/O*

HummelScape: (Mark #1017–D). The issue price for the collectors set was $139.50 (plus shipping) in 1999. Note: figurine has been available in the European market in 2003 and continuously since. Also available as an ornament.

☐ 2094......4.00".....(**TW**).....**❽**.....$150—200
☐ 2094......4.00".....(**OE**)......**❽**.....European market only
☐ 2094/O..3.25".....(**OE**)......**❽**......$69.50

HUM 2095 — Proclamation

First appearance was in September of 2005, available to attendees of the 2005 M.I. Hummel Club Convention held in Boston, MA., with "Boston: M.I. Hummel Club 2005 Convention" written on the scroll, and incised 1999 copyright date and the (TM 8) trademark, but no first issue marking, priced $259. First released in Spring of 2006, with an original issue price of $259, at Spring 2006 Artist Events, where the figurine could be personalized on the blank scroll. The artist event edition has Special Edition 2006 and Bell backstamps, the (TM 8) trademark, and incised 1999 copyright date, but no first issue marking. Now available without Special Event markings, ready for personalization.

*Proclamation -
2005 MI Hummel Club Convention,
Boston MA*

Proclamation

☐ 2095 ....5.25" ......(**OE**) ....❽ $259

HUM 2096/A — Angelic Conductor

Modeled by master sculptor Helmut Fischer in 1999. First year of release figurines have "First Issue 2000 MILLENNIUM" backstamp. Has a 1999 incised copyright date along with (TM 8) trademark. The original issue price was $135 in 2000. Part of the "Angel Orchestra".

☐ 2096/A ....4.00" ......(**OE**) ....❽ $139

HUM 2096/B — Heavenly Harpist

First released in 2003 with an original issue price of $155 and a "First Issue 2003" backstamp. Has a 1999 incised copyright date and the (TM 8) trademark. Part of the "Angel Orchestra". Sculpted by master sculptor Helmut Fischer.

☐ 2096/B....4.00".........(**OE**)....❽....$179

HUM 2096/C — Celestial Drummer
Modeled by master sculptor Helmut Fischer in 1999. First year of release figurines have "First Issue 2000 MILLENNIUM" backstamp. Has a 1999 incised copyright date along with (TM 8) trademark. The original issue price was $135 in 2000. "Celestrial Drummer" was permanently retired at the end of 2005 and will not be produced again. The 2005 production bears a special "Final Issue 2005" backstamp and a "Final Issue 2005" hangtag. Part of the "Angel Orchestra".

☐ 2096/C ....4.00" ....(CE).... ❽ ....$135—$150

FINAL ISSUE
2005

HUM 2096/D — String Symphony
Modeled by master sculptor Helmut Fischer in 1999. First year of release figurines have "First Issue 2001" oval backstamp. Has an incised 1999 copyright date along with (TM 8) trademark. The original issue price was $135 in 2000. (TW) "Temporarily Withdrawn" at the end of 2005. Part of the "Angel Orchestra".

☐ 2096/D ....4.00" ....(TW).... ❽ $135

HUM 2096/E — Heavenly Rhapsody
Modeled by master sculptor Helmut Fischer in 1999. First year of release figurines have "First Issue 2000 MILLENNIUM" backstamp. Has an incised 1999 copyright date along with (TM 8) trademark. The original issue price was $135 in 2000. Part of the "Angel Orchestra".

☐ 2096/E ....4.00" ....(OE).... ❽ $139

Final Issue

HUM 2096/F — Celestial Strings
Modeled by master sculptor Helmut Fischer in 1999. First year of released figurines have "First Issue 2000 MILLENNIUM" backstamp. Has an incised 1999 copyright date along with (TM 8) trademark. The original issue price was $135 in 2000. Part of the "Angel Orchestra". "Celestial Strings" will be permanently retired at the end of 2006 and will not be produced again. The 2006 production bears a special "Final Issue 2006" backstamp and "Final Issue 2006" hangtag.

☐ 2096/F ....4.00" ....(**CE**)...❽...$139

FINAL ISSUE
2006

HUM 2096/G — Celestial Reveille
Modeled by master sculptor Marion Huschka in 1999. First year of release figurines have "First Issue 2002" oval backstamp. Has an incised 1999 copyright date along with (TM 8) trademark. The original issue price was $135 in 2002. Part of the "Angel Orchestra".

☐ 2096/G....4.00" ....(**OE**)..❽ ..$139

HUM 2096/H — Millennium Bliss
Annual Angel 2000 – First in "Annual Angel Series". Modeled by master sculptor Helmut Fischer in 1999. Has a rose colored gown, a yellow wooden star shaped base marked 2000. "Annual Angel 2000" decal on bottom of figurine. Original issue price was $140 in 2000. Part of the "Angel Orchestra". Available as a commemorative of Miller's Expo 2000 with the wording "Miller's Expo 2000" on the front of the Hummel base.

☐ 2096/H ....4.00" ....(**CE**)..❽ ..$140—150

HUM 2096/J — Heavenly Horn Player
Modeled by master sculptor Helmut Fischer in 1999. First year of release figurines have "First Issue 2000 MILLENNIUM" backstamp. Has an incised 1999 copyright date along with (TM 8) trademark. The original issue price was $135 in 2000. Part of the "Angel Orchestra".

☐ 2096/J ....4.00" ....**(OE)**..❽...$139

HUM 2096/K — Joyful Recital
Annual Angel 2001 — Second in "Annual Angel Series." Modeled by master sculptor Helmut Fischer in 1999. Has an incised 1999 copyright date along with (TM 8) trademark. Has a light green gown and a yellow wooden star shaped base marked 2001. "Annual Angel 2001" decal on the bottom of the figurine. Original issue price was $140 in 2001. Part of the "Angel Orchestra". Available as a commemorative of Miller's Expo 2000 with the wording "Miller's Expo 2000" on the front of the Hummel base.

☐ 2096/K ....4.00" ....**(CE)**..❽...$140—150

HUM 2096/L — Heavenly Harmony
Modeled by master sculptor Helmut Fischer in 1999. First year of release figurines have "First Issue 2001" oval backstamp. Has an incised 2000 copyright date along with (TM 8) trademark. The original issue price was $135 in 2001. Part of the "Angel Orchestra".

☐ 2096/L ....4.00" ....**(OE)**..❽ ..$139

HUM 2096/M — Divine Drummer
Modeled by master sculptor Marion Huschka in 1999. First year of release figurines have "First Issue 2001" oval backstamp. Has an incised 2000 copyright date along with (TM 8) trademark. The original issue price was $135 in 2001. Part of the "Angel Orchestra". (TW) "Temporarily Withdrawn".

☐ 2096/M....4.00" ....(**TW**)....❽....$135—150

HUM 2096/N — Zealous Xylophonist
Modeled by master sculptor Marion Huschka in 1999. First year of release figurines have "First Issue 2002" oval backstamp. Has an incised 2001 copyright date along with (TM 8) trademark. The original issue price was $135 in 2002. Part of the "Angel Orchestra".

☐ 2096/N....4.00" ....(**OE**)....❽....$135—150

HUM 2096/P — Heavenly Hubbub
Modeled by master sculptor Helmut Fischer in 1999. First year of release figurines have "First Issue 2001" oval decal backstamp. Has an incised 2000 copyright date along with (TM 8) trademark. The original issue price was $135 in 2001. Part of the "Angel Orchestra". (TW) "Temporarily Withdrawn".

☐ 2096/P ....4.00" ....(**TW**)....❽....$135

HUM 2096/Q — Heaven and Nature Sing
Modeled by master sculptor Helmut Fischer in 1999. First year of release figurines have "First Issue 2002" oval decal backstamp. Has an incised 2001 copyright date along with (TM 8) trademark. The original issue price was $155 in 2002. Part of the "Angel Orchestra".

☐ 2096/Q....3.75" ....(OE)....❽....$155

HUM 2096/R — Seraphim Soprano
Modeled by master sculptor Marion Huschka in 1999. First year of release figurines have "First Issue 2001" oval decal backstamp. Has an incised 2000 copyright date along with (TM 8) trademark. The original issue price was $135 in 2001. Part of the "Angel Orchestra".

☐ 2096/R....3.75" ....(OE)....❽....$135

HUM 2096/S — Triumphant Trumpeter
Modeled by master sculptor Marion Huschka in 1999. First year of release figurines have "First Issue 2002" oval decal backstamp. Angel sits on a painted wooden cloud. "Hummel" only incised on bottom of figurine. Has NO model number and NO copyright date (that I could find). My cello name tag is "Trumpet Player." Original issue price was $135 in 2002. Part of the "Angel Orchestra". Note similarity to HUM 2096/T "Heavenly Time".

☐ 2096/S...3.25"..(OE)..❽..$139

Limited Edition

First Issue

HUM 2096/T — Heavenly Time

First released in 2004 in the North American market as a Sequentially Numbered (LE) Limited Edition of 5000, with a ceramic Joy angel wings pin, a wooden Cloud Display, and an original issue price of $165. The (LE) Limited Edition has a 2001 copyright date decal and the (TM 8) trademark, and is distinguished by a brown horn and a (LE) Limited Edition backstamp (no first issue marking). First released in 2004 in the European market as a first issue figurine with a wooden Cloud Display (no Joy angel wings pin). The first issue figurine has a 2001 copyright date decal and the (TM 8) trademark, and is distinguished

by a yellow horn and a First Issue 2005 backstamp. Part of the "Angel Orchestra". Similar to HUM 2096/S, but the "Triumphant Trumpeter" sits on the other side of his Cloud Display and holds his horn pointed upward. Sculpted by master sculptor Helmut Fischer.

☐ 2096/T.......3.25".......(OE).....❽.....$165

HUM 2096/U — Cymbals of Joy

Annual Angel 2000–Third in "Annual Angel Series" that began in 2000. Modeled by master sculptor Helmut Fischer in 2000. Has an incised 2001 copyright date along with (TM 8) trademark. Has a light purple gown, a yellow wooden star shaped base marked 2002. "Annual Angel 2002" decal on bottom of figurine. The original issue price was $135 in 2002. Part of the "Angel Orchestra".

☐ 2096/U.......3.75".....(CE).....❽......$135

HUM 2096/V — Bells On High

Modeled by master sculptor Helmut Fischer in 1999. First year of release figurines have "First Issue 2002" oval decal backstamp. Has an incised 2001 copyright date along with (TM 8) trademark. The original issue price was $135 in 2002. Part of the "Angel Orchestra".

☐ 2096/V.......3.25".......(OE).....❽.....$139

HUM 2097 — Can I Play?

First released in January of 2006 with an original issue price of $1250. Fifth in "Moments in Time" Collection. Sequentially numbered worldwide (LE) Limited Edition of 3000. Limited to year of production. Has incised 2003 copyright date, the (TM 8) trademark, and "Moments in Time" and (LE) Limited Edition backstamps. Sculpted by a team of Goebel sculptors. A mixed media figurine, with twine ropes for the swing. The figurine captures the image of motion, but the seated girl in the figurine is not free to swing. She is held fast, attached to the girl standing behind her. Note resemblance to HUM 2228 "Can't Catch Me".

☐ 2097........11" x 10.25" x 6.25"........**(LE)** ....❽ $1250

HUM 2098 — Annual Christmas Tree Ornaments

Original issue price — $20—$22.50 each

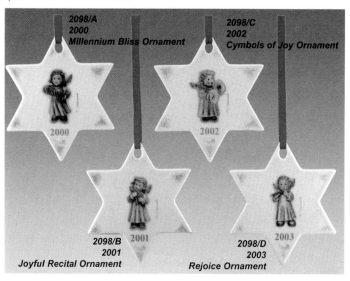

2098/A
2000
Millennium Bliss Ornament

2098/C
2002
Cymbols of Joy Ornament

2098/B
2001
Joyful Recital Ornament

2098/D
2003
Rejoice Ornament

HUM 2099/A — Saint Nicholas Day, Ornament

Modeled by master sculptor Helmut Fischer in 1999. Has a decal 2000 copyright date and the (TM 8) trademark. The original issue price was $20 in 2000.

☐ 2099/A....3.25" ....**(OE)**....❽....$20

481

HUM 2100 — Picture Perfect

M.I. Hummel Club 25th Anniversary Commemorative Figurine, with "Commemorative" backstamp, black wooden base, porcelain plaque, sequentially numbered worldwide (LE) Limited Edition of 2500 pieces. A few Artist Proofs were also made. Modeled by master sculptor Helmut Fischer in 2000. The original issue price was $3495 in 2001.

☐ 2100........8.25".......(CE).....❽.....$3500—4000

HUM 2101 — Girl's Best Friend, A — (2101/A)
Boy's Best Friend, A — (2101/B)

Both figurines were released in the fall of 2000 with "First Issue 2001" backstamp. The original issue price was $140 each in 2000. Modeled by master sculptor Helmut Fischer in 1999. They both have an incised 1999 copyright date along with the (TM 8) trademark.

☐ 2101/A.........4.00".......(OE)....❽.....$139
☐ 2101/B.........4.00".......(OE).....❽.....$139

HUM 2102 — My Heart's Desire — (2102/A)
Secret Admirer — (2102/B)

Both figurines were released in the summer of 2002 with "First Issue 2002" oval backstamp. The original issue price was $140 each in 2002. Modeled by master sculptor Helmut Fischer in 2000. They both have an incised 2001 copyright date along with the (TM 8) trademark. HUM 2102/A "My Heart's Desire" was released in a new small size in 2004 with an original issue price of $59.50.

☐ 2102/A.........3.75".......(OE)....❽.....$140
☐ 2102/A 4/0...3.25".......(OE).....❽.....$69.50
☐ 2102/B.........4.00".......(OE).....❽.....$140

HUM 2103/A — Puppet Princess (EE)
First released in the U.S. market in spring of
2001 as a FREE gift for renewing membership in the M.I. Hummel Club for the
2001/2002 club year. Modeled by master
sculptor Marion Huschka in 1999. It has an
incised 1999 copyright date along with the
(TM 8) trademark and bears the "Club"
exclusive backstamp. A $90 value.

☐ 2103/A ......3.75" ....(**EE**)....❽....$85—90

HUM 2103/B — Puppet Prince (EE)
First released in the U.S. market in the
spring of 2001 as an (EE) Exclusive Edition
for members of the M.I. Hummel Club only
and not sold as an (OE) Open Edition to the
general public. Modeled by master sculptor
Marion Huschka in 1999. It has an incised
1999 copyright date along with the (TM 8)
trademark and bears the "Club Exclusive"
backstamp. The official issue price was $100
in 2001, plus the member's redemption card.

☐ 2103/B ......4.00" ....(**EE**)....❽....$100

HUM 2104 — Sunflower Friends (EE)
Announced in 2000 "Sunflower Friends" will
be an (EE) Exclusive Edition available to
"M.I. Hummel Club" members only, who
have belonged to the Club continuously for
5 years. Modeled by master sculptor Helmut
Fischer in 1999. It has an incised 1999
copyright date along with the (TM 8) trademark. The original issue price was $195.

☐ 2104 ....3.50" ....(**EE**)....❽....$195

HUM 2105 — Miss Beehaving (EE)

Annunced in 2000 "Miss Beehaving" will be an (EE) Exclusive Edition available to "M.I. Hummel Club" members only, who have belonged to the Club continuously for 10 years. Modeled by master sculptor Helmut Fischer in 1999. It has an incised 1999 copyright date along with the (TM 8) trademark. The original issue price was $240 in 2000. A suitable companion for HUM 612 2/0 "Lazy Bones'.

☐ 2105......2.75" ....(**EE**)............❽............$240

2106   2106/O

HUM 2106 — Christmas Time

First released in the U.S. market in 2000, in a (LE) Limited Edition of 25,000 pieces and sold exclusively on QVC on 7 November 2000. Came with a "Christmas Time" Hummelscape: (Mark #1038-D). The price was $239.50 plus shipping in 2000. The ornament was first available as a FREE gift with purchase during one holiday season. It is HUM 2106/O, one of the "Tree Trimmer Ornament" Series. Note: figurine by itself has been available in the European market in 2003 and continuously since.

☐ 2106....4.00"....(**TW**)...❽...$150—200
☐ 2106....4.00"....(**OE**)...❽....
    European market only
☐ 2106/O..3.25"....(**CE**)...❽...$69.50

HUM 2107/A — Bee Hopeful (LE)

A (LE) Limited Edition of 25,000 sequentially numbered pieces worldwide. Modeled by master sculptor Helmut Fischer in 1999. In a collector set with the resin replica Lane hope chest (Mark #1046-D) priced $198 for the Fall 2000 Special Event. The (LE) Limited Edition figurine also available separately. Figurine has NO "First Issue" marking, but does have an incised 2000 copyright date along with the (TM 8) trademark.

☐ 2107/A........4.00"........(**LE**) .... ❽ $185

Bee Hopeful and Quilting Bee Collectors Sets

HUM 2107/B — Little Knitter (LE)

A (LE) Limited Edition of 25,000 sequentially numbered pieces worldwide. Modeled by master sculptor Helmut Fischer in 1999. In a collector set with the "Quilting Bee" Hummelscape (Mark #1047-D) priced $198 for the "Spring 2001" Special Event. The (LE) Limited Edition figurine also available separately. Figurine has NO "First Issue" marking, but does have an incised 2000 copyright date along with the (TM 8) trademark.

☐ 2107/B........4.00"..............(**LE**)....❽....$185

HUM 2108/A — Musik, Please (LE)

A Limited Edition (LE) of 25,000 sequentially numbered pieces worldwide. Modeled by master sculptor Helmut Fischer in 1999. In a collector set with the Volkfest Accessory priced $198 for the "Spring 2002" Special Event. Companion to HUM 2108/B "Alpine Dancer with Marktplatz" Hummelscape. The (LE) Limited Edition figurine also available separately. Figurine has NO "First Issue" marking, but does have an incised 2000 copyright date along with the (TM 8) trademark and limited edition backstamp. Available in collector set with "Bavarian Village" Plaque (No. 818251), priced $189 in 2006. Companion to HUM 2108/B "Alpine Dancer with Marktplatz" Hummelscape.

☐ 2108/A.......4.00"................(**LE**)....❽....$185

HUM 2108/B — Alpine Dancer (LE)

A (LE) Limited Edition of 25,000 sequentially numbered pieces worldwide. Modeled by master sculptor Helmut Fischer in 1999. In a collector set with the Marktplatz Hummelscape (Mark #1065-D) priced $198 for the "Fall Fest 2001" Special Event. Companion to HUM 2108/A Musik, Please with Volkfest Accessory. The (LE) Limited Edition figurine also available separately. Figurine has NO "First Issue" marking, but does have an incised 2000 copyright date along with the (TM 8) trademark and limited edition backstamp. Companion to HUM 2108/A Musik, Please with Volkfest Accessory.

☐ 2108/B ....4.00"..........(LE)....❽....$185

Musik, Please & Alpine Collector Sets

HUM 2109 — (ON) OPEN NUMBER

HUM 2110/A — Christmas Delivery, Ornament

This star-shaped ornament was modeled by master sculptor Helmut Fischer in 1999. Has a decal "M. I. Hummel" signature, a (TM 7) trademark, but NO copyright date. Both sides are identical. The original issue price was $20 in 2000.

☐ 2110/A ..3.50"..............(CE)....❼....$20

HUM 2111/A — Making New Friends, Ornament

This snowflake-shaped ornament was modeled by master sculptor Helmut Fischer in 1999. Has a decal "M. I. Hummel" signature, a (TM 7) trademark, but NO copyright date. Both sides are identical. The original issue price was $20 in 2000.

☐ 2111/A....3.50"..............(CE)....❼....$20

HUM 2112 — (ON) OPEN NUMBER

HUM 2113 — Extra! Extra!

First released in the U.S. market in the fall of 2001 with "First Issue 2001" backstamp. The original issue price was $240 in 2001. Modeled by master sculptor Helmut Fischer in 1999. It has an incised 2000 copyright date along with the (TM 8) trademark. Many different variations—can also be personalized.

☐ 2113......5.25".......(OE)....❽....$240

HUM 2114 — Declaration of Freedom

Fourth in "Ambassadors of Freedom" Series sold through AAFES catalog and US Military Post Exchanges. New in 2004. A sequentially numbered (LE) Limited Edition of 3000, with a red, white and blue flying eagle backstamp and "Ambassadors of Freedom" inscription. Has incised 2004 copyright date, limited edition backstamp, and the (TM 8) trademark. Includes wooden display with brass plaque inscribed "Declaration of Freedom/ Ambassadors of Freedom", and a 60 page booklet of patriotic passages by Michael W. Smith and a CD of patriotic music and readings by President George W. Bush and Rev. Billy Graham. Figurine with wooden base stands 9.00" tall.

☐ 2114/II....9.00"....(LE)...❽...$300-400

HUM 2115 — Lantern Fun

First released in 2004 with an original issue price of $110. Price reduction to $99 announced in Summer 2004 *INSIGHTS* magazine. Has incised 2003 copyright date, the (TM 8) trademark, but no first issue marking. Mixed media figurine – wooden stick with ceramic lantern. In North American market, part of "Create-A-Gift" Collection when paired with a "Sentiment Occasion" base. In European market, bearing "Lantern" backstamp, part of Hummel Figurines "Through the Year" Collection, with available wooden showcase and ceramic month plaques for making a figural calendar.

Shown with Be Mine Sentiment Occasion base

☐ 2115/B 4/0.......3.25".....(OE)....❽....$99

HUM 2116/A — One Cup of Sugar

First released in the U.S. market in mid-2001, with the (TM 8) trademark and "First Issue 2001" oval decal backstamp, for the original issue price of $140. Modeled by master sculptor Helmut Fischer in 2000. It has an incised 2000 copyright date. A version with new colors became available in 2004, bearing a 2004 Special Edition backstamp and priced $129, sculpted by Marion Huschka. (TW) "Temporarily Withdrawn.

□ 2116/A.....3.75 to 4.00"....(**TW**)....❽....$139

HUM 2116/B — Baking Time

First released in the U.S. market in mid-2001 "First Issue 2001" oval decal backstamp. Modeled by master sculptor Helmut Fischer in 2000. It has an incised 2000 copyright date along with the (TM 8) trademark. The original issue price was $140 in 2001. Companion to HUM 2116/A "One Cup of Sugar".

□ 2116/B.....3.75 to 4.00"....(**OE**)....❽....$139

HUM 2117–2119 — (ON) OPEN NUMBERS

Little Miss Mail Carrier with Decorated Base

Little Miss Mail Carrier

HUM 2120 — Little Miss Mail Carrier

First released in 2004 with an original issue price of $250 and "First Issue 2005" backstamp. Has incised 2000 copyright date and (TM 8) trademark. She resembles HUM 2194, "Duty Calls". Suitable companion for HUM 119 "Postman". The first 2500 released in the North American market in Fall 2004 have Goebel artist signature, "First Issue 2005" backstamp, incised 2000 copyright date and (TM 8) trademark, and a display base decorated with envelopes sealed with a heart, priced $250.

□ 2120.....4.75".....(**OE**)....❽....$250

HUM 2121 — Soap Box Derby (LE)
First Edition of the "Moments in Time" Series. Limited to one year's (2002) production only. Modeled by master sculptor Marion Huschka in 2001. Has a special "Moments in Time 2002 XXI" backstamp. Released in the Fall of 2001 with an incised 2001 copyright date, along with the (TM 8) trademark. The original issue price was $1250 in 2001.

☐ 2121......6.50".......(LE)...**❽**...$1250

HUM 2122–2123 — (ON) OPEN NUMBERS

HUM 2124 — Summer Adventure (EE)
Third and Final Edition of "Wonder of Childhood" series. Members' Exclusive for Club year 26 of the M.I. Hummel Club. Modeled by master sculptor Helmut Fischer in 2001. It has an incised 2001 copyright date along with the (TM 8) trademark. Comes with a wooden base and engraved brass plaque. It has the Club "Exclusive Edition 2002/2003" backstamp—and Black bumble bee. The original issue price was $695 in 2002.

☐ 2124 ....5.75" ....(EE) ....**❽** $695

HUM 2125 — Teacher's Pet
First released in the U.S. market in mid-2001 "First Issue 2002" oval decal backstamp. Modeled by master sculptor Helmut Fischer in 2000. It has an incised 2000 copyright date along with the (TM 8) trademark. The original issue price was $175 in 2001.

☐ 2125......4.75 to 4.50"........(**OE**).....**❽**.....$175

HUM 2126–2128 — (ON) OPEN NUMBERS

HUM 2129/A — Ring in the Season, Ornament

This pinecone shaped ornament was modeled by master sculptor Helmut Fischer in 2001. Has a decal "M. I. Hummel" signature, a "First Issue 2001" date under the (TM 8) trademark. Both sides are identical. The original issue price was $20 in 2001.

☐ 2129/A.....3.50".....(CE).....❽.....$20

HUM 2130 — Nutcracker Sweet

Released in the U.S. market in the fall of 2001 in a (LE) Limited Edition of 10,000 sets worldwide with a real Steinbach (LE) Limited Edition nutcracker (5.50" tall). The figurine was modeled by master sculptor Marion Huschka in 2000. It has a "First Issue 2001" backstamp, an incised 2000 copyright date along with the (TM 8) trademark. Set includes an heirloom wooden box for the nutcracker. The original issue price for the set was $375 in 2001. Figurine also marketed with Wooden Tree Display.

☐ 2130.....6.00".....(OE).....❽.....$250

HUM 2131 — (ON) OPEN NUMBER

HUM 2132 — Camera Ready

Released in the spring of 2001 in celebration of the "25th Anniversary" of the M. I. Hummel Club, as an (OE) Open Edition available to the general public as well as Club members. It has a "Special Commemorative" backstamp (25 years 1977-2002). Modeled by master sculptor Helmut Fischer in 2000. Has an incised 2000 copyright date along with the (TM 8) trademark. The original issue price was $525 in 2001.

☐ 2132........5.50"...(CE)...❽...$525

HUM 2133 — Bashful Serenade

Modeled by master sculptor Marion Huschka in 2000. Has an incised 2000 copyright date. First sold on 5 July 2001 exclusively on QVC through 1 January 2002, in "Bashful Serenade" Collectors Set. With "First Issue 2002" backstamp, the (TM 8) trademark, and display "Bashful Serenade" (Mark #1064-D). The original issue price of the collector's set was $475 in 2001. Figurine alone priced $529 on 2005 Goebel NA suggested retail price list.

☐ 2133.....5.25".....(**OE**)....❽....$529

Bashful Serenade Collector Set

HUM 2134 — Winter Time Duet

First sold on QVC from early October through 1 December 2001. Modeled by master sculptor Helmut Fischer in 2000. It has an incised 2000 copyright date, the (TM 8) trademark, but <u>NO</u> "First Issue" date. The original issue price was $175 in 2001.

☐ 2134 ....4.00" ....(**OE**)......❽......$175

HUM 2135/A — Angelic Drummer

First released in January 2005 with an original issue price of $139 and "First Issue 2005" backstamp. Has incised 2000 copyright date and the (TM 8) trademark. Part of the "Angel Orchestra". Sculpted by master sculptor Helmut Fischer.

☐ 2135/A......4.00" ....(**OE**) ....❽ $139

HUM 2135/C — Precious Pianist

First released in January 2005, with an original issue price of $219 and "First Issue 2005" backstamp. Consists of three parts: wooden cloud base, ceramic piano, and ceramic seated angel. Has incised 2001 copyright date decal and the (TM 8) trademark. Part of the "Angel Orchestra". Sculpted by master sculptor Helmut Fischer.

☐ 2135/C......3.25" ....(OE) ....❽ $219

HUM 2135/D — Melodic Mandolin

First released in 2003 with an original issue price of $135 and "First Issue 2003" backstamp. Sculpted by master sculptor Helmut Fischer. Has incised 2001 copyright date and the (TM 8) trademark. Part of the "Angel Orchestra". Available with "Christmas Ribbon" base (Mark #1110-D) which is musical, playing "Joy to the World." The "Christmas Ribbon" base is also available separately, listed at $20 on the 2005 Goebel NA Suggested Retail Price List.

☐ 2135/D.....3.25".....(OE).....❽....$139

Melodic Mandolin

HUM 2135/E — Celestial Dreamer

First released in 2003 with an original issue price of $135 and a "First Issue 2003" backstamp. Has incised 2001 copyright date and the (TM 8) trademark. Part of the "Angel Orchestra". Sculpted by master sculptor Hel-

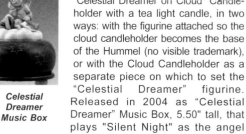

Celestial Dreamer Music Box

mut Fischer. Released in 2004 as "Celestial Dreamer on Cloud" Candleholder with a tea light candle, in two ways: with the figurine attached so the cloud candleholder becomes the base of the Hummel (no visible trademark), or with the Cloud Candleholder as a separate piece on which to set the "Celestial Dreamer" figurine. Released in 2004 as "Celestial Dreamer" Music Box, 5.50" tall, that plays "Silent Night" as the angel revolves on top of the wooden music box; currently priced $199.

Celestial Dreamer

☐ 2135/E......3.25".....(OE)....❽....$139

HUM 2135/F — Sounds of Joy

First released in 2003 with an original issue price of $155 and "First Issue 2003" backstamp. Has 2001 copyright decal and the (TM 8) trademark. Part of the "Angel Orchestra". Sculpted by master sculptor Helmut Fischer.

☐ 2135/F ......3.25" ....(TW) ....❽ $179

HUM 2135/G — Rejoice

Annual Angel 2003 – fourth in "Annual Angel" Series that began in 2000. First released in 2002 with an original issue price of $145 and an "Annual Angel 2003" backstamp. Has incised 2002 copyright date and the (TM 8) trademark. Includes yellow wooden star base marked 2003, measuring 4.00" across. Part of the "Angel Orchestra". Sculpted by master sculptor Helmut Fischer.

□ 2135/G......4.00" ....(**CE**)......❽......$145

HUM 2135/H — Angelic Trumpeter

Annual Angel 2004 – fifth in "Annual Angel" Series that began in 2000. First released in 2003 with an original issue price of $145 and an "Annual Angel 2004" backstamp. Has incised 2003 copyright date and the (TM 8) trademark. Includes yellow wooden star base marked 2004, measuring 4.00" across. Part of the "Angel Orchestra". Sculpted by master sculptor Helmut Fischer.

□ 2135/H......4.00" ....(**CE**)......❽......$145

HUM 2135/J — Spirited Saxophonist

Annual Angel 2005 – sixth in "Annual Angel" Series that began in 2000. First released in 2004 with an original issue price of $165 and an "Annual Angel 2005" backstamp. Has incised 2004 copyright date and the (TM 8) trademark. Includes yellow wooden star base marked 2005, measuring 4.50" across. The first 2500 released in the North American market in Fall 2004 have Goebel artist signature, "Annual Angel 2005" backstamp, incised 2004 copyright date, the (TM 8) trademark, and yellow wooden star base marked 2005 measuring 4.50" across, priced $165. Part of the "Angel Orchestra". Sculpted by master sculptor Helmut Fischer.

□ 2135/J ......4.00" ....(**CE**)......❽......$165

HUM 2135/K — Angel with Triangle

Annual Angel 2006 – seventh in "Annual Angel" Series that began in 2000. First released in 2005 with an original issue price of $165 and an "Annual Angel 2006" backstamp. Has incised 2005 copyright date and the (TM 8) trademark. Includes yellow wooden star base marked 2006, measuring 4.50" across. Part of the "Angel Orchestra". Sculpted by master sculptor Helmut Fischer.

□ 2135/K......4.25" ....(**CE**)......❽......$165

HUM 2136 — Cat's Meow, The

Modeled by master sculptor Helmut Fischer in 2000. Listed as part of the "M.I. Hummel 2003 Premiere" Collection but released in the fall of 2002 with "First Issue 2003" oval decal backstamp. Has 2001 copyright date applied by decal under the (TM 8) trademark. The original issue price was $310 in 2002. In January 2003 Goebel announced the color of the cat was meant to be gray, not black as on the first 5000 figurines released, and so a variation with a gray cat became available, with the (TM 8) trademark and "First Issue 2003" backstamp, priced $310 in 2003. The price adjusted to $279 in 2005.

☐ 2136 ....3.50"..........(OE)....❽....$279

HUM 2137–2142 — (ON) OPEN NUMBERS

HUM 2143/A — Season's Best

Released in the U.S. market in mid-2002 with the "First Issue 2002" backstamp attached to the figurine on cello tape. Modeled by master sculptor Helmut Fischer in 2001. It has the 2001 copyright date under (TM 8) trademark. Includes a small cold cast porcelain ice rink display. The original issue price was $220 in 2002. (TW) "Temporarily Withdrawn".

☐ 2143/A......3.75"..........(TW) ..❽....$220

HUM 2143/B — Let's Take to the Ice

Released in the U.S. market in mid-2002 with "First Issue 2002" backstamp attached to the figurine on cello tape. Modeled by master sculptor Helmut Fischer in 2000. It has the 2001 copyright date under (TM 8) trademark. Includes a small cold cast porcelain ice rink display. The original issue price was $220 in 2002. (TW) "Temporarily Withdrawn".

☐ 2143/B......4.00"..........(TW) ..❽....$220

HUM 2144–2147 — (ON) OPEN NUMBERS

HUM 2148/A — Wait For Me

First released in the U.S. market in mid-2002 as an (EE) Exclusive Edition for members of the M. I. Hummel Club only and not sold as an (OE) Open Edition to the general public. Modeled by master sculptor Helmut Fischer in 2000. It has an incised 2001 copyright date along with the (TM 8) trademark and bears the "Club Exclusive" backstamp. "Exclusive Edition 2002/2003." The original issue price was $100 in 2002. Companion to HUM 2148/B "First Mate."

☐ 2148/A..4.25" ....(CE) ....❽ ....$100—110

HUM 2148/B — First Mate

First released in the U.S. market in spring of 2002 as a FREE gift for renewing membership in the M. I. Hummel Club for the 2002/2003 Club year. Modeled by master sculptor Helmut Fischer in 2000. It has an incised 2001 copyright date along with the (TM 8) trademark and bears the Club Exclusive backstamp and Membership Year 2002/2003 M. I. Hummel Club. A $90 value.

☐ 2148/B..4.00" ....(CE) ....❽ ....$100—110

HUM 2149–2151 — (ON) OPEN NUMBERS

HUM 2152/A — Dearly Beloved Trinket Box

First released in 2003 with an original issue price of $50. A heart-shaped ceramic treasure box with a heart design along the sides. Features a depiction of HUM 2003 "Dearly Beloved" applied by decal over raised detail. Has a decal M.I. Hummel signature, the (TM 8) trademark, and a 2002 copyright date decal. Available in "Dearly Beloved" Gift Set (Large), in presentation box, with HUM 2178/A "Dearly Beloved" Framed Picture, HUM 2179/A "Dearly Beloved" Certificate, and HUM 2163/A "Dearly Beloved" Ornament; set priced $197.50 in 2003. Available in "Dearly Beloved" Gift Set (Small), in presentation box, with HUM 2003 2/0 "Dearly Beloved" figurine, set priced $250 in 2003.

☐ 2152/A..1.75 x 3.25" ....(TW)....❽ $50

| Special Event | Example of Parade of States | United We Stand |

HUM 2153 — Big Announcement

First released in 2003 with an original issue price of $230. Featured in 2003 as a Special Event piece with "First Issue 2003" backstamp, incised 2001 copyright date, and (TM 8) trademark. The Special Edition figurine has a "Special Edition" backstamp and the signboards may be personalized. Price reduced to $219 on 2005 Goebel NA Suggested Retail Price List. Available for each of the 50 US states in "Parade of States" Edition, with a heart-shaped American flag, the state name and motto on the front and a US-shaped flag and The United States of America on the back signboard. The "Parade of States" Edition has Special Edition and First Issue 2003 backstamps, incised 2001 copyright date and the (TM 8) trademark, priced $245. Available as Big Announcement – United We Stand, with tri-color ribbon and United We Stand on the front, and American flag with words "God Bless America" on the back. Available in Europe as Big Announcement – Philharmonie der Nationen, with Philharmonie der Nationen backstamp and hangtag, in support of an international orchestra promoting peace. Sculpted by master sculptor Helmut Fischer and Eber.

☐ 2153 ....4.50" ....(OE) ....❽ $219

HUM 2154/A — Patriotic Spirit

First released with First Issue 2002 (EE) Exclusive Edition backstamp and an original issue price of $198. Has incised 2001 copyright date and (TM 8) trademark. The girl is 4.00" tall, 6.00" tall including the flag. Companion to HUM 2154/B "Celebration of Freedom". Sculpted by master sculptors Helmut Fischer and Tamara Fuchs.

☐ 2154/A ......4", 6" with flag ......(TW) ....❽ $198

HUM 2154/B — Celebration of Freedom
First released in Fall of 2002, with First Issue 2003 (EE) Exclusive Edition backstamp, and an original issue price of $198. Has incised 2001 copyright date and (TM 8) trademark. The boy is 4.00" tall, 6.00" tall including the flag. Companion to HUM 2154/A "Patriotic Spirit". Price reduced to $179 on 2005 Goebel NA Suggested Retail Price List. Sculpted by master sculptors Helmut Fischer and Tamara Fuchs.

☐ 2154/B..4", 6" with flag...(**TW**)....❽....$179

HUM 2155 — Teddy Tales
First released in July 2006 as part of "Teddy Tales" Collector's Set, set priced $199, (LE) Limited Edition of 1000 sets. Figurine in set has "Red Bow" and "Special Edition" backstamp, the (TM 8) trademark, and incised 2005 copyright date. The "Red Bow" backstamp matches the bow in the girl's hair. "Teddy Bear Picnic" Hummelscape, Mark #1132-D, is musical, playing "Oh Where Has My Little Dog Gone," and includes a Certificate of Authenticity stating the Hummelscape is a (LE) Limited Edition of 1000.

☐ 2155 ....3.50" ....(**OE**)....❽....$199

Teddy Tales Collector Set　　　　*Teddy Tales*

HUM 2156 — (ON) OPEN NUMBER

Full Speed Ahead

HUM 2157 — Full Speed Ahead aka When I Grow Up

First released midyear in 2003 with an original issue price of $300 and "First Issue 2003" backstamp. Has incised 2002 copyright date and (TM 8) trademark. A mixed media piece with black wooden train. Available as variation called "When I Grow Up", with "First Issue 2003" backstamp, distinguished by a "Special Edition" backstamp and a wooden red fire truck instead of train. Available in Europe in a "Gold" Collector Set, in a (LE) Limited Edition of 2000, with gold colored wooden train and working gold-toned HO train engine. "Gold" Edition figurine has "First Issue 2003" and "Sonderausgabe Marklin" backstamps.

☐ 2157 ....4.75" ....(OE) .... ❽ $319

Gold Collector Set

When I Grow Up

HUM 2158–2161 — (ON) OPEN NUMBERS

HUM 2162 — Baker's Delight

First released in January of 2004 with an original issue price of $1200. Third Edition in "Moments in Time" Collection. Sequentially numbered worldwide (LE) Limited Edition of 5000. Limited to one year of production. Has incised 2002 copyright date, the (TM 8) trademark, as well as "Moments in Time" and limited edition backstamps. A striking detail on the figurine is the dusting of "flour" on the tabletop and rolling pin. Companion to HUM 2167 "Mixing the Cake" and HUM 2168 "Today's Recipe".

☐ 2162..........7.00"............(LE) ....❽ $1200

HUM 2163/A — Dearly Beloved Christmas Ornament

First released in the January of 2003 with an original issue price of $22.50. Priced $25 on 2005 Goebel NA Suggested Retail Price List. A white heart-shaped ornament with a light blue ribbon for hanging. Has a decal M.I. Hummel signature, the (TM 8) trademark, and a 2002 copyright date decal. Features a depiction of HUM 2003 "Dearly Beloved" applied by decal over raised detail. Both sides of the ornament are identical. Available in "Dearly Beloved" Gift Set (Large), in presentation box, with HUM 2178/A "Dearly Beloved" Framed Picture, HUM 2179/A "Dearly Beloved" Certificate, and HUM 2152/A "Dearly Beloved" Trinket Box; set priced $197.50 in 2003. Fits in HUM 2152/A "Dearly Beloved" Trinket Box, for giving as a gift.

☐ 2163/A ......3.50"............(TW)....❽ $25

HUM 2164 — Me and My Shadow (LE)

First released in the U.S. market in the spring of 2002 in a Numbered and (LE) Limited Edition of 10,000 sets worldwide. Came in a "Commemorative" Collector's Set which included a Steiff Teddy Bear made exclusively for Goebel, a porcleain medallion and a White, Numbered (LE) Limited

Edition Button-in-the-Ear Tag in a worldwide (LE) Limited Edition of 10,000 pieces. The M. I. Hummel figurine was modeled by master sculptor Marion Huschka in 2001 to celebrate the "100th Anniversary of the Teddy Bear". It has an incised 2001 copyright date along with the (TM 8) trademark. The original issue price was $450 in 2002.

☐ 2164 ....5.50 to 5.75".........**(LE)** ..❽ $450

HUM 2165 — Farm Days

First released in January of 2003 with an original issue price of $1200. Second edition in "Moments in Time" Collection. Sequentially numbered worldwide (LE) Limited Edition of 5000. Has incised 2002 copyright date, the (TM 8) trademark, "Moments in Time" and Limited Edition backstamps. Sculpted by master sculptor Helmut Fischer. Resembles HUM 2231 "Friendly Feeding".

☐ 2165 ....7.50"....................**(LE)** ..❽ $1200

HUM 2166 — Circus Act

First appearance was in January of 2003, available in the North American market as a special preview edition available to M.I. Hummel Club members. The $230 price included a donation supporting the "Big Apple Circus" pediatric hospital clown project and a free apple pin. Preview Edition has a 2001 copyright date decal, "Commemorative" backstamp, and (TM 8) trademark, and is distinguished by "Big Apple Circus" on the clown's suitcase.  Regular issue first released in 2003 with an original issue price of $230. Has 2001 copyright date decal, (TM 8) trademark, and the Hummel name label on side of suitcase. Price reduced to $199 on 2006 Goebel NA Suggested Retail Price List. Available in 2005 as European Club Edition, bearing "Special Edition 2005" M.I. Hummel Club backstamp, (TM 8) trademark, and 2004 copyright decal. The European Club Edition is distinguished by the Hummel name label on his back, and new lighter and brighter colors of the clown's wardrobe and accessories – tan pants rather than dark brown, light blue jacket rather than black, green umbrella rather than orange, for example.

☐ 2166 ....4.25" ......(**OE**).....❽.....$199

Regular issue

European Club Edition

HUM 2167 — Mixing the Cake

First released in 2004 with an original issue price of $320 and a "First Issue 2004" backstamp. Has incised 2003 copyright date and (TM 8) trademark. Companion to HUM 2162 "Baker's Delight" and HUM 2168 "Today's Recipe". Note the flour spill – down her apron to her foot. Available in European market in a collector set with HUM 2168 "Today's Recipe" and a German language cookbook. "Mixing the Cake" in the collector set has "First Issue 2004" backstamp, incised 2003 copyright date, and (TM 8) trademark.

☐ 2167 ....5.75" ......(**OE**).....❽.....$320

HUM 2168 — Today's Recipe

First released in 2004 with an original issue price of \$320 and a "First Issue 2004" backstamp. Has incised 2003 copyright date and (TM 8) trademark. Companion to HUM 2162 "Baker's Delight" and HUM 2167 "Mixing the Cake". Note the cookbook he holds. Available in European market in a collector set with HUM 2167 "Mixing the Cake" and a German language cookbook. Today's Recipe in the collector set has "First Issue 2004" backstamp, incised 2003 copyright date, and (TM 8) trademark.

☐ 2168 ....5.50" ......(OE) ..❽ \$320

HUM 2169–2170 — (ON) OPEN NUMBERS

HUM 2171/A — Pretty Performer

First released in Spring of 2003 as part of the "Musical Medley" Collector Set along with HUM 2171/B "Serenade of Songs". The original issue price of the set was \$250, with a declared value of \$385. Both figurines, "Serenade of Songs" and "Pretty Performer", are sequentially numbered in worldwide (LE) Limited Editions of 7500, with 5000 for North America. The collector sets feature figurines with matched (LE) Limited Edition numbers. The wooden piano base included in the collector set is brown in the North American version and gold in the European version. "Pretty Performer" has an incised 2001 copyright date, the (TM 8) trademark and (LE) Limited Edition backstamp.

☐ 2171/A ....4.00" ......(LE)....❽ \$185

Pretty Performer

Musical Medley Collector Set - North American Version

HUM 2171/B — Serenade of Songs

First released in Spring of 2003 as part of the "Musical Medley" Collector Set along with HUM 2171/A "Pretty Performer". The original issue price of the set was $250, with a declared value of $385. Both figurines, "Serenade of Songs" and "Pretty Performer", are sequentially numbered, in worldwide (LE) Limited Editions of 7500, with 5000 for North America. The collector set features figurines with matched (LE) Limited Edition numbers. The wooden piano base included in the collector set is brown in the North American version and gold in the European version. "Serenade of Songs" has an incised 2001 copyright date, the (TM 8) trademark and (LE) Limited Edition backstamp.

□ 2171/B ....4.00" ......(**LE**)....❽ $185

HUM 2172 — (ON) OPEN NUMBER

HUM 2173 — First Flight

Commemorating the "Centennial of Aviation", the "100th Anniversary" of Orville and Wilbur Wright's first airplane flight on December 17, 1903. Sculpted by master sculptor Helmut Fischer. First released in 2003 for $200 in a Special Edition of 2000 with an "American Flag" and "bi-plane" backstamp, the (TM 8) trademark and a wooden display base with brass plaque reading "M.I. Hummel First Flight". Available in a "Kitty Hawk" variation featuring a rectangular wooden base with patriotic plaque, the figurine with Special Event markings, and an oval ceramic Kitty Hawk, NC Commemorative plaque. Available without a wooden base, the figurine marked with a "Commemorative Edition" backstamp and the (TM 8) trademark.

□ 2173 ....4.50" ......(**CE**) ..❽ $200

Serenade of Songs

Musical Medley Collector Set - European Version

Special Edition

First Flight

Pretty Posey

HUM 2174/A — Pretty Posey

First released in 2004 as part of the "Pocket of Posies" Collector Set along with HUM 2174/B "Pocket Full of Posies" and "Blooming Delights "Hummelscape (Mark #1086-D). Price for the Collector Set was $320 in 2005. The Hummelscape is a (LE) Limited Edition of 10,000 with a numbered certificate. The Hummelscape features a place for a candle behind the shop windows, motion that rotates the figurine placed by the shop door, and music, playing "Let Me Call You Sweetheart." Figurine in collector's set has an incised 2002 copyright date, the (TM 8) trademark, "Special Edition" backstamp, and flower detail on side of base matching the flowers she holds. Figurine also available with "First Issue 2004" backstamp and plain base, instead of the "Special Edition" backstamp and flower detail on the side of the base. Figurine alone priced $110 in 2005 US Retailer Catalog.

☐ 2174/A....3.50"............**(TW)**.....❽.....$110

**Pocket of Posies
Collector Set**

HUM 2174/B — Pocket Full of Posies

First released in 2004 as part of the "Pocket of Posies" Collector Set along with HUM 2174/A "Pretty Posey" and "Blooming Delights" Hummelscape (Mark #1086-D). Price for the Collector Set was $320 in 2005. The Hummelscape is a (LE) Limited Edition of 10,000 with a numbered certificate. The Hummelscape features a place for a candle behind the shop windows, motion that rotates the figurine placed by the shop door, and music, playing "Let Me Call You Sweetheart." Figurine in collector's set has an incised 2002 copyright date, the (TM 8) trademark, "Special Edition" backstamp, and flower detail on side of base matching the flowers he holds. Figurine also available with "First Issue 2004" backstamp and plain base, instead of the "Special Edition" backstamp and flower detail on the side of the base. Figurine alone priced $110 in 2005 US Retailer Catalog.

Pocket Full of Posies

☐ 2174/B....3.50"............**(TW)**.....❽.....$110

HUM 2175 — From the Pumpkin Patch
First released in Fall 2006 with an original issue price of $169, as a Fall 2006 Artist Event and Customer "Appreciation Days" figurine. Has special markings and the (TM 8) trademark. Companion to HUM 2011 :Little Landscaper with Pumpkin: with ceramic display base which was the Artist Event figurine in Fall 2005.

☐ 2175/0 ....4.50" ......(OE).....❽.....$169

HUM 2176 — (ON) OPEN NUMBER

HUM 2177 — Shall We Dance
First released in July, 2003 in the "Shall We Dance" Collector Set including "Time To Dance" Hummelscape. Set priced $300 on 2004 Goebel NA Suggested Retail Price List. The Hummelscape is a (LE) Limited Edition of 3000 and features motion as the record revolves, and music, playing "Brahm's Waltz." The figurine in the set has inscribed 2002 copyright date, the (TM 8) trademark and "Premier Edition" backstamp. Figurine first appeared separately on 2004 Goebel NA Suggested Retail Price List, priced $250.

☐ 2177 ....5.50" ......(OE).....❽.....$279

Shall We Dance Collector Set   *Shall We Dance*

In blue/gray frame *In sandy/light frame*

**HUM 2178/A —
Dearly Beloved
Framed Picture**
First released in 2003 with an original issue price of $75. A ceramic 4.00 x 6.00" plaque in wooden 5.50" x 7.25" frame with loop for hanging. Features a depiction of HUM 2003 "Dearly Beloved" applied by decal over raised detail. Has a decal M.I. Hummel signature on front of framed picture. Has Hummel name, number, the (TM 8) trademark, and 2002 copyright date printed in blue ink on felt backing of plaque. Available in more than one color of frame. Available in "Dearly Beloved" Gift Set (Large), in presentation box, with HUM 2163/A "Dearly Beloved" Ornament, 2179/A "Dearly Beloved" Certificate, and HUM 2152/A "Dearly Beloved "Trinket Box; set priced $197.50 in 2003.

☐ 2178/A ..7.25" x 5.50" ......(OE)........❽........$75

**HUM 2179/A —
Dearly Beloved
Certificate**
First released in 2003 with an original issue price of $50. A book-shaped plaque, able to stand on its own. With clear film over right-hand page, suggesting how to personalize it. Film is removable so plaque may be personalized. Features a depiction of HUM 2003 "Dearly Beloved" applied by decal over raised detail. Has a decal M.I. Hummel signature, the (TM 8) trademark, and a 2002 copyright date decal. Available in "Dearly Beloved" Gift Set (Large), in presentation box, with HUM 2163/A "Dearly Beloved" Ornament, HUM 2178/A "Dearly Beloved" Framed Picture, and HUM 2152/A "Dearly Beloved" Trinket Box; set priced $197.50 in 2003.

☐ 2179/A ..3.00 x 5.50" ....(OE).........❽........$50

HUM 2180 — The Final Sculpt (LE)

(LE) Limited Edition of 8000 sequentially numbered pieces worldwide (7,500 for the North American market). Modeled by master sculptor Gerhard Skrobek in 2001 exclusively for his "North American Farewell Tour" in the fall of 2002. He visited only 37 cities, autographing his figurine and visiting with collectors and friends. The figurine is a self-portrait of sorts, in M. I. Hummel style, of a young Gerhard doing his final sculpt and waving good-bye, a copy of Gerhard's book: "*Hummels and Me — Life Stories*" can be seen at his feet. The figurine has an incised 2001 copyright date along with the (TM 8) trademark. The original issue price was $350 in 2002.

☐ 2180 ....5.25" ....(**CE**) ....❽ ....$350—400

507

HUM 2181 — Clear As A Bell

First released in Spring of 2004, as a free gift for membership in the M.I. Hummel Club for the 2004/2005 Club year. Has incised 2002 copyright date, the (TM 8) trademark, and the "Club Exclusive" backstamp, Exclusive Edition 2004-2005. Sculpted by master sculptor Helmut Fischer. Part of Second Year of "Kinder Choir". Companion to HUM 846 "Hitting the High Note with Lamppost". Currently available for $50 from Goebel NA to permit M.I. Hummel Club members to complete their "Kinder Choir". A $100 value.

☐ 2181 ....3.75" ....(EE)......❽.......$100

HUM 2182 — First Solo

First released in Spring of 2003, as an (EE) Exclusive Edition for the 2003/2004 Club year, for members of the M.I. Hummel Club. Includes wooden display base with room for "First Solo" and three other "Kinder Choir" figurines. Has incised 2002 copyright date, the (TM 8) trademark, and the "Club Exclusive" back-stamp, Exclusive Edition 2003-2004. Sculpted by master sculptor Helmut Fischer. Part of "First Year of Kinder Choir". Companion to HUM 845 "Too Shy to Sing". Official issue price in 2003 was $105.

☐ 2182 ....3.50" ....(EE)......❽......$105

First Solo

First Solo with Wooden Base

HUM 2183 — Keeping Time

First released in Spring of 2006, as a free gift for membership in the M.I. Hummel Club for the 2006/2007 Club year. Has incised 2002 copyright date, the (TM 8) trademark, and the "Club Exclusive" backstamp, Exclusive Edition 2006-2007. Sculpted by master sculptor Helmut Fischer. Part of (final) Fourth Year of "Kinder Choir". Companion to HUM 847 "Lamplight Caroler". Currently available for $50 from Goebel NA to permit M.I. Hummel Club members to complete their "Kinder Choir". A $100 value.

☐ 2183 ....3.75" ....(EE) ..❽ $100

HUM 2184 — First Violin

First released in Spring of 2005 as an (EE) Exclusive Edition for the 2005/2006 Club year, for members of the M.I. Hummel Club. Includes wooden display base with room for "First Violin" and three other "Kinder Choir" figurines. Has incised 2002 copyright date, the (TM 8) trademark, and the "Club Exclusive" backstamp, Exclusive Edition 2005-2006. Sculpted by master sculptor Helmut Fischer. Part of Third Year of "Kinder Choir". Companion to HUM 848 "Steadfast Soprano". Official issue price in 2003 was $110.

☐ 2184 ....3.75" ....(EE) ..❽ $110

First Violin with Wooden Base

First Violin

HUM 2185 — Winter's Here

First released in 2003 with an original issue price of $250, with "First Issue 2003" backstamp, the (TM 8) trademark and incised 2002 copyright date. The base has the appearance of a mound of snow. A suitable companion for HUM 2037 "Star Light, Star Bright".

☐ 2185 ....5.25"..........(**OE**).....❽.....$259

HUM 2186 — (ON) OPEN NUMBER

HUM 2187 — Benevolent Birdfeeder, The

First released in 2003 with an original issue price of $400 and a "First Issue 2004" backstamp. Has the (TM 8) trademark and incised 2002 copyright date. In October 2003 a (LE) Limited Edition of 150 Arbeitsmuster Editions were made available in North America to M.I. Hummel Club members. These painters' samples bear a crimped metal "Arbeitsmuster Series" tag and are signed by master sample painter Frank Knoch. The Arbeitsmuster Edition has an incised 2002 copyright date, "First Issue 2004" backstamp, and the (TM 8) trademark, and was priced $400 in 2003. Sculpted by master sculptor Helmut Fischer. Regular issue was priced $399 on 2005 Goebel NA Suggested Retail Price List.

☐ 2187 ....5.50"..........(**OE**).....❽.....$399

HUM 2188—2189 — (ON) OPEN NUMBERS

HUM 2190 — Harvest Time

First released in Fall 2003, with an original issue price of $3000. A worldwide sequentially numbered (LE) Limited Edition of 1000, with 500 for North America. Has limited edition backstamp and the (TM 8) trademark. Sculpted by master sculptor Helmut Fischer. Includes ceramic plaque also bearing the limited edition number, and wooden display base. Measures 13.50" long, 6.25" wide and 8.75" tall. In addition, 100 Artist Proofs were specially numbered and made available to collectors in North America in the Fall 2003. The Artist Proof Edition was priced $3000. Companion to HUM 2200 "Autumn Time".

☐ 2190 ....8.75" ....(**LE**) ....❽ $3000

HUM 2191–2192 — (ON) OPEN NUMBERS

HUM 2193 — Flowers for Mother

First released in 2004 with an original issue price of $59.50. Has incised 2003 copyright date, the (TM 8) trademark, but no first issue marking. In North American market, part of "Create-A-Gift" Collection when paired with a "Sentiment Occasion" base. In European market, bearing "Bouquet" backstamp, part of Hummel Figurines "Through the Year" Collection, with available wooden showcase and ceramic month plaques for making a figural calendar. The boy holds a fistful of flowers with a small red heart on top.

☐ 2193 4/0....3.25"....(**OE**)....❽....$69.50

Shown with Happy Valentine's Day Sentiment Occasion base

Flowers for Mother

HUM 2194 — Duty Calls

Third in "Ambassadors of Freedom" Series for AAFES catalog and US Military Post Exchanges. New in 2003. A sequentially numbered (LE) Limited Edition of 3000, with a red, white and blue flying eagle backstamp and "Ambassadors of Freedom" inscription. Has incised 2003 copyright date, limited edition backstamp, and the (TM 8) trademark. Includes wooden display with brass plaque inscribed "Duty Calls/ Ambassadors of Freedom", and a ceramic plaque showing a reproduction of the famous recruiting poster by James Montgomery Flagg, of Uncle Sam pointing and saying "I Want You." Figurine measures 7.50" and with wooden base stands 8.25" tall. Sculpted by master sculptor Helmut Fischer.

Resembles HUM 2120 "Little Miss Mail Carrier".

☐ 2194 ....7.50", 8.25" with display ......(**LE**) ....❽ $300-400

HUM 2195 — Sunflower Girl

First released in 2004 with an original issue price of $69.50. Has incised 2003 copyright date, the (TM 8) trademark, but no first issue marking. In North American market, part of "Create-A-Gift" Collection when paired with a "Sentiment Occasion" base. In European market, bearing "Sunflower" backstamp, part of Hummel Figurines "Through the Year" Collection, with available wooden showcase and ceramic month plaques for making a figural calendar. Companion to HUM 2219 "Sunflower Boy".

☐ 2195 4/0........3.25"........(**OE**)....❽.....$69.50

HUM 2196 — (ON) OPEN NUMBER

Shown with Happy Mother's Day Sentiment Occasion base

Sunflower Girl

HUM 2197 —
American Spirit
First released in 2003
with an original issue
price of $275.
Includes US flag.
Sculpted by Marion
Huschka in 2001.
Has the (TM 8) trade-
mark.

☐ 2197 ......4.75" ....(TW)..... ❽ $279

**HUM 2198 — Melody
– Conductor**
The "Kinder Choir" con-
ductor. First released in
Spring of 2006, as a
free gift during the 2006-
2007 Club year, for
members of the M.I.
Hummel Club who have
acquired the eight fig-
urines in the "Kinder
Choir": HUM 845 "Too
Shy to Sing", HUM 846
"Hitting the High Note
with Lamppost", HUM
847 "Lamplight Caroler",
HUM 848 "Steadfast
Soprano", HUM 2181

"Clear as a Bell", HUM 2182 "First Solo" with
Wooden Base, HUM 2183 "Keeping Time", and
HUM 2184 "First Violin" with Wooden Base. Has the
(TM 8) trademark and the Club Exclusive back-
stamp. A $110 value.

☐ 2198 ......4.00" ....(EE)..... ❽ $110

HUM 2199 — (ON) OPEN NUMBER

HUM 2200 — Autumn Time

First released in 2005 with an original issue price of $3000. A worldwide sequentially numbered (LE) Limited Edition of 1000, with 400 for North America. Has limited edition backstamp, incised 2005 copyright date and the (TM 8) trademark. Sculpted by the Goebel sculpting team of Anette Barth, Tamara Fuchs, and Helmut Fischer. Includes ceramic Certificate of Authenticity also bearing the (LE) Limited Edition number, and wooden display base. Companion to HUM 2190 "Harvest Time".

☐ 2200 ,,,...9.50 x 12.50".....(LE).....❽.....$3000

HUM 2201–2202 — (ON) OPEN NUMBERS

HUM 2203 — Hope – With Pink Ribbon Bow Base

First released in October of 2004 in the North American market with an original issue price of $99. Has "National Breast Cancer Foundation" backstamp, the (TM 8) trademark, and incised 2004 copyright date, no "First Issue" marking. Includes "Pink Ribbon Bow" base, also with "National Breast Cancer Foundation" backstamp. A mixed media figurine, the girl holds a bouquet of real fabric flowers. For each "Hope" figurine purchased, Goebel NA pledges a donation to benefit breast cancer research. First in a series, followed by HUM 2233 "Light of Hope" released in 2005 and HUM 2240 "Heart of Hope" released in 2006.

☐ 2203 ......3.50" ....(OE).....❽.....$99

HUM 2204 — Holiday Fun

First released in Fall of 2004 as part of "Bavarian Christmas Market" Collector Set with "Bavarian Christmas Market" Hummelscape (Mark #1098-D). Hummelscape depicts a Christkindlmarkt, and features lights and music, playing "Twelve Days of Christmas". Collector set offered at $179 special introductory price through December 31, 2004 and full price of $330 from January 1, 2005. Figurine in set has "2004 Holiday Edition" and "holly" backstamp, incised 2004 copyright date and (TM 8) trademark. The girl holds a real glass ball ornament. Figurine also available without special backstamp. Figurine alone listed for $230 in US Retailer Catalog in 2005.

☐ 2204 ......4.25" ....(OE) ....❽ $230

Holiday Fun

Bavarian
Christmas
Market
Collector Set

HUM 2205 — Troublemaker

First released in January of 2005 with an original issue price of $1200. Fourth edition in "Moments in Time" Collection. Sequentially numbered worldwide (LE) Limited Edition of 5000. Has incised 2004 copyright date, the (TM 8) trademark, "Moments in Time" and "Limited Edition" backstamps. Sculpted by master sculptor Helmut Fischer. Companion to HUM 2214 "What a Smile" and HUM 2215 "Gotcha!" The dog has the girl's slipper in his mouth, and her toe has slipped through a hole in her sock.

☐ 2205 ......7.25" ....(LE)......❽ $1200

HUM 2206–2208 — (ON) OPEN NUMBERS

Puppet Pal

HUM 2209/A — Puppet Love

First released in 2004 with "First Issue 2004" backstamp, the (TM 8) trademark, and incised 2004 copyright date, with original issue price of $145. Sculpted by master sculptor Helmut Fischer. Part of "Puppet Theater" Collector Set with HUM 2209/B "Puppet Pal", (Mark #1094-D) "Puppet Theater" Hummelscape and a storybook titled "An Enchanted Afternoon"; set priced $390 in 2004. The Hummelscape is 7.75" tall and features motion, with puppets going up and down in the theater, and music, playing "Pop Goes the Weasel." Also available by itself (no "Puppet Pal" figurine) with the same Hummelscape and storybook in "Puppet Love" Collector Set, priced $245 in 2004. Storybooks available in 2004 while supplies last. Available in the European market in "Puppet Theater" Collector Set with HUM 2209/B "Puppet Pal" and Wooden Theater. Wooden theater stands on its own and measures 5.00" tall, 4.00" wide and 1.75" deep.

☐ 2209/A.......3.50"......(**OE**)......❽.....$145

HUM 2209/B — Puppet Pal

First released in 2004 with "First Issue 2004" backstamp, the (TM 8) trademark, and incised 2004 copyright date, with original issue price of $145. Sculpted by master sculptor Helmut Fischer. Part of "Puppet Theater" Collector Set with HUM 2209/A "Puppet Love", (Mark #1094-D) "Puppet Theater" Hummelscape and a storybook titled "An Enchanted Afternoon"; set priced $390 in 2004. The Hummelscape is 7.75" tall and features motion, with puppets going up and down in the theater, and music, playing "Pop Goes the Weasel." Also available by itself (no "Puppet Love" figurine) with the same Hummelscape and storybook in "Puppet Pal" Collector Set, priced $245 in 2004. Storybooks available in 2004 while supplies last. Available in the European market in "Puppet Theater" Collector Set with HUM 2209/A "Puppet Love" and Wooden Theater. Wooden theater stands on its own and measures 5.00" tall, 4.00" wide and 1.75" deep.

Puppet Pal

☐ 2209/B ....3.50" ....(**OE**).....❽....$145

HUM 2210 — (ON) OPEN NUMBER

Puppet Theater Collector Set with Hummelscape

Puppet Theater Collector Set with wooden theatre

HUM 2211 — Fancy Footwork

First released in Fall of 2005 with an original issue price of $199 with First Issue 2006 backstamp, incised 2004 copyright date and the (TM 8) trademark.

☐ 2211........4.25" ....(OE) ....❽ $199

HUM 2212–2213 — (OE) OPEN NUMBERS

HUM 2214 — What A Smile

First released in January of 2005 with an original issue price of $320, with "First Issue 2005" backstamp, incised 2004 copyright date and the (TM 8) trademark. Companion to HUM 2205 "Troublemaker" and HUM 2215 "Gotcha!" Sculpted by master sculptor Helmut Fischer in 2004.

☐ 2214 ......6.25" ....(OE) ....❽ $320

Fancy Footwork

HUM 2215 — Gotcha!

First released in January of 2005 with an original issue price of $320, with "First Issue 2005" backstamp, incised 2004 copyright date and the (TM 8) trademark. Companion to HUM 2205 "Troublemaker" and HUM 2214 "What A Smile". Sculpted by master sculptor Helmut Fischer in 2004.

☐ 2215 ......5.75" ....(OE) ....❽ $320

What A Smile

Gotcha!

HUM 2216 — Homecoming

Fifth in "Ambassadors of Freedom" Series for AAFES catalog and US Military Post Exchanges. New in 2005. A sequentially numbered (LE) Limited Edition of 3000, with a red, white and blue flying eagle backstamp and "Ambassadors of Freedom" inscription. Has incised 2004 copyright date, (LE) Limited Edition backstamp, and the (TM 8) trademark. Includes wooden display with brass plaque inscribed "Homecoming/Ambassadors of Freedom", and wooden tree tied with a yellow ribbon. Includes certificate which states "A tribute to those who have served their country in support of the fight against terrorism: W. Goebel Porzellanfabrik presents the "Homecoming" set, with a special version of a popular M.I. Hummel figurine, made with the service members from Operation Iraqi Freedom in mind." Figurine measures 8.00" and with wooden base stands 9.25" tall.

☐ 2216/II ....8.00", 9.25" with display.........(LE).....❽.....$400—500

Do You Love It! - personalizable

HUM 2217/A — Do You Love It!

First released in Spring of 2005 with an original issue price of $109 as the Spring 2005 Artist Event piece. Has Hummel number, 2004 copyright date and (TM 8) trademark applied by decal and incised "Hummel" signature on the back of the frame she holds, due to limited room on the base of the figurine. No first issue markings. May be personalized. Comes with instructions for sending it away for personalization, at an additional fee. Companion to HUM 2217/B "Look What I Made!" Variation available in Spring of 2006 in North American market for $109 with "I Love You" message and design of red roses already applied.

Do You Love It!
with I Love You
message

☐ 2217/A ....3.25" ....(OE) ....❽ $109

HUM 2217/B — Look What I Made!

First released in Spring of 2005 with an original issue price of $109 as the Spring 2005 Artist Event piece. Has Hummel number, 2004 copyright date and (TM 8) trademark applied by decal and incised "Hummel" signature on the back of the frame he holds, due to limited room on the base of the figurine. No first issue

Look What I Made! with I Love You message

markings. May be personalized. Comes with instructions for sending it away for personalization, at an additional fee. Companion to HUM 2217/A "Do You Love It!" Variation available in Spring of 2006 in North American market for $109 with "I Love You" message and design of yellow sunflowers already applied.

Look What I Made! - personalizable

☐ 2217/B....3.25" ....(**OE**)....❽....$109

HUM 2218 — Springtime Friends

First made available in July of 2005, with "Chick" backstamp in the "Springtime Splendor" Collector Set, representing Spring in a "Four Seasons" Collector Set that includes a wooden display shelf for all four seasons. Available from Fall 2005 in European market in "Spring" Landscape: Hummel Source, with HUM 2227 "Morning Call", HUM 661 "My Little Lamb", HUM 197 4/0 "Be Patient" and three Spring accessories (Fountain, Wagon and Spring Tree); the set representing Spring in a "Four Seasons" Collector Series. The figurine has incised 2004 copyright date, "Lamb Laying" backstamp, and the (TM 8) trademark, no first issue markings. She has a flower in her hand.

☐ 2218 ......3.25" ....(**OE**)....❽....$99

HUM 2219 — Sunflower Boy

First made available in July of 2005, with "Sunflower" backstamp in the "Summer Days" Collector Set, representing Summer in a "Four Seasons" Collector Set that includes a wooden display shelf for all four seasons. Available from Fall 2005 in European market in Summer Landscape: Hummel Pond, with HUM 136 4/0 "Friends", HUM 547 4/0 "Bunny's Mother", HUM 2226 "Shepherd's Apprentice" and three Summer accessories (Wayside Cross, Fence and Bench); the set representing Summer in a "Four Seasons" Collector Series. The figurine has "Watering Can" backstamp and the (TM 8) trademark, no first issue markings. Companion to HUM 2195 4/0 "Sunflower Girl".

☐ 2219........3.25" ....(OE) ....❽ $99

HUM 2220 — School Days

First made available in July of 2005, with "Pumpkin" backstamp in the "Autumn Delights" Collector Set, representing Fall in a "Four Seasons" Collector Set that includes a wooden display shelf for all four seasons. Available for sale separately as of July of 2006. The figurine has "Pumpkin" backstamp and the (TM 8) trademark, no first issue markings.

☐ 2220 ....3.25" ....(OE) ❽ $99

HUM 2221 — All Bundled Up

First made available in July of 2005, with "Snowflake" backstamp in the "Winter Magic" Collector Set, representing Winter in a "Four Seasons" Collector Set that includes a wooden display shelf for all four seasons. Available for sale separately as of July 2006 as part of the "Wintertime Wonders" Series. The figurine has "Snowflake" backstamp and the (TM 8) trademark, no first issue markings. Resembles HUM 2026 "Good Tidings". Notice in Summer 2006 *INSIGHTS* that Snowflake backstamp will change to a Snowman backstamp in 2007.

☐ 2221 ....3.25"..........(OE).......❽.......$99

HUM 2222 — A Star For You

First released in Fall of 2005 with an original issue price of $359. A sequentially numbered worldwide (LE) Limited Edition of 7500. Has incised 2005 copyright date, the (TM 8) trademark and Limited Edition backstamp. With matching round presentation tin. Third of mixed media pieces with Swarovski crystal – features a Swarovski crystal star. Also see HUM 856 "A Heartfelt Gift", HUM 902 "Sunflowers, My Love", and HUM 2248 "Special Delivery". A one-of-a kind HUM 2222 "A Star For You" figurine was presented to Robert and Ruth Miller on the occasion of their 80th birthdays in the Spring of 2005, with an "80" in place of the crystal star.

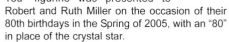

☐ 2222 ......5.00" ....(**OE**) ....❽ $359

HUM 2223 — Practice Makes Perfect, Girl

First released in July 2005 with an original issue price of $139. Has Hummel number, 2004 copyright date, the (TM 8) trademark applied by decal under the base and inscribed "Hummel" signature across back of her skirt. Includes Black Wooden Base. Companion to HUM 771 2/0 "Practice Makes Perfect", Boy with Black Wooden Base. Suitable for display with "Kinder Choir".

☐ 2223 ......3.25" ....(**OE**) ....❽ 139

HUM 2224–2225 — (OE) OPEN NUMBERS

HUM 2226 — Shepherd's Apprentice

First made available in Fall of 2005, with "Goat" backstamp in European market in Summer Landscape: Hummel Pond, with HUM 136 4/0 "Friends", HUM 547 4/0 "Bunny's Mother", HUM 2219 "Sunflower Boy" and three Summer accessories (Wayside Cross, Fence and Bench); the set representing Summer in a "Four Seasons" Collector Series. Available on the North American market from January 2006 as part of the "Animal Friends" Collection with an original issue price of $139. The figurine has incised 2005 copyright date, "Goat" backstamp, and the (TM 8) trademark, no first issue markings.

☐ 2226 ......3.25" ....(**OE**) ....❽ $139

HUM 2227 — Morning Call

First made available in Fall of 2005, with Rooster backstamp in European market in Spring Landscape: Hummel Source, with HUM 661 "My Little Lamb", HUM 2218 "Springtime Friends", HUM 197 4/0 "Be Patient" and three Spring accessories (Fountain, Wagon and Spring Tree); the set representing Spring in a "Four Seasons" Collector Series. Available on the North American market from June 2006 as part of the "Animal Friends" Collection with an original issue price of $139. The figurine has incised 2005 copyright date, "Rooster" backstamp, and the (TM 8) trademark, no first issue markings. Resembles HUM 2085 "Little Farmhand" and HUM 199 "Feeding Time".

☐ ..2227.......3.25".......(**OE**).....❽.....$139

HUM 2228 — Can't Catch Me

First made available in Fall of 2005, with "Goose" backstamp in European market in Fall Landscape: Hummel Garden, with HUM 2229 "Puppy Pal", HUM 2231 "Friendly Feeding", HUM 2232 "Let's Be Friends" and three Fall accessories (Scarecrow, Apple Tree, Wheelbarrow); the set representing Fall in a "Four Seasons" Collector Series. Available on the North American market from April 2006 as part of the "Animal Friends" Collection with an original issue price of $129. The figurine has incised 2005 copyright date, "Goose" backstamp, and the (TM 8) trademark, no first issue markings. Resembles HUM 2097 "Can I Play?"

☐ 2228.......3.25".......(**OE**).....❽.....$129

HUM 2229 — Puppy Pal

First made available in Fall of 2005, with "Puppy" backstamp in European market as part of Fall Landscape: Hummel Garden, with HUM 2228 "Can't Catch Me", HUM 2231 "Friendly Feeding", HUM 2232 "Let's Be Friends" and three Fall accessories (Scarecrow, Apple Tree, Wheelbarrow); the set representing Fall in a "Four Seasons" Collector Series. Available on the North American market from January 2006 as part of the "Animal Friends" Collection with an original issue price of $109. The figurine has incised 2005 copyright date, "Puppy" backstamp, and the (TM 8) trademark, no first issue markings.

☐ 2229........3.25" ....(**OE**).....❽.....$109

HUM 2230/A — Mary

First released in Fall of 2005 with an original issue price of $149, incised 2005 copyright date, the (TM 8) trademark, and no first issue markings. Has incised M.I. Hummel signature on back of her cape. Part of "Children's Nativity Set". Available in "Holy Family" Set with HUM 2230/B "Joseph" and HUM 2230/C "Baby Jesus" with Straw Manger, and free "Children's Christmas Pageant" Center Stage with base and ceramic creche featuring stained glass background. An introductory price of $299 was offered on the "Holy Family Set" through December 31, 2005. Full price, $347.50, as of January 1, 2006.

☐ 2230/A ....3.50" ....(**OE**) ....❽ $149

Mary

HUM 2230/B — Joseph

First released in Fall of 2005 with an original issue price of $149. Has Hummel number, 2005 copyright date and the (TM 8) trademark applied by decal, no first issue markings. Has incised M.I. Hummel signature on back of his cape. Part of "Children's Nativity Set". Available in "Holy Family" Set with HUM 2230/A "Mary" and HUM 2230/C "Baby Jesus" with Straw Manger, and free "Children's Christmas Pageant" Center Stage with base and ceramic creche featuring stained glass background. An introductory price of $299 was offered on the "Holy Family" Set through December 31, 2005. Full price, $347.50, as of January 1, 2006.

☐ 2230/B ....4.25" ....(**OE**) ....❽ $149

Joseph

Holy Family Set for HUM 2230/A; HUM 2230/B and HUM 2230/C

Jesus with Straw Manger

Side view

HUM 2230/C — Baby Jesus With Straw Manger

First released in Fall of 2005 with an original issue price of $49.50 Has Hummel number, M.I. Hummel signature, 2005 copyright date and the (TM 8) trademark applied by decal, no first issue markings. Part of "Children's Nativity" Set. Available in "Holy Family" Set with HUM 2230/A "Mary" and HUM 2230/B "Joseph", and free Children's Christmas Pageant Center Stage with base and ceramic creche featuring stained glass background. An introductory price of $299 was offered on the "Holy Family" Set through December 31, 2005. Full price, $347.50, as of January 1, 2006. Manger is wooden, filled with bits of loose straw. "Baby Jesus" figurine is separate from manger.

☐ 2230/C....2.50" ....(**OE**) ....❽ $49.50

Holy Family Set for HUM 2230/A; HUM 2230/B and HUM 2230/C

HUM 2230/D — Shepherd with Staff

First released in Fall of 2005 with an original issue price of $149. Has Hummel number, 2005 copyright date and the (TM 8) trademark applied by decal, no first issue markings. Has incised "Hummel" on seat of his pants. Named Franz. Part of "Children's Nativity" Set. Available in Three Shepherd Set with HUM 2230/E "Shepherd with Milkjug" and HUM 2230/F "Shepherd with Flute", and free Children's Christmas Pageant Right Stage with base and background; set priced $447 in 2006. See photo of set on page 525.

☐ 2230/D....4.00" ....(**OE**) ....❽ $149

Shepherd with Staff

HUM 2230/E — Shepherd with Milkjug

First released in Fall of 2005 with an original issue price of $149. Has Hummel number, 2005 copyright date and the (TM 8) trademark applied by decal, no first issue markings. Has incised "Hummel" on his back. Named Sepp. Part of "Children's Nativity" Set. Available in Three Shepherd Set with HUM 2230/D "Shepherd with Staff" and HUM 2230/F "Shepherd with Flute", and free Children's Christmas Pageant Right Stage with base and background; set priced $447 in 2006.

☐ 2230/E ....4.25" ....(**OE**) .... ❽ $149

Three Shepherds Set for HUM 2230/D; HUM 2230/E and HUM 2230/F

Shepherd with Milkjug

HUM 2230/F — Shepherd with Flute

First released in Fall of 2005 with an original issue price of $149. Has Hummel number, 2005 copyright date and the (TM 8) trademark applied by decal, no first issue markings. Has incised "Hummel" on side of his left leg. Named Hans. Part of "Children's Nativity" Set. Available in Three Shepherd Set with HUM 2230/D "Shepherd with Staff" and HUM 2230/E "Shepherd with Milkjug", and free Children's Christmas Pageant Right Stage with base and background; set priced $447 in 2006.

☐ 2230/F ....3.00" .....(**OE**).....❽....$149

Shepherd with Flute

King Melchior with Open Box

HUM 2230/G — King Melchior

First released in Fall of 2005 with an original issue price of $149. Has Hummel number, 2005 copyright date and the (TM 8) trademark applied by decal, no first issue markings. Has incised "Hummel" on the back of his cape. Part of "Children's Nativity" Set. He holds an open box. Available in Three Kings Set with HUM 2230/H "King Balthazar" and HUM 2230/J "King Gaspar", and free Children's Christmas Pageant Left Stage with base and background; set priced $447 in 2006.

☐ 2230/G....4.75".....(OE).....❽...$149

Three Kings Set for HUM 2230/G; HUM 2230/H and HUM 2230/J

HUM 2230/H — King Balthazar

First released in Fall of 2005 with an original issue price of $149. Has Hummel number, 2005 copyright date and the (TM-8) trademark applied by decal, no first issue markings. Has incised "Hummel" on the back of his cape. Part of "Children's Nativity" Set. He is kneeling. Available in Three Kings Set with HUM 2230/G "King Melchior" and HUM 2230/J "King Gaspar", and free Children's Christmas Pageant Left Stage with base and background; set priced $447 in 2006.

☐ 2230/H ....3.75" ....(OE) ....❽ $149

King Balthazar kneeling

HUM 2230/I — (OE) OPEN NUMBER

HUM 2230/J — King Gaspar

First released in Fall of 2005 with an original issue price of $149. Has Hummel number, 2005 copyright date and the (TM 8) trademark applied by decal, no first issue markings. Has incised "Hummel" on the back of his cape. Part of "Children's Nativity" Set. He wears a feather headdress. Available in Three Kings Set with HUM 2230/G "King Melchior" and HUM 2230/H "King Balthazar", and free Children's Christmas Pageant Left Stage with base and background; set priced $447 in 2006. See photo of set on page 526.

☐ 2230/J ....4.00" ....(**OE**) .... ❽ $149

HUM 2230/K — Angel with Lantern

First released in Fall of 2005 with an original issue price of $149. Has Hummel number, 2005 copyright date and the (TM 8) trademark applied by decal; has no first issue markings. Has incised "Hummel" on the back hem of gown. Part of "Children's Nativity" Set. Available in "Angel" and "Animals" Set with HUM 2230/M "Young Calf", HUM 2230/N "Donkey", HUM 2230/O "Sheep Laying" and HUM 2230/P "Sheep Standing"; set priced $309 in 2006.

☐ 2230/K....4.25" ....(**OE**) .... ❽ $149

HUM 2230/L — Angela

First released midyear in 2006, with an original issue price of $99, as an addition to the "Children's Nativity" Set. Has the (TM 8) trademark.

☐ 2230/L ....3.25" ....(**OE**) .... ❽ $99

King Gaspar with Feather Headdress

Angel With Lantern

Angela

HUM 2230/M — Young Calf

First released in Fall of 2005 with an original issue price of $55. Has 2005 copyright date and the (TM-8) trademark applied by decal; has no first issue markings. Does not have Hummel number or M.I. Hummel signature on the figurine. Part of "Children's Nativity" Set. Available in "Ange"l and "Animals" Set with HUM 2230/K "Angel with Lantern", HUM 2230/N "Donkey", HUM 2230/O "Sheep Laying" and HUM 2230/P "Sheep Standing"; set priced $309 in 2006.

☐ 2230/M ..3.25" ....(**OE**) ....❽ $55

HUM 2230/N — Donkey

First released in Fall of 2005 with an original issue price of $55. Has Goebel mark, not a Hummel trademark, and no first issue markings. Does not have a copyright date, Hummel number, or M.I. Hummel signature on the figurine. Part of "Children's Nativity" Set. Available in "Angel" and "Animals" Set with HUM 2230/K "Angel with Lantern", HUM 2230/M "Young Calf", HUM 2230/O "Sheep Laying" and HUM 2230/P "Sheep Standing"; set priced $309 in 2006.

☐ 2230/N....4.00" ....(**OE**) ....❽ $55

HUM 2230/O — Sheep, Laying

First released in Fall of 2005 with an original issue price of $25. Has Goebel mark, not a Hummel trademark, and no first issue markings. Does not have a copyright date, Hummel number, or M.I. Hummel signature on the figurine. Part of "Children's Nativity" Set. Available in "Angel" and "Animals" Set with HUM 2230/K "Angel with Lantern", HUM 2230/M "Young Calf", HUM 2230/N "Donkey" and HUM 2230/P "Sheep Standing"; set priced $309 in 2006.

☐ 2230/O....1.75" ....(**OE**) ....❽ $25

HUM 2230/P — Sheep, Standing

First released in Fall of 2005 with an original issue price of $25. Has Goebel mark, not a Hummel trademark, and no first issue markings. Does not have a copyright date, Hummel number, or M.I. Hummel signature on the figurine. Part of "Children's Nativity" Set. Available in "Angel" and "Animals" Set with HUM 2230/K "Angel with Lantern", HUM 2230/M "Young Calf", HUM 2230/N "Donkey" and HUM 2230/O "Sheep Laying"; set priced $309 in 2006.

☐ 2230/P ....2.50" ....(**OE**) ....❽ $25

Children's Christmas Pageant Display

Children's Christmas Pageant Display shown with 14 piece Children's Nativity Set

Children's Christmas Pageant Display

First released in 2005 for the "Children's Nativity" Set. Consists of three parts that fit together. Available free with purchase of "Children's Nativity" sets. The Children's Christmas Pageant Left Stage is free in Three Kings Set. The Children's Christmas Pageant Center Stage and Creche are free in "Holy Family" Set. The Children's Christmas Pageant Right Stage is free in "Three Shepherds" Set.

Children's Christmas Stable, shown with accessories Bridge and Trees

*Children's Christmas Stable, shown with accessories Bridge and Trees, and
14 piece Children's Nativity Set*

HUM 2230/S — Children's Nativity Stable and Accessories: Bridge and Five Trees
First released in 2005 in the European market for the "Children's Nativity" Set. Consists
of two parts: a stable and a set of accessories. Stones weight down the roofing on the
stable. The wooden stable includes two bales of hay, and wooden pieces: swing gate for
the animal pen, ladder, shutters for the window, and shooting star. The set of accessories includes the wooden bridge and five rough hewn trees.

☐ 2230/S..................12.75 x 26.75" ....(**OE**)............$215

HUM 2231 — Friendly Feeding

First made available in Fall of 2005, with "Calf" backstamp in European market as part of Fall Landscape: Hummel Garden, with HUM 2228 "Can't Catch Me", HUM 2229 "Puppy Pal", HUM 2232 "Let's Be Friends" and three Fall accessories (Scarecrow, Apple Tree, Wheelbarrow); the set representing Fall in a "Four Seasons" Collector Series. Available on the North American market from June 2006 as part of the "Animal Friends" Collection with an original issue price of $139. The figurine has incised 2005 copyright date, "Calf" backstamp, and the (TM 8) trademark, no first issue markings. Resembles HUM 2165 "Farm Days".

☐ 2231 ....3.25" ....(**OE**) .... ❽ $139

HUM 2232 — Let's Be Friends

First made available in Fall of 2005, with "Squirrel" backstamp in European market as part of Fall Landscape: Hummel Garden, with HUM 2228 "Can't Catch Me", HUM 2229 "Puppy Pal", HUM 2231 "Friendly Feeding" and three Fall accessories (Scarecrow, Apple Tree, Wheelbarrow); the set representing Fall in a "Four Seasons" Collector Series. Available on the North American market from June 2006 as part of the "Animal Friends" Collection with an original issue price of $129. The figurine has incised 2005 copyright date, "Squirrel" backstamp, and the (TM 8) trademark, no first issue markings. Resembles HUM 2053 "Playful Pals".

☐ 2232 ....2.50" ....(**OE**) .... ❽ $129

HUM 2233 — Light of Hope with Pink Ribbon Base

First released in October of 2005 in the North American market with an original issue price of $109. Has "National Breast Cancer Foundation" backstamp, the (TM 8) trademark, and incised 2005 copyright date, no "First Issue" marking. Includes "Pink Ribbon" Bow Base, also with "National Breast Cancer Foundation" backstamp. A mixed media figurine, the girl holds a lantern by a metal chain. For each "Light of Hope" figurine purchased, Goebel NA pledges a donation to benefit breast cancer research. Second in "Hope" Series, with HUM 2203 "Hope" released in 2004 and HUM 2240 "Heart of Hope" released in 2006.

☐ 2233 ....3.50" ....(**OE**) .... ❽ $109

Night Before Christmas

HUM 2234 — Night Before Christmas

First released in Fall of 2005 as part of "Night Before Christmas" Collector Set with "Night Before Christmas" Hummelscape (Mark #1122-D); set priced $249. Hummelscape measures 7.00" tall, 7.00" wide and 6.00" deep, and features fiber optics that light the tree, star and fireplace. Figurine in set has "Holiday 2005 Special Edition" and "Red Bow" backstamp, incised 2005 copyright date and (TM 8) trademark, no first issue marking. Figurine alone lists for $230 in 2006 Goebel NA U.S. Suggested Retail Price List.

Night Before Christmas Collector Set

☐ 2234 ....4.00" ....(OE) .... ❽ $230

HUM 2235 — Lucky Friend

First released in July 2006 with an original issue price of $199, bearing the (TM 8) trademark, one of four Hummels in the "Heart of Hummel" Collection. "Heart" backstamp and heart on basket. Worldwide (LE) Limited Edition of 5000, sequentially numbered. Just 2500 "Heart of Hummel" Collection Sets are available with matching (LE) Limited Edition numbers on all four Hummels. The Collection Set features HUM 624 "Fresh Blossoms", HUM 908 "Gone-A-Wandering", HUM 2235 "Lucky Friend", and HUM 2237 "Sunday Stroll" in a blue rectangular collector tin; set priced $795.

☐ 2235 ....4.50" ....(LE) .... ❽ $199

HUM 2236 — Sleigh Ride

First made available in Fall of 2005, with "Snowflake" backstamp in European market in Winter Landscape: Hummel Hill, with HUM 2035 4/0 "First Snow", HUM 59 4/0 "Skier", HUM 421 4/0 "It's Cold" and three Winter accessories (Winter Tree, Snowman and Birdhouse); the set representing Winter in a "Four Seasons" Collector Series. Available on the North American market from January 2006 as part of the "Wintertime Wonders" Series with an original issue price of $139. The figurine has incised 2005 copyright date, "Snowflake" backstamp, and the (TM 8) trademark, no first issue markings. She resembles the girl at the front of the sled in HUM 2072 "Winter Days".

☐ 2236..3.25" ....(OE) .... ❽ $139

HUM 2237 — Sunday Stroll

First released in July of 2006 with an original issue price of $199, bearing the (TM 8) trademark, one of four Hummels in the "Heart of Hummel" Collection. "Heart" backstamp and heart on dog's collar. Worldwide (LE) Limited Edition of 5000, sequentially numbered. Just 2500 "Heart of Hummel" Collection Sets are available with matching (LE) Limited Edition numbers on all four Hummels. The Collection Set features HUM 624 "Fresh Blossoms", HUM 908 "Gone-A-Wandering", HUM 2235 "Lucky Friend", and HUM 2237 "Sunday Stroll" in a blue rectangular collector tin: set priced $795.

☐ 2237 ....4.50"..........(LE) ....❽ $199

HUM 2238–2239 — (ON) OPEN NUMBERS

HUM 2240 — Heart of Hope

First released in October 2006 with an original issue price of $109, and a Pink Ribbon Bow Base. Third in "Hope" Series with HUM 2203 "Hope" released in 2004 and HUM 2233 "Light of Hope" released in 2005. Has the (TM 8) trademark. A mixed media figurine. Continues Goebel's support of breast cancer awareness and research.

☐ 2240 ....3.50"..........(OE) ....❽ $109

HUM 2241 — Holiday Dreaming
Collector Set

A new "Holiday Dreaming" Collector Set has been announced for release in November 2006 with an original issue price of $259. The collector set includes a figurine of a boy dragging home the Christmas tree and a Hummelscape depicting a toy shop decked out with greenery for the holidays. The figurine has the (TM 8) trademark.

☐ 2241.......4.50".........(OE).....❽.....$259

HUM 2242–2247 — (ON) OPEN
NUMBERS

HUM 2248 — Special Delivery
Released in September 2006 in (TM 8) in a (LE) Limited Edition with an original issue price of $359. Fourth in a series of mixed media pieces with Swarovski crystal – features a Swarovski crystal gift box in the hands of the shorter girl. Also see HUM 856 "A Heartfelt Gift", HUM 902 "Sunflowers, My Love", and HUM 2222 "A Star For You".

☐ 2248.........5.75".........(LE).....❽....$359

HUM 2249–3011 — (ON) OPEN NUMBERS

HUM 3012 — Celestial Musician Ceramic Ball Ornament
The ornament has a true ball shape and features the same design on the front and the back. One in a set of eight such ball ornaments depicting angels. Has incised M.I. Hummel signature. Features a depiction of HUMI 188 "Celestial Musician" in bas relief. Produced for Goebel by a firm in China, not produced by W. Goebel Porzellanfabrik. Has Hummel number, Goebel mark and 1996 copyright date applied by decal on the bottom. Made of fine, smooth ceramic, includes gold thread for hanging. Sometimes sold with gold ring base for display. Price in 2004 was $49.

☐ 3012 ....3.00"..........(TW) $49

HUM 3013 & 3014 — Angel Candleholders, see page 571.

HUM 3015 — Christmas Angel Ceramic Ball Ornament
The ornament has a true ball shape and features the same design on the front and the back. One in a set of eight such ball ornaments depicting angels. Has incised M.I. Hummel signature. Features a depiction of HUM 301 "Christmas Angel" in bas relief. Produced for Goebel by a firm in China, not produced by W. Goebel Porzellanfabrik. Has Hummel number, Goebel mark and 1998 copyright date applied by decal on the bottom. Made of fine, smooth ceramic, includes gold thread for hanging. Sometimes sold with gold ring base for display. Price in 2004 was $49.

☐ 3015 ....3.00" ....(TW)....$49

HUM 3016 — Angel Duet Ceramic Ball Ornament
The ornament has a true ball shape and features the same design on the front and the back. One in a set of eight such ball ornaments depicting angels. Has incised M.I. Hummel signature. Features a depiction of HUM 261 "Angel Duet" in bas relief. Produced for Goebel by a firm in China, not produced by W. Goebel Porzellanfabrik. Has Hummel number, Goebel mark and 1999 copyright date applied by decal on the bottom. Made of fine, smooth ceramic, includes gold thread for hanging. Sometimes sold with gold ring base for display. Price in 2004 was $49.

☐ 3016 ....3.00" ....(**TW**)....$49

HUM 3017 — Angel Serenade Ceramic Ball Ornament
The ornament has a true ball shape and features the same design on the front and the back. One in a set of eight such ball ornaments depicting angels. Has incised M.I. Hummel signature. Features a depiction of HUM 83 "Angel Serenade with Lamb" in bas relief. Produced for Goebel by a firm in China, not produced by W. Goebel Porzellanfabrik. Has Hummel number, Goebel mark and 1999 copyright date applied by decal on the bottom. Made of fine, smooth ceramic, includes gold thread for hanging. Sometimes sold with gold ring base for display. Price in 2004 was $49.

☐ 3017 ....3.00" ....(**TW**)....$49

HUM 3018 — Christmas Song Ceramic Ball Ornament
The ornament has a true ball shape and features the same design on the front and the back. One in a set of eight such ball ornaments depicting angels. Has incised M.I. Hummel signature. Features a depiction of HUM 343 "Christmas Song" in bas relief. Produced for Goebel by a firm in China, not produced by W. Goebel Porzellanfabrik. Has Hummel number, Goebel mark and copyright date applied by decal on the bottom. Made of fine, smooth ceramic, includes gold thread for hanging. Sometimes sold with gold ring base for display. Price in 2004 was $49.

☐ 3018 ....3.00" ....(**TW**) $49

HUM 3019 — Festival Harmony with Flute Ceramic Ball Ornament
The ornament has a true ball shape and features the same design on the front and the back. One in a set of eight such ball ornaments depicting angels. Has incised M.I. Hummel signature. Features a depiction of HUM 174 "Festival Harmony with Flute" in bas relief. Produced for Goebel by a firm in China, not produced by W. Goebel Porzellanfabrik. Has Hummel number, Goebel mark and 1999 copyright date applied by decal on the bottom. Made of fine, smooth ceramic, includes gold thread for hanging. Sometimes sold with gold ring base for display. Price in 2004 was $49.

☐ 3019 ....3.00" ....(**TW**) $49

HUM 3020 — Festival Harmony with Mandolin
Ceramic Ball Ornament

The ornament has a true ball shape and features the same design on the front and the back. One in a set of eight such ball ornaments depicting angels. Has incised M.I. Hummel signature. Features a depiction of HUM 172 "Festival Harmony with Mandolin" in bas relief. Produced for Goebel by a firm in China, not produced by W. Goebel Porzellanfabrik. Has Hummel number, Goebel mark and 1999 copyright date applied by decal on the bottom. Made of fine, smooth ceramic, includes gold thread for hanging. Sometimes sold with gold ring base for display. Price in 2004 was $49.

☐ 3020 ....3.00" ....(**TW**).....$49

HUM 3021 — Heavenly Angel
Ceramic Ball Ornament

The ornament has a true ball shape and features the same design on the front and the back. One in a set of eight such ball ornaments depicting angels. Has incised M.I. Hummel signature. Features a depiction of HUM 21 "Heavenly Angel" in bas relief. Produced for Goebel by a firm in China, not produced by W. Goebel Porzellanfabrik. Has Hummel number, Goebel mark and 1999 copyright date applied by decal on the bottom. Made of fine, smooth ceramic, includes gold thread for hanging. Sometimes sold with gold ring base for display. Price in 2004 was $49.

☐ 3021 ....3.00" ....(**TW**).....$49

HUM 3022 — Ride Into Christmas Puff Ornament

A tan star-shaped ornament, made of ceramic, with red ribbon for hanging. M.I. Hummel signature in brown and Goebel mark in blue applied by decal. Hummel number, Hummel name and copyright date do not appear on ornament. Features a depiction of HUM 396 "Ride Into Christmas" applied by decal over raised detail. Both sides of the ornament are identical. Companion to HUM 3023 "Christmas Delivery" Puff Ornament. Also found marked 2005 at the top of the star as an annual ornament for 2005.

☐ 3022 ....4.50" ....(**TW**).....$25

HUM 3023 — Christmas Delivery Puff Ornament

First released in 2004 as an annual ornament for 2004 in a limited edition of 1,500. A tan star-shaped ornament, made of ceramic, with red ribbon for hanging. M.I. Hummel signature in brown and Goebel mark in blue applied by decal. Hummel number, Hummel name and copyright date do not appear on ornament. Features a depiction of HUM 2014 "Christmas Delivery" applied by decal over raised detail. Both sides of the ornament are identical. Companion to HUM 3022 "Ride Into Christmas" Puff Ornament. Also found without 2004 marked at the top of the star.

☐ 3023 ....4.50" ....(**TW**).....$25

Other Hummel Related Items

Unnumbered
"M.I. Hummel" Figurine
"Madonna With Wings"

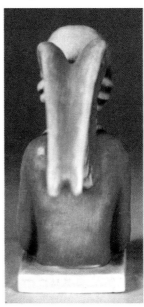

This very rare, unusual, signed "M.I. Hummel" figurine is truly a collector's item. Found several years ago in Munich, Germany, this beautiful "Madonna with Wings" figurine had been in the possession of a German family for many years, but they could not remember its background or from where it came. The figurine is not numbered nor does it have a trademark—only an incised "X" on the bottom, in addition to the "M.I. Hummel" signature on the back. Research reveals that this piece was in all probability modeled by master sculptor Reinhold Unger in the late 1930s or early 1940s. For some unknown reason it was not approved for production by the Siessen Convent or possibly by Sister Hummel herself. This piece, however, is found pictured in an old 1950 Goebel catalogue listed has "Mel 08" and priced at 11 DM. It is not known whether it was actually produced and marketed at that time. If they were produced, they would not have the "M.I. Hummel" signature. It is the signature that makes this figurine unique, rare and fascinating.

Bust of Sister M.I. Hummel

The large white bisque bust in the likeness of Sister Maria Innocentia Hummel was created by master sculptor Gerhard Skrobek in 1965. It was originally used as a display piece for showrooms or dealer displays featuring Hummel items. It has the signature of "Skrobek 1965" in addition to "HU1" incised on the back. In recent years it has become a collector's item and is sought after by many avid "M.I. Hummel" lovers. They were originally given to dealers at no cost; but we did, however, purchase two of these large busts in the early 1970s from a store in New York at a cost of $30 each. A smaller version of the same bust with the "M.I. Hummel" signature incised on the front of the base was first put on the market in 1967 with the incised number "HU2" and the (TM 4) trademark. These originally sold for $6 each. This same small-size

bust was again put on the market in 1977 for a brief time, retailing for $15 to $17 each, but was once again discontinued from production. A third variation of the Sister Hummel bust was issued in 1979 as: "EXCLUSIVE SPECIAL EDITION No. 3 FOR MEMBERS OF THE GOEBEL COLLECTORS' CLUB" only. This piece has an incised "HU 3" as well as 1978 incised copyright date on the bottom. It is in full color with the "M.I. Hummel" signature painted in white on the front. While these busts are not officially classified as true Hummel figurines, they do make a nice addition to any Hummel collection. A commemorative HU2 was available in 2005 to mark the "70th Anniversary" of Hummels (1935-2005), with the (TM 8) trademark and a wooden display base with brass plaque reading "Sr. M.I. Hummel", priced $49.

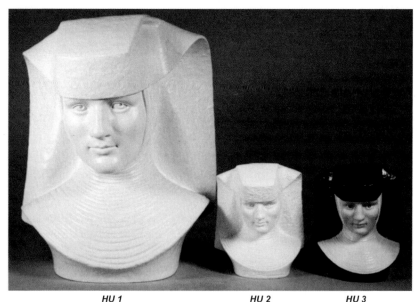

| | HU 1 | | HU 2 | | HU 3 |

☐	HU1	13.00"	(CE)	❹	$2500—2750		
☐	HU2	5.50"	(CE)	❹	$175—200		
☐	HU2	5.50"	(CE)	❺	$150—175		
☐	HU2	5.75"	(CE)	❽	$49	(70th Anniversary)
☐	HU3	5.50"	(CE)	❺	$350—400		

Factory Workers Plate

This anniversary plate was produced by W. Goebel Porzellanfabrik, by and for the workers at the factory where the Goebel annual plates are manufactured. Probably as few as 100 were produced and were not made available to the general public. The "M.I. Hummel" signature is on each of the ten individual plates.

☐ Factory Workers Plate ....$1500—2000　(Uncolored)
☐ Factory Workers Plate ....$2000—2500　(Colored Variation)

Early Goebel Plaque

Early Goebel plaque (front view)　　　　*Early Goebel plaque (back view)*

Produced in hard porcelain, both in light blue background and a chocolate brown color. Measures 2.50 x 4.75" on a beveled base. The embossed inscription on the back reads:

W. GOEBEL
Porzellanfabrik Oeslau
und Wilhelmsfeld
Oeslau b. Coburg

☐ Goebel Plaque (Blue)..................2.50" x 4.75" ....$750—1000
☐ Goebel Plaque (Brown) ....2.50" x 4.75" ....$750—1000

Goebel Animals:
Traditionally Used With "M.I. Hummel" Nativity Sets

These three Goebel camels were designed to be used with the "M.I. Hummel" Nativity Sets, either HUM 214 or HUM 260. The standing camel HX306/0 has an incised 1960 copyright date and has been on the market since the early 1960s. The kneeling camel (Dromedary) and the lying camel (Bactrian) were both released in 1980 for the first time. All three have been produced both in full color and white over-glaze (unpainted) finishes. All models are in current production and are usually found wherever the "M.I. Hummel" figurines are sold. Currently being produced in color only. In 1991 three smaller versions of the same camels were added to the line to go with the new smaller size nativity sets, HUM 214/0.

- ☐ HX 306/0 .... 8.50" .... (OE) .... Standing .... (color) $279
- ☐ HX 306/0 .... 8.50" .... (**TW**) .... Standing .... (white) $275–300
- ☐ 46 820–12 .... 5.50" .... (OE) .... Kneeling .... (color) $279
- ☐ 46 820–12 .... 5.50" .... (**TW**) .... Kneeling .... (white) $275–300
- ☐ 46 821–11 .... 4.50" .... (OE) .... Lying .... (color) $279
- ☐ 46 821–11 .... 4.50" .... (**TW**) .... Lying .... (white) $275–300
- ☐ 46 837 .... 6.50" .... (OE) .... Standing .... (color) $230
- ☐ 46 838 .... 4.00" .... (OE) .... Kneeling .... (color) $230
- ☐ 46 839–09 .... 3.25" .... (OE) .... Lying .... (color) $230

HUM 46-013-01-7 — Horse
The Horse is a Goebel figurine, suitable as part of Hummel Nativity Set 260. Has Goebel mark, not a Hummel trademark. Available on the European Market.

☐ 46-013-01-7 ......9.50".................(**OE**) $285

HUM 46-012-01-9 — Elephant
The Elephant is a Goebel figurine, suitable as part of Hummel Nativity Set 260. Has Goebel mark, not a Hummel trademark. Available on the European market.

☐ 46-012-01-9 ......10.75"...............(**OE**) $485

The "Mel" Signature Hum"mel"

A collector will occasionally happen on to a "Hummel"-like figurine that does not have the usual "M.I. Hummel" signature on it. The figurine will have all of the general appearances of an older genuine "M.I. Hummel" figurine, including the Goebel factory trademark, in addition to the letters "Mel" (the last part of "Hummel") incised on it.

To the best of my knowledge, these items have been designed from original drawings by Sister M.I. Hummel, but for some undetermined reasons were not approved by the Siessen Convent for inclusion in the "M.I. Hummel" line of figurines.

Notice the photo of the "Child in Bed" candy dish. Goebel master sculptor Arthur Moeller modeled this piece in 1945. Since it did not win convent approval, it was later marketed with "Mel 6" incised on the bottom of it. Several other "Mel" items have appeared through the years. The most common of these are the Mel 1, Mel 2 and Mel 3 candlestick holders, modeled by former master sculptor Reinhold Unger in 1939. In the mid-1950s, these items were remodeled by master sculptor Gerhard Skrobek and assigned the model numbers HUM 115 "Girl with Nosegay," HUM 116 "Girl with Fir Tree" and HUM 117 "Boy with Horse" candlesticks with the "M.I. Hummel" signature.

Also modeled by master sculptor Arthur Moeller were Mel 4 "Box with Boy on Top" in 1942, Mel 5 "Box with Girl on Top" in 1942, Mel 6 "Box with Child in Bed on Top" in 1945 and Mel 7 "Box with Sitting Child on Top" in 1946. All "Mel" items were discontinued in 1962, according to Goebel factory information.

Apparently, the "Mel" designation must have been a "catch-all" label intended as a way of marketing these rejected items. I am of the opinion, however, that it was also used to designate experimental items. In our years of research, we have accidentally "stumbled" on two other figurine models with the "Mel" label. Both of them were "International" designs. How many more "Mel" designs will show up in the future is anyone's guess.

Mel 6

Mel 7

Listing of "Mel" Items

The following is a listing of "Mel" items recently found in old factory records (sculpting diaries) at W. Goebel Porzellanfabrik in Roedental, Germany—thanks to the efforts of Veronika Schmidt, research specialist at the factory. Please note that Mel 6, Mel 7 and Mel 8 were used twice: in 1940 and then again in 1945 and 1946.

					Sculptor	Year	Value
☐ Mel 1	=	HUM	115	girl w/nosegay	R. Unger	1939	$300—500
☐ Mel 2	=	HUM	116	girl w/fir tree	R. Unger	1939	$300—500
☐ Mel 3	=	HUM	117	boy with horse	R. Unger	1939	$300—500
☐ Mel 4		box with boy on lid		A. Moeller		1942	no known examples
☐ Mel 5		box with girl on lid		A. Moeller		1942	no known examples
☐ Mel 6		box w/ child in bed on top			A. Moeller	1945	$2000—3000
☐ Mel 7		box w/ sitting child on top			A. Moeller	1946	$2000—3000
☐ Mel 8		angel bust/madonna w/wings			R. Unger	1945	$5000—7000
☐ Mel 6	=	HUM	806	Bulgarian	A. Moeller	1940	$10,000—15,000
☐ Mel 7	=	HUM	807	Bulgarian	A. Moeller	1940	$10,000—15,000
☐ Mel 8	=	HUM	808	Bulgarian	A. Moeller	1940	$10,000—15,000
☐ Mel 9	=	HUM	809	Bulgarian	A. Moeller	1940	$10,000—15,000
☐ Mel 10	=	HUM	810	Bulgarian	R. Unger	1940	$10,000—15,000
☐ Mel 11	=	HUM	811	Bulgarian	R. Unger	1940	$10,000—15,000
☐ Mel 12	=	HUM	812	Serbian	R. Unger	1940	$10,000—15,000
☐ Mel 13	=	HUM	813	Serbian	R. Unger	1940	$10,000—15,000
☐ Mel 14	=	HUM	137/B	Plaque	A. Moeller	1940	$2000—3000
☐ Mel 15	=	HUM	138	Plaque	A. Moeller	1940	$2000—3000
☐ Mel 16	=	HUM	139	Plaque	A. Moeller	1940	$2000—3000
☐ Mel 24	=	HUM	824	Swedish	A. Moeller	1940	$10,000—15,000
☐ Mel 25	=	HUM	825	Swedish	A. Moeller	1940	$10,000—15,000
☐ Mel 31	=	HUM	831	Slovak	R. Unger	1940	$10,000—15,000
☐ Mel 32	=	HUM	832	Slovak	R. Unger	1940	$10,000—15,000
☐ Mel 41	=	HUM	841	Czech	R. Unger	1940	$10,000—15,000
☐ Mel 42	=	HUM	842	Czech	R. Unger	1940	$10,000—15,000
☐ Mel 51	=	HUM	851	Hungarian	A. Moeller	1940	$10,000—15,000
☐ Mel 52	=	HUM	852	Hungarian	A. Moeller	1940	$10,000—15,000
☐ Mel 53	=	HUM	853	Hungarian	A. Moeller	1940	$10,000—15,000
☐ Mel 54	=	HUM	854	Hungarian	A. Moeller	1940	$10,000—15,000

.... HUM TERM ....

HUM NO.: Mold number or model number incised on the bottom of each "M.I. Hummel" figurine at the factory. This number is used for identification purposes.

Copies from Around the World

It has been said that one of the most sincere compliments that can be given to an artist is to have his work copied. I think this holds true when it comes to the "M.I. Hummel" figurines. W. Goebel Porzellanfabrik of Rödental, Germany, has had the exclusive right to produce Hummel figurines, based upon the artwork of Sister Maria Innocentia Hummel, since 1935. The figurines have become so popular over the years that many countries around the world have tried to copy these designs. Korea, Taiwan, Japan, Germany, England and even the United States have all made copies. Most of these are quite inferior in quality when compared to the originals made by Goebel. But a few of the copies are better than others—namely, the Japanese and the English—and we've chosen to show you some of these better copies.

The Japanese have probably succeeded in making the best copies, with the English running a close second. The Japanese finish and colors are more like the originals and sometimes, at first glance, they may fool even an experienced collector. The Japanese have copied the designs but, to my knowledge, have never gone so far as to copy the familiar "M.I. Hummel" signature. On the other hand the English finish is quite shiny and they did copy the signature on their early production models. The English figurines were made by "Beswick" during the war years of 1940 and 1941.

It is, of course, most unethical, if not always illegal, to make copies of Hummel figurines. The question of copies, look-alikes, fakes and their legality is a lengthy and complicated subject and it is not our intention here to delve into that issue. We want only to show readers a few of the better examples of copies that have been done, so as to show how closely they may resemble the originals.

Top photo: HUM 97 (far left) beside English copy #903; HUM 5 (far right) beside English copy #906. Middle photo at left, HUM 71 (far left) with English copy #908; photo at right, HUM 184 (far right) with Japanese copy. HUM 201 with Japanese copy at left.

Bottom view typical Beswick markings

This English "Beswick" figurine was found in England. A copy of HUM 86 "Happiness." It does have an incised "M.I. Hummel" signature as well as the incised number 990.

545

RARE/UNIQUE SAMPLE VARIATIONS OF "M.I. HUMMEL" FIGURINES

Pictured here are six very rare early sample pieces—four having been located in Germany and two found in the United States.

Webster's definitions—RARE: marked by unusual quality, merit, or appeal. Distinctive, superlative or extreme of its kind, seldom occurring or found, uncommon. UNIQUE: being the only one, sole, being without a like or equal.

I truly believe that four of these six examples fit Webster's definitions of both rare and unique at this point in time! "Little Hiker" and "Joyful" have been found in duplicates, so they would only be considered rare.

For some unknown reason, the Sisters at Siessen Convent, who must approve for production all figurines based upon Sister M.I. Hummel's artwork, did not approve these variations. Possibly they felt it would lessen the value of the original artwork when using it in a utilitarian item. This is only speculation on my part because they did approve useful items such as ashtrays, candy bowls, lamp bases, book ends, candleholders and wall vases. Possibly only a whim, impulse, or passing fancy prevented these unique pieces from being produced and sold on the open market.

Whatever the reason, I, for one, am extremely pleased that these four pieces are in our collection and the other two are in a very good friend's collection in the Midwest.

HUM 16/1 with pot

HUM 17/0 with attached pot

546

HUM 47/0 with attached bowl

HUM 53 with attached pot

A ccording to the Goebel factory product book, the following "M.I. Hummel" figurines with attached pots/bowls were produced as samples only in 1935 and 1936. Unfortunately, Goebel did not retain any of these samples for their archives.

☐ HUM II/1	Puppy Love	w/pot from ZF 9	A. Moeller 1935
☐ HUM II/4	Little Fiddler	w/pot from ZF 9	A. Moeller 1935
☐ HUM II/5	Strolling Along	w/pot from ZF 9	A. Moeller 1935
☐ HUM II/11/0	Merry Wanderer	w/pot from ZF 9	A. Moeller 1935
☐ HUM II/13/0	Meditation	w/pot from ZF 9	R. Unger 1935
☐ HUM II/13/0	Meditation	w/bowl from KZ 27/I	R. Unger 1935
☐ HUM II/16/I	Little Hiker	w/pot from ZF 9	A. Moeller 1935
☐ HUM II/17/0	Congratulations	w/pot from ZF 9	R. Unger 1935
☐ HUM II/47/0	Goose Girl	w/pot from ZF 9	A. Moeller 1936
☐ HUM III/47/0	Goose Girl	w/bowl from KZ 27/I	A. Moeller 1936
☐ HUM II/49	To Market	w/bowl from KZ 27/I	A. Moeller 1936
☐ HUM II/53	Joyful	w/pot from ZF 9	R. Unger 1936
☐ HUM II/57	Chick Girl	w/pot from ZF 9	A. Moeller 1936
☐ HUM II/58	Playmates	w/pot from ZF 9	R. Unger 1936

The above chart has a complete listing of the 14 items that the factory has recorded. Six of the 14 we know about, have examples of, and pictures of. We know now that there can be duplicates of these extremely rare pieces, since two of the HUM 16/0 "Little Hiker" figurines with attached pots are now in private collections. We have no photos of the other missing pieces, so just what they look like is not known at this time. Whether they have a normal figurine base like "Meditation," or whether they are without the bases, such as "Little Hiker" or "Congratulations," is unknown. They might not necessarily have a model number or a signature, but will probably have the Goebel "crown" trademark.

Now that you have this exciting information, go out there and scour the countryside, visit garage sales, flea markets and antique shops for the eight remaining "M.I. Hummel" figurines with attached pots or bowls. If you find one, give me a call—maybe we can make a deal! Good luck!

547

"M.I. HUMMEL" FAIENCE

A BRIEF HISTORY OF GLAZES

Colored glazes have been used on ceramics since 3,000 B.C. (Glazes applied to pottery not only serve as a form of decoration, but also make the objects watertight.) The Chinese developed lead glazes in the third century B.C. Tin glazes are believed to have originated in Mesopotamia in the ninth century A.D.; they were used in the Near East, China and India to cover tiles and handcrafted art objects. The Moors brought the tin-glazing technique with them to Spain, where Valencia became famous for it.

In the 15th century, Italian potters at Faenza began using the technique to make majolica. Their majolica was highly popular, and the term Faience was named for the town. Soon, this method for decorating ceramics was used in Florence, Urbino and Venice. France and, later, The Netherlands also produced tin-glazed wares in such famous places as Nevers, Rouen and Delft.

HUM 4 (TM 1)   HUM 7/1 (TM 1)   HUM 9 (TM 1+1)

As you may know, Franz Goebel of W. Goebel Porzellanfabrik first conceived the idea of producing porcelain figurines based on the drawings of Sister M.I. Hummel in 1934. Upon being granted the right to create such figurines, the Rödental, Germany, porcelain company began experimenting with various materials (including porcelain and terra cotta) and decorative techniques for making these new pieces. The goal of these experimentations was to find the best way for Goebel artists to create and finish pieces in colors that would most closely match those found in Sister M.I. Hummel's original art.

Aware of this brief trial-and-error period, Sister M.I. Hummel requested that samples of the various materials and finishes be made and exhibited at international trade fairs, such as the one held in Leipzig, Germany, to test the public's reaction to them. For this reason, we have very early M.I. Hummel figurines in porcelain and terra cotta (such as the HUM 136/V "Friends"), as well as pieces decorated in the Faience technique (such as the HUM 33 "Joyful" ash tray and HUM 113 "Heavenly Song" candleholder). Public acceptance of these pieces was very limited, so their production never advanced beyond the sample stage.

Faience (pronounced fay-ontz or fi-ons) is a term for earthenware decorated with opaque colored glazes. (While now used for all kinds of glazed pottery, Faience is the French word for the porzellana di Faenza— fine tin-glazed and painted earthenware made in Faenza, Italy.) Faience pieces, made of white earthenware or colored clays, were either shaped on a potter's wheel or formed in molds and assembled by hand. After open-air drying, these pieces were kiln-fired at temperatures of 900 to 1100 degrees Centigrade. Still porous after firing, they were then dipped into a liquid tin glaze, which gave the pieces an overall white covering.

Colored glazes were then applied, and the pieces were refired at a lower temperature. (In some factories, firing methods were reversed; the first firing was at a temperature about 100 degrees lower than the second firing.) To prevent the pieces from sticking to the capsule in the round kilns, which were fired with coal, the tin glaze was wiped off the bottom of the bases before firing.

Goebel's Faience pieces based on Sister M.I. Hummel's artwork were fired in small muffles that the company used exclusively for samples. The colors of these pieces are soft and flow into one another; some have a more or less messy appearance. Also, the solid tin glaze may have left the "M.I. Hummel" signature partly illegible. The Faience technique permitted only a narrow range of colors and the surface was glossier than desired. The company felt that it detracted

This "Hear Ye, Hear Ye" Faience figurine is 7.25 inches high and was found in Germany.

from the unique character of the original art, so only a very small quantity of these items was produced.

Very few of these early Faience pieces are known to exist in private collections. Their prices have varied greatly, due to public ignorance about just what they are. The uninformed sold them for a mere fraction of their true value. Items this rare, in my opinion, should be valued from $5000 to $10,000 each, depending on the size and condition of the example. So, here's a new game for lovers of M.I. Hummel figurines: now that you are informed, look for these rare faience pieces—and hope that you find one being offered by a seller who has no idea of what he or she possesses.

GOEBEL
CRYSTAL "M.I. HUMMEL" FIGURINES

First released in Europe as a test market item early in 1991 and then in the U.S. market in the summer of 1991. These twelve models, rendered in 24 percent lead crystal with a silky matte finish, are replicas of the original ceramic "M.I. Hummel" figurines. They have an incised "M.I. Hummel" signature and the Goebel (TM 6) trademark with a 1990 date. They do not have an incised model number. Now listed as (CE) Closed Editions:

☐ Apple Tree Girl	3.75"	(CE)	❻	$50—60
☐ Botanist	3.125"	(CE)	❻	$50—60
☐ Visiting An Invalid	3.75"	(CE)	❻	$50—60
☐ Meditation	3.50"	(CE)	❻	$50—60
☐ Merry Wanderer	3.50"	(CE)	❻	$50—60
☐ Postman	3.875"	(CE)	❻	$50—60
☐ Coloiot	3.00"	(CE)	❻	$30—40
☐ Little Sweeper	2.875"	(CE)	❹	$30 40
☐ Village Boy	3.00"	(CE)	❻	$30—40
☐ For Mother	2.875"	(CE)	❻	$30—40
☐ Sister	2.875"	(CE)	❻	$30—40
☐ March Winds	2.875"	(CE)	❻	$30—40

The following six items were originally sold only in Europe, but were available in the U.S. also. Now listed as (CE) Closed Editions:

☐ Apple Tree Boy	3.75"	(CE)	❻	$75—100
☐ For Father	3.75"	(CE)	❻	$75—100
☐ Kindergartener	3.50"	(CE)	❻	$75—100
☐ School Boy	3.50"	(CE)	❻	$75—100
☐ Grandma's Girl	3.50"	(CE)	❻	$75—100
☐ Grandpa's Boy	3.50"	(CE)	❻	$75—100

Several crystal pieces were produced exclusively for the Avon Company as promotional items. They all have the "M.I. Hummel" signature and year of issue:

☐ For Mother (trinket box)	4.25"	1993	$50—75
☐ Soloist (crystal bell)	5.50"	1994	$50—75
☐ Song of Praise (candleholder)	3.75"	1995	$50—75
☐ Watchful Angel (plate)	8.50"	1996	$50—75

BERLIN AIRLIFT MEMORIAL EDITION WITH AUF WIEDERSEHEN

In 1993 a special limited edition (25,000 sets worldwide) was produced as a memorial to the Berlin Airlift. The three-piece set includes the M.I. Hummel figurine "Auf Wiedersehen" HUM 153, with a special backstamp featuring the flags of the U.S., Germany, Britain and France. It stands beside a porcelain replica of the Airlift Memorial that is located at Templehof Airport in Berlin. The 7.375" high memorial replica bears a special commemorative backstamp and sets on a wooden base with an engraved brass plaque which reads: "In commemoration of the Berlin Airlift—a heroic effort to keep a city free, June 26, 1948 to September 30, 1949," in both English and German. The original issue price was $330 in 1993.

☐ 153/0 ....3 piece set Berlin Airlift ....(CE) ....❼ ....$350—400

CHECKPOINT CHARLIE LIMITED COMMEMORATIVE EDITION

A Rare Variation of this set

In 1994 a special limited edition of 20,000 individually numbered sets worldwide was produced and sold only through U.S. military base exchange stores, as a tribute to military personnel, a symbol of the cold war, and a guarantee of freedom for West Berlin. The three piece set includes the M.I. Hummel figurine "Soldier Boy" HUM 332, with special backstamp, a 4.00" high Checkpoint Charlie replica with wooden base and 8.625" wide plaque with wood posts. The brass plaque on the base reads: "We are defending the freedom of Paris, London and New York when standing up for liberty in Berlin" (John F. Kennedy). Original military issue price was $195 in 1994.

☐ 332............3 piece set Checkpoint Charlie ....(CE) ....❼ ....$350—400

WOODEN DEALER PLAQUE

☐ Wooden Dealer Plaque ....33.00" x 22.50" x 2.50" ....$5000—10,000

These large wooden dealer plaques were made by a woodworking shop in the Goebel factory area of Rödental, Germany in the mid-1950s. According to factory records, about 100 plaques were made and given to good customers for display purposes. They were hand decorated with artist's oil paints by Messrs. Gunther Neubauer and Harald Sommer. The plaques weigh approximately twenty pounds and measure 33 inches long by 22.50 inches high. They vary in thickness from .875 inch to 2.50 inches at the thickest part. Most of plaques have been found in Germany, but many years ago we purchased one in the Boston area. There is no Goebel trademark, only a large "A" within a circle and a bolt of lightning running through the "A" incised on the back.

FLYING "FULL BEE" DISPLAY

This blue three-dimensional ceramic and plastic version of the Goebel 1950 trademark (TM 2) was used for display purposes. It has the incised number "WZ 1" and the (TM 2) "full bee" trademark on the bottom.

☐ "Full Bee" Display ......4.75" x 5.00"........❷........$2000—2500

"M.I. Hummel"
FOUR SEASONS MUSIC BOX SERIES

This series of four limited edition music boxes was first released in 1987, then one each succeeding year. Called the "Four Seasons Music Box" series with a worldwide limited production of 10,000 pieces individually numbered. Originally sculpted by master sculptor Gerhard Skrobek and chief master sample painter Gunther Neubauer, who created the model, which was then carried out in the woodcarving by Anri of Italy. Inside the box is a gold-plated 36-note Swiss movement by Reuge. Each piece carries the M.I. Hummel signature carved in wood on the top.

1987 Winter

1988 Spring

1989 Summer

1990 Fall

Issue Price

☐ 1987 Ride into Christmas	$390	(CE)	$800—1000
☐ 1988 Chick Girl	$400	(CE)	$600—750
☐ 1989 In Tune	$425	(CE)	$600—750
☐ 1990 Umbrella Girl	$450	(CE)	$800—1000

ARS AG—CHRISTMAS PLATES 1987–1990

Celestial Musician
1987

Angel Duet
1988

Guiding Light
1989

Tender Watch
1990

This series was first issued in 1987 as a four part, decal produced, Christmas plate. Each plate was limited to 20,000 consecutively numbered pieces. Produced in the Goebel factory depicting original drawings of Sister M.I. Hummel under license of ARS AG, Switzerland, owner of the copyrights of the original paintings.

☐ 1987	7.50"	(CE)	❻	$60—75
☐ 1988	7.50"	(CE)	❻	$50—60
☐ 1989	7.50"	(CE)	❻	$50—60
☐ 1990	7.50"	(CE)	❻	$50—60

M.I. HUMMEL "PEN PALS"

First released in the U.S. market in 1996, this set of six "name card table decorations" is actually made of "mini-mini" M.I. Hummel figurines cemented to a small porcelain base. They come with a special wipe-off pen for personalizing each with a name, date or special greeting. Each figurine has its own incised model number on the bottom of the figurine's base, but that cannot be seen since the figurine has been securely cemented to a separate base. This base has only the (TM 7) trademark applied by blue decal; nothing else. The only way to see the model number is to separate the two pieces. This is extremely difficult to do and is really not necessary since I have already done this for you (and me); curiosity got the better of me! Goebel found a strong, hard cement (not rubber base) for joining these two pieces. The company did not intend for them to come apart! The original issue price was $55 each in 1996.

View of the base and figurine when separated.

View of the bottoms of base and figurine.

☐ 43 5/0	...........March Winds	3.00"	..............3.25" with base
☐ 51 5/0	...........Village Boy	3.00"	..............3.25" with base
☐ 98 5/0	...........Sister......................................	2.875"	...........2.875" with base
☐ 135 5/0	..........Soloist	3.00"	..............3.25" with base
☐ 257 5/0	..........For Mother......................................	3.00"	..............3.25" with base
☐ 482 5/0	..........One For You, One For Me	2.25"	...........2.50" with base

A RARE VARIATION
YOU BE THE JUDGE!
UNSIGNED "M.I. HUMMEL" FIGURINE

"Sunny Days" signed "Ugr"　　　　*"Stormy Weather" HUM 71 (TM 1)*

The figurine on the left was located in the City of Coburg, Germany, approximately five miles from Rödental where the Goebel factory is located. It does not have the usual "M.I. Hummel" signature nor the Goebel trademark. The only markings is the incised "Ugr." on the bottom, which undoubtedly stands for Reinhold Unger, one of the first Goebel master sculptors to translate Sister M.I. Hummel's artwork into three dimentional form. Unger also created "Stormy Weather" based upon another Hummel drawing. This figurine, based upon the drawing of "Sunny Days," apparently was rejected by the sisters at Siessen Convent. It is now part of the Robert L. Miller collection.

.... HUM TERM ....

DOUBLE FULL BEE: This term is used to describe the Goebel Company trademark found on some "M.I. Hummel" figurines. On "double full bee" pieces the full bee trademark is found both incised and stamped.

A RARE VARIATION

Rare Variation HUM 203 HUM 203 (TM 1)

As I have always said, you can never tell when or where a rare "M.I. Hummel" figurine will turn up. This is a good example. This rare prototype (four post version) of HUM 203 "Signs of Spring" was recently found in Arizona. Sold by a retired military man who had served in Europe during WW II. He was stationed close to the area of Germany where the Goebel factory was located—that a young German girl would visit the Army quarters each week and would sell "M.I. Hummel" figurines as souvenirs. He had purchased a number of figurines and had kept them all through the years until recently, when he decided to dispose of some of his old items. He sold 39 figurines to a local antique shop. An alert "Hummel" dealer spotted them and purchased all 39 items. Noticing the difference between this old "Signs of Spring" and the current model, he gave me a call for my opinion. I stated that I had never seen or heard of a major variation of this figurine and requested a photograph for comparison. After receiving the photos and several phone calls later, this rare prototype "Signs of Spring" is now part of the Robert L. Miller collection. I would be remiss if I did not commend the alert dealer, Ron Brixey, for his professional, business-like and ethical handling of the sale of this figurine.

.... HUM TERM ....

PROTOTYPE: This term as used by Goebel means the "one and only sample" (first out of the mother mold) that is presented to the Siessen Convent of any newly developed "M.I. Hummel" figurine.

"M.I. Hummel"
Calendars/Kalenders

M.I. Hummel Kalenders (German) were first published by Goebel in 1951 in the German version only. Each *kalender* contained thirteen color photographs of M.I. Hummel figurines with varying backgrounds. The first English version calendar was published for the 1954 year using the same photographs that were used in the 1953 German version. This continued on with few exceptions, (note 1964 German/1965 English and 1975 German/1976 English) until the 1988/1989 years when the size, style and format were drastically changed. These older Calendar/Kalenders are now highly collectible and bring from $50 to $2000 on the secondary market.

☐   *1951 German*

☐   *1952 German*

☐   *1953 German*

☐   *1954 English*

☐   *1954 German*

☐ *1955 English*

☐ *1955 German*

☐ *1956 English*

☐ *1956 German*

☐ *1957 English*

☐ *1957 German*

☐ *1958 English*

☐ *1958 German*

☐ *1959 English*

☐ *1959 German*

☐ *1960 English*

☐ *1960 German*

☐ *1961 English*

☐ *1961 German*

☐ *1962 English*

☐ *1962 German*

☐ *1963 English*

☐ *1963 German*

☐ *1964 English*

☐ *1964 German*

☐ *1965 English*

☐ *1965 German*

☐ *1966 English*

☐ *1966 German*

☐ *1967 English*

☐ *1967 German*

☐ *1968 English*

☐ *1968 German*

☐ *1969 English*

☐ *1969 German*

☐ *1970 English*

☐ *1970 Greman*

☐ *1971 English*

☐ *1971 German*

☐ *1972 English*

☐ *1972 German*

☐ *1973 English*

☐ *1973 German*

☐ *1974 English*

☐ *1974 German*

☐ *1975 English*

☐ *1975 German*

☐ *1976 English*

☐ *1976 German*

☐ *1977 English*

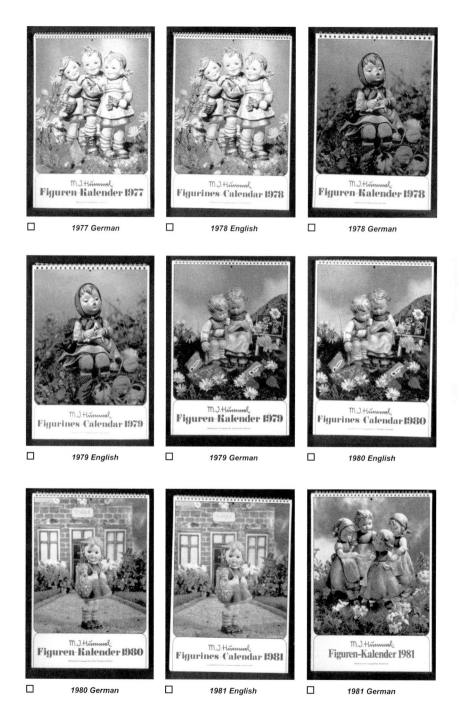

☐   *1977 German*

☐   *1978 English*

☐   *1978 German*

☐   *1979 English*

☐   *1979 German*

☐   *1980 English*

☐   *1980 German*

☐   *1981 English*

☐   *1981 German*

☐ *1982 English*

☐ *1982 German*

☐ *1983 English*

☐ *1983 German*

☐ *1984 English*

☐ *1984 German*

☐ *1985 English*

☐ *1985 German*

☐ *1986 English*

☐ **1986 German**

☐ **1987 English**

☐ **1987 German**

☐ **1988 English**

☐ **1988 German**

☐ **1989 English**

☐ **1989 German**

☐ *1990 English*

☐ *1990 German*

☐ *1991 English*

☐ *1991German*

☐ *1992 English*

☐ *1992 German*

☐ *1993 English*

☐ *1993 German*

ENGLISH = <u>C</u>alendar   GERMAN = <u>K</u>alender

☐   *1994 German*   ☐   *1994 English*

☐   *1995 German*   ☐   *1995 English*

☐   *1996 German*   ☐   *1996 English*

☐   *1997 German*   ☐   *1997 English*

ENGLISH = <u>C</u>alendar   GERMAN = <u>K</u>alender

☐ *1998 German*

☐ *1998 English*

☐ *1999 German*

☐ *1999 English*

☐ *2000 German*

☐ *2000 English*

☐ *2001 German*

☐ *2001 English*

ENGLISH = <u>C</u>alendar   GERMAN = <u>K</u>alender

☐ *2002 German*

☐ *2002 English*

☐ *2003 German*

☐ *2003 English*

☐ *2004 German*

☐ *2004 English*

☐ *2005 German*

☐ *2005 English*

☐   *2006 German*   ☐   *2006 English*

Cover of German Kalender
matches English Calendar

☐   *2007 German*   ☐   *2007 English*

ENGLISH = Calendar   GERMAN = Kalender

EXPRESSIONS OF YOUTH

Many collectors have been fascinated and intrigued by the unfinished "white-ware" figurines. These are simply unfinished figurines about half way through the normal production process. This is the condition of each M.I. Hummel figurine as it reaches the painting department. In order to satisfy this urge to own a figurine in "white-ware," in 1992 Goebel issued seven popular items in this finish with only the facial features painted in addition to a little shadow on the base. All items bear the (TM 7) trademark and the 1991 copyright date applied by blue decal, and the words: Expressions of Youth in red letters. Now listed as (CE) "Closed Editions".

					Issue Price	Current Price
☐ HUM 2/1	Little Fiddler	7.50"	(CE)	$230	$200—250
☐ HUM 7/1	Merry Wanderer	7.00"	(CE)	$230	$200—250
☐ HUM 13/V	Meditation	13.75"	(CE)	$720	$720—750
☐ HUM 15/II	Hear Ye, Hear Ye	7.50"	(CE)	$230	$200—250
☐ HUM 21/II	Heavenly Angel	8.75"	(CE)	$230	$200—250
☐ HUM 47/II	Goose Girl	7.50"	(CE)	$230	$200—250
☐ HUM 89/II	Little Cellist	7.50"	(CE)	$230	$200—250

"Made in China"

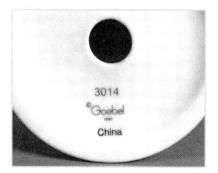

I never thought I would see the day that any M.I. Hummel figurine would be labeled "China." But, I guess we really do live in a changing world!

Back in September 1998 I responded to an advertisement from Danbury Mint of Norwalk, Connecticut, and ordered two sets of M.I. Hummel angel candlesticks at $111 per set.

The first set to arrive was comprised of two beige-colored candlesticks that were identical in shape, measuring 5.75 inches tall, with a different "Hummel" angel on each of the two sides (front and back). By facing them side by side (front of one and back of the other) I had a pair!

The second set was designed the same way: two angels, one on each side. Thus, my four candlesticks, lined up side by side, do have four different M.I. Hummel motifs.

They are well made and have the

incised M.I. Hummel signature on the front and back of each candlestick. However, they do not have the usual incised HUM model number on the bottom. The only marks are the "Goebel" blue decal name with the copyright sign, "1996" directly underneath, and "China" applied with a cello sticker in a reddish-brown color. Two of the four candlesticks have the number "3014" in a blue decal directly above Goebel—nothing else.

The candlesticks measure 5.75" high, having a 3.50" wide round base with a .625" round hole in the center. They appear to be formed from the usual "ceramic" material as used in their German-made counterparts.

The Danbury advertisement states: "fine glazed porcelain." The artwork seems to be hand painted, and is in bas-relief (like other M.I. Hummel plates, bells, vases, etc.), rather than flat decals.

The fact that the candlesticks were produced in China rather than Germany, and that they do not have the incised HUM model numbers on the bottom was disappointing to me. But, all in all, I am satisfied with my purchase and the price I paid.

I re-read the Danbury advertisement and could find no mention of just where the candlesticks were manufactured. I guess I just assumed they were made in Germany.

I am glad that I now have some of the "first?" M.I. Hummel items produced in China.

Plaques Honoring U.S. Military

Five military plaques honoring the U.S. Military have been released and sold exclusively through the U.S. Military Post Exchanges. The five represent the separate branches of service. Each plaque is actually a three-piece set. It consists of the 4.75" figurine HUM 720 "On Parade" (one half of HUM 50 "Volunteers"), a round stand-up plaque with either U.S. Army, Navy, Air Force, Marines or Coast Guard emblem in brilliant colors, and a wooden base with a brass plate reading: "Tribute To A Proud Heritage." The 4-inch round plaque has the incised number "030" along with the Goebel (NOT HUMMEL) trademark. The retail price through the military for each three-piece set was only $119 plus $3 shipping. HUM 720 "On Parade" retails for $180 on year 2004 Suggested Retail price list, but is now (TW) "Temporarily Withdrawn" as of January 1, 2005.

☐   *U.S. Navy*

☐   *U.S. Air Force*

☐   *U.S. Marines*

☐   *U.S. Coast Guard*

☐   *U.S. Army*

M.I. HUMMEL DOLLS
by Don & Beth Woodworth

M.I. Hummel doll production began in 1950 with seven dolls in Hummel motifs, sculpted by Karl Wagner. They were made in two sizes 16.5" and 10.25", and introduced at the Nuremberg Doll Fair in March 1951. At first the doll bodies were made by the Hermann Steiner firm in Neustadt, Germany, and then painted and dressed by Goebel craftsman. The clothing was designed and sewn by Goebel craftsman. In 1952 Goebel assumed full production of the doll bodies as well as clothing. The first material for the dolls was a hard rubber, which was changed shortly thereafter to a soft rubber. Then in 1964 vinyl replaced rubber as the material of choice, and in 1983 porcelain dolls were introduced. This porcelain is actually the same fine earthenware used to make the Hummel figurines. The baby dolls were introduced in 1953. To identify a M.I. Hummel doll, look for the M.I. Hummel signature or Goebel name and the Hummel trademark usually incised or molded in the back of the neck. Older dolls may have a sticker on the shoe, and in some cases tags have been sewn to the dolls and the clothing. The doll may be marked with the series number or year of production and may bear a M.I. Hummel hangtag on its wrist or about its neck.

500 Series   1950-1952

Description: The first seven M.I. Hummel doll motifs. Soft-stuffed jointed doll with rubber head, hand-painted face.

501	Gretl (Sister)	16.5"	CE	$150—250
502	Seppl (Brother)	16.5"	CE	$150—250
503	Bertl (Little Shopper)	16.5"	CE	$150—250
504	Hansl (Little Hiker)	16.5"	CE	$150—250
505	Liesl (Happy Pastime)	16.5"	CE	$150—250
506	Max (Brother)	16.5"	CE	$150—250
507	Wanderbub (Merry Wanderer)	16.5"	CE	$150—250

1500 Series   1951—1958

Description: The first seven M.I. Hummel doll motifs. Rubber doll with rubber head; modeled hair; hand-painted face; head, arms and legs moveable.

1501	Gretl (Sister)	16.5"	CE	$125—250
1502	Seppl (Brother)	16.5"	CE	$125—250
1503	Bertl (Little Shopper)	16.5"	CE	$125—250
1504	Hansl (Little Hiker)	16.5"	CE	$125—250
1505	Liesl (Happy Pastime)	16.5"	CE	$125—250
1506	Max (Brother)	16.5"	CE	$125—250
1507	Wanderbub (Merry Wanderer)	16.5"	CE	$125—250

1600 Series   1951—1963

Description: The first seven M.I. Hummel doll motifs, and Chimney Sweep added in 1952. Marked M.I. Hummel and Hummel trademark 3. Rubber doll with rubber head; modeled hair; hand-painted face; head and arms moveable; legs immovable.

1601	Gretl (Sister)	10.25"	CE	$125—250
1602	Seppl (Brother)	10.25"	CE	$125—250
1603	Bertl (Little Shopper)	10.25"	CE	$125—250
1604	Hansl (Little Hiker)	10.25"	CE	$125—250
1605	Liesl (Happy Pastime)	10.25"	CE	$125—250
1606	Max (Brother)	10.25"	CE	$125—250
1607	Wanderbub (Merry Wanderer)	10.25"	CE	$125—250
1608	Felix (Chimney Sweep)	10.25"	CE	$125—250

1101 Series   1953—1960
Description: Rubber baby doll with rubber head; modeled hair; hand-painted face; head, arms and legs moveable; hand-painted eyes. Sold with cradle.

| 1101 A—J | Baby (with dress variations) | 13" | CE | $100—200 |

V 101 Series   1958—1960
Description: Same baby doll as 1101, but made of vinyl; vinyl doll; modeled hair; hand-painted face; head, arms and legs moveable; hand-painted eyes. Sold with cradle.

| V 101 A—J | Baby (with dress variations) | 13" | CE | $100—200 |

V 103 Series   1960—1968
Description: Same baby doll as V 101, but with glass eyes; vinyl doll; modeled hair; hand-painted face; head, arms and legs moveable; glass eyes. Sold with cradle.

| V 103 A—W | Baby (with dress variations) | 13" | CE | $100—200 |

V 203 Series   1964—1967
Description: Same baby doll as V 103, but with sleeping eyes; vinyl doll; modeled hair; hand-painted face; head, arms and legs moveable; sleeping eyes. Sold with cradle.

| V 203 A—W | Baby (with dress variations) | 13" | CE | $100—200 |

V 105 Series   1961—1965
Description: Vinyl baby doll; hair sewn in; hand-painted face; head, arms and legs moveable; glass eyes. Sold with cradle.

V 105 A—L	Baby (with dress variations)		13"	CE	$100—200

V 205 Series   1964—1969

Description: Vinyl baby doll; hair sewn in; hand-painted face; head, arms and legs moveable; sleeping eyes. Sold with cradle.

V 205 A—L	Baby (with dress variations)	13"	CE	$100—200

1102 Series   1954—1960

Description: Rubber baby doll with rubber head; modeled hair; hand-painted face; head, arms and legs moveable; hand-painted eyes. Sold with cradle.

1102 A—J	Baby (with dress variations)	10.25"	CE	$100—200

V 102 Series   1958—1960

Description: Same baby doll as 1102, but made of vinyl; vinyl doll; modeled hair; hand-painted face; head, arms and legs moveable; hand-painted eyes. Sold with cradle.

V 102 A—J	Baby (with dress variations)	10.25"	CE	$100—200

V 104 Series   1960—1975

Description: Same baby doll as V 103, but in a smaller size; vinyl doll; modeled hair; hand-painted face; head, arms and legs moveable; glass eyes. Sold with cradle.

V 104 A—W	Baby (with dress variations)	10.25"	CE	$100—200

V 204 Series   1964

Description: Same baby doll as V 104, but with sleeping eyes; vinyl doll; modeled hair; hand-painted face; head, arms and legs moveable; sleeping eyes. Sold with cradle.

V 204 A—W	Baby (with dress variations)	10.25"	CE	$100—200

1700 Series   1953—1975

Description: Doll made first of rubber, then of vinyl; modeled hair; hand-painted face; head, arms and legs moveable.
Marked M.I. Hummel and Hummel trademark.

1701	Gretl (Sister)	11"/12"	CE	$125—250

1702	Seppl (Brother)	11"/12"	CE	$125—250
1703	Bertl (Little Shopper)	11"/12"	CE	$125—250
1704	Hansl (Little Hiker)	11"/12"	CE	$125—250
1705	Liesl (Happy Pastime)	11"/12"	CE	$125—250
1706	Max (Brother)	11"/12"	CE	$125—250
1707	Wanderbub (Merry Wanderer)	11"/12"	CE	$125—250
1708	Felix (Chimney Sweep)	11"/12"	CE	$125—250
1709	Rosi (School Girl)	11"/12"	CE	$125—250
1710	Peterle (School Boy)	11"/12"	CE	$125—250
1711	Mirel (Girl Baby Doll)	11"/12"	CE	$125—250
1712	Franel (Boy Baby Doll)	11"/12"	CE	$125—250
1713	Mariandl (Favorite Pet)	11"/12"	CE	$125—250
1714	Jackl (Little Goat Herder)	11"/12"	CE	$125—250
1715	Christl (Weary Wanderer)	11"/12"	CE	$125—250
1716	Schorschl (Farm Boy)	11"/12"	CE	$125—250
1717	Ganseliesl (Goose Girl)	11"/12"	CE	$125—250
1718	Anderl (Accordion Boy)	11"/12"	CE	$125—250
1719	Nachwachter (Hear Ye, Hear Ye)	11"/12"	CE	$125—250
1720	Brieftrager (Postman)	11"/12"	CE	$125—250
1721	Schusterjunge (Boots)	11"/12"	CE	$125—250
1722	Skihaserl (Skier)	11"/12"	CE	$125—250
1723	Konditor (Baker)	11"/12"	CE	$125—250
1724	Radibub (For Father)	11"/12"	CE	$125—250
1725	Puppenmutterchen (Doll Mother)	11"/12"	CE	$125—250

1800 Series

1001—1006:   1067   1076

Description: Vinyl doll; modeled hair; hand-painted face; head, arms and legs moveable. Two variations: 1. with glass eyes and hair sewn in, 2. with sleeping eyes and hair sewn in.

1801	Rosl (Little Sweeper)	8"	CE	$100—200
1802	Rudi (Home From Market)	8"	CE	$100—200
1803	Vroni (Meditation)	8"	CE	$100—200
1804	Seppl (Boy with Toothache)	8"	CE	$100—200
1805	Mariandl (Favorite Pet)	8"	CE	$100—200
1806	Jackl (Happy Traveler)	8"	CE	$100—200

1809—1812:   1953—1958

Description: Rubber doll; modeled hair; hand-painted face; head, arms and legs moveable.

1809	Rosi (School Girl)	14"	CE	$125—250
1810	Peterle (School Boy)	14"	CE	$125—250
1811	Mirel (Little Gardener)	14"	CE	$125—250
1812	Franzl (Little Farm Hand)	14"	CE	$125—250

1900 Series   1972—1985

Description: Vinyl doll; vinyl head and body; modeled hair; hand-painted face; head, arms and legs moveable. The Boy and Girl Baby Dolls are found in many different outfits.

1901	Gretel (Sister)	11"	CE	$100—150
1902	Seppl (Brother)	11"	CE	$100—150
1903	Rosa (Boy Baby Doll)	11"	CE	$100—150
1904	Rosa (Girl Baby Doll)	11"	CE	$100—150
1905	Liesl (Happy Pastime)	11"	CE	$100—150
1906	Wanderbub (Merry Wanderer)	11"	CE	$100—150
1908	Felix (Chimney Sweep)	11"	CE	$100—150
1909	Rosi (School Girl)	11"	CE	$100—150
1910	Peterle (School Boy)	11"	CE	$100—150
1914	Ganseliesl (Goose Girl)	11"	CE	$100—150
1917	Radibub (For Father)	11"	CE	$100—150
1925	Lauterbach (Weary Wanderer)	11"	CE	$100—150
1926	Strupf Verloren (Lost Stocking)	11"	CE	$100—150
1927	Krankenbesuch (Visiting An Invalid)	11"	CE	$100—150
1928	Auf Heimlichen Wegen (On Secret Path)	11"	CE	$100—150

1960 Series   1958—1963

Description: Doll made first of rubber; hair sewn in; hand-painted face; head, arms and legs moveable; hand-painted eyes. Later dolls made of vinyl; hair sewn in; head, arms, and legs moveable; glass eyes. Do not resemble Hummel figurines.

1960/A	Sonny	14"	CE	$100—200
1960/B		14"	CE	$100—200
1960/C	Gabi	14"	CE	$100—200
1960/D		14"	CE	$100—200
1960/E	Reni	14"	CE	$100—200

1961 Series   1959—1965

Description: Doll made first of rubber, then in vinyl; hair sewn in; head, arms and legs moveable; glass eyes. Do not resemble Hummel figurines. Found in many different outfits.

1961/A	Helga	14"	CE	$100—200
1961/B		14"	CE	$100—200
1961/C	Rotkappchen	14"	CE	$100—200
1961/D	Angelika	14"	CE	$100—200
1961/E	Astrid	14"	CE	$100—200
1961/F	Fred	14"	CE	$100—200
1961/G	Anke	14"	CE	$100—200

1961/H		14"	CE	$100—200
1961/K		14"	CE	$100—200
1961/M		14"	CE	$100—200
1961/N		14"	CE	$100—200

2961 Series   1964

Description: Same as 1961 vinyl doll, but with sleeping eyes. Doll made of vinyl; hair sewn in; hand-painted face; head, arms and legs moveable; sleeping eyes. Do not resemble Hummel figurines.

2961/C	Rotkappchen	14"	CE	$100—200
2961/H		14"	CE	$100—200
2961/K		14"	CE	$100—200
2961/M		14"	CE	$100—200
2961/N		14"	CE	$100—200

Porcelain Dolls I   1983—1989

Description: Sculpted by Helmut Fisher in 1982. Doll with soft stuffed body and porcelain head, hands and feet, hand-crafted by Goebel. Doll has M.I. Hummel incised on back of neck and labels sewn into the clothing with the M.I. Hummel signature and name of the doll. With wooden stand and certificate of authenticity. Original issue price $175. Withdrawn from production December 1989.

719	Postman	15.75"	CE	1983	❻	$200—300
718	Birthday Serenade/Boy	15.75"	CE	1983	❻	$200—300
717	Birthday Serenade/Girl	15.75"	CE	1983	❻	$200—300
716	On Holiday	15.75"	CE	1983	❻	$200—300
443	Lost Sheep	15.75"	CE	1985	❻	$200—300
446	Signs of Spring	15.75"	CE	1985	❻	$200—300
465	Carnival	15.75"	CE	1985	❻	$200—300
444	Easter Greetings	15.75"	CE	1985	❻	$200—300

Porcelain Dolls II   1988—1994

Description: Doll with soft stuffed body and porcelain head, hands and feet, hand-crafted by Goebel. Doll has "Goebel" and M.I. Hummel hallmark incised on back of neck. Certificate of authenticity. Original issue price $175—$200. Sculpted between 1986—1989. Each doll has its own mold, making each doll distinct. (See also Hummels 512—519 in main body of book.) Doll 519 "Ride Into Christmas" is distinguished from Doll 960 "Ride Into Christmas" by a porcelain Christmas tree with snow capped branches, no snow on top of lantern. Doll 519 "Ride Into Christmas" includes sled for display.

512	Umbrella Girl	8"	CE	1988	⑥	$175—250
513	Little Fiddler	14.25"	CE	1988	⑥	$175—250
514	Friend or Foe?	7.5"	CE	1989	⑥	$175—250
516	Merry Wanderer	14.5"	CE	1990	⑥	$175—250
517	Goose Girl	14.5"	CE	1990	⑥	$175—250
518	Umbrella Boy	9.5"	CE	1989	⑥	$175—250
519	Ride Into Christmas	13"	CE	1989	⑥	$175—250

Porcelain Dolls III 1996 —1999

Description: Doll with soft stuffed body and porcelain head, hands and feet, hand-crafted by Goebel. Original issue price $200—$250. Each doll has its own mold, making each doll distinct. (See also Hummels 515—524 and 950—960 in main body of book.) Dolls 515 "Kiss Me" and 960 "Ride Into Christmas" were sculpted by Gerhard Skrobek, and the others were sculpted by Marion Huschka. Doll 524 "Valentine Gift" was a M.I. Hummel Club Exclusive in Club Year 1998—1999 and features a glass wine bottle in wicker basket, embroidered fabric heart, and Club backstamp. Doll 960 "Ride Into Christmas" is distinguished from Doll 519 "Ride Into Christmas" by an artificial Christmas tree in basket with wine bottle, and porcelain snow-capped open lantern. Doll 960 Ride Into Christmas includes a sled for display. Dolls 950 "Apple Tree Girl" and 951 "Apple Tree Boy" include a ceramic tree display. The others include a wooden stand.

515	Kiss Me!	14"	CE	1998	⑥	$175—250
521	School Girl	13.5"	CE	1996	⑥	$175—250
522	Little Scholar	14.5"	CE	1996	⑥	$175—250
524	Valentine Gift	16"	CE	1998/1999	⑥	$175—250
950	Apple Tree Girl	14"	CE	1998	⑥	$175—250
951	Apple Tree Boy	14"	CE	1998	⑥	$175—250
960	Ride Into Christmas	11"	CE	1999	⑥	$175—250

Vinyl Dolls 1995—2000

Description: Vinyl M.I. Hummel doll made for Goebel by the firm Engel—Puppen GmbH in Rodental, Germany, in a worldwide limited edition of 20,000. Modeled hair, hand-painted. Priced $94—$140 in 2000.

272012K	Baby Girl	10.5"	CE	1995	⑦	$90—150
272029K	Baby Boy	10.5"	CE	1995	⑦	$90—150
292010K	Peterle (School Boy)	11.5"	CE	1995	⑦	$125—225
292027K	Rosi (School Girl)	11.5"	CE	1995	⑦	$125—225
292034K	Krankenbesuch (Visiting an Invalid)	11.5"	CE	1995	⑦	$125—225
292041K	Hansl (Brother)	11.5"	CE	1995	⑦	$125—225

292058K	Strickliesl (Happy Pastime)	11.5"	CE	1995	❼	$125—225
292065K	Lauterbach (Weary Wanderer)	11.5"	CE	1995	❼	$125—225
292089K	Radi—Bub (For Father)	11.5"	CE	1995	❼	$125—225
292072K	Ganseliesl (Goose Girl)	11.5"	CE	2000	❽	$125—225
292096K	Felix (Chimney Sweep)	11.5"	CE	2000	❽	$125—225
	Gretl (Little Shopper)	11.5"	CE			$125—225
292102K	Strupf Verloren (Lost Stocking)	11.5"	CE			$125—225

70th Anniversary Collection: 1935-2005

Goebel created special Hummels in celebration of the 70th Anniversary of Hummels in 2005. HUM 45/III "Madonna with Halo", HUM 184 "Latest News" - Leipzig Fair, and all of the 70th Anniversary Collection figurines have an incised crown mark and the (TM 8) trademark, a 70th Anniversary backstamp, and a rectangular ceramic 70th Anniversary Plaque that is crimped to the Hummel. They were made with historical casting and painting techniques and colors, using original molds hidden in Siessen Convent for safekeeping during World War II.

70th Anniversary Collection

					Issue Price
☐ 28/III	Wayside Devotion	8.75"	(LE of 1,935)	❽	$799
☐ 12/I	Chimney Sweep	6"	(LE of 1,935)	❽	$379
☐ 24/I	Lullaby CH	3.5"	(LE of 1,935)	❽	$329
☐ 20	Prayer Before Battle	4.5"	(LE of 1,935)	❽	$259
☐ 14 A	Bookworm Bookend, Boy	5"	(LE of 1,935)	❽	$429
☐ 14 B	Bookworm Bookend, Girl	4.5"	(LE of 1,935)	❽	$429
☐ 6/0	Sensitive Hunter	4.75"	(LE of 1,935)	❽	$339
☐ 11/0	Merry Wanderer	5"	(LE of 1,935)	❽	$339
☐ 43	March Winds	5.25"	(LE of 1,935)	❽	$289
☐ 15/0	Hear Ye, Hear Ye	5.75"	(LE of 1,935)	❽	$339

70th Anniversary Commemoratives

☐ 45/III	Madonna with Halo	16"	(LE of 1,935)	❽	$429
☐ 184	Latest News - Leipzig Fair	5"		❽	$429
	(Limited to production in 2005 only, not sequentially numbered)				
☐ HU2	Bust of M.I. Hummel	5.75"		❽	$49
	(Limited to production in 2005 only, not sequentially numbered)				
☐ 969	Puppy Love Wooden Case Clock	10.25"		❽	$250
	(Limited to production in 2005 only, not sequentially numbered)				

M.I. HUMMEL MINIATURES
by Don & Beth Woodworth

The Pre-Goebel Miniatures

From 1977 to mid-1979 artist Robert Olszewski crafted miniatures in his own studio, including five based on Hummel motifs, but unauthorized by W. Goebel Porzellanfabrik. Alerted to his breach of Goebel's copyright, Olszewski contacted Goebel in 1978. Goebel recognized his unique talent, which led to the formation of the Goebel Miniatures Studios in Camarillo, California in July 1979, with Robert Olszewski as Master Artist. The "pre-Goebel" Hummel miniatures made by Olszewski are highly prized by collectors, and bring $1000—2000 each. They were made of handcast bronze, handpainted and signed. One, "Pocketfull of Posies", was a numbered (LE) Limited Edition of 200. In addition to the quantities of painted figurines reported below, a small number of each motif were made as charms in silver or gold, and a small number of "Rainy Weather" figurines were made in sterling silver.

PRE-GOEBEL HUMMEL MINIATURES

			Issue Price	Qty	
PG-04	Rainy Weather	"Stormy Weather"	$36 in 1977	439	CE
PG-05	Farmyard Hero	"Barnyard Hero"	$30 in 1977	489	CE
PG-07	Child With Doll	"Kiss Me"	$30 in 1978	388	CE
PG-11	Pocketfull of Posies	"Ring Around the Rosie"	$90 in 1978	200	CE
PG-12	Bringing Home the Tree	"Ride Into Christmas"	$34 in 1978	343	CE

The first authorized M.I. Hummel miniature was special for members of the Goebel Collectors Club. It was a miniature of the first club piece, "Valentine Gift", in a 14kt gold-plated pendant. The second M.I. Hummel miniature was also a club exclusive, a miniature of the club piece "What Now?", in an 18kt gold over silver (vermeil) pendant. A very small number of 14kt gold "Valentine Gift" and "What Now?" tie tacs were made as gifts for officials of Goebel and as a sales award for an employee of Goebel. The popularity of the first two pendants led later to a third, with a miniature of the club piece "Honey Lover" in an 18kt gold-plated pendant. The miniatures may be removed from the pendants by removing the small screw from the bottom of the jewelry cage, so that they may be displayed as miniature figurines. Each of the miniatures for the pendants was made in limited quantity, handcast in bronze and hand-painted, with the M.I. Hummel signature affixed via a tiny decal. The studio mark included the item number and year of issue.

JEWELRY

			Issue Price	Club Exclusive		
248-P	Valentine Gift Pendant	.875"	$85 in 1983	1983-1984	CE	$150—250
249-P	What Now Pendant	.875"	$125 in 1986	1986-1987	CE	$100—175
247-P	Honey Lover Pendant	.875"	$165 in 1994	1994-1995	CE	$100—175

What followed, to the delight of collectors, was a whole community of familiar Hummel figurines in miniature, with domed displays and a miniature German village called KinderWay for displaying them. Each of the miniature figurines was handcast in bronze and hand-painted, with the M.I. Hummel signature affixed via a tiny decal. The studio mark included the item number and year of issue. The first 10,000 of each motif were marked First Edition under the base of the figurine and on the box. Additional quantity of any motif were marked Second Release and the year of production. "Morning Concert" was a club exclusive, and therefore limited in production. It was marketed in the Morning Concert Vignette, which included the miniature of "Morning Concert", its own bandstand, and glass-domed display. The base of miniature "Morning Concert" was marked Club Edition 1991 Goebel USA.

FIGURINES — Issue Price

			Issue Price		
250-P	Little Fiddler	.875"	$ 90 in 1988	CE	$75—125
251-P	Stormy Weather	.875"	$115 in 1988	CE	$100—140
252-P	Doll Bath	.875"	$95 in 1988	CE	$80—130
253-P	Little Sweeper	.875"	$90 in 1988	CE	$75—125
254-P	Merry Wanderer	.875"	$95 in 1988	CE	$75—125
255-P	Postman	.875"	$95 in 1989	CE	$80—130
256-P	Visiting An Invalid	.875"	$105 in 1989	CE	$90—140
257-P	Apple Tree Boy	.875"	$115 in 1989	CE	$100—150
262-P	Baker	.875"	$100 in 1990	CE	$85—125
	Also in Bakery Day Vignette				
263-P	Waiter	.875"	$100 in 1990	CE	$85—125
	Also in Bakery Day Vignette				
264-P	Cinderella	.875"	$115 in 1990	CE	$100—150
	Also in Flower Market Vignette				
265-P	Serenade	.875"	$105 in 1991	CE	$90—140
266-P	Accordion Boy	.875"	$105 in 1991	CE	$90—140
267-P	We Congratulate	.875"	$130 in 1991	CE	$100—150
268-P	Busy Student	.875"	$105 in 1991	CE	$90—140
269-P	Morning Concert	.875"	Not sold separately	CE	$85—125
	Part of Morning Concert Vignette				
279-P	Ride Into Christmas	.875"	Not sold separately	CE	$100—150
	Part of Winterfest Vignette				
280-P	Plaque—English	.875"	$130 in 1991	CE	$110—155
280-P	Plaque—German	.875"	$130 in 1991	CE	$110—175
	Available in Europe				
281-P	School Boy	.875"	$120 in 1992	CE	$110—155
282-P	Wayside Harmony	.875"	$140 in 1992	CE	$120—160
283-P	Goose Girl	.875"	$130 in 1992	CE	$120—170

Production of Hummel miniatures at Goebel Miniatures Studios was suspended at the end of 1992. Consequently, the three miniatures that had just been released in 1992, School Boy, Wayside Harmony, and Goose Girl, were on the market only briefly, resulting in them being more difficult for collectors to locate. Two special edition miniature

Hummels were released later, "The Mail is Here" in 1993 and "Ring Around the Rosie" in 1994. "The Mail is Here" miniature was marketed in "The Mail is Here" Vignette which included a handcrafted clocktower with working clock, and a glass-domed display with hardwood base. "The Mail is Here" miniature was marked "First Year of Issue 1993", Goebel USA. The miniature "Ring Around the Rosie" was part of the "Ring Around the Rosie" Vignette, with a musical base that played "Springtime" while rotating the miniature, and a glass-domed display with hardwood base. The "Ring Around the Rosie" miniature was marked (LE) Limited Edition—10,000 Pieces, 1994, Goebel Germany. Goebel has no current plans for any further Hummel miniatures.

285-P	The Mail Is Here	1"	Not sold separately	CE	$275—350
	Part of The Mail Is Here Vignette				
286-P	Ring Around the Rosie	3"	Not sold separately	CE	$350—500
	Part of Ring Around the Rosie Vignette				

Robert Olszewski designed charming scenes in miniature for the display of the Hummel miniatures. Each of the domed displays, known as vignettes, consisted of hand-painted scenery for one or more miniatures, with a glass dome and a round base of burnished metal, with the exception of the hardwood bases for "The Mail is Here" and "Ring Around the Rosie" vignettes. The KinderWay village pieces were modeled after the look of villages in the Bavaria area of Germany. Olszewski planned for flexibility in the use of the displays. Pieces were made to mix, match and be interchangeable, to allow collectors to devise a setting for their miniatures according to their own liking, and then be able to change it whenever they wish. Production of the displays was suspended at the end of 1992.

VIGNETTES

37355   Bavarian Cottage, with its base, in Solitaire Display Dome
$45 issue price in 1988. For display of one or more miniatures.
4.625" CE $40–60

37726   Bakery Day Vignette with Baker and Waiter Miniatures
$225 issue price in 1991. Display limited to 3000 worldwide. Figurines marked First Edition 1990. 4.625" CE $100–185

37728   Winterfest Vignette with Ride into Christmas Miniature
$195 issue price in 1991. Display limited to 5000 worldwide. Figurine marked First Edition 1991. 4.625" CE $185–225

37729   Flower Market Vignette with Cinderella Miniature
$135 issue price in 1991. Display limited to 3000 worldwide. Figurine marked First Edition 1990. 4.625" CE $125–185

030   Morning Concert Vignette with Morning Concert Miniature

$175 issue price in 1991. 1991-1992 club exclusive. Figurine marked Club Edition 1991 Goebel USA.   4.625" CE $125–175

826504   Mail Is Here Clock Tower Vignette with Mail Is Here Miniature
$495 issue price in 1993. Display limited to 3000 worldwide. Working clock in clocktower. Figurine marked First Year of Issue 1993 Goebel USA. 7.75" CE $430–525

826101   Ring Around the Rosie Vignette with Ring Around the Rosie Miniature
$675 issue price in 1994. Limited Edition of 10,000 worldwide. Figurine marked Limited Edition—10,000 Pieces, 1994, Goebel Germany. Musical base turns the miniature while playing tune, "Springtime." 9.5" CE $500–700

KINDERWAY
953-D   Bavarian Cottage
$60 issue price in 1988. Fits in Bavarian Village Display or with its base in Solitaire Display Dome.   4" CE $40–60

954-D   Bavarian Village
$100 issue price in 1989. Has village building and place for Bavarian Cottage. 5" CE $80–110

960-D   Bavarian Marketsquare with Marketsquare Bridge
$110 issue price in 1990. Has bakery and restaurant, and place for Hotel, Flower Stand, Band Stand, Shrine or Church.   4.75" CE $100–130

961-D   Marketsquare Hotel
$70 issue price in 1990. Fits in Bavarian Marketsquare or Countryside School Displays.   4.75" CE $65–100

962-D   Marketsquare Flower Stand
$35 issue price in 1990. Fits in Flower Market Vignette or in Bavarian Marketsquare or Countryside School Displays.   1.75" CE $30–45

963-D   Marketsquare Bridge
$30 issue price in 1990. Spans between two of Bavarian Marketsquare, Countryside School and Bavarian Village displays.   .625" CE $15–25

974-D   Countryside School—with Marketsquare Bridge
$100 issue price in 1991. Has school building and place for Hotel, Flower
Stand, Band Stand, Shrine or Church.   4.75" CE $90–130

975-D   Wayside Shrine
$60 issue price in 1991. Fits in Bavarian Marketsquare or Countryside
School Displays.   4" CE $50–75

977-D   Bavarian Band Stand
Part of Morning Concert Vignette (1991-1992 club exclusive), or fits in
Bavarian Marketsquare or Countryside School displays.   Not sold
separately.   3.25" CE $40–50

993-D   Bavarian Alps
$100 issue price in 1992. Stands alongside rest of KinderWay.
7.125" CE $85–120

994-D   Trees
$40 issue price in 1992. Stands alongside rest of KinderWay.
4.5" CE $35–60

995-D   Bavarian Church
$60 issue price in 1992. Fits in Bavarian Marketsquare or Countryside
School Displays.   6.5" CE $55–80

"Mail Is Here Clock Tower" Vignette

"Ring Around the Rosie" Vignette

"HUMMEL-HUMMEL"

We regularly receive many letters and phone calls regarding HUMMEL-HUMMEL. This figurine actually has no connection at all with the "M.I. Hummel" figurines made by W. Goebel Porzellanfabrik of Rödental, Germany. A very good German friend of ours, who now lives in Kansas City, Missouri, gave us a copy of this story many years ago when we had asked him about HUMMEL-HUMMEL.

"HUMMEL-HUMMEL"

"MORS-MORS"

THE HUMMEL-HUMMEL STORY

"About 100 years ago, there lived in the German city of Hamburg a man by the name of Hummel. Since Hamburg, like a lot of cities along the German coast, did not have good drinking water and very few wells with pure water, Mr. Hummel made a living by catering water to the well-to-do citizens of that town.

"He was a gruff, gaunt looking character, dressed in a soot-black suit and wearing a stove-pipe hat. With the two wooden buckets hanging from the yoke across his shoulders, he was one of the most familiar sights in Hamburg at that time. People, especially children, used to taunt him by hollering 'Hummel-Hummel' when they passed him; his short retort always was 'Mors-Mors' (kiss my fanny).

"Over the years this has become a sort of greeting for Hamburg citizens wherever they meet in the world. It is their good-natured way of saying 'Hello' and striking up new friendships. The man with the water buckets and the "HUMMEL-HUMMEL" has become the symbol of the city of Hamburg, and the likeness of this man can be found in various shapes and materials in the shops of Hamburg."

The city of Hamburg has even erected a large granite statue as a monument of "Old Mister Hummel' to help perpetuate this legend.

The photographs illustrating this page are of a figurine that was actually produced by the Goebel company and is sold in the shops of Hamburg.

"Slash" Mark
# Denotes Second Choice

For your information: At one time, an imperfect or flawed figurine produced by W. Goehel Porzellanfabrik that was detected during final inspection, was so marked by grinding a small groove or "slash" mark through the trademark. These pieces were then sold to factory employees as "seconds." Occasionally a round, red decal also was used on these seconds.

Pictured with this column is the bottom of a figurine bearing both a slash mark through the trademark, and the round decal reading: "For staff members only - seconds," plus a numeral "2." and the word "Wahi." My German dictionary defines the word "wahi" as meaning a choice or alternative.

These round decals were produced in various sizes, but I have only seen them in the color red. They are usually very difficult or next to impossible to find, unless a factory employee sells or gives away the second. Such a piece does make a nice addition to M.I. Hummel figurine collection.

The words "Goebel, Germany" on this figurine clearly have a white slash mark ground through the type, accompanied by a round, red decal labeling this figurine as a factory second. (Photo: Robert L. Miller)

Insurance Claim for
Hummel Boxes(?)!

I recently received an interesting phone call from an insurance agent. His reason for calling was that I had been referred to him as an expert on M.I. Hummel figurine collectibles. His company had a client that had stored his Hummel figurine collection in the basement of his home, where it had suffered water damage. The figurines themselves were all O.K., but all of the boxes were ruined by the water.

The client had submitted a claim for $14,000 (400 boxes x $35 = $14,000) and the insurance agent wanted to know if this could be possible. I was dumbfounded!! In all my years of collecting and writing articles about M.I. Hummel figurines, I had never heard anything so ridiculous!!!

I wrote a column in March 1995 on this very same subject and feel that this is still very much accepted as the true situation today. The following is a partial reprint from the March 1995 magazine:

Original Boxes - Valuable?

A lady called me the other day; she was very unhappy. She had sent her M.l. Hummel figurine to a conservation laboratory to have her figurine restored (repaired). She was quite satisfied with the restoration of the figurine, but the problem was that the restorer had not returned it to her in the original styrofoam box!

The restorer eventually located her box and sent it to her by a postal delivery service. The package containing the empty box was delivered to her apartment complex. But, before she could pick up the package at the complex office, it was discovered missing! Whomever appropriated the package must have been extremely disappointed when he discovered all it contained was an empty box!

I tried to console the collector, telling her that she had lost absolutely nothing! The empty box had no value! The collector, however said her dealer always told her that the original boxes added greatly to the value of her figurines. I tried my best to convince her that this was not so.

I explained that my wife, Ruth, and I have several thousand M.I. Hummel figurines in our personal collection (an accumulation of over 25 years), but we have no boxes. Most of them did not even come in a box.

The purpose of a box is simply to deliver the figurine in an undamaged condition to the eventual owner. I cannot imagine what size storage area we would need had my wife saved all the boxes...

Today, over 20 years later, we know of no dealers who will pay more for the plates with or without a box. I will admit that the plates are easier to handle if they are in boxes — which only points out the original intention for which the box was designed!

Now, if the owner of a collection of M.I. Hummel figurines moves quite often (such as being in the military), the boxes are handy and convenient for safely moving a collection. Again, this emphasizes the original purpose for the box!

Recently, articles have been written addressing this very subject. I would like to quote from one of the articles, which I think is correct and to the point:

"The issue for collectors on what to do regarding the storage of the 'packaging' for their collectibles continues to mount with every new box they have to store. When the closets and cupboards all become piled high with empty boxes, questions (and other things) begin to tumble out: What will I do with any more boxes? Do I really need to keep these boxes? Are these empty boxes really worth anything?

"If we are to apply some kind of logic to this quandary, a good starting point would be an analysis of the 'box-is-valuable' myth. When did the myth begin? There's no certain answer, but one can easily imagine that some sales associates in retail settings have used the phrase, 'By all means, save this original box, because it makes your figurine much more valuable.

"To whom would it make the figurine more valuable?, have never heard of a collector refusing to purchase a collectible because the box produced from storage was not pretty enough or collectable enough.

"It is conceivable that perpetration of the 'box-Is-valuable' myth could reach ridiculous proportions for both collectibles dealers and collectors alike. For example, if boxes were considered important on the secondary market, what would determine the value of each box? Would the size of the box relate to the price — small value for small boxes, greater value for larger boxes? And what about condition of the boxes? How much would you deduct for a scratch, a tear, a dent, or a cut somewhere on the box? And what happens if the box no longer has its original packaging papers or enclosures?

"Manufacturers of collectibles have provided the finest quality of packaging in order to get these items safely into our homes. However, that does not justify our turning boxes into items to be revered.

"A collector friend of mine once suffered the breakage of a retired piece of crystal when the bottom of the container gave way. In that instance the box's sole function was to safely transport a piece of beautiful, valuable crystal. Having failed this test, the box is hardly to be considered valuable!

"Wouldn't it be great if we could all just somehow agree collectively to adopt a philosophy that says we collect figurines — not boxes!! Think about it, and keep on collecting — figurines."

P.S. I have not heard the out come of this claim, but I feel certain that it was in all probability, disallowed. Most insurance companies insure the figurines — not the boxes!

"M.I. Hummel" Mini Plates

1971–1976

1976–82 Sample

This set of six 1-inch miniature plates were put on the market in 1987 and were produced by Ars Editibn of Zug, Switzerland, and were distributed by Schmid Brothers, Inc. of Randolph, Massachusetts. They are replicas, in decal form, of the Goebel "M.I. Hummel" bas-relief annual plates produced by Goebel from 1971 through 1976. The details on the plates (and their boxes) were faithfully duplicated in ceramic form. Each plate has the M.I. Hummel signature on both the front and back. The back decal reads: "Made in West Germany, ANNUAL PLATE, M.I. Hummel, 1971" (etc.) and what appears to be a combination of the TM 4 and TM 5 Goebel trademarks. The front decal is an exact color version of the larger counterpart. The miniature cardboard boxes are a delightful part of the entire set.

The collection of six miniature plates came as a complete display in an oval wooden frame, along with a magnifying glass with which to appreciate the craftsmanship. The original issue price was $150 per set, limited to 15,000 sets worldwide. To my knowledge, they were not sold in Canada. At the time, they seemed to be overpriced, and to my recollection, did not sell very well. It is doubtful, in my mind, that the full 15,000 sets were ever produced.

Today, these sets can sometimes be found for sale at flea markets, antique shows, and collectors fairs. I have seen them priced from $75 to $150 per set. Be sure to ask for the miniatured boxes, as they add greatly to the uniqueness of the set.

A second set of six miniature plates, 1977 to 1982, was planned, but, according to Ars Edition of Zug, Switzerland, was never produced or sold in the United States market.

.... HUM TERM ....

ARS: The shortened form of ARS EDITION GmbH of Munich, Germany. Ars Edition was formerly known as Ars Sacra Josef Mueller Verlag, a German publishing house, selling postcards, postcard-calendars and prints of M.I. Hummel, which first published the Hummel Art. Today Ars Edition GmbH is licensee for Hummel books, calendars, cards and stationery. Owner: Mr. Marcel Nauer (grandson of Dr. Herbert Dubler).

AUSTRALIAN DEALER'S PLAQUES

The Australian Dealer Plaques were produced in the early 1970s at the request of F. R. Barlow & Sons, Melbourne, Australia, the exclusive importer of "M.I. Hummel" figurines for all of Australia at that time. The factory could not locate the pertinent records for that time period, but learned that the Barlow Company went out of business in the mid-1970s. At the present time, we have no idea how many stores received these personalized dealer plaques. They are normal HUM 187 (5.50 x 4.00") dealers plaques. I am sure there are many more just waiting to be found! You Australian collectors get busy! The Wallace plaque was purchased in Perth, Australia several years ago.

KNOWN TITLES
- ☐ Light & Shade Pty Ltd..........(CE)
- ☐ Carmosino's ....(CE)
- ☐ J. R. Wallace & Co ....(CE)
- ☐ Demasius Stores Pty Ltd ....(CE)
- ☐ Ches Louise ....(CE)

The Back Half of the Figurine

Half of all M.I. Hummel figurines are "interpretations" or "extensions" of Sister Hummel's original artwork. I'm referring to the "back half" of each figure.

Sister Maria Innocentia drew only in <u>flat</u>, two-dimensional form. She did not draw front, back and side views of each subject, as an architect would do. I think she actually wanted to leave the back half, or unseen portion, to our imagination! Otherwise, she would have provided a back view of each drawing!

All Goebel modelers, from Moeller and Unger to Skrobek and Fischer, have used their "imagination" or "interpretation" for the back half or unseen portion for each and every creation they modeled three-dimensionally. For example: Sister Hummel's drawing of "Angel Duet" (postcard H 411) shows only a front view of two angels (we can see the wings of only one angel) holding a red candle. What did she intend for the back view?

Master sculptor Reinhold Unger, in 1948, thought that one angel should have an arm on the shoulder of the other (angel?). In 1958, master sculptor Theo R. Mertzenbach decided this should be changed to a lower position for the arm. When I questioned Theo about this change, he personally told me that, in his view, it would be easier for the artists to paint, that it would look better, and it is a more natural position. Two master sculptors - two interpretations. Both were approved by the Sisters of Siessen Convent!

Sister Hummel's drawing of HUM 47 "Goose Girl" — a little girl with three geese in front of her, is all that we can see from her drawing. What is the little girl doing with her hands behind her back? Did she have a bag of bread crumbs for the geese, a rag doll, a bunch of flowers, a stick, or nothing at all? Master sculptor Arthur Moeller "imagined" that she was holding a bouquet of flowers.

Every <u>two</u>-dimensional drawing of Sister Hummel must of necessity be "interpreted" by a master sculptor before it can be produced into a <u>three</u>-dimensional M.I. Hummel figurine. This is what they do!

I personally feel that none are better qualified to do this than the master sculptors at W. Goebel Porzellanfabrik in Germany. I am sure that Sister Maria Innocentia would approve.

Some collectors do not like Goebel's interpretations. I think the best way to express dissatisfaction is — if you don't like it, don't buy it. That keeps the focus on our true love, the hobby of collecting!

M.I. Hummel postcard with the original artwork for the "Angel Duet" sculpture.

M.I. Hummel postcard "The Little Goose-Girl," bearing the original art for that sculpture.

GOEBEL PRODUCED MINIATURE WWII MILITARY VEHICLES

I did not know this until early in 1991, when I received two different letters inquiring about Goebel-produced miniature military vehicles. I, of course, called both men and informed them that I had no experience with Goebel miniature tanks, but I would do a little research at the factory on my next visit to Germany. Some months later, while visiting the factory archives, we were shown a large wooden tray full of these miniature models. Possibly 100 to 150 pieces in various sizes, colors and shapes. Our guide through the archives explained that these miniature vehicles had been made during the war years and were used by the German military for use on their plotting boards or maps. The locations of various army units and their bases, both German and enemy, were followed by positioning the miniature vehicles on these boards. As the positions changed, the miniatures were moved with a long stick, similar to a pool cue, to the new location, thus assisting leaders in studying their military strategies. I had remembered seeing these plotting boards in the photos published during the war years.

The little ceramic or clay Goebel vehicles measure approximately 2.50 to 2.75" in size. Some have movable turrets and are quite good reproductions of different military vehicles. Others have names incised on the bottom, such as Sherman, Churchill, Panther, Tiger, etc., representing vehicles from Germany, France, England, Russia and the United States. Colors vary from gray or green to olive drab. One collector now has over thirty different items in his collection. He has purchased them from former U.S. Army personnel who picked them up as souvenirs during the war years. He has even found them in Germany and Poland! We have approximately twenty items in our personal collection.

Bottom views

USA Sherman

The M.I. Hummel Club®
(Formerly: Goebel Collectors' Club)

F ounded in 1977 as the Goebel Collectors' Club, the first of its kind, this important organization continues its early established tradition as a collector's information service.

The services it imparts are many. By having constant access to its members through its quarterly magazine, *INSIGHTS*, personal correspondence between members and Club staff, and one-on-one discussions at various collectors' shows and in-store promotions, the Club is constantly aware of the needs of its members and seeks to respond in as much depth as possible.

There are a variety of aspects to Club membership, enough to satisfy collectors at all levels. Whether one owns one M.I. Hummel figurine, or 100, or any number in between, the pages of *INSIGHTS* can open doors of knowledge.

The special articles focus on the history of the figurines, the life of Sister Maria Innocentia Hummel, the intricacies of production, and helpful hints on how to decorate with your figurines. Its pages are filled with pleasurable reading and full-color photographs.

For the intermediate and advanced collector there is the knowledge that any question, no matter how obscure, will be thoroughly researched by the Club, calling on the available records at the factory as well as its own files developed over the years.

All members can share in the Club's expanded opportunities by joining a local chapter, comprised of members in any given regional area who meet on a regular basis for the purpose of sharing and imparting knowledge, and having a great deal of fun while doing it. The Club publishes a quarterly chapter newsletter called *Chapter & Verse*.

There are exclusive purchase opportunities for Club members as well. In each year of membership, M.I. Hummel treasures are produced for members only, with the Club's own backstamp attesting to that exclusivity. These handcrafted motifs are available for purchase by members at select stores throughout North America or direct from the Club.

A winsome M.I. Hummel figurine gift is presented from the Club to each new member; through this unique welcome gift, members can already feel the specialness of the organization they have just joined. Renewing members also receive a gift figurine each year, a warm thanks from the Club.

A custom designed fact-filled binder, each member's introduction to knowledge, is another exciting benefit. The Club also holds a fun-filled biennial convention for members only.

The Club offers an extensive travel program as well. Thousands have traveled on these trips designed for lovers of M.I. Hummel figurines, and their guests. Each trip to Europe includes a behind-the-scenes tour of the Goebel factory in Bavaria, Germany (the home of the figurines), available only to members on these trips. (Members who travel on their own know to carry their membership cards with them; the card, their "passport" to many pleasures, is their free ticket to lunch when visiting the factory.)

The European M.I. Hummel Club was introduced and the International M.I. Hummel Club was launched. Members have the opportunity to make fascinating contacts with members from around the world.

The M.I. Hummel Club—your open door to enjoyment, fascination and a fulfilling experience.

For more information, please call or write the M.I. Hummel Club, Goebel Plaza, P.O. Box 11, Pennington NJ 08534-0011. 1-800-666-CLUB (2582). You can also e-mail the Club at memsrv@mihummel.com or visit the Club at www.mihummel.com.

PREVIEW EDITIONS (PE) (Ended with Club Year No. 22)

☐ Cheeky Fellow	HUM 554	16		1992/93	$120
☐ Sweet As Can Be	HUM 541	17		1993/94	$125
☐ Little Troubadour	HUM 558	18		1994/95	$130
☐ Strum Along	HUM 557	19		1995/96	$135
☐ One, Two, Three	HUM 555	20		1996/97	$145
☐ What's That?	HUM 488	21		1997/98	$150
☐ The Poet at the Podium	HUM 397/3/0	22		1998/99	$150

Figurines Issued Exclusively for Members of The M.I. Hummel Club
(Formerly: The Goebel Collectors' Club)

				Issue	Price
☐ Valentine Gift	HUM 387	No. 1	1977		$45
☐ Smiling Through, Plaque	HUM 690	No. 2	1978		$50
☐ Oister M.I. Hummel Bust	HU 3	No. 3	1979		$75
☐ Valentine Joy	HUM 399	No. 4	1980		$95
☐ Daisies Don't Tell	HUM 380	No. 5	1981		$80
☐ It's Cold	HUM 421	No. 6	1982		$80
☐ What Now?	HUM 422	No. 7	1983		$90
☐ Coffee Break	HUM 409	No. 8	1984		$90
☐ Smiling Through	HUM 408	No. 9	1985		$125
☐ Birthday Candle	HUM 440	No. 10	1986		$95
☐ Morning Concert	HUM 447	No. 11	1987		$98
☐ The Surprise	HUM 431	No. 12	1988		$125
☐ Hello World	HUM 429	No. 13	1989/90		$130
☐ I Wonder	HUM 486	No. 14	1990/91		$140
☐ Gift from a Friend	HUM 485	No. 15	1991/92		$160
☐ My Wish Is Small	HUM 463/0	No. 16	1992/93		$170
☐ I Didn't Do It	HUM 626	No. 17	1993/94		$175
☐ Little Visitor	HUM 563/0	No. 18	1994/95		$180
☐ Country Suitor	HUM 760	No. 19	1995/96		$195
☐ Celebrate With Song	HUM 790	No. 20	1996/97		$295
☐ Playful Blessing	HUM 658	No. 21	1997/98		$260

☐ At Play ....HUM 632 ....No. 22 ....1998/99 .....$260
☐ Private Conversation ....HUM 615 ....No. 23 ....1999/00 .....$260
☐ Will It Sting? ....HUM 450/0 ....No. 24 ....2000/01 .....$260
☐ Looking Around....................................HUM 2089/A ......No. 25 ....2001/02 .....$230
☐ Rolling Around ....HUM 2088/B ......No. 26 ....2002/03 .....$230
☐ Playing Around ....HUM 2088/A ....No. 27 ....2003/04 .....$230
☐ Waiting Around ....HUM 2089/B ....No. 28 ....2004/05 .....$230
☐ Miniature Valentine Gift Necklace ....1983 ....$85
☐ Miniature What Now? Necklace ....1986 ....$125
☐ Miniature Honey Lover Pendant ....1994 ....$165
☐ At Grandpa's.......................................HUM 621 ....1994 ....$1300
☐ A Story from Grandma ....HUM 620 ....1995 ....$1300
☐ Valentine·Gift Plaque ....HUM 717...........1996 ....$250
☐ Valentine Gift Doll................................HUM 524...........1998/99 ....$200
☐ Lucky Charmer ....HUM 2071.........1999/00 ....$90
☐ Hummele ....HUM 365...........1999/00 ....$145
☐ Merry Wander Plaque with Bee ....HUM 900 ....1999/00 ....$199
☐ Sharpest Student ....HUM 2087/A ....2000/01 ....$95
☐ Wishes Come True...............................HUM 2025/A ....2000/01 ....$625
☐ Puppet Prince......................................HUM 2103/B ....2001/02 ....$100
☐ Scooter Time ....HUM 2070 ....2001/02 ....$695
☐ Picture Perfect ....HUM 2100 ......2001/02 ....$3495
☐ Extra, Extra - Club 25th Anniversary ......HUM 2113 ......2001/02 ....$240
☐ Wait For Me ....HUM 2148/A ....2002/03 ....$100
☐ Summer Adventure ....HUM 2124 ......2002/03 ....$695
☐ I Brought You a Gift ....HUM 479 ....1989–90 ....FREE GIFT
☐ Merry Wanderer Pendant ....Sterling Silver ..1990–91 ....FREE GIFT
☐ Two Hands, One Treat ....HUM 493 ....1991–92 ....FREE GIFT
☐ Lucky Fellow ....HUM 560 ....1992–93 ....FREE GIFT
☐ A Sweet Offering ....HUM 549/3/0 ..1993–94 ....FREE GIFT
☐ For Keeps ....HUM 630 ....1994–95 ....FREE GIFT
☐ From Me To You ....HUM 629 ....1995–96 ....FREE GIFT
☐ Forever Yours ....HUM 793 ....1996–97 ....FREE GIFT
☐ Nature's Gift ....HUM 729 ....1997–98 ....FREE GIFT
☐ Garden Treasures ....HUM 727 ....1998–99 ....FREE GIFT
☐ Pigtails ....HUM 2052 ......1999–00 ....FREE GIFT
☐ Honor Student ....HUM 2087/B ....2000–01 ....FREE GIFT
☐ Puppet Princess...................................HUM 2103/A ....2001–02 ....FREE GIFT
☐ First Mate ....HUM 2148/B ....2002–03 ....FREE GIFT
☐ Too Shy To Sing..................................HUM 845 ....2003-04 ....FREE GIFT
☐ Clear As A Bell....................................HUM 2181 ....2004-05 ....FREE GIFT
☐ Steadfast Soprano ....HUM 848 ....2005-06 ....FREE GIFT
☐ Keeping Time......................................HUM 2183 ....2006-07 ....FREE GIFT
☐ Melody-Conductor ....HUM 2198 ....2006-07 ....FREE GIFT
☐ First Solo ....HUM 2182/B ....2003-04 ....$105
☐ First Love ....HUM 765 ....2004-05 ....$945

☐ Hitting the High Note	HUM 846	2004-05	$110
☐ Sad Song	HUM 404	2005-06	$295
☐ April Showers	HUM 610	2005-06	$745
☐ First Violin	HUM 2184	2005-06	$110
☐ Gifts of Love	HUM 909	2006-07	$350
☐ Togetherness	HUM 753	2006-07	$745
☐ Lamplight Caroler	HUM 847	2006-07	$110

CELEBRATION PLATE SERIES

☐ Valentine Gift	HUM 738	1986	$90
☐ Valentine Joy	HUM 737	1987	$98
☐ Daisies Don't Tell	HUM 736	1988	$115
☐ It's Cold	HUM 735	1989	$120

ANNIVERSARY FIGURINES

☐ Flower Girl (5 years) RETIRED	HUM 548	1990	$105
☐ Sunflower Friends (5 years)	HUM 2104	2000	$195
☐ Little Pair (10 years) RETIRED	HUM 449	1990	$170
☐ Miss Beehaving (10 years)	HUM 2105	2000	$240
☐ Honey Lover (15 years)	HUM 312/I	1991	$190
☐ Behave! (20 years)	HUM 339	1996	$350
☐ Relaxation (25 years)	HUM 316	2001	$390
☐ Forget-Me-Not (30 years)	HUM 362/I	2006	$350

Glossary of Terms

AIR HOLES: Air holes are tiny holes intentionally made in the figurines during production to prevent the pieces from exploding during the firing process. These air holes are usually placed so carefully in the figurines that often times they go unnoticed by the casual observer.

ANNIVERSARY EXCLUSIVES: Figurines offered exclusively to M.I. Hummel Club members of 5, 10, 15, 20, 25 or 30 years of membership.

ANNIVERSARY PINS: In the Club year in which you celebrate your 5th, 10th, 15th, 20th, 25th or 30th anniversary, you will receive a special pin to mark the occasion.

ARS: The shortened form of ARS EDITION GmbH of Munich, West Germany. Ars Edition was formerly known as Ars Sacra Josef Müeller Verlag, a German publishing house, selling postcards, postcard-calendars and prints of M.I. Hummel, which first published the Hummel Art. Today Ars Edition GmbH is licensee for Hummel books, calendars, cards and stationery. Owner: Mr. Marcel Nauer (grandson of Dr. Herbert Dubler).

ARS AG: A corporation based in Zug, Switzerland holding the two-dimensional rights of original M.I. Hummel drawings as well as the two-dimensional rights for reproductions of M.I. Hummel products made by Goebel. "Ars" is the Latin word for art.

ARTIST'S MARK: The artist's mark is the signature of the face painter, the artist who paints the face of the figurine. This signature is usually in the form of a set of initials accompanied by the date. These artist's marks almost always appear in black on the underside of the figurine's base.

ASSEMBLERS NUMBER: The small incised number (usually two digits) on the bottom of the figurine identifies the person who assembled the individual soft clay parts of the figurine. Smaller than the incised model number or the copyright date. Has no real meaning to the collector, only for Goebel production control.

AUTHORIZED M.I. HUMMEL CLUB RETAILER: A merchant granted the authority by an official "M.I. Hummel" distributor to redeem M.I. Hummel Club exclusive editions and promote the Club.

BACKSTAMP or TRADEMARK: The official legal mark that Goebel places on the bottom of all "M.I. Hummel" products.

BAS RELIEF: Sculptural relief in which the projection from the surrounding surface is slight. This type of raised work is found on the annual and anniversary "M.I. Hummel" plates.

BESWICK: The Beswick Company of England produced some copies of "M.I. Hummel" figurines around the WW II time period. There are approximately eleven known models of "Beswick Hummels." The Beswick pieces usually have a very shiny appearance and are marked on the underside with a model number incised into the base and the Beswick trademark which reads "Beswick England" set in a circle. A facsimile of the "M.I. Hummel" signature was used along with the term "Original Hummel Studios." The Beswick Company was acquired by the Royal Doulton Company of England. No records are known to exist of any agreement or contracts which might have given the Beswick Company the right to produce "M.I. Hummel" figurines.

BISQUE: This is a term used to describe ceramic pieces which have not been glazed, but are hard-fired and vitreous.

CHIP: The term used to describe a flaw in a ceramic figurine which reaches beyond the painted surface and the glazing. A chip in a ceramic figurine is usually rough to the touch and greatly affects the value of the item.

CLOSED EDITION: Pieces formerly in W. Goebel production program but no longer produced. In 2006 Goebel began to use the term "Closed Edition" to indicate the Hummel has been retired in that size and will never be produced again. Such a Closed Edition (retired) Hummel figurine has a Closed Edition hangtag.

CLOSED NUMBER: An identification number in W. Goebel's numerical identification system that was used to identify a design or sample models for possible production, but then for various reasons never authorized for release.

CLUB YEAR: The M.I. Hummel Club year spans from 1 June to 31 May. Membership year dates from the time you first joined the Club through the end of the M.I.Hummel Club year.

COPYRIGHT DATE: This is the date that is oftentimes incised into the bottom of an M.I. Hummel figurine. This date represents the year in which the figurine design was registered with the United States copyright office. Many M.I. Hummel figurines are registered and then do not go into general production for several years after the initial copyright is registered. The incised date is NOT the date that the figurine was necessarily produced or painted.

CRAZING: This is the term used to describe the existence of several minute cracks in the glaze of a figurine. This is a natural condition that develops as the ceramic material ages. Some pieces will become "crazed" at a faster rate than others. Many factors of production as well as the humidity of the environment where the figurine is displayed can play a part in this process.

CURRENT PRODUCTION: The term used to describe those items currently being produced by the W. Goebel Porzellanfabrik Rödental, Germany.

CURRENT TRADEMARK: Designates the symbol presently being used by the W. Goebel Porzellanfabrik to represent the company's trademark.

DECIMAL POINT: This incised "period" or dot was used in a somewhat random fashion by the W. Goebel Porzellanfabrik over the years. The decimal point is and was primarily used to reduce confusion in reading the incised numbers on the underside of the figurines. Example: 66. helps one realize that the designation is sixty-six and not ninety-nine.

DOUBLE CROWN: This term is used to describe the Goebel Company trademark found on some "M.I. Hummel" figurines. On "double crown" pieces the crown trademark is usually found incised and stamped.

DOUGHNUT BASE: A term used to describe the raised circular support on the underside of a figurine. Many figurine bases with a circle inside the regular circular base gave rise to the term, but has now been used to describe many bases with the circular support on the underside.

DUBLER: A "Dubler" figurine is one produced during the WW II time period by the Herbert Dubler Co. Inc. of New York City. These pieces were substitutes for genuine Goebel "M.I. Hummel" figurines when Goebel "Hummels" were not coming into the U.S. The Dubler figurines were made of plaster of paris and were distributed by the Crestwick Co. of New York which later became Hummelwerk and ultimately the present Goebel United States firm, Goebel of North America.

ENGOBE: Engobe is a special glaze which is used on certain size "4/0" figurines only, to achieve a matte finish. This glaze has the advantage that details on such small figurines do not get lost, as would be the case if the regular Hummel glaze was used.

EXCLUSIVE EDITION: (EE) Figurines created only for M.I. Hummel Club members. This edition bears a special Club backstamp and will never be released to the general public, but can usually be purchased on the secondary market.

FAIENCE: (pronounced fay-ontz or fi-ons) is a term for earthenware decorated with opaque colored glazes. A few early samples were produced experimentally by Goebel on "M.I. Hummel" figurines using this technique.

FINAL ISSUE: A term used by Goebel to refer to a figurine that has been permanently retired from production and will not be produced again.

FIRST ISSUE: A term used by Goebel since 1990 on all newly released figurines during the first year of production.

FULL BEE: The term "Full Bee" refers to the trademark used by the Goebel Co. from 1950 to 1957. Early usage of this trademark was incised into the material. Later versions of the "full bee" were stamped into the material.

GOEBEL BEE: A name used to describe the trademark used by the Goebel Company from 1972 until 1979. This trademark incorporates the GOEBEL name with the V and bee.

GOEBEL COLLECTORS' CLUB: The name given to the organization formerly located in Tarrytown, New York, for collectors of items produced by the W. Goebel Porzellanfabrik of West Germany. In 1989 the name was officially changed to the "M.I. Hummel Club."

HERBERT DUBLER, INC: Founded in 1934 in New York, importing products from the publishing house "Ars Sacra Joseph Mueller Munich," named after Dr. Herbert Dubler, son in law of Mr. Joseph Mueller. During WW II and thereafter this company distributed Hummel products such as cards, calendars and books. During that time the "Dubler Figurines" were put on the market. Herbert Dubler, Inc. was renamed "CHRESTWICK, INC." honoring the president, Mr. Alfred E. Wick. In 1956 the company was sold to W. Goebel Porzellanfabrik and became known as "Hummelwerk, Inc." and later changed to "Goebel United States", now Goebel of North America.

HOLLOW MOLD: The term used by "M.I. Hummel" collectors to describe a figurine that is open on the underside of the base. With these particular bases the collector can visually see into the cavity of the figurine.

HUM NO.: Mold number or model number incised on the bottom of each "M.I. Hummel" figurine at the factory. This number is used for identification purposes.

HUMMELSCAPE: According to Websters, a "scape" is a scene, as of land, sea, clouds, etc. — back-foundation, landscape. Hummelscape is a back-formation, made in China, to enhance the display of Hummel figurines. Oftentimes made to help carry out a thought, idea or season. A decorative piece of cold cast ceramic, usually very well made and highly detailed to display Hummel figurines.

"INTERNATIONAL": This name is given to the group of M.I. Hummel figurines that were produced in 1940 with the national dress of other countries. Master sculptors Reinhold Unger and Arthur Moeller translated Sister Hummel's sketches into Goebel M.I. Hummel figurines. The "Internationals" are highly sought-after by collectors.

LIMITED EDITION (LE): A figurine that is produced for a specific time period or in a limited quantity.

LOCAL CHAPTERS: Groups of M.I. Hum-

mel Club members who meet locally to study "M.I. Hummel" figurines and contiinue charitable work of Sister Hummel.

MEL: A Goebel-produced figurine with the letters "MEL" incised somewhere on the base of the piece. These pieces were designed from original drawings by Sister M.I. Hummel, but for some undetermined reasons were not approved by the Siessen Convent for inclusion in the "M.I. Hummel" line of figurines.

MIXED MEDIA: A mixed media figurine incorporates other artistic media in additionto the basic earthenware or ceramic material of the Hummel figurine. Use of the mixed media can enhance the realism of an M.I. Hummel, such as the wooden sled on Hum 2074 "Winter Sleigh Ride". It can allow for the inclusion of a detail that could not be carried out in earthenware, such as the glass balloon on a metal string in Hum 2089/B "Waiting Around". It can also make the Hummel more special, such as the Hummel figurines which incorporate Swarovski crystal items.

MODEL: This term most often refers to a particular "M.I. Hummel" figurine, plate, bell or other item in the line. When not used in reference to a specific motif, the word model also can refer to the sculptor's working model from which the figurines are made.

MOLD GROWTH: In the earlier days of figurine production the working molds were made of plaster of paris. As these molds were used, the various molded parts became larger due to the repeated usage. With modern technology at the Goebel factory and the use of acrylic resin molds, this problem has been eliminated and today the collector finds very few size differences within a given size designation.

MOLD INDUCTION DATE (MID): A coined or invented term used by the uninformed—never used by Goebel. The correct term is "copyright date" (CRD). The incised date on the bottom of your figurine is the year of creation date. This creation date is used for the U.S. copyright recordation. The copyright law says that the year of creation date has to be part of the product and incised with the respective year. It can vary between two and three years from the completion of the clay model by the Goebel master sculptor to the final creation respective copyright year. In some instances the creation date and the copyright application are in the same year, in others not. EXAMPLE: HUM 559 "Heart and Soul" was modeled by master sculptor Helmut Fischer in 1988, but has the incised 1989 copyright date on the bottom of the figurine, and was released in the U.S. market in 1996.

MOTHER MOLD SAMPLE: This term used by Goebel refers to the original samples out of the mother mold. The very FIRST piece out of the mother mold is what Goebel refers to as a "prototype"—the one and only sample that is presented to the Siessen Convent of any newly developed "M.I. Hummel" figurine. All others are "mother mold samples".

MUSTERZIMMER: The German word meaning sample model designating that this piece is to be held at the W. Goebel Prozellanfabrik in the "sample room" to be used for future reference by production artists.

OESLAU: Name for the village where the W. Goebel Porzellanfabrik is located. Oeslau is now a part of the City of Rödental, Germany. The name Oeslau appears on Hum 348 "Ring Around The Rosie."

OPEN EDITION: Pieces currently in W. Goebel's production program.

OUT OF PRODUCTION: A term used by the Goebel Company to designate items that are not currently in production, yet have not been given an official classification as to their eventual fate. Some items listed as out of production may become closed editions, remain temporarily withdrawn, or ultimately return to current production status.

OVERSIZE (OE): This description refers to a piece that has experienced "mold growth" size expansion. A figurine that measures larger than the standard size is said to be "oversized."

PAINT FLAKE: The term used to designate a flaw in a ceramic figurine whereby the paint has been chipped. This type flaw does not go beyond the glazed surface.

PAINT RUB: A general wearing away of the paint surface of a figurine in a particular spot. This condition is usually caused by excessive handling of a figurine, thin paint in a given area of the figurine, or the excessive use of abrasive cleaners.

PAINTER'S SAMPLE: A figurine used by the painters at the Goebel factory which serves as a reference figurine for the painting of subsequent pieces. The painters of "M.I. Hummel" figurines attempt to paint their individual pieces to match the painter's sample as precisely as possible. Painter's Samples are sometimes marked with a red line around the side of the base.

POSSIBLE FUTURE EDITIONS (PFE): Figurines that have been modeled but not yet released for sale to the public.

PREVIEW EDITION (PE): Figurines with an M.I. Hummel Club backstamp offered exclusively to members for a special preview period. After its first two years of production, it may become an open edition (OE) available to the general public, bearing a regular Goebel backstamp only.

PROTOTYPE: This term used by Goebel means the "one and only sample" (first out of the mother mold) that is presented to the Siessen Convent of any newly developed "M.I. Hummel" figurine.

RATTLE: All "M.I. Hummel" figurines are hollow on the inside. Occasionally, when the figurine is fired, a small piece of clay will drop off on the inside. This little bit of clay when dry will cause a slight rattle. Actually, it does not hurt the figurine or affect the value one way or the other. I would not even call it a flaw, as it does not detract from the appearance. Actually, it is one means of identification that might come in handy sometime!

REINSTATED: The term used to indicate that a figurine has been placed back into production by the W. Goebel Porzellanfabrik after some prior classification of non-production.

RETIRED: A term used by Goebel to refer to a figurine that has been permanently removed from production. The molds are broken and the figurine will never be produced again.

RÖDENTAL: The town in Germany where the W. Goebel Porzellanfabrik is situated. Rödental is located near Coburg and lies only a few miles from the former East German border. In 1981 Rödental became the official Sister City of Eaton, Ohio, due to the longtime "Hummel" relationship with Robert L. Miller and the International "Hummel" Festival held annually at Eaton, Ohio and then in Dayton, Ohio.

SAMPLE MODEL: Generally a figurine that was made as a sample only and not approved by the Siessen Convent for production. Sample models (in the true sense of the term) are extremely rare items and command a premium price on the secondary market.

SCHMID: A former distributor of "M.I. Hummel" figurines and related items. Schmid Brothers, Inc. of Boston was one of the earliest importers of "Hummel" figurines in 1935. Of course, no figurines were imported from Germany during the war years. Immediately after the end of WW II, Schmid once again became one of the chief distributors along with the Ebeling & Reuss Company of Devon, Pennsylvania in the 1960s and early 1970s. At the end of 1968, Goebel terminated their agreement with Schmid in favor of their distribution company called "Hummelwerk" headquartered at Elmsford, New York. In 1988, after a lengthy court battle, Schmid temporarily became the sole distributor of "M.I. Hummel" products in the U.S. In 1994 Goebel purchased from Schmid the exclusive rights to be the sole distributor of "M. I. Hummel" products in the U.S. Schmid Brothers, Inc. of Boston is no longer in business.

SECONDARY MARKET: The buying and selling of items after the initial retail purchase has been transacted. Oftentimes this post-retail trading is also referred to as the "after market." This very publication is intended to serve as a guide for the secondary market values of "M.I. Hummel" items.

SIESSEN CONVENT: Located in Wuerttemberg region of Germany near Saulgau. This facility is where Sister M.I. Hummel resided after taking her vows. She continued to sketch in a studio inside the convent until her untimely death at the age of 37 in 1946. The Siessen Convent houses the Sisters of the Third Order of St. Francis. Sister Hummel is buried in the cemetery located on the Convent grounds.

"SLASH" MARK: At one time, an imperfect or flawed figurine produced by Goebel and found during final inspection was marked by grinding a small groove or "slash" through the trademark. These pieces were then sold to factory employees as "seconds." Some of these "slash" marked pieces eventually found their way on to the secondary market and sold to uninformed collectors.

STYLIZED TRADEMARK: The symbol used by the Goebel Company from 1957 until 1964. It is recognized by the V with a bumblebee that has triangular or "stylized" wings.

TEMPORARILY WITHDRAWN (TW): A designation assigned by the W. Goebel Porzellanfabrik to indicate that a particular item is being withdrawn from production for some time, but may be reinstated at a future date. This actually means, withdrawn from the U.S. market only, but, however, it could still be produced for the European market, or other World markets.

TERRA COTTA: A reddish clay used in an experimental fashion by artisans at the W. Goebel Porzellanfabrik. There are a few sample pieces of "M.I. Hummel" figurines that were produced with the terra cotta material. These terra cotta pieces have the look of the reddish-brown clay and were not painted.

THREE LINE TRADEMARK: The symbol used by the W. Goebel Porzellanfabrik from 1964 until 1972 as their factory trademark. The name for this trademark was adopted to recognize that the V and bee was accompanied by three lines of print to the right of the V. Also known as TM4.

TM: Abbreviation for trademark.

TW: Abbreviation for temporarily withdrawn.

UNDERGLAZE: The term used to describe especially the number 5 trademark that appears actually underneath the glaze as opposed to the later version of the number 5 trademark that appears on the top of the glaze.

U.S. ZONE: The words "U.S. ZONE—GERMANY" were used on figurines produced by the W. Goebel Porzellanfabrik after W.W. II when the country of Germany was yet undivided and the Goebel factory was part of the U.S. Zone. The U.S. ZONE marking was used either alone or with the Crown trademark from 1946 until 1948. Once the country was divided into East and West, the W. Goebel Porzellanfabrik used the Western or West designation.

WAFFLE BASE: Another term to describe the quartered or divided bases.

WHITE OVERGLAZE: The term used to designate an item that has not been painted, but has been glazed and fired. These pieces are completely white. All "M.I. Hummel" items are produced in this finish before being individually hand painted.

About the Artists

H andmade in the W. Goebel Porzellanfabrik studios in Rödental, Germany, "M.I. Hummel" figurines enjoy a unique advantage. This art form has been developed in close cooperation with and through the personal assistance and advice of the artist herself, Sister Maria Innocentia Hummel, both at the factory and at the Convent of Siessen. Though gentle and gifted with a fine sense of humor, she was very demanding when it came to her art. Master sculptors Arthur Moeller and Reinhold Unger had many discussions with her, and she commented in detail in her bold, clear handwriting when she looked at samples. She did not hesitate to take up the modeler's stick or the painter's fine brush to make her intentions understood. Millions of collectors and friends all over the world have loved and revered the outcome of this artistic collaboration which continues today, long after the death of Sister Maria Innocentia, through the art authorities at the convent.

The sculptors, known for so masterfully transforming two-dimensional art into this new dimension, brought varied experience and training to their work. **Arthur Moeller** was born in 1885 at Rudolstadt in Thuringia. After completing basic studies of modeling at a fine arts studio, he left home to work with a number of porcelain factories. He developed his talents at the Arts and Crafts Academy in Dresden and afterwards at the Academy for Applied Arts in Munich, the same school where Sister M.I. Hummel was to enroll one generation later. From his artistic hands and imagination came works that were shown in Paris and Munich. In 1911, Max Louis Goebel, third-generation head of the company, became aware of this talented young artist and invited him to work with the company. When Moeller died in 1972 in the 86th year of his life, he had been with the company for nearly 50 years. Besides his demanding tasks at the Goebel atelier, Moeller found time to exhibit at fine art shows in Munich, Coburg and Kulmbach. He was a master of the small form. This very special gift enabled him to contribute an immense wealth to the Goebel range. When the time came to create charming

Arthur Moeller

figurines from Sister M.I. Hummel's artwork, he and his equally gifted colleague, Reinhold Unger, were the right men for the task.

Reinhold Unger also came from Thuringia where he was born in 1880, near where the Goebel factory owned its ancestral porcelain factory. Unger studied at the Fine Art School of Professor Hutschenreuther in Lichte and worked afterwards with the Kunstanstalt Gaigl in Munich.

His works were shown at fine art exhibitions in Munich and he came to work in the Goebel atelier upon the invitation of Max Louis Goebel in 1915. After a fine and fruitful collaboration of 50 years, Unger died in 1974 in the 94th year of his life. His work was highly praised by the press and fine art authorities. On special trips into Upper Bavaria he had absorbed impressions of both the folk art and the deep religious feelings of the area, all of which were incorporated into his artwork. This ability enabled him to develop, through close collaboration with Arthur Moeller and Sister M.I. Hummel, those lovely figurines which were to conquer the hearts of millions. In general, it can be said that most of the religious items incised "M.I. Hummel" and made before 1958 were sculpted by Unger.

Reinhold Unger   *Gerhard Skrobek*

Third in this prestigious line of "M.I. Hummel" sculptors is **Gerhard Skrobek**, who joined Goebel in 1951. After his birth in Silesia in 1922, his parents, who thrived in an environment of music and painting, soon moved to Berlin where young Gerhard was exposed to a wealth of museums. He would go to the zoological gardens and sit for hours observing and sketching the animals. His decision to turn to sculpture led him to the renowned Reimannschule where he studied under the prestigious Melzer. In 1946, Skrobek went to Coburg to continue his art studies with the well-known sculptor Poertzel, who created many porcelain pieces for W. Goebel Porzellanfabrik. Skrobek travelled extensively at this time and exhibited in Coburg and Munich. In 1951 he joined Goebel and soon became one of its leading sculptors. He was entrusted to continue the tradition of sculpting the "M.I. Hummel" figurines, and under his talented and guiding hands much of the original artwork was turned into figurines. He also contributed the "M.I. Hummel" plates and bells to the line and created the eight-foot "Merry Wanderer," the famous landmark in front of the Goebel Collectors' Club Gallery and Museum in Tarrytown, New York. "Today's Children" and "Co-Boy" figurines are his creations, and many Goebel series such as Charlotte Byj and the Wildlife Collection attest to his talents.

Traditions of quality continue, and the closeness between the Convent of Siessen and the sculptor's atelier at Goebel is strongly maintained.

Karl Wagner was born on March 30, 1900 in Holenbrunn/Oberfranken. At the age of 16, he entered the Nuernberg School of Arts where his work won one award and six commendations. From 1920 to 1922 he studied at the Art Academy of Stuttgart. After completing his studies, he entered the ceramics industry as an artist and sculptor. In 1936 he joined W. Goebel Porzellanfabrik.

From 1936 until 1972, when the sculptor retired, he created many figurines for Goebel including several in the **M.I. Hummel** and **Disney** lines. In 1949, Wagner was named master sculptor for Goebel's new toy division, **Hummelwerk-Spielwaren KG**. He was responsible for the modelling and technical preparations of all of the products, including animals and the M.I. Hummel dolls.

Two years after his retirement, Karl Wagner died on December 4, 1974.

Guenthur Neubauer was born on February 3, 1932 in Noerdbohmen, in what is today Czechoslavakia. When he was a schoolboy the war brought him to Coburg, Bavaria, where he began his apprenticeship with W. Goebel Porzellanfabrik in March 1948.

Karl Wagner

Gunther Neubauer

Mr. Neubauer's tremendous creative talent, especially evident in his drawings, was recognized and encouraged by his teacher, master sculptor Arthur Moeller. After three years of schooling in the factory, Neubauer passed the arduous ceramic and porcelain tests. The most artistically talented graduate of his class, he was immediately brought into production to decorate the more difficult figurines. During this time, he accomplished the rare feat of becoming an expert in both under and overglaze decorating.

The following years were marked by Neubauer's rapid advancement through the artistic ranks at Goebel. In 1953 he became the sample painter for a group of approximately 30 artists. Two years later he assumed the responsibility for the design development of new products and of new production methods. After passing the state exams in 1961, he was certified as a master of ceramics.

Since 1960 Neubauer has participated in both the teaching of apprentices and the development of production methods. As department manager and chief master sample painter, he is responsible for the decoration of all underglazed and overglazed collectibles. As a teacher, he instructed all of the apprentices in the fine ceramic division from 1966 through 1974, and today he is the prime instructor for the underglaze painting education of all apprentices.

In 1956 Neubauer married another talented sample painter with Goebel, who died after a long illness in 1985. Their only daughter, Heike, has inherited her parents' artistic aptitude, and is an interior decorator.

In addition to being an active sportsman, participating in swimming, walking and skiing, Mr. Neubauer enjoys painting in both watercolors and oils, and he is an accomplished photographer. He has retired from Goebel after almost 50 years.

Franz Kirchner was born on September 12, 1935 in Neersof, a town not far from W. Goebel Porzellanfabrik in Rödental, Bavaria. Upon graduation from junior high school, he decided to pursue a career as an artist and, on August 8, 1949, entered the three-year apprentice program at Goebel.

After the successful completion of the program in 1952, he began work in Goebel's decorating department. Through continued schooling and expanded artistic experience, he became a qualified master of under and overglaze painting.

Due to his artistic talent and conscientiousness, Mr. Kirchner was made a master sample painter in 1955. Today as assistant manager of the decorating department, he is responsible for the sample decoration of new pieces.

604

Franz Kirchner   *Helmut Fischer*

Mr. Kirchner has travelled throughout Germany and in the U.S. demonstrating his craft. On one trip to the U.S. he appeared at the Hunter Mt., New York, German Alps Festival and at the International Plate and Collectibles Exposition in South Bend, Indiana.

In his spare time, he develops his talents as a fine artist, specializing in landscapes. He is also a musician, and is an active member of a band focusing on traditional German music, in which he plays both the clarinet and saxophone. He also enjoys walking and working in his garden.

Helmut Fischer   As a master sculptor at W. Goebel Porzellanfabrik (WGP), Germany, Helmut Fischer is entrusted with the difficult task of transforming the two-dimensional art of Sister M.I. Hummel into the world-famous figurines that bear her name.

Highly imaginative and talented, Helmut combines his creativity and sculpting expertise to create a wide range of M.I. Hummel® figurine motifs. Fourth in a prestigious line of M.I. Hummel sculptors, Helmut continues the Goebel tradition of quality and handcraftsmanship.

Born in Coburg in 1950, Helmut comes from a family of skilled craftsmen who recognized his talent and encouraged his development. At the age of 14, Fischer followed his father's suggestion and enrolled in the Goebel apprenticeship program as a sculptor. Three years later, he passed the difficult exam given by the Chamber of Commerce and Industry in Coburg. After joining Goebel, he utilized his talent and skills to create numerous models of porcelain, fine earthenware and glass.

In the 1980s, Helmut created several series including Serengeti, a true-to-nature collection of animal sculptures, the DeGrazia collection, based on the artwork of Ted DeGrazia, as well as Goebel's line of Walt Disney figurines, based on the artwork of the Disney Company. His works have been exhibited in the *Museum der Deutschen Porzellanindustrie* in Hohenberg an der Eger, Germany, and he was recognized as a "Works-of-Art" artist in the United States in 1986.

Since 1988, Helmut has been entrusted with the development and sculpting responsibilities of M.I. Hummel figurines including the Century Collection figurine "We Wish You the Best." With his unique artistic talents and over 20 years of experience with the company, Helmut has also assumed the reins of M.I. Hummel Master Sculptor position at WGP.

Helmut lives in Neustadt, Germany, and enjoys drawing, photographing nature, kayaking and riding his mountain bike. He speaks English, though not fluently, and is looking forward to his next trip to the U.S.

Marion (Müller) Huschka

Marion (Müller) Huschka was born on October 15, 1959 in Rödental, Germany. She is the fourth generation in her family to be employed with W. Goebel Porzellanfabrik. Her father is presently supervisor in the whiteware department, her mother works in the office and her sister is in the painting department. Marion started her employ-ment in 1976 with her apprenticeship and examination in 1979 as a sculptor (WGP and occupational training centre for ceramic art in Selb, Germany) was complete. In 1982 she participated in a Study Trip to Italy. She was also a student of Master Sculptor Gerhard Skrobek whose guidance and artistic instructions prepared her for sculpting M.I. Hummel figurines. Since 1981 she has been a "Sculptor-Trainer" of new students at Goebel. Due to the support she is giving the young trainee sculptors, she was called into the board of examiners for sculptors at the Chamber of Commerce and Trade in Coburg for ceramic vocations in 1982. In 1984, Marion participated in the Goebel Facsimle Factory Promotion Tour in California. She has been responsible for most of the Disney/Hummel look-alike figurines, including the large seven figure Disney "Adventure Bound" figurine. This was the most complicated Disney figurine ever produced by W. Goebel Porzellanfabrik which was limited to 25 pieces. Along with Mr. Skrobek and Mr. Fischer, Ms. Huschka has recently achieved "Works of Art" status. Marion has a good knowledge of the English language and speaks fluent English. She lives in Rödental with her husband and daughter. Her hobbies include landscape drawing, riding, gardening and hiking with her family. Marion Elke Huschka is a very talented, personable lady.